Lecture Notes in Computer Science 10281

Commenced Publication in 1973
Founding and Former Series Editors:
Gerhard Goos, Juris Hartmanis, and Jan van Leeuwen

Editorial Board

More information about this series at http://www.springer.com/series/7409

Pei-Luen Patrick Rau (Ed.)

Cross-Cultural Design

9th International Conference, CCD 2017
Held as Part of HCI International 2017
Vancouver, BC, Canada, July 9–14, 2017
Proceedings

 Springer

Editor
Pei-Luen Patrick Rau
Tsinghua University
Beijing
China

ISSN 0302-9743   ISSN 1611-3349   (electronic)
Lecture Notes in Computer Science
ISBN 978-3-319-57930-6   ISBN 978-3-319-57931-3   (eBook)
DOI 10.1007/978-3-319-57931-3

Library of Congress Control Number: 2017938162

LNCS Sublibrary: SL3 – Information Systems and Applications, incl. Internet/Web, and HCI

Printed on acid-free paper

This Springer imprint is published by Springer Nature
The registered company is Springer International Publishing AG
The registered company address is: Gewerbestrasse 11, 6330 Cham, Switzerland

Foreword

The 19th International Conference on Human–Computer Interaction, HCI International 2017, was held in Vancouver, Canada, during July 9–14, 2017. The event incorporated the 15 conferences/thematic areas listed on the following page.

A total of 4,340 individuals from academia, research institutes, industry, and governmental agencies from 70 countries submitted contributions, and 1,228 papers have been included in the proceedings. These papers address the latest research and development efforts and highlight the human aspects of design and use of computing systems. The papers thoroughly cover the entire field of human–computer interaction, addressing major advances in knowledge and effective use of computers in a variety of application areas. The volumes constituting the full set of the conference proceedings are listed on the following pages.

I would like to thank the program board chairs and the members of the program boards of all thematic areas and affiliated conferences for their contribution to the highest scientific quality and the overall success of the HCI International 2017 conference.

This conference would not have been possible without the continuous and unwavering support and advice of the founder, Conference General Chair Emeritus and Conference Scientific Advisor Prof. Gavriel Salvendy. For his outstanding efforts, I would like to express my appreciation to the communications chair and editor of *HCI International News*, Dr. Abbas Moallem.

April 2017   Constantine Stephanidis

HCI International 2017 Thematic Areas and Affiliated Conferences

Thematic areas:

- Human–Computer Interaction (HCI 2017)
- Human Interface and the Management of Information (HIMI 2017)

Affiliated conferences:

- 17th International Conference on Engineering Psychology and Cognitive Ergonomics (EPCE 2017)
- 11th International Conference on Universal Access in Human–Computer Interaction (UAHCI 2017)
- 9th International Conference on Virtual, Augmented and Mixed Reality (VAMR 2017)
- 9th International Conference on Cross-Cultural Design (CCD 2017)
- 9th International Conference on Social Computing and Social Media (SCSM 2017)
- 11th International Conference on Augmented Cognition (AC 2017)
- 8th International Conference on Digital Human Modeling and Applications in Health, Safety, Ergonomics and Risk Management (DHM 2017)
- 6th International Conference on Design, User Experience and Usability (DUXU 2017)
- 5th International Conference on Distributed, Ambient and Pervasive Interactions (DAPI 2017)
- 5th International Conference on Human Aspects of Information Security, Privacy and Trust (HAS 2017)
- 4th International Conference on HCI in Business, Government and Organizations (HCIBGO 2017)
- 4th International Conference on Learning and Collaboration Technologies (LCT 2017)
- Third International Conference on Human Aspects of IT for the Aged Population (ITAP 2017)

Conference Proceedings Volumes Full List

1. LNCS 10271, Human–Computer Interaction: User Interface Design, Development and Multimodality (Part I), edited by Masaaki Kurosu
2. LNCS 10272 Human–Computer Interaction: Interaction Contexts (Part II), edited by Masaaki Kurosu
3. LNCS 10273, Human Interface and the Management of Information: Information, Knowledge and Interaction Design (Part I), edited by Sakae Yamamoto
4. LNCS 10274, Human Interface and the Management of Information: Supporting Learning, Decision-Making and Collaboration (Part II), edited by Sakae Yamamoto
5. LNAI 10275, Engineering Psychology and Cognitive Ergonomics: Performance, Emotion and Situation Awareness (Part I), edited by Don Harris
6. LNAI 10276, Engineering Psychology and Cognitive Ergonomics: Cognition and Design (Part II), edited by Don Harris
7. LNCS 10277, Universal Access in Human–Computer Interaction: Design and Development Approaches and Methods (Part I), edited by Margherita Antona and Constantine Stephanidis
8. LNCS 10278, Universal Access in Human–Computer Interaction: Designing Novel Interactions (Part II), edited by Margherita Antona and Constantine Stephanidis
9. LNCS 10279, Universal Access in Human–Computer Interaction: Human and Technological Environments (Part III), edited by Margherita Antona and Constantine Stephanidis
10. LNCS 10280, Virtual, Augmented and Mixed Reality, edited by Stephanie Lackey and Jessie Y.C. Chen
11. LNCS 10281, Cross-Cultural Design, edited by Pei-Luen Patrick Rau
12. LNCS 10282, Social Computing and Social Media: Human Behavior (Part I), edited by Gabriele Meiselwitz
13. LNCS 10283, Social Computing and Social Media: Applications and Analytics (Part II), edited by Gabriele Meiselwitz
14. LNAI 10284, Augmented Cognition: Neurocognition and Machine Learning (Part I), edited by Dylan D. Schmorrow and Cali M. Fidopiastis
15. LNAI 10285, Augmented Cognition: Enhancing Cognition and Behavior in Complex Human Environments (Part II), edited by Dylan D. Schmorrow and Cali M. Fidopiastis
16. LNCS 10286, Digital Human Modeling and Applications in Health, Safety, Ergonomics and Risk Management: Ergonomics and Design (Part I), edited by Vincent G. Duffy
17. LNCS 10287, Digital Human Modeling and Applications in Health, Safety, Ergonomics and Risk Management: Health and Safety (Part II), edited by Vincent G. Duffy
18. LNCS 10288, Design, User Experience, and Usability: Theory, Methodology and Management (Part I), edited by Aaron Marcus and Wentao Wang

19. LNCS 10289, Design, User Experience, and Usability: Designing Pleasurable Experiences (Part II), edited by Aaron Marcus and Wentao Wang
20. LNCS 10290, Design, User Experience, and Usability: Understanding Users and Contexts (Part III), edited by Aaron Marcus and Wentao Wang
21. LNCS 10291, Distributed, Ambient and Pervasive Interactions, edited by Norbert Streitz and Panos Markopoulos
22. LNCS 10292, Human Aspects of Information Security, Privacy and Trust, edited by Theo Tryfonas
23. LNCS 10293, HCI in Business, Government and Organizations: Interacting with Information Systems (Part I), edited by Fiona Fui-Hoon Nah and Chuan-Hoo Tan
24. LNCS 10294, HCI in Business, Government and Organizations: Supporting Business (Part II), edited by Fiona Fui-Hoon Nah and Chuan-Hoo Tan
25. LNCS 10295, Learning and Collaboration Technologies: Novel Learning Ecosystems (Part I), edited by Panayiotis Zaphiris and Andri Ioannou
26. LNCS 10296, Learning and Collaboration Technologies: Technology in Education (Part II), edited by Panayiotis Zaphiris and Andri Ioannou
27. LNCS 10297, Human Aspects of IT for the Aged Population: Aging, Design and User Experience (Part I), edited by Jia Zhou and Gavriel Salvendy
28. LNCS 10298, Human Aspects of IT for the Aged Population: Applications, Services and Contexts (Part II), edited by Jia Zhou and Gavriel Salvendy
29. CCIS 713, HCI International 2017 Posters Proceedings (Part I), edited by Constantine Stephanidis
30. CCIS 714, HCI International 2017 Posters Proceedings (Part II), edited by Constantine Stephanidis

Cross-Cultural Design

Program Board Chair(s): **Pei-Luen Patrick Rau, P.R. China**

- Na Chen, P.R. China
- Zhe Chen, P.R. China
- Yu-Liang Chi, Taiwan
- Paul L. Fu, USA
- Zhiyong Fu, P.R. China
- Sung H. Han, Korea
- Toshikazu Kato, Japan
- Pin-Chao Liao, P.R. China
- Dyi-Yih Michael Lin, Taiwan
- Rungtai Lin, Taiwan
- Yongqi Lou, P.R. China
- Liang Ma, P.R. China
- Alexander Mädche, Germany
- Katsuhiko Ogawa, Japan
- Chun-Yi (Danny) Shen, Taiwan
- Pei-Lee Teh, Malaysia
- Yuan-Chi Tseng, Taiwan
- Lin Wang, Korea
- Hsiu-Ping Yueh, Taiwan

The full list with the Program Board Chairs and the members of the Program Boards of all thematic areas and affiliated conferences is available online at:

http://www.hci.international/board-members-2017.php

HCI International 2018

The 20th International Conference on Human–Computer Interaction, HCI International 2018, will be held jointly with the affiliated conferences in Las Vegas, NV, USA, at Caesars Palace, July 15–20, 2018. It will cover a broad spectrum of themes related to human–computer interaction, including theoretical issues, methods, tools, processes, and case studies in HCI design, as well as novel interaction techniques, interfaces, and applications. The proceedings will be published by Springer. More information is available on the conference website: http://2018.hci.international/.

General Chair
Prof. Constantine Stephanidis
University of Crete and ICS-FORTH
Heraklion, Crete, Greece
E-mail: general_chair@hcii2018.org

http://2018.hci.international/

Contents

Cultural Foundations of Design

Transforming Traditional Paper Cutting into LINE Stickers   3
    Tzu Chiang Chang and Shu Hui Huang

A Systemic Approach to Concrete Constructions.   15
    Bernardino Chiaia, Alessandro Fantilli, and Pier Paolo Peruccio

Western vs. Eastern: A Reflective Research on the Development
of Chinese Animation   25
    Wen Ting Fang, Po-Hsien Lin, and Rungtai Lin

A Study of Communication in Turning "Poetry" into "Painting".   37
    Ya-Juan Gao, Li-Yu Chen, Sandy Lee, Rungtai Lin, and Yige Jin

The Impact of Chinese Traditional Cultural on the Gesture
and User Experience in Mobile Interaction Design   49
    Ren Long, Xu Liu, Tian Lei, Xue Chen, and Ziliang Jin

What is a System?: A Lesson Learned from the Emerging Practice
of DesignX   59
    Jin Ma

A First Speculation on Cultural Experiments as Design Research Methods. . .   76
    Francesca Valsecchi, Roberta Tassi, and Elena Kilina

Waterfall Flow vs. Fixed Grid Webpage Layout Design – The Effects
Depend on the Zhong-Yong Thinking Style   94
    Man-Ying Wang and Da-Lun Tang

Transforming Concepts of a Taiwanese Twin Cup
into Social Design Activities   104
    Ning-Hsien (aka Vincent) Yang

Applying the Story of *The Dream of the Butterfly* in Creative Design   121
    Mo-Li Yeh, Chun-Ming Lien, and Yi-Fang Kao

Cross-Cultural Product and Service Design

Research and Application of Service Design Thoughts in Subway
Advertisement Design   133
    Xing Fang, Yangshuo Zheng, Heng Liu, Yongzhen Zou, and Xiaoqin Cao

Consistency of Use Flow Improving User Experience
of Service-Oriented Websites   146
  Canqun He, Xu Yang, Zhengsheng Li, Zhangyu Ji, Jiaojiao Wang,
  and Shuya Ni

Independent Bathing for Older Adults: The Conceptualization
of the iMagic-BOX Portable Walk-In Bathtub   161
  Chew Kien Ming and Jeffery Yeow Teh Thiry

The Integration of Personal and Public Transportation in Creating
Seamless Experience   171
  Qiao Liang, Miaosen Gong, Linghao Zhang, and Anran Qin

Integration and Innovation: Learning by Exchanging Views - A Report
of the Cross-Cultural Design Workshop for Stone Craving   181
  Po-Hsien Lin, Ya-Juan Gao, Taihua Lan, and Xiaoge Wang

The Item-Based Fashion Matching Experience in Online Platform Service
Design: A Case Study from Chinese Customers   192
  Hao Tan, Wei Li, Zhengyu Tan, Shijing Fang, and Shihui Xu

The Interdisciplinary Collaboration of Innovational Design   204
  Shu-Huei Wang, Shyh-Huei Hwang, and Ming-Shean Wang

Research on the Service Design of the Museum Visiting   216
  Yanyun Wang and Junjie Chu

Implementation of Service Design on Innovation Development
of Traditional Handicraft: A Case Study of Yongchun Lacquered Basket   232
  Yan Wu, Li-Yu Chen, and Lei Ren

Designing a Cross-Cultural Interactive Music Box Through
Meaning Construction   241
  Yongmeng Wu, Nick Bryan-Kinns, Wei Wang, Jennifer G. Sheridan,
  and Xiang Xu

RETRACTED CHAPTER: Design for Meaningful Materials Experience:
A Case Study About Designing Materials with Rice and Sea-Salt   258
  Liang Yin, Ziyu Zhou, and Hang Cheng

Research on the Design of Bicycle Service System in Colleges
and Universities Based on Contact Mining   269
  Yi-qian Zhao and Ya-jun Li

SDIV: Service-Defined Intelligent Vehicle Towards the 2020
Urban Mobility   288
  Bo Zhou, Xiaohua Sun, and Binhui Zhang

Cross-Cultural Communication

Investigating the Comprehension of Public Symbols for Wayfinding
in Transit Hubs in China   301
  Dadi An and Edwin H.W. Chan

Interpretation of Space: From Images to Vocabulary   312
  Li-Yu Chen, Ya-Juan Gao, Wun-Cong Yen, and Ching-Hui Huang

A Study on Signage Design and Synesthesia in Senior Residences   324
  Miao-Hsien Chuang, Tong-Fang Ni, and Jui-Ping Ma

Chinese Migrant Food Business in Italy and Design Researches
for Intercultural Dialogue   334
  Shushu He

Collaborative Service for Cross-Geographical Design Context:
The Case of Sino-Italian Digital Platform   345
  Chenhan Jiang and Yongqi Lou

A Pilot Study of Communication Matrix for Evaluating Artworks   356
  Rungtai Lin, Fengde Qian, Jun Wu, Wen-Ting Fang, and Yige Jin

Family, Friends, and Cultural Connectedness: A Comparison Between
WeChat and Facebook User Motivation, Experience and NPS Among
Chinese People Living Overseas   369
  Chunhui Xie, Jagannadha Sri Harsha Putrevu, and Chelsea Linder

Design for Social Development

Design for Neighborhood Amateur Cultural Club – A Community
Regeneration Practice in Qinglong Hutong   385
  Zhiyong Fu and Xue He

Design to Improve Medication Adherence for the Elderly in China   399
  Long Liu, Chu Wang, Qian Zhou, and Ziying Yao

Open Your Space: A Design Activism Initiative in Chinese
Urban Community   412
  Minqing Ni

Designing Architectural Space Using Service System Design Approach   432
  Jintian Shi and Xiaohua Sun

Web Content Analysis on Power Distance Cultural Presence
in E-Government Portal Design   441
  Wan Adilah Wan Adnan, Nor Laila Md Noor, Fauzi Mohd Saman,
  and Farez Mahmood

Designing to Support Community Gardens by Going Beyond
Community Gardens   451
   Xiaolan Wang and Ron Wakkary

Sewing for Life: The Development of Sewing Machine
in the Tune of Women Life Experience in Taiwan   469
   Ju-Joan Wong and Hsiao-Hua Chen

The Design Thinking Leading to Different Levels of Change:
Example of the Togo Village in Southern Taiwan   482
   Cecile Ching-yi Wu

Discussion on the Dynamic Construction of Urban Public Space
with Interactive Public Art   495
   Ping Zhou and Zhiyong Fu

Cross-Cultural Design for Learning

DanMOOC: Enhancing Content and Social Interaction in MOOCs
with Synchronized Commenting   509
   Yue Chen, Qin Gao, and Quan Yuan

Exploring Factors Influencing Knowledge Sharing of International Students
at Chinese University   521
   Zhe Chen, Shunong Deng, Adila Mamtimin, Jiaxin Chang, Feng Liu,
   and Lin Ma

Breakout: Design and Evaluation of a Serious Game for Health Employing
Intel RealSense   531
   Jimmy Chhor, Yun Gong, and Pei-Luen Patrick Rau

Instructional Design and Teaching Effectiveness of SPOCs in Chinese
Higher Education   546
   Ka-Hin Lai, Lili Dong, and Pei-Luen Patrick Rau

Exploration on Education Practice Based on Employment
and Entrepreneurship in Higher Institutes of China   554
   Jing Li, Lin Ma, Xin Wu, and Zhe Chen

Design for Learning Through Play. An Exploratory Study
on Chinese Perspective   565
   Maria Luce Lupetti, Yuan Yao, Jing Gao, Haipeng Mi,
   and Claudio Germak

Teaching Older Adults to Use Gerontechnology Applications Through
Instruction Videos: Human-Element Considerations   582
   Pei-Lee Teh, Chee Wei Phang, Pervaiz K. Ahmed, Soon-Nyean Cheong,
   Wen-Jiun Yap, Qi Ma, and Alan H.S. Chan

A Preliminary Study on the Learning Assessment in Massive
Open Online Courses.   592
   Quan Yuan, Qin Gao, and Yue Chen

Culture and User Experience

Busting the Myth of Older Adults and Technology:
An In-depth Examination of Three Outliers   605
   Robert Beringer

Evaluating the Use of LINE Software to Support Interaction During
an American Travel Course in Japan.   614
   Dave Berque and Hiroko Chiba

Research on Car Gesture Interaction Design Based on the Line Design   624
   Jing Chunhui and Jing Zhang

The Role of Trust with Car-Sharing Services in the Sharing Economy
in China: From the Consumers' Perspective   634
   Shang Gao, Jia Jing, and Hong Guo

A Critique on Participatory Design in Developmental Context:
A Case Study.   647
   *Ulemba Hirom, Shyama V.S., Pankaj Doke, Sylvan Lobo, Sujit Devkar,
   and Nikita Pandey*

Understanding Users' Acceptance of Money Gifting in a Social Game   659
   Hanjing Huang and Pei-Luen Patrick Rau

The Role of Socially Assistive Robots in Elderly Wellbeing:
A Systematic Review   669
   Reza Kachouie, Sima Sedighadeli, and Amin B. Abkenar

A New Method for OTAs to Analyze and Predict Users' Online Behavior
Patterns and Preferences.   683
   Rui Kang and Pei-Luen Patrick Rau

A Pilot Study of Mining the Differences in Patterns of Customer Review
Text Between US and China AppStore   693
   Lisha Li, Liang Ma, Pei-Luen Patrick Rau, and Qin Gao

The User's Performance Study for Different Layouts of Car's Dashboards. . .   703
   Linghua Ran, Xin Zhang, Huimin Hu, Chaoyi Zhao, and Taijie Liu

Do Consumption Values and Environmental Awareness Impact
on Green Consumption in China?   713
   Lebohang Sekhokoane, Nan Qie, and Pei-Luen Patrick Rau

A User Experience Study for Watching Delay Interrupted Video
in the Context of Mobile Network.   724
    Hao Tan, Jiahao Sun, Bin Wang, Qiyong Zhao, Wei Li,
    and Zhengyu Tan

Driver's Information Needs in Automated Driving   736
    Huining Xing, Hua Qin, and Jianwei Niu

Retraction Note to: Design for Meaningful Materials Experience:
A Case Study About Designing Materials with Rice and Sea-Salt E1
    Liang Yin, Ziyu Zhou, and Hang Cheng

Author Index   745

Cultural Foundations of Design

Transforming Traditional Paper Cutting into LINE Stickers

Tzu Chiang Chang[✉] and Shu Hui Huang

Graduate School of Creative Industry Design, National Taiwan University of Arts,
Banqiao District, New Taipei City 22058, Taiwan
chang.tc0214@msa.hinet.net, shhuang@textiles.org.tw

Abstract. The development of technology not only has sped up our interpersonal communication, but has also brought about mixed emotions. The reason why LINE mobile communication software (mobile application) is welcomed is because it has all kinds of lively stickers. These stickers convey delicate emotions that are difficult to convey through texts to message recipients, enriching the contexts of interpersonal communications. However, since designers started to design their own images, negative semantic behaviors have also been created. This has led to message recipients feeling psychologically uncomfortable. With regard to this and based on five stickers with negative semantic meanings among personal creations in Taiwan, we specifically carried out our study through three cultural design properties – external, functional, and psychological. We hope that through Value-added designs, the decent model of technological application can be completed. Hopefully, the positive semantic meanings of the word "Shii" (喜) in traditional paper cutting and its extensions including "happiness", "sadness", "anger" and "without joy" can correct the behaviors of these stickers. Further-more, in doing so, modern elements could be infused into arts, and tech fashion could be manifested.

Keywords: LINE sticker · Negative semantics · Traditional paper cutting · Character "Shii" (喜)

1 Introduction

"Culture" is a valuable asset of mankind. "Innovation", on the other hand, ensures the extension of culture. However, as time passes and changes, when we get to communicate with distant relatives and enjoy the convenience brought by technology, it actually reflects the extent of our lives' richness. LINE mobile communication application (mobile application) software is the product of this era. To achieve the purpose of exchange, users can communicate through transmitting "texts" and "stickers" via the Internet. This has made communications between people simpler and faster. It has also brought negative semantic behaviors. Until 2015, there were more than 17 million registered user accounts, accounting for approximately 70% of Taiwan's population (LINE BLOG 2015). This data shows that using LINE to transmit messages has made interpersonal communication of account users in Taiwan more

© Springer International Publishing AG 2017
P.-L.P. Rau (Ed.): CCD 2017, LNCS 10281, pp. 3–14, 2017.
DOI: 10.1007/978-3-319-57931-3_1

rapid and intimate. Moreover, it has deepened the importance of the application of this software in modern life.

However, in the Chinese culture, there is a sticker behavior that conveys "good" semantic meanings, and that is traditional "paper cutting" art. "Shii" is the most commonly used word. It is a kind of art that conveys simple emotions through paper and scissors or knives in the hands of women in rural areas. The content of its images is deeply influenced by Chinese philosophical thinking, forming a unique "semantic" form of culture. Finally, based on people's habits and behaviors, stickers are displayed on windows or objects. It applies cultural aesthetics into interpersonal communication in a specific way. This is consistent with the message transmission approach of LINE's "stickers". However, this mode of transmitting messages through traditional paper-cut stickers will be severely challenged by modern life. With regard to this, we hope that the negative use of words of LINE stickers could be transferred into positive messages through the semantic word of "good" in paper cutting. In addition, we hope that through modern Value-added design models, a new life could be given to our culture.

As time passes, even if people's mentality remains unchanged, the tools, things, and cultures of the world will continue to change. Technology will continue to move forward. Although the principles of design will not change, the method of applying these principles will change according to new human activities, new technologies, and new ways of communication and interaction (Norman 2014). Therefore, we understand that culture must grasp the contexts of era by seeking changes in traditions and seeking breakthroughs in contents. With a broader perspective, paper cutting art will have a bright future.

Lin et al. (2007) believes that, on the cultural level, culture is the evolution of human civilization. It is a product created through joint activities. Generally speaking, culture is defined as the overall activities of human life, including languages, customs, religions, arts, ways of thinking, and living habits. It is a way of living, interpersonal relationship, and value system generated from the application of wisdom in order to mitigate the issue of human race survival and continuation. Culture consists of social activities that are characterized by creativity, inheritability, and comprehensiveness. Design is based on the foundation of the science of "seeking realness", through the art of "seeking aesthetics" as a form of expression to achieve the innovative behavior of "seeking goodness". With regard to this, we need to bring "traditional paper cutting" into this century. At the same time, through the use of semantic word "good" in sticker messages, negative semantic meanings of LINE may be corrected. In addition, it is hoped that through Value-added design models, sticker creations that meet "modern" demands could be designed based on the three specific properties including external-transfer, functional-transit and internal-transform, as shown in Fig. 1.

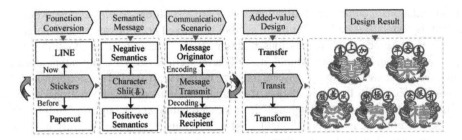

Fig. 1. The procedure of traditional paper cutting design

2 Semantic Communications and Paper-Cut "Shii" (喜)

In terms of interpersonal communication, the core of human communication is the exchange of messages. "Message" refers to the expression of verbal words and non-verbal behaviors. Through message channels, speakers' thoughts, feelings, and attitude inclinations are transmitted. The course of messages is formed by the process of choosing these verbal words and non-verbal behaviors, which is known as "encoding". Then, "decoding" is completed through the process of interpretations by message recipients. Finally, "feedback" is completed through sending responses by message recipients to message originators. Message originators can ensure whether message recipients understand the original message based on this message, which marks the completion of the feedback channel. In this scenario, we complete the message sharing of semantic meanings (Verderber et al. 2004) as shown in Fig. 2.

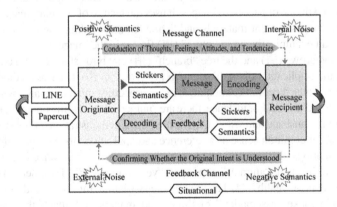

Fig. 2. The scenario for message transmission

Human emotion is a kind of meaningful relationship that exists between personal and meaningful environments. Behaviors and physiology are merely compositions among these. In terms of phenomenon, the environment is full of meanings. From the perspective of observation, emotions are reactions. From the perspective of experience, emotions are meaningful perceptions (Fell 1977). In addition, stimuli are various representations, conflicts, and situations. They are also things of physiological basis, which is "symbol". On the other hand, symbol is a mixed body of various internal and external conscious and subconscious representations. Therefore, if a situation were perceived through a form of symbol, it would arouse emotions. This shows that it is an integration of external expressions and internal states. It is also a kind of energy transfer. This transfer comes from stimulation of external communications on emotional states (Hillman 1960). However, "language" is an explicit habit, and "thought" is an implicit habit. Therefore, language is "thought". When we cannot communicate fully through language, we often need to use other ways of expression to make our language communication more complete (Watson 1930). "Non-verbal communication" is a method. In fact, we are "the message itself". Its purpose, in fact, is to express the insufficiency in our language message transmission, allowing message recipients to understand more clearly the semantic content that message originators want to express. Moreover, through interactions, they can have a better understanding of each other. Through responding to each other, communication behaviors can build common grounds and acceptance in the process.

2.1 The Regularity of Traditional Paper-Cut Semantic Meaning Compositions

The theme of paper cutting is different from the realism of western arts. It is even more different from freehand painting in traditional Chinese style. Art works are completed through personal intuition, impression, and imagination. In fact, they have certain implied meanings. Through cultural heritage, a kind of collective rules are formed. Tao (2003) believes that the regularity of mascots' formation includes: (1) The method of homophonization: application of the Chinese "homophonic" words. This is the "main" method of application in the theme of paper-cut images. It uses the feature of "similar imagery sounds" to convey the images content materials and theme features. Taking the Chinese character "Shii" (喜) as an example, the word "plum" (梅) flower in the image uses the homophonic sound form "eyebrow" (眉) and the tree "branch" (梢) that birds stand on as a combination that conveys the implication of "radiance with joy" (喜上眉梢). (2) The method of representation: people attach certain connotations to the properties of animals and plants and the forms of object and matter. For instance, there are "numerous seeds" in pomegranates, which represents "loving husband and wife". (3) The method of demonstration: people use familiar matters that are of common sense as a reference and apply them to everyday life. Furthermore, representations of forms and arts are attached to them. For instance, "ancient coins" represent "wealth", and "animals" represent "year after year". Together, they signify "consecutive years of wealth". (4) The method of association: through wonderful, touching legends, people make "association" of things and matters and attach the meanings of images. For instance, the legend of "hopewell" (和合) two individuals have the metaphor of "loving husband and wife". (5) The method of integration: it is a "combined" image derived from "multiple" auspicious factors. It gives images themselves richer connotative meanings. Taking "monkeys" as an example, the combined image of the word "Shii" and "lotus" implies "greetings in the year of monkey", as shown in Fig. 3.

1. Homophonization   2. Representation   3. Demonstration   4. Association   5. Integration

Fig. 3. The generation of the regularity of paper-cut "Shii" (喜)

2.2 Definition of the "Joy" and Its Extended Implications

The word "Shii" (喜) is known as "double joy" (囍). It represents of joyful, cheerful, and happy. When "double joy" is placed side by side, it implies joy on top of joy. Looking from the word itself, "Shii" is a joint ideogram. In Shou Wen, the shape of "one" is similar to a drum placed on a platform, signifying celebration through music performances. When there is "mouth" at the bottom, it conveys the meaning of "laughter" and "happiness" when one hears about happiness. In addition, the word "Shii" is also known as "delight," implying matters of "joy" and "happiness".

In terms of the model of the word, its text structure is symmetrical, which is highly perceptible to changes and is easily recognized. Combined with imagery themes, it has become the most auspicious sign of folk celebrations. This shows that the word "Shii" includes two connotations. The first one simply conveys the emotional "happiness" or "joy" of our inner state. Second, it is a general representation of the conditions between people, and between people and things such as wedding and fun. Therefore, when we are "not happy" or "not joyful", we can use "without joy" to explain our "upset" emotional reaction. The other implication of "without joy" is "not joyful". It is an external "angry" emotion stimulated from the mood. Therefore, the word "anger" represents roar, for example. "Not happy" is the emotion of "sorrow". Thus, the word "sorrow" is used. With regard to this, the word "Shii" has extended meanings including "happiness", "anger" and "sadness" Fig. 4.

Fig. 4. Categories of emotions extended from the word "Shii"

3   Design Transfer and the Creation of the Word "Shii"

There are three steps in the transfer of design. The first step involves using LINE as the platform for design transfer. Second, in the category of personal created stickers in Taiwan "Mainstream/Dialect Language", five stickers with negative semantic meanings were chosen to be decoded as the basis for design transfer. Third, through the three properties - external (tangible) transfer of cultural product design, mid (behavioral) transit of function, and internal (psychological) transform, the word "Shii" was transferred and served as the basis for the extensions including joy, anger, sorrow, and happiness. In doing so, the positive sticker design model could be carried out.

3.1 Design Platform and Sticker Decoding

Following 2015, after LINE released the platform LINE Designers Market on May 8th, designers can individually design stickers that are in line with their own personal styles and earn profits from them. By January 13th, retrieved information shows that there are a total of 170,509 sets of work on the shelf for sale. Among them, there are 4,807 sets, categorized under "Mainstream/Dialect Language". Since sticker creation is considered a personal creative expression, there are stickers that display negative expressions, making message recipients feel emotionally uncomfortable. Therefore, this study chose LINE as the platform for design transfer.

By decoding LINE stickers, it is hoped that the characteristics of stickers with negative semantic meanings can be grasped in terms of design transfer properties. Furthermore, the positive semantic meanings brought by paper-cut word "Shii" can be further adjusted. In this step, the five stickers with negative semantic meanings under the originally created sticker category "Mainstream/Dialect Language" are first semantically decoded. At the same time, the three main categories of symbol of Peirce are used as a reference for designing stickers: icon, index, and symbol, as shown in Table 1.

Table 1. Sticker categories with negative semantic meanings in LINE

Category	Forms of Image				
LINE Icon	超爽的	卡稱!!!	歸懶趴火		乾!
Title	Super comfortable	Ass	B**ls of raging fire	Sorrow of the b**ls	Dry
Sound	Homophone	Homophone	Homophone	Homophone	Homophone
Index	Smile, opened mouth	Opened mouth	Raging fire, opened mouth	Crying, Opened mouth	Gripped fist, opened mouth
Implication	Comfortable	Very nice	Angry	Sad	Cursing
Symbol	Joyful (Joy)	Happy (Happiness)	Angry (Anger)	Sorrow (Sadness)	Not joyful (Without Joy)

*Source of data: Mainstream/Dialect Language Category of personal creative stickers on LINE

From the content analysis of Table 1, we know that these are negative semantic meanings derived from the application of "homophones" in Chinese. For instance, super comfortable is a reaction from interactions between males and females, implying very comfortable and enjoyable, which is used to illustrate "joy". "Ass" which in Chinese refers to "ass" is used for "cursing" others, but makes oneself feel very pleased and happy. "B**ls of raging fire" uses "testicles on fire" to convey the external emotion of extreme "anger". "Sorrow of the b**ls" is derived from the homophones of "slight" sorrow and "b**ls" of the bottom, which conveys the uncomfortable feeling of the private part. Through this, the inner "sorrow" is transferred. "Dry" and "f**k" words are homophones. Without directly using abusive words to curse others, the emotion of "not joyful" is conveyed. Through the features of Chinese language and exaggerated non-verbal facial expressions and body language, these stickers present specific expressions of correct behaviors. Although the purpose of message is achieved, the imagery design of this approach must be corrected.

3.2   The Properties of Design Transfer

When the message transmission of modern technology LINE stickers is focused on function, we must transfer our technology-centered technical discipline in the past to a sentimental state of mind that is humanity and culture-centered. In other words, this involves considering changes in people's affections and the depth of culture. In addition to promoting the interactions between products and users, cultural connotations are included into the realm of design thinking, forming a pleasant state of communication. Therefore, there are three levels of design transfer properties in this study: (1) outer or tangible level includes: color, texture, shape, surface decoration, lines, detailed handling, and structural composition properties and etc.; (2) middle or behavior level includes: function, operability, convenience of use, security, and integrated relationship properties, etc.; (3) inner or psychological level includes: special implications of products, story-inclined, emotional, and cultural characteristics, etc. (Lin 2004) Through the complete three levels of properties, in addition to the achievement of a better understanding of cultural characteristics, cultural essence is acquired in the process of design, as shown in Fig. 5.

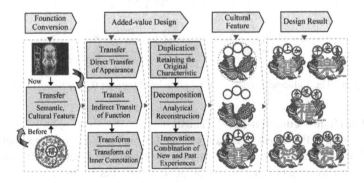

Fig. 5. The transfer model of cultural graphic design

3.2.1   The Whole Tangible-Level Transfer

The first step-transfer of the tangible level considers the outer transfer application of cultural characteristics. Among the LINE sticker samples, outer forms range from figurative to abstract figures or to exaggerated facial expression and body language. They present irregular forms of external patterns transmit the meanings of the images intuitively. In terms of color, to match the outer features, bright colors are used. Therefore, we see designers' personal styles and techniques in these images, but we cannot see the application of deep, cultural connotations. With regard to this, using "cultural connotation" as the basis of design thinking, we carry out thinking processes of accepting or rejecting and reconstruction through the features, color implications, and line properties of paper cutting. In this way, cultural art characteristics are grasped, presenting a new aspect of Value-added design.

In the philosophical ideas of Chinese people, "round" represents perfection and completeness. It is the perfect symbol of everything. Furthermore, "round shape" is one of the important features in modeling: "Advocating perfection". The so-called perfection refers to both wholeness and completeness. When individuals feel as if they cannot be in harmony, the nature of beauty is within its form, "seeking for unity in diversity". This objective basis reflects the perfection of the universe. This concept has formed a complete idealized mindset toward things. Thus, in the folk art works, what it seeks is a "whole and complete" image feature. Paper cutting is one of the examples (Zuo 1998). "Goldfish" is an incarnation of auspicious animals. In terms of color, "red" represents a symbol for vitality and vigor. With respect to this, the transfer of the external level uses "round shape" combination and the image element of "goldfish" in paper cutting. At the same time, "red" is used as the main color scheme for the design composition to show cultural essence and feature, as shown in Fig. 6.

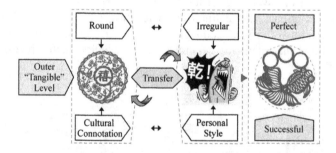

Fig. 6.   The Value-added design of tangible level transfer (Color figure online)

3.2.2   The Hollow Function-Level Transit

The second step is the transit of behavioral level, which is based on users' behavioral mid-level. It emphasizes the indirect feature transit between functions. Through resolution or reconstruction of function, the purpose of transit is achieved.

The artistic style of "paper cutting" is unique. It is different from other three-dimensional, exaggerated image forms of LINE sticker contents. A pair of scissors or a knife neatly trim the edges and create a "hollow" silhouette, creating works of images that are extremely simple, neat, fresh, and pure. In a flat, neat silhouette, a body of various sizes is symmetrically incorporated. This feature has become an exclusive characteristic of paper cutting art. Therefore, in the mid function level transit of stickers, we apply the unique "hollow" feature of silhouette in paper cutting art into images and texts such as joy, happiness, anger, sorrow, and without joy. It is hoped that with the simple and neat style of paper cutting, values can be clearly and directly added onto designs, thereby reflecting the ordinary spirit of internet users and cultural features, as shown in Fig. 7.

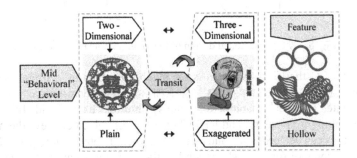

Fig. 7. The Value-added design of function-level transit

3.2.3   The Auspicious Inner-Level Transform

The third phase is the transform of intangible level. This is a level that is based on inner appeals. Emphasis is on the transform of images with special connotations, stories, and cultural features. It is also the main level of transform of this study.

In traditional Chinese culture, paper-cutting art is a kind of phenomenon that is based on the concept of "good fortune". The cultural significance that it implies surpasses oral language. It is even applied in prayers such as "everything goes well with prosperity, happiness and goodness". This feature is pursued for a kind of aesthetics of "fullness, wholeness, brilliance, and radiance". In terms of composition, emphasis is placed on symmetry, whole and complete perspective, and incompleteness is avoided. Most images are in pairs because symmetry and evenness imply calmness and perfection. In terms of color, red, gold and yellow are commonly used in the folk community. In terms of lines, simple and neat lines are full of rhythm and order of life (Tong 1996). With respect to this, this study uses this as the basis of the intangible-level transfer. In the image, "goldfish" is the homophone of "gold" and "jade", which symbolize wealth. The word "Shii" has extended meanings including "happiness", "sadness", "anger", and "without joy". The results of transform are the auspicious language features comprised from Chinese language idioms as shown in Fig. 8.

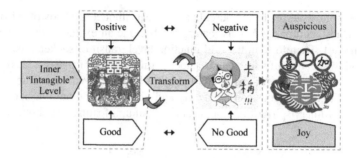

Fig. 8. The Value-added design of the intangible-level transform

With regard to the word "Shii", it is the symbol for "joyful". A combination of "double Shii" (囍) is "joy on top of joy" (喜上加喜), which represents a "very joyful" emotional state. The word "happiness" is the symbol for "happy" and "blissful". Its semantic meaning is "peaceful and happy" (平安喜樂), which conveys the meaning that if all things can be "peaceful" and well, it is a very "happy" enjoyment. The word "anger" is the symbol for "angry", which has the semantic meaning of "rage out of humiliation" (惱羞成怒). It explains that although people external emotional reac-tion such as anger, if we transfer our mood, we will obtain the same "good" result. The word "sorrow" is the symbol for "sadness", which has a semantic meaning of "extreme happiness followed by sorrow" (樂極生哀). It indicates that people must have a sense of alertness and have a grateful heart to avoid the feeling of sorrow. The two words "without joy" express the emotion of "not happy" or "not joyful". It is also a collec-tive way of expressing "anger" and "sorrow". Its semantic meaning is presented through "resentment without joy" (忿恨有不喜), indicating that when people feel unhappy because things turn out badly, we should transfer our negative emotions into the driving force for success. These are all positive thinking in culture and the "auspi-cious" semantic manifestation of paper cutting.

For this reason, "goldfish" and "roundness" are used as the theme of creation in the design of stickers because "gold" and "jade" are applications of Chinese homophones. They symbolize wealth. "Roundness" represents the expectation that all things will turn out "well". Inside the circle, auspicious texts are placed on the images. The auspicious texts show the "stable" and "harmonious" state of the image, specifically transferring cultural connotations onto stickers. It shows "whole" (圓滿) and "perfect" (完美) sticker design, as shown in Fig. 9.

Fig. 9. The complete diagram of Value-added design of paper-cut transfer (Color figure online)

4 Conclusion

When the traditional meets the modern, whether it is ancient historical culture or new-found style of hundred-year-old arts, all of these are for the glorious mission of maintaining cultural traditions. These are manifestations of fashion for the purpose of infusing modern elements into arts.

Through five LINE negative semantic stickers, this study uses traditional paper-cutting "Shii" (喜) word and its extensions - "happiness", "sadness", "anger" and "without joy" words. Through the semantic meanings and characteristics of Chinese characters, positive cultural elements are blended in. In the process of design transfer, three steps of cultural properties - outer tangible form, mid behavior, and inner emotion, three specific conclusions are obtained:

1. With respect to the external level: Using "whole" outer features as the basis of transfer, "round" paper-cut tangible form represents the auspicious outlook of "perfection" and "wholeness". With regard to this, the goldfish-like round shape design and arrangement serve as the foundation of transferring stickers' outer appearance. Red is used as the main color scheme. In addition to emphasizing the symbol of vitality, it also symbolizes perfection in all things.
2. With respect to the behavioral level: The foundation of transfer is based on the function of paper cutting's "hollowness". The simple and neat cutting of the image's edges not only emphasize the simplicity of the work and clearness of the image, the imagery features of "vagueness" and "realness" of "hollowness" also specifically apply humanistic philosophy of silhouette in design. This allows the audience to experience more cultural imaginations and fun through a flat perspective. This is the most significant feature of paper cutting function. Through this, we can clearly and directly reflect spiritual characteristics in cultural connotations.
3. With respect to the internal level: The foundation of transform is based on the cultural connotation of "auspicious" mentality. "Round shape" is a complete, isolated line. It is a symbol for perfectness. The homophone of goldfish is "gold" and "jade". It is a symbol for wealth, which is combined with "roundness" and forms the body of the composition. Next, texts are placed inside the circle to manifest auspicious connotations. For instance, the arrangement of the word "joy" and "joy on top of joy" indicates the text implication of "very joyful". When "happiness" is arranged with "peace and happiness", it conveys simplistic and plain stability. It is something that makes people feel "joyful" and "happy" about. On the other hand, the word "anger" can be presented as "rage out of humiliation" to convey the emotional reaction of anger. However, with the transfer of the mind, one can also obtain a "good" result. "Sorrow" is presented as "extreme pleasure followed by sorrow", which indicates that people must have a grateful heart and be prepared for sorrow. The words "without joy" are presented as "resentment without joy", indicating that when people feel unhappy because things turn out badly, we should transfer our negative emotions into the driving force for success. Last, the texts are used as the theme that emphasizes harmonious and stable perspective in life. Finally, paper-cutting features and cultural connotations are specifically transferred onto stickers with an outer

appearance of the complete "round shape". They are unique, meaningful sticker creations that show that everything is completed with "wholeness".

Acknowledgements. The authors would like to thank Professor John Kreifeldt for offering valuable suggestions. The authors also wish to thank those who contributed to the research.

References

Barthes, R.: Elements of Semiology. Macmillan, London (1977)

Fell, J.P.: The phenomenological approach to emotion. In: Emotion. Brooks/Cole, Monterey (1977)

Gamble, T.K., Gamble, M.W.: Interpersonal Communication: Building Connections Together. SAGE Publications, Thousand Oaks (2013)

Hillman, J.: Emotion. Routledge & Kegan Paul, London (1960)

Han, C.Y.: Image Communication. Wiseman, Taipei (2005)

Hsu, C.-H., Lin, C.-L., Lin, R.: A study of framework and process development for cultural product design. In: Rau, P.L.P. (ed.) IDGD 2011. LNCS, vol. 6775, pp. 55–64. Springer, Heidelberg (2011). doi:10.1007/978-3-642-21660-2_7

Huang, M.F.: Application of pet therapy to healing style design: a case study of LINE stickers design. (Unpublished master's thesis). Department of National Taipei University of Technology, Taipei (2004)

Kreifeldt, J., Lin, R., Chuang, M.-C.: The importance of "feel" in product design feel, the neglected aesthetic "DO NOT TOUCH". In: Rau, P.L.P. (ed.) IDGD 2011. LNCS, vol. 6775, pp. 312–321. Springer, Heidelberg (2011). doi:10.1007/978-3-642-21660-2_35

Lin, R., Sun, M.X., Chang, Y.P., Chan, Y.C., Hsieh, Y.C., Huang, Y.C.: Designing "culture" into modern product: a case study of cultural product design. In: Aykin, N. (ed.) HCII 2007. LNCS, vol. 4559, pp. 146–153. Springer, Heidelberg (2007). doi:10.1007/978-3-540-73287-7_19

Lin, R.: Cultural creativity, value-added design. Art Apprec. **1**(7), 26–32 (2004)

LINE Taiwan: LINE-Blog (2015). http://official-blog.line.me/tw/archives/38020960.html

Norman, D.A.: Emotional Design: Why We Love (or Hate) Everyday Things. Basic Books, New York (2004)

Norman, D.A.: The Design of Everyday Things: Revised and Expanded Edition. Basic Books, New York (2014)

Strongman, K.T.: The Psychology of Emotion from Everyday Life to Theory. Wiley, Hoboken (2003)

Tao, S.Y.: Chinese Mascots. Dong Da, Taiwan (2003)

Tong, W.E.: Auspicious patterns of children play. Natl. Palace Mus. Month. Chin. Art **1**(157), 4–6 (1996)

Verderber, K., Beebe, S.A., Verberber, K.: Inter Act: Interpersonal Communication, Concepts, Skills and Contexts. Oxford University Press, Oxford (2004)

Watson, J.B.: Behaviorism, revised edn. University of Chicago Press, Chicago (1930)

Zheng, Z.M.: Cognitive Psychology. Laureate, Taipei (2004)

Zuo, H.Z.: Chinese Folk Art Modeling. Hu Nan, Chinese (1998)

A Systemic Approach to Concrete Constructions

Bernardino Chiaia, Alessandro Fantilli, and Pier Paolo Peruccio$^{(\boxtimes)}$

Politecnco di Torino, Turin, Italy
{bernardino.chiaia,alessandro.fantilli,
pierpaolo.peruccio}@polito.it

Abstract. In recent years the term design has been overexploited in popular magazines, newspapers and on television. Schools and universities have increased the courses on offer which now include very different design disciplines, from social design to systemic design. The latter, in particular, is the ability to outline and plan the flow of matter and energy from one system to another, within metabolization processes which reduce the ecological footprint and generate a remarkable economic flow. Today designers are asked to strategically design a scenario that doesn't focus only on product innovation as an end in itself, but involves developing broader issues which require the input and expertise of other fields of learning. These issues necessarily include non-traditional economic and industrial models (i.e. Circular Economy, Blue Economy and Bioeconomy). This paper aims to create bridges between the world of construction engineering and design practices based on non-linear industrial models. It stimulates a discussion about systemic design challenges in relation with the concrete structures, evidencing some challenges, open questions and possible new directions.

Keywords: Concrete structures · Systemic design · Construction · Environment

1 Introduction

Systemic Design (SD) is the ability to outline and plan the flow of matter and energy from one system to another, within metabolization processes which reduce the ecological footprint and generate a remarkable economic flow [1]. Its roots are in cybernetics and the complexity of systems and it regards the study of industrial and agricultural processes with an eye to transforming the output of a process in a chain mechanism whose goal is the total elimination of manufacturing waste. The final objective is providing benefits for the whole community: total reduction of the production output, creation of new job placements, new virtuous cooperation among people and better environmental quality. This model takes the inspiration from the foundations of the generative science. More than ever before we need to design products, systems and services efficiently and in an ecologically correct manner. We cannot ignore anymore the complex relationship between action and reaction in natural and artificial systems. Architects and Engineers were already aware of this in the fifties, when they realised how complex and difficult design actually was: "(...) problems have

© Springer International Publishing AG 2017
P.-L.P. Rau (Ed.): CCD 2017, LNCS 10281, pp. 15–24, 2017.
DOI: 10.1007/978-3-319-57931-3_2

a background of needs and activities which is becoming too complex to grasp intuitively" Christopher Alexander wrote in his milestone book Notes on the Synthesis of form [2]. Too many variables became involved and an interdisciplinary approach was needed with the input by experts from more than one field of learning. The process that gradually developed and grew during that period helped to break down disciplinary barriers and moved in the opposite direction to the monodisciplinary and specialist approach of the first half of the nineteenth century, an approach that had been adopted to counter the boom in knowledge, especially scientific knowledge. Today designers are asked to strategically design a scenario that doesn't focus only on product innovation as an end in itself, but involves developing broader issues which require the input and expertise of other fields of learning. These issues necessarily include non-traditional economic and industrial models.

This paper aims to create links between the world of construction engineering and design practices based on non-linear industrial models. It tackles the issue of sustainability in the field of concrete structure applying a systemic approach to satisfy both sustainable and mechanical requirements. The paper offers a critical reading of some case studies and stimulates a discussion about systemic design challenges in relation with the concrete world, evidencing some challenges and new directions toward sustainability.

2 Challenges in Concrete Structures

As shown in Fig. 1, concrete is a composite material made of cement (the binder), water, stone aggregates, and additives. Although concrete is the most widely used material on the earth after water, it is not environmental friendly. Indeed, the production of cement requires high amounts of energy, water and natural resources [3]. Thermal energy usually constitutes around 90% of total energy and is used for activities such as the clinker burning unit and to dry out raw materials. Producing clinker entails carbonizing limestone, which takes place at about 900 °C during which the limestone decomposes into CaO and CO_2. Temperatures of around 1400 °C are needed to decarbonize and later sinter raw meal (Fig. 2). The remaining 10% of the energy is electricity, which is mainly needed to grind coal, raw meal and cement. Water consumption in the cement plant is due to the preparation of the slurry in wet-process kilns. Water is fundamental also for the treatment of the exhausted gas, the quenching of the cement, the cooling down of engines and the dust abatement. It must be remarked that also the other components of concrete are consumed faster than they can be replenished

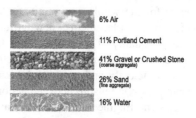

Fig. 1. Composition of concrete

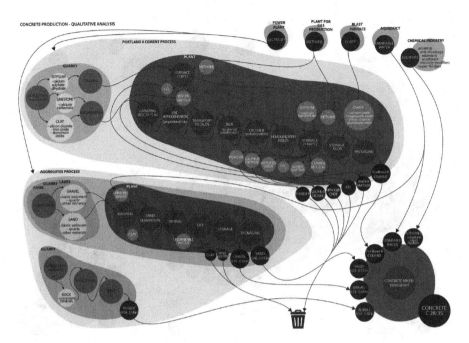

Fig. 2. Concrete production: qualitative analysis

(resource depletion). The world consumption of aggregates exceeds 40 billion tonnes per year, which is twice the amount of sediment carried by all the rivers in the world. Thus, to reduce the impact of concrete on biodiversity, land losses, water supply, climate changes, extreme events, etc., clean technologies need to be applied to concrete production. For these reasons, several efforts are directed to reduce the use of natural raw materials for cement production (limestone, marl, clay, sand, schist, gypsum and pozzolana) or substitute them with byproducts and non hazardous wastes. The literature review provides some interesting examples of "new" materials deriving from external production processes: fly ash, slag, sludge, chemical gypsum, incinerator slag, mill scales and alumina dust. These are all outputs of production processes transformed in input for the cement industry satisfying quality requirements.

Cement manufacturing is highly energy and produces intensive CO_2 emissions. This industry is one of the major causes of global warming on the planet: the direct emission factor of CO_2 in the cement plant mainly depends on the extreme heat required to produce clinker. Therefore it seems urgent reducing its quantity or replacing it with secondary raw materials. Cement, as seen above, could be an interesting repository of industrial, and even agricultural, waste products: i.e., silica fume, steel slag and husk ash. In particular, ash from burning of rice husks is one of the most cutting-edge product deriving from agricultural waste, even if its limited availability. The rice husks are burned without oxygen at a temperature of 800 °C. The product resulting from this process is practically pure silicon. 20% of cement conventionally used in the preparation of concrete could be replaced with this silicon of vegetable origin, which moreover provides protection against corrosion and strengthens the concrete (Fig. 3).

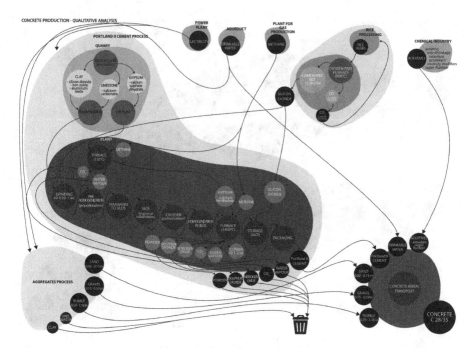

Fig. 3. 20% of cement conventionally used in the preparation of concrete could be replaced with silicon of vegetable origin

Regarding the energy field, cement manufacturing plant demands thermal energy provided by incineration of mainly fossil based fuels. This heavy amount of energy is often integrated by a contribution from the slaughterhouse waste (animal meal). Meal derived from animal meat and bones has a high calorific value to fuel kilns generating significant amounts of calcium salts, which may also be used in replacement of raw materials [4].

2.1 New Breakthroughs in Construction Engineering: The Frejus Highway Security Tunnel

A systemic design approach to building engineering was applied at the beginning of this century to the preliminary study for the construction of a security gallery (second tube) of the Frejus highway tunnel. This 12.9 km long infrastructure connecting the towns of Modane (France) and Bardonecchia (Italy) is one of the main Alpine crossings between France and Italy. It is still under construction and it will enter into service in 2019.

The systemic approach developed by Sitaf spa (Italian society managing the A32 highway and the Frejus Tunnel), Zeri Foundation, Università di Torino (Agricultural Sciences) and Politecnico di Torino (Design, Materials and Mechanical Engineering) raised by the necessity of finding systemic solutions to the excavation of tons of rocky materials and the impact of logistics activities on environment and society.

The main point of this project (unfortunately never implemented) consists in increasing the value of the rock chips (muck) which is mainly a waste and rarely used for construction applications [1]. Physical and chemical analysis of the rock demonstrates the presence of significant amount of calcareous schists potentially used in rice fields to cover the soil. This material has a potential of 230,000 tons of calcite and 150,000 tons of miche, that compensates for the lack of silicon caused by an intensive rice cultivation. The design research leads to a series of considerable benefits: better use of material properties, reversed decline of the impoverishment of soil quality, reduced use of plant protection products (pesticides) and improvement of the soil water retention.

The project provides solutions for placing the material extracted from the tunnel. The approach changes the usual perspective of things: waste becomes resource and resources are used to generate new products. At the same time it works for preventing the soil impoverishment in the areas of Novara and Vercelli (Piedmont region). Generally, the intensive rice cultivations are focused on the maximum output of the plant, taking into account only the grain and not the whole plant. The objective is to increase the value of the whole rice biomass. The analysis of the cycle referred to the rice production shows two products which are not considered at all: the chaff (husk of grains) and the straw. The former is rich in silicon and germanium, the latter in cellulose and lignin. All these high value materials are obtained by the chaff steam explosion process. Germanium could be used in electric and electronic equipments, lignin is a great combustible material which produces clean energy: it comes from season crops and the combustion process produces an amount of carbon dioxide equal to the amount absorbed by the plant during its whole life. Finally, cellulose could be used as a row material in the production of "non oil" plastic material, while silicon could be exploited as semi-conductor in the production of photovoltaic panels.

Summing up, chaff and straw, first considered as a waste, useful only for combustion, are now row materials for applications in several technical fields. Even the muck, rich in natural substances, originally used as a filling material, could be exploited to avoid the excessive use of plant protection products.

3   The Ecodesign of Concrete Structures

Unlike other construction materials, it is impossible to tailor a concrete mixture that can be universally considered the most sustainable. This is due to the following reasons:

- The composition of structural concrete depends on the required performances (or functions), which are not always the same (e.g., one-way or two-way slabs are designed to resist to bending actions, whereas columns are mainly compressed).
- For a specific function, concrete is tailored in different ways, because the availability of natural resources is not the same in all the zones of the Earth.

Recently, rubber from end-of-life tires has been used to achieve a more favorable Life Cycle Assessment (LCA) of structural concrete [5]. In some European Countries, rich of stone quarries but poor of oil fields, such as Italy, it is more convenient to produce the clinker by burning this rubber. Whereas, in the Middle East (e.g., Qatar), where a large quantity of oil can be found, but aggregates for concrete are very scarce, it seems more appropriate the use of rubber in substitution of the natural stone aggregates. In the latter case, the so-called rubber concrete does not perform as the traditional concrete does, and sometimes it is not suitable for structural applications. Thus, LCA can only compare group of concretes available in a specific marked and tailored to fulfill specific requirements, or functions. Moreover, concretes should always be associated to a functional unit, which provides a reference for the inputs and outputs of LCA.

In the case of structural concrete, Damineli et al. [6] suggest the use of a functional unit of performance - the compressive strength f_c - instead of the unit of concrete volume or weight - 1 m^3 or 1 kg. The following indexes can therefore be used in the comparative analysis [6]:

- the Binder intensity indicator (bi_{cs}), which measures the total amount of binder, contained in a cubic meter of concrete, necessary to deliver 1 MPa of compressive strength,
- the CO_2 intensity indicator (ci_{cs}), defined as the amount of CO_2 released for the production of a cubic meter of concrete, to deliver 1 MPa of compressive strength.

As both bi_{cs} and ci_{cs} decrease with f_c (see Fig. 4a), high-strength concretes are in principle more sustainable than normal-strength concretes.

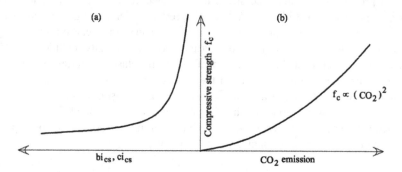

Fig. 4. Concrete strength as the functional unit of LCA: (a) the binder and the CO_2 intensity indicators *vs.* f_c [2]; (b) the amount of CO_2 released for the production of a cubic meter of concrete (with a strength f_c) [3].

The same results can also be obtained through the so-called material performance strategy, which consists of improving the performances to reduce the impact of concrete [7]. Indeed, the amount of concrete, and of the released CO_2 as well, reduces when concrete strength increases, although f_c is proportional to the power 2 of the CO_2 emissions per cubic meter of concrete (Fig. 4b). As an example, the environmental impact of two columns, made respectively with concrete of strength 40 MPa (type 1) and 60 MPa (type 2), are compared in Fig. 5a. The higher the strength, the larger the amount of CO_2 released by a cubic meter of concrete, but the lower the cross-sectional area A and the volume (of concrete and CO_2) of the entire column.

To increase f_c, the content of cement must be increased, whereas the amount of water should remain the same, or reduced by adding superplasticizers to concrete

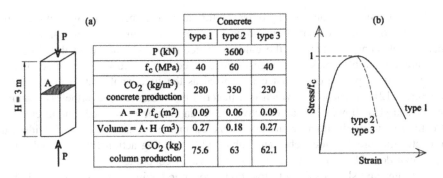

Fig. 5. The environmental impact of three concrete columns: (a) the production of carbon dioxide; (b) the stress-strain relationship of the concretes subjected to uniaxial compression.

mixtures. In addition, the porosity needs to be reduced by using, for instance, fine pozzolanic admixtures [8]. Such additives can also substitute Portland cement, the major responsible of the CO_2 production, without compromising the strength. This is the case of type 3 concrete (Fig. 4a), in which a part (18% in weight) of the cement contained in type 1 concrete has been substituted by the same amount of fly ash and silica fume [9]. In accordance with the substitution strategy suggested by Habert and Roussel [7], the impact of the type 3 column is lower than that of type 1 concrete, despite the same strength and volume of the column.

Nevertheless, concrete mixtures with higher strength show a more brittle behavior. Thus, the performance strategy (applied to type 2 concrete) causes a steeper softening response of concrete, as illustrated in the stress-strain diagrams reported in Fig. 5b. As a result, the column cast with type 2 concrete requires a larger amount of transversal rebar (whose area is in direct proportion to f_c [10]), with respect to the same column made with type 1 concrete. In such cases, the environmental advantage of decreasing the volume of concrete (due to the increment of strength) vanishes, because more stirrups or spirals are needed in compressed columns.

Similarly, the substitution of cement with pozzolanic admixtures can lead to a reduction of the mechanical performances. In particular, in concrete where part of cement is replaced by silica fume and fly ashes (i.e., type 3 concrete), the strength does not change (with respect to type 1 concrete) but the post-peak stage is more brittle, as in high strength concrete (i.e., type 2 concrete) [9].

The above-mentioned brittle response indicates that, in some structures, compressive strength cannot be used as the functional unit of LCA, although f_c is adopted to classify structural concrete. Conversely, as suggested by Fantilli and Chiaia [9], the fracture toughness in compression must be the functional unit of the concretes used to cast columns. When referred to this mechanical property, the use of steel or plastic fibers also produces environmental advantages, because they bridge the cracks and increase the residual stresses in the post-peak stage of Fig. 5b. Conversely, with respect to the compressive strength, fibers do not produce any environmental benefit, because the production of CO_2 increases (a volume of steel is added to the mass of concrete) without modifying f_c [11].

22   B. Chiaia et al.

The necessity of considering other performance parameters is also evident in reinforced concrete (RC) structures prone to cracking in aggressive environments. In such RC elements, to increase the chloride penetration resistance (and therefore the structural durability), cracks in the tensile zones need to be narrow. Hence, crack width is the structural performance that can be used as the functional unit of cracked RC structures [12], instead of f_c (which is a material performance). Nevertheless, Fantilli and Chiaia [13] showed that an effective LCA can also be performed among cracked structures by using the fracture energy of concrete in tension, instead of crack width. In concrete structures without rebar and subjected to bending actions, the optimal functional unit depends on the post-cracking response of concrete.

In beams and slabs made with traditional concrete having a strain softening in the post-cracking stage, flexural strength is more representative than compressive strength. In lightweight concrete slabs investigated by Fantilli et al. [14], the better performances can be observed when granulated rubber substitutes the traditional expanded clay

Table 1. The functional units of some concrete structures.

Type of concrete structure		Functional unit	Ref.
Compressed		Compressive strength	[2, 5]
		Fracture toughness in compression	[5, 9]
RC elments prone to crack in aggressive environments		Crack width	[8]
		Fracture toughness in tension	[9]
Beams and slabs without rebar		Flexural strength in strain softening concretes	[10]
		Maximum bending moment in strain hardening concretes	[11]

aggregate. On the contrary, if the comparative analysis is limited to the compressive strength, the use traditional aggregates (stone or expanded clay) is always more convenient than the rubber from end-of-life tires.

If high performance concretes are used to cast elements subjected to bending actions, the functional unit must be again a structural performance and not a material property (i.e., compressive or flexural strength). As in the case of high strength concrete (type 2 in Fig. 5a), the environmental cost (in term of CO_2 produced per cubic meter) is remarkably higher than that of traditional concrete. Thus, to assess the environmental benefit, the input and output of LCA must be referred to the ultimate (or the maximum) bending moment of beams and slabs made with ultra-high performance concrete [15].

It must be finally remarked that both the flexural strength and the ultimate bending moment depend on the post-peak behavior (and on the ductility) of concrete in tension. For this reason, the possible functional units of structural concrete, as summarized in Table 1, always take into account the fracture toughness of concrete, in a direct or indirect manner.

4 Conclusions

The analysis reported in the previous sections has mainly pointed out four conclusions:

- it does not exist a concrete which can be universally considered the most sustainable. Moreover, the design of concrete structure cannot be only based on the mechanical performances: a systemic approach is necessary when concrete structures have to satisfy both sustainability and mechanical requirements.
- when we talk about production in a SD perspective, we do refer not only to industrial production but also to agricultural production. Within the same territorial context, we need to ensure that agriculture, industry, and the community at large blend harmoniously with the natural system: this is the key to a production model of sustainable growth.
- in SD physical objects could disappear while the methodological process and metaproject become much more important. Open industrial systems are designed to avoid production waste: the focus moves to production in which the output becomes a resource (input) for another production process. Considering the all elements of a system (such as the one applied to the second tube of the Frejus Highway Tunnel), the next challenge would be to design links among different sectors, from agriculture to the cement industry. Is it really possible to trace a line between the tons of muck from the mountain and the rice husks burned to produce green cement? Who are the main professionals to be involved in the project? Where is the limit of a system?

References

1. Bistagnino, L.: Systemic Design. Slow Food, Bra (2011)
2. Alexander, C.: Notes on the Synthesis of Form. Harvard University Press, Cambridge (1964)

3. Van Oss, H.G., Padovani, A.C.: Cement manufacture and the environment. Part II: environmental challenges and opportunities. J. Ind. Ecol. **7**, 93–126 (2003)
4. Ferraro, R., Nanni, A., Vempati, R.K., Matta, F.: Carbon neutral off-white rice husk ash as a partial white cement replacement. J. Mater. Civ. Eng. **22**(10), 1078–1083 (2010)
5. Siddique, R., Naik, T.R.: Properties of concrete containing scrap-tire rubber - an overview. Waste Manage. **24**(6), 563–569 (2004)
6. Damineli, B.L., Kemeid, F.M., Aguiar, P.S., John, V.M.: Measuring the eco-efficiency of cement use. Cem. Concr. Compos. **32**, 555–562 (2010)
7. Habert, G., Roussel, N.: Study of two concrete mix-design strategies to reach carbon mitigation objectives. Cem. Concr. Compos. **31**, 397–402 (2009)
8. Mehta, P.K., Monteiro, P.J.M.: Concrete - Microstructure, Properties, and Materials. McGraw-Hill, New York (2006)
9. Fantilli, A.P., Chiaia, B.: Eco-mechanical performances of cement-based materials: an application to self-consolidating concrete. Constr. Build. Mater. **40**, 189–196 (2013)
10. ACI 318-14 Building Code Requirements for Structural Concrete and Commentary. American Concrete Institute (2014)
11. Fantilli, A.P., Chiaia, B.: The work of fracture in the eco-mechanical performances of structural concrete. J. Adv. Concr. Technol. **11**, 53–67 (2013)
12. Van den Heede, P., Maes, M., De Belie, N.: Influence of active crack width control on the chloride penetration resistance and global warming potential of slabs made with fly ash + silica fume concrete. Constr. Build. Mater. **67**, 74–80 (2014)
13. Fantilli, A.P., Chiaia, B.: Evaluating the eco-mechanical performances of fiber-reinforced concrete. ACI Spec. Publ. **299**, 1–12 (2015)
14. Fantilli, A.P., Gorino, A., Chiaia, B.: Ecological and mechanical assessment of lightweight fiber-reinforced concrete made with rubber or expanded clay aggregates. Constr. Build. Mater. **127**, 692–701 (2016)
15. Fantilli, A.P., Kwon, S., Mihashi, H., Nishiwaki, T.: Eco-mechanical performances of UHP-FRCC: material vs. structural scale analysis. In: Sustainable Built Environment (SBE) Regional Conference, Zurich, 15–17 June 2016 (2016)

Western vs. Eastern: A Reflective Research on the Development of Chinese Animation

Wen Ting Fang[(⊠)], Po-Hsien Lin, and Rungtai Lin

Graduate School of Creative Industry Design,
National Taiwan University of Arts, New Taipei City, Taiwan
f_wenting@163.com, t0131@ntua.edu.tw,
rtlin@mail.ntua.edu.tw

Abstract. Animation in China, stretching across a century, has been through many vicissitudes. In view of the current development of Chinese animation industry, animators imitate the styles of America and Japan excessively, which contain a large number of western elements from character modeling to story building. It has showed a serious lack of confidence, and entered into an erroneous zone with a general over-reliance on imitation. The literature review of this research consists of the comparison of the animated films from different cultures and eras and discuss the related research models. This research is based on animation study model with the method of attribute evaluation, the questionnaire survey and MDS, and will make a large-scale comparative study of domestically and abroad-produced animated films, with the special focus on technical level, semantic level and effectiveness level to deeply investigate the connotation based on the differences between Chinese and Western cultures. To re-produce folk and re-shape traditional art, creators show prominent Chinese unique oriental charm in value, customs, aesthetic concepts, and so on. To raise feasible countermeasures on how to enhance core competitiveness of animated films, it is urgent to grasp the opportunity to regain confidence of Chinese animation.

Keywords: Chinese animation · Western animation · Cultural industry · Technical level · Semantic level · Effectiveness level

1 Introduction

Since first Chinese animated film of Studio scene designed in 1926, Chinese animation have passed centuries progress (Jin 2004). Wan brothers, the early Chinese animators, started a new chapter of Chinese animation with persistent dream and unlimited creativity, although they had the backward technology and equipment and key technology was monopolized. Since Shanghai Animation Film Studio established, a series of classic animated movies with Chinese traditional special features were created, such as ink animation, paper-cut animation and puppet animation. Their animation works got good reputations both at home and abroad, and also create a nationalization model for Chinese animation (Jia and Yan 2012). Chinese animation went down for the impact of market economy and the entrance of foreign animated films. The animation development

© Springer International Publishing AG 2017
P.-L.P. Rau (Ed.): CCD 2017, LNCS 10281, pp. 25–36, 2017.
DOI: 10.1007/978-3-319-57931-3_3

stagnates and the related industrial chain lost. Till 1999, the release of Lotus Lantern reversed the embarrassing situation, becoming the magnum opus which represented the transformation of Chinese animation from arts to markets and also started the reconstruction road for Chinese nationalization animation (Liu 2001).

China has a profound cultural heritage, which has given birth to myriad of unique material. In view of the current domestic development of animation industry, animators imitate the styles of America and Japan excessively, which contain a large number of Western elements from character modeling to story building. Chinese animation has been deeply influenced by the ideological trend of America and Japan, and it has been impacted by commercial consideration (Wang 2011). It has showed a serious lack of confidence, and entered into an erroneous zone with a general over-reliance on imitation, including the excessive worship of the Hollywood and the Disney style, and then gradually lost themselves. Cultural products tend to be uniform; personality has become a fantasy.

Capitalist culture, with its strong economic power of developed countries, has a strong influence on the cultures of other countries, becoming the primary force for culture globalization. In the spread of animations made in the USA, Japan, Britain and other countries, their cultures are introduced as well. With the purpose of opening the world market, the culture transmission is not only an introduction of a national culture but also a transplantation of the values of western hegemony from social, psychological, artistic, and other perspectives. Culture globalization and localization have transformed into a two-way interactive process.

To take up with great challenges with Chinese animation, we should explore how we can boost the development, and meanwhile maintain national characteristics. Accordingly, since there is a huge market potential of Chinese animation, making a breakthrough in the mode of traditional thinking is indeed important to upgrade the domestic cartoon industry. The artistic and technical levels of film assure long-term vitality, while good market returns also offer funding for artistic re-creation, and because of this, it is worthy of value if we can find a perfect fit to combine art and business systematically. If Chinese animation wishes to develop normally, the core of the question is to create the excellent works based on Chinese mainstream culture. The animation creation will increase its value for creating from reality, to grasp the direction and form of the core of Chinese culture, which is a very important factor in finding the road to nationalization (Jia and Yan 2012).

The purpose of this research includes: (1) discuss the core elements of excellent animation; (2) analyze different characteristics of animation among China, American and Japan, to explore the development of Chinese animation; (3) deeply analyze the problems of the development of Chinese animation; (4) state the countermeasures of solutions for the problems.

2   Literature Review

Wu (2015) arranged the information of Chinese animation vertically from the beginning, development and integration, adherence and construction, confrontation and intensification. Animation in China, stretching across an 80-year period, has had many milestones, including what have been described as the two golden ages (1957–1966) and for about a decade from 1978 to the late 1980s (Lent and Ying 2003). According to the study, the process of animation is divided into six phases: the development (1920–1949), the classics (1950–1980), the integration (1980–1990), the adherence (1990–2000), the confrontation (2000–2010), and the exploration (2010–2017).

From 1920 to 1949, Chinese animation film began with the experiment of a combination of live-action and animation since 1920s. In American, the animators got rid of the sideshow and the game at last when the first feature length animation of Snow White and the Seven Dwarves was made by Disney in 1937, which took a substantial step forward in narrative art. Meanwhile, Chinese animation also followed the narrative style of Disney, such as Princess Iron Fan (Bi and Chen 1982).

From 1950 to early 1980, Chinese animation had made great achievements, with many films winning awards in the world such as The Monkey King (1964), Little Tadpole Looking for Mummy (1961) and Ne Zha Nao Hai (1979) (Jin 2004). It was the most glorious parts of Chinese animation, with special style, mystical imagination and classical works. At that time, the most typical feature of American animation was the entertainment like the movie Tom and Jerry. American intends to spread their own national view and values to the audience to reach similar cultural identity.

From 1980 to 1990, there were some excellent works in this decade, which were with profound internal organs and superior quality. But Chinese animation neglected the expansion of markets, with the single sales patterns and the limited creative thoughts, which resulted all followed the creation concepts by the older generations in the 80s (Wu 2015). In terms of creative content, Chinese animation still remained in children education essentially, which lacked of the understanding of contemporary concept for children's education and research of markets in this period. In contrast, the role dispositions of American and Japanese animation were more youthful, vitality and rebellious, which precisely catered to the youngsters' pleasure and occupied a considerable portion of Chinese animation market share (Lin 2012).

Till 1990s, the once-grand Shanghai Animation Film Studio almost didn't have magnum opus. There were some reasons about this phenomenon such as the popular of the processing animation, the impact of foreign TV cartoons and the hysteresis of the management system, resulted in the brain that drained sharply (Lin 2012). In the meanwhile, Lotus Lantern designed in 1999 as a return work for national culture and elaborate works, whereas it also had drawbacks on story structures, characters and scenarios. This film drew on Chinese style but also adapted Disneyesque animal animation, whilst Lotus Lantern was particularly dependent on Pocahontas (1995) for its indigenous (Stephanie 2005).

From 2000 to 2010, the popular Chinese animated films of this period nearly imitated the foreign cartoons, specifically, lack of innovation. In order to let audience be curious about the works and transmit its culture, American was adept at creating with exotic cultures and reorganizing the cultural symbols in shape, narrative and technology by American style (Mi and An 2011). Kung Fu Panda, an animated film produced and distributed by Dream Works in 2008, has attracted worldwide attention. There is a popular tendency in Hollywood movies that Chinese elements have been gradually adopted with a feature of intense cultural impressions and Chinese values (Guo 2010).

From 2010 to 2017, Chinese animation (e.g., Monkey King: Hero is Back, Quebec Pull and Big Fish & Begonia) starts to explore and develop in the progress of cultural globalization. Monkey King: Hero is Back is the modern exploitation of traditional cultural resources, with Chinese spirit in audio-visual language area and cultural expression, and it contains the idea of modernity between a docking with pop culture and visual effects (Yang 2015). The same year, American framers had created masterpieces of different styles under constantly attempt, such as Kubo and two strings.

For the communication theory, Chen et al. (2014) built the research framework of turning poetry into painting, as shown in Fig. 1. from artist (addresser) creating art works (message) to audience (addressee), and the communication process should meet three aspects that are the external perception of technical level, the meaning cognitive of semantic level and the inner feelings of effectiveness level, combined with artist's creation mode and audience's cognitive mode, analyzing communication factors and function to explore audience cognition process (Lin 2015), and providing theoretical foundation for the animation model.

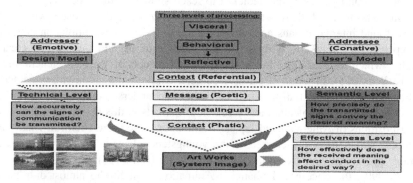

Fig. 1. The research framework of turning poetry into painting

3   Methodology

3.1   Animation Research Model

This research is based on animation study model with the method of attribute evaluation, the questionnaire survey and MDS, and will make a large-scale comparative study of domestically and abroad-produced animated films, with the special focus on technical level, semantic level and effectiveness level to deeply investigate the connotation based on the differences between Chinese and Western cultures. Based on the previous studies (Lin 2014), the animation research model which combining communication theory with animation evaluation factors, was proposed to explore the model of animation research as shown in Fig. 2. A visual and acoustic communication of animation is a process of coding through the the artists' creation and letting the audience decode. To discuss the differences between different times and places of the animation

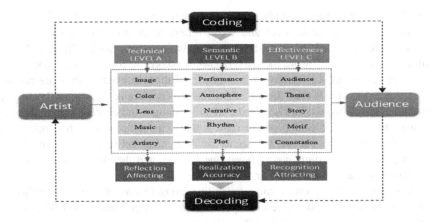

Fig. 2. The animation research model

through image, color, lens, music and artistry on technical level; performance, atmosphere, plot, narrative and rhythm on semantic level and audience, theme, story, motif
and connotation on effectiveness level.

3.2 Procedure

This study consisted of 4 steps:

Step1. Through initial literature review, taking the historical time as the axis, the
researcher selected 13 animated films in three countries from the 6 stages. Every
film is closely related to the factors of the cultural background, the economic
environment, the political system and the social values with the same period, as
shown in Table 1.

Table 1. 13 animated samples

1920—1949		1950—1980		
P1	P2	P13	P3	P4
1980—1990		1990—2000		
P5	P9	P6		P7
2000—2010		2010-2016		
P10	P11	P8		P12

P1 Princess Iron Fan	P2 Snow White and the Seven Dwarfs	P3 The Monkey King	P4 Tom and Jerry
P5 The Nine-Clored Deer	P6 Lotus Lantern	P7 The Lion King	
P8 Monkey King: Hero is Back	P9 Zaze no tani no Naushika	P10 Pleasant Goat and Big Wolf	
P11 Kung Fu Panda1	P12 Kubo and the Two Strings	P13 Baby Tadpoles Look for Their Mother	

Step2. Through animation study model, five relative attributes were found out from technical level, semantic level and effectiveness level, and then the descriptive words were presented to establish the questionnaire. There are 13 films, and each film has 15 questions, using the scale of 5-order score. According to the content of the subjects, subjects subjectively evaluated and thought whether they are consistent, and selected 1 if they thought the content was extremely consistent with the meaning of left words, and selected 5 if they thought the content was extremely consistent with the meaning of the right words. The subjects were 60 undergraduates from National Taiwan University of Arts, aged between 18–30 years old. During the test, the films were played one by one, and the subjects evaluated 15 questions of each animation after watching.

The reliability of the questionnaire: reliability refers to consistency or stability of measurement results, and the reliability of this study coefficient was 0.801, so the reliability of this study has reached the standard.

Step3. Through the MDS analysis, the films were recombined. This study used MDS to explore the similarity and the dissimilarity of 13 films so as to understand the characteristics of each animation, and displayed the relative position of individuals in two-dimensional space.

Step4. Through the data analysis, to summarize the list, to sum up the three aspects of the evaluation by subjects, so as to compare the different characteristics of animation in China, American and Japan, this study deeply dug into the current problems of Chinese animation.

4   Results and Discussions

4.1   The Construction of Attribute Assessment

Based on the research model, this research cited two relative adjectives from the attributes on three levels, to explore the differences between the animated films. After extensive collection of information about relevant adjectives of Animation assessments, through consultation with relevant experts, they were converted into 15 adjective groups, as shown in Table 2.

Table 2. The attribute assessment of 15 adjective groups

The Attribute Assessment		
Technical Level	Semantic Level	Effectiveness Level
F4 Image: Abstract — Realistic	F7 Performance: Lively — Boring	F1 Audience: Kid — Adult
F5 Color: Colorful — Gray	F13 Atmosphere: Warm — Cold	F2 Theme: Educational — Entertaining
F6 Lens: Normal — Original	F8 Narrative: Variant — Single	F11 Story: Clear — Obscure
F15 Music: Passionate — Melodious	F9 Plot: Dramatic — Straightforward	F3 Motif: Romantic — Lifelike
F14 Artistry: Traditional — High-tech	F10 Rhythm: Tight — Soft	F12 Connotation: Moral — Social

4.2 The Cognition of The Spatial Distribution

Through MDS analysis, its purpose is to use the perceptual map for the analysis of perceptual position, and then we can see the evaluation of animation from technical level, semantic level, effectiveness level and the distribution of animation in the two-dimensional space. 13 films were evaluated by 15 criteria, and the evaluation matrix of the mean was taken as the basis of the reference analysis.

According to the Fig. 3, (1) early Chinese classic animation p3 and Disney animation p2 formed a cluster. Furthermore, two films that were the first colorful feature-length animation in their countries had high value in the history of world animation, and they had similar attributes in style. (2) Chinese animation p5, p1, p13, p6 compared with American and Japanese had different distribution area, which belonging to the fourth quadrant. The attributes of Chinese early animation were significantly different from the foreign animation, and ethnic style was sui generis. (3) p11, p7, p8, p12 that had the similar attributes from the perspective of division formed a cluster, and study tried to explore the reason that the recent return of p8 was combined with other excellent animation. (4) p4 and p10 had many commonalities, but also had great differences. (5) p9 that was distributed separately in a single region was obviously different from other films with a unique personality characteristics.

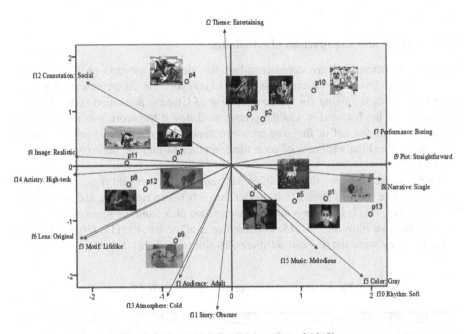

Fig. 3. The spatial distribution map of 13 films

Group1. p2 and p3, with high artistic value and distinctive national characteristics, were early colorful feature-length animation. p3 of Chinese classical myths created a fabulous romantic atmosphere, and p2 from Grimm's fairy tales was easy to understand and colorful. So it was named: Early Classic.

Group2. Even though there was no cluster between p6, p5, p1 and p13, they possessed attributes of traditional skills, single narrative and simple plot. The four cartoons have obvious national characteristics, which emphasized the importance of using national methods and drew on Chinese painting, folk art, Peking Opera, traditional frescoes and modern technology. So it was named: Traditional Skill.

Group3. p11, p7, p8 and p12 all used a superb technical means from two-dimensional, three-dimensional till stop-motion to reflect inheritance and innovation in lens language, character design, narrative and plot. So it was named: Cutting-edge Technology.

Group4. p4 and p10 could be compared with each other because they were all short sketch animation and extremely humorous. But they have big difference on the artistic quality. For instance, p10 that had rough production methods and it was hard to reach p4 on visual effect. So it was named: Humor and Entertainment.

Group5. p9 was a highly stylized Japanese animation. Director Hayao Miyazaki's works contained the reflective issues of dream, environmental protection and existence, with beautiful image, variegated scene and imaginative color. His animation of the unique world view and the humanistic values influenced the trend of Japanese animation in past ten years, and he was good at using animated techniques to reflect human civilization. So it was named: Unique style.

4.3 Analysis and Comparison of Attributes

Through tabulation analysis, comprehending the views of subjects on the technical level, semantic level and effectiveness level, to compare the differences among three countries, and then looking for the development of Chinese animation context. 3 was the average in the list, and it was the greater tendency if the score was much less or bigger. The numeric list of the gray area represented the scores are similar. Another table summarized the attributes of each film, in order to find the differences from the three levels.

Early Classic: it shows that two films had similar attributes and typical features by themselves. The score of f6 and f8 is greater than 3 between two films, and the score of f1, f5, f11, f14, f9, f7, f12 is less than 3 between two films, and the score of f2 is closer to 3 between two films. P2: f4, f15, f3 at both ends of the list, P3: f15, f10 at both ends of the list, they were the obvious attributes, as shown in Table 3.

Table 3. The evaluation of the sorts by Early Classic

	f15<	f14<	f12<	f10<	f11<	f1<	f5<	f7<	f9<	f13<	f4<	f3<	f2<	f8<	f6
P3	1.63	1.88	1.92	2.08	2.12	2.14	2.18	2.31	2.35	2.78	2.78	2.78	3.04	3.14	3.27
	f11<	f7<	f3<	f5<	f1<	f14<	f13<	f12<	f9<	f10<	f2<	f6<	f8<	f15<	f4
P2	1.39	1.92	1.94	2.10	2.20	2.24	2.24	2.31	2.45	2.98	3.08	3.20	3.24	3.33	3.41

Country	Animation	Technical level(A)		Semantic level(B)		Effective level(C)	
		Similarity	Difference	Similarity	Difference	Similarity	Difference
China	p3 *The Monkey King*	Color-Colorful, Artistry-Traditional, Lens-Original	Music-Passionate, Image-Abstract	Performance-Lively,	Rhythm-Tight	Audience-Kid, Story-Clear,	
America	p2 *Snow White and the Seven Dwarfs*		Music-Melodious, Image-Realistic	Plot-Dramatic, Narrative-Single	Atmosphere-Warm	Connotation-Moral	Motif-Romantic

Traditional Skill: p1, p5, p13, and p6 had the similar attributes such as f14, f12, f11, f3 and f1 which belonged to effectiveness level. Therefore, the four films formed their own distinctive artistic features with different skills through the creation of technical and semantic level. Among which, the unique attributes of p1 were f8, f5, f15 and f10, and the unique attributes of p5 were f5 and f4, and the unique attributes of p13 were f13, f2, f5 and f15. P6 was the 90's animation work and its unique attributes were f2 and f9, which was regard as the regression of National creation and delicate art. But p6 had the defect that imitated with Hollywood animation from the design of character and the structure of the story, as shown in Table 4.

Table 4. The evaluation of the sorts by Traditional Skill

P1	f14<	f12<	f15<	f10<	f11<	f7<	f1<	f9<	f6<	f3<	f4<	f2<	f13<	f8<	f5
	1.59	2.20	2.22	2.35	2.59	2.63	2.76	2.76	2.86	2.88	3.02	3.18	3.22	3.43	4.00
P5	f14<	f2<	f11<	f5<	f3<	f12<	f7<	f4<	f1<	f13<	f9<	f6<	f15<	f10<	f8
	1.90	2.08	2.35	2.35	2.37	2.39	2.51	2.53	2.82	2.90	2.94	2.96	3.06	3.06	3.10
P13	f14<	f13<	f11<	f2<	f12<	f1<	f4<	f3<	f6<	f7<	f8<	f9<	f10<	f15<	f5
	1.86	2.06	2.10	2.16	2.22	2.27	2.39	2.49	2.84	2.92	3.55	3.63	3.65	3.78	4.20
P6	f12<	f2<	f14<	f11<	f7<	f9<	f10<	f1<	f5<	f3<	f15<	f13<	f8<	f4<	f6
	1.98	2.02	2.08	2.10	2.14	2.29	2.29	2.31	2.57	2.65	2.65	2.86	2.94	3.16	3.22

Country	Animation	Technical level(A)		Semantic level(B)		Effectiveness level(C)	
		Similarity	Difference	Similarity	Difference	Similarity	Difference
China	p1 *Princess Iron Fan*	Artistry-Traditional	Color-Gray, Lens-Original, Music-Passionate	Performance-Lively	Narrative-Single, Rhythm-Tight, Plot-Dramatic,	Audience-Kid, Story-Clear,	
	P5 *The Nine-Clored Deer*		Color-Colorful, Lens-Original		Plot-Dramatic, Rhythm-Tight	Connotation-Moral, Motif-Romantic	Theme-Educational
	P13 *Baby Tadpoles Look for Their Mother*		Color-Gray, Image-Abstract, Lens-Normal, Music-Melodious		Atmosphere-Warm, Narrative-Single, Plot-Straightforward, Rhythm-Soft		Theme-Educational
	P6 *Lotus Lantern*		Color-Colorful, Lens-Original, Music-Passionate		Plot-Dramatic, Rhythm-Tight,		Theme-Educational

Cutting-edge Technology: four films used similar technical level (f5, f15, f14, f6) and semantic level (f7, f9, f10, f8) to reach the different effectiveness level. The score of P8(f14) was 4.39 which was close to p11, the high tendency of cutting-edge technology, and it indicated that subjects thought the level of technology of p8 had been comparable with Hollywood. At semantic level, the scores of the four films were close. At semantic level, p8 was suitable for adults to watch with the romantic theme and the moral story. Moreover, p11 and 12 all had cultural connotations, p11: Chinese elements, p12: Japanese elements, which used Hollywood narrative style to convey the mainstream values of the United States under the cultural form, as shown in Table 5.

Humor and Entertainment: according to the Table 6, it showed that p4 and p10 had the same market position at effectiveness level. The scores of f11, f1 and f2 were close, but p4 (f2) was higher than p10 (f2). By contrast, the humor of p4 was better than p10. There were quite differences between p4 and p10 at technical level and semantic level, and it could be clearly seen from the scores of f6, f4, f15, f7, f9 and f10 that the original lens language, the memorable characters, the vivid performance and the fleshy plots were the features of p4. By comparison, there were some defects of p10 such as the single lens language, the stiff performance and the boring plots.

Table 5. The evaluation of the sorts by Cutting-edge Technology

P8	f5<	f7<	f9<	f10<	f11<	f12<	f15<	f2<	f8<	f13<	f1<	f3<	f4<	f6<	f14
	2.00	2.04	2.24	2.29	2.37	2.39	2.47	2.84	2.86	3.00	3.06	3.43	3.57	3.73	4.39

P7	f7<	f11<	f9<	f5<	f1<	f15<	f2<	f13<	f10<	f3<	f14<	f8<	f12<	f4<	f6
	1.45	1.76	2.04	2.04	2.29	2.39	2.55	2.59	2.63	2.76	2.78	2.86	3.06	3.45	3.69

P11	f7<	f9<	f11<	f5<	f10<	f13<	f15<	f12<	f1<	f8<	f3<	f2<	f4<	f6<	f14
	1.73	2.02	2.04	2.16	2.31	2.39	2.55	2.61	2.69	2.80	3.10	3.14	3.49	3.96	4.45

P12	f7<	f9<	f5<	f11<	f10<	f15<	f12<	f2<	f8<	f3<	f4<	f13<	f1<	f6<	f14
	1.88	2.06	2.20	2.31	2.35	2.51	2.59	2.59	2.76	2.80	2.98	3.00	3.16	3.92	4.12

Country	Animation	Technical level(A)		Semantic level(B)		Effectiveness level(C)	
		Similarity	Difference	Similarity	Difference	Similarity	Difference
China	P8 *Monkey King: Hero is Back*	Color-Colorful, Music-Passionate, Artistry-High-tech, Lens-Original	Image-Realistic	Performance-Lively, Plot-Dramatic, Rhythm-Tight, Narrative-Variant	Atmosphere Between Warm and Cold	Story-Clear	Connotation-Moral, Theme-Educational, Motif-Romantic, Audience Between Kid and Adult
America	P7 *The Lion King*		Image-Realistic		Atmosphere-Warm		Theme-Educational, Audience-Kid, Motif-Romantic
	P11 *Kung Fu Panda1*		Image-Realistic		Atmosphere-Warm		Connotation-Moral, Theme-Entertaining
	P12 *Kubo and the Two Strings*		Image Between Abstract and Realistic		Atmosphere Between Warm and Cold		Connotation-Moral, Theme-Educational, Audience-Adult, Motif-Romantic

Table 6. The evaluation of the sorts by Humor and Entertainment

P4	f11<	f10<	f1<	f7<	f15<	f9<	f5<	f8<	f14<	f13<	f3<	f12<	f6<	f4<	f2
	1.41	1.69	1.84	1.84	1.98	2.02	2.37	2.43	2.57	2.59	2.90	3.18	3.35	4.43	

P10	f11<	f1<	f6<	f5<	f3<	f4<	f14<	f13<	f10<	f12<	f8<	f15<	f9<	f7<	f2
	1.59	1.65	2.12	2.31	2.49	2.67	2.67	2.69	2.76	3.14	3.18	3.18	3.43	3.57	3.84

Country	Animation	Technical level(A)		Semantic level(B)		Effectiveness level(C)	
		Similarity	Difference	Similarity	Difference	Similarity	Difference
America	P4 *Tom and Jerry*	Artistry-Traditional, Color-Colorful	Lens-Original, Image-Realistic, Music-Passionate	Atmosphere-Warm	Performance-Lively, Rhythm-Tight, Plot-Dramatic, Narrative-Variant	Story-Clear, Audience-Kid, Theme-Entertaining	
China	P10 *Pleasant Goat and Big Wolf*		Lens-Original, Image-Abstract, Music-Melodious		Performance-Boring, Plot-Straightforward, Narrative-Single,		

Unique Style: As can be seen from the Table 7, f4, f5, f6 and f14 were the higher propensity of attributes of p9 at technical level, which was very appealing with the somber tinge, the distinctive style and the excellent lens language. f7, f9, f8, f10 and f13 were the higher propensity of attributes at semantic level, with "time and space cross " construction and the multiple perspectives narrative. Finally, it achieved the subject cognition on the effect level, which reflected the reflection of the social reality, and had the function of educational influence.

Table 7. The evaluation of the sorts by Unique Style

P9	f7<	f9<	f2<	f8<	f10<	f5<	f14<	f11<	f3<	f15<	f13<	f12<	f1<	f4<	f6
	1.76	1.98	2.02	2.51	2.73	2.88	2.90	2.94	3.16	3.18	3.29	3.35	3.49	3.51	4.00

Country	Animation	Technical level(A)	Semantic level(B)	Effectiveness level(C)
Japan	P9 *Zaze no tani no Naushika*	Image-Realistic, Color-Gray, Lens-Original, Artistry-Traditional	Atmosphere-Cold, Performance-Lively, Narrative-Variant, Rhythm-Tight, Plot-Dramatic	Theme-Entertaining, Audience-Adult, Connotation-Social

Chinese early classic animation with the elegant artistry, the exquisite conception and the elegant color had a lower proportion of favorite by subjects. There were some problems of these cartoons, such as the simple plot, the single lens language and the kid audiences. If national tradition wants to be accepted by the modern audiences, it should add modern elements appropriately, such as support of advanced technology and the contemporary humanities. Monkey King: Hero is Back was the exploration of the cultural regression to realize the modern mining of cultural elements.

Pleasant Goat and Big Wolf which earned good ratings in China with easy understanding cartoon mode, had grasped a group of young audiences. This animation, which had the commercial success, cannot conceal a wide gap with Tom and Jerry in artistry. Tom and Jerry could be classic because of rich imagination, vivid expression and subtle actions. If Chinese animation intends to gain praise by public, it should enhance the artistic aesthetic value.

5 Summary

The core elements of excellent animation: exquisite craftsmanship, vivacious character design, elegant and meticulous color collocation, gripping background music and proceed from the camera language on Technical level; appropriate situation atmosphere, living performance, rich storyline, pluralistic narrative technique and unique rhythm on semantic level; the clear theme, the cultural connotation or reflect reality on effectiveness level.

At present, Chinese animation is still at the stage of exploration, and there is a big gap between America and Japan. On technical level, it's lack of modeling diversity and innovation, and it has younger-age trend; on semantic level, role performance is not good at creating a favorable atmosphere, and the plot of the narrative is single and simple; On effectiveness level, lack of emotional touching, it didn't pay attention to the mining of traditional art and culture connotation. But at present there are also several exploratory animation powerful return, such as the Monkey King: Hero is Back, which has a successful exploration on cultural context in terms of technology.

There are some reasons for the lack of Chinese animation. For instance, "China School " emerging from 1960s to 1980s showed a serious limitation for artistic creation, such as the variation for traditional culture and the shortage of national culture education. Thus, younger generations are not familiar with local culture and traditional artistic form lack of ideas, values and imagination on the using of Chinese cultural elements. Another factor is the loss of the talented, which is the key to the competition between current Chinese animation and foreigner's. Still another factor concerns the swift development of modern society and economical transition as well as the expansion of national animation market. Under such circumstances, animators still have to satisfy the various demands of the public, and as a result, they have been lost in blind imitation.

According to the analysis, we can see that early Chinese animation has strong ethnic characteristics, whereas they are gradually disappeared after the 90's. It is the key to restore national tradition that we should focus on potential talents, train them to be more culturally-oriented in education, and pay attention to the integration of tradition and modern. The animation talents must be cultivated in the aspects of the script, the design, the performance, etc.

The creation of Chinese animation still depends on imitation from technical level to effectiveness level. The government must support the originality, which will become the strong backing for animation industry. Moreover, it is important to expand perfect animation markets and substantially build up successful brands and Monkey King: Hero is Back has provided a successful reference.

Acknowledgements. The authors would like to thank Professor Rungtai Lin for offering the research framework and valuable suggestions. The authors also wish to thank those who contributed to the research.

References

Bi, C.Y., Chen, Z.C.: China's first animated cartoon and several first. Movie Rev. **2**, 29 (1982)

Chen, S.J., Lin, C.L., Lin, R.: The study of match degree evaluation between poetry and paint. In: The 5th Asian Conference on the Arts and Humanities (ACAH 2014), April 2014

Guo, H.: Re-exploration of the founding of Chinese animation in 1920s. Journal. Q. **103**(1), 106–112 (2010)

Jia, F., Yan, H.: The artistic spirit of the animator – retrospecting the faith, efforts and achievements of the animator of Shanghai art and film factory. Film Lit. **18**, 4–7 (2012)

Jin, T.Y.: The founding and maturity of "Chinese school of animation". Film Art **01**, 57–60 (2004)

Lin, C.L., Chen, C.L., Chen, S.J., Lin, R.: The cognition of turning poetry into painting. J. US-Chin. Educ. Rev. B **5**(8), 471–487 (2015)

Liu, X.: The nationalization and modernization of Chinese animation. Chin. Telev. **06**, 38–42 (2001)

Lent, J.A., Ying, X.: China's animation beginnings: the roles of the wan brothers and others. Asian Cinema **14**, 56–69 (2003)

Lin, Q.: Chinese Animated Movies. Ph.D. dissertation, Shanghai Normal University (2012)

Mi, G.F., An, R.: The value export of American animated cartoon and the strategy of cultural communication. Chin. Telev. **05**, 69–72 (2011)

Stephanie, D.: Little Friends: Children's Film and Media Culture in China. Md.: Rowman & Littlefield Publishers, Lanham (2005)

Yang, X.Y.: A phenomenal film: the symposium review of Chinese animated film monkey king: hero is back. Contemp. Cine. **09**, 198–200 (2015)

Wang, F.: Analysis of the lack of animation creation in China today. Film Lit. **06**, 54–55 (2011)

Wu, X.: Chinese animation on history studies from a comparing perspective. Ph.D. dissertation, Chinese National Academy of Arts (2015)

A Study of Communication in Turning "Poetry" into "Painting"

Ya-Juan Gao[3(✉)], Li-Yu Chen[2], Sandy Lee[3], Rungtai Lin[1], and Yige Jin[4]

[1] Graduate School of Creative Industry Design,
National Taiwan University of Arts, No. 200, Zhongshan Rd., Zhongli District,
Taoyuan City 320, Taiwan
rtlin@mail.ntua.edu.tw
[2] Department of Interior Design, Chung Yuan Christian University,
No. 16-28, Ln. 36, Guizi Rd., Taishan District, New Taipei City 243, Taiwan
chenly99@gmail.com
[3] Sandy Art Studio, No. 59, Sec. 1, Daguan Rd., Banqiao District,
New Taipei City 220, Taiwan
78343821@qq.com, slee@mail.mcut.edu.tw
[4] School of Fashion & Craft, Shanghai Art and Design Academy,
851 Jiahang Rd., Jiading District, Shanghai 201808, China
yigeqll@sina.com

Abstract. This study proposed a research framework to study the communication of turning poetry into painting by using 21 paintings with their poetic titles. A total of 57 graduate students participated in the study. Subjects were asked to evaluate the fitness of paintings with their poetic title based on the six functions of communication theory. The results showed that the approach can be applied for evaluating the painting effectively and provide artists with an idea how to concentrate their efforts at the creation stage, and it is easy to communication with audience. In addition, the research framework seems to be a better way to explore the understanding of turning poetry into painting, which is clearly worthy for further research.

Keywords: Communication · Cognitive human factors · Poetry · Painting

1 Introduction

Recently, artistic literature citizens apply to a variety of artistic media, symbols, and metaphors; in order to independently create and perform expressions about their own ideas and communicate their life experience. For every artist was first an amateur (Emerson 1883), thus, the arts are the media which provide powerful and essential means of social communication. Taking poetry as an example, poetry is a form of verbal art that uses the aesthetic qualities of language. Poetry has been more generally regarded as a fundamentally creative act employing language. Poetry uses forms and conventions to suggest different interpretations of words or to evoke emotive responses (Lin et al. 2015). On the other hand, painting and graphic design are the forms of visual

© Springer International Publishing AG 2017
P.-L.P. Rau (Ed.): CCD 2017, LNCS 10281, pp. 37–48, 2017.
DOI: 10.1007/978-3-319-57931-3_4

art, which is a mode of creative expression consisting of representational, imaginative, or abstract designs produced by the application of color to two-dimensional artwork. Turning poetry into painting deals with complex objects which are interdisciplinary in their own nature. This nature appears to be suitable for an opening to "read" in different ways and multiple perspectives are available to analyze them (Chen et al. 2014, 2015).

In the early 20th century, artists began to experiment with nonrepresentational art, in which formal qualities such as line, color, and form were explored rather than subject contents. Today, painting vacillates between representational and nonrepresentational forms (Beatty 2011; Beatty and Ball 2010; Mare 2010). Frankel (1957) stated that in Chinese literary tradition, the Chinese character of "writing" has been used in the dual sense of "to write" and "to paint", and that the expression of "to look" at a painting literally means "to read" a painting. The idiom of "idyllic" (詩情畫意, shiqinghuayi), which literally means a quality suggestive of poetic and picturesque, used as the criteria to evaluate a Chinese painting (Yeh and Lin 2014; Yeh et al. 2014).

A poem creates visual images in the reader's mind, just as a painting creates images in the viewer's eyes. A great painting has much more below the surface than the first impression. When a viewer is faced with a painting, the audience is presumably required to interpret the elements provided by decoding and then constructing meaning by encoding (Fiske 1990). Thus, the audience has to discover or construct a meaning and then attribute that meaning to what is in the painting (Laude and Denomme 1972; Cantoia and Antonietti 2000). A poem is a painting made with words. In the analysis of poems and paintings, it is important to consider whether or not the texts are situated in the poems in a way that is analogous to the illustrations of the paintings (Laude and Denomme 1972). It has been argued that the idea of turning poetry into painting should be interdisciplinary, as well as mentally challenging and creative (Michel 1999). Mare (2010) explored whether or not visual images and works of art can be "read," and raised important questions as to whether the description and interpretation of a work of visual art can be referred to as the "reading" of that work.

Thinking about art as a process of social communication, this article intends to understand how the relationship between the artist and the audience has potentially altered in social communication. For the communication between artist and audience, three levels are identified to the study of communication, namely technical, semantic and effectiveness levels (Fiske 1990; Lin 2007). Based on the communication studies and previous studies (Lin 2007; Lin et al. 2015), therefore, this study proposed a research framework which could be used for a continuous research of a deeper understanding to explore the nature of turning poetry into painting.

2 Framework for Turning "Poetry" into "Painting"

Based on Lin's studies (2007), a framework was proposed for turning poetry into painting as shown in Fig. 1 which consists of three main parts: poetic works, creation model and artwork. The creation model focuses on how to extract the semantic features from poetic works and then transfer these features into the painting. The creation model consists of three steps; *identification* (extract semantic features from original poetry), *translation* (transfer them to drawing elements) and *implementation* to finally create a painting. The

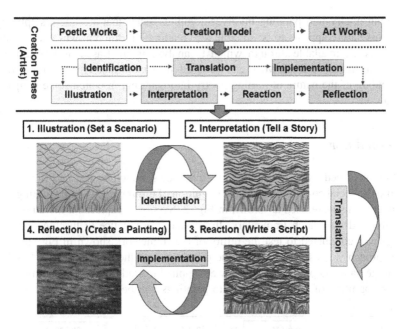

Fig. 1. Framework for turning "Poetry" into "Painting"

creation model is described as follows: (1) Identification phase: The semantic features are identified from original poetry, then painter uses their experience to obtain, evaluate, and utilize drawing elements from the poetry. (2) Translation phase: painter translates the semantic features to the painting within a chosen poetry. The painter achieves some depth and experience of practice in these semantic features and produces artwork for the interaction between artist and poetry. (3) Implementation phase: the implementation phase expresses the drawing elements with the semantic features, the meaning of poetry, an aesthetic sensibility, and the flexibility to fit the painting with the poetry.

Based on the creation model and previous studies (Michel 1999; Lin 2007), the turning poetry into painting model is used by scenario and story-telling approaches. In a practical process, four steps are used to design a cultural product, namely; illustration (set a scenario), interpretation (tell a story), reaction (write a script), and reflection (create a painting) as shown in the bottom of Fig. 1. The four steps of the cultural product design process are described as follows: (1) Illustration/set a scenario: this step seeks to analyze the semantic features in order to determine the key features to represent the scenario. (2) Interpretation/tell a story: based on the previous scenario, some interactions should be explored in this step. According to the interaction, a user-experience approach is used to describe the features of the painting by a story-telling. (3) Reaction/write a script: this step is to develop an idea sketch in text or pictograph form based on the developed scenario and story. During this step, the scenario and story might require modification in order to transform the semantic meaning into a painting. (4) Reflection/create a painting: this step deals with previously identified semantic features and the context of the painting. At this point, all semantic features should be listed in a matrix table which will help artist check the cultural features in the creation process (Lin 2007).

Turning poetry into painting involves complex issues that are interdisciplinary in nature. This nature appears to be suitable for "reading" in different ways, and multiple perspectives are available through which to analyze them. Based on the above discussions, the research framework can be used in a continuous search for a deeper understanding of the nature of turning poetry into painting, in which some conjectures can be tested.

3   Methodology

This study involved using questionnaires, interviews, matching test and fuzzy ratings to explore the social communication and cognition of turning poetry into painting. Three different sessions were used as shown in Fig. 2. Session 1 explored a literature review and established a research framework. In Session 2, a practice of turning poetry into paintings was conducted to test the utility of the framework shown in Fig. 2. Then, a rating approach was used to evaluate the paintings with their poetic title in Session 3. Multivariate data and protocol analysis were applied to study the social communication and the recognition of turning poetry into paintings will be explored (Lin et al. 2015).

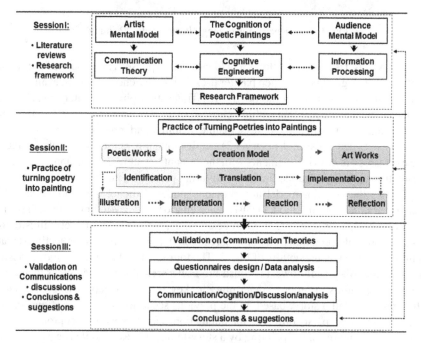

Fig. 2. Method for studying the communication of turning poetry into painting

3.1   Research Framework

An artwork must reach three functions to express its significance through the symbol system including (1) Signification: the art work can express a kind of significance; that is, the artist's intentions can indeed be expressed through the art work; (2) Expression: the art work may represent the artist's feelings; that is, through the art works, the artist's imaginations thoughts and feelings can be reproduced; (3) Communication: the results of signification and expression can be sent to the viewer only when the artist's thoughts and the viewer's ones are identical (Fiske 1990; Jakobson 1987).

In the communication model, Jakobson (1987) proposed six constitutive factors with six functions in an act of communication. The six constitutive factors are as follows: addresser, addressee, context, message, contact, and code. Each of these factors determines a different function in each act of communication: emotive, conative, referential, poetic, phatic, and metalingual. For the mental model of cognitive engineering, Norman (2013) proposed a conceptual model that includes three parts: design model, user's model, and system image. For emotional design, Norman (2002) proposed three levels of processing: visceral, behavioral, and reflective for emotional design. Therefore, a research method combining the previous studies was proposed to explore the issue of turning poetry into painting as shown in Fig. 3.

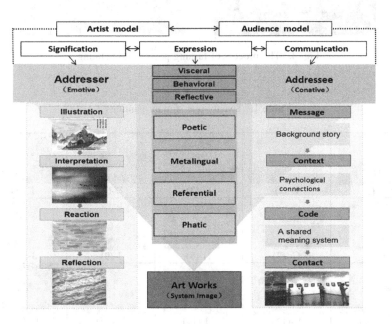

Fig. 3. Research framework for study turning poetry into painting

3.2   Practice of Turning Poetry into Painting

The amateur painter Ms. Lee conducted the practice of turning poetry into painting. The painter was asked to read the paper entitled – Turning Poetry into Paintings: An Experiment in Visualization by Michel (1999) and two related papers (Hsu et al. 2011; Lin 2007). Then, the twelve abstract paintings were painted according to the selected poetry following the four steps of illustration, interpretation, reaction and reflection for turning poetry into paintings. She developed the poetic title based on the framework

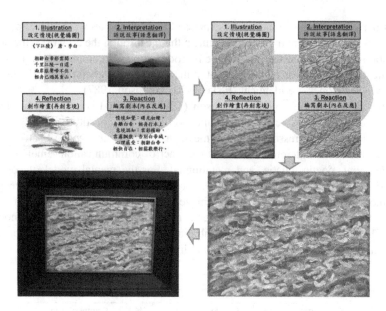

Fig. 4. The process of turning poetry into painting

Table 1. Twenty-one stimuli paintings

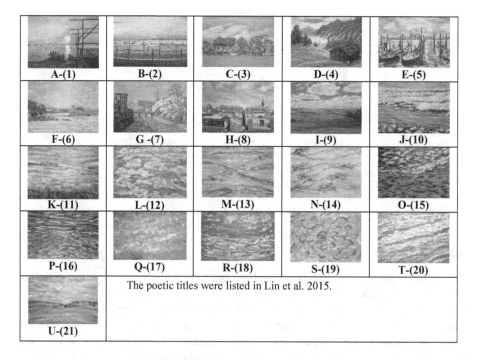

shown in Fig. 1 and expressed her own feeling of the painting and focused on whether the poetic title expressed the mood of the painting. For example, Fig. 4 showed the process of turning a poem entitled – *I set out with a farewell to Bai-Di Town glittered with morning clouds*, to a painting (Lin et al. 2015).

The study was based on the Lee's 21 paintings as shown in Table 1, which includes nine landscape paintings (A1 to I9) and twelve abstract paintings (J10 to U21). The nine landscape paintings, which were comprised of nature scenes containing clouds, were used as the base from which the author proposed poetic titles related to clouds. The key factor for the proposal of these poetic titles was that they had to help the audience to more easily understand the mood of each painting. Therefore, in creating the titles, the first thing that had to be done was to associate viewers' main visual impressions of the paintings with their life situations. Meanwhile, the poetic titles developed by the author were also recognized by the painter as sufficiently similar to the painter's intentions (Lin et al. 2015).

3.3 Validation on Turning Poetry into Painting

This study involved using questionnaires' interviews and design and recognition. Two schools and fifty-seven college students served as the subjects. Based on the research framework (Fig. 3), questionnaire used the six functions of communication theory to rating the fitness of painting with its poetic title as shown in Table 2. Question is a numerical open-ended question, the first item in the question asked the fitness between the painting and its title from 0% (not fit) - 100% (complete fit) to fill in; the remaining six questions are about the feelings of the intensity from 1 (not agree) to 100 (very agree) to fill in, so do the questionnaire data input by the original value of the statistical analysis. All subjects were university student volunteers from the northern and southern regions of Taiwan. A total of 57 subjects: 24 males and 33 females between the ages from 28 to 41 participated in the study. Subjects were told the purpose of the experiment. Then they were asked to rate each painting with its poetic title according to the questions (Chen et al. 2014, 2015).

Table 2. The rating of fitness of idyllic image and six functions

* I set out with a farewell to BaiDi Town glittered with morning clouds, to a painting.

1. Rating the fitness of "Idyllic image" between the painting and title.

2. Rating the fitness of "Emotive" between the painting and title

3. Rating the fitness of "Poetic" between the painting and title.

4. Rating the fitness of "Referential" between the painting and title

5. Rating the fitness of "Phatics" between the painting and title.

6. Rating the fitness of "Metalingual" between the painting and title

7. Rating the fitness of "Conative" between the painting and title.

4 Results and Discussion

4.1 Comparisons Between Landscape and Abstract Paintings

The mean and standard deviation of fitness of idyllic image are 76.20 and 11.90. For the six functions, their mean and standard deviation are Emotive (73.7/14.5), Poetic (73.4/12.0), Referential (69.2/12.9), Phatic (68.5/14.2), Metalingual (68.5/13.2) and Conative (72.1/12.8), respectively. Through the Pearson Correlation analysis, the functions of communication to each other were positively related as showed in Table 3. The stimulus paintings include landscape paintings and abstract paintings. Through the independent t-test analysis, in order to analyze whether there are differences in the cognition of communication elements between landscape and abstract paintings, as shown in Table 4. For the total image of idyllic, the result showed significance which indicates that the idyllic image of landscape painting is better than that of abstract painting (80.0 vs. 72.4; $t(57) = 6.50$, $p < 0.001$). For the six functions of communication, the results (Table 4) showed the differences between the landscape and abstract paintings are significant, and the fitness of the landscape paintings are obviously higher than those of the abstract paintings.

Table 3. The correlation analysis of the communication functions

	Idyllic	Emotive	Poetic	Referent.	Phatic	Metalin.	Conat.
Idyllic	1						
Emotive	0.71**	1					
Poetic	0.73**	0.83**	1				
Referential	0.66**	0.81**	0.79**	1			
Phatic	0.70**	0.82**	0.85**	0.90**	1		
Metalingual	0.73**	0.78**	0.80**	0.90**	0.91**	1	
Conative	0.72**	0.85**	0.90**	0.84**	0.88**	0.88**	1

**Correlation is significant at the 0.01 level (2-tailed).

Table 4. Paired samples t-test of landscape painting (L) and abstract painting (A)

	Mean difference (L vs. A)	T-test
Idyllic image	80.0 vs. 72.4	6.50***
Emotive	75.9 vs. 71.6	3.05**
Poetic	76.1 vs. 70.7	4.40***
Referential	71.3 vs. 67.0	3.00**
Phatic	72.1 vs. 64.9	5.85***
Metalingual	71.8 vs. 65.2	4.46***
Conative	75.2 vs. 69.0	4.17***

*$p < 0.05$, **$p < 0.01$, ***$p < 0.001$

The highest and lowest paintings of fitness rating of landscape and abstract paints are listed in Table 5. For the landscape paintings, the highest rating is painting A-1 and the lowest rating is painting C-3. The paired-sample t-test was used to compare the

Table 5. Paired samples t-test of landscape painting (L) and abstract painting (A)

	Mean (A1vs C3)	t-test	Mean (J10 vs R18)	t-test
Emotive	81.8 vs. 71.6	5.27***	74.2 vs. 68.4	2.54*
Poetic	81.7 vs. 75.0	4.03***	74.0 vs. 70.8	1.62
Referential	80.9 vs. 66.6	6.58***	70.4 vs. 63.3	2.78**
Phatic	76.6 vs. 69.9	3.01**	68.4 vs. 62.6	2.51*
Metalingual	78.0 vs. 67.2	5.00***	68.1 vs. 62.0	3.02**
Conative	81.0 vs. 72.0	3.98***	73.1 vs. 65.3	2.75**

*$p < 0.05$,**$p < 0.01$,***$p < 0.001$

difference between painting A-1 and C-3, and the result showed that painting A-1 is higher than painting C-3. In addition, the six functions of painting A-1 and C-3 was compared using the paired-sample t-test and the results showed in Table 5 and Fig. 5. For example, the emotive function of painting A-1 is significantly higher than the painting C-3 (81.8 vs. 71.6; $t(57) = 5.27$, $p < 0.001$). The other functions are poetic function (81.7 vs. 75.0; $t(57) = 4.03$, $p < 0.001$), referential function (80.9 vs. 66.6; $t(57) = 6.58$, $p < 0.001$), phatic function (76.6 vs. 69.9; $t(57) = 3.01$, $p < 0.01$), metalingual function (78.0 vs. 67.2; $t(57) = 5.00$, $p < 0.001$) and conative function(81.0 vs. 72.0), $t(57) = 3.98$, $p < 0.001$), respectively. Thus, for the six functions of communication, the highest degree of fitness with landscape painting are significantly higher than the lowest degree of fitness.

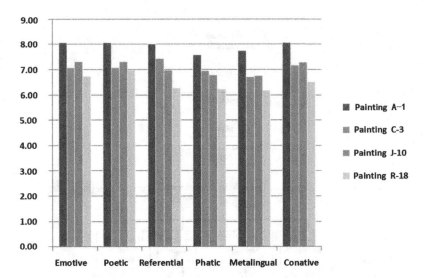

Fig. 5. The comparisons of the six functions of communication

For the abstract paintings, the highest rating is painting J-10 and the lowest rating is painting R-18. The paired-sample t-test was used to compare the difference between painting J-10 and R-18, and the result showed that painting J-10 is higher than painting

R-18. In addition, the six functions of painting J-10 and R-18 was compared using the paired-sample t-test and the results showed in Table 5 and Fig. 5. For example, the emotive function of painting J-10 is significantly higher than the painting R-18 (74.2 vs. 68.4; $t(57) = 2.54$, $p < 0.05$). The other functions are poetic function (74.0 vs. 70.8; $t(57) = 1.62$, $p = 0.11$), referential function (70.4 vs. 63.3; $t(57) = 2.78$, $p < 0.01$), phatic function (68.4 vs. 62.6; $t(57) = 2.51$, $p < 0.05$), metalingual function (68.1 vs. 62.0; $t(57) = 3.02$, $p < 0.01$) and conative function (73.1 vs. 65.3; $t(57) = 2.75$, $p < 0.01$), respectively. Thus, for the six functions of communication, the highest degree of fitness with abstract painting are significantly higher than the lowest degree of fitness with emotive function, referential function, phatic function, metalingual function and conative function. Hence, only the poetic function is no different in the abstract painting group that may need further studies to explore.

4.2   Discussion

This study used communication theory as a technique for evaluating paintings which based on the poetry. The rating focused the six functions of communication of turning poetry into painting. The results showed that the six functions of communication could be applied for evaluating the paintings effectively and could provide artists with an idea of how to concentrate their efforts at the creation stage of turning poetry into paint communication easily with the audience. Some results are summarized as follows: (1) There are positive correlations among the functions of communication. The results

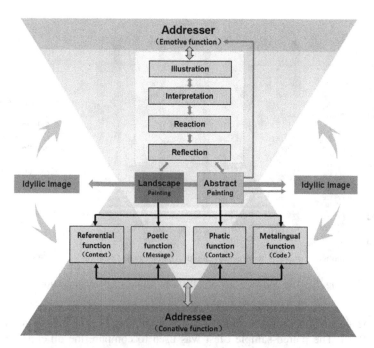

Fig. 6. A framework for exploring the process of turning poetry into painting

show that the emotional, poetic, referential, phatic, metalingual and conative function are related to each other in turning poetry to painting. (2) When compared landscape paintings with abstract paintings, landscape paintings are higher than abstract paintings in emotive function. Thus, how to enrich the artist's emotion for the expression of emotive function needs to be studied in further study. (3) In the study of the degree of fitness between poetry and painting, the functions of communication with the highest degree of fitness in landscape paintings are higher than those with the lowest degree of fitness. But for the abstract painting, the poetic function showed no significant difference that needs to explore the reason for understanding.

5 Conclusion

For the turning poetry into painting, the painter (addresser) wanted successfully communicate with the audience (addressee), and from the functions of communication were studied to understand the conceptual difference between artist and audience. The communication approach appears to have an advantage over the subjective interpretation of artwork. A framework for exploring the process of turning poetry into painting was proposed as shown in Fig. 6.

Although the idea of using a communication approach to explore the evaluation of artwork is quite simple, this study is only the first step in testing the utility of communication functions as an approach for understanding the creation and recognition of turning poetry into painting and is clearly worthy of more in-depth study.

Acknowledgments. The authors would like to thank Professor Rungtai Lin for directing the research. Special thanks to Sandy Lee of Sandy Art Studio for authorizing the use of her paintings in this study.

References

Beatty, E.L.: The intersection of poetry and design. In: Proceedings of the 8th ACM Conference on Creativity and Cognition (C&C 2011), pp. 449–450. ACM, New York (2011)

Beatty, E.L., Ball, L.J.: Poetic design: an exploration of the parallels between expert poetry composition and innovation design practices. In: Proceedings of the 1st DESIRE Network Conference on Creativity and Innovation in Design, pp. 62–71. Desire Network, Lancaster (2010)

Cantoia, M., Antonietti, A.: To see a painting versus to walk in a painting: an experiment on sense-making through virtual reality. Comput. Educ. **34**(3), 213–223 (2000)

Chen, S.J., Lin, C.L. Lin, R.: The study of match degree evaluation between poetry and paint. In: Proceedings of the 5th Asian Conference on the Arts and Humanities (ACAH 2014), Osaka, Japan (2014)

Chen, S.J., Lin, C.L., Lin, R.: A cognition study of turning poetry into abstract painting. In: The Fifth Asian Conference on Cultural Studies (ACCS 2015), Kobe, Japan (2015)

Emerson, R.W.: Poetry and imagination. Lett. Soc. Aims **8**, 3–4 (1883)

Frankel, H.H.: Poetry and paintings: Chinese and western views of their convertibility. Comp. Lit. **9**(4), 289–307 (1957)

Fiske, J.: Introduction to Communication Studies. Routledge, London (1990)

Hsu, C.H., Lin, C.L., Lin, R.: A study of framework and process development for cultural product design. In: Rau, P.L.P. (ed.) IDGD 2011. LNCS, vol. 6775, pp. 55–64. Springer, Heidelberg (2011). doi:10.1007/978-3-642-21660-2_7

Jakobson, R.: Language in Literature. The Belknap Press of Harvard University Press, Cambridge (1987)

Laude, J., Denomme, R.: On the analysis of poems and paintings. New Lit. Hist. 3(3), 471–486 (1972)

Lin, R.: Transforming Taiwan aboriginal cultural features into modern product design: a case study of a cross-cultural product design model. Int. J. Des. 1(2), 45–53 (2007)

Lin, C.L., Chen, J.L., Chen, S.J., Lin, R.: The cognition of turning poetry into painting. J. US-Chin. Educ. Rev. B 5(8), 471–487 (2015)

Mare, E.A.: Can one "read" a visual work of art? S. Afr. J. Art Hist. 25(2), 58–68 (2010)

Michel, K.F.: Turning poetry into paintings: an experiment in visualization. Art Educ. 52(3), 6–12 (1999). The Practice of Art Education

Norman, D.A.: Emotional Design – Why We Love or Hate Everyday Things. Basic Books, New York (2002)

Norman, D.A.: The Design of Everyday Things: Revised and Expanded Edition. Basic books, New York (2013)

Yeh, M.L., Lin, P.H.: Beyond claims of truth. J. Arts Humanit. 3(1), 98–109 (2014)

Yeh, M.L., Lin, R., Wang, M.S., Lin, P.H.: Transforming the hair color design industry by using paintings: from art to e-business. Int. J. E-Bus. Dev. 4(1), 12–20 (2014)

The Impact of Chinese Traditional Cultural on the Gesture and User Experience in Mobile Interaction Design

Ren Long[✉], Xu Liu, Tian Lei, Xue Chen, and Ziliang Jin

Department of Industrial Design,
Huazhong University of Science and Technology, Wuhan, China
longren@hust.edu.cn

Abstract. Many designer using traditional cultural elements in mobile application interaction design, this design concept enhance user's cognitive and emotion. Users will be inspired by an inner cultural identity when using App, and they will feel delighted about the operation. So integrate the traditional cultural elements into the interactive system is necessary, however, how to design the cultural element can conform to the user's mental model, and have a positive impact on the user experience, that is the direction of the paper.

This paper is focused on the impact of integration of the traditional cultural elements into the interactive system on the user experiences. Research is divided into two parts, part 1 for the extraction of characteristics of traditional cultural elements, the part 2 for cultural elements into the different model (Design Model, User Model, and System Model) of the effects on the user experience.

Keywords: Mobile HCI · Traditional culture · Mental model · User experience

1 Background

Traditional culture is overall characterization of ideological culture, ideology in national history. With the development of China's economic, the heritage of traditional cultural began to be national attention. A lot of mobile application that have traditional culture characteristics become the indispensable tool in people's life.

Many designer using traditional cultural elements in mobile application interaction design, this design concept enhance user's cognitive and emotion. Users will be inspired by an inner cultural identity when using App and they will feel familiar about the operation and also feel delighted. But in the process of practical, many mobile Apps just embedded culture elements through the way like duplicate, blend etc. The designer did not fully consider that there is a gap between user's understanding of cultural elements and gestures, this will lead to different degree of user experience problems.

Integrated the traditional cultural elements into the interactive system is necessary, however, how to design the cultural element can conform to the user's mental model, and have a positive impact on the user experience, that is the direction of the paper.

© Springer International Publishing AG 2017
P.-L.P. Rau (Ed.): CCD 2017, LNCS 10281, pp. 49–58, 2017.
DOI: 10.1007/978-3-319-57931-3_5

2 Literature Review

The famous American economist, Toffler said: "human need high technology, more need high emotional, people is not only need the satisfaction of material needs, but also need the spiritual and cultural needs. Once the products are given a good emotion, will shorten the distance of people and products on the emotional, behavioral cultural identity, it will convey different cultural background groups demand for cultural emotion". Cultural identity will affect people cognitive and emotional to products, product design should be in accordance with the cultural values of the Times, through the design product to influence the culture of human society, to guide the formation of a new culture form [1].

Tradition is a process of accumulation, in this process formed many cultural phenomena, cultural style, cultural material, these elements which influence the development of traditional culture and art design, the traditional Confucian aesthetic concept in the form of a subtle infection native concept of life and aesthetic perception [2].

The Confucian traditional culture elements integrated into the APP interaction design, can close the distance between the user cognition and the APP, when users see or use in the APP will be inspired by an inner identity, will generate cheerful, familiar with the operation of the psychological [3].

However, the traditional culture elements of integrated into the APP, will indirect effect on the information, about the user's selection, receiving, cognitive, operation. And cultural elements should be in what form integrated into the interactive system, can enhance the function of the elements and cultural affinity, and not to a user's cognitive burden.

"Mental Model", the concept was first put forward by Kenneth Craik, he thinks that mental Model is used to interpret the individual's perception of the internal relations of things in the real world [4]. Then, many scholars from different angles to improve and complement the concept, such as Indi Young thinkmental model is the change of emotion and thought when people trying to execute an action [5]. Due to mental model application in various fields, so the definition is different priorities. But after a summary can be found, most of the cognitive scientists or scholars to define mental model descriptive definitions and purposes. In short, mental model is the way of thinking and ideas which hidden in the human brain, it represents the external reality mapping model which is formed by the internal representation in the brain, these models affect the person's external behavior.

The formation of a mental model mainly relies on the anticipation of memory. When faced with new information, previously stored in the brain of a background, experience, will be out one by one, when these form a system, mental model was formed. When in contact with new things, mental models will be guiding behavior [6].

In the field of human-computer interaction, mental model can help designers a better understanding of the user, also can help users to better understand and use the product. Norman try to split interaction process into three models related to the mental model: Design Model, User Model, and System Model [7]. Design model is a bridge between the system model and user model, it determines the usability of the product. Design models tend to be more user mental models, the higher the usability of the product, the user will feel program easier to understand and use, the users learning and using cost will be reduced [8].

When we are in the APP design on traditional culture, the role of mental models is particularly important, designer based on the understanding of traditional culture, and integrate the traditional cultural elements into the interface and interaction design, then the form the Design model of the product. And user access to cultural APP scenario, their behavioral logic in this scene is influenced by the cultural background, the user for the understanding of traditional culture to build a mental model, affect their understanding of the cultural elements of the interface and interactive operation. If the design of cultural elements of the metaphor is not in conformity with the user's mental model, the user may use the wrong gestures, unable to accomplish its task, as a result affect the user experience.

This paper is focused on the impact of integration of the traditional cultural elements into the interactive system on the user experiences. Research is divided into two parts, part 1 for the extraction of characteristics of traditional cultural elements, the part 2 for cultural elements into the different model (Design Model, User Model, and System Model) of the effects on the user experience.

3   Experiment I - The Traditional Culture Element Feature Extraction

The goal for this part is to select typical ones from multiple Chinese cultural elements to be candidates for the integration into mobile apps.

Traditional elements is not only the Chinese ancient pattern, design, artifacts, also including sounds, smells, scene, many experts put the traditional culture elements into the recessive and dominant characteristics. Recessive characteristics through the value identity and aesthetic to express, dominant characteristics through the appearance shape, color, totem and so on. In this paper, the research object for the dominant characteristics of cultural elements.

We choose 6 typical cultural representations with various forms, based on cultural identity, semantic and symbolic meaning, and the relationship with interaction. These representations were Chinese Calligraphy, Pippa, Ink Painting, Kung Fu, Chinese Chess, and Chinese Opera. These representations contain visual characteristics, tactility, can represent the typical Chinese culture and nationality.

We used these cultural representations as the samples in Experiment I (shown in Fig. 1), and invite 20 student aged 17–30 to evaluate these samples according to the aspects of "Typicality of Chinese Culture", "Element -Gesture Correlation", "Semantics", "Identification", "Easy-to-use", "Memorability" and "Degree Of Preference", using 5-point scale.

The results indicate that:

- These 6 culture representations have significant differences in "Typicality", "Semantics", "Identification", "Easy-to-use" and "Memorability", with the corresponding α values smaller than the threshold 0.01 (Shown in Table 1).

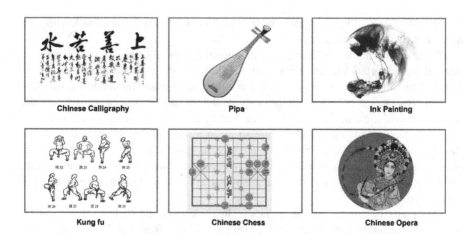

Fig. 1. Chinese culture representations

Table 1. Results of one-way ANOVA

ANOVA

		Sum of squares	df	Mean square	F	Sig.
Typicality	Between groups	17.767	5	3.553	6.320	.000
	Within groups	64.100	114	.562		
	Total	81.867	119			
Semantics	Between groups	22.267	5	4.453	9.543	.000
	Within groups	53.200	114	.467		
	Total	75.467	119			
Identification	Between groups	23.767	5	4.753	9.659	.000
	Within groups	56.100	114	.492		
	Total	79.867	119			
Easy to use	Between groups	23.875	5	4.775	8.634	.000
	Within groups	63.050	114	.553		
	Total	86.925	119			
Memorability	Between groups	19.842	5	3.968	6.839	.000
	Within groups	66.150	114	.580		
	Total	85.992	119			

- Participants feel more familiar to Ink painting, it is very close to the scenes of life, ink painting are compatible to utilize in interaction design, Ink painting shown a high score in "Typicality of Chinese Culture", "Element -Gesture Correlation", "Semantics", "Identification", "Easy-to-use" and "Memorability". The probably reason lead to this results are: (1) Ink painting is more common in scenes of life, it has a higher identification level; (2) Ink painting have the attributes and characteristics of Confucian culture; (3) Ink painting is the elements that can be directly control and influence by action, it can naturally utilize into interactive system.

Based on the experimental results, we confirm choose Ink Painting as experimental material (Fig. 2).

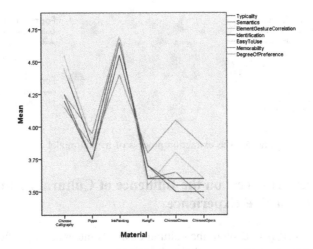

Fig. 2. Chinese culture representations' scores in dependent variables

4 Experiment II Materials-The User Mental Model and the Design Model Extraction

First, let ordinary users and professional designers to express their understanding of Ink Painting element, and then extract the user's mental model and design model, and use the two models in experiment II, to test the matching degree between the System Model, User Mental Model, and Design Model, and their relationship with the user experience.

This experiment mainly use User Interviews and Think Aloud Protocol, to understand the user and designer how to think about Ink Painting element. Reference Indi Young of construct a mental model method, this research will be summarized the mental model of the extraction steps as follows:

User stories - sort out mental information (from the interview recording video and Think Aloud Protocol) - mental information extracted from "character description"- put same properties of "features" together - form a "stack", and name it - put the same attribute features "stack" together - form the "mental model", and the graphic performance.

Experimental invite 20 students, ask each participant some questions, including describing the understanding of Ink Painting element, recall the Ink Painting application scenarios at ordinary time's life, and the behavior of the interaction process. Let the participants in the case of without prompt situation, repeat to complete the above questions, write and make records.

Based on the extraction of mental information, clear up the interview results of 20 students, to map the user and designer mental model figure of Ink Painting, the process as shown Fig. 3. The user's and designers mental model of Ink Painting will be used in the experiment II as materials.

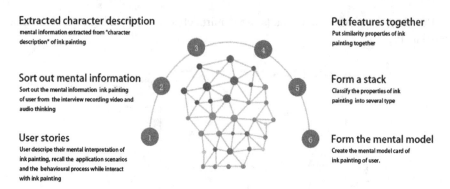

Extracted character description
mental information extracted from "character description" of ink painting

Sort out mental information
Sort out the mental information ink painting of user from the interview recording video and audio thinking

User stories
User descripe their mental interpretation of ink painting, recall the application scenarios and the behavioural process while interact with ink painting

Put features together
Put similarity properties of ink painting together

Form a stack
Classify the properties of ink painting into several type

Form the mental model
Create the mental model card of ink painting of user.

Fig. 3. The extraction process of mental model

5 Experiment II – Test on the Influence of Cultural Elements on the Interactive Experience

The goal of this part is to explore the cultural elements integrate into different models could affect the user experience in the mobile apps.

The independent variables in this experiment are "Different Product Model", and "Task Type". According to the extraction model, we divided "Product Model" into 3 conditions: "System Model", "User Model" and "Design Model". "System Model" means that the practical operation of the machine and software model, can be understood as a model of the engineer. "User Model" means the users of Ink Painting element model of cognition. "Design Model" means the designers of Ink Painting element model of cognition. We choose our phones commonly used functions and operations, such as unlock, dial-up, writing, viewing articles, Ink Painting elements can be natural integrate into these operations, so the four operations as the experiment tasks.

The controlled variables include "experimental facilities", "Experimental environment", "and Interface elements design form". We designed 12 kinds of experiment materials (shown in Fig. 4) and designed the questionnaire based on the PACMAD mobile usability model. Test subjects including Feedback Clarity, Memorability, Easy to Understand, also contains the emotional factors, for example, the degree of innovation, satisfaction. Integrated these factors, this experiment involved with the 11 items to measure the various aspects of the user experience.

The subjects are 20 young people aged 18–30, in which half are male and half are female, 12 are from department of industrial design, and the other 8 are from other areas. All subjects are experienced iOS users.

The results indicate that:

- When ink painting integrate in Design Model and User Model with different level and form, the design model shown significant impact on "Satisfaction For Culture Element", "Easy To Use", "Degree Of Preference", this results state that integrate culture elements in design model can enhance the user experience, at the same time, the usability of interface and the rate of user successfully finish the task both improved;

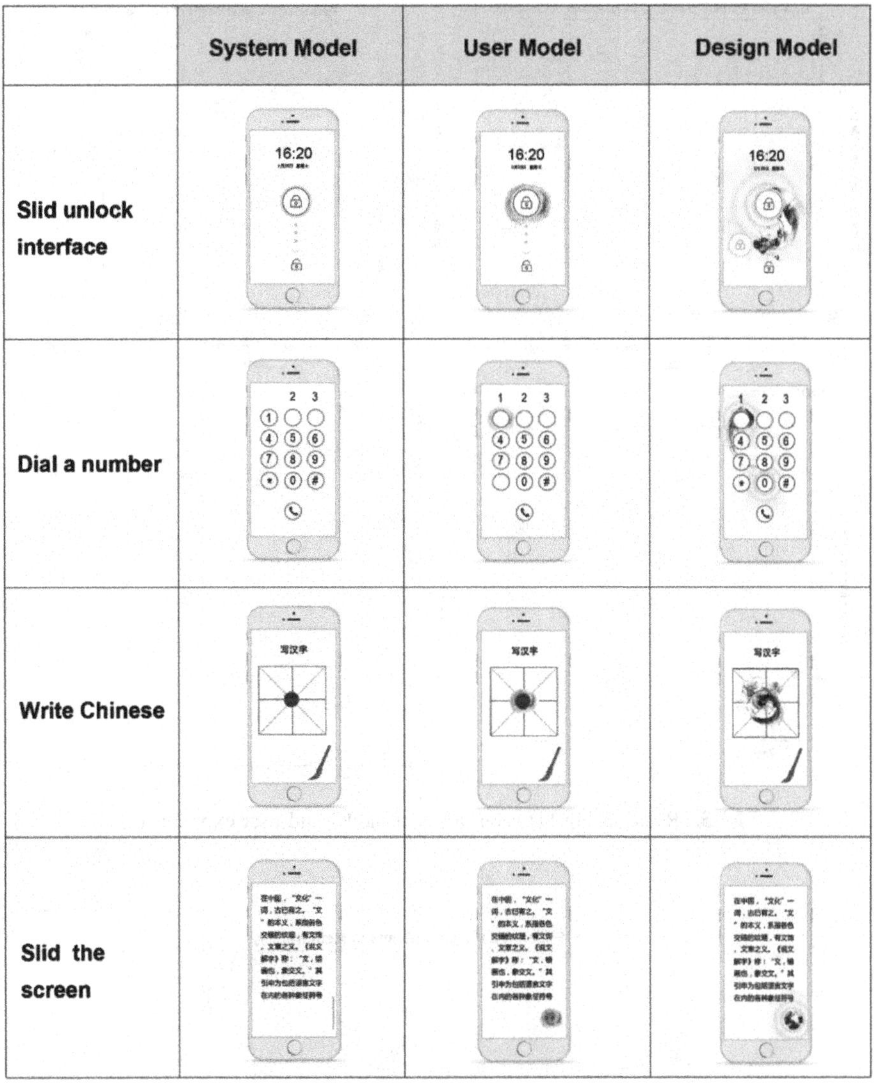

	System Model	User Model	Design Model
Slid unlock interface			
Dial a number			
Write Chinese			
Slid the screen			

Fig. 4. Materials for experiment II

when the effect of design model exceeded expectations of user, user will be impressive to our product and clearly feeling the innovation and interesting (Fig. 5);

- In three models, the "Memorability" affects the user experience significantly, other 5 evaluations are the best in the System Model, the median in Design Model and User Model. The reason of this result may be the design elements in the System Model is more simple, easy to remember, and other two models have the rich form of elements in the design, also combined with a variety of interactive effect, it may be a burden to user's memory; This result indicates that the integration of cultural elements promoted the user experience, even though it reduced the "Memorability" (Fig. 6).

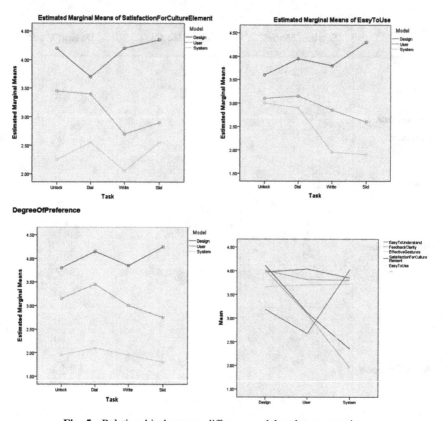

Fig. 5. Relationship between different model and user experience

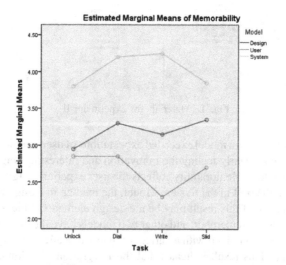

Fig. 6. Relationship between different model and user experience

- Different complexity of task type, there is no bigger difference influence on user experience; the "Easy to Understand", "Feedback Clarity" affects the user experience significantly, it indicates that Ink Painting element fit into multiple functions and interface design scenario (Fig. 7).
- "Effective Gestures" has very limited influence on the interaction experience. May be because the user do an operation used gestures are familiar, such as clicking, sliding gesture, so the user gestures have a weak influence on different model (Fig. 8).

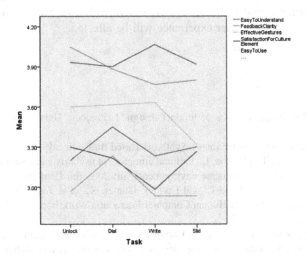

Fig. 7. Relationship between task and user experience

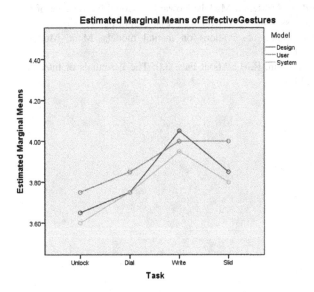

Fig. 8. Relationship between different model and user experience

6 Conclusion

Mental models still have high guiding significance in the interaction design of mobile Internet products, the user's understanding of cultural elements significantly affects the interaction experience. Traditional culture elements integrate into interaction design improving the emotional and operational experience.

When the elements implementation effect beyond user expectations of the Design Model, the usability of the product will be high, the user experience will be better. Users can clearly realize the product innovative and interesting, and can have more impressive. When the System Model is inconsistent with User Mental, the usability of the product is reduced, the user experience will be affected.

References

1. Xihua, X.: The cultural essence of product design. J. Zhejiang Univ. (Humanit. Soc. Sci.) (2009)
2. Chinese Calligraphy Character Image Synthesis Based on Retrieval
3. Minocha, S., French, T., Dawson, L.: Cultural attractors of usability and customer relationship management in (B2C) e-commerce environments. In: 2003 6th Conference on Culture and HCI: Bridging the Cultural and Digital Divides. Gunter, K., et al. (eds.) Proceedings of the 2nd British Computer Society Human Computer Interaction Workshop, pp. 37–47. University of Greenwich, London (2003)
4. Craik, K.: The Nature of Explanation. Cambridge University Press, Cambridge (1943)
5. Young, I.: Mental Models: Aligning Design Strategy with Human Behavior. Rosenfeld Media, New York (2008). Hofstede, G.: Cultures and Organisations: Software of the Mind. McGraw-Hill, New York (1991)
6. Johnson Laird, P.N.: Mental Models: Towards a Cognitive Science of Language. Inference and Consciousness. Harvard University Press, Cambridge (1983)
7. Norman, D.A.: Some observations on mental models. Ment. Models. **7**, 7–14 (1983). Erlbaum, Hillsdale, US
8. Cooper, A., Reimann, R.M.: About Face 3.0: The Essentials of Interaction Design. Wiley, New York (2007)

What is a System?: A Lesson Learned from the Emerging Practice of DesignX

Jin Ma[⊠]

College of Design and Innovation, Tongji University, Shanghai, China
majin.poly@gmail.com

Abstract. The scope of design continues to expand and designers have been increasingly dealing with issues arising from systems. DesignX as inquiry into the approaches how to design for complex, sociotechnical system started in 2014, and emerging practices have been inspired ever since. However, it is observed that DesignX focuses on "How" issues without sufficiently addressing the fundamental question "What is a system?" Divergent from DesignX's dominant focus, Richard Buchanan proposed a schema of systems. With references to Buchanan's earlier work on the strategies of inquiry and the nature of interaction, a holistic framework of systems was synthesized. Using this framework, the author further analyzed the case of "Design for Healthcare in the Community," which was an explorative step of a DesignX project. In this paper, the author attempted to reflect on the developing trajectory of DesignX dialogue by employing Buchanan's ongoing work on systems as a reference framework. It is argued that Buchanan's framework of systems provides a valuable theoretical tool to enrich the DesignX dialogue and practice.

Keywords: The nature of systems · DesignX · Complexity · Design for healthcare

1 Introduction

While design does not have its own subject matter, the scope of the subject matters of design stretches across the areas ranging from signs and symbols, tangible objects, and activities to systems [1]. Richard Buchanan maintains, "the common subject matter of design is variously described as the artificial or the human-made or products that support human beings in all of their individual and collective activities [4]." This commonality allows us to understand the significant transformation of design emerging over the past decade: design is moving beyond the conventional artifact-centered practice and starting to tackle larger matters of greater complexity, for example, sociotechnical systems [15]. This is also the origin of the emerging DesignX exploration.

DesignX is an initiative promoted by a group of scholars with genuine curiosity about how design could address the complex issues the world faces today [10]. The initial Manifesto [7] emphasized that design must change in order to tackle complex

P.-L.P. Rau (Ed.): CCD 2017, LNCS 10281, pp. 59–75, 2017.
DOI: 10.1007/978-3-319-57931-3_6

problems. The DesignX Conference in 2015 as a follow-up was planned to advance the understanding about how designers could play a role in designing for complex sociotechnical systems. It was in that Conference, an impromptu dialogue was triggered and thus disclosed to the participants a plain fact: we lacked basic understandings of the system that would allow us to address the DesignX problems.

In this paper, I attempt to reflect on the developing trajectory of DesignX dialogue through synthesizing Buchanan's work on systems as a reference framework. Employing this framework, I will further analyze a DesignX project to demonstrate how the understanding of the nature of systems could be a powerful theoretical tool to improve our practice.

2   The DesignX Dialogue

During October 10–11, 2015, a small working conference on "DesignX," organized by the Don Norman and Pieter Jan Stappers, two key members of the DesignX Collaborative, was held at the Tongji University College of Design and Innovation (Shanghai, China). As a follow-up to the DesignX Manifesto, this conference was designed, before its kickoff, to harvest the preliminary common understandings about the nature of DesignX problems, the principles of DesignX approach, and possibly tools and methods. During the discussion, one of the participant—Richard Buchanan—raised a simple, yet provocative question: "What is a system?" The room become quiet.

The first response from Don Norman was, "a system is a set of interacting parts." When situated in the social context of greater complexity, the idea of a system becomes further blurry as Don Norman noticed that: "actually I don't know how to define a system ... it's one of those 'I know when I see it.' It's all of the components that come together to make possible whatever it is that we are interested in. It's really easy to talk about the mechanical process, but it's really hard when you start to talk about the social, complex system, because—where to draw the boundary? ... How to draw the line to define a system is part of the problem [9]."

This was an unusual moment to a gathering whose participants' background exhibiting a deliberate mixture ranging from design to systems theory, cybernetics, computer science, education, business and management, and industries. What did it mean that a group of experts familiar with systems thinking and working on system design were not sure about what a system was?

In addition, John Flach borrowed a view from general systems theory that, according to Gerald Winberg [19], a system is a way of thinking about the world: "That the idea there is an extrinsically defined object down there as the system that exists in the world is a mistake. The system is where we choose—as scientists—to draw the boundary. It's our definition of the problem that makes it a system."[1]

---

[1] John Flach commented on the idea of "system" during Don Norman's presentation "A Brief Introduction of DesignX History and Goals of the Conference," at the DesignX Conference, Tongji University, Shanghai, October 10–11, 2015.

The inspirational, generic definitions of system sensitized DesignXers' curiosity to know more about systems, given that designing (for) complex sociotechnical systems was focused on. Hence, "systems" was added as a theme in the group discussion. The statements and questions teased out during the discussion are summarized in Appendix.

Instead of addressing the *How* questions emphasized by the organizers, most of the considerations focused on *What* and *Why*—What a system is when viewed from different perspectives and Why that matters. The DesignXers were impressed by the pluralism of understandings of systems but were unable to frame the pluralist positions. It also signaled that, in order to deal with complex, larger design issues, it was too ambitious to solely focus on the *Hows* without giving the *Whats* and *Whys* ample considerations.

Buchanan's question "Do we actually understand the meaning of a system?" is a rhetorical one. The point is that, although each of us may have a certain definition for a system, we are neither aware of the perspective we hold to obtain the definition, nor do we pay attention to other definitions and the perspectives implied, not to mention the relationships between them. As one of the participants of the DesignX Conference, I was fascinated by the different, sometimes conflicting, understandings of system, and was curious to know their implications for how design has been practiced. Hence, a review on the idea of system was conducted.

3   The Idea of a System

In Merriam-Webser's Collegiate Dictionary [18], one of the most significant meanings of "system" is "a regularly interacting or interdependent group of items forming a unified whole." This entry includes a set of variations including: "a group of interacting bodies under the influence of related forces"; "an assemblage of substances that is in or tends to equilibrium"; "a group of body organs that together perform one or more vital functions"; "the body considered as a functional unit"; "a group of related natural objects or forces"; and "a group of devices or artificial objects or an organization forming a network esp. for distributing something or serving a common purpose." Considering sociotechnical systems where human beings become part of the system, it would be interesting to ask, what it means by a human being, being a component of a system, as, for example, a "natural object," or a "body organ" in a metaphorical sense.

This dictionary definition goes in concert with the received view of systems in the systems thinking discipline. Similar to Norman's definition at the Conference, Donella H. Meadows [17] began her renown treatise *Thinking in Systems* with: "A **system** is an interconnected set of elements that is coherently organized in a way that achieves something.... [A] system must consist of three kinds of things: elements, interconnections, and a function or purpose."

This is what Richard Buchanan [5] called "a commonplace definition," which is full of uncertainty as it consists of solely variables—relationship among "X" in a process of "Y" that achieves "Z." By grasping this definition alone does not help one understand what a system really is. For Buchanan [5], to understand what "a system" means, one must ask him/herself 3 questions:

(1) What is being systemized? (What's the content?)
(2) How does the interaction or the relationship actually happen? (How do they work together?)
(3) What holds the system together? (What are the principles/goals/purposes/values?)

In addition, Buchanan's earlier work on the nature of interaction [6, 8] and the strategies of inquiry [3] would make a useful expansion to that list by considering:

(4) What is the nature of the interaction?
(5) What is the underlying strategy of seeing the system as so?

After years of systematic exploration of the meaning of system, Richard Buchanan [5] developed a schema that accommodates four big kinds of understandings of a system, each implying a significant philosophical stance. First, and the most common definition is: "A system is an *assemblage* of interacting parts or bodies under the influence of (natural) forces"; second, a system can be seen as "a *set* or arrangement of things so related as to form a unity"; third, a system is "a *group* of units to form a whole and to operate in unison"; and fourth, a system is "a *condition* of harmonious, orderly interactions." In addition, "system as an assemblage" has a sense of contingency, controlled by the natural forces; "system as a set" is arbitrary in that it is an intentional choice made by human; "system as a group" is a biological metaphor indicating a functioning organic whole; and "system as a condition" overcomes conflicts to achieve harmonious, orderly interactions of unlimited number of parts [5].

This schema of systems echoes two different but corresponding schemata that Buchanan developed to describe strategies of inquiry and the nature of interaction. Considering these two will allow us to better understand the underlying position that each kind of system definitions indicates.

In his seminal article "Thinking about Design: An Historical Perspective," Buchanan [4] pointed out that "the strategy of inquiry is to seek the resolution of theoretical, practical or productive problems and move toward to advancement of knowledge in the various branches of human learning and activity." He further introduced four strategies [3, 4]: the strategy of design science seeks the underlying elements or parts of complex phenomena so as to investigate mechanisms of combination; the strategy of rhetoric focuses on communication through formulating persuasive arguments; the strategy of poetics (productive science) focuses on the analysis of essential elements and the creative synthesis of these elements as a unified whole; and the strategy of dialectic is to identify and to overcome conflicts, contradictions, and oppositions by accommodating them within a system or a bigger whole (see Fig. 1).

Based on an equivalence of the modes of thought, Buchanan [6, 8] also established a schema of interaction. He identified four kinds of interactions: the "thing to thing" interaction, the "person to person" interaction; the "person to environment" interaction, and the "person to idea (cosmos)" interaction.

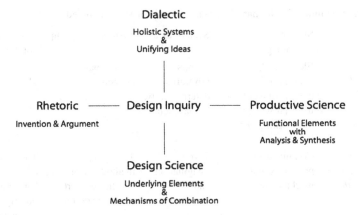

Fig. 1. Four strategies of inquiry. (Source: Richard Buchanan [3])

With the above two schemata as a reference framework, the distinctions between the kinds of systems can be further clarified. Seeing a system as an assemblage of interacting parts for a certain goal has a root in the pursuit of "the basic elements that underlie the complexities of the material world and the workings of the mind [4]," and is directed to combining those elements into processes and mechanisms. The thing-thing interaction dominates in this kind of systems. Seeing a system as a set of things arbitrarily decided by human beings, instead, follows the rhetorical strategy that focuses on argumentation and communication, where person-person interaction prevails. Seeing a system as a group of functioning units within an organically unified whole reflects the poetic strategy of analyzing essential elements and creatively synthesizing them into a whole by means of person-environment interaction. And, seeing a system as a condition indicates the dialectical position [8, 16] that calls for a process, characterized by person-idea interaction, of assimilation in which unlimited number of parts with conflicts or contradictions may find something in common and thus get closer to the truth.[2]

Bearing the five key questions about a system in mind, I summarize Buchanan's schema of kinds of systems in Table 1. Based on this framework, it is clear that the popular understanding of a system from the systems thinking doctrine stems from the tradition of design science as it largely focuses on identifying the basic parts and then process and mechanisms. And the general systems theorist's interpretation of system as a way of thinking about the work is true, but what remained unarticulated then is that the different ways of thinking about the world are not randomly and subjectively individual-based, but instead their fundamental philosophical positions can be characterized.

---

[2] For more explanation about the mode of thought where the dialectic strategy rests upon, see Richard McKeon's work "Philosophic Semantics and Philosophic Inquiry"; Miso Kim also provided a nice clarification on dialectic in her dissertation "Design for Participation: An Inquiry into the Nature of Service."

Table 1. A summary of Richard Buchanan's kinds of systems based on his work [3–6].

	System as an assemblage	System as a set	System as a group	System as a condition
What is being systemized?	Elements that underlie the complexities of the material world and the workings of human mind	Things arbitrarily determined by human beings	Functional elements	Underlying ideas
How do they work together? (How does the interaction happen?)	Combined in processes and mechanisms	Through imagination and argumentation	The discipline of methods of making and the properties of the made-thing	The condition of harmonious, orderly interactions
What holds the system together?	Natural forces	Human intention to communicate	An organic whole	To overcome conflicts and to assimilate them into a broader context
What's the nature of the interaction?	Thing to thing	Person to person	Person to environment	Person to idea
What's the underlying strategy/position?	Design Science (Science in its reductive sense)	Rhetoric	Poetics/Productive Science	Dialectic

4   The Challenge to DesignX

As design evolves, the kinds of systems that designers work with/for vary. When design is mainly focused on making artifacts and giving form to technology, the first kind of systems is the largest whole that the designer attempt to grasp. However, when design begins to intervene in sociotechnical systems such as healthcare, education, and transportation, human actors become a significant part of the kinds of systems that designers work with, and various principles, goals, purposes, and values emerge. A subtle but crucial change happens: If it was sufficient for the designer to work as an objective observer overseeing the process and mechanisms of an assemblage of interacting parts when working with the first kind of systems, it is no longer the case for the rest three kinds because designing has become part of the system resulting from designers' intervention and the interaction between designers and all the other parts of the system including other human actors are wide and profound.

The *What* question is oftentimes entangled with the *Why* question. It is natural to ask, "Why do we discuss the idea of a system?" Aside from to satisfy the genuine curiosity toward the distinct philosophic significances the idea of a system implies,

Buchanan's inquiry into the pluralistic understanding of a system is timely to the design field because such understanding sheds light on different ways design has been practiced and why.

This is particularly relevant to the emerging DesignX inquiry. Although the discussion about "system" was included ad hoc into the group discussion during the DesignX Conference, it was short and underdeveloped, and was absent from the rest agenda. However, the more people talked about the practices, the tools and processes, the less clear it became what the unique contribution DesignX would bring in to the design field. Puzzled by the difficulty of advancing the knowledge about DesignX, Norman and Stappers [10] tentatively concluded that the major challenges facing DesignX do not "stem from trying to understand or address the issues, but rather arise during implementation, when political, economic, cultural, organizational, and structural problems overwhelm all else."

When viewed with reference to the nature of systems, one may argue differently. The problematic DesignX issues are the content of the system that designers attempt to deal with; by designing in such systems, however, designers' implementation becomes exactly part of the intrinsic interactions of the system; and in order to make solutions work, both the solutions as new constructions and the design implementation process must pay respect to the principle that holds the system as a whole. None of the three aspects could be treated as an independent task, because the three together constitute a system. Therefore, the understanding of kinds of system could serve a powerful complement to the agenda of DesignX, because while Norman and Stappers promote to seek new approaches how to design the complex systems, Buchanan's schema provides insights about What a system is and Why it works or doesn't work when designing in a system.

When focusing on the *How* issues, Norman and Stappers [10] called for the exploration of implementation using modular approach and incrementalist strategy of "muddling through." The un-spelt simplistic strategy of Design Science and its influence is manifested. The challenge rises from that the principle of seeing the system following the natural forces that influence the material world and the working of the mind does not apply to the kinds of systems other than an assemblage of interacting objective parts. The design science view of a system is not enough for DesignX.

The confusion prevails not only in theoretical conversations, but in practices inspired by the ethos of DesignX. It was challenged that both the tangible and intangible design products that were seen as great achievements from the design perspective may not work at all in the aimed system. In the rest part of this paper, I will investigate a project on design for healthcare, using Buchanan's schema of systems to analyze the predicaments the designers encountered during the process.

5 The Case of Designing for Healthcare in the Community

The Tongji University College of Design and Innovation (D&I), Shanghai, focuses on studying and improving the burning issues facing today's China by using design as an agent [11–13]. Being the place where DesignX was first voiced, D&I has been actively promoting practices that deal with DesignX issues. Healthcare is one of the areas of special interest to this college.

Healthcare in China is undergoing a crucial transitional phase—the Healthcare Reform promoted by a series of national policies since 2009 introduces a hierarchical diagnosis and treatment system to be supported by establishing the primary care service system [14]. The current healthcare system is characterized by its institutionalized uneven distribution of medical resources. The top-tiered hospitals tend to be patients' first choice unconditionally, regardless of what is needed: advanced medical treatment or primary care. Given that Chinese population is huge, almost every top-tiered hospital runs on an overloaded basis providing limited resources to unlimited demands. As a consequence, numerous conflicts occur including the increasingly deteriorating doctor-patient relationship. In contrast to overcrowded big hospitals, community hospitals that are purported to be responsible for primary care remain largely invisible to most of the public.

Situated in this context, shortly after the DesignX Conference my colleague Dr. Hao Yang and PhD candidate Dongjin Song invited me to work with them to plan a master's studio project—"Design for Healthcare in the Community." Its aim was to understand the status and emerging needs of the transitional healthcare system on the community level in Shanghai. And hopefully it could become a preliminary step of a long-term healthcare service system design initiative grounded in the community where the school is located.

First, we reached out to the Community Healthcare Service Center (CHSC)—the community hospital that shares the neighborhood with D&I, seeking their collaboration and basic information the plan the project. In spring 2016 thirteen Year 1 master's students, divided into 4 groups, participated in the 5-week project. Each group worked respectively on one division of the services offered by CHSC: family doctor, outpatients, hospice care, and children health services. The medical professionals were engaged in the entire process providing expert knowledge about their daily work. In the following section, I will describe some of our memorable pathways in systems during the project and will analyze them by means of the framework of systems.

5.1 The Principle of a DesignX System Is Emergent Through Conflicts

The first impressive pathway came from the supervisor group during project planning. Based on the desktop research on the medical systems in China and a field study in CHSC, the supervisor group were surprised to realize that the medical resources accessible to the public provided by the community hospitals are much richer than we previously knew. How strange that we, as the residents of this community, were blind to what we already have? We arrived at a hypothesis that, in order to implement the nationwide hierarchical diagnosis and treatment system, it must be supported by making the primary care distributed on the community level become visible to people when needed. In short, the goal of our project should be "How to make community hospital based healthcare services visible and attractive to more patients?"

However, when we approached the Vice Director of CHSC and asked for his opinion, his response was a surprise to us. The VD maintained that the community hospital was a state-owned institution and that the greatest challenge to this hospital was the lack of financial allocation and policy supports from the government. The problem was that the community hospital doctors overwork, too, but their salary was too poor to support them to lead a decent life in the city of Shanghai. In short, the community hospital did not need to attract more patients.

This was the first time that we reflected on the question "What is *the* system that we are trying to intervene?" The community hospital is undoubtedly a system in itself, but it is at the same time a part in *the* healthcare service system that could possibly be available to the residents living there. To expand the scale and to enhance the quality of the medical service was not of interest to the current hospital. In the meanwhile, the reason why residents put the top-tiered big hospitals as their first choices also seemed reasonable: the big hospitals are equipped with the best doctors, best facilities, and best resources. Nonetheless, should these two parts of *the* system continue to function the way as is, the contradiction between the limited resources possessed by top hospitals and the increasing demands for quality healthcare from the public would grow even worse. This is also the reason why National Healthcare Reform was first planned and promoted by the government. Although it seemed well justified for the community hospital, the local residents, and the government to interact with the rest components of *the* system in their current manners, none of them are happy with their gains from *the* system. What if the private hospitals, social workers, the families of the patients, and social enterprises/associations were to be considered? There is obviously no exhaustive list of components of *the* system at all. Bewildered by our ignorance of the system, we reshaped the project topic into "How to improve community healthcare experience based on the relationship between medical professionals and patients." By shifting back to the "home domain" of human-centered design and experience design, we gave up the idea of describing the system before the study of experience revealed the system to us.

With hindsight, it would be helpful to see this unknown system of the community-based healthcare service as a condition of potential harmony if the conflicts of the ideas could be overcome and be assimilated into a bigger whole. When the designer enters such a system in order to understand the system's goal, the person-to-idea interaction occurs. A dialectical strategy should be employed to develop the possible common goal through dialogues with different actors involved. The conflicts of ideas and values cannot be resolved by merely studying the organizational structure of the hospital, the procedures of the diagnosis and treatment, the experience of the patients, or by proposing pre-determined argument. The designer must allow him-/herself to be exposed to the variety of conflicting ideas and seek the common principle so that all these ideas can be well absorbed into a whole. Although CHSC is a major part of the studied system, the hospital administrator's voice is not sufficient to establish the principle how the more preferred community-based healthcare service system works. Adopting the co-creation approach in an experience design project may be a sufficiently good starting point, however, to design for a system it requires the supervisor group to work more on establishing the principle of the system by reaching out to more relevant actors.

5.2   Pathways of Human Experience Lead to Possible Constructions in the System

The second pathway was from the group that worked on family doctor service. Family doctors work at the networked small clinics subordinated to the community hospital. Their responsibilities consist of two main parts: offering daily outpatient services at the clinic and visiting patients who live in family wards at their homes. The family doctor group worked closely with family doctor Shen by immersing themselves in Dr. Shen's work environment, accompanying and observing the doctor at both the clinic and patients' homes. Because of such immersion, the students entered the environment where Dr. Shen resided in his work time. They recorded, by notes and photos, the shabby clinic, the patients (mostly the elderly) suffering from chronical diseases and confined to beds, the anxious family members, Dr. Shen's encounters in the street on his way to the medical rounds, etc. They talked with the doctor as well as the people the doctor communicated with. More importantly, sliding into the environment and experiencing the tedious but professional encounters between Dr. Shen and his patients allowed this group of students to empathize with the doctor. During the tutorials, the students spoken for medical professional's concerns by stepping into the shoes of Dr. Shen. They took pictures that have emotional impact in order to let people know more about family doctors' work (Figs. 2 and 3). They admired the doctor's way of communicating with his patients, the families, and the helpers, always ready to provide detailed information, usually repeatedly, in order to release their anxiety, but they also observed that such communication physically and emotionally exhausted the doctor, not to mention the piles of paper work after the rounds back to the clinic.

Fig. 2. The family doctor and his clinic. Photo taken in field study. Courtesy of Shengyu Huang, Chi Zhang, and Yiting Hu.

The final proposal from this group was an information management system that connected the family doctor, the patient's helper, and the patient's family member in terms of the reconstructed information flow (Fig. 4). The students discovered that the patient's biggest concern was that he/she or the helper who took care of him/her would

Fig. 3. Family doctor's visit. Photo taken in field study. Courtesy of Shengyu Huang, Chi Zhang, and Yiting Hu.

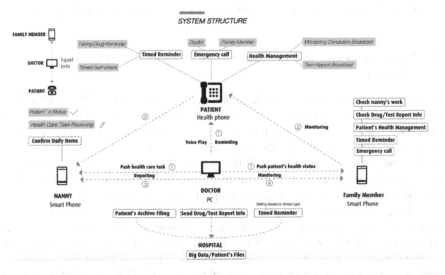

Fig. 4. The proposed information management system for family doctor and patient. Courtesy of Shengyu Huang, Chi Zhang, and Yiting Hu.

forget or confuse the doctor's order after the doctor left; the patient's adult sons and daughters who live elsewhere would be eager to be updated on their parent's conditions. Both lead to that the family doctor was overburdened by having to repeat his/her orders whenever approached by the patient side. On the other hand, the doctor nonetheless must record such information in the patient's chart saved in hospital's database. Aided by an online platform, the doctor's diagnosis and prescription updates in the database could be turned into a resource and be sent to different people in customized ways. Hence, the new service would be able to satisfy the needs of communicating clear and timely information by using the existing resource, without creating any extra work for the doctor.

This is an example of approaching the system from the poetic perspective. The detailed observation of the interaction between a person and his/her environment allowed the students to draw the boundary of the family doctor-based healthcare service system in their project. It also enabled them to identify the possible tangible objects that could serve as useful touch point in the new system. The previous surroundings of the doctor became a part of a unified whole. It is notable that the students used pathways of their own experiences to reveal such interactions. Without entering Dr. Shen's working environment and later becoming part of his could-be-changed environment (by prototyping), the deeper concerns of the doctor—his compassion for the patients, dignity about his profession, and helplessness about the current situation— would be hardly addressed in one resolution.

Using pathways of human experience is widely used in human-centered design, however. It merits further exploration when the subject matters of human-centered design are complex systems that human beings cannot experience the whole. The boundary of the aimed system could be melted down when new elements are taken into account. In this case, the CHSC VD's feedback was, this system was technologically feasible but did not work because it might involve leaks of patients' privacy information.

5.3   Tracing Elements and Interconnections Alone Does Not Grasp a System

The most challenging pathway in this project occurred to the group that worked with the hospice care department at CHSC. During the field study, the students found that nursing workers played an important role in providing hospice care as they were the ones closely interacting with the dying patients—they not only looked after but lived with the patients in the same space. Employed by independent labor companies, the nursing workers were outsiders to the hospital and therefore worked and lived without being able to use the resources as the hospital employed nurses and staff do. The students argued that, should the value of the nursing workers be appreciated by the hospital and their working and living condition improved, the patients would get better comfort care. This idea was however rejected straightaway by the hospital during the interim presentation as the hospital administrator saw it impossible and unreasonable to spend anything more on these third-party employees: it called for additional investment that the currently limited finance barely afforded. This encounter sensitized the students' curiosity to know how the hospice care service system currently ran.

The students then set about mapping the community hospital based hospice care service system in the hope that the significant problem and new opportunity could be identified. Their approach was to identify all possibly involved elements of this service system, and to trace the interconnections between the elements. Because of the complexity of the system, they categorized the elements and their interconnections into different layers with each layer depicting one type of connections, for example, financial relationship, reputation network, personal relationships, etc. To present the whole system, they merged these layers into one system map. (See Figs. 5, 6 and 7.)

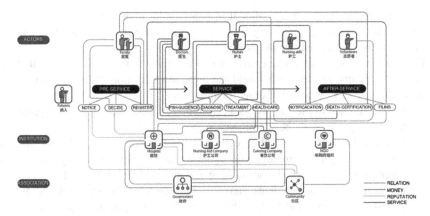

Fig. 5. The map based on the service process and activities. Courtesy of Xin Guan, Li Qian, Yuhong Ma, and Ottla Arrigoni.

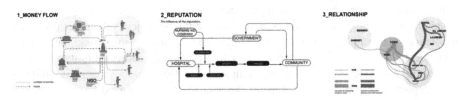

Fig. 6. Layers of the system based on financial connections, reputation network, and personal relationships. Courtesy of Xin Guan, Li Qian, Yuhong Ma, and Ottla Arrigoni.

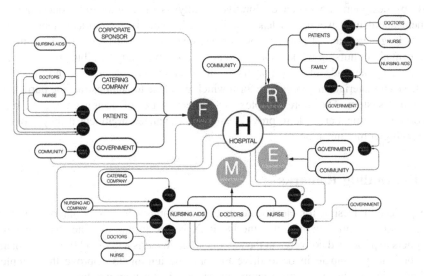

Fig. 7. The merged system map of community hospital based hospice care service. Courtesy of Xin Guan, Li Qian, Yuhong Ma, and Ottla Arrigoni.

By doing so, the students were confident in maintaining their argument of improving nursing workers' working and living conditions to enhance the entire service, but this idea was still not welcomed by the hospital.

Despite the effort of describing each part of the system, it was challenged that the system still appeared unclear: What held the detached snapshots together? What were the principles, values, goals, or visions for the future?

With the reference to the framework of systems, at least three significant problems of the designing process can be identified.

First, when the students aimed to convince the hospital of the value of nursing workers, unknowingly they embarked on a journey of wrestling with a system from a dialectic perspective. Instead of approaching the stakeholders who held distinct and often conflicting ideas, the students analyzed the needs of the stakeholders mostly based on desktop research and logical elaboration. The dialogue directed to achieving the condition to assimilate all the conflicts and contradictions never happened.

Second, although the students were originally inspired by their experiences of the interactions happening in the ward, they became alienated from human experiences during the system mapping stage. They treated each actor as a thing, instead of as a human being, a thing with material inputs and outputs. The system was regarded as an assemblage of things whose interconnections could be objectively described. The problem is, they employed a stance of design science to analyze the system, but did not implement the scientific analysis by calculating the inputs and outputs through systematically collecting facts and figures, employing statistics tools, or applying models from cognitive science. Instead, most of the analysis was conducted based on logical elaboration and subjective judgment. This is the reason why the claimed design opportunity was perceived as arbitrary imaginations.

Third, the more the students worked on mapping a complex system, the lesser they were aware of that they were designers with the expertise of making. The products made by designers, no matter explorative prototypes or manufactured ones, are "argument about how we should lead our lives [2]." This is a rhetorical stance to see design in general, and it also applies to designing for complex systems. Holding the argument about nursing workers, the students did not make any tangible prototypes and use them to persuade the key players in the very system. There was no creatively synthesized materials in appropriate form which was able to demonstrate the purpose of the aimed system. The more complex the subject matter of design grows, the more important designers are able to provide tangible, visualized argument if they aspire to convincing communication.

6   Concluding Remarks

The project of Design for Healthcare in the Community is a preliminary step of a designer-driven initiative to tackle the DesignX issues around us. The challenges the designers experienced converge at the key question: What is a system? If we, designers, are about to participate in or to drive the practice aiming to improve the complex sociotechnical systems, we must know our objects better than we did.

As inquiry into the approaches of how to design for complex systems, DesignX initiated in 2014 is successful in bringing together people from different disciplines and domains to examine this issue. It nonetheless exhibits the lack of sufficient interest in reflecting on the nature of the system in the purported endeavor of addressing *Hows*. In my view, the lack of understanding the nature of a system will impact the significance of DesignX, both on theoretical and practical levels.

Richard Buchanan's exploration of the schema of systems, when combined with his persistent work on the strategies of inquiry and types of interaction, provides a valuable holistic framework to enrich the DesignX dialogue and practice. The framework allows the designer to position the kinds system that he/she is working on and therefore to choose strategies and methods and tools that are consistent with the principle of that system they try to map, synthesize, and design for.

The community based healthcare design project was conducted before Buchanan's presentation of "Systems and Pathways of Human Experiences." By synthesizing Buchanan's framework of systems and applying it in the analysis of the problems encountered during this project, it sheds light on how our practice could be improved in terms of design attitudes, methods and tools, processes, and ability to seek knowledge from relevant disciplines. All these will be influenced by understanding the nature of the system that we are working on.

What we learned from this project can be summarized as follows:

(1) A system is greater than components and interconnections between the components; it is principles, values, goals and purposes that hold everything together. However, the approach to seeking principles or purposes must go concert with the principles or purposes that kind of system implies.

(2) A system is inherently dynamic, and different types of interactions could be traced when the system is viewed from different perspectives.

(3) It is unlikely for a human being to grasp the totality of a system due to two reasons: (a) the relationship of parts-and-wholes makes the boundary of a system relative—while a system contains components, each component as well as the system per se can be a part of a bigger whole; (b) there can be more than one kind of systems that are involved in one design project, and the boundary and content of the system change when the view shifts.

(4) The process of designing for a system involves the designer entering that system and interacting with the components of the system. Such interactions are determined by which kind the system is viewed. When the type of interaction is not consistent with the kind the system is treated, it is likely that the system that the designer thought he/she is dealing with does not hold.

How to design for complex systems will be further studied with the above findings well taken into account.

Appendix: Viewpoints About a System from the Group Discussion at the DesignX Conference 2015

What is a system?	What constitute a system?	Why systems?	Relationship between systems and human beings (Why systems now?)
– As a way to see the world, systems imply actions or perspectives; – System is a man-made thing (or concept) including elements which work; – System is a net of relations which influence each other; – A system is a variable composite; – Are systems organizations/structures?; – What's the opposite side of systems thinkin/designing? Provocative/speculative design?	– A system has a goal; – Does a system have a culture/values? – What is the relationship between a system and a structure?	– System is a helpful tool to understand existing things; – A system is not still; – The system articulates/frames the problem; – What is a system about: management or facilitation?; – What is the difference between a system and the world where we live in, if the boundary is an artificial construction?; – Knowledge from physics helps us understand systems; – [If] system is always more than we can understand or design, why don't we speak about context instead?	– Humans do a bad job of making systems; – Nobody can experience a full (the totality of a) system; – How do we make systems adapt to people (not the other way around)?; – How do we make people adapt to systems, and be happy?; – Is system about the humanity?; – What is the role of business in the forming/designing of the system?

References

1. Buchanan, R.: Rhetoric, humanism, and design. In: Buchanan, R., Margolin, V. (eds.) Discovering Design: Explorations in Design Studies, pp. 23–66. University of Chicago Press, Chicago (1995)
2. Buchanan, R.: Design and the new rhetoric: productive arts in the philosophy of culture. Philos. Rhetoric **34**, 183–206 (2001)
3. Buchanan, R.: Strategies of design research: productive science and rhetorical inquiry. In: Michael, R. (ed.) Design Research Now, pp. 55–66. Birkhäuser Basel, Basel (2007)
4. Buchanan, R.: Thinking about design: an historical perspective. In: Meijers, A. (ed.) Handbook of the Philosophy of Science. Volume 12: Philosophy of Technology and Engineering Sciences, pp. 409–453. Elsevier, London (2009)
5. Buchanan, R.: Systems and the pathways of human experience: an emerging challenge for design. (Keynote speech presented at the Emerging Practices Conference on Design Research and Education, Tongji University, Shanghai, 15–16 October 2016)
6. Buchanan, R.: The structure of inquiry. (Lecture, Tongji University, China, 10 October 2016)

7. Friedman, K., Lou, Y., Norman, D., Stappers, P.J., Voûte, E., Whitney, P.: DesignX: a future path for design, jnd.org: http://www.jnd.org/dn.mss/designx_a_future_pa.html. Accessed 4 Dec 2014

8. Kim, M.: Design for participation: an inquiry into the nature of service. Ph.D. dissertation, Carnegie Mellon University (2015)

9. Norman, D.: A brief introduction of DesignX history and goals of the conference. (Presentation at the DesignX Conference, Tongji University, Shanghai, 10–11 October 2015)

10. Norman, D., Stappers, P.J.: DesignX: complex sociotechnical Systems. She Ji: Int. J. Des. **1**, 83–94 (2015). doi:10.1016/j.sheji.2016.01.002

11. Lou, Y.: Enabling society: new design processes in China the case of chongming. J. Des. Strat. **4**, 22–28 (2010)

12. Lou, Y., Valsecchi, F., Diaz, C.: Design Harvests: An Acupunctural Design Approach Towards Sustainability. Mistra Urban Futures, Gothenburg (2013)

13. Lou, Y., Ma, J.: A 3D "T-shaped" design education framework. In: Bast, G., Carayannis, E. G., Campbell, D.F.J. (eds.) Arts, Research, Innovation and Society. ARIS, pp. 123–136. Springer, Cham (2015). doi:10.1007/978-3-319-09909-5_7

14. Lü, J.: Improvement of hierarchical diagnosis and treatment system under deepening medical and health reform (论深化医改进程中分级诊疗体系的完善). Chin. Hosp. Manag. **34**, 1–3 (2014)

15. Ma, J.: When human-centered design meets social innovation: the idea of meaning making revisited. In: Rau, P.L.P. (ed.) CCD 2015. LNCS, vol. 9180, pp. 349–360. Springer, Cham (2015). doi:10.1007/978-3-319-20907-4_32

16. McKeon, R.: Philosophic semantics and philosophic inquiry. In: McKeon, Z.K. (ed.) Freedom and History and Other Essays: An Introduction to the Thought of Richard McKeon, pp. 242–256. University of Chicago Press, Chicago (1990)

17. Meadows, D.H.: Thinking in Systems: A Primer. Chelsea Green Publishing, White River Junction (2008)

18. Merriam-Webster's Collegiate Dictionary, 11th edn., s.v. "system."

19. Winberg, G.: An Introduction to General Systems Thinking, 25th Anniversary edn. Dorset House Publishing, New York (2001)

A First Speculation on Cultural Experiments as Design Research Methods

Francesca Valsecchi[1,2,3(✉)], Roberta Tassi[1,2,3], and Elena Kilina[1,2,3]

[1] Tongji University College of Design and Innovation, Shanghai, China
francesca@tongji.edu.cn, roberta.tassi@polimi.it,
lena.kilina@gmail.com
[2] Politecnico di Milano, Milan, Italy
[3] UNICAMP, Campinas, Brazil

Abstract. This paper offers a reflection on design research and its forms and methods of cultural interventions, with the aim of contextualising it into the frame of complexity. The paper seeks to restate culture as a necessary element in the construction of a qualitative analytic that informs design discipline, in a contemporary moment where the strategic insights and discoveries valuable to innovation are more and more associated with artificial intelligence in its variety of forms, and cumbersome data processes. In the first part, we discuss the definitions of transculturality, context, and story, within the frame of design and complexity and, specifically, in the methods and tools we use to conduct design research, both in the way of developing the research process and conducting original design inquiries in the field.

In the second part, we discuss culture practices in design research, presenting four experiments that we have been conducting in a transcultural context, and framing which use of culture is necessary to the production of research insights. The examples are discussed as ethnographic exercises in which transculturality is a process of subjective negotiation, when relative and progressive framing defines the context, and where stories include pluralism and allow diversity of interpretations. Because we aim to transform these cases of cultural exploration into structured research methods, we will discuss how ultimately they help to inform if and how the design that we do might be genuinely necessary.

Keywords: Transculturality · Cultures · Design research · Cultural experiments

This paper offers a reflection on design research and its forms and methods of cultural interventions, with the aim of contextualising it into the frame of complexity, which we acknowledge as the current epistemological paradigm, and to which we grant the scope of being itself an ongoing cultural process. We will do so discussing culture practices in design research, meaning some experiments that we have been conducting in a transcultural context, and framing which use of culture is necessary to the production of research insights.

© Springer International Publishing AG 2017
P.-L.P. Rau (Ed.): CCD 2017, LNCS 10281, pp. 76–93, 2017.
DOI: 10.1007/978-3-319-57931-3_7

1   Introduction. Statements on Analytics in Design Research

With daily pace, we observe that strategic insights and discoveries valuable to innovation are more and more associated with artificial intelligence in its variety of forms, and cumbersome data processes. Therefore this paper firstly restates culture (intended as the immaterial set of values connected to social, emotional, and relational environments) as the necessary element in the construction of a qualitative analytic that informs design discipline.

Of course, we do not disavow the relevance of technological contribution at a macro level, but at the same time, we feel the urge to deepen the reflection on how the micro-practices need to be improved as well as intensely studied and implemented.

Analytics is by definition the process of obtaining an optimal and realistic decision based on existing data. If we contextualise this in design research, analytics is the phase that informs design decision, what we produce, and how we deliver it to users. In all the creative discipline, and more recently much more in strategic business and user experience as examples, the word "analytics" is widely used and involves a dichotomy between quantitative and qualitative, between what we can measure and what could be observed. Qualitative and quantitative analytics both are essential to industry, from start-ups to mid-size companies, to inform their decisions, and quantitative information has never been as accessible as in the most recent times. Even small businesses who have been monitoring behaviours on their web platforms for the past one or two years, for example, have suddenly in their hands large set of data that could be explored to understand better their users.

Quantitative analytics looks at actual numbers. It is used to get hard data on how people behave (blurred boundaries between market and business analysis). It can be done with semi-automatic processes regarding data generation and requires to know basics of statistics analysis for the interpretation and use of the information.

Qualitative analytics—this usually means looking at the intangibles. It is far more subjective and interpretative, and you use it to understand why people behave in a certain way (blurred boundaries with user-centered design and applied ethnography). It requires to immerse in the context of interest, and to develop and conduct research sessions and in-depth conversations, to gather stories that can be mapped and processed to inform the innovation process.

They differ in the kind of insights they can provide, often referred as the "what/when/where" in contrast with the "how/why". What people say as opposed to what people truly do, think, and feel. There is an abundance of 'what' 'where' and 'when' of statistics, and thus the deep, actionable insights about the 'why' and 'how' aspects coming from qualitative analytics get often ignored or lost. Using mixed methods overcome the dilemma, combining the rigorous, scientific view of the relationship between two or more variables (quantitative, that yet it doesn't tell us much about why those relationships exist), with the possibility to access to the big picture and what people think and feel (the qualitative - with the limit that we can't really implement and test theories scientifically).

We often define research as a set of activities whose purpose is to inform and inspire the design process where information and inspiration are equally important to establish the vision. Our concern is that relying only on automation of the research process (at the stage of analysis, but also in the application of methods of inquiry) would sacrifice inspiration and reduce the depth of information, as studying human behaviours through analytics is different than immersing in their context, life and motivations. Big data and artificial intelligence can illuminate certain gaps and facilitate initial orientation but needs to be combined with a direct contact with human beings and context to gain deep understanding and inspirations.

The need of both of them is evident, and we read widely in academic and dissemination publications that data scientists love numbers, yet not all data is numerical. In design terms, qualitative analysis is the scientific study of data that can be observed, but not measured: it includes the analysis of context, human behaviour, emotions and other factors that are hard to digitise without losing any meaning; in fact, it concerns with cataloguing the qualities of what is studied. Quantitative analysis is the study of data that can be measured, the quantities of a category of data. Often in design the need of stronger qualitative analytics is affirmed, because it allows us to measure things we can't count and define in numbers, like the overall user experience - where undoubtedly knowing "the how and why" people behave, is more crucial than what they do.

In design terms, to include culture framing as one of the assets of qualitative analytics, help to ultimately overcome one of the most common myths: that it would be useful only for academic researchers in selected fields such as social sciences and marketing. Instead, by looking at the complex world, almost all innovation problems have a qualitative aspect, and thus, quantitative analysis alone would never be able to tell the complete story and frame complexity in an understandable way. Methods and tools for qualitative analysis inspired by the ethnographic practice have been widely applied as a way to engage people in the design process (whether you refer to a design thinking, user-centered design, user experience or service design methodology), with the idea that knowing the user in depth is the only way for companies to acquire a competitive advantage on the market and to push the boundaries of technological innovation. But methods and tools are not exhaustive, not enough, to enable any person to conduct qualitative inquiries - they can guide and support, but a shift in the perspective is still needed to develop useful insights and capture interesting stories.

As a consequence, in a moment in which we are assisting to a desperate run after users to discover their behaviours and needs, we are also experiencing a reduction of quality of research and stories we hear, which flatten the way in which we see the world around us, reduce our projective possibilities, and raises concerns about the relevance of research itself. "*Just because you can measure something doesn't mean it is important*" it's becoming almost a *meme* (that can be widely found in online citations) in the literature and conversations about how balance quantitative and qualitative. "*Things that might be*" should be the new *meme* – if we limit this projective capacity of design research, we are limiting the analytics (possibility of taking the informed decision) with the analysis (comprehension of existing structure and components), reducing the creative power of interpretation, and narrowing its relevance, as described in the following elements:

- **Adjust the value proposition in design** - which information is more or less meaningful may not emerge directly from analysis, whereas one of the assets of the researcher is the capability to highlight interesting connections between data points and raise attention to what is more relevant to drive design decisions, without getting lost in less valuable (yet measurable) details. *What information matters most?*
- **Choose the appropriate language for them** - the audience we are communicating research insights to, and the purpose that brings us in the field may assume a predominant role in the study: instead of feeling in the position of capturing and representing the unknown, researchers may get stuck into what the audience expects to hear or is expecting to question. *Is that what we really heard?*
- **Methods and tools have become a commoditised vehicle** - research is not merely a matter of conducting interviews, building journey maps and listing user needs to proceed to the next step in the design process. Research requires a shift in perspective and deep understanding of the importance of establishing a connection with people, to design for and with them, and tweak existing tools according to our scope. *What is our real research objective?*
- **There is little space for cultural nuances** - the speed imposed to research and all of the listed things above result in an inquiry practice that scratches the surface of behaviours and doesn't have time (or interest) to pay attention to all those elements that can't be immediately understood or easily mapped into existing frameworks. *Are we discovering - and then saying - anything new?*

Analysis and analytics are ways to think in terms of past and future. Analysis looks backwards over time, providing a historical view of what has happened, existing models and practices. On the other side, analytics typically look forward to shape the future or predict a result, highlight a pattern and project a behaviour. Sometimes design research limit to produce analysis but not analytics. In these considerations, we believe the role of culture is essential to criticise and challenge existing practices, by embracing that culture is evolutionary and so oriented to the future by nature. Plus of course culture cannot be measured. Still, we are using it here as a generic term, that we want to unfold into a few crucial definition when we consider culture into design research (in the next paragraphs, through a combination of instances of theory and practice). We believe that the way in which we conduct research, and we teach it, has to be redefined and continuously criticised. *Are the insight we determine really useful? Are they useful to what extend and towards which purposes? How can we improve the dialogue between quantitative and qualitative information to fully leverage their potential bridging analysis with analytics?*

2 Key Concepts for Design Research

The paper reflects on these definitions within the frame of design and complexity, and specifically, in the methods and tools, we use to conduct design research, both in the way of developing the research process and conducting original design inquiries in the field. We believe that to do relevant, valuable, insightful research, we do need to embrace diversity instead of oversimplifying reality, and look at culture as a powerful concept, a conversation to be continuously unfolded among global and local complexity. We therefore propose statements of meaning that help to frame these ideas, namely (1) transculturality, (2) context, (3) stories.

The concept of transculturality is lent from anthropology, where it has been established as the paradigm through which looking at cultures (Valsecchi 2015): it overcomes the prefix of inter- and multi- by suggesting a playground where (cultural) differences can encounter and further transform into an alternative entity. In previous publications, authors underlined the importance of trans- as a prefix with creative power.

For over seventy years anthropology has been studying the concept of transculturation, how the specificity of multiple, variable, dynamic and unequal statement identity of the modern man clearly manifested, located in the complex relationship with the general known and legitimised acculturation (cultural contact) model. Most scholars interpret transculturation as a process of changing the material of culture, customs and beliefs of a particular socio-cultural group, which takes place when it is a prolonged close contact with another group – an adept of their cultural traditions (Malinowski 1944). In the term *"transculturation"* there is the important Latin prefix "trans" which means "above", "super", "through", "on the other side" (Beals 1955). The last two values are particularly relevant, because they imply the inclusion of none, but several cultural reference points, the intersection of several cultures, between them and the running of a special state of cultural state- according to the individual that experiences this condition. By Ortiz's definition, "acculturation" is the acquisition of culture in unidirectional process and transculturation involves two phases - the loss or deculturation and the creation of a new culture (neo-culturation). Thus, it is equally important the destruction of cultural elements and the creation of the new cultural alliances (Ortiz 1995). Following this reasoning, in design, the anthropological notion of transculturality come to place when we think of cultures as dynamic entities whose encounter allow creation: in this sense transculturality implies the respect of diversities before their analysis (knowing before the analytics, and not vice-versa, when analytics is used singularly toward the knowledge production/decision making – perhaps this is this a design specificity).

Here it comes the definition of context, crucial to design discipline, and to situate creative actions into reality. Bounded contexts inform and allow the design to take place and impact. Thus design actions boundaries do not overlap with context framing. John Gero, quoting and elaborating on Benerencetti, reminds that although it is very common to say that representation (in the form of research activity or design projection) are context-dependent, the contents of such representation cannot be established solely composing the parts together. In some way, context also includes what we decide to discard, to leave aside the impact of design projection, being this process completely determined and intentional, or simply outside of the scope of actions. Research should bring us *"outside of the box"*: Gero and Smith recall that *"something inside the box is context-dependent when you need something outside of the box to determine what it means"* (Gero and Smith 2007). They underline that context is not the abstract external projection of a situation, but it's the result of representations that include design agents (in this case, designers acting research). Framing the context is a necessary step to understand where the deconstructive and reconstructive moments of culture emerge: there is where we can actually study them, and there is where decisions take place at first. What we think, what we discover belong to defined contextual framing, as well as what we would produce and create. Globalisation may enlarge the design scope but gives no help in breaking the boundaries where knowledge and actions can be indeed unfolded. A sophisticated use of context as a design notion implies recognising the role of sensitivity and respect towards localism and specificities as what help us to frame our actions - yet also determine their limit.

Finally, the definition of story, or storytelling, as it is recently acknowledged as a general, often the preferable, design outcome. Often we look at stories as an authorial contribution, as an easy-to-be-consumed form of creative ideas, as a trigger to "users engagement", and we value stories for their marketing value because they collect attention to pre-determined propositions. We have been discussing already in previous publications (Valsecchi and Tassi 2016) that the designers capacity of telling stories is rather an interpretative outcome, which conveys the result of an action of active listening, and whereas ultimately stories can articulate common ground is because they give voice to the alternatives that have been captured in reality. The meaning of designing stories is to respect pluralities rather than offering the univocal narration. Each of us is the narrator; we use stories to communicate with others, to convince them, inspire or simply entertain. For designers creating stories - it is an essential part of the creative process, because the story is what determines the interaction with the users, and how effective this interaction will be. While experimenting with different ways of how to integrate storytelling into design, we gradually framed our view of the storytelling approach. Understanding and framing under the influence of an interdisciplinary research team consisting of the areas of design services, fine and visual arts, social sciences, media and communication. Particular emphasis has been put on the different areas of application and characteristics of storytelling. Yiannis argues that "*stories open valuable windows into emotional, political and symbolic lives in organizations*". In addition, the stories can be called "*one part of the process of adoption of sense*" and that "*the truth of the story is not on the facts, but in the meaning*" (Yiannis 2000). Our goal is to experiment with different ways of how to integrate storytelling and storytelling inspired approaches to design. We want to experiment with different applications and features of the narrator in the course of the projects, switching focus between the story that we tell (as creation), and the stories that are happening (as discovery).

3   Cases from Teaching and Research Practice

Underlining that the relationship between culture and research has to be unfolded through a transcultural practice, by the development of stories from the culture, and within a contextual frame of those, the primary focus is to reflect on how culture intensely affects our design activities. Moreover, we want to highlight how designing within complexity means much more than designing in or for a global landscape: it means to design within the continuum of cultural transformation.

We would like to discuss here some unconventional practices of cultural exploration, considering if and how they might be developed into more structured research methods that helps accounting for transculturality, context and stories. Namely, they are:

(a) a tea house occasionally built as a TAZ of conversation based on tea gifting and performed in public spaces;
(b) a series of qualitative media and communication actions that act in the domain of cultural heritage inside the contradiction of past and future urban development;
(c) a programme of workshops by which citizens are called to participate in the activity of envisioning and produce imagery of future cities based on subjective beauty;
(d) "For us by us", a design process used to stimulate a dialogue between residents of informal settlements to discuss and conceive tech-based solutions to everyday risks in their neighborough (e.g. fire)

These practices have been developed as teaching and research activities in a setting itself transcultural (authors writing as foreigners living in not motherland countries, and with students and participants of different intellectual, geographical, and social background). Three of them have been developed in mainland China, grounded therefore on local settings but with a view on their possible impact. One story comes from Africa, and enlightens how we can orient research towards community empowerment and the design of sustainable solutions with their end-users (not for the end-users).

(a) Serendipitea

In China, the habit of drinking tea is not only a consumption; it is often connected to rituals that involve emotional and spiritual communities, family tradition, and healthcare wisdom - for instance, think about family gathering during festivity, as well as ceremonies in temples and sacred occasions. Everybody is familiar with tea rituals, and everybody is able to appreciate the quality of good tea, its importance not only as a product but in the capacity of carrying the values of a whole production chain (including workers, techniques, and environment). Serendipitea is a friendly and gifting-based tea house that has been created as an intimate performance for art festivals with high community spirit, festivals that cherish a DIY approach, and that practices decommodification: the efforts of organising, maintaining, and performing are collective and collaborative although mostly played by strangers. It has been ideated by a group of friends with deep knowledge about tea production, to share the pleasure of excellent quality teas, to contribute to the spirit of inclusive gathering, and to offer a space where new forms of a community could emerge. It looks like a simple table with a tea set, installed for a few hours or days, as a quiet spot where people can stop, have a seat, and taste the brews as well as the conversation with the other passer-by. We have been performing the tea house in a few festival situations, that in design terms we can recognise as communities of practice, but still, they are gated communities. Then, the thought of expanding the context of this performance emerged, along with the desire to offer the pleasure of this temporary setting outside the festivals' boundaries; by this we aimed to push the goal of the spontaneous conversations beyond the serendipity forms in which they happen, towards a more explicit interest in knowing people and their how and why. We moved Serendipitea to public places, and we performed it as a TAZ of conversation based on tea gifting, that is the ultimate core value that we want to pursue. Gifting is a ritual, often demonised as waste, it's a practice hidden - if not disowned - in current consumerist society: conversation, also, is often an opportunistic encounter, in the society where creating networks is valued for the material benefit they bring and out of a sense of pleasurability. Cities are open spaces, yet often empty of the value of the real discovery since efficiency and productivity drive their development and wealth. In the interest of provoking this mainstream status, we moved serendipity in the middle of urban parks and city gathering, to be an occasional temporary open tea-house: it become an open set-up that is public in its existence (it wouldn't have any meaning without the participants) and scope (it wouldn't have any meanings without a free, unselfish, and undriven pleasure in the sharing). By opening a space of spontaneous conversation, and creating the condition of listening to these conversation without the need of orienting them to specific research goals, we are collecting fragments about how surprisingly citizenry can be, and how various and multiform it appears. We achieve to know better the city through the experience of its creatures. More structured research questions are emerging from the open interaction with the humans being in the city; the forms in which the tea-house is being put in place is gradually evolving to give more space to activity, to interact with the context in which is performed, and to welcome more exchange (sometimes someone brought sweets and candies to share, crafts and games to play, tools for storytelling, etc.). We have been performing the tea-house in 2016 about ten times, being able to expand significantly the perception of how city inhabitants looks like - people we would have never met anywhere else - and we are using this immaterial knowledge for a more reflective ground - about what "users" can represent, not only as a stakeholders of design plans but firstly as inspirators of creative actions that still need to be unfolded (Fig. 1).

Fig. 1. The installation of Serendipitea in Kenting, Taiwan, performed at Springscream festival, April 1–4 2016

(b) "From Material waste to Cultural Energy". Archaeology of the future

This project has been developed in the context of an MA design studio course at Tongji D&I in winter 2016[1], as a series of qualitative media and communication actions in the domain of cultural heritage, leveraging on the contradictions among past and future within urban development. This design studio belongs to a series exploring the potential of communication design tools in approaching, understanding, and talking about the complexity of urban changes. In particular, it aims to reflect and design around cultural and social issues, building a strong connection with the physical environment and experimenting with field research.

Students have been sent to look for abandoned objects in areas of the city where great transformation is undergoing, navigating the city across the traces of the past and its decadence, and the landmarks of the future and its opulence. They had to search things that have been forgotten, leftovers, fragments, items from the material culture that could inspire us to find deeper stories within the urban transformation. The brief of the studio was to find those objects, using them as the trigger for more in-depth research and inquiries, and as the spark of a storytelling activity about the present of Shanghai. The role of archaeology is metaphorical: *which kind of story do we tell if we could choose to pass on something to the future? Which is the message that we can dig out from the complexity of the present, and that is worth to preserve? How many layers of reality and transformation can we observe, or discover, or appreciate, when we invest time in wandering around, crossing the discontinued boundaries between old and new?*

In communication design theories, we called macroscopes the visual artefacts that convey knowledge about a complex, social issues (data visualisation are as such, together with mapping and storytelling tools, and co-creation devices). The course produced macroscopes that talk about the transformation of heritages along the process of the transformation of the city and would build narratives about the forms, the aesthetics, the participants and the meanings of how such change is happening.

Abandoned places and objects indicate the "deadness" of modern architecture, and they hide unexpected forms of life. We discovered that the diversity and beauty of Shanghai are nothing but a creative use of space. Limited resources and population density make people adapt the city to themselves. The activity in the design studio has been conceived to break the rules of time, space, and linear communication between message and users. Instead of producing media for a commercialized user-scape, the stories created used media in a very broad sense: students produced artefacts that embed the complexity of the present, and transfer it in a synthetic way into forms to be received and consumed in the future, building messages that can generate resilience, overcoming the disruption of time, space and culture. By producing outcomes for the future, we aim to use media and design tools to focus on the nature and the quality of the messages, reflect on the contradiction between preservation and innovation, and disrupt the constraint of the aesthetics using instead the transcultural environment of urban development as a stage where new (design) languages can occur.

---

[1] Tongji University, College of Design and Innovation - MA Design Studio 1/2016 - Projects names: Memories of Shanghai, Hidden in the City, Lilong's Memories, Lights and Shadows, See Me - projects will be available online by the time of the conference.

Research had been the stage to re-frame the relationship between the message and the possible recipients: the devices discovered, being abandoned, unused, trashed, wasted, forgotten, dismantled, are out of a cycle of life and use, whereas they enter a new cycle of possible symbolic meanings. Media wasn't the catalyst of descriptive narration. Instead, they serve the purpose to research beyond the sense of displacement that urban change naturally embeds, and they led to a critical analysis of the potential transculturality that urban change may unfold: *"Producing knowledge about the loss that is happening. Give to the loss of history a meaning. Building knowledge out from memory. Activate envisioning and share visions. Transform the abandoned in preferable"* (course syllabus).

Finally, a temporary exhibition of the projects had been created inside one of the most ancient traditional residential neighborhood of Shanghai, currently under demolition (manifesting itself at the edge of a private area and public place of interest), where they serve as scenography for the storytelling of Mr. Chen, the last member of a family living there for more than one hundred years. He is currently opening the house to passers-by, displaying numerous and ancient heritage relics and fragments, books, newspapers, pictures, unassembled pieces of a history that are not only in the people living there but in all the architectural and material elements of the surrounding. It would be fair to say that by living in the city, no one can avoid the use of public places. Furthermore, this means that it is impossible not to visit them as social scene, although it is not focused, and sometimes unwillingly. Urban public space is a constitutively social situation, especially considering the interactions among urban residents. It is also a historical phenomenon, which means that it varies over time depending on the social and societal conditions. City streets, parks, squares, are regarded as symbols of collective well-being, and they represent the opportunities to discuss the progress and the utility of public management; they are sites of public discourse that facilitate the growth of civic culture and the awareness of political debate and reforms; thus the role of public space within the increasing urbanization and the consequent social problems has changed.

Generally speaking, at the end of the nineteenth century under the influence of the significant economic, political and cultural changes, the city became a place for a new phase of modernization, as the urban population rose, internal migration and movement within the city grew, and new forms of social and cultural interaction between space and people appeared. Public space is defined when it's not private, when it has facilities available for public access, and exists without a commercial basis and not under the control of state power authority; places where people meet each other, regardless of their social status or role in society (Smith and Low 2006). The issues of place, belonging, and citizenship have been highly debated in the intellectual agenda since the early 1990s, yet most of these studies take "the West" as their focus point. The Asian turn may urge us to rethink these notions with the emergence of alternative functions of some spaces, and the re-imagination of public space by what it may be named global modernities. Although citizenship has always been defined as a legal and political relationship between the subject and the state, recent studies propose a broader concept of the citizenry: *"the dynamics underpinning the way in which globalisation affects placemaking can be seen as articulating new definitions of cultural citizenship"* (Fox 1977). Though there are continuous changes and transformations in how public and private places are categorized, as values that they possess, always depending on their contexts, the distinction of public/personal space can be hardly recognized because one space can become a part of another. With this action, our media contribute to return to the city an active public space, whose value can be out of its physical borders and there can be an emotional value that creates the connection between the status of the space and its inhabitants (Figs. 2 and 3).

Fig. 2. Students presenting two of the group projects during the final temporary exhibition in the traditional house of Mr. Chen

Fig. 3. Discussion and interaction in Mr. Chen house

(c) **Cities After Cars. Imagining, designing and visualizing future city spaces.**

Cities After Cars is a research project[2] started in 2016 and with approved funding for 2017. It is a programme of workshops by which citizens are called to participate in activity of envisioning, imagery producing of future cities based on subjective beauty.

Through the workshops, we engage groups of citizens in a visionary, hands-on experiment to re-visualize those urban spaces currently organised around cars;

---

[2] Refer to http://citiesaftercars.org for a complete project outline.

imagining an open canvas where unexplored communal aesthetic perspectives and landscapes will be built. Cars are not simply the first mobility instruments of contemporary society; they remain the most powerful symbol of what citizens everywhere in the world call 'development'. Car-based mobility, however, should not restrict the way we think about the cities we'd like to live in. Changing the conditions of current urban reality in China and beyond requires developing new ideas and imagined possibilities for future cities. The research engages citizens and civil society stakeholders into a process of envisioning and self-positioning in such a car-free future, and ultimately to develop policies and guidelines that can serve government and industries interest in developing future mobility services, as well as plans for public space management.

The research is currently in the phase of data gathering through the workshops and will be followed by data dissemination through public exhibitions, and data analysis through policy guidelines development. The research will eventually benefit civil society groups through the activity of engagement, citizens at large through public dissemination, and political and industrial stakeholders through the implementation of strategies for urban change.

We define this research as experimental because the workshops are based on a cultural challenge, and are grounded on research as a way to activate cultural inquiries. In fact, regardless best practices and innovation in sustainable mobility that is getting introduced across urban settings, a car-free future is not yet on the global agenda, neither in the industry nor political trends. Instead, cars are still markers of industrial, economical, and personal wealth. That means, we believe there are so many cars around us because people want them; or, they are unable to think otherwise. Through the workshops, participants are on the front-line of city imagination: they are encouraged to consider beauty over functionality, to cherish meaningfulness versus convenience, as well as to reclaim individual wishes and collective inspirations over technical needs and necessities. Workshops represent a systematic exercise of the "what if" through which the city after cars can be imagined, unfolded, and – eventually – created by the inspiration of minor alternatives, and without the uniformity of the major technological systems. We believe this research can largely affect design implementation of urban planning: talking about beauty in cities can be considered as utopian; thus rather we express the interest of exploring the vision of how a city without cars might spring not from planning or management point of view, but in the choice and imaginary of its citizenry. Motivated by cases study and ongoing experiments all over the world that reduced cars, we acknowledge that intimate and collective visions cannot exclusively derive from planning: they have to be stimulated in order to transform the hidden dreams into actual needs, and then they need to be integrated into it.

Moreover, workshops are experimental because they are not concerned with services or mobility systems. Research yet is leading to language based design outputs, aiming to advance imaginary and vision by the production of visual representations – in the form of postcards, posters, sketches, collage, pop-ups, models, etc. – through images and craft tools. How to fill the spaces not utilised for car-based mobility? What would everybody like to see? How do we find, diffuse, and inject beauty at the micro level of the city landscape? How do these aesthetic visions overlap or converge?

Each workshop will produce a series of images that will be collected into a gallery of visions of future cities as seen through the eyes of their citizens and the workshop participants; reflecting upon these outcomes provides a vibrant starting point to raise innovative collaborative research questions and actions about aspirations for future cities. By running the workshops in urban settlements of different scale, nature, and geography we will collect a variety of visual artefacts that are the seeds of a conversation about what the city we want might look like. Produced artifacts are being coded through grounded theory, and insights will be produced about the qualities that individuals and social network embed with the vision of the future, including needs, aspiration, and missing values. The dissemination of this material in the form of public exhibition will stimulate discussion and critique of the insights whereas they can be developed within a common ground of values and qualities that can be taken into account into future strategies of urban planning.

These language-based design outputs are devices of further design research. Regarding visual disciplines, they are discussed as a toolkit of visual ethnography; as contents, they are coded into narrative patterns and visual taxonomies. They can be modelled to assess the efficacy of envisioning methods in citizens' engagement and scenario building, and this would contribute to a very active literature and practice in the global debate about design for social innovation: referring to the cone of Potential Futures developed by Joseph Voros, a role for emotional - rather than cognitive and informational – knowledge is reclaimed as asset in designing with positive impact. From urbanism point of view (and mainly urban design), it will be discussed how these visions of beauty and possible new space configurations could realistically be integrated into the existing urban landscapes and design. The main focus here would be on the three critical spatial dimensions of 'visual', 'social' and 'perceptual'. The study would also link to theories developed by Jan Gehl, on the progression from occupied space (mainly by cars) towards reclaimed space (primarily by users). From this perspective, we conduct studies on two/three distinct zones in the studied cities, with same parameters for comparison. From a social science point of view all materials can be employed to inquire into "socio-technical imaginaries" (Jasanoff 2016) of urban infrastructures: replacing the car opens up a chance to redesign the city, so how do large scale infrastructures look different? What kind of wishes, hopes, values, etc. about physical infrastructures and urban spaces does this envisioning reflect and provoke? What is the cultural identity ordinary citizens are looking for in urban infrastructures (after the cars)? How do these socio-technical imaginaries of beauty help to rethink future metropolitan design as a social construction of urban space?

At the current state of the art of the project, approved funding will cover the workshops phase (about ten workshops until summer 2017), and more applications are being submitted to extend the workshop into policy feeding actions. Although the factors affecting climate change are systemic and cannot be reduced to car consumption in the cities, the social role of cars affects in a very direct ways citizens behaviours: re-discussing the social need of cars in urban environment will build awareness of individual and participative roles into climate change related actions. Without doubts, the reduction of vehicle mobility will directly mitigate climate change and offer practical evidence of how behavioural changes are at the root of larger urban development actions. By building visions of cities without cars, the promotion of sustainable consumption patterns and the activation of citizens in the process of city management are swifted. Having the citizens engaged in directly tackling climate change embeds the cultural challenge of connecting individuals with urban stakeholder, as well to connect their emotional needs to the system of resources and implementation policies that might help the vision to become a reality. The analysis will be discussed and integrated into urban local strategic priorities and reorientation into current business practices and network. While cars are an ever-present landmark that shapes urban landscapes, best practices and disruptive cultural innovation in sustainable mobility could be introduced across urban settings to develop a car-free future, and a citizens supported urban management (Figs. 4 and 5).

Fig. 4. Projects discussion among participants at the end of Cities After Cars (Shanghai Himalayas Museum, December 11th, 2016)

Fig. 5. Participants in action during Cities After Cars workshops

(d) **For us by us - community engagement to bring tech-based innovation in informal economies**

A design process structured around three key phases of work with community groups to help them designing their own design solutions, with the intent of making affordable tech-based services available to populations that typically don't have access to innovation. The process aims at enabling communities not only to shape the service model around the new tech product, but also to define how the business model could work in order to make that innovation sustainable and scalable in their reality, so that it can really improve their lives on regular basis (instead of relying on donations and humanitarian aid). This fully integrated in-field research and design approach shifts research from exploration to action, and the design researchers themselves become tools for the community to express their needs, challenges and desires, and turn them into tangible solutions.

The process was tested in the context of a project around fire sensors promoted by American Red Cross with the communities of Mukuru (Nairobi) and Khayelitsha (Cape Town) and has lead to the creation of a full service (named Fire Club) that is now piloted in several cities across Africa and Asia. The For us by us process don't just give to people ownership and control on what services are provided and how - but can generate learnings during the process that have direct influence on the life of those individuals and groups.

When we were working on the fire project, all the activities we did together with the more motivated community members contributed to raise awareness about the specific problem, and distributed information that then stayed within the communities themselves (Cisero and Tassi 2016). For example, during the fire sensors workshops, people learned how to prevent better fire outbreaks and what to do to extinguish them, save their belongings and protect their kids. The groundwork had been set for a potential multiplicative learning approach as some of them promised to start training peers and increase their fire prevention awareness. As an organization, it is possible to also deliver training certificates along the journey that legitimize what the community members are doing and learning, which could potentially help them find jobs (e.g. a training certificate on fire response or human-centered design training certificates to the students who have been working with us to moderate the participatory design sessions) (Figs. 6 and 7).

Fig. 6. Experience Mapping and Role Playing exercises during a community workshop in Cape Town (November 2015)

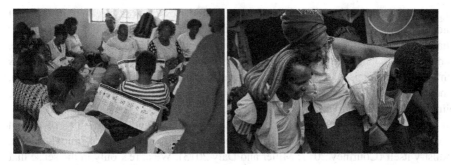

Fig. 7. Fire safety service simulation in Nairobi (December 2015): community members studying their role based on a scenario they elaborated in a previous workshop, and then acting out the response journey.

4 Relevance and Discussion

In design industry and curricula, there is a general practice of anticipating the concept and ideation phases with research, but we are here discussing that design research is more than users engagement, and is different that performing interviews seeking for insights. We send students to talk with people, although often those inquiries are the dry repetition of techniques through which students, in reality, search for confirmation to concept pre-sets more than achieve fundamental discoveries. Tasks are accomplished, but insights are shallow. This can happen sometimes also in ready-to-made research in industry and business. It's not a critique to competences, whilst a reflection on the reason for research, that shouldn't serve ideation, rather it should ground it. In this sense, we discuss how research produces analysis but is not sustained by adequately meaningful analytics. When research is performed as a reductive implementation of tasks, it ultimately doesn't get too far. It limits in fact to be a technical exercise with no criticism. It produces stories as a way to silver lining what we already have in mind; it considers context as a way to frame where we already are; it discusses cultures from the limited perspective of a language-based setting (whether nationalities, origin, social status). Pragmatic qualitative research is done through a variety of methods (Creswell 2013): while some of them are simple such as surveys and interviews, the very crucial ones seem to be complex structures of ethnography and phenomenology, they are not composition of task, rather systematic implementation of reflective and critical practice. Moreover, in design research, thus practice are consolidated, the toolkit is mutable and adaptive to the complexity of the research settings and scope: therefore we claim that research and development upon practices and methods is the fundamental step to enter the journey towards discovery and insights. Considering complexity as the framework where design can take inspiration from, but also has to give a contribution to, we value the middle ground between the micro and macro perspective. Designers can work in a complex world (the "what") because they do start from recognising the complexity of the inner possibilities (the "how"); thus in being researcher within a creative domain means performing exploration rather than applying technical procedures. Our first challenge is to imagine and finalize tools that may help in framing the complexity and setting the boundaries of possible, and meaningful understanding. The value of research is not amounting to the data collected – either quantitative or qualitative – but in understanding which the right question might be, and in which language it can be posed. Therefore, the examples are discussed as ethnographic exercises in which transculturality is a process of subjective negotiation, when relative and progressive framing defines the context, and where stories include pluralism and allow diversity of interpretations.

A lot of writing is being produced about the limits and the inutility of design research, as a large slice of budget that does not get to the point of innovating the industry itself (Courtney 2017; Miller and Daly 2013). We agree, only in the sense that research methods is what need to be questioned and advanced, not research purposes and scope. We claim that better design research can emerge from fewer interviews to users, and more conversations with human beings; better insights when valuable data from automatic analytics can be integrated by meaningful documenting of the complexity of design problems, recognizing in this way that the value of research transcends the goal of having efficiently profitable outcomes. Design might serve innovation but it also has a social and cultural role on offering dense and critical outlooks on the nuances and the variety of the realities that exist. For this purpose we have been describing experiments where typical qualitative interviews are substituted by visual conversations, open setting for strangers exploration, values based confrontation, and tools for handling the immaterial, the psychological, the visionary; all elements of culture of which we can say very little outside of subjective perspective of the researchers, yet elements that define the reality of what we research in a very situated way. We believe automatism and repetition of methods should be discouraged in front of complexity because they inform the design that we want (or that we have to do, as students or practitioners) but not at the all the design that might be genuinely necessary. Instead hypothesis are the creative agent of any meaningful decision and can be inspired by unconventional research practices. The cases discussed are not established methodology yet, but all are useful to give value to qualities over quantities, to diversity over similarities, to the specific over the generic: these are all feature that we believe are pertinent of a healthy look into complexity with a beneficial impact to social knowledge before the innovation growth.

References

Beals, R.: Acculturation. In: Anthropology Today: An Encyclopedic Inventory, Chicago (1955)

Cisero, C., Tassi, R.: Market creation through community engagement: combining ethnographic and business thinking to bridge life-changing technologies to emerging economies. In: Ethnographic Praxis in Industry Conference Proceedings, vol. 2016, issue 1 (2016). Accessed 29 Nov 2016

Courtney, J.: User Research is Overrated (2017). https://medium.muz.li/user-research-is-overrated-6b0fe101d41#.ywt19qvca. Accessed 20 Feb 2017

Creswell, J.W., Creswell, J.W.: Qualitative inquiry and research design: choosing among five approaches. SAGE Publications, Los Angeles (2013)

Fox, R.G.: Urban Anthropology: Cities in Their Cultural Settings. Prentice Hall, Englewood Cliffs (1977)

Gero, J.S., Smith, G.J.: Context and design agents. In: Kokinov, B., Richardson, D.C., Roth-Berghofer, T.R., Vieu, L. (eds.) CONTEXT 2007. LNCS (LNAI), vol. 4635, pp. 220–233. Springer, Heidelberg (2007). doi:10.1007/978-3-540-74255-5_17

Miller, E., Daly, E.: Understanding and measuring outcomes: the role of qualitative data. White Paper, IRISS (Institute for Research and Innovation in Social Services) (2013)

Ortiz, F.: Cuban Counterpoint: Tobacco and Sugar. Duke University Press, Durham (1995)

Malinowski, B.: A Scientific Theory of Culture and other Essays. University of North Carolina Press, Chapel Hill (1944)

Pu, M.: Public Places in Asia Pacific Cities: Current Issues and Strategies. The Geojournal Library. Springer, Dordrecht (2011)

Smith, N., Low, S.: Introduction: the imperative of public space. In: Low, S., Smith, N. (eds.) The Politics of Public Space, pp. 1–16. Routledge, New York, London (2006)

Valsecchi, F., Tassi, R.: The listening capability: three insights around and about a design way to storytelling. In: Bertolotti, E., Daam, H., Piredda, F., Tassinari, V. (eds.) The Pearl Diver: The Designer as Storyteller. DESIS Network (2016)

Valsecchi, F.: Cultural translations as design capability. Lessons learnt from the European-Asian encounter in understanding and creating embedded meanings. In: Meroni, A., Galluzzo, L., Collina, L. (eds.) The Virtuous Circle: Design Culture and Experimentation, Cumulus Conference Milano, 3–7 June 2015. McGraw-Hill Education, Italy (2015)

Yiannis, G.: Storytelling in Organizations: Facts, Fictions, and Fantasies. Oxford University Press, Oxford (2000)

Jasanoff, S.: The Ethics of Invention: Technology and the Human Future. W. W. Norton & Company, New York (2016)

Waterfall Flow vs. Fixed Grid Webpage Layout Design – The Effects Depend on the Zhong-Yong Thinking Style

Man-Ying Wang[1(✉)] and Da-Lun Tang[2]

[1] Department of Psychology, Soochow University, Taipei, Taiwan
mywang@scu.edu.tw
[2] Department of Mass Communication, Tamkang University, Taipei, Taiwan
daluntang@gmail.com

Abstract. This study examines how the perception of information layout of webpages is influenced by users' thinking style, namely, Zhong-Yong (Median) thinking. The waterfall flow and the fixed grid layout were used to present woman's clothing information in an online store context. Participants rated the classical aesthetics, expressive aesthetics and attractiveness of the webpages after they browsed the webpage under different goals (i.e., leisure viewing vs. target search). Both layout and the mode of use affected the classical aesthetics and attractiveness ratings for low Zhong-Yong but less so for high Zhong-Yong thinking individuals. These findings were interpreted by Zhong-Yong's influence on users' controlled vs. guided information search behavior during web browsing. Implications for the roles of culture and individual differences on the design of webpage information layout were also discussed.

Keywords: Information layout · Classical aesthetics · Expressive aesthetics · Webpage attractiveness · Waterfall flow · Fixed grid · Eye tracking

1 Introduction

Culture affects online users' perception and experience towards websites and contents [3, 11, 13]. Previous studies showed that Easterners and Westerners may differ in their approaches to information representation [12, 14]. It was demonstrated recently that such cultural differences are actually related to the division of geographic regions and the associated life styles [17]. As thinking style is critically underlying one's representation of the visual environments, its effects on website information layout design are expected. Research efforts directed to the study of thinking style on information layout design in specific, user interface and webpage/website design in general are relatively limited, nevertheless.

This study examines whether the *Zhong-Yong* or *Median* thinking style – a prevalent Chinese Confucian rooted world view or life philosophy - contributes to the aesthetic preferences for web page information layout. Specifically, we created web store pages of woman's clothing in either the waterfall flow or the fixed grid layout. Participants browsed through these pages to engage in either a leisure viewing or target

© Springer International Publishing AG 2017
P.-L.P. Rau (Ed.): CCD 2017, LNCS 10281, pp. 94–103, 2017.
DOI: 10.1007/978-3-319-57931-3_8

search task and rated the classic and expressive aesthetic experiences for these web pages as well as webpage attractiveness and product likings. We found the Zhong-Yong thinking style affected viewers' aesthetic experiences and preferences as the function of page layout the mode of use. These findings had various implications for webpage information design.

1.1 Zhong-Yong (Median) Thinking Style

Zhong-Yong or the *Median* thinking style is a historically rooted behavioral code in the Chinese culture [9, 25]. It dictates against impulsive or extreme reactions and encouraged individuals to actively maintain an emotional neutral point for emotional equilibrium. Individuals are prompted to take an encompassing view of the ongoing situations before taking actions in a situationally appropriate and optimal manner. Previous studies demonstrated that high Zhong-Yong thinking individuals exhibited higher processing capacity and controlled their attentional processing efficiently so that they were not easily affected by the emotionality of attentional cues in a cueing paradigm [2, 22].

High Zhong-Yong individuals also adopted a global processing scheme. [7] demonstrated that the Navon-type global precedence effect was exhibited for high than low Zhong-Yong individuals. [23] examined and compared the viewing behaviors of high vs. low Zhong-Yong individuals. High Zhong-Yong individuals were able to more efficiently shift from the global to the local mode of processing. They also exhibited larger scan paths as the information complexity was low. These findings suggested that the high Zhong-Yong thinker is characterized by an active visual attentional control tendency including actively integrating information across spatial extent when necessary. These visual strategies support high Zhong-Yong individuals to be able to observe/think before they take the appropriate actions.

Taking a global scheme in visual processing has implications for webpage design. [4] found visual patterns during webpage viewing depended on whether the participant was Chinese, Korean, or American. When the participant came from the culture that encourages holistic thinking (e.g., Chinese and Korean), [4] found that he was likely to view webpages using circular scan patterns (as recorded by an eye tracker), i.e., scan across the whole page. Analytically-minded participants (e.g., Americans) more readily read from the center to the periphery. [4] suggested design guidelines devised to cater the browsing behaviors of holistic thinkers. For example, as the holistic thinkers tend to scan the whole page to obtain the big picture, contents could be placed more freely on the page.

1.2 Web Store Design and Aesthetics

Web store design affected shoppers' attitudes through emotion and tasks [16, 24]. Visual aesthetics constitutes an important emotional aspect that may impact subjective usability as evidenced by the over-cited quote "Attractive things work better" [15, 20]. Although aesthetics has always been an influential dimension of product design, we know very little on how beauty and use are associated. For example, will usable things also look pretty?

[10] distinguished between "classical aesthetics" and "expressive aesthetics". The classical aesthetics emphasizes orderly and clear design while the expressive aesthetics dimension pertains to the creativity and originality dimension of design. [10] evaluated classical aesthetics by measuring aesthetic, pleasant, clear, clean and symmetric features in design while the measures were creative, fascinating, special effect, original, sophisticated for the expressive aesthetics. While both aesthetic dimensions exhibited reasonable correlations with perceived usability, pleasure of interaction and service quality, classical aesthetics correlated with perceived usability and pleasure higher than the expressive aesthetics.

Findings by [10] suggested that the experience of classical aesthetics may be intrinsically related to the process of use while expressive aesthetics pertains to independent evaluation of visual and other properties. However, [17] created website designs that followed the principles of classical and expressive aesthetics respectively but found little difference in their respective usability. It is not clear which design element(s) and the associated usability of a website is affected by the classical and expressive aesthetics. As classical aesthetics may draw on information related to the processes of using or interacting, the nature of such process is also revealed by users' viewing behavior recorded by eye trackers.

1.3 Hypothesis

High Zhong-Yong thinkers exhibit controls over their visual processing and adopt global processing schemes. The overall information layout on a webpage is either ignored or adopted when needed by them. Low Zhong-Yong thinking individuals, in contrast, are less actively controlling their browsing of webpages. Their visual attention is guided in a bottom up manner by the specific information layout on the webpage they are viewing. This subtle difference between the active ignore and/or use vs. passive guidance by the webpage layout could be exhibited by comparing viewers' behavior for the fixed grid vs. waterfall flow webpage layout.

The waterfall flow layout, popularized by Pinterest.com and other websites, is characterized by flows of grids of uneven sizes across the page. The fixed grid layout, in contrast, is comprised by grids that are orderly aligned and of similar sizes (see Fig. 1 for examples). The neighboring contents on a webpage compete for visual attention with the currently processed information. In the fixed grid layout, neighboring grids are similarly sized and located with the currently attended grid and create stronger competition than the waterfall flow layout as the neighboring grids in the latter tend to differ in sizes and locations with the current grid. As such, the waterfall flow layout supports a leisure viewing mode of processing [6] in which the viewer may dwell on specific grids of contents with little competition from neighboring grids. In the fixed grid layout design, the competition for attentional processing from the neighboring grid, nevertheless, enhances the sequential and orderly search behavior that serves the attainment of the target search goal [6].

Fig. 1. Examples of waterfall layout (left) and grid layout (right) webpages used in this study

High Zhong-Yong thinking individuals actively control their visual processing of the webpage and are less easily affected by either the layout or the mode of use. The visual attention of low Zhong-Yong individuals, on the other hand, is captured in a bottom up manner by information layout if the task goal is leisure viewing. Low Zhong-Yong individuals exert stronger control over their visual processing when the task is target search and, as such, the effect of webpage layout may diminish. The classical aesthetic rating and webpage attractiveness rating are related to the process of viewing and is affected by Zhong-Yong. In contrast, the expressive aesthetic rating is expected to be higher for the waterfall flow than the grid layout because the irregularity spaced and located grids in the former result in novelty. Expressive aesthetics is not affected by Zhong-Yong as it is associated with the visual properties and contents of the webpage, not viewing process.

H_1. The classical aesthetic rating and webpage attractiveness rating for the waterfall flow layout are higher than those for the fixed grid layout during leisure viewing. The reverse is true during target search. This pattern is expected for low but not high Zhong-Yong individuals.

H_2. The expressive aesthetic rating for the waterfall flow layout is higher than the fixed grid layout regardless of the tendency in Zhong-Yong thinking.

The fixed grid layout may prompt non-deliberate shifts of fixations due to competition from neighboring grids. Regressive viewing (i.e., regress towards earlier locations of fixation) is deployed by the user in order to gather more information from the previous grid. More regressive views are thus expected for the fixed grid than the waterfall flow layout. This difference occurs only for low Zhong-Yong thinking individuals as their visual processing is guided by the information layout in a bottom-up manner.

H_3. Recursive viewing is more prevalent in the fixed grid than the waterfall flow layout, for low but not high Zhong-Yong individuals.

2 Method

2.1 Participants

Fifty-five participants took part in the experiment. They were undergraduate students of various majors. All participants were females to ensure they would be engaged by the online store clothing merchandise used in the study. The background questionnaires they completed showed all had online shopping experiences and 86% had recent (within three months) online shopping experience for clothing. Half was randomly assigned to the leisure view and half to the target search condition.

2.2 Design and Materials

The experiment is a layout (2) x mode of use (2) x Zhong-Yong (2) mixed design, with layout (grid vs. waterfall layout) as a within-subject factor and the mode of use (viewing leisurely vs. looking for a product that one likes) and Zhong-Yong as a between subject factor. Four different types of women's clothing (shirts, blouses, jackets, and sweaters) were used to formulate the webpages with each webpage constituting 48 clothing of the similar type (e.g., shirts). These 48 clothing were placed in 4 × 12 webpages with four clothing in each row and 12 clothing in each column in the grid layout and approximately so in the waterfall layout condition (see Fig. 1). All webpages were of similar sizes, i.e., 1024 × 5000 pixels. There are four different webpages for each layout. Cares were taken to counterbalance the clothing so that the set of clothing used were similar for grid and waterfall layout across participants. Each participant viewed eight webpages (4 in waterfall layout and 4 in grid layout) presented in random orders.

Seven rating questions measured the classical aesthetic (clean, pleasant and aesthetic) and expressive aesthetic (sophisticated, creative and fascinating) responses as well as webpage attractiveness [19] using seven-point scales. Participants of the target search condition answered two additional questions for the clothes they picked – "This clothing is nice" and "I like this clothing". The Zhong-Yong Belief Value Scale [8] was used to measure the propensity towards Zhong-Yong thinking.

2.3 Procedure

The stimuli were presented on a 23 inch color monitor at the resolution of 1024 × 768 in a quiet room. Participants viewed the webpage by scrolling up and down using the arrow keys and they pressed the "esc" key to end the viewing of the current webpage. They were allowed to view as long as they like but no longer than one minute for each webpage. The rating questions appeared on the center of the screen to replace the webpage and the participants responded to the rating questions using mouse. Eye movements were also recorded using the remote mode of Eyelink 1000 system, sampling pupil locations at 500 Hz.

Participants were asked to imagine they browsed the web store for new looks and styles as a pastime (leisure viewing). They simply viewed the webpages and signal when they were done viewing. Others were asked to imagine they were taking the time to search for good winter clothing (target search) and were asked to pick one clothes in the current webpage that they liked the most.

3 Results

A median split at 40 on the Zhong-Yong Questionnaire score was used to divide participants into high and low Zhong-Yong groups. ANOVAs were performed on dependent measures.

3.1 Classical and Expressive Aesthetic Ratings

The first analysis treat the classical vs. expressive aesthetics as a variable and performed the layout (2) x mode of use (2) x aesthetic dimension (2) ANOVA separately for high and low Zhong-Yong individuals. For high Zhong-Yong individuals, layout interacted with the aesthetic dimension ($F(1,30) = 23.78$, $p < .0001$). The fixed grid layout was rated higher on the classical aesthetic dimension than the waterfall flow layout while the reverse was true when rating on the expressive aesthetic dimension. These effects interacted with the mode of use only marginally ($F(1,30) = 3.01$, $p = .09$). During leisure viewing, the fixed grid layout was rated higher than the waterfall flow layout on the classical aesthetic dimension. Differences between these two types of layouts were not significant in the rest of the conditions (see Fig. 2).

For low Zhong-Yong thinking individuals, layout interacted with the mode of use ($F(1,24) = 5.24$, $p < .05$). The waterfall flow layout was rated prettier than the grid layout when the mode of use was leisure view but the two layouts did not differ when the mode of use was target search. Layout also interacted with the aesthetic dimension ($F(1,31) = 9.8$, $p < .005$). Similar to the responses of high Zhong-Yong individuals, the waterfall flow layout was rated higher on the expressive aesthetic dimension than the fixed grid layout. Different from high Zhong-Yong individuals, the two types of layouts did not differ on the classical aesthetic dimension (see Fig. 2). The mode of use interacted with the aesthetic dimension ($F(1, 24) = 6.51$, $p < .05$). The classical aesthetic dimension was rated higher than the expressive aesthetic dimension when the mode of use was leisure view while the ratings on the two dimensions did not differ for target search.

To summarize, the Zhong-Yong disposition affected the viewer's classical but not the expressive aesthetic experience. Layout affected the expressive aesthetic experiences regardless of Zhong-Yong individual differences. On the classical aesthetic dimension, the high Zhong-Yong individual preferred the fixed grid layouts during leisure viewing. These findings support H_1 and H_2.

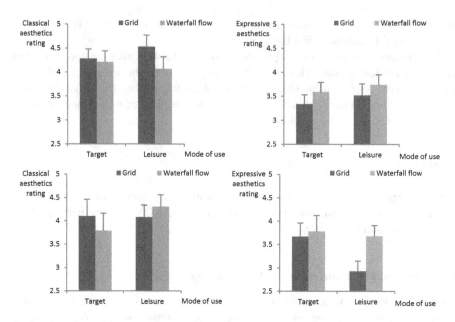

Fig. 2. The effect of layout and mode of use on classical and expressive aesthetics ratings for high (top) and low (bottom) Zhong-Yong individuals

3.2   Webpage Attractiveness

The analysis of webpage attractiveness found a three-way interaction between layout, mode of use and Zhong-Yong ($F(1,54) = 7.33$, $p < .01$) (Fig. 3). For low Zhong-Yong thinking individuals, planned comparisons showed that the waterfall flow layout was rated more attractive than the fixed grid layout if the mode of use was leisure view. The two types of layouts did not differ in rated attractiveness when the goal was target search or if the individual was high Zhong-Yong thinking. These findings support H_1.

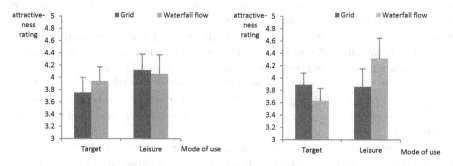

Fig. 3. The effect of layout and mode of use on webpage attractiveness rating for high (left) and low (right) Zhong-Yong individuals

The analysis of product attitude did not find any significant effect.

3.3 Viewing Time and Eye Tracking Measures

The analysis of the viewing time found a significant effect of layout ($F(1,53) = 6.08$, $p < .05$). The fixed grid layout was viewed longer than the waterfall flow layout. Regressive viewing was analyzed using object-based recurrence measure [1]. The analyses using the first 15 s of viewing data found no interaction between Zhong-Yong and layout. There was significant main effects of layout ($F(1,54) = 4.98$, $p < .05$) and task ($F(1,54) = 13.41$, $p < .001$). Greater regressive viewing occurred for the fixed grid than the waterfall flow layout and leisure view than target search. As there was an effect of layout on regressive viewing but the effect did not interact with Zhong-Yong, these findings partially support H$_3$.

4   Discussion

Current findings call attention to the potentials of adapting webpage design to user's thinking style as a means to enhance users' positive experience toward the website. Previous studies have demonstrated that users perform information seeking task better using websites designed by designers from their own culture. Uncovering information design elements related to thinking style may thus serves as a useful approach to the design of culturally congruent websites [5, 21]. As mentioned earlier in this article, [4] suggested to scatter information on a webpage as a way to match with the visual processing style of holistic thinkers such as Chinese and Japanese. The holistic thinking style has also been shown to associate with the geographical regions of southern China that farm rice, in contrast to the northern China regions that farm wheat [18]. As such, the optimal webpage design could be more accurately delivered according to the linked geographic regions, not just countries.

The Zhong-Yong thinking style studied in the current study is related, though not equivalent, to the much studied holistic thinking style. The individual differences in Zhong-Yong thinking influences whether the user is actively using visual attentional control or is largely guided by information layout of and current task goal when he browses through a webpage. When low Zhong-Yong thinking individuals browsed webpages as a leisure pastime, they rated the aesthetics and attractiveness of webpages higher if the information was presented in a waterfall flow layout rather than the fixed grid layout. Low Zhong-Yong thinkers did not exhibit preferences for a specific type of information layout when they were engaged in target search. Although both high and low Zhong-Yong individuals rated the waterfall flow layout higher along the expressive aesthetic dimension regardless of the mode of use, high Zhong-Yong individuals rated the regularly ordered fixed grid layout more classically aesthetic than the waterfall flow layout after performing the leisure viewing task but not after the target search task. These findings suggested that an information layout driven by a clear rule (such as the fixed grid) may serve high Zhong-Yong individual well while the innovative, novel layout (such as the waterfall flow) is better received by low Zhong-Yong individuals when they browses for enjoyment or pastime.

It should be noted that the current study is a laboratory study, though demonstrating detailed processing differences, the findings and interpretations of which are limited by the small sample sizes. The current study also did not measure the usability dimension to associate the aesthetic and subjective experience with actual webpage use. Larger scale online studies will be needed to help verify if the fit between webpage layout and Zhong-Yong thinking style may actually predict the online performance such as navigation, purchase decision, ad click-through.

References

1. Anderson, N.C., Bischof, W.F., Laidlaw, K.E., Risko, E.F., Kingstone, A.: Recurrence quantification analysis of eye movements. Behav. Res. Methods **45**(3), 842–856 (2013)
2. Chang, T.Y., Yang, C.T.: Individual differences in Zhong-Yong tendency and processing capacity. Front. Psychol. **5** (2014). doi:10.3389/fpsyg.2014.01316
3. Cyr, D.: Website design, trust and culture: an eight country investigation. Electron. Commer. Res. Appl. **12**(6), 373–385 (2013)
4. Dong, Y., Lee, K.P.: A cross-cultural comparative study of users' perceptions of a webpage: with a focus on the cognitive styles of Chinese, Koreans and Americans. Int. J. Des. **2**(2), 19–30 (2008)
5. Faiola, A., Matei, S.A.: Cultural cognitive style and web design: beyond a behavioral inquiry into computer-mediated communication. J. Comput.-Mediat. Commun. **11**(1), 375–394 (2005)
6. Hassenzahl, M., Ullrich, D.: To do or not to do: differences in user experience and retrospective judgments depending on the presence or absence of instrumental goals. Interact. Comput. **19**(4), 429–437 (2007)
7. Huang, J.L., Chung, Y.J., Lin, Y.C.: Forest before trees when needed: global processing and ZhongYong. In: Wei, C.W., Yang, C.F. (eds.) Chinese Social Psychological Review - Psychological Studies of ZhongYong-II, vol. 8, pp. 49–65 (2014)
8. Huang, C.L., Lin, Y.C., Yang, C.F.: Revision of the ZhongYong belief-value scale. Indig. Psychol. Res. Chin. Soc. **38**, 3–41 (2012)
9. Ji, L.J., Lee, A., Guo, T.: The thinking styles of Chinese people. In: Bond, M.H. (ed.) The Oxford Handbook of Chinese Psychology, pp. 155–167 (2010)
10. Lavie, T., Tractinsky, N.: Assessing dimensions of perceived visual aesthetics of web sites. Int. J. Hum.-Comput. Stud. **60**(3), 269–298 (2004)
11. Marcus, A., Gould, E.W.: Crosscurrents: cultural dimensions and global web user-interface design. Interactions **7**(4), 32–46 (2000)
12. Miyamoto, Y., Nisbett, R.E., Masuda, T.: Culture and the physical environment holistic versus analytic perceptual affordances. Psychol. Sci. **17**(2), 113–119 (2006)
13. Moura, F.T., Singh, N., Chun, W.: The influence of culture in website design and users' perceptions: three systematic reviews. J. Electron. Commer. Res. **17**(4), 312–339 (2016)
14. Nisbett, R.E., Peng, K., Choi, I., Norenzayan, A.: Culture and systems of thought: holistic versus analytic cognition. Psychol. Rev. **108**(2), 291 (2001)
15. Norman, D.A.: Emotional Design: Why We Love (or Hate) Everyday Things. Basic Books, New York (2004). doi:10.1145/966012.966013
16. Porat, T., Tractinsky, N.: It's a pleasure buying here: the effects of web-store design on consumers' emotions and attitudes. Hum. Comput. Interact. **27**(3), 235–276 (2012)
17. Sonderegger, A., Sauer, J., Eichenberger, J.: Expressive and classical aesthetics: two distinct concepts with highly similar effect patterns in user-artefact interaction. Behav. Inf. Technol. **33**(11), 1180–1191 (2014)

18. Talhelm, T., Zhang, X., Oishi, S., Shimin, C., Duan, D., Lan, X., Kitayama, S.: Large-scale psychological differences within China explained by rice versus wheat agriculture. Science **344**(6184), 603–608 (2014)
19. Tractinsky, N., Cokhavi, A., Kirschenbaum, M., Sharfi, T.: Evaluating the consistency of immediate aesthetic perceptions of web pages. Int. J. Hum.-Comput. Stud. **64**(11), 1071–1083 (2006)
20. Tractinsky, N., Katz, A., Ikar, D.: What is beautiful is usable. Interact. Comput. **13**(2), 127–145 (2000)
21. Vyncke, F., Brengman, M.: Are culturally congruent websites more effective? An overview of a decade of empirical evidence. J. Electron. Commer. Res. **11**(1), 14 (2010)
22. Wang, M.Y., Lin, S.J., Yeh, Y.Y.: Unexpressed pleasure, anger, sorrow and joy – the implementation of Zhong-Yong thinking through attentional and memory processing of emotional stimuli. In: Wei, C.W., Yang, C.F. (eds.) Chinese Social Psychological Review - Psychological Studies of ZhongYong-II, vol. 8, pp. 28–48 (2014)
23. Wang, M.-Y., Tang, D.-L., Kao, C.-T., Sun, V.C.: Banner evaluation predicted by eye tracking performance and the median thinking style. In: Marcus, A. (ed.) DUXU 2013. LNCS, vol. 8013, pp. 129–138. Springer, Heidelberg (2013). doi:10.1007/978-3-642-39241-2_16
24. Wang, Y.J., Minor, M.S., Wei, J.: Aesthetics and the online shopping environment: understanding consumer responses. J. Retail. **87**(1), 46–58 (2011)
25. Yang, C.F.: Multiplicity of Zhong Yong studies. Indig. Psychol. Res. Chin. Soc. **34**, 3–96 (2010)

Transforming Concepts of a Taiwanese Twin Cup into Social Design Activities

Ning-Hsien (aka Vincent) Yang[✉]

National Taiwan University of Arts, New Taipei City, Taiwan
vincentyang2006tw@gmail.com

Abstract. To promote personal body-mind-soul (BMS) wellness is very basic in life around the world. Via theoretical and practical concepts of cultural ergonomics (CE), designers develop products and services in the culture creativity industry (CCI) to transform and bring users not only cultural contexts, but interactive experiences. This paper then places focuses on transforming concepts of a Taiwanese twin cup into a BMS buddy activity design created from the literature review about CCI, applied CE, LOHAS and BMS industry. For developing the users' interactive experiences, CE includes excellent theories which are also methodological approaches that carry interaction- and experience-based benefits to people. The research case is about the transformation from linnak which is a typical cultural object in the Taiwanese Paiwan tribe into a series of buddy partner activities conducted at 2015 Asian Pacific Playback Theatre Conference. At the end, the research results will show the conference participants' feedback and cultural meaning of working together and sharing valuable experiences with each other in groups from the researcher's design. Most importantly, the results will confirm the scholarly theories, follow methodological approaches, and present practical values in the future social design activities.

Keywords: Cultural ergonomics (CE) · Culture creativity industry (CCI) · Body mind and spirit (BMS) · Paiwan Linnak · Buddy partner & social design activities

1 Significant Research Journey Introduction

Body Mind and Spirit Connection is designed to show you how the connection between the body, the mind and the spirit is so important and how it can help you to maintain a totally healthy "being". Maintaining our health is the best gift we can give ourselves. (Body Mind and Spirit Connection Wellness and Learning Center [1])

It's been very vital for people to promote personal wellness in life around the world. Most people often pursue their financial satisfaction and economical success, but forget their own peace of minds. Recently people have encountered political, economical, and educational changes in their current transition. Thus, the introduction of paper focuses on four parts such as (1) research backgrounds, (2) research purposes, (3) research question, (4) research methods in procedure, and (5) research contribution.

© Springer International Publishing AG 2017
P.-L.P. Rau (Ed.): CCD 2017, LNCS 10281, pp. 104–120, 2017.
DOI: 10.1007/978-3-319-57931-3_9

1.1 Research Backgrounds

Match with Environmental Background. For the political, economical, and educational reasons in society, people need some spaces (e.g. secret gardens) to well promote their body-mind-soul (BMS) connection, and designers shall also consider those social factors as Stevens [2] states its importance of the promotion of individual wellness. The same scenarios apply to people in Taiwan. In the past, Taiwan's unstable political dispute, chaotic economical dropdown, and arguable educational policies under such a rapidly vibrant environment affected people in many ways. Thus, from Maslow's [3] hierarchy of five levels of human needs, most people in Taiwan shall not only fulfill their basic needs, but long for inspirations from higher human motivations.

Current Situational Problems. Current situational problems obviously appear in the world. For example, politicians always fight for their final "wins" to take political spots and advantages. Business persons also earn whatever they can benefit from the society, and forget their initial missions for underrepresented groups. Educators in school tend to teach ways of success in order for their students to well survive in the future competitive world. Those things have happened in Taiwan, resulted in some others' imbalanced well-beings, and brought local residents unhealthy thoughts, bodies and minds. Thus, people have tended to swiftly search for any religious comfort, instead of the choice of constantly establishing their personal scales of peaceful minds. So people shall pay attention to their BMS connection and wellness.

Therefore, the idea of BMS wellness may be changed according to some new concepts. In medical and therapeutic fields of treatment, DK [4] addresses that concepts, projects and methods have been effectively utilized for promoting clients' health and wellness in many ways (e.g. spa, green garden, nature, facility, yoga, tai chi, etc.). For new discoveries and current problems, traditional BMS methods need new theories and practices of healing peoples' wounds in order to satisfy peoples' further needs, or discover new concepts (e.g. products/services, or programs/activities) for innovative designs in society. Hence, the research tends to provide another angle to see problems in Taiwan, offer new ideas from professional fields, including the incorporation of expressive work (e.g. dance, theatre, arts, music, etc.) stated by Krout [5] and Sajnani [6], mindfulness activities in active communities from Doyle et al. [7], and harmonic life such as eudaimonia around the world as Albanese [8] states to strengthen human bodies, promote minds' growth, contain experiences in spiritual ways, and create a possible case of services, programs and activities via changed or transformed concepts from culture creativity industry (CCI).

Research Relevancy. The applied cultural ergonomic (CE) theory was utilized in the research. Lots of research results have focused on theories and practices of LOHAS industry, CCI, Applied Theatre (AT) activities and BMS wellness, but little has found from both applications transformed from CCI and even further mixture of topics between expressive events and mindfulness activities in the BMS business. Hence, the research is very relevant. Using the Paiwan Linnak—a Taiwanese twin cup design from an aboriginal tribe is a great example from the concepts of CE. The research finally adapted the applied CE theories and framework and presented a transformed buddy activity design that makes participant partners closer in Hong Kong at Asian Pacific Playback Theatre Conference (APPTC) workshop in November, 2015.

Narrative Motives. Researcher's personal motives led the research to reach another level in academia. For example, the researcher has been motivated by more professional playback practitioners' work in AT, academic scholars' practical concepts in BMS, and field practitioners' successfully experiential cases via expressive activities and mindful events to connect peoples' wellness. Adapting examples from CE, the researcher utilized an activity plan in the conference. Hence, one of the research motives is to check whether the original concepts of CE are good to transform Paiwan Linnak into a buddy partner activity design to combine between theory and practice, and whether the activity plan works for the conference participants in purpose.

1.2 Research Purposes

Buddy Partner Relationships. Through the academic literature, the research first provides a clear picture of BMS and LOHAS industries, importantly illustrates theories of CE, additionally presents CCI, and frames the twin cup transformation from CE into social activity designs. Next, the researcher describes, designs, and utilizes the buddy partner activities from three levels of the framework created by Lin, Lin, Chen, & Hsiao [9] as the major methodology. Lastly, the research purposely describes a curve of buddy partner activity plan and participants' feedback.

1.3 Research Question

Research Question. One research question is posted: "What will be new findings from conference workshop participants' feedback under such a social activity design after the research utilizes transformed concepts via three levels of a modified framework of cultural ergonomics?"

1.4 Research Methods in Procedure

Specific Research Methods. The researcher first makes sure of research motives and purposes. Utilizing the existing literature about CCI, CE, LOHAS and BMS industry, and concepts of Paiwan Linnak is the second step. At last, the research employs the theories and frameworks of CE to create a modified framework, a curve of activities, lesson plans, academic references, and receives participants' feedback to come up a new perspective regarding social design activities in the future BMS business, or self-healing programs.

1.5 Research Contribution

Based on the results, this paper offers its unique benefits. The research paper was going to first contribute to the participants at 2015 APPTC. Then, the researcher would lead the similar activity for playbackers at Taiwan Playback Theatre Association (TPTA) in

2016. Furthermore, the research results brought more academic and practical values to the general public or underrepresented groups in the society when the researcher brought topics into doctoral classes from 2016 to 2017.

2   Transformed Body-Mind-Soul Literature Review

In the faith of respect to the culture and the profession of creativity, the association help people with talents and industries to enter into the proper creativity, innovation and own business, so as to assist society to identify the cultural originality. (TCCA Taiwan Cultural & Creative Association [10])

From the literature part, there are four parts such as (1) culture creativity industry, (2) applied ergonomic studies, (3) future LOHAS industry, and (4) Body-Mind-Spirit industry that are reviewed in the following.

2.1   Culture Creativity Industry

The definition of an industry is explained differently according to the scale of national development. Basically, it is defined to be the final production of goods, services, or creativities within a financial, cultural, and political system. Thus, a group of business sectors work on the similar management activities within an industry such as food, texture and high-tech businesses. Based on the cultural factors, any industry is able to promote its products with creativity into the market to produce potential wealth for local people. From Ministry of Culture, Republic of China (Taiwan) [11], the following functions clearly state the visions of cultural & creative industry.

Cultural policy and its implementation must serve the people by helping to expand culture into the international realm and build the nation's soft power. Policies should also employ the latest technology to more effectively spread the knowledge of Taiwan's unique culture and customs both domestically and internationally.

Except for the cultural policy, the contents and ranges of cultural and creative industry were revised on March 19th, 2014. There are sixteen categories of cultural and creative industry. Particularly Category Fourteen—Creative Life Industry integrates core knowledge and creativity of life industry, offers experiential practices and appreciates aesthetics of life. Furthermore, more products have been created through applied ergonomic studies in the CCI emphasized by Lin [12, 13], Lin et al. [14] and Lin et al. [9].

2.2   Applied Ergonomic Studies

Cultural ergonomics (CE) is a practical method to evaluate products/services. Lin et al. [9] well defines it. "Cultural ergonomics extends our understanding of cultural meaning and our ability to utilize such understanding for design and evaluate everyday products" (p. 242). In addition, Lin et al. [9] also provides a theoretical approach for product/service/creativity transformation.

Cultural ergonomics is an approach that considers interaction- and experience-based variations among cultures. Designers need to develop a better understanding of cultural ergonomics not just to participate in cultural contexts but also to develop interactive experiences for users (p. 242).

Taiwanese aboriginal craft products present a pretty style with powerful arts of design in their daily life. Lin et al. [9] states "Taiwan aboriginal culture has great potential to enhance design value and gain recognition in the global market" (p. 242) to serve as an embryonic form and a fundamental function. Additionally, the transformed product/service/creativity combines CE and interactional design to allow users to get in touch with humanity, explore local cultures, and provide interactive experiences. From the recent study results, Lin et al. [9] takes the linnak as a represented aboriginal cultural object in Taiwan.

From the tradition to modern design, the linnak is one of the great examples of product transformation in the current market. The design of linnak of the Paiwan tribe is so valuable that it has been used in the Paiwan tribe's daily life to share cultural meanings with others and work together for closeness by Lin [12, 13] and Lin et al. [14]. Mainly, Lin et al.'s [9] page 245 and Lin [12] point out four genuine steps for designing a cultural product. "In a practical design process, four steps are used to design a cultural product: investigation (setting a scenario), interaction (telling a story), development (writing a script), and implementation (designing a product)." Please also read the page 245 of Lin et al.'s [9] article about "Scenarios in the development of the linnak" and "A framework for cultural ergonomics in product design" that are also shown in this paper section three: "Cultural Ergonomics Design Methodology."

According to the cultural product design model, the concepts of three cultural levels are applied to cultural product/service/creativity transformation that depends on the designers' transformed and utilized concepts from the outer, middle or inner level and focus. For example, the cultural product/service/creativity design would be applied in the future LOHAS and BMS industries.

2.3 Future LOHAS Industry

Based on the concepts of self-supply, people in the LOHAS industry care about consumption in health. Further speaking, people will consider self and family health and their responsibilities for the existing environments. LOHAS is a conceptual word formed by the initial letter of the following words such as Lifestyles Of Health And Sustainability. From 1986 to 2001, Paul Ray and his research team had surveyed more than 150,000 people. Ray [15] published a book which is called The Cultural Creatives: How 50 Million People are Changing the World in 1998, and defined the meaning of LOHAS. People in the LOHAS industry consider values more than price in consumption. They affect others' consumption behaviors and value life quality in the environment. Thus, surrounding-friendly and social responsibility are very important factors for suppliers to pay attention to. For LOHAS areas of studies, American LOHAS magazine Executive Director, Ning [16] also confirms the above concepts under such industrial pollution and negative effects on our living environment. In general, there are five LOHAS areas of studies such as (1) self-growth, (2) optional therapy, (3) healthy diet, (4) health lifestyle, and (5) ecological sustainability. Even though there are five areas of studies about LOHAS life businesses for people in Taiwan, they have lacked further practices in life, especially on their individual development of bodies, minds and spirits which would be explained for individuals and groups in the BMS industries.

2.4 Body-Mind-Spirit Industry

For the definition of BMS industry, target audiences are motivated to consume goods, services and creativities, and then feel satisfied from many aspects on their body, mind and spirit development. From academic research on physio-psycho-spiritual (e.g. PPS) integration from the public views, not many people have heard about PPS, but pointed out that spiritual experiences have been related to religious faiths to someone who is greater than self, and to the mystery in the world. In Taiwan, most PPS or BMS businesses or industries focus more activities on religious, mystical, and traditional approaches which have allowed the audiences to be immersed in their own spiritual experiences and religious beliefs.

However, some PPS or BMS businesses or industries have offered their participants more experiential activities with non-religious advocate. For example, there are expressive, experiential activities on bodily, mindful and spiritual practices such as drama, dance, music, art, therapeutic work, human potentials, applied drama & theatre elements, etc. These approaches have recently become the other options for the audiences. Among hundreds of companies, foundations or associations, Miranda, iReborn, Uho, Jade, PsyGarden, etc. are PPS or BMS examples in Taiwan. PsyGarden's [17] mission statement well states. "To catalyze ideological transformations … To witness cultural meanings … To model indigenous experiences … To nurture the local narratives of humanity", the research findings were analyzed to explain the workshop activities for networking opportunities, holistic learning and pursuit of quality in life.

3 Cultural Ergonomics Design Methodology

Cultural product design is a process of rethinking or reviewing cultural features and then redefining them to design a new product that satisfies modern consumers by way of cultural and aesthetic features. (Lin et al. [9], p. 252)

The methodology includes four parts: (1) adapted research framework, (2) extended research process, (3) conference workshop participants, and (4) multiple research tools.

3.1 Adapted Research Framework

Theoretical and Applied BMS Case. For the adapted research framework, Lin et al. [9] have studied CE in product design for a long time and utilized figures to illustrate their research framework. From their great points, CE will turn out to be a significant issue in product design for target audiences to interact with and experience what designers' creative ideas mean in CCI in society. "While product design has been user-centered for some time, there is now greater emphasis specifically on user experience, with ergonomics increasingly becoming a part of interactional design" Lin et al. [9] address the above from page 244. In CE product designs, scholars have had systematic approaches to codify cultural influence. Lin et al.'s [9] two figures (P. 245) show three cultural levels of CE product design to explain their research framework.

For instance, Fig. 1 scenarios in the development of the linnak illustrates key points of three cultural levels, factors and scenarios as Lin et al. [9] indicate its scenarios in the development of the linnak of Paiwan tribe culture.

(1) the outer level (user) focuses on linnak formation associated with user demand, lifestyle, and immediate feeling; (2) the middle-level (tool) focuses on function, usability, and consumer behavior regarding the linnak in everyday life; and (3) the inner-level (task) focuses on cultural meaning, including ceremony, reflection, and emotion. (p. 244)

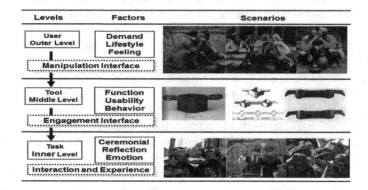

Fig. 1. Scenarios in the development of the linnak.

Except for the scenarios from the Lin et al.'s [9] article, scholars from Hsu et al. [18], Lee [19], Lin et al. [20], Murovec and Prodan [21], and Norman [22] also confirm the scenarios. From Fig. 1, the outer level (user) with manipulation interface describes that people in the Paiwan tribe culture drank together to feel closer. The linnak is designed at the middle level (tool) to focus on its function for engagement interface and use of intimacy in life. Lastly, the inner level (task) shows how the Paiwan tribe people utilize the linnak in diverse ceremonies, weddings and celebrated rituals to interact with others and experience the cultural meaning.

The above comprehensive figure has also formed the framework. From Lin et al.'s [9] page 245, Fig. 2, a framework for cultural ergonomics in product design shows the whole process in different layers to come up with CE in interactional and experiential design. The framework includes three major layers which contain (1) the conceptual model from cultural ergonomics, design transformation model to cultural products, (2) research method from identification (cultural objects), translation (design information and elements) to implementation (creative products), and (3) human system design from cultural layers, cultural levels to design features.

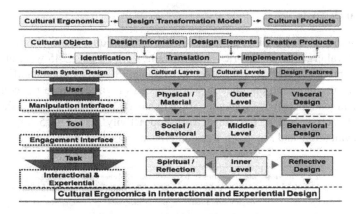

Fig. 2. A framework for cultural ergonomics in product design.

The above framework was adapted and modified as the main research tool for the research case. The research processes, participants and tools would be described next.

3.2   Research Process

Experimental Research Process. The researcher set up research purposes, then reviewed the relevant literature, and finally adapted Lin et al.'s [9] framework as the main research base of methodology. Moreover, the modified CE framework with evaluative were utilized for the research transformation in 2015. Furthermore, the specific case about the concepts of Paiwan Linnak transformed into buddy partner activities was conducted on November 29th, 2015 in Hong Kong for the APPTC 2015 workshop target audience. However, the length of preparation time and research period had lasted from September 2015 to January, 2017, and the research results were from on-line play-backers' constructive feedback. Finally, the research showed the research's overall analysis, reflection and conclusion in 2016.

3.3   Participants

APPTC 2015 Workshop Participants. The research participants mainly came from the 2015 playback conference. One of the accepted workshop proposals led by the researcher was conducted at 2015 APPTC. Because the conference planning committee tried to balance the number of participants for each workshop which was taken place at the same time, the participants should register and would be arranged by their own workshop interests. Thus, the original number from the conference arrangement was about 12 playbackers who were from Macau, Hong Kong and some provinces of Mainland China. As for research roles, the researcher had taken many jobs as the workshop planner, instructor, feedback collector, researcher, writer, translator and analyst in the process of research. Regarding the research tools and contents, they all depended on a framework modification of CE with some evaluation forms.

3.4   Research Tools

A Modification of Cultural Ergonomics with Evaluation Forms. Lin et al.'s [9] original cultural ergonomics theories and the framework on page 245 were utilized to design the conference workshop in order to evaluate all activity contents. Figure 3 a modification of cultural ergonomics in workshop was revised to plan the conference workshop and lead its activity contents. Some evaluative tools for the workshop were value-added such as Fig. 4, five-stage workshop activity plan, Fig. 5, two-question workshop evaluation, and Fig. 6, on-line conference workshop questionnaire.

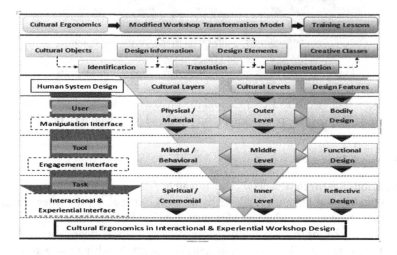

Fig. 3. A modification of cultural ergonomics in workshop

	Warm-up	Exploration	Work	Closure	Feedback
NO.	2:00-2:20	2:20-2:40	2:40-3:20	3:20-3:40	3:40-4:00
1	PPT pictures + music • Basic information • Title	Circle of whispering • Purposes: Buddy, 4-grid & magic • Any surprise	Pair-up PT work • Buddy partner chatting • Solo playback • 4-step feedback • Draw my past picture	King's and queen's words • Create words • Read them aloud • PS: Show PPT and skip this activity	Evaluation • Index of happiness • Index of sweetness
2	Walk around: • Physical greetings • Park, market, zoo, quiet place	Simple name game (e.g. balls)	Double buddy talk • The future magic room • PT still picture • Group feedback time	Three items • Trash can • Treasure box • Questions	One action • Group picture
3	• Name & need • Indian humming sound	Sociometry • Living distance, playback history, feeling and needs	Buddy partner time • Your future picture about treasures in your magic room • Red threads		Online feedback (Questionnaire) • Best learning • Questions with confusion • Future applications
4	Draw my current feeling	Three circles • A Taiwanese twin cup • Cultural Ergonomics in PT • Three colors in your life			Any question(s) • Extra work: Six-Part Story Making (6PSM) • Ending
5		Pair-up • Draw a cooperative picture with partners			

Integrating the Essence of Three Novel Circles Utilized in Self Future Exploration of Company Practice

A Modified Workshop Activity Plan

Fig. 4. Five-stage workshop activity plan (Color figure online)

Fig. 5. Two-question workshop evaluation

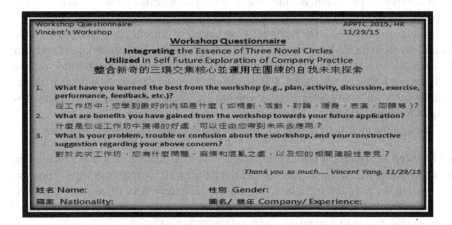

Fig. 6. On-line conference workshop questionnaire

4 Playback Workshop Case Analysis

The application of cultural features is a powerful and meaningful approach to product design. Consumers nowadays require a design that is not only functional and ergonomic but also able to stimulate emotional pleasure. (Lin [13], p. 14)

Next, the case analysis—workshop contents, results & feedback includes four parts.

4.1 Workshop Contents, Results and Feedback

The case analysis touches upon four parts: (1) a modification of research framework: to describe the framework for activity plan of the conference workshop, (2) a five-step workshop plan: to execute the plan which provided the details, curve of activities, lesson plans and practical references, (3) the conference participants' in-workshop responses: to quickly receive the participants' responses to gain overall workshop results, and (4) three on-line feedback questions: to utilize three survey questions to get the participants' after-workshop feedback.

A Modification of Research Framework. A modification of research framework is significant for the researcher to form the research structure which guides the research process, Fig. 3. A modification of cultural ergonomics in workshop work describes each layer transformed from the Lin et al.'s [9] original CE framework. For the first layer, the researcher used the concepts and practices of CE, modified the contents to become the workshop transformation model, and designed some training lessons. As for the second layer, through cultural objects, like an aboriginal twin cup, the researcher would identify objects' utilization, collect design information, translate meaning of scenarios, add design elements, implement ideas and finally come up with creative classes for the conference workshop participants. For the last layer, the readers read the figure column information vertically and horizontally to reach the goal and process of CE in interactional & experiential design. Besides, the human system design allows us to experience a workshop design from three steps such as user (manipulation interface), tool (engagement interface) and task (interactional & experiential interface). Additionally, three cultural layers in the BMS workshop design include (1) physical (material), (2) mindful (behavioral), and (3) spiritual (ceremonial). Cultural levels describe from the outside circle to core which contain outer, middle and inner levels. At last, the workshop design features start with bodily design, come with functional design and end up with reflective design for the participants.

Based on the modified framework, the researcher created a five-step workshop plan.

A Five-Step Workshop Plan. A five-stage workshop activity plan was prepared for the workshop participants. Figure 4 states the topic and its activity contents. There are five steps in the plan that includes (1) warm-up, (2) exploration, (3) work, (4) closure, and (5) feedback. Each activity title was posted; however, the activity in red was deleted in the workshop due to limited time and the researcher's choice.

The Conference Participants' In-Workshop Responses. Whether the workshop succeeds or not, it mainly depends on the participants' evaluative feedback. Results from the short survey would be explained after Fig. 5, two-question workshop evaluation.

From the conference arrangement, the original participants should be 12. But, one was missing because the Pilipino team went to an outdoor playback performance; one Cantonese left earlier for her urgent need. Two workshop volunteers came to join the workshop to still maintain 12 participants. The results of the two in-workshop responses were close to 93% (e.g. 4 participants circled 4; 8 persons circled 5). The audience seemed to feel happier after attending the workshop. Some participants felt confused with the survey of index of sweetness. Thus, the percentage of results was about 85% (e.g. 3 separated participants circled 3 and 4; 6 persons circled 5). The audience needed more relevant and value-added activities to gain their sweetness.

Three One-Line Feedback Questions. To utilize three survey questions to get the participants' feedback, the researcher prepared hard copies. Due to insufficient time, the feedback comments were noted. After the workshop, the researcher sent out the modified workshop PPT with Fig. 6 in both English and Chinese to the participants.

From the 12 participants, some written feedback in brief sentences translated in English by the researcher was posted in italic and analyzed in terms of three categories such as application, time and creativity. The feedback is listed in the following.

In terms of application.

1. I never thought of playback applications this way. I like Vincent's 3 novel circles of activities that gave me ideas to work on my own BMS and buddy relationships.
2. I like the idea and practices of doing solo playback.
3. I need time to think of Vincent's workshop [framework] about CE. It was so quick that I couldn't see the figure clearly. But, I know this in my teaching career.
4. The five-step workshop plan was clear to me, and I know the workshop flow.
5. It was a great idea to incorporate expressive activities into a playback workshop.
6. Vincent's workshop activities were offered for us to taste a portion of his design. I would like to continue to work on the six-part story making that seems to be fun to understand my own story and others in society.

In terms of time.

1. Vincent utilized many activities, but time was short. I wanted to have more activities. Two hours were short. The organizers shouldn't cut the workshop short.
2. I needed more time to talk to my buddy partner about my stories. Time was short.
3. Vincent might arrange some time to explain cultural ergonomics. The time was not enough for him so he might come to China to conduct some workshops.
4. It is interesting. After the workshop, we still have homework to do. But, there was no time for us to work on the six-part story assignment. I wish we had more time.

In terms of creativity.

1. Vincent's workshop was creative: lighting-up candle, drawing, exercising, posting questions for thought, showing PPT, playing music, giving homework, etc.
2. Lots of Vincent's workshop activities were very creative and relevant to my life. I will learn more creativity from him for my underrepresented groups in our society.

5 Research Discussions, Suggestions and Conclusions

When designing "arts" into "business", we need a better understanding of human-art interaction not just for taking part in the humanity context, but also for developing the interactive experience of arts. (Lin [23], p. 1)

The significant conclusion includes (1) research findings for discussions, (2) research limitations for extensions, (3) research suggestions for implications, (4) researcher's expectations from inspirations, and (5) research creativity towards conclusions.

5.1 Research Findings for Discussions

Several discussions from the research findings were proposed for the future research. There are four pieces such as further theoretical tests, step-by-step guidelines, more creative explorations, and pre-workshop communication.

Further Theoretical Tests. First of all, it is good to discuss an existing theory, or a framework to be constantly tested and utilized after any researcher decides to follow and treat the theory as a good tool, methodology, or approach. Since this research was a prior study by taking CE theories from Lin et al. [9], the modified research framework has indicated its future applications in any BMS study and social activity.

Step-by-Step Guidelines. Secondly, it is a must to describe a step-by-step plan that a trainer shall conduct an applied BMS workshop after the framework. From the research case, the workshop plan was designed by following not only human system design, concerning about cultural layers, cultural levels and design features, but a workshop curve, including activities from each step. The researcher also planned many physical, mindful and spiritual activities, examined exercises from outer, middle and inner levels, and allowed the participants to interact with each other and experience the designed workshop from bodily (e.g. walking around the room with purposes from the warm-up step), functional (e.g. buddy and 4-step feedback work with solo playback performances from the work step) and reflective viewpoints (e.g. three items and two questions of reflective feedback from the closure and feedback steps).

More Creative Explorations. Thirdly, from the participants' research results, their words will lead more creative explorations in the future. For example, creative BMS activities will be great to make strong impacts on the participants as a male participant from China said. "Lots of Vincent's workshop activities were very creative and relevant to my life. It never occurred to me. I will learn more creativity from him." In addition, adding some activities from other fields is also a thoughtful idea. A female participant from Macau described her opinion. "It was a great idea to incorporate expressive activities into a playback workshop." The last example is to explore the participants' stories through some creative ways. Two female participants from Hong Kong and Canton in China expressed their thoughts. "I would like to continue to work on the six-part story making that seems to be fun to understand my own story…. I like the idea and practices of doing solo playback."

Pre-workshop Communication. At last, workshop time is always crucial so communication to the conference organizers shall be important for attention. For instance, four participants addressed that time was short. A female American Chinese even stated her strong point. "I want to have more activities. Two hours are short for the workshop. The organizers shouldn't cut the workshop short." The researcher had communicated with the organizers for a long time. But, the projector didn't work in the beginning; the volunteer reminded the researcher to cut 15 min short due to the last workshop. For the above reasons, the researcher had to decide to skip some activities and made the feedback and questionnaire short. Thus, the pre-workshop communication should be an issue to be raised for reference, especially within a short amount of workshop preparation time. A better communication will be the main key for the workshop organizers, participants and researchers in any future conference. From the above, the research is limited by its nature.

5.2   Research Limitations for Extensions

The research was limited due to its nature of study. The research participants were a few in terms of workshop participation, and research time was divided within years.

The Size of Workshop Participants. The size of workshop participants was small for the research in the conference. However, it was a prior study. The research limitation will become extended studies. The researcher already applied the research framework, workshop plan and adapted activities to a drama in education (DiE) conference for K-12 teachers and Taiwanese Playback Gathering (TPG) for TPTA members in 2016. There will be more participants to join the social activity design work.

The Length of Research Time. The length of the workshop time was short. The given conference workshop had been conducted for two hours. The research was done earlier in semester from September, 2015 to January, 2016. It will be extended to a long-term base research. More non-religious BMS activities, playback applications and expressive work shall be considered in the future. The researcher will be able to collect more local and international data to develop a new theory, framework, method, or approach for people with self-healing abilities in 2017.

5.3   Research Suggestions for Implications

From the findings, research suggestions for implications were proposed for the future researchers. There are theoretical, methodological and practical applications.

Theoretical Applications. From the literature review, the scholars' CE theory is able to be applied in the training service fields. CE is not only a theory, but a research approach. The later scholars are still working on the framework modification. It has been utilized for the Taiwanese aboriginal twin cup scenarios. Therefore, the theory shall be extended and applied in terms of academic research such as aboriginal fabrics, clothes, and textiles. CE has been proved in product design; it shall be theoretically applied in invisible products, services and programs, too as shown in this study.

Methodological Applications. The theories with frameworks for CE in product design provide a clear picture. This study utilized figures to transform main research structures and frameworks to be this research methodology. After modifying the original framework, the process presented detailed steps and contents. For methodological applications, the researcher will continue to apply the concepts of CE in the field of self-healing programs and businesses with Lin et al.'s scholars [9, 14, 18, 20].

Practical Applications. There are four practical research implications. The research offered the playbackers new insights individually, in group and society such as life-long learning, expressive applications, buddy partner relationships, and company practices. First, for the participants' life-long learning, the workshop lesson contents and activities would assist them in planning their future teaching careers, working on academic theories, leading creative work for underrepresented groups in society, and telling life stories.

As for the second point, some participants agreed to work on something about expressive applications, have multiple activities in workshop, and do solo playback in life in the future. Thirdly, for developing buddy partner relationships, some participants gave the research positive feedback *"to work on my own BMS work and buddy relationships"* so any person in society won't feel alone. At least, there is someone there to support each other via buddy partner relationships. Besides, there is an extra piece of homework. This research finally brings in new concepts to the future company practices for underrepresented groups and BMS organizations in society.

5.4 Researcher's Expectations from Inspirations

When the research came to almost the end, the researcher suddenly found out that the researcher has been inspired by several significant turning points: (1) too many activities, (2) only prior studies, and (3) modified theoretical framework.

Too Many Activities. Within a time limit, the workshop shouldn't offer too much. There were many activities at one time in two hours. In fact, any BMS activities shall bring the participants a piece of mind. Hence, slowing down the workshop speed, cutting off some activities, and focusing on the core work will be the main improvement for the researcher's future applications. The researcher also carried too many tasks at one time as the workshop instructor, researcher, observer, evaluator, listener, computer technician, and notetaker. For the workshop, the roles shall be simple.

Only Prior Studies. The research was a prior study. As a result, the research findings and new learning knowledge should be the future contents and materials for further studies. Based on this study, the researcher collected more quantitative participants' feedback and voices in society via the self-healing questionnaire in 2017.

Modified Theoretical Framework. The playbackers preferred practices to theories. From the researcher's observation, most playbackers would like to put theories into practices rather than come up with academic theories. The researcher has had a strong belief that a good framework, theory, or an approach will provide people a clearer picture beyond their daily practices. Finally, the small steps from the research would make research dreams bigger. Therefore, a combined framework among CCI, CE, LOHAS and BMS shall be developed soon for playback practitioners in our society.

5.5 Research Creativity Towards Conclusions

Any research journey seems to come to the conclusion. For the research creativity towards conclusions, there are three positive viewpoints and ending thoughts to make.

First, CE has been an academic theory and practical approach to be tested and transformed for products. It shall work for the services, trainings, classes, programs and workshops for different participants in society to receive invisible benefits. Secondly, it will be a new exploration for the playbackers in the world. For the playback instructors and participants, the researcher will not only devote time, money and effort in finding new knowledge for the playback and BMS development in Taiwan, but create practical healing workshops and activities in Taiwan and the world. Finally, for the researcher, it was not an end, but another new start in the research journey. How to transform existing theories into personal academic theories will be main concerns and research issues for the researcher to think and work in the doctoral studies.

For research missions, the researcher will try to fulfill participants' both expressive and mindful needs, allow them to receive colorful experiences, join newly social design activities, reach their own goals of self-growth, maintain healthy BMS wellness, find optional choices from resources, shorten the gap between theory and practice, and moti-vate various levels of learners, participants or consumers to work on small projects to make meaningful transformation so does the research topic—*Transforming a Taiwanese Twin Cup into a BMS Buddy Activity Design.*

Acknowledgements. I really appreciate it because of Professor R. T. Lin's generosity for me to adapt his theories and research frameworks to my research. Next, this paper is also dedicated to him, APPTC participants and my wife in the research process.

References

1. Body Mind and Spirit Connection: Wellness and Learning Center. Welcome to body mind and spirit connection (2001–2012). http://www.hmie.gov.uk/documents/publication/hmiepcie.html
2. Stevens, M.: The promotion of wellness. Landsc. Architect. **85**(1), 64–67 (1995)
3. Maslow, A.H.: A theory of human motivation. Psychol. Rev. **50**(4), 370–396 (1943)
4. DK: Spas in airports. Hosp. Des. **26**(6), 44 (2004)
5. Krout, R.E.: Music listening to facilitate relaxation and promote wellness: integrated aspects of our neurophysiological responses to music. Arts Psychother. **34**(2), 134–141 (2007)
6. Sajnani, N.: The body politic: the relevance of an intersectional framework for therapeutic performance research in drama therapy. Arts Psychother. **40**(4), 382–385 (2013)
7. Doyle, S., Kelly-Schwartz, A., Schlossberg, M., Stockard, J.: Active community environments and health. J. Am. Plann. Assoc. **72**(1), 19–31 (2006)
8. Albanese, F.: New wellness for new bodies (English). Domus (919), 1–2 (2008). ISSN: 00125377
9. Lin, R., Lin, C.L., Chen, S.J., Hsiao, W.H.: Cultural ergonomics in interactional and experiential design: conceptual framework and case study of the Taiwanese twin cup. Appl. Ergon. **52**, 242–252 (2016)
10. Taiwan Cultural & Creative Association TCCA: The Aims of the Association (2012). http://www.culture.org.tw/TCCAfrom.html
11. Ministry of Culture, Republic of China (Taiwan): Functions (2013–2015). http://english.moc.gov.tw/article/index.php?sn=239
12. Lin, R.: Transforming Taiwan aboriginal cultural features into modern product design: a case study of a cross-cultural product design model. Int. J. Des. **1**, 45–53 (2007)
13. Lin, R.: Designing Friendship into modern products. In: Toller, J.C. (ed.) Friendships: Types, Cultural, Psychological and Social. Nova Science Publishers Inc., Hauppauge (2009)
14. Lin, R., Lin, P.-H., Shiao, W.-S., Lin, S.-H.: Cultural aspect of interaction design beyond human-computer interaction. In: Aykin, N. (ed.) IDGD 2009. LNCS, vol. 5623, pp. 49–58. Springer, Heidelberg (2009). doi:10.1007/978-3-642-02767-3_6

15. Ray, P.: The Cultural Creatives: How 50 Million People are Changing the World. Three Rivers Press, New York (1998)
16. Ning, T.: Lohas (2010). http://www.lohas.com/forum/speakers/ted-ning
17. PsyGarden Publishing Company: About us (2015). http://www.psygarden.com.tw/about.php?func=english
18. Hsu, C.-H., Lin, C.-L., Lin, R.: A study of framework and process development for cultural product design. In: Rau, P.L.P. (ed.) IDGD 2011. LNCS, vol. 6775, pp. 55–64. Springer, Heidelberg (2011). doi:10.1007/978-3-642-21660-2_7
19. Lee, S.L.: Garments culture of Taiwan aborigines. Hist. Objects **87**, 14–28 (2000)
20. Lin, R., Cheng, R., Sun, M.X.: Digital archive database for cultural product design. In: Aykin, N. (ed.) HCII 2007. LNCS, vol. 4559, pp. 154–163. Springer, Heidelberg (2007)
21. Murovec, N., Prodan, I.: Absorptive capacity, its determinants, and influence on innovation output: cross-cultural validation of the structural model. Technovation **29**, 859–872 (2009)
22. Norman, D.A.: Emotional Design: Why We Love (Or Hate) Everyday Things. Basic Books, New York (2004)
23. Lin, R.: Turning "art work" into "interior design"—a case study of Mondrian style. Paper Accepted to Present at the 2016 HCI International Conference, Toronto, Canada, 17–22 July 2016

Applying the Story of *The Dream of the Butterfly* in Creative Design

Mo-Li Yeh[1]([⊠]), Chun-Ming Lien[2], and Yi-Fang Kao[1]

[1] Graduate School of Product and Media Design,
Fo Guang University, Jiaoxi, Taiwan
1101moli@gmail.com, g9730810@gmail.com
[2] Department of Commercial Design and Management,
National Taipei University of Business, Taipei City, Taiwan
cmlien@ntub.edu.tw

Abstract. In recent years, traditional cultural material has been creativity applied to increase the value of artistic designs and expand aesthetic economies worldwide. Cultural creative designs involve extracting and transforming cultural elements and symbols to create new aesthetic meanings in artworks. This study extracts the intangible cultural elements of the Chinese fable, *The Dream of the Butterfly*, through analyzing its literary meanings to provide inspirational concepts for cultural creative designs. The experience in *The Dream of the Butterfly* was a turning point in the life of Chuang Tzu. In response to increasing stresses of modern living, soothing emotional designs have become trendy. The light-hearted writing style of Chuang Tzu and the erratic portrayal of the butterfly are ideal inspiration for creative designs. This study aggregates practices based on theories of cultural creative designs and organizes various interpretations of *The Dream of the Butterfly* through the Chuang Tzu aesthetic theory and by scholars worldwide. The fable was interpreted on three interpretative levels (namely the dreamlike state, the integration between the thing and the self, and the sympathetic circulation of mind and matter) to analyze existing artworks inspired by the fable. Thus, spiritual reflections in the process of creative transformation have been clarified, and a reference for transforming the philosophy of *The Dream of the Butterfly* into creative designs has been established.

Keywords: The Dream of the Butterfly · Cultural creativity · Creative design

1 Introduction

Most of the classical Chinese literary works, which have been handed down the generations over thousands of years, are well-refined masterpieces. Not only do they capture the essence of ancient culture and wisdom, but they also correspond to numerous aspects of creative design. These classical works can be used to create memorable creative designs and enable new generations to experience the distinctive legacy of Chinese culture, thereby achieving cultural preservation. Therefore, this study explored *The Dream of the Butterfly*, a fable from *Qi Wu Lun* (*Discussion on Making All Things Equal*) in the *Chuang Tzu*. The fable is as follows:

© Springer International Publishing AG 2017
P.-L.P. Rau (Ed.): CCD 2017, LNCS 10281, pp. 121–130, 2017.
DOI: 10.1007/978-3-319-57931-3_10

Once Chuang Chou dreamt that he was a butterfly, a fluttering butterfly which was pleased with himself and did not know that he was Chuang Chou. Soon, he woke up and found himself an unmistakable Chuang Chou. However, he didn't know if he was Chuang Chou who had dreamt he was a butterfly, or a butterfly dreaming he was Chuang Chou. There must be a distinction between Chuang Chou and a butterfly! This is called the Transformation of Things.

Through considering the meaning of this work, this study explores the cultural context and design of the Chuang Tzu's aesthetics. It aggregates and analyzes various interpretations of *The Dream of the Butterfly* and existing related artworks to provide a theoretical basis for transformative designs and applications, as well as specific creative design methods. Understanding the realms of *The Dream of the Butterfly* enhances the poetic and artistic moods and aesthetic values of artworks. Therefore, this study examines the applicability of *The Dream of the Butterfly* in modern design to facilitate the preservation of culture and enhance the depth and significance of cultural creative designs.

Cultural design involves creating emotional products through the use of cultural elements to facilitate a spiritual consumer experience that draws on beliefs, memories, or emotions and satisfies consumers' cultural-level psychological needs. An outstanding product can communicate with people through emotional images and inspire their sensations in a similar approach to that of an artwork. According to Norman [13] emotional elements are central to the success of product design, and the soul-touching power of a product is maximized through empathy, which is based on the truest resonance to the life experience of each individual. Thus, creative inspiration from *The Dream of the Butterfly* can provide an empathetic concept for generating artistic and cultural designs.

2 On Applying the Philosophy of *Chuang Tzu*

Given the stresses of modern life, soothing emotional designs have become trendy. This study aims to expand imagination through the fantasy world created by the fables in the *Chuang Tzu*. No matter how treacherous the world has been, plants, animals, and strange, changing worlds constitute the emotional universe in of the Chuang Tzu. The fables are richly imaginative, featuring effective literary techniques, fantastic descriptions of scenery and characters, and minimalistic yet meaningful writing. These fables also exhibit diverse genres, complex content, and charming forms and art that are not restricted to any specific format. This literary achievement is unrivaled among pre-Qin literature, thus making the *Chuang Tzu* an outstanding work when compared to literary works worldwide [12].

Since the early 1900s, there have been interpretations of the *Chuang Tzu* by Friedrich Nietzsche, Henri Bergson, existentialism, phenomenology, hermeneutics, and deconstructionism, which expand on its philosophy and add new depth; the *Chuang Tzu* has been interpreted from the perspectives of metaphysics, aesthetics, philosophy of art, and ecoenvironmental philosophy [15]. The fables of Chuang Tzu have also attracted the attention of numerous artists and writers over time, because the creative freedom inherent in these fables has considerably influenced aesthetic philosophy and artistic creations among them [11]. The rhetoric and use of rich metaphors in the

Chuang Tzu has broadly influenced the literature of subsequent eras; in particular, the appreciation of the arts and craftsmanship in the *Chuang Tzu* has shaped later literary and artistic works. When aesthetic creators transcend their sense of gains and losses, their spirits and creativity are freed, affording them scope for liberty and pleasure in their artistic creations [20].

Chu [4] claimed that imagination is the fundamental capability required for artists and writers, and that people who lack imagination may only become artisans or literati. Moreover, the breadth of imagination defines the value of artistic works. Arts are appreciated through their creativity, which is founded on imagination. Creativity involves integrating, organizing, and tailoring existing constructs into new order or forms; in other words, artists arrange, organize, and tailor their observations of nature or life experience into coherent works. Imagination also plays a key role in aesthetics. The rich literary grace and beauty of the *Chuang Tzu* arise from its unpredictable, imaginative spaces rendered without the restrictions of specific forms. Plants and animals feature in the emotional world portrayed by Chuang Tzu, corresponding to the current trend in design, which stresses the use of emotional elements.

Chu [4] indicated that Chuang Tzu transferred his emotions to a fish in the *Chiu Shui* chapter (*The Chapter of Autumn Flood*) to share the life of the fish. This inter-action between Chuang Tzu and the fish is a form of psychological empathy. In the famous *Fable of Kunpeng*, Chaung Tzu opened an infinite space for the human spirit through the transforming fish and birds in his experiential world. His philosophical writing is "limitless and uninterrupted (*Tian Hsia*, literally *The World*)" and similar to "the water of the Yellow River that descends from the Heaven." The concept of "tours" employed by Chuang Tzu has profoundly influenced later literary, aesthetic, and artistic works. "Heart tours," which involve transcending all human relationships and interests in the tangible world and observing things aesthetically, are the core of the psycho-logical activities in traditional Chinese aesthetics. The concept of "the usefulness of the useless" bears a striking similarity with the modern European aesthetic theory of transcending human interests and utilitarianism [2].

In summary, the fables of *Chuang Tzu* have profoundly influenced later literary, aesthetic, and artistic works. The aesthetic psychological activities involved in the fables transcend the human relationships and interests in the tangible world. The observance of the world through this artistic mindset constitutes the core of the psy-chological activities promoted in the traditional Chinese aesthetics. The school of thought involved in the fables bears a considerable similarity with modern European aesthetic theory, which transcends human interests and utilitarianism. This makes *Chuang Tzu*, which can be used in developing the modern literature, aesthetics, and philosophies, suitable for the theoretical transformation as discussed in this paper.

3   On the Levels of the Realms in *The Dream of the Butterfly*

In this study, three interpretations of *The Dream of the Butterfly* were employed and examined in three artworks. In "On the Annotation Orientations of *The Dream of the Butterfly* and their Utilities," Lin [9] distinguishes between the mainstream interpre-tation of the fable adopted in the days of Guo Xiangzhu (Jin Dynasty) and Chengxuan

Yingshu (Tang Dynasty) versus the new philosophical interpretation of *Chuang Tzu* through the introduction of modern European–American aesthetics and the discourse on related aesthetic experience by modern scholars. Although enriching *The Dream of the Butterfly*, the various new interpretations may confuse readers. These diverse interpretations can be categorized into three major orientations, namely the traditional "dreamlike state" interpretation, the integration between the object and the self, and the sympathetic circulation of mind and matter. In this study, these three interpretive levels were investigated according to the characteristics of the related artworks. The decision of how to interpret the key subjects of the fable concerns not only the variations among interpretive approaches, but also the diversity of the interpreters' understanding of the philosophy of Chuang Tzu. These three levels of interpretations are detailed as follows.

3.1   Dreamlike State

In his "Preliminary Study on the Meaning of the Dream in *Chuang Tzu*," Hsu [7] divided *The Dream of the Butterfly* into the dream phase (when Chuang Tzu dreamed of being a butterfly without being aware of his identity as Chuang Tzu) and the waking phase (after Chuang Tzu woke up from the dream), thereby helping readers distinguish time and place within the fable. However, scholars over time have proposed divergent interpretations and focal points. Some have focused on interpreting the dream phase; some have argued that the waking phase is the true focal point of the fable; others have addressed Chuang Tzu and the butterfly themselves as the center of the entire story. Most of the scholars who interpret the fable through the dreamlike approach have divided the story into the dream and waking phases according to the plot progression and explained both phases as dream states on the basis of the following line: "He didn't know if he was Chuang Chou who had dreamt he was a butterfly, or a butterfly dreaming he was Chuang Chou." Accordingly, the dreamlike interpretation approach was designated as the first level of the realm of *The Dream of the Butterfly*.

3.2   Integration of the Object and the Self

According to Chen [2], Chuang Tzu used this fable to describe the state of humans enjoying themselves and doing as they pleased. To Chuang Tzu, the universe is a massive garden, where butterflies fly around joyfully without constraints; humans should similarly roam around the universe with freedom and without constraints. The transformation into a butterfly is a reflection of arts. In other words, the aesthetic experience is used to reflect upon the changes of objects, eliminate the distance between the object and the self, and attain the integration of the two entities. Kao [8] maintained that the sense of infinite space involves first the confusion caused by the environment, then the emotions caused by sensations, and finally the perfect integration between the emotions and the environment. This process of assimilation is caused by the continuation of self, which leads to an expanding world with no barriers. The transformation into the butterfly involves the experience of an object by the self through its mind, a self-metaphor through the use of the object, and ultimately the elimination of the distinction between the object and the self. According to *The Aesthetics and Literature of Chuang Tzu*, aesthetic experience is a realm of the actualization of the object and the self. When Chuang Tzu dreamed of becoming a butterfly, he did not know whether he was Chuang Tzu who dreamed of being a butterfly or a butterfly that dreamed of being Chuang Tzu. Such is the transition between the object and the self [4].

Whether dreams are real or virtual is explored in *Chuang Tzu*. Chuang Tzu recorded the dream of being a butterfly and analyzed it as in line with his own aspirations (being happy with himself and doing as he pleased). In that dream, Chuang Tzu completed his transformation into a butterfly, and the dream was not only a dream. Therefore, Chuang Tzu was unaware of his identity as Chuang Tzu. When he woke up, he had to recognize that he did not truly become a butterfly. This experience led to a major change in the life of Chuang Tzu [1].

Scholars who have interpreted the fable as the integration between the object and the self generally focus on the aesthetic experience of self-actualization, pleasure, and freedom as described in the lines "flitting and fluttering around," "happy with himself and doing as he pleased," and "he didn't know he was Chuang Chou." The experience of the integration of the object and the self in the dream was used to directly verify the accessibility of the happiness and free spirit in life. In *The New Discourse on Laotzi and Chuang Tzu*, Chen [2] indicated that the concept of the transformation into the object does not only indicate the process of Chuang Tzu's transformation into a butterfly but also symbolizes the disappearance of the border between the object and the self, the sympathy between the subject and the object, and thereby their mutual integration. The concept directly refers to the spiritual harmony between the object and the self. Accordingly, the concept of the integration of the object and the self was designated as the second level of the realm of *The Dream of the Butterfly*.

3.3   Sympathetic Circulation of Mind and Matter

The sympathetic circulation of mind and matter, which is an extension of the dreamlike approach and the concept of the integration between the object and the self, is a new concept used to describe Chuang Tzu's transcendence of the realms of life in *The Dream of the Butterfly* [9]. This concept also describes the absence of independent reality and the attainment of spiritual transcendence and freedom through the overcoming of the borders between life and death and between the self and the others as described in the *Qi Wu Lun* (*Discussion on Making All Things Equal*).

In "*True People Do Not Dream* and *The Dream of the Butterfly*: The Preliminary Study on the Meaning of Dreams in *Chuang Tzu*," Hsu [6] interpreted the concept of the transformation into the object through the thorough sympathetic circulation of the object and the self (separation → integration → separation). Hsu [7] emphasized the aesthetic experience of pleasure and freedom in the realm of integration, and the reflection and realization of the subject of the oneness between the dream and reality and between life and death in the realm of separation. This fable signifies these things in the mind of the subject. The interactive circulation between the aesthetic experience and spiritual realization leads to the transformation into the object.

According to the concept of the sympathetic circulation of mind and matter, Chuang Tzu attained the highest realm of life through the separation, integration, separation circulation of mind and matter. The transformation into the object involves the aesthetic experience in the realm of integration and the reflection and realization of life in the realm of separation. This is a continuous process of circulation between separation and integration. This circulation process enables an individual to continually transcend the realms of life and achieve *Tao* (literally "the way") [10].

According to Kao [8], the emotional (e.g., internalized images and physical, sensual, and emotional reactions) and intellectual (e.g., conceptual relationships based on representations or symbols) substance of aesthetic experience simultaneously exist in the consciousness of each individual and continuously interact with each other. This enables individuals to fulfill not only personal interests through their experiences but also their personal aesthetic sensibilities. External phenomena are a starting point or a border to the processes and realms of aesthetic experience, and can only be converted to personal experience through internalization. This corresponds to the concept of the sympathy between mind and matter. Therefore, the sympathetic circulation of mind and matter was designated as the third level of the realm of *The Dream of the Butterfly*.

4 Transitioning and Interpreting the Story in Design

According to Chin [3], art is inseparable from constructs, which are acquired through experience and typically generated from the imagination. Continual imagining leads to the generation of multiple constructs, which are then integrated and expressed to form the artistic connotation and appeal of an artwork. Artists must put emotions into everything, giving life to their imagined universe, and construct in line with their zeitgeist, to create extraordinary works and attain the infinite realm in which life and art are one. Regardless whether an artwork is based on dreams, mysteries, satire, or religion, transformations can be traced within the basis of the artwork. According to *The History of Chinese Esthetics*, as evidenced in its evolution from capturing images from observation in the early Qin era to the fusion of subjective thoughts and emotions into objective items and the vital imaginations during the Wei, Jin, Northern, and Southern dynasties, classical Chinese aesthetics involves the exploration of psychological activities in aesthetic creations. Accordingly, the examination of the artworks in this study is based on interpretations of the diverse abstract and specific elements in *The Dream of the Butterfly*.

A fundamental consensus on creative transformations in Chinese philosophies, ideologies, and cultures was preliminarily established through intensive promotion by scholars such as Charles Fu, Yu-Sheng Lin, and Zheng-Tung Wei in the 1980s [15]. These scholars selected *Chuang Tzu*, which contains abundant original philosophical writings and has considerably impacted Chinese philosophy, as the basis of artistic transformation. The writings of *Chuang Tzu* were expanded upon and restated through the employment of modern knowledge. According to Fu, not only should the possible connotations described by the original author be stated, but the maximum potential of the knowledge in the text must be discovered. According to *Innovative Meanings*, transformative creative narratives can be applied to give the Chuang Tzu philosophy a new life and form. The philosophical techniques of phenomenology, Heidegger's ontology, and deconstructionism can be used to perform the transformative creations based on *Chuang Tzu*. Such creative procedures lead to an expansion of the possibilities embedded within the original works. Thus, the original works are no longer limited to recapitulating their original meanings, but are instead incorporated in a new contemporary perspective, thereby inspiring more creative transformations of ancient philosophies [17–19].

According to Fu [5], the hermeneutics of creativity originated from interpretative studies of the classical philosophical and religious works of *Tao Te Ching* (*The True Classic of the Way and the Power*). Because this hermeneutics is a general methodology, it can be applied to continue, inherit, reconstruct, transform, and modernize an ideological tradition (e.g., Confucianism or Buddhism). According to the hermeneutics of creativity, carrying forward ideological and cultural traditions enables modern scholars to develop appropriate attitudes in processing said traditions. This hermeneutics can also be applied in literary appreciation and criticism as well as studies on the history of philosophy and ideas. The theory of interpreting and transforming classical literary works involves the process of reading, interpreting, absorbing, and transforming the said works. Fu maintained that the hermeneutics of creativity involves constructing a comprehensive theory through the appreciation, criticism, and creative transformations of classical works. Generally, hermeneutics encompasses studies of the humanities such as literature and the arts, and incorporates the essences of various European and American philosophies. The process of the transformative applications of classical works can be generalized into the following five levels:

1. *Actual meaning:* what the original author *actually* said. This requires collating and researching the original texts.
2. *Intended meaning:* what the original author intended to say. This requires semantic clarifications, contextual studies, biographical studies, and logical analyses.
3. *Implied meaning:* what the original author could have implied in the text. This requires referencing relevant analyses and interpretations by scholars over time.
4. *Deeper meaning:* what the original author should have said without being aware of it themselves. This may be related to deeper or fundamental meanings under the surface of the text, which require hermeneutical insights to identify.
5. *Creative meaning:* what the original author might say today to preserve the original thoughts in the text. This requires creativity from the interpreters to identify.

Wong [14] suggested that the aforementioned modern Chinese hermeneutics provides true creative opportunities and particularly emphasized the deeper and creative meanings among the five levels of hermeneutics proposed by Fu [5]. These subjective meanings involve transforming the implied meanings as interpreted by other people into one's own contemporary, perceptive creative thinking and incorporating Gadamer's antecedent structure. In other words, works of the past are questioned through the perspective of the present, thereby increasing the possibility of the interactions between the works of the past and the creators of the present. The questioning and transformation of classical works through modern creative design fulfills the concept of embedding modern elegance within the emotional recall of ancient times in cultural and creative industries. An outstanding artwork must be appropriately interpreted to induce its appreciators into its artistic world. Gadamer described hermeneutics as an envoy of all thinking, thus alluding to its mediating role in creative activities. Yeh [16] addressed hermeneutics as the basis for interpreting and applying classical aesthetics in modern designs. This enables designers to examine the interpretation phases and contents of classical literature corresponding to their creative works. Thus, the applicability of the systematic development of literary interpretation in the transformative designs based on the literature can be expanded, and designers can understand and adjust the interpretative positions of their works.

The artworks investigated in this study can be analyzed and correspond to the interpretative levels of *The Dream of the Butterfly*. Figure 1 shows the metal sculpture created by Pei-Chun Chen, which compares interpersonal interactions to the integration between Chuang Tzu and the butterfly and from seeing others to seeing oneself. The transformation within the work resembles both a ring of flowers and a circle of butterflies. The flowers and butterflies are similar to yet distinct from each other. Such an ambiguous combination is a form of the winding between the dream and the reality. Figure 2 depicts the illustration by Yuan-Chian Liu, which reveals the distinct constructs of Chuang Tzu and the butterfly within the same image. To overcome the restraints of this conventional art style, Liu focused on the frequently overlooked concept of the transformation into the object (the butterfly) by turning the arms of Chuang Tzu into butterfly wings and removing Chuang Tzu's outerwear, which signifies the transcendence of the secular reality. The mist represents the illusory realm of the dream. Thus, the integration between the object and the self was conveyed. Figure 3 illustrates the poster created by Dai-Qiang Jin for an international festival of dance based on the concept of *The Dream of the Butterfly*. A picture that ambiguously resembles either a butterfly or a dancer is used to convey the expression, "Is it the dancer who dreams of being a butterfly, or the butterfly that dreams of being a dancer?" Thus, the state of mind of the dancer and the harmony between the mind and the art are portrayed; the sympathetic circulation between the mind and matter is achieved.

Fig. 1. Dreamlike state (by Pei-Chung Chen 2013)

Fig. 2. Integration between the object and the self (by Yuan-Chian Liu 2015)

Fig. 3. Sympathetic circulation of mind and matter (by Dai-Qiang Jin 1989)

5 Conclusion

The key meanings, structures, and sensory cognitive relationships in *The Dream of the Butterfly* were examined to clarify diverse understandings of the fable by scholars in their own interpretations. Because of these divergent understandings, the fable has been interpreted in numerous orientations, thus enriching its significance. This study investigates the cultural contexts and design of the Chuang Tzu's aesthetics to formulate a theoretical basis for transformative designs and applications. According to the characteristics of the three artworks explored, the interpretative realms of *The Dream of the Butterfly* were divided into three levels: the dreamlike state, the integration between the object and the self, and the sympathetic circulation of mind and matter. Thus, a reference for analyzing the artworks based on the fable was created for practitioners in the cultural and creative industries.

Acknowledgment. This study was partly sponsored with a grant, NSC 105-2410-H-431-011, from the National Science Council, Taiwan.

References

1. Chao, W.M.: The Windy Spirit of Chuang Tzu: From the Butterfly to the Climate. Linking, Taipei (2010)
2. Chen, K.Y.: The New Discourse on Laotzi and Chuang Tzu. Wunan, Taipei (2007)
3. Chin, C.: New Discourse on Aesthetics and Literature. Commercial Press, Taipei (2003)
4. Chu, R.C.: The Aesthetics and Literature of Chuang Tzu. Mingwen, Taipei (1992)
5. Fu, C.W.H.: From the Hermeneutics of Creations to the Mahayana Buddhology. Tungta, Taipei (1990)
6. Hsu, S.H.: The genealogy of Chuang Tzu's pro-confucianism: an 'other' reading of Chuang-Tzuology. Chin. J. Natl. Taiwan Univ. **17**, 21–65 (2002)
7. Hsu, S.H.: True people do not dream and the dream of the butterfly: the preliminary study on the meaning of dreams in Chuang Tzu. Res. Chin. Lit. (5) (1991)
8. Kao, Y.K.: Study on the Chinese Aesthetics and Literature. National Taiwan University, Taipei (2004)
9. Lin, H.P.: On the annotation orientations of the dream of the butterfly and their utilities. Dong Hwa J. Chin. Stud. **1**, 31–54 (2002)
10. Li, M.Y.: Discussion of the materialization of Chuang-Tse from the butterfly dream of Chuang-Chou. J. Pingtung Teach. Coll. **10**, 355–370 (1997)
11. Li, Z.H., Liu, G.J.: History of Chinese Esthetics. Anhui Arts, Hefei (1999)
12. Liu, Y.Q., Yeh, M.L.: Application of Zhuangzi in 2D animation. In: Asian Foundation Design Conference, Tainan, Taiwan (2015)
13. Norman, D.A.: The Design of Everyday Things. Basic Books, New York (2002)
14. Wong, W.X.: Creation Opportunity. Tangshan, Taipei (1998)
15. Oh, C.C.: Chuang Tzu and Deconstructionism. Showwe Information, Taipei (2010)
16. Yeh, M.L.: Application of poetry in creative design. Ph.D. thesis, Graduate School of Creative Industry Design, National Taiwan University of Arts (2014)

17. Yeh, M.L., Chien, C.W., Lin, R.T.: Employing poetry culture for creative design with six-standpoints. In: Design Research Society 2014 Conference, Umeå University, Sweden (2014)
18. Yeh, M.L., Lin, P.H., Wang, M.S.: Employing poetry culture for creative design with a polyphonic pattern. USA. In: Rau, P.L.P. (ed.) CCD 2013. LNCS, vol. 8023, pp. 269–278. Springer, Heidelberg (2013). doi:10.1007/978-3-642-39143-9_30
19. Yeh, M.L., Wang, M.S., Lin, P.C.: Applying the time and space forms of poetry to creative design. In: Rau, P.L.P. (ed.) CCD/HCII 2014. LNCS, vol. 8528, pp. 798–807. Springer, Cham (2014). doi:10.1007/978-3-319-07308-8_76
20. Yeh, M.L., Liu, Y.Q., Lin, P.H.: Design and application of the illustrations of *Zhuangzi*. In: Rau, P.L.P. (ed.) CCD 2016. LNCS, vol. 9741, pp. 397–405. Springer, Cham (2016). doi:10.1007/978-3-319-40093-8_40

Cross-Cultural Product and Service Design

Research and Application of Service Design Thoughts in Subway Advertisement Design

Xing Fang[1], Yangshuo Zheng[1(✉)], Heng Liu[1], Yongzhen Zou[1],
and Xiaoqin Cao[2]

[1] Wuhan University of Technology, Wuhan, Hubei, China
zhengyangshuo@163.com, 867624024@qq.com
[2] Zhongkai Agricultural Engineering College, Guangzhou, Guangdong, China

Abstract. This paper explores the design of subway space advertising forms from the perspective of service design. Firstly this paper analyzes the concept of service design. On this basis the necessity of applying the design method to design subway advertising forms are analyzed. Secondly, through the analysis of the subway space and population factors, find where and when we should use the method of service design to design subway space advertising forms, and the application of service design methods in the field is explored. At last, combined with the case of a specific subway advertisement design, summed up the innovation points and follow-up research direction.

With the development of smart city and the arrival of service-oriented society, subway system, as a vehicle responsible for urban residents travel will further extend and develop in smart city construction and will be closely related to people's daily life. Subway advertisement, as a significant part of subway, has a great influence on passengers' travel experience. Most existing subway spaces adopt traditional advertisement as their media form, whose thoughts embodied in the design little meet passengers' real demands. Therefore, the lack of originality leads to passengers' less satisfaction. On the basis of the service-oriented thoughts and ideas, this paper explores new ways and thoughts for subway advertisement design and strives to tightly combine design and service together by breaking through traditional thoughts. Furthermore, this paper tries to create maximal benefits and the best solution based on limited resources.

Keywords: Service design · Subway space advertisement design · Subway service

1 Introduction

1.1 Concept of Service Design

The combination of the two concepts "service" and "design" as a relatively new field in the development of design is a new concept put forward after Modernism. Service-oriented design mainly studies how to systematically apply the theories and methods of design into the creation, definition and planning of service. Its design philosophy is built on interactive service, creative service and service economy. To explore the social value and commercial value of service-oriented design in social

P.-L.P. Rau (Ed.): CCD 2017, LNCS 10281, pp. 133–145, 2017.
DOI: 10.1007/978-3-319-57931-3_11

development by the collaborative design of user group is a concentrated reflection of "people-oriented" design philosophy in the aspects like user experience, value creation and social innovation.

Service design means to create useful and applicable experience for users by innovation or integration and establish an efficient and distinctive service from the perspective of service provider so as to create a better experience and deliver greater value for users. The application of exact approaches and tools of service-oriented design can help us figure out how to realize these principles and objects in corresponding stages of service design and how to make service-oriented design meet or even surpass users' demands. Different stages of service-oriented design ask for corresponding tools and approaches.

(1) Establish role models: The establishment of a role model may help the designer to have an intensive understanding of users from the perspective of design. To learn about users' lifestyle, living habit, attitudes toward life and users' experience and the pattern they adopt in service plays a significant role in service-oriented design.

(2) Draw a user experience map: user experience map as a tool to understand the interaction between users and product, service and system, aims to assist to clearly analyze the problems emerging in service so as to improve user experience based on this. An experience may can directly reflect user operation flow, expectation, their specific goal, emotion and the whole experience chain and determine the potential touch points between the user group and service product so as to actively and entirely control and assess the experience that a product provides.

(3) Analyze service touch point: in the thought of service-oriented design, it is just the design of service touch point that embodies the value of design. There is a wide range of forms of touch point: from the communication among people, the details in users' interaction on platform products to the activities in specific scenes. All of these may trigger service touch points. And touch points are usually made up of four aspects: people, object, process and environment.

(4) Service blueprint: Service blueprint is a kind of planning map describing the realization of system function in details, which can also concretely show the value orientation in service. Service blueprint shows its service in the following aspects at the same time: describes the process of service implementation, the place for user reception, the role that service provider plays and other elements that may appear in service-oriented design. Service blueprint provides an approach to dividing service into several blocks and then describes the steps, tasks, methods and the tangible exhibitions that customers can feel one by one.

Service design has various approaches and tool kits. In daily service design, designers have to select the ones they need based on practical problems so as to properly solve the problems emerging in service-oriented design.

1.2 Information Transmission Analysis in Subway Space

In the information society, information and knowledge have become the strategic resources and basic elements of economic industrial development. The value of information depends on the extent to which it is used and how is transformed. The advertisement communication in the subway public space plays a carrier role for video, text and graphic information. The information transmission of advertising from the sender to the receiver in the subway space is a propagation phenomenon. Advertising information dissemination is the process of transferring advertising information between the communication subject, passengers and the advertising media.

From the present situation, the main problem of subway public space information dissemination is the information asymmetry between advertisers and recipients, which is mainly caused by the following reasons:

(1) The information dissemination media diversification caused by information overload. Print media, electronic media, online media and face to face interpersonal communication are involved in the dissemination of subway advertising information, resulting in a substantial increase in the amount of information, information overload become an inevitable phenomenon.

(2) From the theory and practice on the subway advertising information seriously inadequate. From the view of the subway travel attribute, the formation process of the subway advertisement information dissemination effect is the process which affects passengers cognition and guide passengers behavior, involves the communicator, the media, the information contents, the passenger itself, the physical environment and many kinds of elements, Subway advertising information dissemination effect is complex and unstable.

(3) Ignore the subway advertising information users, the effective dissemination of subway advertising information feedback is not sufficient. Subway passenger's interest, the level of understanding, social status and other individual factors and social factors will have an impact on the dissemination of advertising information. Passengers not only accept information but also use information, not only selectively receive advertising information, and can explain its information feedback to the advertising information management department.

In order to solve the problem of poor communication of advertising information in the subway public space, firstly we need more cross-application with information technology so as to speed up the dissemination of advertising information, reduce the cost of advertising information and optimize the dissemination of advertising information. For subway passengers, advances in information technology have resulted in more flexible, centralized and interactive communication between subway passengers and subway advertising management department. Taking "interactive advertising" as an example, the media can publish advertising contents and deeper functions (transactions, payments, etc.), users also can participate in modifying the form and contents of real-time media environment.

More importantly, it's need to make clear service design as a subway space advertising design methodology, "user-centered design" no longer stay on the surface, through design tools such as user experience map, service touch points, service blueprint and other tools to guide the overall promotion of the subway advertising information dissemination of the overall effects and optimization user experience constantly.

2 The Significance of the Service Design Thought into Subway Advertisement Design

In the actual subway context, the revolutionary development of information technology changes both the form of advertisement and the service philosophy. The diversity of the original carrier, structure and marketing mode of subway advertisement and the appearance of equipment like new light box and interactive touch screen make subway passenger- participation design possible. With the arrival of the era of "experimental service", the function of subway advertisement has gradually changed into providing in-demand information to passengers, which realizes customized autonomous service mode.

Centering on improving passenger experience, the service-oriented design easily stimulates the participation and initiative of subway service-provider and passenger group. To discuss subway advertisement design from the perspective of service-oriented design, the design should be based on passengers' actual demands and the elements including user characteristic, feature of technique and environment so as to provide valuable and high-quality service that passenger group needs.

The application of service-oriented thought into subway advertisement design makes the designer more thoroughly understand passenger's behavior and lets the design provide different advertisement functions and experience to passengers through the integration of sense judgment, emotional experience, thought experience, action experience and relevance experience into subway advertisement.

Driven by service design, not only the development strategy of subway advertisement will be innovated based on current situation, but also the commercial value of subway and the overall quality of city will be improved. Furthermore, the subway advertisement itself will be given a more meaningful form; moreover, the specific context of subway and interaction pattern will be given brand new definitions.

3 The Application Path of Service Design Thought into Subway Advertisement

The fundamental attribute of service-oriented design is a system design for the relationship among people, thing, behavior, environment and society. Located in the subway system, subway advertisement not only creates commercial value, but also great user value and social value. In the era of the experience of service-oriented economy, subway advertisement can adopt multiple ways to attract passenger group's attention, provide the service in demand and produce better subway-taking experience. Therefore, the design of subway advertisement from the perspective of service-oriented design has to take the functions and features of subway and passenger's psychological and behavioral traits into overall consideration. Furthermore, based on various elements of subway, this kind of design lets passengers directly experience, feel and participate and makes the subway advertisement have much benefit of advertisement.

3.1   Analysis of Subway Environment

Subway space generally falls into station hall, platform, pedestrian path, tunnel, train and elevator. With the rapid growth of urban population and the improvement of subway, the capacity of subway space is continually expanding. Subway advertisement plays an important role in increasing economic benefit, shaping city image and improving passenger's travel experience. Different subway spaces have different forms of advertisement. For example, the advertisement forms used on the ground of stair in subway include carpet decal advertisement, ground projection advertisement, integrated design covering both ground and wall etc. (as shown in Fig. 1). Based on the

Fig. 1. Subway advertisement integrated design

Other	Elevator	Elevator
		Escalator
	Train	Body
		Carriage
	Top surface of subway station	Subway platform top
		Subway channel top
	Subway station cylindrical	Column
		T card
	Wall of subway station	Channel U shape space
		Channel on both sides of the wall
		Tunnel wall
		Screen door wall
	Subway station ground	Blind ground
		Platform floor
		Channel ground
		Stair floor
	Subway space	Advertising media

Fig. 2. Categories of subway advertisements

spatial position and the characteristics of media, the categories of subway advertisements in form have been shown in Fig. 2.

3.2   User Role Model of Subway Passengers

To more thoroughly understand the status of the development of the subway advertisement in Wuhan, we handed out some questionnaires about Wuhan Subway Line 3 by the way of O2O and sampled 500 valid ones for study. The result shows that the age range of subway passengers is fairly wide mainly from 15–60. Most of the passengers have received high school education or above; the majority of them are middle-income office workers and students. Their purposes of travel mainly include commuting, going to school, going shopping, joining a party etc. And almost all passengers have a specific purpose of travel. Affected by the features of subway environment, passengers sometimes are nervous while sometimes relaxed with the characteristics of their behaviors changing from free ones to orderly ones. When a passenger is relatively relaxed with free actions, the attention he pays on subway advertisement usually improved greatly.

In our survey, we also found out that the advertisement in the carriage of subway and the light box advertisement on the platform more easily raises passengers' concern. And passengers generally pay attention to public benefit and tourism advertisement, especially show great interested in dynamic and interactive advertisements. The previous user study and situational analysis lay a foundation for the following designs.

3.3   Study of User Behavior and Deficiencies

Passengers' behaviors in subway are always uniform with similar purposes. The analysis of passengers' path and passenger's path-finding behavior is a significant component of the study of subway passengers flow. To determine the main flow in subway can help us understand the features of subway passengers' behavior. The survey shows that subway passengers' behavior flow includes three steps: enter into the station and get on the subway, transfer, get off the subway and walk out of the station. These three steps form a complete experience of taking the subway (as shown in Fig. 3).

Fig. 3. Complete experience of taking subway

Although subway passengers' behaviors are generally similar, in different stages and steps, not only passengers' physical and mental state changes continuously, but also the communication effect of subway advertisement is influenced to some degree.

Subway advertisement, as an important component of subway, can improve or weaken passengers' experience of taking the subway. To further explore the potential deficiencies in subway service, we thoroughly analyze passengers' physical and mental state, their actual demands and the problems in subway service after passengers complete tasks.

Through the detailed analysis of the deficiencies in subway service, we find out that passengers' mental expectation produced on pedestrian way, platform, subway and station is greater than the service supplied, which is reflected in four aspects: (1) passengers spend relatively long time in passing pedestrian way and the frequency is fairly high; (2) the service facility provided on platform is insufficient; the elderly and the weak physiological status is relatively weak; while other people are fairly relaxed and free, who always feel bored when waiting for subway; (3) time spent on taking subway is quite long; the chair for rest is insufficient, which may make passengers bored and anxious; (4) exits and passageways for passenger to walk out of station or transfer are numerous with chaotic guidance information which makes passengers nervous.

Based on the analysis and conclusion above, we find out that the improvement in the overall level of service is the main way to improve passengers' experience of taking the subway. Subway infrastructure has significant functions which cannot be changed randomly. Thus, to improve infrastructure is not a sensible choice. While, subway advertisement, as a part of subway, can be improved from the perspective of service experience in its form so as to improve the overall quality of service.

3.4   Service Touch Points

With regard to passengers' experience of taking the subway, the main flow of taking the subway mainly includes three aspects: enter into the station and get on the subway, take subway, get off the subway and walk out of the station. The service touch points in the first aspects include conductor, self-service ticket machine, ticket checking machine etc.; touch points in taking subway include broadcast, arrival information board, subway environment, chair, etc.; and touch points in the last aspect include ticket checking machine, map outside station etc. Since passengers' activities are carried out inside subway, the ubiquitous service touch point in subway is spatial environment including wall, ground, post, shielded gate, tunnel, subway, chair, guidance system, and carry-on smart equipment and article. As for the type of advertisement media, light box advertisement, interactive screen and mobile TV are all the objects considered to improve (as shown in Fig. 4).

What needs to be emphasized is that different subway stations have different functions, which include the station in business district, station for transferring, station in key culture district, characteristics station etc. Therefore, the behaviors and mental profiles of passengers in these stations are greatly different. In subway advertisement design, we have to analyze the touch points in a specific environment and explore design opportunity based on specific advertisement content and passenger features so as to continually improve subway's service quality (as shown in Fig. 5).

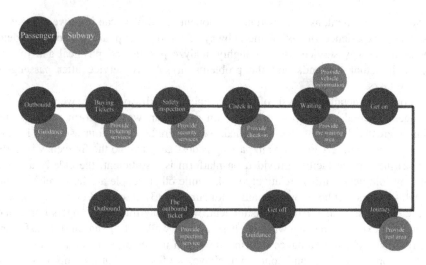

Fig. 4. Service design blue prints

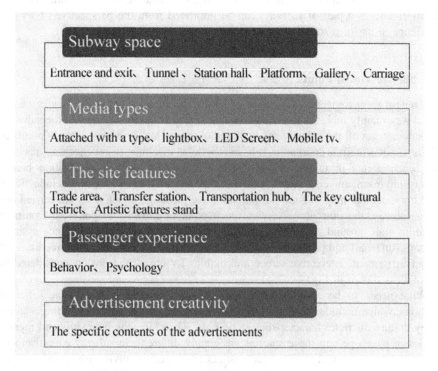

Fig. 5. Information analysis of design touch points

4   Service Design in Subway Advertisement—A Case Study of Wuhan Subway Line 3

In previous survey, we have found out that if passengers spend a long time in passing pedestrian path or pass many times, it may cause passenger anxiety. If there are many exits or passageways with disordered guidance information, it may cause passenger nervousness. To deal with the questions above, we choose the stair and passageway in subway as the place for advertisement design and propose an innovative scene-based designing plan.

4.1   "Hongtu Boulevard Station" Case Study

Take Wuhan Subway Line 3 as an example, one of the stations named Hongtu Boulevard is not only a transfer station, but also a junction station and a characteristic station with distinctive features. It covers a large area whose width is twice the size of typical stations also with a number of passageways. Due to this special environment, it is better to include environmental change in space design so as to clearly guide passenger's activity and travel path. Therefore, based on the characteristics of the stairs and passageways in subway, the fundamental function we have to realize first is to lead passenger enter into and walk out of the station, transfer and buy tickets. Moreover, Hongtu Boulevard, as a transfer station, can realize airport transfer and lead passenger to polar ocean world. Thus we decide to design a theme for the subway advertisement in this station. Through giving a feeling of freshness to passengers, we avoid passenger's boredom and tediousness produced in taking subway; instead, we give passengers a sense of belonging and identity of their destination (Fig. 6).

Fig. 6. The original design of subway advertisement environment

Taking into account the Hongtu Boulevard station set transfer station, traffic hub station, art stand in one, as designers we should give full consideration to this more complex spatial characteristics in the design implementation. In addition to providing passengers with safe, punctual, comfortable and pleasant environment, but also should meet the emotional needs of passengers and individual needs. In addition to the closed space, mobility and stability of the subway transfer channel space, the lack of natural flavor, easy to lose sense of direction is the most urgent problem to be solved. Therefore, the overall environment of the channel environment design is the main way, that is, the combination of wall and advertising design. Wall decoration materials, environmental protection, between stations and the recognition of the environment and the shaping of the atmosphere is our main consideration.

Hongtu Boulevard Station - Polar Ocean World's export channel functional attributes to determine the area is a full use of the scene design of the subway space, staircase aisle on both sides of the wall can use 3D stickers to create a blue ocean fantasy atmosphere, Advertising box can be used diving courtyard of the circular shape, in order to increase of interest and attractiveness. In Hongtu Avenue station transfer airport line transfer channel, the same can be used to identify the way to shape the functional attributes and environmental atmosphere, the wall design for the cabin effect, advertising frame shape in accordance with the aircraft window design. It can be found that different sites should be designed according to different actual needs. This needs to balance the commonality and individuality according to the site function and passenger demands, and build a diversified metro visual culture on the basis of uniform subway line identifications (Fig. 7).

Fig. 7. The new design of subway advertisement environment

4.2   Design Evaluation of New Subway Site Scheme

To alternative to the original "gray space" atmosphere, passenger repression has been improved by the new design scheme, not only in the passenger senses to give a more profound spatial transition information, but also for advertising interest and attractiveness has also increased. Compared with the traditional design of subway space transfer, the new design scheme pays more attention to the personalized and humanized design of advertising design. According to the location function of the station, the spatial characteristics of the corridor, and the psychological characteristics of passengers in the subway space environment, in the design process should pay more attention to passengers in the station or transfer their psychological feelings. In the provision of visual guidance at the same time, through the theme, the scene of the space advertising design, to give passengers a different experience, we not only create higher service value but also raise attention of the advertisement.

For passengers, the new design scheme not only completed the transition of service functions, provides passengers a waiting, rest and transit sites, but also help passengers complete the user experience optimization, relax before the psychological characteristics of tension. As for the subway system, the personalization subway environment design try to bring more possibilities for future development. According to local conditions, user-oriented design to comprehensively upgrade the value of the subway service, for shaping and dissemination of the subway cultural value also have obvious effects and meanings.

From the design evaluation point of view, with feedback from the current interview information can be learned, the new design has been widely recognized by subway management side, subway engineering side, the representative passengers. Follow-up evaluation of the data details are in the process in order to further improvement and constant optimization.

5   Contribution

Based on the service design concept and research method, combined with advertising communication and environmental psychology, this paper points out that service design thinking should be an important dimension to be followed in the process of subway space advertisement design, In the specific analysis process, this paper analyzes the design principles and key points of the subway space advertisement design through the study of the behavior psychology of the passengers, the relationship between cognitive laws and the subway space environment, and puts forward relevant design methods and strategies. And selected typical cases for analysis. Through the combination of theory and practice, this paper explores the feasible methods and strategies for the future design of subway advertisement space. So as to achieve high-quality subway space advertising design provides a new thinking way.

6 Conclusion

With the continuous development of society and the improvement of life, the rich material of modern society and the highly developed science and technology, making that passengers needs of subway space advertising are rising. The public role of subway space will have more and more important social significance. From the perspective of urban sustainable development, it is necessary to locate the subway space advertisement design and its interactive mode from the perspective of service design, pay more attention to the study of subway environmental impact and human behavior needs. In the subway space advertising design under service design ideas, will be able to focus on the subway passenger physical, psychological, cultural and other aspects of the real needs. Service design adhere to the "user-oriented" orientation, emphasizing the comprehensive study of multi-disciplinary, for the subway space advertisement design is very urgent need.

Compared with other public spaces, the space of subway advertisement has its distinctive features. To discuss the design of subway advertisement from the perspective of service-oriented design, we have to make analysis of subway environment and user characteristics and take the value created by service design and the expected user experience as the objective. Combining with mature new media and interactive technique, we provide a brand new experience and feeling to passengers by the application of sense judgement, emotional experience, thought experience, action experience and relevance experience in subway advertisement. The study of service design thought into subway advertisement design will promote the construction and development of urban subway service and put forward a service solution with social value, user value and economic value.

Acknowledgements. This paper was supported by research funds: "The Fundamental Research Funds for the Central Universities (WUT:2016VI056)", "Hubei Technology Innovation Soft Science Research Project (2016ADC092)", "Guangdong Soft Science Research Project (2016A070706009)".

References

1. Xin, X., Cao, J.: Service design driving public affairs management and organizational innovation. Design 126 (2015). Hai, J.: Service design case study. Decoration (06), 28 (2010)
2. http://wiki.mbalib.com/wiki/%E6%9C%8D%E5%8A%A1%E8%AE%BE%E8%AE%A1
3. Liu, G.: Design Methodology, p. 3. Higher Education Press, Beijing (2011)
4. Liang, F.: Interactive Advertising. Tsinghua University Press, Beijing (2007)
5. Shedroff, N.: Information interaction design. In: Jacobsen, R. (ed.) A Unified Field Theory of Design in Information Deisgn, pp. 267–292. The MIT Press, Cambridge (1999)
6. Kelly, K.: What Technology Wants. CITIC Publishing House, Beijing (2011). Preamble
7. Jonathan, S.: Defining virtual reality: dimensions determining telepresence. J. Commun. **42**, 73–93 (1992)

8. John, D.L., Li, H.: From the editors: why we need the journal of interactive advertising. J. Interact. Advert. **1**(Fall), 1–3 (2000)
9. Liuyi: User experience design in Chinese market. Packag. Eng. 04 (2011)
10. Dan, P.: Research on user experience based on C2C network shopping platform. Jiangnan University, p. 126 (2011)
11. Nielsen, J.: Usability Engineering. Academic Press, Burlington (1994)
12. Garrett, J.J.: The Elements of User Experience: User-Centered Design for the Web, pp. 13–20. New Riders Publishing, New York (2003)
13. Garrett, J.J.: User Experience Elements, p. 9. Mechanical Industry Press, Beijing (2007)

Consistency of Use Flow Improving User Experience of Service-Oriented Websites

Canqun He[1(✉)], Xu Yang[1], Zhengsheng Li[2], Zhangyu Ji[1],
Jiaojiao Wang[3], and Shuya Ni[4]

[1] College of Mechanical and Electrical Engineering of Hohai University,
Changzhou, China
hecq@163.com
[2] School of Automotive and Traffic Engineering of Jiangsu University,
Zhenjiang, China
[3] VAIM Industrial Design, Qingdao, China
[4] College of International Languages and Cultures of Hohai University,
Nanjing, China

Abstract. Based on the theories of user experience and mental model, the paper takes two representative E-banks of China for case study. Method of questionnaire is used to determine research object and contents, observation is used to obtain mental model of users and actual model of E-banks, and path search is applied to verify the relationship between mental model and actual model. An innovative research of E-banks' login, transfer and remittance by usability test has been done to analyze participants' task completion time, task completion rate, heat map, scan path and other indicators affecting user experience, in which case the assumption that consistency of use flow can improve user experience of service-oriented websites is validated.

Keywords: Service-Oriented websites · E-bank · Use flow · Consistency · Mental model · User experience

1 Introduction

Nowadays people are getting more and more accustomed to the Internet with its popularization. Online shopping, online transfer and online ordering have become a common way of life while websites have gradually become the most important carrier for people to acquire information and to interact with others and the society, which provides a sufficient space for the development of service-oriented websites. Currently, there exist rich theories of interaction design and user experience home and abroad such as user-centered design, goal-oriented design and user mental model. However, studies on website use flow are in great shortage, let alone studies on use flow of service-oriented websites.

In-depth study is needed when users get to the websites at the beginning and several practices will lead to a fixed use flow model. Mental model of user operation, as a fixed using habit, will certainly be constructed after using similar use flow models. Robert Hoekman put forward the concept of user mental model and designed pattern library

© Springer International Publishing AG 2017
P.-L.P. Rau (Ed.): CCD 2017, LNCS 10281, pp. 146–160, 2017.
DOI: 10.1007/978-3-319-57931-3_12

from the perspective of user experience to provide standard solutions for the same or similar issues, thus creating consistent user experience across multiple sites [1].

At present, service-oriented websites in China differ greatly from each other due to different image orientation and cultures of enterprises. Consistent use flow of service-oriented websites makes it possible for the implementation model to be more similar to the user mental model, which requires less cognitive time for users to use websites [1]. Under such circumstances, it will not only save users' cognitive and learning time but also be more in line with the user's habits and psychological expectations. Besides, websites' versatility, re-utilization, efficiency and usability will be greatly enhanced.

1.1 Service-Oriented Websites

Websites can be divided into three overlapped types according to their functions: content-based websites, service-oriented websites and e-commerce websites. The service-oriented website, as its name implies, is to focus on providing service. It serves as the main carrier to realize the functions of websites to meet users' demands of seeking particular help or completing special tasks with a very specific purpose, to name a few, Industrial and Commercial Bank of China (ICBC) and China Mobile Online Business Office.

According to the definition of service-oriented website, it mainly aims at providing particular service for users. There are four main features of these service-oriented websites. Firstly, service-oriented websites can provide users with more specific services because the information they contain only relates to one certain field [2]. Secondly, users who visit service-oriented websites usually have a strong sense of purpose [2]. Thirdly, design of service-oriented websites must consider usability. Fourthly, use flow of the same or similar modules in the service-oriented websites tends to be consistent. As Joshua Porter put it, the most appealing application is the one which enables people to accomplish a specific task excellently [3]. And service-oriented website is exactly the application.

1.2 User Experience

The concept of user experience was first proposed by Donald Arthur Norman, which has gradually affected all fields of human activity with the infiltration of computer science in mobile and graphics technology [4]. User experience refers to the behavior, thoughts and personal feelings of the user in the use process of a product or a service, including rational and sensible experience provided by the product or service [5]. Design brings both practical products and improved service, experience and value. User experience reflects the user-centered and people-oriented design philosophy [6]. User experience of web interface is the subjective psychological feelings which are formed when the user interacts with the interface, including user's acceptance of the website, the degree of pleasure when using it and the degree of tolerating website vulnerability [7]. When mapped to the web interface design, user experience covers functional design, information structure design, interactive design, visual design and so on. Humanization and rationality of web interface design have a direct impact on user experience [8].

1.3 Mental Model

Mind is all the spiritual activity of mankind. Kenneth Craik, a Scottish psychologist, was the first one to put forward mental model in 1943 to explain individual's cognitive process of the operation of something in real world [9, 10]. It was Johnson Laird who started to take mental model into real practice to describe the way of problem-solving and the thinking patterns of deductive reasoning [10]. Mental model is established when the individual is disrupted by external stimuli, then the brain recognizes and picks up needed information to process, and finally rules or experience are preserved.

Mental model of service-oriented websites can be divided into macro and micro levels. Macro-level refers to the users' cognitive structure and content on attitude and activity level, including key concepts, product expectations, task flows and related models of service-oriented websites [9]. Micro-level refers to the prospective cognition when users complete a specific operation or task. It is an internal concept record when users interact with the websites [11]. It is also an indispensable part of website design to study its internal mental model through observation and analysis of users objective behaviors [12].

1.4 The Effect of Mental Model on User Experience of Service-Oriented Websites

Norman proposed three models in interaction design: (1) Mental model. It is the cognition of function and behavior on service-oriented websites that users should have in their brains. (2) Represented model. It is the way that the designer chooses to present the service-oriented websites to users [13]. (3) Implementation model. It is a real working model of websites when service-oriented websites are in use. During the whole designing process of service-oriented websites, mental model determines design direction of web interface. Represented model of clear and concrete service-oriented websites which correspond to users' mental model should be developed by investigating needs of target users [14]. It will be much easier for users to accept it when final implementation model matches well with mental model [15].

Generally speaking, effects on user experience of service-oriented web interface by mental model involve three parts. Firstly, it removes learning and cognitive burdens of users. Secondly, it improves the efficiency of the user to complete the task. Thirdly, it promotes user satisfaction. However, there are still some limitations when mental model functions on service-oriented websites due to its own restrictions. For instance, mental models differ from one another in that every environment is unique, which results in complicated research contents as well as high requirements for researches.

2 Research on Mental Models of Service-Oriented Websites: Taking E-Banks as an Example

We may infer from the effects of mental model on user experience of service-oriented websites that such user experience can be improved when implementation model is consistent with mental model. Therefore, it is deduced that consistent design may contribute to better user experience of the website. Similarly, consistency of use flow can enhance user experience of service-oriented websites.

In order to know whether the reference is feasible or not, the study takes E-banks as an example from the perspective of user experience to analyze the function of consistent use flow by means of researching implementation model and mental model of E-banks.

2.1 Identification of Target Users and Research Contents of E-Banks

According to the study on mental model of E-banks, we have distributed a questionnaire entitled *Personal Use of E-Banks* online and totally received 102 valid copies. On the basis of the data obtained, people aged under 30 with bachelor degree or above have been chosen to be our target users for observation and interviews. Then we take Industrial and Commercial Bank of China (ICBC) and Agricultural Bank of China (ABC) as research objects and we set transfer, remittance, registration and login as research contents.

2.2 Acquisition of User Mental Information of E-Banks

Interview to Obtain User Mental Model. According to investigation results, three users with obvious characteristics were selected to have an in-depth interview with the results recorded to acquire users' subjective demands for e-banks and to establish mental models to complete the three tasks. Based on the correspondence between user mental model and user experience elements, specific needs of users are respectively matched with five levels of user experience proposed by Jesse James Garrett [6] (Table 1).

Table 1. User requirements corresponding to user experience elements

User experience elements	User's specific requirements
Surface	Clear website interface; Consistent performance style
Skeleton	Accurate and reasonable navigation classification; Accurate and consistent language expression
Structure	Timely feedback; Provide boot and helpful information; Allow undo action
Scope	With account inquiries, transfer and remittance, shopping, payment, wealth management and other functions
Strategy	Provide users with financial services

Based on the above analysis, mental models of user completing registration, login and transfer and remittance are extracted, including key page jumps and operation behavior, as shown in Figs. 1 and 2.

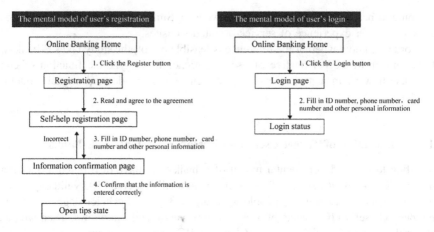

Fig. 1. The diagram of mental model of user's e-bank registration and login

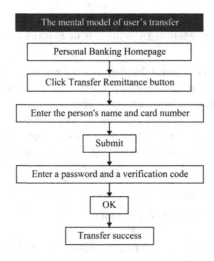

Fig. 2. The diagram of mental model of user's transfer and remittance

Observation to Obtain Implementation Model of E-banks. 20 people among target users were invited to respectively use ICBC and ABC to complete three tasks including registration, login, and transfer and remittance. The implementation models of three tasks were concluded by observing and recording the users' operation process (including key pages and operation behavior). (1) The diagram of implementation model of ICBC and ABC registration (Fig. 3). (2) The diagram of implementation model of ICBC e-bank login (Fig. 4). The diagram of implementation model of ABC e-bank login (Fig. 5). (3) The diagram of implementation model of ICBC and ABC e-bank transfer and remittance (Fig. 6).

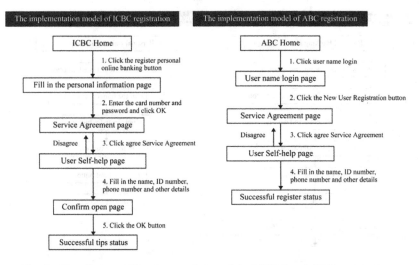

Fig. 3. The diagram of implementation model of ICBC and ABC registration

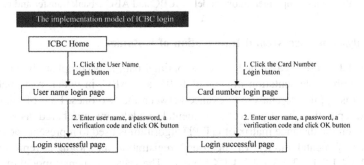

Fig. 4. The diagram of implementation model of ICBC e-bank login

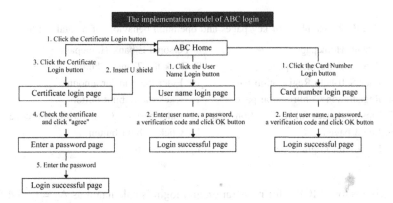

Fig. 5. The diagram of implementation model of ABC e-bank login

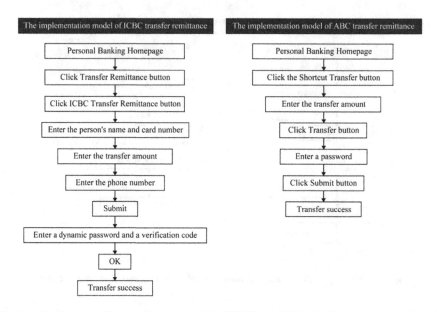

Fig. 6. The diagram of implementation model of ICBC and ABC e-bank transfer and remittance

2.3   Analysis of User Mental Information of E-Banks

Mental model of user is assumed to be the optimal path to accomplish the task and is compared with implementation models of ICBC and ABC, in which case method of path search is applied to analyze relevance between the two ones. First of all, the key pages and operation behavior of user mental models are numbered as shown in Table 2. Then the distance matrix of GT-PD algorithm is used to represent each model. The vector of mental models of the users' registration and login is represented as A_1 = (1 2 3 4 1 2 1 2 3 2 3 1 2 3 4 1 4 5 5 6 1). The vector of mental model of transfer and remittance is represented as B_1 = (1 2 3 4 5 6 1 2 3 4 5 1 2 3 4 1 2 3 1 2 1). We can calculate $\bar{a}_1$ = 2.667 and $\bar{b}_1$ = 2.667 (Table 3).

Table 2. Numbers of key pages and operation behaviors of mental model

1. E-bank Homepage	8. Personal E-bank Homepage
2. Service Agreement page	9. Click the Transfer button
3. User Self-help Registration page	10. Enter the transfer amount
4. Registration Confirmation page	11. Click the Submit button
5. Tips of Successful Registration page	12. Enter password and verification code
6. Login page	13. Click Submit button
7. Successful Login page	14. Successful Transfer

Matrix vector of ICBC for registration and login is calculated as A_2 = (2 3 4 5 1 2 1 2 3 3 4 1 2 4 5 1 5 6 6 7 1); matrix vector of ICBC for transfer and remittance is

Table 3. Numbers of model distance matrix

	User mental model	ICBC	ABC (Card number or user name login)	ABC (Certificate Login)
Registration and login	A_1	A_2	A_3	A_4
Transfer and remittance	B_1	B_2	B_3	B_4

calculated as B_2 = (1 4 6 7 8 9 3 5 6 7 8 2 3 4 5 1 2 3 1 2 1). Then conclusion is drawn as $\bar{a}_2$ = 3.2381 and $\bar{b}_2$ = 4.1905. Matrix vector of ABC when the user registers and selects the card number or user name to login is calculated as A_3 = (2 3 4 5 1 2 1 2 3 1 2 1 2 2 3 1 3 4 4 5 1); matrix vector of ABC when the user registers and selects certificate login is calculated as A_4 = (2 3 4 5 3 5 1 2 3 5 6 1 2 6 8 1 7 9 8 10 2); matrix vector of ABC for transfer and remittance is calculated as B_3 = (1 3 4 5 6 7 2 3 4 5 6 1 2 3 4 1 2 3 1 2 1). Then conclusion is drawn as $\bar{a}_3$ = 2.4762 $\bar{a}_4$ = 4.4286 and $\bar{b}_3$ = 3.1429.

SPSS is used to calculate global correlation coefficient between A_1 and A_2, A_1 and A_3, A_1 and A_4 and to analyze the correlation between various distance matrices. The conclusion comes out as $N_1 > N_3 > N_2$, which indicates that implementation model of ICBC when completing registration and login is the closest to user mental model and can most satisfy users' psychological expectations. According to researches mental model's effect on user experience of service-oriented websites, it is predicted that users will be most satisfied using ICBC to register and log in (Table 4).

Table 4. Global correlation coefficients between registration and login models

	ICBC A_2	ABC (Card number or user name login) A_3	ABC (Certificate Login) A_4
User mental model A_1	N_1 = 0.9789	N2 = 0.8731	N_3 = 0.9167

SPSS is used to calculate global correlation coefficient between B_1 and B_2, B_1 and B_3 to ensure accuracy. The conclusion comes out as $M_1 < M_2$, which indicates that implementation model of ABC when completing transfer and remittance is the closest to user mental model. According to researches on mental model's effect on user experience of service-oriented websites, it is predicted that users will be most satisfied using ABC to complete transfer and remittance (Table 5).

Table 5. Global correlation coefficient between each model of transfer and remittance

	ICBC B_2	ABC B_3
User mental model A_1	M_1 = 0.9231	M_2 = 0.9723

3 Assumption and Experimental Verification on Use Flow Consistency of E-Banks

3.1 Experimental Hypotheses and Experimental Purposes

Experimental Hypotheses. The previous research has revealed that a consistent design of service-oriented websites can provide a better user experience. If implementation model of e-bank is consistent with users' mental model, whether it can be inferred that implementation models of all e-banks are also consistent, which means use flow of all e-banks needs to be consistent.

E-banks serve as an example to solve the problem above and to verify the correctness of the inference objectively by means of usability test, which shows whether the assumption of "use flow consistency of e-banks" is valid.

Experimental Purposes. The usability test studies for specific operations of e-banks. It mainly analyzes completion degree, completion efficiency, completion time and user satisfaction degree of the given task through the information recorded by the eye movement apparatus, the experiment video and the post-experiment interview, with the aim to analyze whether the consistency of use flow is conducive to enhancing user experience of e-banks (Figure 7).

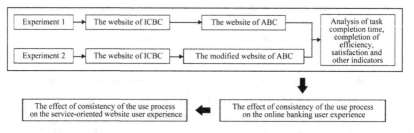

Fig. 7. Usability test of e-banks use flow consistency

3.2 Experimental Design

Determination of the Experimental Subjects, Objects and Tasks. The test involves 39 participants who have used two or more kind of e-banks and are familiar with the interface. Experimental scope is determined as follows (Table 6):

Experimental Tasks. Contrast test method is adopted in the experiment: Usability tests are respectively conducted using consistent flow and inconsistent flow as a comparison. Experiment 1 is to test on the original website interface, that is prototype interface with inconsistent flow (Prototype A and Prototype B). While in experiment 2, the modified web interface is tested using a consistent flow prototype (Prototype A 'and Contrast Prototype B').

Registration of personal account of e-banks and transfer and remittance are included in the experimental tasks. Each is required to complete the experimental task in order.

Table 6. Summary of experimental subjects, objects and test tasks

Factors	Results	Determine the scope
Age and education of subjects	(1) 51.8% of the surveyed users were under 30 (2) 82.4% of the users education is undergraduate or above	(1) Aged 30 or below (2) Bachelor degree or above
Objects	(1) ICBC accounted for 50% (2) ABC accounted for 26.2%	(1) ICBC (2) ABC
Testing tasks	(1) E-bank operations first need to log in personal accounts (2) Transfer and remittance accounted for 25.22%	(1) Log in a given personal account (2) Transfer to an account

Note: Testers are those who have used two or more kind of e-banks and are familiar with use flow of them.

3.3   Experimental Prototype Design

The first experiment is to operate the existing websites of ICBC and ABC, which differ greatly from each other. There is only one way to log in ICBC by account while three different login methods are allowed in ABC (Figure 8).

Fig. 8. Comparison of login method between prototype A and prototype B

The premise of experiment 2 is to make operation flow of the test object remain consistent. According to the preceding analysis of user mental model of e-banks—implementation model of ICBC is the closest to user's login mental model, the prototype A'—use flow of ICBC website, is set to remain unchanged. And Dreamweaver is used to produce a prototype B' which is the same as prototype A' in use flow. That is to assimilate the operation process of ICBC into ABC on the basis of original use flow of ABC. In order to make experimental results not affected by other factors, this change is under the premise that other aspects remain unchanged. The interface of the final prototype B' is shown in Figs. 9 and 10.

Fig. 9. Modified login interface of ABC

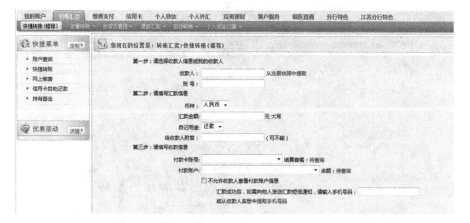

Fig. 10. Modified transfer interface of ABC

3.4   Analysis of Experimental Results

Task Completion. As is shown in the experiment result, there are altogether 20 people going through the experiment, among which only 14 experiments are valid ones. Eight participants have completed all the tasks which accounts for 57.14% and two participants succeeded nothing. Task completion rates of prototype A and prototype B are 71.43% and 64.29%, respectively. In experiment 2, 19 people took part in the test with 16 experiments in the end turning out valid ones. Task completion rate of prototype A' and prototype B' are 93.75% and 100%, respectively. To conclude, original website interface of experiment 1 has more usability problems than those of experiment 2.

Task Completion Time. Firstly, SPSS is used to analyze time samples of each task to verify if the emergence of experimental data can be promoted to the overall scope of service-oriented websites. Then, according to the significant variance and the average value of task completion time, it is analyzed whether the changes of use flow will affect task completion, and whether the user's experience with ICBC (the former operation of the test object) will affect the user's later use of ABC (the latter operation of the test object).

Assuming that there is no big difference of task completion time between prototype A' and prototype A, and the average time prototype A took for task 1 $\bar{N} = 52.21$. The results of the single-sample T test for prototype A' task 1 (Table 7) show significant value p = 0.979 > 0.05 with the SPSS calculation to set the test value = 52.21 and the confidence interval to 95%. Therefore, it is reasonable to accept the null hypothesis that the completion time of prototype A' task 1 has no significant difference from that of prototype A task 1. Similarly, there is no significant difference as is shown in Table 8 significant value p = 0.707 > 0.05.

Table 7. Results of the single-sample T-test for prototype A 'task 1

	Test value = 52.21 (time average of prototype A task 1)					
	t	df	Sig.(Bilateral)	Mean difference	95% confidence interval of the difference	
					Lower limit	Upper limit
Prototype A 'task 1	.027	15	.979	.16500	−12.6841	13.0141

Table 8. Results of the single-sample T-test for prototype A 'task 2

	Test value = 185.27 (time average of prototype A task 2)					
	t	df	Sig.(Bilateral)	Mean difference	95% confidence interval of the difference	
					Lower limit	Upper limit
Prototype A' task 2	−.384	14	.707	−7.07000	−46.5498	32.4098

One-sample T-test analysis is also used to verify whether task 3 and task 4 of prototype B' are significantly different from those of prototype B. As is shown in Tables 9 and 10, the significant difference between Task 3 and Task 4 is less than 0.05, so there is a 95% or more possibility that significant difference of task completion time exists between Prototype B' and Prototype B.

Table 9. Results of the single-sample T-test for prototype B 'task 3

	Test value = 98.80					
	t	df	Sig. (Bilateral)	Mean difference	95% confidence interval of the difference	
					Lower limit	Upper limit
prototype B' task 3	−16.788	15	.000	−50.86250	−57.3201	−44.4049

Table 10. Results of the single-sample T-test for prototype B 'task 4

	Test value = 98.80					
	t	df	Sig. (Bilateral)	Mean difference	95% confidence interval of the difference	
					Lower limit	Upper limit
Prototype B' task 4	−8.937	15	.000	−120.92000	−149.7580	−92.0820

The experimental results are not accidental according to the analysis above and they can be extended to a larger scale of service-oriented websites, while changes to use flow will affect the time for users to complete the tasks. Combined with the above data and eye movement experimental video analysis, the following conclusions can be drawn.

3.5   Experimental Results

According to the experimental results, the following conclusions can be reached:

Users' operation can be affected by previous experience.

Consistent use flow can significantly improve users' operating efficiency. To further explain this phenomenon, SPSS is used to calculate the global correlation coefficient between the corresponding tasks in the two experiments respectively, with results shown in Table 11. It can be inferred that the global correlation coefficient $N_1 = -0.439$ (negative correlation) between task 1 and task 3 in experiment 1, while the global correlation coefficient $N_2 = 0.305$ (positive correlation) for task 1 and task 3

Table 11. Global Correlation Coefficients for Login Tasks in Two Experiments

	Prototype A (ICBC)	Prototype B (ABC)	Correlation coefficient
Login (inconsistent)	Task 1	Task 3	$N_1 = -0.439$
	Prototype A' (ICBC)	Prototype B' (Modified ABC)	
Login (consistent)	Task 1	Task 3	$N_2 = 0.305$

in the second experiment. It is thus possible to determine that a consistent login flow facilitates the users' operation while inconsistent login flow hinders it.

User experience of e-banks can be improved by recording the account information automatically.

When it comes to the same or similar functional modules, users tend to choose a consistent using method to reduce cognitive and learning time. From the perspective of e-banks, the consistency of use flow can help users successfully complete the task, improve their efficiency and finally enhance the availability and user experience of e-banks.

4 Summary and Discussion

In this study, the problem of how to improve user experience of websites is refined to the research es on use flow of web site under the premise of ensuring the functions of service-oriented websites. Combined with the theory and research method of user mental model, it is verified that consistency of use flow is helpful to enhance user experience of websites by taking e-banks as an example.

Although this study summarizes the usability problems related to login and transfer and remittance of ICBC and ABC, there are many types of websites in service-based websites and e-bank is only one of them. Therefore, more research subjects will be considered into test in future researches and research scope will be extended to many other types of websites.

Acknowledgment. This study is financially supported by Basic Study Funding of Central University (2013B34214).

References

1. Hoekman Jr., R.: Design the Obvious: A Common Sense Approach to Web Application Design. China Machine Press, Beijing (2008)
2. Lan, Z.: Research on the usability of functional website design. Tianjin University, Tianjin (2009)
3. Porter, J.: Designing for the Social Web. Posts & Telecom Press, Beijing (2010)

4. Zheng, Z.: Research on Mobile Publication Oriented to User Experience. Suzhou University, Suzhou (2012)
5. Lucas, D.: Understanding user experience. Web Tech. **5**(8), 42–43 (2000)
6. Garrett, J.J., Fan, X.: The Elements of User Experience–User-Centered Design for the Web. China Machine Press, Beijing (2007)
7. Chen, Y.: Research on web interface design method for user experience. Chongqing University, Chongqing (2010)
8. Xiao, H.: Design of university portal based on user experience. Silicon Val. **20**, 103 (2011)
9. Zhao, C.: Application of Mental Model in User - Centered Design. Tsinghua University, Beijing (2013)
10. Yu, M.: Research on consistency of mental model and information construction and its application in mobile internet software. Zhejiang University, Hangzhou (2011)
11. Li, H., Song, L.: Selection and application of mental model measurement methods for users using websites. Theor. Appl. **38**(2), 11–16 (2015)
12. Huang, M.: Research on natural user interface design based on mental model. GongShang University, Zhejiang (2015)
13. Zhu, J.: Research on the user mental model understood by the e-commerce website classification system. Nanjing University of Science and Technology, Nanjing (2010)
14. Preece, J.: Interaction Design: Beyond Human-Computer Interaction. Electronic Industry Press, Beijing (2003)
15. Norman, D.A.: The Design of Everyday Things. CITIC Press, Beijing (2010)

Independent Bathing for Older Adults: The Conceptualization of the iMagic-BOX Portable Walk-In Bathtub

Chew Kien Ming[1(✉)] and Jeffery Yeow Teh Thiry[2]

[1] Inventor, iMagic-BOX, Kuala Lumpur, Malaysia
stefan@imagic-box.com
[2] Researcher, iMagic-BOX, Kuala Lumpur, Malaysia
jeffery@imagic-box.com

Abstract. The rising issue of world population ageing has brought about increasing concern for the well-being and healthcare needs of older adults. With the unfortunate current state of professional elderly healthcare, the duty of caring for their needs often falls to family members. With current trends pointing towards a shift to a more independent lifestyle for older adults, it becomes increasingly important that technologies are developed to assist their daily living. This paper describes issues involving the everyday task of bathing in tandem with the advent of the walk-in bathtub concept. Unfortunately, due to severe design flaws, conventional market offerings of walk-in bathtubs tend to cause more harm than good, prompting a need for an overhaul of the design concept. Hence, this paper outlines the conceptualization and design methodology of the iMagic-BOX portable walk-in bathtub, a series of mobile, walk-in bathing and shower units designed to assist older adults to be able to independently and comfortably bathe on their own. The goal of this paper is to showcase the individual design elements of these specialized walk-in bathtub units in hopes of inspiring other inventors to appreciate the role of gerontechnology in improving the lives of older adults worldwide.

Keywords: Gerontechnology · Invention · Healthcare · Walk-in bathtub

1 Introduction

Amongst the various demographic complications seen in recent years, the significant demographic shift in population ageing stands in prominence. Various factors, such as the rise in life expectancy rates at birth have increased the proportion of older adults aged 60 years or over to significantly higher levels [10]; this number was projected to more than double itself from projected numbers of 901 million in 2015, to 2.1 billion in 2050. In other words, if this projection becomes a reality, the world will have more than 830 million persons aged 80 years or over by the end of the 21th century. The United Nations also reported that 40 percent of the older adults aged 60 years or above live independently, and this number is projected to increase consideration into the future [10]. Altogether, this rapid age spike holds far-reaching implications for not just these

© Springer International Publishing AG 2017
P.-L.P. Rau (Ed.): CCD 2017, LNCS 10281, pp. 161–170, 2017.
DOI: 10.1007/978-3-319-57931-3_13

individuals, but for all others in the population, as this increases the duty of caring for the older population.

In modern times, the changing social needs of older adults cause them to suffer from difficulties in physical functioning as a natural part of aging. Due to these underlying social circumstances, new challenges impair these individuals' ability to maintain a comfortable, yet independent lifestyle in spite of their physical difficulties. These individuals now face greater needs for social support, but at the same time face greater risks of social isolation; as they require social support for a better living situation, the danger of also becoming prone to overreliance on said support leads to a lack of independence. This issue becomes compounded with their need for proper healthcare, where hospital visits become more common and last longer, where healthcare issues stem from health complications that tend to be chronic and long-term in nature. Older adults will naturally be encouraged to spend more time at home, and thus are in dire need of effective home care services as well, provided either by professional agencies or more commonly, fellow family members.

It is here that the field of gerontechnology holds the most promise. Fozard et al. describes gerontechnology as a combination of the separate elements of *gerontology* and *technology*, where the former describes scientific study of aging whereas the latter is the development and implementation of technological products, services and physical environments [7]. Gerontechnology's scope is concerned with utilizing technology as a means to support a better life for aging people, hence the connection between the two fields of study [3]. This naturally relates to the potential that the usage of technology can bring about benefit to both aging and aged people [6, 8, 11], which positions it as a vital field of study in supporting older adults going forward.

While gerontechnology focuses on the impact of different technologies within five domains of human activity [8, 11], for the purposes of this paper, the domain concerned with housing and daily living (technology supporting independence, convenience and safety of daily activities among the elderly people) is of particular note. As a direct result, it is through the marriage of technology with careful consideration of aging that various issues faced within domains such as housing and daily living can be addressed.

The goals of this paper are as follows: to outline the specific issue of bathing as a healthcare concern for older adults, and the conceptualization of the iMagic-BOX portable walk-in bathtub, a series of mobile, walk-in bathing and shower units designed to assist older adults to be able to independently and comfortably bathe on their own.

2 The Problem with Bathing

2.1 The Lack of Proper Healthcare Facilities

For the average older adult suffering from mobility issues, the question of healthcare comes to light. As described by the United Nations, there is a rising trend of late for older adults to live independently, and this brings about various socio-cultural implications [10]. In other words, the demand for nursing/old folks' homes are likely to see a decline in demand in the coming future. Indeed, the Association of American Medical Colleges has declared shortages regarding the supply and demand of physicians to provide medical care for all the facilities across the United States of America [2]. A similar situation is being seen in the supply and demand of nurses as well [1]. These developments, alongside the alarmingly poor conditions of well-established healthcare providers for the old such as those seen in the vast majority of NHS England Hospitals [5, 9], forces an ultimatum: for the average older adult wanting independence in their healthcare, without reliance on medical centres and facilities, it will necessitate opting for either homecare or family support if their physical condition ever worsens.

With this situation becoming the norm, it is often the case that for these older adults, as time progresses, it becomes increasingly likely that they will be unable to fully care for themselves. Many will either be unable to afford or simply prefer not to opt for homecare services, so the duty of caring for them falls to the rest of the family. Unfortunately, this is understandably, not possible in most circumstances, as family members have their own lives to lead and commitments to their own nuclear families, so family support can never be truly full-time.

2.2   The Inability to Conduct Self-care

In this situation, older adults will be left to tackle basic, everyday activities by themselves, despite their physical complications. In the case of ever-increasing physical difficulty, carrying out such activities such as bathing or taking a shower becomes increasingly challenging, and even dangerous. During the conceptualization of the iMagic-BOX portable walk-in bathtub, various such activities were considered, in an attempt to identify where the need for assistive technology was most needed, and eventually the answer became clear. For the sake of long-term care, bathing quickly turns into one of the commonplace activities that becomes increasingly unfeasible to carry out independently. One of the most common places of accidents occurring in the household is the washroom - a combination of wet surfaces and movement difficulties usually results in unfortunate accidents.

In a "Morbidity and Mortality Weekly Report" by the Centres for Disease Control and Prevention, they identified that in the United States of America in 2008, approximately 21.8 million persons aged 15 years or above were involved in nonfatal, unintentional injuries, incurring approximately $67.3 billion in lifetime medical costs [4]. The key finding of the report however was that injury rates increased with age, and coincidentally, most injuries in the washroom (81.1%) were caused by falls. While these statistics do include injuries occurring on or near the toilet among others, injuries occurring in or around the tub or shower increased markedly, from 49.7 per 100,000 among persons aged 15–24 years to 200.2 among persons aged 85 years or above. In summary, these findings point the extreme dangers that come about when older adults are carrying out the act of bathing. The washroom is dangerous enough to warrant that the standard convention is for nursing home patients to only receive only a single bath per week to reduce the likelihood of accidents, while some facilities provide at least two a week [9], and this occurs in professional facilities with trained caregivers, let alone untrained family members.

2.3   The Design Failures of the Conventional Walk-In Bathtub

Market forces have been savvy to these complications, and have in the past attempted to solve the dangers of bathing with a bathtub through the concept of a "walk-in bathtub". As such this concept is not a new one, with many existing designs, providing a large variety of such products currently available for purchase in the marketplace. The unfortunate fact is, after some analysis, several design flaws of standard designs were identified, and are as follows (Fig. 1):

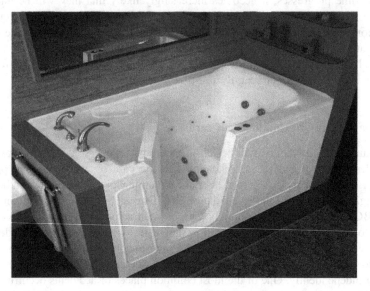

Fig. 1. A standard-design walk-in bathtub currently in market

First and foremost, the walk-in bathtub's entryway- conventionally, an inwards-opening door in the sidewall of the bathtub, a design choice that poses several difficulties. Most designs require the user to raise their feet over a step, or pass through an uncomfortably narrow doorway. This can be particularly difficult, given the physical weakness often experienced in the users' legs during the physical motion. The inwards-opening door also poses a safety hazard, not allowing a person to vacate the bathtub in the case of an emergency without first draining the water out.

The classic-style walk-in bathtubs are also guilty of long waiting times, referring to the time taken for water to both fill and drain. This issue does not merely affect the time taken in waiting, but also negatively affect the user's comfort as they will usually be undressed while waiting, meaning the user can be stuck waiting, wet and cold for long periods before being able to vacate the bathtub. Moreover, as these bathtubs are designed so that the user is forced into a sitting position, yet the actual water height limit will hardly reach the users' breast, leaving their entire upper body unsubmerged. Hence, users would not be having a proper full-body bath, and this complicates self-cleaning.

Additionally, walk-in bathtubs are primarily permanent installations, installed like a regular bathtub in the washroom and are not designed for mobile usage. This forces the user to travel to the washroom to take a bath, which, as obvious as it may seem, can be incredibly inconvenient for certain older adults. For example, if an individual happens to be relatively immobile, the process of making the journey from their current location in the home (for instance, the bedroom) to the washroom where the conventional/walk-in bathtub is installed can be arduous or even dangerous in some cases.

Furthermore, the standard pricing for walk-in bathtubs ranged from $5,000 for low-end models to $17,000 for high-end models. These demanding prices are oftentimes the result of the high installation costs that are coupled with the actual price of the bathing unit itself. Altogether, the substantial monetary investment required in purchasing a walk-in bathtub is arguably unjustified as the buyer is likely to receive a product whose design elements make it unsuited to their needs. An individual could have instead used these funds elsewhere for greater benefit, as for the same cost, one could renovate their washroom to have a fully-featured walk-in shower unit, which as an added benefit, raise the value of the property.

3 Designing the iMagic-BOX Portable Walk-In Bathtub

3.1 Initial Concept Development

The authors of this paper began development of the experiential product design that would eventually become the iMagic-BOX portable walk-in bathtub in its current form. The initial design concept was straightforward: to redesign the walk-in bathtub so that it would effectively serve its supposed function, because the concept of a walk-in bathtub if well-realized held the potential to positively impact the lives of many older adults worldwide. The authors sought inspiration for its design by studying the entire process of bathing, from aspects of mobility to reach the bathtub as well as the act of bathing with a bathtub itself (Fig. 2).

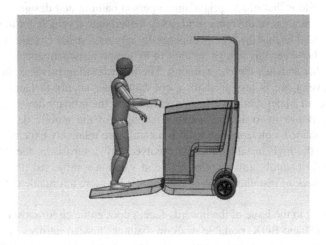

Fig. 2. An early 3D rendition of the iMagic-BOX portable walk-in bathtub

The primary inventor soon realized that the inability to self-bathe, and having to rely on another person's assistance for such a menial task could damage an older adult's pride, which could condition their bathing behavior. In extreme cases, some individuals may actively avoid the act of bathing, perhaps as an avoidance of the anxiety associated with the activity, leading to declining hygiene, putting their continued health and welfare at risk. With this in mind, the iMagic-BOX portable walk-in bathtub design was to overhaul the walk-in bathtub concept with the addition of various built-in facilities/conveniences that would accommodate for the mobility difficulties of its user.

The design methodology is straightforward: inspect each design component of conventional walk-in bathtubs and attempt to overhaul it, thus resulting in a complete overhaul of the entire product. For example, regarding the installation of conventional walk-in bathtubs, which are permanent, and the issues this causes regarding the transportation of patients, the design overhaul of this aspect was to eliminate installation altogether and make the bathing unit fully mobile instead. From here, quality assurance testing would be performed to evaluate the efficacy of the design overhaul.

Altogether, the iMagic-BOX portable walk-in bathtub was meant to cater to the same demographic as those targeted by conventional walk-in bathtub producers, primarily older adults, which usually includes the physically frail and a subset of the physically disabled such as wheelchair-bound individuals. As a direct result, specific features of the overall design were tuned to be more user-friendly to such individuals, such as ensuring very little physical ability would be required to operate the unit's controls, or that any instructional wording is of gerontological standard for easy reading.

3.2 The iMagic-BOX Portable Walk-In Bathtub Feature-Set

With consideration of the various flaws of the conventional walk-in bathtubs in mind, the defining feature of the iMagic-BOX portable walk-in bathtub design was a focus on mobility. Its build is that of an upright single-person bathing unit designed to be easily carted to different areas of the home, and easily loaded onto a vehicle for transport. The only caveat would be that the unit must generally rely on a stable electricity source and water supply, however this allows the unit to be temporarily/permanently installed in any location that satisfies these conditions. The main limiting factor is the electricity supply, however there is less need for a constant water supply (a factor which will become clearer in a later section). Thus, by eliminating the primary flaw of a permanent installation, this ties in to another inherent strength of the mobile design, cost. As previously explained, conventional walk-in bathtubs are relatively expensive products, mostly due to the high installation costs involved. By comparison, the iMagic-BOX portable walk-in bathtub aims to offer high-end value at a projected price of $9,000, owning to the lack of installation costs, making it a far more affordable option (Figs. 3 and 4).

With regards to the issue of the inwards-facing door entrance for most conventional designs, the iMagic-BOX portable walk-in bathtub instead utilizes a drawbridge design, and has its forward-facing wall as an actual drawbridge that extends outwards

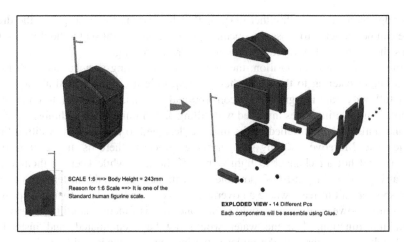

Fig. 3. The 3D-model of the iMagic-BOX portable walk-in bathtub used for 3D printing individual components

Fig. 4. 3D models comparing separate size renditions of iMagic-BOX portable walk-in bathtub units

as a ramp leading up to the unit. Hence, instead of having to step over the tub-wall/step, the user is able to walk directly into the bathtub as if it were a doorway without hindrance and sit comfortably on the high-traction bath chair within the unit. To ensure that the user is properly secured, the bath chair comes with belt restraints as an option to prevent sliding or falling off from the seat, another common hazard in conventional walk-in bathtubs. As an alternative, for wheelchair-bound users, an alternative model has the bath chair removed and the internal compartment enlarged to fit an entire wheelchair and its user, which can easily roll backwards into the bathtub using the drawbridge as a ramp. With either design, after the user is safety in place, the draw-bridge can be retracted to close the opening, forming an airtight seal to hold water; this dodges the concern of navigation through a narrow opening.

With the user now in position, the unit can began taking in water and will fill to desired height catering to the sitting height of specific user, which will allow for the proper full-body bath not granted by conventional designs. In addition, to counter the infamous long waiting times involved with filling and draining such bathtubs, the water inlet and outlet valves installed in the unit are designed to reduce these waiting times significantly. Moreover, during the draining process, there is the option of a user-activated hot air channel to lightly dry off the user while keeping them warm. Alternatively, the iMagic-BOX portable walk-in bathtub could instead be used a seated-shower unit instead, where an overhead shower head can be activated to provide a refreshing shower if the user would prefer one. If this function is utilized instead of the bathtub function, then the water would not be accumulated, and instead be immediately drained through the outlet valve instead to prevent build-up.

Furthermore, to assist with personal mobility of the user, the interior of the unit is ergonomically-designed, with grooves and handles built into its structure to be used to assist in the sitting-down and standing from a seated position movements in the non-wheelchair model. Additionally, the interior houses most of the control interfaces including a drawbridge toggle, shower/bath toggle, water elevation settings, water temperature settings, controls to begin filling/draining water while in bath mode, and finally an emergency water release. As added support, a bar located is on top of the back walk of the unit if the user would rather grasp it to help with sitting or pulling themselves upwards to stand.

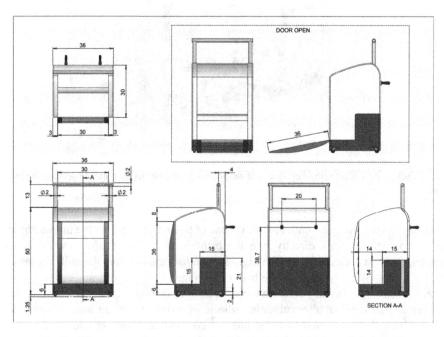

Fig. 5. Dimensions of a version of the iMagic-BOX portable walk-in bathtub

Finally, the design seeks to go above and beyond mere adherence to environmentally-friendly design; its construction allows it to take advantage of green technologies to reduce water usage and wastage. The unit is designed to utilize an external water storage tank (of varying capacity) that requires an approximate of 30 L (or 8 Gallons) of water for a shower spray bath, and double that for a full-soak bath. As an added benefit, this allows the unit to still be fully usable during the event of a water shortage, or if there is no direct water supply, with a full tank providing enough water for at least one more full-soak bath, while remaining a mobile unit. To improve this water efficiency further, the interior is outfitted with an efficient membrane water filter that is capable of cleaning and filtering used bathwater. It is efficient enough that the same bathwater can be reused several times while still being fully hygienic if needed, with the used bathwater being drained back into the storage tank for further use, instead of drainage to be expunged from the unit instead (Fig. 5).

4 Practical Implications and Conclusion

Through the combination of these specialized designed features seeking to overcome the failing of previous attempts at walk-in bathtubs, the iMagic-BOX portable walk-in bathtub aims to assist older adults in bathing independently in the comfort of their own homes, without worrying about the need to burden family members. Furthermore, although it was not the inventor's original intention, there was the realization that this design concept could not only serve older adults but also any individual inflicted with physical functioning limitations, regardless of age. While the numbers involved may not be as staggering as those for older adults, these individuals still represent a significant portion of adults in the world [12]. While not all who are accounted for in this category may be severely impacted in their daily functioning, this does not underplay the significant proportion of individuals who are. Many such individuals suffer from varying degrees of problems that range across a wide variety of daily activities, and as such are in need of specialized treatment or technologies to assist in their daily living. The real danger comes from when such individuals themselves become older, and have to contend with their already existing ailments, in addition to the general issues that come with old age. At the very least, the iMagic-BOX portable walk-in bathtub may prove useful for these individuals' bathing needs.

Moreover, the mobile nature of the unit's design has highlighted the opportunity for this style of design to be implemented in professional nursing centre settings. Considering how these facilities currently struggle with bathing their patients/clients on a regular basis, there is an opportunity to utilize several units as mobile, shared bathing units within the centre. The units' water storage tanks could be pre-filled and then the entire units moved to the location of each patient/client (their personal rooms for instance) where they can be provided a shower/bath without the need to endanger/inconvenience the patient/client with unnecessary travel.

Despite the design decisions made for the iMagic-BOX portable walk-in bathtub's current design, the authors of this paper recognize that no one design is ever one-size-fits-all, for designs must be catered to specific contexts and circumstances of its usage. With this in mind, efforts have already been made to create alternative versions of the unit, by making drastic design changes to suit different operating conditions. The most prominent of these being the RotoBATH, a model that eschews the drawbridge design in favor of a rotating bath-only unit which would allow for the user to go from a standing position into a lying position, that being the same position a conventional bathtub utilizes.

It is this paper's authors' hope that by sharing the conceptualization process and the methodology that lead up to and during the iMagic-BOX portable walk-in bathtub's development as a fully-realized product, so that other inventors may see the increasing need for the interplay between technology and aging, and the potential that the growing field of gerontechnology possesses in combating the rising issue of ageing in populations around the world.

Acknowledgements. The authors sincerely thank the Gerontechnology Lab of Monash University Malaysia for their kind assistance in the preparation of this paper.

References

1. American Association of Colleges of Nursing: Nursing Shortage Fact Sheet (2014). http://www.aacn.nche.edu/media-relations/NrsgShortageFS.pdf. Accessed 10 Nov 2016
2. Association of American Medical Colleges: The Complexities of Physician Supply and Demand: Projections from 2014 to 2025: Final Report (2016 Update). IHS Inc., Washington (2016)
3. Bouma, H., Fozard, J.L., Bouwhuis, D.G., Taipale, V.: Gerontechnology in perspective. Gerontechnology **6**, 190–216 (2007)
4. Centers for Disease Control and Prevention: Nonfatal bathroom injuries among persons aged $\geq$ 15 years. Morb. Mortal. Wkly Rep. **60**(22), 729–733 (2011)
5. Centre for Analysis of Social Exclusion: Older People's Experiences of Dignity and Nutrition During Hospital Stays: Secondary Data Analysis Using the Adult Inpatient Survey (2015)
6. Chen, K., Chan, A.H.S.: The ageing population of china and a review of gerontechnology. Gerontechnology **10**(2), 63–71 (2011)
7. Fozard, J.L., Rietsema, J., et al.: Gerontechnology: creating enabling environments for the challenges and opportunities of aging. Educ. Gerontechnol. **26**, 331–344 (2000)
8. Fozard, J.L.: Impacts of technology interventions on health and self-esteem. Gerontechnology **4**, 63–76 (2005)
9. The Canadian Press: Seniors in Alberta Nursing Homes to Get At Least Two Baths a Week (2013). http://www.huffingtonpost.ca/2013/03/05/alberta-seniors-bathing-standards-nursing-home_n_2813862.html. Accessed 10 Nov 2016
10. United Nations, Department of Economic and Social Affairs, Population Division. World Population Ageing (2015). ST/ESA/SER.A/390
11. van Bronswijk, J.E.M.H., Bouma, H., Fozard, J.L.: Technology for quality of life: an enriched taxonomy. Gerontechnology **2**, 169–172 (2002)
12. World Health Organisation: World Report on Disability 2011. WHO Press, Geneva (2011)

The Integration of Personal and Public Transportation in Creating Seamless Experience

Qiao Liang[(⊠)], Miaosen Gong, Linghao Zhang, and Anran Qin

School of Design, Jiangnan University, Wuxi, People's Republic of China
liangqiao@jiangnan.edu.cn,
{miaosen.gong,anran.q}@foxmail.com, wowo.zlh@163.com

Abstract. Seamless experience has becoming a major focus in industrial design, including transportation design. It can be argued that to create this kind of "seamless" feeling calls for consideration from three levels: product, system and service, as product being the carrier, system being the logic lying beneath while service being the process of co-creation with users. It is also proposed that the integration of personal and public transportation become crucial in creating a seamless experience with the process of urbanization and complexity of transportation system. Then, the different nature of personal and public transportation is analyzed and four possible design models, or design methods, are proposed. Furthermore, a design case is illustrated as an initial design attempt in application. It is shown that the integration process involves complicated design elements and calls for deep collaboration.

Keywords: Seamless experience · Personal transportation · Public transport · Integrated innovation

1 Introduction

Experience has been a major focus in product design—both physical and internet product. Also, as experience seems to become increasingly diversified, to create a seamless experience become a crucial issue. In general, seamless experience comes from a variety of aspects. (1) Among different products. This part contains two aspects: the appearance of products and the interaction of product. The former one focuses on the appearance of the product. For example, car companies have been trying to maintain some key features in car styling. BMW's "Double Kidney" grille and "flaming surface" are classic representatives. This is called "brand DNA" [1, 2], which uses specific styling features to create a similar cognition and further to form a seamless experience. For the latter one, apple devices are good examples. Although iphone, ipad and Macbook have similar system and interaction model, one still have to reopen a task or an app when he/she changes to another device. What Apple tries to do is, besides keeping continuity across multiple devices by interface and apps, to "jump" for one device to another while continuing the same task. For example, If one is reading a web

© Springer International Publishing AG 2017
P.-L.P. Rau (Ed.): CCD 2017, LNCS 10281, pp. 171–180, 2017.
DOI: 10.1007/978-3-319-57931-3_14

site on MacBook, he/she can walk over to iPad, swipe up, and continue reading the same site. If one is writing an email on iphone, he/she can hand it off just as easily to Mac and finish typing it on a real keyboard. This is to create, as Tim Cook said, "an integrated and continuous experience across all apple products" [3]. (2) Online and Offline experience. Since multichannel retailing is becoming widespread and popular, how to create seamless experience for customer has been a major concern. For example, companies should correspond between their online and offline channels in terms of convenience and availability, customer comprehension and uniform company identity [4]. (3) Web and mobile experience. Since many software applications are available in both web and mobile version, some gaps of interacting show as the app is designed first or only for one of these two platforms. Thus some approaches have been taken to mitigate such an issue and create seamless experience when users shift between platforms [5].

Whereas daily travelling is always a huge part of human life, this kind of seamless experience is also gaining more attention in transportation design. For example, some car companies have adopted smart operating system in their cars, so the drivers can mirror the content of their mobile phone onto the in-car screen and use those apps such as map or music player in a manner which they are familiar with. However, as the current and changing nature of society and lifestyle patterns generate diversified travel needs [6], a more holistic way of creating this seamless experience is needed, integrating personal and public transportation being one of the feasible solution. Also, from the cases above it can be seen that, all of those seamless experiences seems to have something in common—to keep some key factors such as styling, interface, manipulation in certain continuity while the user transit among various platforms. So the importance is the existence of platforms and to have something continuous in between. In transportation design, the platform can be product, system and service.

2 Experience of Transportation

2.1 Interrelationship of Product, System, Service and Experience

According to the new definition of Industrial Design by WDO, "Industrial Design is a strategic problem-solving process that drives innovation, builds business success and leads to a better quality of life through innovative products, systems, services and experiences." The definition shows the trend that industrial design is now way beyond function and form [7], but is an integration of product, system, service and experience. From certain perspective, this integration can be understood as—product is the carrier, tangible or intangible; system is the logic lying beneath; service is the process of co-creation with user [8]; while experience is the pursued value, as shown in Fig. 1.

The implication of this figure is that, to gain a valuable experience, the design should take product, system and service into consideration at the same time. This is especially the case when it comes to transportation design.

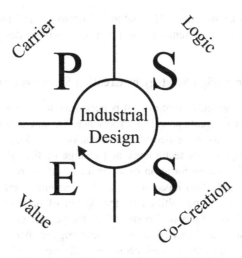

Fig. 1. The hierarchy of industrial design

2.2   Product, System and Service of Transportation Design

Generally, transportation includes personal transportation and public transportation, which seems mutual exclusive. Due to their nature, the different characters of these two can be summarized as below (Fig. 2).

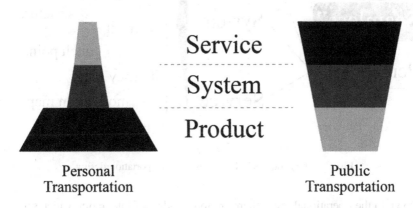

Fig. 2. The different nature of personal transportation and public transportation

For personal transportation, product itself is the most important, because it is closely related to the mobility of single person. On the basis of product, related system is constructed and service provided. It is kind of bottom-up hierarchy. As for public transportation, according to its definition, "a shared passenger-transport service which is available by the general public", means that it is a kind of service in the first place. Then certain system has to be built in order to serve the general public rather than single person. As long as this purpose is achieved, the form of the product varies. So it is more like up-bottom structure. The nature of personal and public transportation determines that they have different starting point and focus in designing.

2.3   Transportation Design Strategy of Creating Seamless Experience

Due to those aforementioned distinctions, it is necessary to get insights of the basis of transportation in order to create seamless experience. On one hand, the essential purpose of transportation is to move people from location A to location B. On the other hand, with the development of technology and change of lifestyle, people now have higher expectation of the transportation experience. For these reasons, the purpose of "seamless" should include two basic sources: physical and perceptual, as shown in Fig. 3. The former one can be fulfilled by the design of product and system which enable a smooth transition of physical body. While the perception of "seamless" comes from product [9], system and service, as each piece triggers perceptual reactions. For either situation, the design elements which lie beneath are closely interrelated.

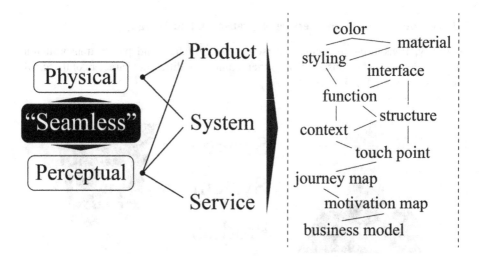

Fig. 3. The "sources" of seamless in transportation design

Down to the operational level, there are four models of integration which serve the purpose of creating "seamless". The first one is "Product+Product", or product-leading. This is the straight-forward way of integrating, which requires the "combination" of product, so that users can transit from one product to another conveniently. A simple example would be a subway with special scooter or bicycle which can be used for "one last mile" after passengers get off. The second one is "Product+System", or system-orienting, which calls for a systematic way of organizing products to make the transit smoothly. This may be seen in future cities with all autonomous cars running on the streets, in which all the cars are controlled by the intellectual system. The third one is "Product+Service". In this case, service can be used as a supplement or even substitution of some products. Nowadays, all kinds of car sharing or car pool services are using this kind of concept. This model also influence some car manufactures directly. "Xiaopeng Motors", a Chinese startup car company that aims at providing electric cars for the youth, takes "half selling and half renting" strategy and encourage long-term renting, which means users don't necessarily have to buy a car, while having the service instead. Last but not least, the fourth model is "Product+System+Service", which is the most comprehensive way of integration (Fig. 4).

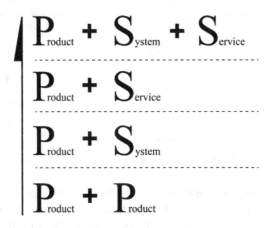

Fig. 4. Four models of integration

3   Design Case

In order to put the research into practice, some designs are done and reflections are made. Here is one of the design case which tries to combine the advantages of personal transportation and public transportation on the basis of H-Bahn.

3.1   Research and Concept

A general research is conducted in order to get a broad look on the current situation of personal and public transportation in the city. It is concluded that with the emerging of environmental and economic problem, more environmental-friendly, comfortable and convenient way of transporting are in demand. New energy vehicles and smart public transportation system have become popular, among which, rail transportation has regaining popularity in recent years, especially in China. It is reported that by the end of 2016, there are 43 Chinese cities whose constructing plan of rail transportation system have been approved by the government, and the trend has extended from first-tier cities to second-and third-tier cities. The whole planned mileage reaches 8600 km, and the expecting yearly subsidy is estimated $130 million from 2016 to 2020. Therefore, rail transportation is chosen as starting point of the design.

As there are several kinds of rail transportation for passenger such as tram and H-Bahn, a comparison is made. Several criteria are used such as construction cost, operating cost, land occupation and line coverage. It can be seen that high punctuality, high security and "green" are the general advantages of public transportation. While, some features such as low flexibility are the disadvantages, which can be used as the starting point of problem-solving (Fig. 5).

Project	Construction cost	Operating cost	Occupied area	Line coverage	Bearing capacity	Operating speed	Flexibility	Punctuality	Security	Green
Tramcar	●●●	●●●	●●●●	●●●	●●●●	●●●	●●	●●●●	●●●	●●●●
Metro	●●●●●	●●●●●	●●	●●	●●●●●	●●●●●	●	●●●●●	●●●●●	●●●
Light Rail Transit	●●●●	●●●●●	●●	●●	●●●●●	●●●●●	●	●●●●●	●●●●●	●●●
H-Bahn	●	●●	●	●●	●●●	●●●●	●●	●●●●●	●●●●	●●●●
Passenger cableway /Elevator	●	●	●	●	●	●	●	●●●●	●●●●	●●●●

Fig. 5. Comparison of different rail transportation

A quick user research is conducted and the dissatisfaction and major expectations for public transportation are collected. Then four personas are constructed including daily commuter, retired people, housewife and tourist. Based on their demands, the concept of this design is defined as "a transportation system based on public railway which have personal features and can be used as personal transportation at certain circumstances, also some services should be provided to meet special needs".

3.2   The Design

Three groups of designers collaborate on the design, focusing on product, system and service respectively. The final design is named "AirPT".

System

The rail network consists of two parts: the main lines and the branch lines. Main lines go across the main part of the city, like the aorta of human body, while the branch lines go deep into communities even buildings, just like capillaries. Accordingly, there will be two kinds of cabins: large one and small one. Large ones are like regular H-Bahn cabin, having the capacity of 50 to 70 people and running only on the main lines. Small ones have capacity of 1 to 4 people, which run both at the main lines and the branch lines. Some platforms are incorporated with office or residence buildings. Different route situations have also been considered and designed in order to make the system adaptive for complicated urban layout, such as single track with three directions and double track with four directions (Fig. 6).

The Figure below shows the information flow of this system. The information among control center, user, station and vehicle is carefully examined and systematically controlled so that the information exchanging is smooth (Fig. 7).

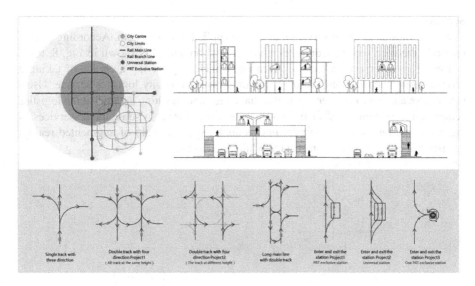

Fig. 6. Line distribution system

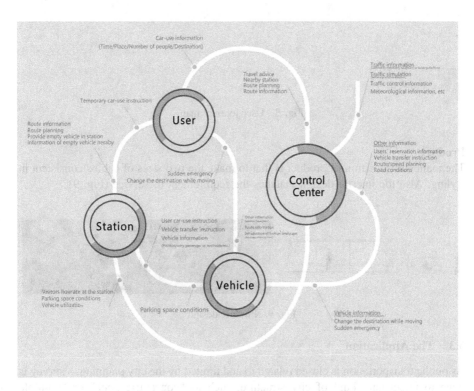

Fig. 7. Information flow diagram

Service

There are various kinds of service that can be applied in this system. According to user research, the core service would be reserving and booking. As shown in Fig. 8, users can use apps to reserve a cabin conveniently, including having a choice of taking a private cabin or shared one. Another important service is city logistics service. Users can reserve a cabin to deliver a parcel or have the cabin fetching a parcel at the logistics center before picking him/her up. Furthermore, there are also some in-car services as the cabin can be used for tourism. For example, with the help of augmented reality, tourists can enjoy explanation service while sightseeing.

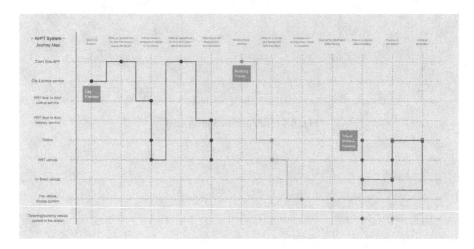

Fig. 8. User journey map

Product

The main consideration of product is that to make the two sizes of cabins consistent in styling. Also the interior design matches the requirement of service (Fig. 9).

Fig. 9. Product design

3.3   The Application

As public transportation is closed related to and limited by the city planning, a survey is done to understand kind of city structure, such as "concentric zone" or "multiple nuclei". Also, some basic development models like Transit-Oriented Development (TOD) and Joint Development (TJD) [10] are also studied. Then the Chinese city

Xiamen is chosen as an ideal location for application. It is thought that the AirPT system would be a good supplement of public transportation there due to the character of this city. By field survey and desktop research, the geography, the functional layout and the general situation of residence are understood. Then the predicted traffic situation and demand is estimated by setting the community, the population of each district, the situation of commuting and travelling. On this basis, the line distribution of AirPT is designed (Fig. 10).

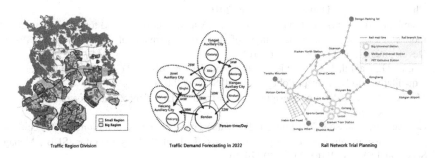

Fig. 10. Attempt for application

4 Discussion

With the accelerated process of urbanization, the way of commuting and travelling become diversified, and people have higher expectation for transportation experience. In this context, the integration of personal transportation and public transportation seems to be a necessary and effective way for creating a seamless experience. In general, there are two ways of doing this. The first one is to make personal mobility "sharable", just like car pool or car sharing. Meanwhile, to make public transportation more personalized is also feasible. According to the analysis and design case above, product, system and service all have the potential to do so, "product leading", "system orienting" and "service guiding" are all possible ways, and there is no clear boundary among them, and all three factors are co-dependent. Actually, integrating personal transportation and public transportation is such a big topic and complicated one, inter-discipline knowledge such as urban planning and architecture design are needed. What design can contribute most is that to understand the problem comprehensively and do the problem-solving holistically. Also, the design case here is a concept design which needs further perfection and testified. But to consider how the elements of product, system and service should be integrated is the right way of problem-solving here.

References

1. Karjalainen, T.M.: It looks like a Toyota: educational approaches to designing for visual brand recognition. Int. J. Des. 1(1), 67–81 (2007)
2. Karjalainen, T.M., Snelders, D.: Designing visual recognition for the brand. J. Prod. Innov. Manag. 27(1), 6–22 (2010)
3. Apple's next big design challenge: a seamless experience across all your devices. https://www.wired.com/?p=991161
4. Kockum, A., Molin, E.: Creating a Seamless Experiences Between Online and Offline Channels. Linnaeus University, Sweden (2016)
5. Brambilla, M., Mauri, A., Franzago, M., et al.: A model-based method for seamless web and mobile experience In: Proceedings of the 1st International Workshop on Mobile Development, pp. 33–40. ACM (2016)
6. Beirão, G., Cabral, J.A.S.: Understanding attitudes towards public transport and private car: a qualitative study. Transp. Policy 14(6), 478–489 (2007)
7. Mitchell, C.T.: Redefining Designing; from from to Experience. Van Nostrand Reinhold, New York (1993)
8. Gebauer, H., Johnson, M., Enquist, B.: Value co-creation as a determinant of success in public transport services: a study of the Swiss Federal Railway operator (SBB). Manag. Serv. Qual.: Int. J. 20(6), 511–530 (2010)
9. Van Rompay, T., Hekkert, P., Muller, W.: The bodily basis of product experience. Des. Stud. 26(4), 359–377 (2005)
10. Cervero, R., Ferrell, C., Murphy, S.P.: Transit-oriented development and joint development in the United States: a literature review. TCRP Res. Results Dig. (52) (2002)

Integration and Innovation: Learning by Exchanging Views - A Report of the Cross-Cultural Design Workshop for Stone Craving

Po-Hsien Lin[1(✉)], Ya-Juan Gao[1], Taihua Lan[2], and Xiaoge Wang[2]

[1] Graduate School of Creative Industry Design,
National Taiwan University of Arts, New Taipei City, Taiwan
t0131@ntua.edu.tw, 78343821@qq.com
[2] Graduate School of Craft and Design, College of Fine Arts,
Fujian Normal University, Fuzhou, People's Republic of China
lantaihua@126.com, wangxiaoge1975@126.com

Abstract. This article reports on a cross-cultural design workshop held at Fuzhou, China, 25–30 December 2015. The workshop was intended to provide a platform that would bring together artists in stone craving, academic researchers, and managers from stone craving industries, in order to focus exclusively on the teaching of creativity in stone craving for the future. Sessions were devoted to works exhibition, cross-disciplinary courses and cross-cultural design workshops. This study focuses on the cross-cultural workshop which included the desirability of creativity throughout the curriculum, and particularly focuses on coaching, learning, and practicing. The purposes of the workshop emphasized interactive learning and addressed the interactions of practicing. Results are presented herein to establish a platform for examining the way artists communicate across culture as well as the interwoven experience of stone craving and culture in the creation process.

Keywords: Stone craving · Cross-cultural · Design workshop · Cultural product design

1 Introduction

Stone carving is one of Chinese historic and profound arts and crafts [17]. As early as in the Stone Age, China's ancestors had mastered the skills of stone processing. The stoneware was both decorative and functional. Its variable ornamentations have been carrying on ancient Chinese civilization. Jade carving, and inheriting the ancient stone processing craft, are the outstanding embodiments of Chinese ancient scientific, technological, and cultural achievements. There were many significant and distinctive stone and jade carvings in every dynasty during the long Chinese history [4]. With the social stability and economic prosperity especially since the Ming and Qing dynasty, the traditional handicrafts did better than before [19]. Many stone carving skills had

© Springer International Publishing AG 2017
P.-L.P. Rau (Ed.): CCD 2017, LNCS 10281, pp. 181–191, 2017.
DOI: 10.1007/978-3-319-57931-3_15

developed, such as protruded carving, circular engraving, shadow carving, hollow carving and openwork carving in the Kangyongqian Prosperity Times (康雍乾盛世).

As carving materials extended further, there emerged the building stone carving, jade carving, ink-stone carving, seal-stone carving and so on. The stone carving art taste promoted as the scholars' artistic concept joined in it. What Chinese stone carving expresses is the pursuit of the spirit of perseverance and the aesthetic thought of profound consideration. Traditional stone carving has gradually entered into a new transitional period with the development of modern processing techniques, the transformation of life style and the diversified aesthetic tendency in the 20th century [3, 8]. On the one hand, the emergence of new tools and new technology has greatly improved the production efficiency and reduced the production cycle and cost; on the other hand, the promotion of public artistic taste has required higher technology and ideas in traditional stone carving [15].

Contemporary stone carving inherits the traditional handicraft, as well as being influenced by contemporary art in creative concepts, process techniques and patterns of manifestation. Young stone carving artists with pioneering spirit and outstanding creativity are emerging in large numbers. They are not only the inheritance of folk culture, but also the pioneers of modern stone carving art [3, 8]. Thus, stone carvings are increasingly broader in spanning geographical and cultural boundaries. The variety and distinction of Chinese culture offers potential application in the field of design. By enhancing the original meaning and images of cultures and taking advantage of new production technology, stone craving will have great potential for enhancing product design value thus increasing cultural product recognition in the global market. Yet little research is available on the influence of culture as it pertains to the creativity of stone craving in cultural product design.

To address these considerations, a forum was organized on Chinese stone craving in 2015, the aim of which was to bring together young and middle-aged inheritors of Chinese stone carving art from a variety of disciplines to present current skill and theoretic issues and contribute to a collaborative in the stone craving field. The forum were devoted to three events: (1) an open works exhibition for displaying skill, material, topics, contents and metrics for selecting participants; (2) organizing discipline-based and cross-cultural disciplinary courses; and (3) conducting a cross-cultural design workshop in stone craving [2].

The works exhibition displayed the masterpieces of 100 stone carving artists from all over the country, involving jade carving, ink-stone carving, seal-stone carving, and so on. It typically reflects the achievements of Chinese contemporary stone carving art, some of which are shown in Fig. 1. The works demonstrate not only the artist's persistence in traditional culture but also the artist's exploration in new materials and new technologies. This exhibition was also an open platform for learning from each other by exchanging views. We are looking forward to driving folk art thought interactions and cross-border exchanges by means of this show of "Chinese stone carving art senior workshop for young and middle-aged artist." We wish to transform heart impulses and thoughts into new creative inspiration and motivation. As the philosopher says; the ideal state of art, is not lost in the past, but found in the future. The future of Chinese stone carving art is in the eyes, hands, dreams and hearts of numerous gifted youths. We have been feeling the booming of the art of stone carving [18].

Fig. 1. Some works display in stone craving exhibition

Then, inter-disciplinary courses were arranged for the participants following the works exhibition. Finally, a cross-cultural design workshop was conducted to provide a platform that would bring together sculptors in stone craving, design researchers, and managers from stone craving industries, in order to focus exclusively on the teaching of creativity in stone craving for the future. This article focuses on the ross-cultural design workshop which has established a cross-cultural design model to provide designers with a valuable reference for designing a successful cultural product. Results presented herein create an interface for examining the way stone craving artists communicate across cross-cultural issues and the interwoven experience of creation and culture in the stone craving [13].

2   Cultural Product Design Model

From the design point of view, designing a product with local features in order to emphasis its cultural value has become a critical issue in the design process. Cultural product design has played an important role in embedding the cultural elements into products and in increasing the cultural value in the global competitive product market [6]. Using cultural features to add extra value to a product not only benefits economic growth, but also promotes unique local culture in the global market. Lin [10] proposed a framework for studying cultural objects summarized in Fig. 1. The cultural product design model in Fig. 1 consists of three main phases: conceptual model, research method, and design process. The conceptual model focuses on how to extract cultural features from cultural objects and then transfer these features to the design model. The design model is composed of three phases: identification (extract cultural features from original cultural objects), translation (transfer them to design information and design elements) and implementation to finally design a cultural product.

Culture can be classified into three layers: (1) Physical or material culture, including food, garments, and transportation related objects, (2) Social or behavioral culture, including human relationships and social organization, and (3) Spiritual or ideal culture, including art and religion, as shown in the bottom of Fig. 2 [10]. These three culture layers can be fitted into Leong's three culture levels given above [9].

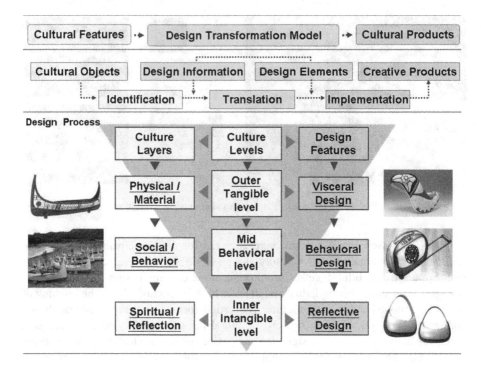

Fig. 2. Cultural product design model

Since cultural objects can be incorporated into cultural design, three design features can be identified as follows: (1) the inner-level containing special content such as stories, emotion, and cultural features, (2) the mid-level containing function, operational concerns, usability, and safety, and (3) the outer-level dealing with colors, texture, form, decoration, surface pattern, line quality, and details [9, 10]. For the design process, three levels are identified as: transfer, transit and transformation, which can be mapped into three levels of design features: visceral design, behavioral design and reflective design [16].

Lin also proposed a cultural product design process using scenario and story-telling approaches. In a practical design process, four phases are used to design a cultural product as shown in Fig. 3, included investigation (set a scenario), interaction (tell a story), development (write a script), and implementation (design a product) that will be discussed in detail in Sect. 3. Process for Cross-Cultural Product Design [10].

To test the utility of the cultural design process, Lin [10] took the "Pinban boat", a canoe, as the cultural object to transfer its cultural features into a modern product. The Tao people are a Taiwan aboriginal people native to the tiny outlying Orchid Island. They are traditionally good at making canoes. The Pinban boat shown in Fig. 4 is a symbol of their tribe. The Tao people live by fishing and usually bring the holy dagger with them while fishing.

Figure 4 shows the final cultural product designed from the Tao's Pinban boat and holy dagger. According to the four steps of the cultural design process, the scenario is

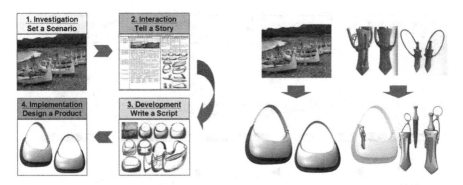

Fig. 3. Four phases of cultural product design   **Fig. 4.** An example of cultural product design

that Tao people ride in their Pinban boat with their holy dagger to protect them and sail to the ocean for fishing. Based on this scenario the Pinban boat was transformed into a modern bag and the holy dagger into a knife-like modern alarm. In modern society, one can imagine a woman holding the modern bag and bringing the modern alarm to protect her while walking down the street, matching the previous scenario of Tao people fishing with their Pinban boat and holy dagger [10, 11].

3   Process for Cross-Cultural Product Design

The cultural product design is a process of rethinking or reviewing the cultural features and then redefining them in order to design a new product to fit into society and satisfy consumers through culture and esthetic [10, 11]. Designing new products by adding unique cultural features would not only benefit economic growth, but also promote unique local culture in the global market. Therefore, transforming cultural features into a cultural product becomes a critical issue. In order to facilitate the understanding of the cultural product design process, the design framework and process are proposed for combining consumer attitudes, cultural levels, cultural attributes, transformation, product semantics and design features as shown in Fig. 5.

A good understanding of cultural attributes will benefit articulating the context between the culture and product design and therefore accelerate concept development. Based on the cultural product design framework and process, the cultural product is designed using scenario and semantics approaches. In a practical design process four phases are used to design a cultural product, namely: investigation (set a scenario), interaction (tell a story), development (write a script), and implementation (design a product) as shown in Fig. 5. Following a review of the literature and expert opinions, design guidelines were developed based on the research of consumers' needs, cultural content and design theories. Ten steps of design procedure would provide designers or students a systematic method to designing a cultural product. The four phases and ten steps of the cultural product design process are further described accordingly as follows [7].

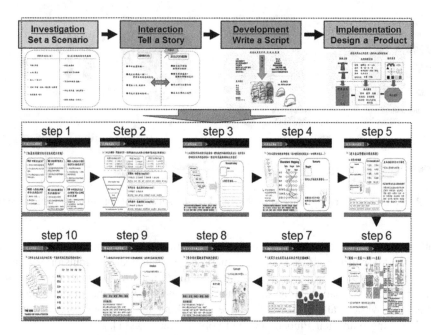

Fig. 5. Design framework and process for cultural products

1. Investigation/set a scenario
   Step 1: Discussing the condition: understanding cultural products through discussions. Designers should have explicit understanding of design aspirations and develop a preliminary prioritized attributes hierarchy.
   Step 2: Recognizing the trend: based on the cultural attributes, observe, compare and incorporate related issues such as economic developments, social trends, technological applications, and related existing products into the new product design.

2. Interaction/tell a story
   Step 3: Targeting the consumer: make a good observation of customer needs and explore the consumer society in order to define a product image with meaning and style derived from culture features concerns.
   Step 4: Describing the scenario: this step allows designers to describe scenarios of users who have a preference for a particular style and identify with the features, meaning, category, and appropriateness of the product.
   Step 5: Establishing the direction: this step establishes design specifications which will identify the goal, function, target group, and limitations of the design. All of these concerns should match attitudes of consumers [12].

3. Development/write a script
   Step 6: Analyzing the culture: Identify original cultural features including tribal affiliation, object, type, image, material, color, characteristic, operation, pattern, form grammar, form construct, formation, using scenario, cultural content, and resource.

Step 7: Connecting the relationships: based on reasonable connections such as product semantics, describe product features and develop a product with these cultural attributes. The analysis and synthesis will be processed back and forth between cultural analyses and design concepts as shown in Table 1.

Step 8: Selecting the rationale: assessing, selecting, and integrating semantically feasible manifestations into expressive wholes. In addition, describe the product performance and sketch the preliminary design image.

4. Implementation/designing a product

Step 9: Developing the concept: this step is the concept development and design realization by figurative product semantics (e.g. metaphor, simile, metonymy, analogy, and allegory), in order to transform the cultural meaning into a logically correct cultural product.

Step 10: Completing the design: examining the details and integrity of the cultural product as product features, supply cultural attributes to transform them reasonably into the product performance.

Based on the foregoing study phase, we specifically propose a design framework and process for cultural product design, proving the effectiveness of this systemic approach by many design examples, some of which are shown in Fig. 6 [7, 10, 11].

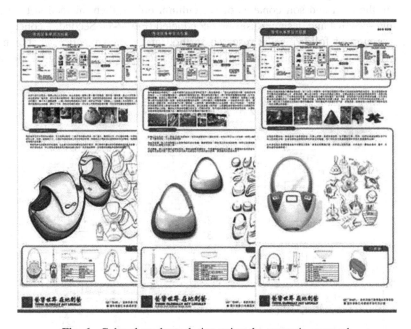

Fig. 6. Cultural products design using the systemic approach

4   Design Practice in Cross-Cultural Creativity Workshop

To conduct the design practices in the cross-cultural workshop, the participants were randomly assigned into 12 groups, each group members diverse in geographical, skill, and material attributes. Each group was asked to design a cultural product based on the previous process. The results are summarized by the process of integration of brain-storming, interaction of design concepts from local culture, and the category of products related to daily-used products. China has many different local features. Each local culture has dissimilarities in their respective features. Therefore the purpose of this workshop was to teach group members how to extract cultural features for demonstrating their craving skills into their works even for daily-used products which could be easy recognized by consumers.

The workshop started with presentations by Professor Lin on the concept of 'culture', cross cultural usability and creativity issues for cultural product design, and studies of design process across cultures as shown in Fig. 7 [7, 10, 11]. The workshop that ensued established a roadmap for artists in cross-cultural design for stone craving in the further development [14].

According to Fig. 7, participants are led through the process for implementing design practices in the cross-cultural creative workshop which include: building a design conceptual model, follow the research approach, format related information, and conduct the scripting method. First: a design concept model was built to help understand both the hard and soft contents of the cultural object, then interaction between both culture-product and designer-user was conducted (Fig. 7-1). Second: a conceptual model was studied following the research method and design practice as shown in Fig. 7-2. Third: a cultural object or a local feature was chosen for exploring the cultural

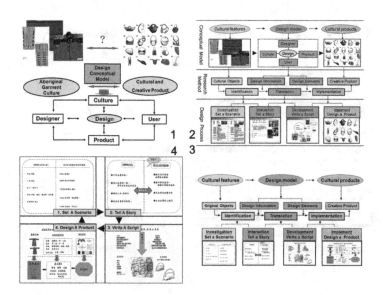

Fig. 7. Process of design practice in cross-cultural creativity workshop

attributes and developing a cultural product (Fig. 7-3). The most important part is the scripting approach for setting a scenario, telling a story, writing a script, and designing a product as shown in Fig. 7-4. The scripting approach simplifies iterations in the design process. In the presentation, an example of using the scripting method to assist in the design of an old picture transformed to a traffic sign was explained and discussed. The result indicated the proposed scripting technique is effective (Fig. 8).

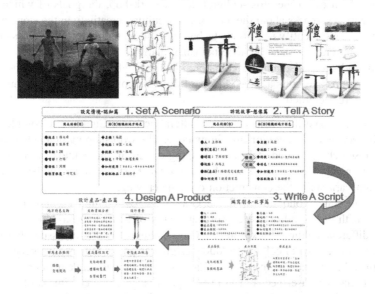

Fig. 8. A scripting approach for designing cultural product design

During the workshop, the participants were involved in the design process (Fig. 9), and modern products were developed using the culture features as examples to explore the feasibility of the design reference from the cultural features. Hence, the workshop provided designers with a valuable reference for designing successful cultural products. In the discussion session, each group presented the concept of the design and sought out the appropriate daily-uses of the products (Fig. 10). The workshop also discussed many questions related to cross-cultural ergonomics and participants agreed that more research is needed in the stone craving field (Fig. 11). Especially important are user behavior studies of culturally diverse user groups for market segmentation [1]. These studies can form the basis for culturally sensitive design for stone craving. Before

Fig. 9. The design practices   **Fig. 10.** Some of the results   **Fig. 11.** The discussion session

leaving, participants made commitments to work toward change at least in their own fields. In addition, participants' specific commitments to future actions were also given.

5 Conclusions

This report focuses on the cross-cultural design workshop, the goals of which were: (1) to increase awareness about the area of cross-cultural creativity in the stone craving community; (2) to identify new tools, techniques and methodologies for cross-cultural study of stone craving, and (3) to establish a platform for generating new research directions and cross-disciplinary collaboration. Through case studies from diverse workshop groups and comparative studies of different contents in stone craving fields, two areas were identified:

1. Stone craving and the preservation of cultural heritage: Culture is a complex issue that is very hard to operationalize in practice. The workshop participants called for more research to be undertaken on defining culture in the context of cultural features as an approach to assess whether and to what extent culture can be considered a design variable in the construction of stone craving.
2. Cross-Cultural ergonomics of Stone Craving: Cross-cultural ergonomics is concerned with the usability and comprehensibility of marketing based on user needs from different cultural backgrounds. Cross-cultural ergonomic issues have been explored in the area of cultural product design; design guidelines have been created, design and evaluation methodologies have been devised to implement cross-cultural and international user needs. The user population of stone craving is often just as international as those of globally marketed cultural products. Designing for culturally diverse users is a challenge that deserves more attention when creating stone craving resources.

One clear outcome of the workshop was the strong need for research on cross-cultural issues in the design and implementation of stone craving fields. It is the intention of the authors to report the results of the workshop and invite the stone craving community to include cross-cultural creativity issues and concerns into its future research. For more information, please visit the platform: http://fj.artron.net/20151223/n803722.html.

Acknowledgements. The authors would like to express their sincere thanks to Professor Lin for designing the courses for the workshop and especially for authoring the use of the teaching materials in this article. The authors also wish to thank those who contributed to the workshop and made publication of this research possible.

References

1. Chang, S.H., Hsu, C.-H., Lin, R.T.: Cultural creativity in experience design model. In: Marcus, A. (ed.) DUXU 2014. LNCS, vol. 8517, pp. 622–630. Springer, Cham (2014). doi:10.1007/978-3-319-07668-3_60

2. Dym, C.L., Wesner, J.W., Winner, L.: Social dimensions of engineering design: observations from Mudd design workshop III. J. Eng. Educ. **92**(1), 105–107 (2003)
3. Hall, S., King, A.: Old and new identities. In: Beyond Borders: In Thinking Critically About Global Issues, pp. 167–173 (2005)
4. Howard, A.F.: Chinese Sculpture. Yale University Press, New Haven (2006)
5. Hsu, C.-H., Chen, R., Lin, R.: Analysis of application of digital archives to value-added design in cultural creative products. In: Rau, P.L.P. (ed.) CCD 2014. LNCS, vol. 8528, pp. 731–742. Springer, Cham (2014). doi:10.1007/978-3-319-07308-8_70
6. Hsu, C.H., Chang, S.H., Lin, R.: A design strategy for turning local culture into global market products. Int. J. Affect. Eng. **12**, 275–283 (2013)
7. Hsu, C.-H., Lin, C.-L., Lin, R.: A study of framework and process development for cultural product design. In: Rau, P.L.P. (ed.) IDGD 2011. LNCS, vol. 6775, pp. 55–64. Springer, Heidelberg (2011). doi:10.1007/978-3-642-21660-2_7
8. Jenkins, H.: Convergence Culture: Where Old and New Media Collide. NYU Press, New York City (2006)
9. Leong, D., Clark, H.: Culture-based knowledge towards new design thinking and practice - a dialogue. Des. Issues **19**(3), 48–58 (2003)
10. Lin, R.: Transforming Taiwan aboriginal cultural features into modern product design: a case study of a cross-cultural product design model. Int. J. Des. **1**, 45–53 (2007)
11. Lin, R.: Designing friendship into modern products. In: Toller, J.C. (ed.) Friendships: Types, Cultural, Psychological and Social, pp. 1–24. Nova Science Publishers, New York (2009)
12. Lin, R., Lin, P.-H., Shiao, W.-S., Lin, S.-H.: Cultural aspect of interaction design beyond human-computer interaction. In: Aykin, N. (ed.) IDGD 2009. LNCS, vol. 5623, pp. 49–58. Springer, Heidelberg (2009). doi:10.1007/978-3-642-02767-3_6
13. Lin, R., Lin, C.L.: From digital archive to e-business: a case study of turning "art" to "e-business". In: Proceedings of 2010 International Conference on E-Business (2010)
14. Lin, C.L., Chen, S.J., Hsiao, W.H., Lin, R.: Cultural ergonomics in interactional and experiential design: conceptual framework and case study of the Taiwanese twin cup. Appl. Ergon. **52**, 242–252 (2016)
15. Michaelson, C., Middleton, A.P.: The identification of carving techniques on Chinese jade. J. Archaeol. Sci. **31**(10), 1413–1428 (2004)
16. Norman, D.A.: Emotional Design: Why we Love (or Hate) Everyday Things. Basic Books, New York (2004)
17. Paludan, A.: Chinese Sculpture: A Great Tradition. Serindia, Chicago (2006)
18. Sax, M., Meeks, N.D., Yu, W.: The parade scene of Fish Wagons on Murals and stone-craving portraits of the Han Dynasty. Archaeol. Cult. Relics **3**, 011 (2013)
19. Wang, J.: The Story of Stone: Intertextuality, Ancient Chinese Stone Lore, and the Stone Symbolism in Dream of the Red Chamber, Water Margin, and the Journey to the West. Duke University Press, Durham (1992)

The Item-Based Fashion Matching Experience in Online Platform Service Design: A Case Study from Chinese Customers

Hao Tan[1], Wei Li[2(✉)], Zhengyu Tan[2], Shijing Fang[2], and Shihui Xu[2]

[1] State Key Laboratory of Advanced Design and Manufacturing for Vehicle Body, Hunan University, Changsha, China
htan@hnu.edu.cn

[2] School of Design, Hunan University, Changsha, China
{liwei2014,sj_fang,xushihui}@hnu.edu.cn

Abstract. In online fashion retail platform, the customer service has played an essential role during the shopping process. In this study we focus on the service design of fashion matching experience in online shopping platform in different service scenarios, which has become one of the key issues of the fashion matching service. Based on the previous research on the matching service during the shopping process, we took the Chinese consumer as an example and focused our research on the fashion matching when the customers make purchase decision. In this paper, a new matching platform was designed based on fashion items and adopted the methods of verbal report and Likert scale to analysis the customer's shopping experience. The experiments results indicate that with the item-based matching platform, the experience of customer online shopping is promoted to some extent, and customers can enjoy the entertainment and practicality of the interactive matching service. Moreover, this item-based service can be used by designers to provide matching references.

Keywords: Matching experience · Online shopping · Fashion retail

1 Introduction

In fashion retail industry, companies are expected to enhance customer shopping experience (CSE) to survive and thrive in competitive sales market. CSE means the customer's interaction with a retail company during the whole shopping process, there are three components in CES: pre-sales, in-store and after-sales (Bikshorn 2011). Moreover, the shopping experience largely have affects on customer's purchase decisions which is particularly crucial to sales profit (Kent 2007). In today's fashion retailing business, the application of internet has extended its business range for more customers by online shopping website and the influence of online product reviews has played an important role in customer's shopping experience.

According to researchers' investigations, the online product reviews has regarded as an electronic equivalent of Word-of-mouth (WOM) which have influenced sales and treated as a valuable asset to retailing companies (Chevalier 2006; Dellarocas 2007;

© Springer International Publishing AG 2017
P.-L.P. Rau (Ed.): CCD 2017, LNCS 10281, pp. 192–203, 2017.
DOI: 10.1007/978-3-319-57931-3_16

Duan et al. 2008). Moreover, study by PowerReviews has found that 59% customers admit that their purchase behaviors are strong influenced by products reviews.

In the past period, the fashion designers designed an amount of fashion products then considered how to matching those items together and present those matched fashion products to the customers. The process of fashion matching was based on the designers' professional skills and experience.

Nowadays, in the fashion retailing business, especially on online shopping platform, some items are matched only after the fashion products have been designed and produced, then the retailers provide those matching fashion products to customers through the salesmen. In this process, the matching fashion products are provided by the salesmen based on the designer's idea without professional skills to evaluate the matched work, hence, this process may lead a result which is the salesmen may not provide the most attractive matched fashion products to the customers. On the other hand, the customers can not find the matched fashion products through thousands of items in an online store and their mindset of fashion shopping is based on the item which means the customers will choose one item and then take a long time to choose other items to matching those items together. All these patterns will lead the online fashion shopping process turns more complicated and the customers under this scenario may over purchase because they can not match the items by professional and rational way. In 2004, Kobayashi use a method to matching the fashion items based on colors. In this study, an item-based fashion matching platform was designed for giving customers matching service in the product reviews, which customers can choose color clues to receive the professional references (Fig. 1).

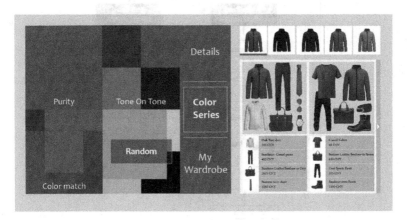

Fig. 1. The interface of item-based fashion matching service through color clues (Color figure online)

To improve online fashion customer service quality, it is important to make customers feel satisfied with the shopping process. Based on common format in Chinese e-commerce platform, the fashion products reviews are based on the advertising picture which shows the item itself. Since the format of online products reviews play an important and necessary role in influencing the customers' purchase decision like a 'sales assistants' (Chen 2008). Meanwhile, customer have to matching the item they purchased with other items by themselves. In this process, customers purchase the items and have to do the matching work without any professional knowledge or guidance. For the usual online shopping process, customers search one item at first, then receive the item information, after they read or watch the specific products reviews they will make a measurement about the product, then make the decision and purchase. For matching the product they brought, customers will repeat the process to purchase the second one, the third one which make the process so complicate and the customer have to do the matching work by themselves all the time. With the designed platform provided in this paper, there are two processes of online shopping (Fig. 2), one is the traditional process which the customers need to repeat the purchase for single item over and over again to finish purchase a suit of fashion apparel. In the second process, customers can use the item-based matching service to find other items and purchase for only once.

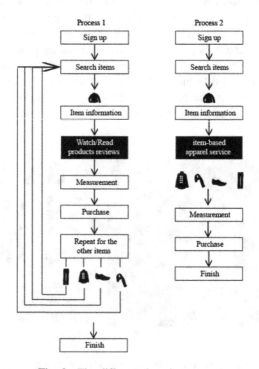

Fig. 2. The different shopping process

With this new matching service, customers may receive professional matching references while in the process of online shopping, moreover, they could finish the whole shopping process with high efficiency. For confirm the new item-based matching service will truly benefit for users, we have done some experiments.

2 Experiment

2.1 Participants

In this research, 100 participants were involved in the experiment which were all familiar with online shopping. The participants consisted of 46 males and 54 females which age ranged from 20 to 48 and they spent various lengths of time on online shopping (M = 30.19, SD = 8.25).

2.2 Experimental Arrangement

The whole research is divided into two experiments. In the first experiment, users were divided into two groups and invited to select products according to the given fashion item from two different shopping platforms. And users needed to score the experimental process. In the second experiment, two sets of clothing that users chose from two platforms were printed to the same size and users were invited to score and evaluate the two sets of clothing they chose.

2.3 Experiments

Experiment 1

In Experiment 1, users were randomly divided into two groups (Group A and Group B), each group with 50 users. There were two sets of experimental materials. The first platform simulated shopping process of the current China's largest online shopping site "Taobao" which user hunted for goods by type keywords and search results. The second platform created page jump mode based on color clues of professional matching cases. In order to rule out the impact of user experience of different operation sequence, users in the group A experienced platform 1 firstly, and then platform 2 at meanwhile group B did the same procedure in the contrary order. All collocations were asked to finished as quickly as possible, and each user needed to choose a set of clothing which would fit a given single product (a white shirt). In order to control the impact of the different types of items on the experimental results, users were proposed to buy an outer wear, a pair of pants, a pair of shoes and a handbag as the target. Throughout the process of clothing choice, the feedback from users were collected as an oral report. At the end of the stage, we invited users to score the complete purchase process on a 5-point Likert scale ranging from 1 (very poorly) to 5 (very well) to evaluate the convenience of the platform. And the shopping time user spent on the experiment was also recorded to compare the convenience of the two platforms.

Experiment 2

In the second phase of the experiment, two sets of clothing that users chose from two platforms were printed to a picture of the same size. Then users were invited to score and evaluate the two choices from the picture to output an oral report as shown in Figs. 1 and 2. Users scored the pictures on a 5-point Likert scale ranging from 1 (very poorly) to 5 (very well) to evaluate the satisfaction of the consequences from two different platforms (Figs. 3 and 4).

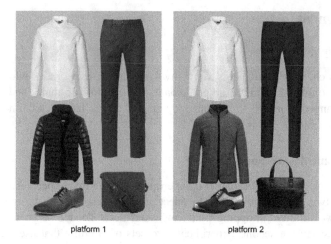

platform 1   platform 2

Fig. 3. Picture of consequence from different platforms (male)

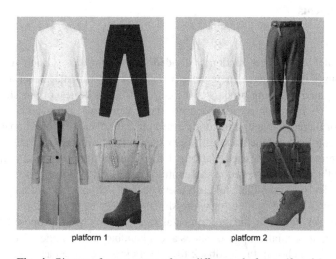

platform 1   platform 2

Fig. 4. Picture of consequence from different platforms (female)

Process Methods and Measurements of Oral Report

Direct extraction method: adjectives and adverbs of degree that appeared explicitly in oral reports were extracted to judge users' attitude toward the platform (Table 1).

Situational Extraction

Sometimes users did not express any explicit adverbs or adjectives. The way judging the users' attitude in this case is to review their oral reports and summarize their attitudes through colloquial descriptions (including exclamatory and interrogative sentences) and intonation in the context. Then users' attitudes and feelings were judged

Table 1. Direct extraction

Participants' words	Extracted adjectives	Adverbs degree	Level
This is so convenient for matching	convenient	so	High level
I think the whole progress is very fast	fast	very	High level
This way is too complex to me	complex	too	Extreme
It is more faster than before	fast	more	Medium grade
Matching in this way is pretty helpful for me	helpful	pretty	High level
Those clothes are really fit me	suitable	really	High level

by taking the physical scene, the language environment and the tone of the users into consideration. The input information was transformed into an expressive form of adjective and adverbs (Table 2).

Table 2. Situational extraction

Participants exact words	Extracted adjectives	The adverbs of degree	Level
How dose it know my style? It is amazing!	suitable	extremely	Extreme
Ah? I have finished the progress?	fast	very	High level
What should I do?	confuse	a little	Lower

Verbal Language Environment Extraction

Another way to judge users' attitude in the case that the statement did not appear any obvious adverbs or adjectives was through the analysis of users' hypothesis, comparisons, suggestions and expectations with the present environment and the current target attitudes or feelings, and translated it into adjective-dominated declarations (Table 3).

Table 3. Verbal language environment extractions

Participants exact words	Extracted adjectives	The adverbs of degree	Level
If there is a platform in real life, I may choose to use it.	useful	incomparable	High level
My husband must love this platform!	suitable	extremely	Extreme
Is there any other choice?	deficient	slightly	Lower
I will waste a lot of time to pick-up without those suggestions	helpful	very	High level

Incidence-Description Extraction

The fourth way we could judge participants' attitude without any obvious adverbs or adjectives was through participants' descriptions of the test process. We considered the movement and mental activity of users to judge the users' attitudes or feelings. Following analysis, the data was also translated into adjective-dominated declarations (Table 4).

Table 4. Incidence-description extraction

Participants exact words	Extracted adjectives	The adverbs of degree	Level
I don't have any special feeling about it.	insentience	slightly	Lower
I didn't spend much time to matching on this platform	convenient	pretty	High level

Classification of Adjectives

The adjectives and adverbs from users' oral report were coded by Ma Shi When Tong. Firstly, adjectives were classified according to the positive or negative meanings. If an adjective expressed a comparatively cheerful position, such as "convenient" or "useful", it was coded as positive (+). If an adjective expressed a comparatively unfavorable position, such as "deficient" or "confuse", it was coded as negative (−). In our experiments, adjectives were picked out and were divided into two parts (positive and negative) by taking the physical scene, the language environment and the tone of the users into consideration.

Classification of Adverbs

Adverbs were coded in a different way. Because our users are from China, so the oral reports were recorded in Chinese, and for the sake of accuracy, analyzed in Chinese, the processing of adverbs made reference to the local grammar. According to the XinHua Dictionary, adverbs of degree can be divided into four categories: extreme, high level, medium grade, and lower. According to these categories, adverbs extracted from the oral report were arranged on a Likert scale with nine levels. If these adverbs modified positive adjectives then adverbs were assigned 4, 3, 2, and 1 points, respectively. On the contrary, these adverbs modified negative adjectives then adverbs were assigned −4, −3, −2, and −1 points, respectively. Neutral adverbs were assigned 0 points (Table 5).

Table 5. Research degree adverbs of degree

Level of gradable adverb	Level of gradable adverb in paper
Extreme	too, extremely
High level	also, very, quite, pretty, especially, utterly, fully, so, fairly, such, particularly, really incomparable
Medium grade	relatively, even more, still more
Lower	slightly, a little

2.4   Experiments Results

Experiment 1

Experiment 1 tested the difference of the convenience level of users' experience of Platform 1 (Platform 1 simulating the current China's largest online shopping site "Taobao" shopping process, and entering keywords is the main search method) and Platform 2 (The platform2 created page jump mode based on color clues according to professional matching cases). Figure 5 shows the shopping time on two platforms. Obviously, users spend more time to pick out what they like on platform 1, the average time is 29.1 min (Min = 10 min, Max = 48 min). When users shopping on platform 2, the average shopping time is 19.61 min (Min = 8 min, Max = 32 min).

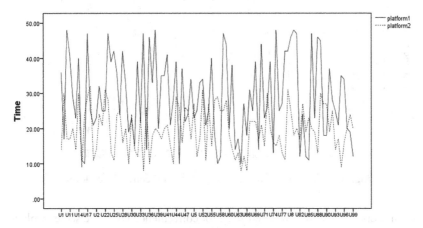

Fig. 5. Shopping time

Of all the 100 participants, by using platform2, 74 users spend less time while only 25 users spend more time and 1 user spend equal time on online shopping. The maximum of time consuming on platform 2 preceding platform 1 is 39 min while the time range is 19 min on platform 1 preceding platform 2. For a more detail statistic of time range on platform 2 preceding platform 1, there are 27 users in 1-10 min, 21 users in 11–20 min and 26 in 21–40, while the percentage form of time ranges can be represented as 36.49%, 28.38% and 35.13% respectively. As for platform 1 preceding platform 2, there are 19 users in 1–10 min, 6 users in 11–20 min and 0 in 21–40 and also the percentage form of time ranges can be represented as 76%, 24% and 0% respectively.

Of all the 100 participants, by using platform2, 74 users spend less time while only 25 users spend more time and 1 user spend equal time on online shopping. The maximum of time consuming on platform 2 preceding platform 1 is 39 min while the time range is 19 min on platform 1 preceding platform 2. For a more detail statistic of time range on platform 2 preceding platform 1, there are 27 users in 1-10 min, 21 users in 11–20 min and 26 in 21–40, while the percentage form of time ranges can be represented as 36.49%, 28.38% and 35.13% respectively. As for platform 1 preceding platform 2, there are 19 users in 1–10 min, 6 users in 11–20 min and 0 in 21–40 and also the percentage form of time ranges can be represented as 76%, 24% and 0% respectively.

The Fig. 6 shows the oral report scores (user experience on convenience level) when users shopping with two different platforms. The score of platform 2 was higher than platform 1. When users shopping on the platform 1, The average oral report score of platform is 0.26. When users shopping on the platform 2, the average oral report score is 1.43.

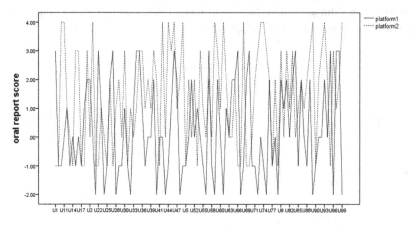

Fig. 6. oral report scores (user experience on convenience level)

When users use the 5-point Likert scale for convenience level, the score of platform 2 was higher than platform 1 (Fig. 7), the average score is 3.92. When users shopping on the platform 1, the average score is 3.17.

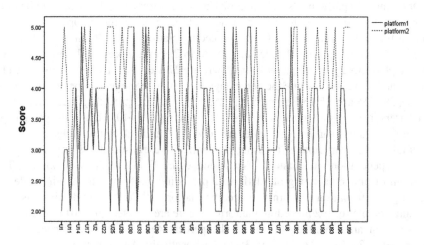

Fig. 7. scores of convenience level

Experiment 2

The experiment 2 tested the difference of users' experience of Item-based Fashion Matching between the Platform 1 and Platform 2. The Fig. 8 shows the oral report scores (users' experience of Item-based Fashion Matching) when users shopping with two different platforms. The score of platform 2 was higher than platform 1. When users shopping on the platform 1, The average oral report score of platform is 0.6. When users shopping on the platform 2, the average oral report score is 0.61.

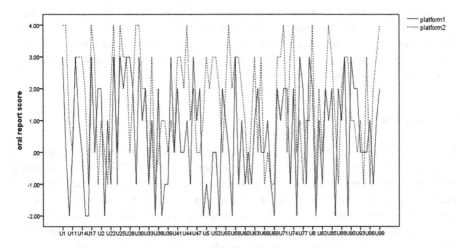

Fig. 8. oral report scores (users' experience of Item-based Fashion Matching)

When users use the 5-point Likert scale for experience of Item-based Fashion Matching, the score of platform 2 was higher than platform 1 (Fig. 9), the average score is 3.72. When users shopping on the platform 1, the average score is 2.99.

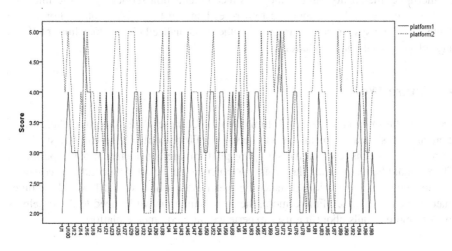

Fig. 9. scores of Item-based Fashion Matching

Experiment 1 shows platform 2 increase user convenience to what extent. Shopping time result states that there are 74% users who considers platform 2 saves their time. For subjective judgment, there are 78% and 81% users who considers platform 2 is more or equally convenient contrast to platform 1 in oral report test and convenience level test respectively. The ones who gives platform 1 a better score are all very familiar with platform 1 and maybe using platform 2 just changes their online shopping habit. So if they get more familiar with platform2, they may change their mind. Experiment 2 shows our item-based fashion matching system does play a positive role in matching clothing. 79% (Item-based Fashion Matching scores test) and 75% (oral scores test) users think platform 1 is better than matching clothing by themselves. And also, almost all of the users who thinks matching clothing by themselves is better are good at online shopping and clothing matching. To sum up, platform 2 could help novices do a better online clothing shopping.

3   Conclusion

As the service received by customer affects the decision of online clothes shopping choice greatly, online service gains a huge importance. On Chinese online shopping platform, various kinds of sell service patterns are explored to promote the experience quality. In this paper, a mode of customer shopping service experience based on online clothes shopping is proposed and a suits matching recommendation service system which recommend suits matching patterns to customers is designed. In this system, a database of customer shopping records is established which together with the clothes purchased at present are leveraged to recommend customers how to comprise suits. On using the system, not only can the customers experience the suits matching service, but also the excessive consumption is alleviated effectively. By using this system, the experience of customer online shopping is promoted to some extent, and customers can enjoy the entertainment and practicality of the interactive suits matching service. Furthermore, merchants can use the suits recommendation service system to integrate clothes resources and push more customer-need and customer-like clothes. For a wide perspective, the system can be applied to other personalized clothes matching platform and related social contact platform.

4   Future Work

Experimental study in this article is limited to the Chinese online shopping platform, so there are still several problems need to be solved. Firstly, only Chinese online shopping customer and mainstream online shopping platform are considered in our experiment. There should be many other platforms, customers to be included. Secondly, accessories are not involved in the clothes matching experiment which would lower the clothes matching entirety effect. Furthermore, there are numerous works need to do to help us explore more details about the user experience on e-commerce platform.

- build suits matching management system to enforce the relationships of online shopping industry.
- consider more clothing factors including scenes, usage and any other customization service.
- Design and compare different interaction ways to abstract customers in the website from different angles, like product introduce, selling strategy then measure its validity.

Acknowledgments. We would like to express our gratitude to Chunshan Deng who helped us during the experiment with his professional skill. The research was supported by National Key Technologies R&D Program of China (2015BAH22F01/2015BAH22F02), National Natural Science Foundation of China (61402159/60903090), Hunan Provincial Social Science Foundation of China (2010YBA054), the State Key Laboratory of Advanced Design and Manufacturing for Vehicle Body Funded Projects.

References

Bikshorn, M.: From customer service to customer experience enhancement, Customer Experience Reporting (2011). http://www.serviceexcellencegroup.com

Kent, T.: Creative space: design and the retail environment. Int. J. Retail Distrib. Manag. **35**, 734–745 (2007)

Chevalier, J.A., Mayzlin, D.: The effect of word of mouth on sales: online book reviews. J. Mark. Res. **43**(3), 345–354 (2006)

Dellarocas, C., Zhang, X.M., Awad, N.F.: Exploring the value of online product reviews in forecasting sales: the case of motion pictures. J. Interact. Mark. **21**(4), 23–45 (2007)

Duan, W., Gu, B., Whinston, A.B.: The dynamics of online word-of-mouth and product sales — an empirical investigation of the movie industry. J. Retail. **84**(2), 233–242 (2008)

Forman, C., Ghose, A., Wiesenfeld, B.: Examining the relationship between reviews and sales: the role of reviewer identity disclosure in electronic markets. Inf. Syst. Res. **19**(3), 291–313 (2008)

Gu, B., Park, J., Konana, P.: Research note—the impact of external word-of-mouth sources on retailer sales of high-involvement products. Inf. Syst. Res. **23**(1), 182–196 (2012)

Hu, N., Sian, K.N., Reddy, S.K.: Ratings lead you to the product, reviews help you clinch it? The mediating role of online review sentiments on product sales. Decis. Support Syst. **67**, 78–89 (2013)

Ye, Q., Law, R., Gu, B.: The impact of online user reviews on hotel room sales. Int. J. Hosp. Manag. **28**(1), 180–182 (2009)

Zhu, F., Zhang, X.Q.: Impact of online consumer reviews on sales: the moderating role of product and consumer characteristics. J. Mark. **74**(2), 133–148 (2010)

PowerReviews: The 2011 Social Shopping Study. http://www.powerreviews.com/assets/download/Social_Shopping_2011_Brief1.pdf2011

Chen, Y.B., Xie, J.H.: Online consumer review: word-of-mouth as a news element of marketing communication mix. Manag. Sci. **54**(3), 477–491 (2008)

Kobayashi, M.: Studies on the color panning of clothing – existence of the "ideal skin color" and the effect of the clothing color. J. Jpn. Res. Assoc. Text. End Uses **45**(3), 56–63 (2004)

Ma, J., Shi, M., Tong, W.: Business Press, Shanghai (2010)

Likert, R.: A technique for the measurement of attitudes. Arch. Psychol. **22**(140), 1–55 (1932)

Xinhua Dictionary Compilation agency. Xinhua Dictionary. The Commercial Press (2004)

The Interdisciplinary Collaboration
of Innovational Design

Shu-Huei Wang[1(✉)], Shyh-Huei Hwang[2], and Ming-Shean Wang[1]

[1] Department of Digital Design, MingDao University,
Wen-Hua Rd, Changhua 52345, Taiwan
angelawang36@gmail.com, wangms@mdu.edu.tw
[2] Graduate School of Design, National Yunlin University of Science
and Technology, Douliu, Taiwan
hwangsh@yuntech.edu.tw

Abstract. The purpose of empathic design is to motivate the empathy of designers to better understand the potential needs of users (including the proprietors). The example of Youth Originality Design Camp of Liouduei in 2011 was used in this research to examine the design procedures of the innovative products for interdisciplinary empathic design of the local industries and to analyze the process of interdisciplinary empathic design conducted by grouped specialists in various fields and the students, design behavior of students from different departments and the influence on design after students experience the local cultures and industries. Thirty-six students participating in the contest were investigated in four phases. According to the findings of the research, recognition from 64(%) to 90% of the students was obtained after allowing them to experience the Liouduei culture and the students, learning from the proprietors on the first stage, benefited from empathic design in learning of the local culture. In phase two, students considered that they stayed at the proprietors' homes for the night, which provided an opportunity for them to have an in-depth understanding of the proprietors' problems. On the third stage, recognition of 87% of the students was acquired after an in-depth interview between the students and proprietors. In the last phase, 84 to 85% of the students identified with brainstorming and prototype production. The results of the research indicate the procedures for innovative interdisciplinary empathic design help the students enhance their empathy basically, and benefit them to better understand the needs of the proprietors and motivate them to form creative ideas; however, there is still a long way to achieve commercialization.

Keywords: Empathic design · Innovational process · Creative design · Interdisciplinary collaboration · Design workshop

1 Introduction

People emphasize the spiritual significance of consumption and emo Design in the 21st century focuses on the emotional needs in the minds of consumers and is characterized with the properties of touching and experiencing. Design changes with the trendy demands in various fields and empathy has been explored in philosophy and aesthetics

© Springer International Publishing AG 2017
P.-L.P. Rau (Ed.): CCD 2017, LNCS 10281, pp. 204–215, 2017.
DOI: 10.1007/978-3-319-57931-3_17

already. Empathy has been applied to design recently to provide more considerate design to users and to discover and satisfy the potential needs of users. Consequently, the example of Youth Originality Design Camp of Liouduei in 2011 was used in this research to examine the design procedures of the innovative products for interdisciplinary empathic design that the students participating in the contest might be empathic to the needs of the proprietors.

Design is empathic since designers are required to have more penetrative ideas that others may not observe for improvement. This kind of observation can be trained and developed through systematic ways. Empathy of designers may be enhanced and the potential needs of users can be disclosed more clearly when applying the concept of empathic design during the process. Empathic design is to create empathy via the design procedures to discover the potential demands of users. Nevertheless, demands usually aim at two targets from the perspective of the industrial chain. One is the proprietors and the other is the users. Innovation of interdisciplinary empathic design in the local industry in Liouduei of southern Taiwan is the theme of this research. Design behaviors of the students in the design department were analyzed and the practical needs of the local industry were observed. Innovative procedures of interdisciplinary empathic design can help students to have an in-depth understanding of the industrial problems for empathic creation.

The example of Youth Originality Design Camp of Liouduei in 2011 was used for the procedures of the interdisciplinary empathic design. Innovative products of the local industry in Liouduei were designed and selected by the host. Thirty-six design young students participated in the contest in addition to design scholars, locally respected grand old men, craftsmen and experts. The purposes of the research are as the follows:

If the interdisciplinary empathic design procedures may develop innovative products that meet the proprietors' needs, if the interdisciplinary empathic design procedures can help students to be empathic to the proprietors' needs, and whether the interdisciplinary empathic design procedures can help students to develop empathy and design from the points of views of the target.

2 Literature Review

2.1 Interdisciplinary Spiritual Design Age

The dramatic changes in the 21st century arouse people to be aware of the environmental, cultural and social demands for a balanced development among the human beings, nature and technology. Natural and man-made disasters for the past few years are frequent in particular. Besides environmental protection, the spiritual need of people is even more important when facing major calamities. Take the natural and man-made disasters in Japan, including the earthquake, the tsunami and the nuclear disaster as an example. The lesson of spiritual reconstruction after disasters should be learned. Nowadays, people stress an emotional and spiritual life and the emphasis on materials in the past has been converted to minds. Though the spiritual needs are as important as the air, they have always been neglected. Empathic design listens to the minds of the consumers and realizes the real needs of the human beings by applying a variety of ways and tools in this spiritual age. Luxury and elegance are no longer considered, but comfort and spiritual communication should be satisfied instead. The time of meeting physical needs earlier is called the physical age and the time of satisfying mental and spiritual needs now is called the spiritual age. Spiritual consumption will be the mainstream and a spiritual economy will be formed in the future (Tsao 2003: 10–11). Henceforth, the spiritual age of empathic design has also arrived.

2.2   Previous and Current Design

Design changes with social, cultural, economic, technological, political and educational variations. In other words, changes are to be made to cope with age demands. How to make changes among past, present and future has become an issue for designers. Design was usually conducted by an individual alone or teamwork in a single field before. However, such model won't be able to solve complicated design problems today. Therefore, an interdisciplinary teamwork model is required for current design (see Fig. 1).

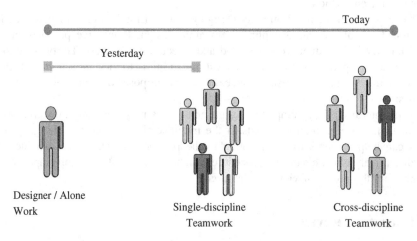

Fig. 1. A comparison of previous and current designers (Pitipanich 2010: 41)

2.3   Changes of Design

Influenced by the internal and external factors of technological and time changes, design needs to be changed as well. Designers used to execute a continuous design process from start to finish of a project in the past. However, an interdisciplinary team at present needs to decide what types of designers and tools are required for the task in the beginning and these designers will take part in the project until completion, which is a linear design process (see Fig. 2).

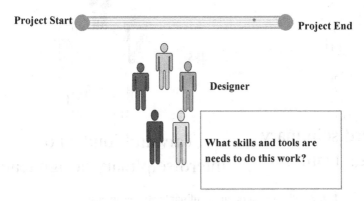

Fig. 2. Changes of design

2.4   The Advent of the Spiritual Empathic Design Age

Waal's mentioned in the preface of his book titled "The age of empathy – Nature's Lessons for Kinder Society" that greed was out and empathy was in. In the financial crisis of 2008, Obama, the newly inaugurated president of the United States presented the issue of empathy in his speech to the Northwestern University in Chicago. He said "I think we should talk more about our empathy deficit.... It's only when you hitch your wagon to something larger than yourself that you will realize your true potential." (Waal 2009). The coming of the empathic age reminds people of the necessity to ponder and reflect the essences of human nature and mother nature especially when tremendous changes happen to the politics, economy and culture so that empathy can be restored and the highest value of human being can be achieved (The 911 event occurred in the US then and the conflicts between Americans and Islamic people were unceasing.).

3   Methodology

3.1   Design Structure

Forming of an interdisciplinary design team: take IDEO as an instance. The members of its interdisciplinary design team consist of ergonomic and anthropologic experts and visual and industrial designers depending on the project requirements, which belongs to a general industrial design process. Nevertheless, to suit the measure to local conditions, the interdisciplinary design team of the Youth Originality Design Camp of Liouduei in 2011 was composed of experts and teachers who were good at leisure and sightseeing, furniture production and design, design culture, community development and crafts along with participating proprietors and artisans. It was expected the combination of the traditional technique and the creativity of young designers might innovate the cultural products in Liouduei, which belongs to a cultural creativity product design process (Fig. 3).

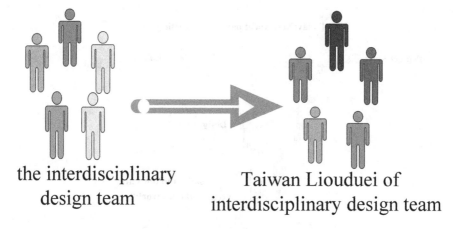

the interdisciplinary design team

Taiwan Liouduei of interdisciplinary design team

Fig. 3. Illustration of an interdisciplinary design team

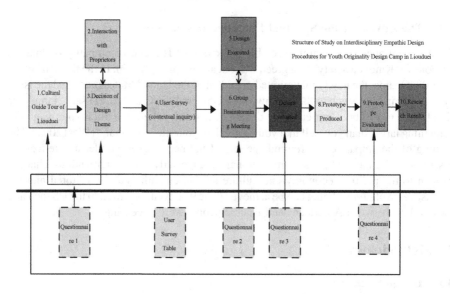

Fig. 4. Structure of interdisciplinary empathic design procedures

The structure of the research on the steps of interdisciplinary empathic design in Taiwan is based on the interdisciplinary design team of the Youth Originality Design Camp of Liouduei in 2011, which was composed by interdisciplinary experts and teachers and was a design process of innovating local industry. To cope with the design competition rules planned for the Youth Originality Design Camp of Liouduei in 2011, five stages were divided for testing and the study frame was illustrated as the following (Fig. 4).

3.2 Innovative Procedures of Empathic Design

Empathic design methods and testing steps are described as follows. On the first day, young designers were given cultural and historic classes about Liouduei as well as lectures on cultural creativity product design and development after signing in to comply with the requirements of the design proprietors. They also had a guided tour in Liouduei and decided the design theme with the proprietors before staying at the proprietors' houses for the night. For the second day, young designers were arranged to observe and record the demands of the proprietors and discussed with the teachers about their preliminary design charts and findings. The design concept of each group could be understood during interactive communication of team brainstorming meeting. On the third day, a design review and a discussion with the interdisciplinary design teachers were made for the completion of a model. For the fourth day, model production and a report were completed and presented. Finally, the judges decided and awarded (Fig. 4).

4 Analysis of Results

4.1 Data Collection

As related experts couldn't be invited like in the case of IDEO, five phases were divided for testing in compliance with the design competition rules planned for the Youth Originality Design Camp of Liouduei in 2011. Data collection of these five stages is described as the following.

1. Phase 1: designers experienced a cultural tour and learned from the proprietors about the design culture (making sure of the design subject with the proprietors) after understanding the culture and communicating with the proprietors (2011/07/07–07/08).
2. Phase 2: observation and survey of the proprietors (users): staying at the proprietors' houses for the night, discussing with the proprietors on the morning of July 8th and returning to the host at noon. Designers might learn observation and interview based on contextual inquiries while staying at the proprietors' homes.
3. Phase 3: what had been learned after observing and interviewing with the proprietors.

4. Phase 4: making a prototype, completing a brainstorming meeting with the inter-disciplinary experts and teachers and designers' feelings during the process of making the prototype.
5. Phase 5: evaluating and displaying the prototype for testing.

4.2   Data Analysis

1. There were 226 respondents for the questionnaire survey on the interdisciplinary empathic design procedures in five phases and 143 valid copies were retrieved.
2. Results of descriptive statistics on the interdisciplinary empathic design steps in five phases for the Youth Originality Design Camp of Liouduei in 2011 are as follows.

(1) Phase 1 (after cultural understanding and communicating with the proprietors): major dimensions of the questionnaire are local cultural recognition, learning from and communicating with the proprietors and design culture. For the dimension of local cultural recognition, 64% of the designers approved and 90% of the designers agreed to the dimension of learning from and communicating with the proprietors. They reveal staying at the proprietors' residences and learning from them are quite helpful for the designers to apply empathy to their design and learning. 85% of the designers made a positive response to the dimension of design culture. It shows designers take local cultural elements into consideration, and imagine themselves as users and ponder long and deeply over the factors of people, things, objects, places and landscape, which helps the designers to project their empathy onto their design a lot (Figs. 5, 6 and 7).

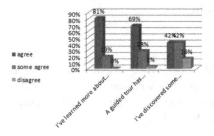

Fig. 5. Questionnaire 1/(dimension 1) local cultural recognition

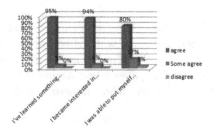

Fig. 6. Questionnaire 1/(dimension 2) learning from and communicating with the proprietors

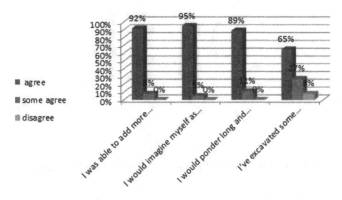

Fig. 7. Questionnaire 1/(dimension 3) design culture

(2) Phase 2 (observing and surveying the proprietors): the design theme needed to be decided with the proprietors and the teams had to discuss with the proprietors and find their problems and opportunities on this stage. The hosting organization selected two people as a team in advance and eighteen teams were formed. There were 18 copies of the questionnaire survey and seventeen copies were retrieved with a retrieval rate of 94%. In the Youth Originality Design Camp of Liouduei in 2011, designers had more time to communicate with the proprietors and had a closer observation of the proprietors' daily life, work habits, family members and the environment by staying at their homes. Therefore, they excavated the proprietors' (users') experiences and problems via applying empathy. Contextual inquiries with the proprietors helped the designers to observe and experience deeply as well as to discover the proprietors' problems and opportunities.

(3) Phase 3 (after investigating the proprietors): designers had a basic understanding after experiencing a cultural trip, staying at the proprietors' places for the night and observing and interviewing them. Designers were tested on this stage if they truly comprehended the problems and opportunities of the proprietors. Thirty-six participants were asked to fill in a questionnaire survey and handed it over the following afternoon. Thirty-two out of a total number of thirty-six copies were retrieved with a retrieval rate of 89%. There were two major parts in this questionnaire, including comprehension of the proprietors (users) and help by observing the proprietors (users) (Figs. 8 and 9).

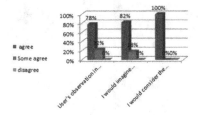

Fig. 8. Questionnaire 2/(dimension 1) understanding of the proprietors

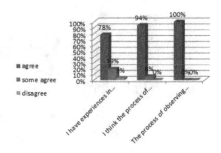

Fig. 9. Questionnaire 2/(dimension 2) help from observing the proprietors

For the dimension of comprehension of the proprietors (users), 87% of the designers agreed to it and 100% of the designers identified themselves with Item 3 (I will put myself in the user's shoes when designing.), which proves designers imagine the user's scenario while designing. 87% of the designers agreed to the dimension of help by observing the proprietors (users) and 100% of the designers identified themselves with Item 7 (The process of observing and interviewing the user helps me a lot on product design.), which shows observing and interviewing the users (by applying the user's survey table) help the designers a lot when designing.

(4) Phase 4 (after producing the prototype): feelings of the designers while producing the prototype were tested on this stage Thirty-six participants were asked to fill in a questionnaire survey and handed it over the following morning. Seventeen out of a total number of thirty-six copies were retrieved with a retrieval rate of 47%. There were two major parts in this questionnaire, including the feelings of producing the prototype and the brainstorming meeting. For the dimension of the feelings of producing the prototype, 84% of the designers agreed to it and 100% of the designers identified themselves with Item 1 (I will imagine myself as the user and put myself in his/her shoes when producing the prototype.). It proves designers truly identify themselves with the users and consider for them by placing themselves in the users' position (applying empathic design), which helps designers a lot when designing. 85% of the designers agreed to the dimension of the brainstorming meeting and 94% of them identified themselves with Items 5 (I can get different creativity ideas by meeting with

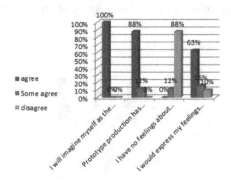

Fig. 10. Questionnaire 3/(dimension 1) feelings of producing the prototype

teachers of various fields.) and 6 (I have a different thought after the brainstorming meeting.), which reveals meetings with teachers from various fields and brainstorming meetings really assist designers in their innovation and creativity (Figs. 10 and 11).

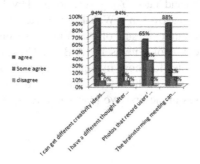

Fig. 11. Questionnaire 3/(dimension 2) brainstorming meeting

(5) Phase 5: thirty-six designers were divided into sixteen teams (two out of the original eighteen teams were combined for display) and exhibited their prototypes. Local people, students, administrative personnel and specialty teachers on site were given the questionnaire survey. Though 100 copies were handed out, only 41 were collected with a retrieval rate of 41% because of a sudden downpour. The main purpose of this questionnaire survey is to understand visitors' opinions about the displayed prototypes. The survey was conducted in the afternoon of July 10th before the announcement of prize winners. The question items were described as follows. 1. Which team's design touches you the most? (Select 1 team.) 2. Which team's design is the most creative? (Select 3 teams.) 3. Which team's design reflects the culture in Liouduei the best? (Select 3 teams.) 4. Which team's design meets the users' requirements the most? (Select 3 teams.) 5. Which team's product you hope you can get on the market? (Select 3 teams.) An analysis was conducted as the following.

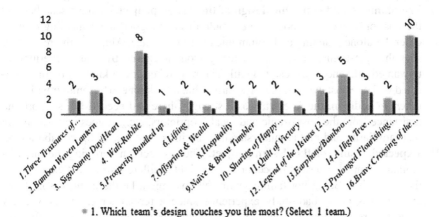

Fig. 12. Bar chart of respondents' choices on question item 1

Ching-yao Liang and Mei-ting Huang's Brave Crossing of the Strait was awarded the prize of Hakka spirit. The best creativity prize went to The Earphone presented by Fu-ying Chang and Wei-ting Chi. The ecological pen named A High Tree Discovered designed by Ching-ren Shih and Ting-yu Chen and the bamboo woven lantern named Lifting made by Li-fang Fan and Yu-su Yang were honored by the prize of the innovated product. Lin-li Huang and Yu-tze Lin's Wali-Rubble was awarded the most popular prize. Compared with the survey result of the fifth phase on the evaluation of the prototype in questionnaire 4, choice items 16 (A Brave Crossing of the Strait) and 13 (The Earphone) got more votes for those five question items. Besides, Choice item 16 (Brave Crossing of the Strait) was in the first two places in four question items and choice item 13 (The Earphone) was in the first two places in three question items (Fig. 12).

5   Conclusion

(1) **The source of the design project.** As the organization hosting the Youth Orig-inality Design Camp of Liouduei was not under control of the researcher, plan-ning and considerations of the host were still respected. However, it is suggested a budget for design projects will be available in the future so that the design process can be controlled completely.

(2) **Personnel participating in the design project.** The organization hosting the Youth Originality Design Camp of Liouduei was not an academic institution but an NGO. Therefore, the personnel taking part in the camp were the members of the organization. The advantage was that this NGO knew very well about the local proprietors and had good interaction with them; however, the shortcoming was the researcher couldn't handle if the participants of the design project were required by the research. Another issue was whether a creativity design camp was suitable to be held outside the school. It was lucky this time since the design department of a certain university gave full support of students, equipment and technology; otherwise, the hosting organization might not be able to hold the Youth Origi-nality Design Camp of Liouduei alone and to present the final design results.

(3) **Pre-planning and empathic design of the design project.** As the researcher met the host only one time, both parties couldn't have a good understanding of each other, let alone planning and communication in advance. Although the researcher sent the questionnaire surveys to the person in charge by mail; nevertheless, unwanted influence was resulted still. The researcher got to know and communi-cated with the host two to three days earlier, but it took time to be familiar with each other. In addition, the research was a stranger there and needed full support and assistance from the host (traffic and local proprietors, etc.). It goes without saying that familiarity and mutual understanding are important factors for collaboration.

(4) **Expected results of the design project.** The research on verifying the interdis-ciplinary empathic design procedures was slightly different from that expected by the researcher. Being not familiar with the host might be the main reason; how-ever, it was not a bad study experience since a researcher can't know every research organization or object. It was lucky this research was successful to a certain extent and the questionnaire survey tables were collected.

(5) **Innovative results of the design project.** Thanks to the efforts of the participant students for four days, some accomplishments were made in the Youth Originality Design Camp of Liouduei. For instance, the Earphone of the best creativity prize will be available on the market after only making slight modification.

References

Tsao, S.: Spiritual Age, pp. 10–11. Foundation of Museum of World Religions, New Taipei City (2003)

Pitipanich, K.: A report of culture and creativity development results. In: International Conference on Culture and Creativity Development. Taipei County Government, 12–14 November 2010, p. 41 (2010)

Waal, D.F.: The Age of Empathy – Nature's Lessons for Kinder Society. Three Rivers, New York (2009). Preface

Research on the Service Design of the Museum Visiting

Yanyun Wang[(✉)] and Junjie Chu

Ocean University of China, Qingdao, Shandong Province, China
15954269878@163.com, chujunjie@ouc.edu.cn

Abstract. With the development of the Internet, the challenge of transition also comes to museums. In this paper, the authors investigate the online and offline situation of museums. Focused on the user pain points found in our investigation, we build the participatory museum service system with the service design tools, such as stakeholder maps, system map, blueprint and so on. Visitors can have more opportunity to interact and communicate with museums. This paper tries to offer some suggestions for improvement of museum service design.

Keywords: Museum · Experience · Service design · Web · Visiting

1 Introduction

As a showcase of history and culture, museums have accompanied us for a long time. However, with the development of society, the role of the museum have also changed from presentation to education and communication. More and more visitors come to museums for self-improvement. Consequently, providing visitors with valuable experience has become a crucial mission for cultural heritage institutions. We have investigated the current situation of museums in China including websites and spaces to give some suggestions for the development of museums.

2 Literature Review

This literature review examined areas of interest relating to user experience of museum visiting.

2.1 User Experience

The international standard on ergonomics of human system interaction, ISO 9241-210 [1] defines user experience as "a person's perceptions and responses that result from the use or anticipated use of a product, system or service". According to the ISO definition, user experience includes all the users' emotions, beliefs, preferences, perceptions, physical and psychological responses, behaviors and accomplishments that occur before, during and after use. The ISO also list three factors that influence user experience: system, user and the context of use [2].

© Springer International Publishing AG 2017
P.-L.P. Rau (Ed.): CCD 2017, LNCS 10281, pp. 216–231, 2017.
DOI: 10.1007/978-3-319-57931-3_18

Donald Norman brought the concept of user experience to wider knowledge in the mid-1990s [3]. He never intended the term "user experience" to be applied only to the affective aspects of usage. A review of his earlier work [4] suggests that the term "user experience" was used to signal a shift to include affective factors, along with the pre-requisite behavioral concerns, which had been traditionally considered in the field.

With the development of mobile, ubiquitous, social, and tangible computing technologies, human-computer interaction has permeated into practically all areas of human activity. This has led to a shift away from usability engineering to a much richer scope of user experience, where users' feelings, motivations, and values are given as much, if not more, attention than efficiency, effectiveness and basic subjective satisfaction (i.e. the three traditional usability metrics [5]) [6].

2.2 User Experience of Museum Visiting

Jessie Pallud and Emmanuel Monod did a research that had investigated a set of phenomenological concepts that serve as a basis for IS evaluation, and more specifically, cultural heritage systems evaluation. They have conducted three focus groups that reveal the importance of a phenomenological experience for museum visitors, and found that technologies can lead to enhance visitor experience [7]. Carly Wickell studied on usability of online museum collections. His study focused on stakeholders of The Henry Art Gallery, located in Seattle, Washington, and provided a model comprised of Usability Testing and Follow-Up Interviews to create a comprehensive view of the user experience as it relates to online collections access. The findings of this evaluation revealed trends in usability and user experience [8]. Lisa Joy Gumerman conducted a project focused on user experience to create a plan for a web application that would increase engagement with the audience of a local museum. Finally they gave the Fort Collins Museum of Discovery a project plan including specific design, content and technology recommendations resulting from research and development [9]. Olav Røtne and Victor Kaptelinin did a design-based study of a mobile museum app and found that higher visual richness and content-related challenge were positive to museum experience, while the effect of information access selectivity was negative [10]. Morten Hertzum did a review of museum websites. This review investigates the process of design that underlies current museum websites and argues that it will be crucial to their future evolution and success to center this process around the users [11].

Zheng Yi, doctor of Fudan University, holds the point that the education information and announcement provided by the web of museums make preparation for visitors' visiting. It also can guide them to have a more reasonable visit [12]. Zhang Ruiying, secretary general of the China museum association of professional committee of the digital museum, said in the interview that information technology would be the drive of the development of museums. It will change the overall condition of museums and improve the visiting quality [13].

2.3 Service Design

In 1991, Prof. Dr. Michael Erlhoff at Köln International School of Design (KISD) first introduced service design as a design discipline [14].

Service design is a new expansion of traditional design field in the post-industrial age, is the comprehensive implementation of the concept of design. Service design is a system design including people, things, behavior, and environment. The purpose of service design is for customers to create a useful, convenient and hope to have, for an organization to create effective, efficient and unique services, and create a better experience, pass a more positive value [15].

3 Present Situation Investigation

With the rapid development of the Internet, the visiting experience of the museum not only includes the field visit but also contains the website. In order to obtain a more complete understanding about visitors and museums, we divided our investigation into three parts: the visiting at museums, the visiting online and the result.

3.1 The Visiting at Museums

Research Methods. In this part, we used three methods of investigation: questionnaire, interview and shadowing. Questionnaire is one of the commonly used methods in user research. It can collect a large number of responses in a short period of time, and can reduce cost, by means of research on Internet [16]. With the help of interview, we can have a thorough understanding of users' behavior and emotions.

Research Place. We chose Qingdao Museum as the research place. Founded in 1965, Qingdao Museum is an integrated local museum of history and arts. It is one of China's first batch of Class-I museums and a key unit for ancient books protection. In 2000, the new Qingdao Museum was officially open to the public in Laoshan. The new museum covers a land area of 105 m^2 and has a floor space totaling 30,000 m^2. The main building of the new museum has three stories above ground and one story underground, and includes 16 exhibition halls and a winding corridor. The total exhibition area exceeds 7,000 m^2. Qingdao Museum has become a cultural landmark and a marvelous cultural spot in Qingdao [17].

Research Result. In order to learn visitors' behavior and idea, we designed Questionnaire (1.0) and (2.0). We distributed 49 Questionnaires (1.0) at Qingdao Museum. Then according to the result of Questionnaires (1.0) recovered, we adjusted questions and distributed Questionnaires (2.0). There are 136 people attended this research. The results are followed (Fig. 1):

When it comes to how often people go to museums a year, about 85% respondents chose 1–3 while only 4% chose above 8 times. As is shown in the pie chart, museums don't have the ability to attract people. Once people are not satisfied with their experience at the first time, they would not like to go anymore (Fig. 2).

From the chart we can see that when asked about why you come to museums, the majority of the respondents chose traveling and learning (Fig. 3).

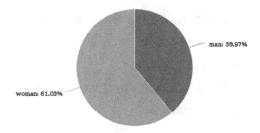

Fig. 1. Gender distribution

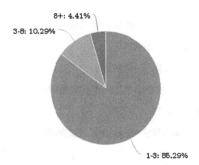

Fig. 2. How often do you go to museums one year

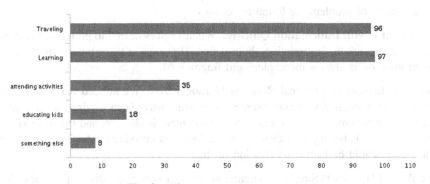

Fig. 3. Why you come to museums

With the development of Internet, except recommend by others, people begin to try other ways to learn information about museums, such as websites of museums, official accounts... (Fig. 4).

When it comes to which ways you would like to choose during visiting, most respondents like just reading introduction, few respondents chose to hire a docent (Fig. 5).

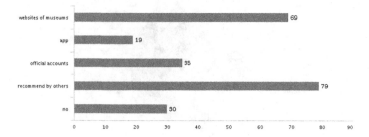

Fig. 4. The ways to learn information about museums

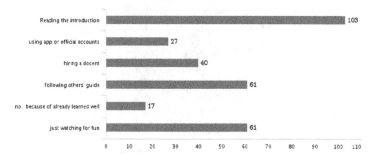

Fig. 5. The ways of explanation

We had interviews one by one with the respondents who filled in the questionnaire. Three aspects of problem are found as follows.

Can't Find Useful Information Quickly. When visitors decide to go to the museum, they would search the information about it first. However, it takes much time because the information is always incomplete and fragmented.

The Introduction of Cultural Relics is Homogenized. We noticed that few people chose to hire docents, so we asked some respondents why. Then we draw a conclusion that there are two main reasons, one is that the content is obscure, and the other is that the explanation is boring. However if visitors just read introduction beside the cultural relics, they would find little information of them.

The Way of Display is Single. No matter how visitors are interested in the relics, they can only see the relics behind a piece of glass at museums. Visitors can't touch them, even can't see the bottom and back of them.

3.2   The Visiting Online

Since 2002, museums has begun to build websites in China. Today almost every museum has its own website. With the increasing dependence on the Internet means that the museum website is quickly becoming the face of the institution. And for some visitors, the websites make the first impression of museums. We investigated 96 national top/first-class museums with the method of content analysis.

Research Methods. Content analysis is one of the most widely used research methods of social science. A large number of empirical studies used this way to collect and process data. Content analysis is a kind of research method that which describes its obvious delivering content objectively, systematically and quantitatively [18].

Here are some researches using the method of content analysis. Wu Yin got the model featured the object of the preliminary study based on the analysis of the content of 52 Local Government Websites in the United States, Japan and China [19]. Wang Zhe, Xiang Rui, and Tao Siyu, from the point of view of the target customers of the railway passenger station portal, constructed an evaluation index system with two levels and 30 items. They selected the representative of the 8 railways passenger station as a sample site, and analyzed the content of the evaluation index of each sample site using the content analysis method [20]. Xiao Liang, Zhao Liming, extracted the image theme of Taiwan tourism destination: natural ecology, vacation, country, culture, city, further analysis, through the content analysis on the two sides of the tourism website, travel agency website and the official website. Wang Yanli, Yang Gaixue expected to sum up the main results and development trends of research on informal learning through the analysis of the informal learning related literature published from1997 to 2010 [21]. Zheng Haoran, analysis the domestic 22 Chinese luxury shopping website, and explore the relationship between the construction of the website and marketing effect through the establishment of the evaluation system in 2014 [22]. Chen Haiping intends to carry on the content analysis to the university website content, in order to discover the university website to be possible to realize each function, look for the university website the main function, and compare the difference between China and the US [23]. Considering we need to judge the experience of the website, we chose content analysis method to avoid man-made subjective factors.

Evaluation System. Websites of museums contain several function modules, but the highest attention people paid to is the module related to visiting in reality. So we build the evaluation system with three parts: the visiting assist, the display exhibits and the interactive operation (Fig. 6).

Research Result. Because there are 8 museums don't have websites, so we investigate 88 museums.

The visiting assist: From the chart we can see that majority of websites do a good job on Service information. Some index can reach above 90%, such as Announcement, Open time, Ticketing policy and so on. But in the response test, only four museums have responsive web (Fig. 7).

The display exhibits: For the index of browsing collections, the result varies from different index. On one hand, almost every museum has index with Exhibition classification and Showing the pictures of the collections. But only about 10% museums have the introduction about the location of the collection. Only 2 museums offer links of literature (Fig. 8).

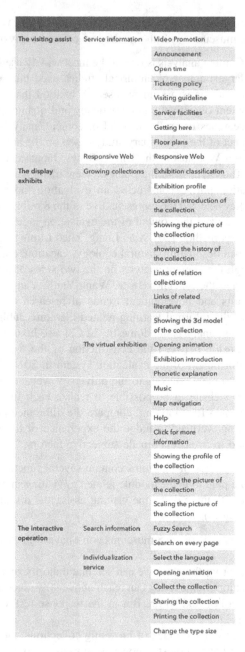

The visiting assist	Service information	Video Promotion
		Announcement
		Open time
		Ticketing policy
		Visiting guideline
		Service facilities
		Getting here
		Floor plans
	Responsive Web	Responsive Web
The display exhibits	Growing collections	Exhibition classification
		Exhibition profile
		Location introduction of the collection
		Showing the picture of the collection
		showing the history of the collection
		Links of relation collections
		Links of related literature
		Showing the 3d model of the collection
	The virtual exhibition	Opening animation
		Exhibition introduction
		Phonetic explanation
		Music
		Map navigation
		Help
		Click for more information
		Showing the profile of the collection
		Showing the picture of the collection
		Scaling the picture of the collection
The interactive operation	Search information	Fuzzy Search
		Search on every page
	Individualization service	Select the language
		Opening animation
		Collect the collection
		Sharing the collection
		Printing the collection
		Change the type size

Fig. 6. Evaluation system

With the continuous development of Internet technology, more and more museums chose to open virtual museum exhibition. By June 10, 2016, there are 43 museums have their own virtual museum exhibition. However, different museum has different

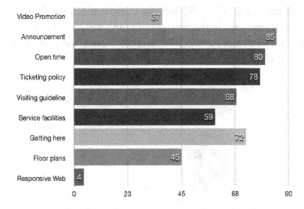

Fig. 7. The visiting assist

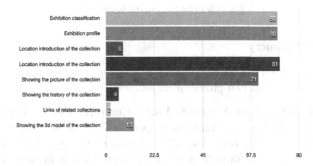

Fig. 8. The display exhibits 1

construction level, and most of them decide to build it with the help of other companies. There are only 16 websites that which offer checking detailed information of the collections. Most virtual museum exhibitions are simple, merely taking panoramic pictures. They still have a long way to go (Fig. 9).

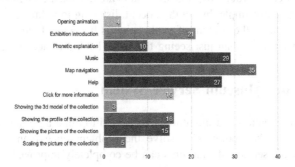

Fig. 9. The display exhibits 2

The interactive operation: Only 52 websites allow users to choose languages. We found that there are differences in the content of some websites between the versions of English and Chinese. There are only 10% websites offer the operation of collecting, sharing and printing (Fig. 10).

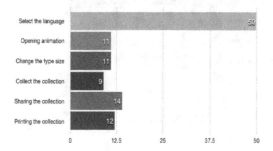

Fig. 10. The interactive operation

3.3 Research Summery

Through the research on the current situation of museum, we found that the museum's service system mainly has two problems as follows.

The Service Experience of Museums Lacks Completeness. Experience happens before, during, and after a visit. But most of us only focus on the experience during a visit ignoring the experience before and after. From the investigation about websites of museums, we can see that though most of museums have built their websites, the availability and usability still need improving. When it comes to the knowledge we can learn from, there is still a certain gap between websites and museums.

There are more problems from the service at the exhibition hall. For example: visitors can't quickly find the collection they interested in and may get lost in the big hall…

The Way and the Content of Explanation Need Change. As the most important part of a visit, explanation should help visitors understand the collections better. But through our research, we found that lots of visitors are not satisfied with the experience. The current ways, for example, hiring the docent, listening to volunteer and so on need to be improved because the content of explanation is boring and the way of display is single. People want more than just seeing the relics behind a piece of glass.

4   Participatory Museum Service System

Based on the investigation and literature, we decided to build a participatory museum service system. The key point is to solve the problem on explanation during the visiting; thereby the service of museums can be completely improved.

4.1 Service Design

Service Design aims to create services that are useful, useable, desirable, efficient and Effective. It is a human-centered approach that focuses on customer experience and the quality of services is the key value for success. It is a holistic approach, considering the integrated way of strategic, systematic, process-oriented and touch point design decisions. It is a systematic and iterative process that integrates user-oriented, team-based, and interdisciplinary approaches and methods in ever-learning cycles [14].

The tools induced by Politecnico di Milano and Domus Academy are used to show our service system.

4.2 Users

Based on the investigation we did, we divided our users into four parts: Common visitor, Common lovers, Fanatics and Professors. They have different levels of knowledge and awareness on collections.

4.3 Stakeholder Maps

There are 8 stakeholders in this service system, divided into three levels according to the importance and influence. The most important stakeholder is visitor as well as web designer and exhibition planners who also play important roles in the system. They make up the first level. Guest service agents, volunteer and docent also affect the visiting experience and they are in the second level. Salesmen and securities are in the last level (Fig. 11).

Fig. 11. Stakeholder maps

4.4 Motivation Matrix

The aim of the motivation matrix is to understand the connection of different actors of the system. Thanks to the motivation of them in the system: each actor expresses what he or she needs or expects from the service. The motivation matrix is an interesting means of investigation of the solution assuming the viewpoint of each stakeholder with his or her own interests [24].

From the chart, we can see that almost every stakeholder is related with others (Fig. 12).

	Visitor	Web designer	Exhibition planners	Docent	Volunteer	Inquiry desk	Salesman	Parking
Visitor		visiting response	visiting response	listening/response	listening/response	ask information	buy souvenir	parking cars
Web designer	showing collections		assist	introduction	introduction	introduction	assist	introduction
Exhibition planners	showing collections	help		offering content	offering content		offering content	
Docent	explanation	assist	assist		example	assist	opportunity	
Volunteer	explanation	assist	assist	assist		assist		
Inquiry desk	offering information		assist	assist	assist			
Salesman	offering souvenir	offering content	offering souvenir					
Parking	parking place							

Fig. 12. Motivation matrix

4.5   Customer Journey Map

The customer journey map is an oriented graph that describes the journey of a user, representing the interaction with the service with the touch points. In this kind of visualization, the interaction is described step by step as in the classical blueprint. There is a stronger emphasis on some aspects as the flux of information and the physical devices involved. At the same time there is a higher level of synthesis than in the blueprint: the representation is simplified trough the loss of the redundant information and of the deepest details.

A visit can divide into 7 stages: online visiting, arrive, entrance, visiting, buy, out and home. Visitors' sad points were focused on entrance and visiting. For example: when the visitor came to the museum for the first time, he didn't know how to plan his visit. So the museum can formulate some certain line for them. When they came to the inquiry desk, the guest service agent would recommend to them (Fig. 13).

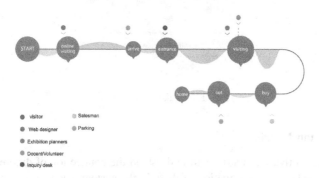

Fig. 13. Customer journey map

4.6 System Map

The system map is a visual description of the service technical organization: the different actors involved, their mutual links and the flows of materials, energy, information and money through the system [24].

We try to break the traditional service system, and build the participatory museum service system. In this system, we consider online and offline service. Visitors can have more opportunities to interact and communicate with museums (Fig. 14).

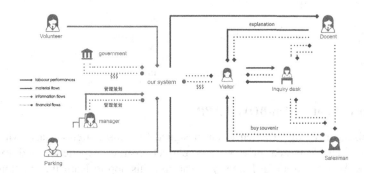

Fig. 14. System map

4.7 Blueprint

The blueprint is an operational tool that describes the nature and the characteristics of the service interaction with enough details to verify, implement and maintain it. It is based on a graphical technique that displays the process functions above and below the line of visibility to the customer: all the touch points and the back-stage processes are documented and aligned to the user experience [24].

Online Visiting. We should consolidate the contact between the website function module and the real visit. Simplify the online booking steps so as to encourage visitors to book online. Then arrange the timetable more reasonably. What's more, try to enhance the virtual display. Give visitors more opportunities to choose and interact, so they can learn more knowledge.

Entrance. At the inquiry desk, visitors can ask related information and rent AR glasses. They can choose the right recommended route to visit with the glasses.

Visiting. When you choose one collection, the glasses will play the introduction video of it. The videos can be uploaded by users. People can tell the stories of the collections by themselves. After watching the video, you can scale and rotate the virtual collection.

Buy. The store of the museum offers the souvenir designed by the museum.

Out. Return the glasses (Fig. 15).

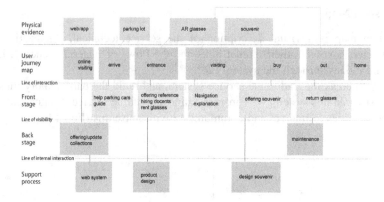

Fig. 15. Blueprint

4.8   Touch Point Design-BOWU APP

A customized browsing experience app designed for Museum enthusiasts who based on AR and UGC. It can give visitors perfect visiting experience and excellent knowledge. When you are at home, you can use this app to learn information about museums and exhibitions. If you want to know more about the collections, you can watch the videos uploaded by other users (Fig. 16).

Fig. 16. BOWU icon

Register/Log in. Information of museums has been added into the page to improve the enjoyment and enhance the function of our app (Fig. 17).

Fig. 17. Register/Log in

Museum/Exhibition. Museums and exhibitions are recommended by app according to the location and interest (Fig. 18).

Fig. 18. Museum/Exhibition

Collection/Explanation. Visitors can choose the videos listed in the page. After watched the videos, you can give a evaluation to this video (Fig. 19).

Fig. 19. Collection/Explanation

Transcribe Explanation. Visitors just need to add pictures and transcribe the video and then they can have their own explanation video (Fig. 20).

Fig. 20. Transcribe explanation

Touch Point Design-AR Glasses. Visitors can rent AR glasses from the inquiry desk. It can recommend visiting lines for you and introduce collections for you. With it, you can have more interaction with the collections (Fig. 21).

Fig. 21. Scene

5 Conclusion

In this paper, we put service concept into the research of museum visiting. It contains certain forward-looking and practical applicability. As a window of showing a city, even a country, the impression of the museum are influenced a lot by the experience. Museums are in a slow transition at present. It is a big challenge for them to follow the development of Internet and give users proper experience.

We investigated the current station of museums and found some pain points which focused on the explanation. So we used service design concept to build a participatory museum service system, and did research with service tools such as persona, stakeholder maps, customer journey map and so on.

6 Future Work

There have been few service design cases focused on museums so although we did some exploration and attempt, it still need to be constantly improved in the future practice and accumulation. In the future, we can do some pilot projects on some certain museums.

This study on the topic intends to arouse more intention to the development of museums, so as to improve the experience of museums.

References

1. Smith, T.F., Waterman, M.S.: Identification of common molecular subsequences. J. Mol. Biol. **147**, 195–197 (1981)
2. User experience. https://en.wikipedia.org/wiki/User_experience
3. Norman, D., Miller, J., Henderson, A.: What you see, some of what's in the future, and how we go about doing it: HI at Apple Computer. In: Proceedings of CHI 1995, Denver, Colorado, USA (1995)
4. Buley, L.: The User Experience Team of One: A Research and Design Survival Guide. Rosenfield Media, LLC, Brooklyn (2013)
5. ISO 9241-11:1998: Ergonomics of Human System Interaction: Guidance on Usability

6. COST Action IC0904-TwinTide: Towards the Integration of IT Design and Evaluation. http://www.cost.eu/COST_Actions/ict/transectorial_it_design_and_evaluation
7. Pallud, J., Monod, E.: User experience of museum technologies: the phenomenological scales. Eur. J. Inf. Syst. **19**(5), 562–580 (2010). Appendix: Springer-Author Discount
8. Wickell, C.: Great Expectations: Researching Usability of Online Museum Collections
9. Gumerman, L.J.: Inspiring engagement through the user experience: a project with the Fort Collins Museum of Discovery. Dissertations and Theses - Gradworks (2014)
10. Røtne, O., Kaptelinin, V.: Design choices and museum experience: a design-based study of a mobile museum app. In: Collazos, C., Liborio, A., Rusu, C. (eds.) CLIHC 2013. LNCS, vol. 8278, pp. 9–13. Springer, Cham (2013). doi:10.1007/978-3-319-03068-5_3
11. Hertzum, M.: A review of museum web sites: in search of user-centred design. Arch. Mus. Inform. **12**(2), 127–138 (1999)
12. Li, X.: The ways to improve the experience of museums. http://www.wenwuchina.com/article/201622/270487.html
13. Zheng, Y.: The research of museum education: the programming and implementation before, during, after, visiting museums
14. Service design. https://en.wikipedia.org/wiki/Service_design
15. Xin X., Cao J.: Service design drives the public affairs management, and organizational innovation. Design (5), 124–128 (2014)
16. Dai, L.: Design Research
17. Qing Dao Museum. http://www.qingdaomuseum.com
18. Berelson, B.: Content Analysis in Communication Research. Free Press, Glencoe (1952)
19. Wu, Y.: About local governments in America, Japan, the comparative study of the home page
20. Jie, W., Rui, X., Siyu, T.: The evaluation of railway web based on the content analysis. Railw. Transp. Econ. **30**(2), 78–81 (2008)
21. Liang, X., Liming, Z.: Content analysis about the web including Taiwan travelling on both sides. Travel J. **24**(3), 75–81 (2009)
22. Yanli, W., Gaixue, Y., Juan, W.: The research on informal learning based on content analysis. Remote Educ. Mag. **29**(4), 71–76 (2011)
23. Haiping, C.: The analysis and comparison of the college web between USA and China. Intell. Mag. **31**(2), 28–29 (2012)
24. Service design tools. http://www.servicedesigntools.org/tools/20

Implementation of Service Design on Innovation Development of Traditional Handicraft: A Case Study of Yongchun Lacquered Basket

Yan Wu[1], Li-Yu Chen[1(✉)], and Lei Ren[2]

[1] Ph.D. Program in Design, Chung Yuan Christian University,
Chung-Li, Taoyuan City, Taiwan
164836866@qq.com, chenly99@gmail.com
[2] College of Fine Art, Huaqiao University,
Quanzhou, Fujian, People's Republic of China
85149584@qq.com

Abstract. In recent years, the protection method the traditional craftsmanship of intangible cultural heritage gradually receives more attention, with the purpose for the protection of intangible cultural heritage and community construction. This study takes Yongchun lacquered basket in Fujian as an example, aiming to analyze the development difficulty of the local traditional handicraft industry, explore the mechanism to promote the traditional handcraft industry by service design, measure the success of the sustainable development with service design as guide, so as to conclude the enlightenment of sustainable development of traditional craftsmanship. Service design is a user-centered design method, to help build innovative service or improve existing products or services, with the aim to make the product or service provided useful, usable and more efficient. Service design, as a discipline, should not be isolated, but be combined with service development, management, operation and marketing together. First of all, the historical development and the production process of Yongchun lacquer basket as intangible cultural heritage should be analyzed, with the field investigation for its present situation. Second, INPD (Integrated New Product Development) can be used with service design as orientation to analyze the opportunity gap of the traditional handcraft industry of Yongchun lacquered baskets through Society, Economic, Technology (SET) and Value Opportunity Analysis (VOA) is used to explore and evaluate the attribute of new product opportunities. Finally, INPD with service design as orientation is taken as our process framework of intangible cultural heritage protection.

Keywords: Service design · Yongchun lacquered baskets · Design method · Traditional handicraft industry · Innovative development

1 Introduction

As the modern industrialization develops rapidly, the traditional handicrafts are replaced by machines, and the transition of the modern way of life, the production diversity, the spread diversity, the sales diversity and consumption form, etc. result in

P.-L.P. Rau (Ed.): CCD 2017, LNCS 10281, pp. 232–240, 2017.
DOI: 10.1007/978-3-319-57931-3_19

the decrease of the desire for traditional handicraft industry. The traditional crafts-manship of Yongchun lacquer basket in Fujian, as a very important factor of the cultural assets and created 500 years ago, is facing the inheritance fault and the loss of valuable traditional craftsmanship and ethnic cultural heritage. In order to protect the intangible cultural heritage, the protection method for the traditional craftsmanship of intangible cultural heritage is getting more and more attention. This study takes tra-ditional Yongchun lacquer basket in Fujian as an example, aiming to analyze the development dilemma and error of the local traditional craftsmanship, explore the mechanism of using service design to promote the development of traditional handcraft industry, and measure the success of the sustainable development of service design as the guide, thus the enlightenment for the sustainable development of traditional craftsmanship is concluded.

2 Status Quo of Lacquer Basket

2.1 History of Yongchun Lacquer Basket

Yongchun lacquer basket is the famous traditional bamboo basket arts and crafts is in Fujian province, created in the period of Mingde between 1506–1506. According to the records of "Yongchun Motto", lacquer basket has 500 years' history, and more than 100 kinds of varieties; it is widely used for folk ancestor worship, marriage basket or god greeting and ancestor worship, etc. [1]. Since Fujian Minnan culture is prevalent, lacquer basket is mainly concentrated in Quanzhou, Shishi and Yongchun. The pro-ducing area of lacquer basket in Yongchun is located in Longshui village, Xianjia town, Yongchun County, Quanzhou city, Fujian province, which is the main base and root of producing lacquer basket. Because of the place name, it is known as Longshui lacquer basket, and very popular in Minnan area in which culture and folk activities are quite prevalent; moreover, it is exported to Southeast Asia and other regions with Chinese people. A poem circulated in one hundred year says, "Hands flutter with dance, warp and weft are into the drawing. Bamboo basket carries water without leakage, small to hide the needle and large to be as cabinet". What is mentioned in the poem is the lacquer basket in Longshui Village. "Longshui lacquer basket" has been included in Quanzhou non-material cultural heritage, and officially listed in Fujian intangible cultural heritage list in June, 2009. Yongchun government, jointly with local residents, declared the national intangible cultural heritage [2] (Fig. 1).

Fig. 1. Yongchun Longshui lacquer basket (Color figure online) (data source: photo by the author)

2.2   Craftsmanship of Yongchun Lacquer Basket

The largest diameter of traditional lacquer basket is half a meter, and the smallest one is only three centimeters. The color is bright red, black and gold, which symbolizes auspiciousness, richness and honor. It is one of the commonly used things in Minnan people's home. Since there are Minnan people that have immigrated to Southeast Asia, the tradition of using lacquer baske thas gradually formed in Southeast Asia. According to the records of Yongchun Motto: "in the period of Mingzhengde (1506–1522), the painters in Longshui put the traditional product of bamboo basket and bamboo plate embryo into lime water for boiling, wiped them and put tung oil ash, and then it was tabled with grass cloth, coated with raw painting, to make lacquer basket, which is durable; after then, it was improved gradually. On handle, cover, and body of the basket, the decorative patterns or designs were added; after 30 working procedures, it turned into valuable lacquer basket." The craftsmanship of Yongchun lacquer basket is quite complicated, with 5 types of working including making basket embryos (bamboo weaving), ash basket, painting, drawing and carving, and 33 procedures, as follows: 1. making basket embryos (bamboo weaving). 2. Adding putty. 3. Painting and carving [3].

2.3   Development Dilemma of Yongchun Lacquer Basket Industry

With the high-degree urbanization and the rapid development of science and technology, the traditional craftsmanship of lacquer basket is facing the unprecedented challenges. Due to the change of modern lifestyle, the problems, for example, the demand for the traditional lacquer basket demand dramatically decreases traditional craftsmanship inheritance suffers from fault, the population outflow appears and the business model cannot keep pace with the times, have impact on the intangible cultural heritage with 500 years' history. First, the inheritance of the traditional craftsmanship of lacquer basket is the most serious problem now. The aging of traditional craftsmen in Longshui is very serious; due to the complexity of the production process and the large length, most of the local young people are unwilling to inherit the traditional lacquer basket craftsmanship. With the development of the modern city and the demise of the traditional handicraft industry, the younger generation is away from Longshui due to study or work, with the smaller possibility of engaging in traditional basket craftsmanship. "There are more than 1000 people in Longshui village; the number of existing practitioners is less than 200, and most of them are engaged in basket retail personally; there are more than 20 people taking a part-time job in the company. There is a lack of the people who can complete all processes of lacquer basket alone." Guo Zhihuang describes the status quo. According to statistics, currently, there are 128 lacquer basket professionals in the village, and according to the type of work, there are 81 bamboo weavers, 33 putty people, 14 lacquer painters; according to gender, there are 69 men and 59 women [4]. In terms of age, the age for the main practitioners of lacquer basket are above 40 years old, many of which are in high age stage, and there are only 6 people under the age of 40, but only 6 people can only make bamboo weaving but cannot make putty and painting. There is no practitioner under the age of 30. That is to say, in Longshui Village that is the production base of lacquer basket, the villagers under the age of 40, have been unable to jointly create a complete lacquer basket.

3 Value Analysis of Traditional Yongchun Lacquer Basket with Service Design as Orientation

3.1 Definition of Service Design

Service design is the most important tool for the service design put forward by G. Lynn Shostack in "European Journal of Marketing" and "Harvard Business Review" — the concept of Service Blueprint applied in marketing management. Based on the definition of British design association, service design simply refers to providing users with the overall experience of design, and your products and services for customers are "more useful, usable, favorable to use, and more convenient, more efficient, and more valuable [5]." Design consultant LIVE | WORK said, "Service design is to use the mature design process and technology to develop the service. It is a kind of innovative and actual way to improve existing services and innovative service [6]." INPD is the product development approach with service design as orientation, composed of four steps, identifying opportunity, understanding opportunity, transforming opportunity into product concept, realizing opportunity. It is the premise of clarify the fuzzy product development process [7] (Fig. 2).

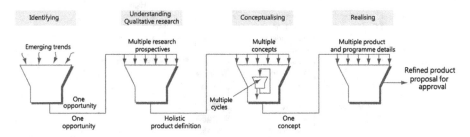

Fig. 2. Four_phase product development process (adapted from Cagan and Vogel (2004))

3.2 Identifying the Product Opportunity Gap Through SET Factor Analysis

Through the existing research of traditional handicraft industry of Yongchun lacquer basket, the SET (Social-Economic-Technology) of service design factor analysis method is used to seek culture value system of the industry, respectively from social, economic and technological aspects [7]. Through the collection of existing results and literature historical data excavation and arrangement, the method of service design and process in the early stage is applied, with the field survey and the qualitative and quantitative research, it mainly focuses on the protection and development of traditional industry of Yongchun lacquer basket to discuss.

The analysis of the social, economic and technical factors can produce product opportunity of traditional lacquer basket handcraft; by the application of the tools of service design as orientation, finding its industry's opportunity gap eventually is transformed into value opportunity. Our goal is to recognize the new trend and to find a matching consumer group and product demand through the analysis of social, economic, and technological factors, and then based on customer needs and expectations of reasonable product or service in organic integration, it aims to develop its new products or services to protect the inheritance and sustainable development of traditional Yongchun lacquer basket handicraft industry.

3.3   Analysis of VOA Value Opportunity Based on Ethnography

Based VOA (value opportunity analysis) of ethnography, it is the key tool for the second stage–"understanding opportunity" of INPD procedure with service design as orientation, and its purpose is to use qualitative research to clarify product value opportunity after "identifying opportunity" in the first stage. Value can be understood as the product attributes to make the product available, usable, and favorable to have. It is these attributes that make function characteristics and value connected to produce VO (value opportunity), which is made up of seven types of value: emotion, ergonomics, aesthetics, characteristics, influence, core technology and quality. Attributes of the first value opportunity "emotion" contain adventure, independence, security, sensibility, confidence and strength. Attributes of the second value opportunity "ergonomics" attributes

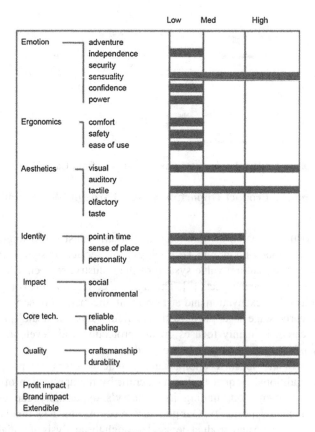

Fig. 3. VOA of lacquered basket

contain comfort, security, easy use. Attributes of the third value opportunity "aesthetics" contain sight, hear, touch, smell, taste. Attributes of the fourth value opportunity "characteristics" contain timing, comfortable, individual character. Attributes of the fifth value opportunity "influence" contain social influence and environmental impact. Attributes of the sixth value opportunity "core technology" contain reliability and availability. Attributes of the seventh value opportunity "quality" contain process and durability [7] (Fig. 3).

From the analysis of value opportunity, the traditional lacquer basket has smaller numerical value in adventure and safety of emotion, as well as in ergonomics; the most obvious one is that the numerical value is significantly smaller in interest effect, brand effect and extensibility; its advantage mainly lies in aesthetics and quality. From the previous SET analysis, it can be concluded that the advantage of traditional lacquer basket is the reflection of its aesthetic and cultural value, and the disadvantage lies in a series of problems with vicious cycle caused by the demand reduce.

4   Innovative Practice of Bamboo Furniture

4.1   Development of INPD Bamboo Furniture with Service Design as Orientation

According to the definition made by UNESCO, "cultural industry" refers to a series of activities in accordance with the industry standard production, reproduction, storage, and distribution of cultural products and services. "Culture" in cultural industry contains the way of life and its economic properties, so one of the most important links for the research on the protection of the cultural industry, and the inheritance of traditional craftsmanship is the study of culture as well as group culture. Cultural value is transformed into commercial value through the innovation of the traditional industries, cultural value and economic value are realized through the product design and service innovation. So, after three years' uninterrupted participatory observation, the author made the local government departments, designers, traditional lacquer basket technicians, design companies and college students majoring in design common basket of traditional industries to jointly attend the lacquer basket products innovation design, and imported INPD based on service design as orientation.

The first stage: the product opportunity identification and selection. In the SET analysis of traditional lacquer basket, the research team used informal interview and

Fig. 4. Bamboo furniture model manufacture (data source: photo by the author)

qualitative research with qualitative research maintenance as priority to summarize three opportunity gaps: 1. through the experience of economy orientation, it makes Yongchun Longshui lacquer basket factory into a sightseeing factory, with sales and experience of weaving technique. 2. Culture creative product design and production.

Item	Category	Yongchun furniture of phyllostachys heteroclada
Basic introduction	Industry characteristics	Traditional bamboo lacquered basket handcraft weaving, materials of primitive ecology
	Main products	Furniture and household products
	Development background of the industry	The traditional lacquered basket that was once well sold declines due to demand decrease, and its industrial resources disappear year by year.
	Development target of the industry	Combined with the traditional handcraft, it helps the innovative development of traditional industry by designing the products that meet the demand of consumers.
	Organization structure of the industry	1.Lacquered basket factory in Yongchun 2.Design company 3. Commercialization development
Upstream creation, research and development	Innovative elements	Traditional craftsmanship, materials of primitive ecology meet the aesthetic demand of modern people.
	Innovative output mechanism	Due to traditional craftsmanship of lacquered basket, combined with the demand for the primitive furniture industry, it integrates innovative design and traditional handcraft.
	Production method of products	1. Traditional craftsmanship weaving in Yongchun.2. Commercialization furniture development .
Midde-stream production and manufacture	Main materials of products	Bamboo
	Manufacture procedure of products	Design plan, drawing, model, traditional lacquered basket weaving method
	Category of products	Furniture, lamps and lanterns, household products
	Derivative products	Display of public area, furniture industry, experience of traditional craftsmanship
	Unit of measurement of product	Piece, set, piece
Downstream sales	Marketing strategies	Design exhibition, business use, furniture shopping place, promoting relevant things of traditional industry
	Main marketing market	China, Europe
	Benefit evaluation of the industry	1.Expand the new field of traditional handcraft industry 2 Help traditional handcraft industry survive and inherit 3. promote and spread traditional craftsmanship and culture 4. create breakthrough products

Fig. 5. Budget and promotion plan for bamboo furniture (made by the author)

3. Fineness of traditional Yongchun lacquer basket weaving and furniture and household products market development. The second stage: product opportunity understanding. In value analysis table, we can conclude the importance of user's demand lies in the industry interest's value opportunity; it is important for the storage and development of the traditional lacquer basket handicraft to make the breakthrough innovation. The third stage: transforming the opportunity into product concept. In the process of the conceptual design of bamboo furniture, designers and traditional lacquer basket technicians jointly produced many preliminary conceptual models, and during this stage, all personnel have a very clear concept on product technology, craft limitation and product modeling (Fig. 4).

The fourth stage: transforming concept into the implementation stage of the model opportunity. The details of a large number of bamboo furniture should be weighted, so that designers and traditional basket technicians together made the products, verified the rationality of furniture modeling and compiling. The market department clarified the market demand and user positioning, began to make production plan and the preliminary market strategy, including product's budget and promotion plan (Fig. 5).

5 Conclusion

The intangible cultural heritage of traditional handicraft industry is very precious cultural assets, and it not only shows the local culture, life and production history, but also is one of the important characteristics of a country's historical process of modernization. With the evolution of socialization, as well as the influence of way of life and national policy, the traditional handicraft industry gradually tends to face the fate of production suspension and the missing inheritance people. Traditional handicraft industry's protection method is taken seriously day by day, with the purpose to protect the intangible cultural heritage and find out its system of cultural value and economic value. This study takes traditional Yongchun lacquer basket in Fujian as an example, aiming to analyze the development difficulty of the local traditional handicraft industry, explore the mechanism to promote the traditional handcraft industry by service design, measure the success of the sustainable development with service design as guide. Field research and analysis of the development of handicraft industry history and the production process of Yongchun lacquer baskets was conducted. Through SET (society, economy, technology), it analyzed opportunity gap of the development of traditional handicraft industry of Yongchun lacquer baskets. Then, VOA (value opportunity analysis) was applied to explore and evaluate the attribute of the new product opportunities. INPD with service design as orientation was used as our intangible cultural heritage protection and development process framework. The implications for the sustainable development of the traditional craftsmanship were concluded, as the basis to deeply research, store and reuse traditional handicraft industry innovation and development.

References

1. Yong chuan county motto edition committee: Quanzhu City Motto, Yongchun County Motto (2016)
2. Baidu encyclopedia. http://baike.baidu.com/subview/2760943/2760943.html
3. Fjian Yongchun. http://www.fjyc.gov.cn/m/show.aspx?ctlgid=272516&Id=106088
4. Fujian Yongchun. http://www.fjycwy.com/a/xijuwutai/20130826/31.html
5. UK Council. http://www.designcouncil.org.uk/news-opinion/video-what-service-design
6. Live|work. https://www.liveworkstudio.com/themes/customer-experience/service-design/
7. Cagan, J., Vogel, C.M.: Creating Breakthrough Products: Innovation from Product Planning to Program Approval. China Machine Press, China (2002)

Designing a Cross-Cultural Interactive Music Box Through Meaning Construction

Yongmeng Wu[1]([envelope]), Nick Bryan-Kinns[1], Wei Wang[2,4], Jennifer G. Sheridan[3], and Xiang Xu[4]

[1] Media and Arts Technology, Queen Mary University of London, London, UK
yongmeng.wu@qmul.ac.uk
[2] School of Industrial Design, Georgia Institute of Technology, Atlanta, GA, USA
[3] b00t Consultants Ltd, London, UK
[4] School of Design, Hunan University, Changsha, People's Republic of China

Abstract. There is growing interest in designing culturally identifiable products for cross cultural consumers. However, literature rarely pays attention to the conflicting needs of these products in terms of cross-cultural usability and their unique cultural identity. This paper presents a design model addressing this problem through a process of meaning construction. By identifying the culture's shared and unique meaning, designers are able to map the target meaning onto the product attributes - the form, content and interaction - thus presenting culturally identifiable and cross-culturally acceptable products to culturally heterogeneous consumers. A case study of designing a meaningful cross-cultural interactive music box with the Kam ethnic minority culture is presented focussing on the detailed process of meaning construction, and implementation and evaluation. Feedback in the field showed that the shared meaning built in the boxes helped outsiders to understand the interaction. The unique meaning helped to attract the attention from participants outside Kam culture, and improved the cultural identity. The results also showed that participants from different culture preferred different product features, for example the story content attract participants outside Chinese culture, while Chinese participants preferred playful interaction on the sound.

Keywords: Meaning construction · Cross-cultural design · Product identity · Interactive music · Design method

1 Introduction

Many regional cultural and traditional communities in China are suffering from transformation because of rapid urbanisation [1]. One of the key challenges that traditional rural communities encounter in modern society is the preservation and maintenance of their original social capital [2]. This issue leads to an important topic of this paper related to design practice: how to preserve and promote traditional cultural heritage of rural communities in the digital age in order to

© Springer International Publishing AG 2017
P.-L.P. Rau (Ed.): CCD 2017, LNCS 10281, pp. 241–257, 2017.
DOI: 10.1007/978-3-319-57931-3_20

sustain and improve local people's cultural identity, as well as to stimulate local economic development? Cultural product design offers solutions by transforming and intensifying traditional cultural feature in consumer products or tourist souvenirs. By embedding local cultural features and emphasising cultural value in product design, product value is enhanced, as well as its identity in the global market [4]. However, an emerging problem for these exotic souvenirs is that culturally diverse users might encounter cultural breakdowns [6], which is especially true for interactive products or systems due to representational variations between cultures [7].

Informed by the "Meaning in Mediated Action" approach of cross-cultural HCI design [7] which highlights the role of "shared meaning" in broad contexts and its use as a base to design shared representations, this paper proposes a more detailed framework integrating the idea of "shared meaning" with "unique meaning" for the purpose of supporting the design of product usability as well as cultural identity across different cultures. Following the design model, this paper presents a case study of designing interactive cultural products for cross-cultural consumers in a remote minority community, detailing the process of designing two meaningful interactive music boxes through identifying the "shared meaning" and "unique meaning" and mapping them to the product attributes: form, content, interaction. By engaging designers with a local community to acquire cultural knowledge, and encouraging innovation from local craftsmen in the design process, two prototypes were designed and implemented in a local mobile maker space using local materials. An agile evaluation method collecting 'in-situ' feedback for further design iterations was carried out with local residents and tourists, followed by a more formal evaluation in London (UK) when the boxes were displayed in a public exhibition. Questionnaires were collected at the exhibition with participants outside Kam culture. Results showed that shared meaning helps outsiders to understand the product interaction, and improved the cultural identity. The results also showed that participants from different culture preferred different product features, for example the story content attract participants outside Chinese culture, while Chinese participants preferred playful interaction on the sound. The model offered a clear idea from the beginning to guide the process on designing a cross-cultural interactive product. And also, it gave a structure to organise the evaluation, by analysing the effectiveness of the two-layer meaning as well as the design attributes.

2   Design Objectives and Methods

2.1   Meaning in Cross-Cultural Design

Meaning is proposed as a central factor in design practice for cross-cultural products for the following two major reasons:

- First of all, meaning construction is an ongoing activity of people when they talk, think and act in everyday situations [5]. Research from Markussen and Krogh [9] focuses on the dynamic process when people creatively reshape and transform pre-existing cultural knowledge when they encounter a new digital artefact that has unexpected structures of experience, or conflicts with their previous knowledge. They use blending theory as a new conceptual framework to unpack the internal configurations and governing principles of meaning construction. Therefore, designing cross-cultural products need to consider the process of user's meaning construction.

– Secondly, communicating meaning is an approach to avoid the culturally determined usability problems of products for culturally heterogeneous users [7]. [8] addresses issues related to product internationalisation and localisation, approaches for designing interfaces for cultural diverse users in early 1990s, through studies of the usability and user experience of interactive interfaces across diverse cultures. The common limitation of this process is that culturally diverse users often encounter cultural breakdowns, "the moment when the user becomes conscious of the properties of the system and has to mentally break down or decompose his or her understanding of the system in order to rationalise the problem experienced" [6].

Through analysis of user's cultural breakdowns, Bourges-Waldegg and Scrivener identified the fundamental problem of designing interfaces for culturally diverse users is to communicate the intended meaning of representations in different cultural contexts [7]. They presented the "meaning in mediated action (MMA)" approach to tackle the main usability issues determined by cultural difference in Human-computer interaction cross-cultural design. This approach starts by determining the contexts shared by the members of a culturally heterogeneous user group and use these as a base to design shared representations. The MMA approach focuses on how representations and meaning mediate action, putting *shared meaning* in the centre position to be a tool for understanding as well as an analytical tool.

In contrast to the emphasis on shared meaning outlined above, studies also indicate the importance of *unique meaning*. For example, Rampino proposed meaning innovation in the process of product innovation [10]. Meaning innovation here concerns the emotional and symbolic aspects of a product, i.e. what a product is able to communicate, which is strictly linked to its cultural context. This is very close to the concept of *design icon*, that "products that gather a cultural meaning that is greater that the sum of their specifications" [11]. As a result of meaning innovation, the product becomes culturally successful. The idea of *unique meaning* is also highlighted as a key point to promote cultural identity and product value in the field of cultural product design described in the following section.

2.2   Cultural Product Design

As opposed to the trend of internationalisation and localisation on global products, an emerging trend is designing cultural product to promote local cultural identity and enhance cultural values and traditions, because "the search for identity includes claiming the right to maintain different values" [12]. Besides the benefit of creating and sustaining cultural identity, emphasising product local features and cultural value has become a critical issue in the design process. It helps to transform traditional objects into modern products that meet the needs of the contemporary consumer market, and in turn helps to enhance product value in the global market [14]. It can also enhance individual experience and memory, and trigger a culture reflection of customers [13].

One branch of study in this field focuses on analysing the cultural factors related to design. The study of cultural layers has expanded from a two-layer framework (visible, and invisible) [19], to a three-layer framework (basic assumptions, values, and artefacts) [20], and finally towards a four-layer framework [21], including the first layer of basic assumptions and values, the second layer of beliefs, attitudes and conventions, the third layer of systems and institutions, and the fourth layer of artefacts, products, rituals and behaviour [22]. Other studies started to relate the cultural levels to attributes of cultural objects. For example, Leong and Clark distinguished three special levels of cultural objects: the outer 'tangible' level, the mid 'behavioral' level, and the inner 'intangible' level [18]. Moreover, Hsu et al. provided detailed cultural factors relating to design attributes: the outer level dealing with colors, texture, form, decoration, surface pattern, line quality, and details; the mid level containing function, operational concerns, usability, and safety; the inner level containing special content such as stories, emotion, and cultural features [17].

Another branch of study focus on methodology for designing cultural products to transform and encode unique culture factors. A culture-centred design approach was proposed by [15] with a cultural filter in order to improve the usability and allow cultural identity, meaning, values and tradition to be truly integrated and conveyed. Similarly, Richie proposed a culture-oriented model to combine and break down the contemporary socio-cultural factors into material, emotional, social practice and technology/design factors [22]. Wang et al. addressed traditional craft and modern design collaboration in brocade products [3]. Tung suggested co-creation as a method to stimulate the development and preservation of a local craft in a sustainable and commercially viable way [16]. Lin provided four steps to design a cultural product, including investigation, interaction, development, and implementation using scenario and story-telling approaches to access to social background, resource constraints and background information [14]. In a later paper, the four phases of cultural product design were expanded into a ten steps framework [17]. Wang et al. summarised three social design paradigms for cultural product design [27]: (i) cultural intermediaries paradigm which mainly adopts quasi-ethnographic approaches, such as participatory observation, interviews and cultural inquiries; (ii) the product–service system paradigm which adopts an artefact oriented development process that with methods such co-design, participatory design; and (iii) the community engagement paradigm which adopts an event-driven process, applying in-situ and iterative techniques such as cultural probes and community performance.

The studies discussed above on cultural factors offered an idea to construct the meaning, including both *shared meaning* and *unique meaning*, through the product attributes in the proposed model. This allows the meaning construction model to offer operationable guidance in design practice. The methods proposed in this field are mainly focused on extracting and encoding the unique culture factors, with less attention on the identifying and implementing the shared meaning. Therefore our proposed model will offer an approach addressing both aspects, as well as an case study illustrating detailed process.

3   Meaning Construction - A Design Model

There are clearly two conflicting needs which emerge in terms of *meaning* when considering the design of a commercial souvenir product from both a cross-cultural product design and the cultural product design perspectives:

- A need for *shared meaning* related to cultural factors, context and representations that culturally diverse users share in order to ensure product understandability and usability across cultures.
- A need for *unique meaning* related to the tangible, behavioural, and intangible culture factors that the culture uniquely possessed so as to cherish and promote the culture.

Therefore, based on the idea of highlighting the role of *shared meaning* from the MMA approach, we proposed to integrate *unique meaning* in cross-cultural product design as a source for meaning innovation.

Building on the cultural factors of cultural products discussed above, we propose three more specific cultural attributes of interactive products: interaction, form, and content. The *interaction* includes the functions, operations, and actions of product, which is directly related to the behavioural level of culture, including cultural factors such as behavioural norms, beliefs, concerns etc. The *form* includes shape, color, material, texture, patterns of product, which is linked with the tangible level of cultural. The *content* includes the visual, sound and emotion experience of product, and is bounded with the intangible level of culture, including the cultural factors such as sound, stories, and emotions.

We propose a model for designing cultural interactive products through mapping the *shared meaning* and *unique meaning* with the design attributes of the interactive systems that relates to the different culture levels, see Fig. 1. Specifically, the mapping involves, on one hand, constructing shared meaning through a process of identification of shared representations, contexts, or factors with relation to the interaction, form and content. On the other hand, the mapping involves constructing unique meaning of product through a process of extraction of featured culture factors in terms of the interaction, form and content. It is necessary to note that the mapping between the meanings and the product attributes are not fixed, the mapping can be varied according to different culture and different products. The idea of mapping the two-layer meaning into product attributes is to construct the abstract meaning through concrete design attributes, in order to offer designers an implementable model to construct the product's meaning.

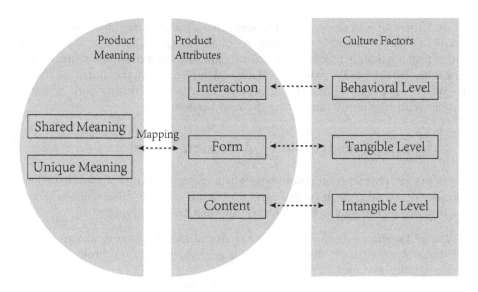

Fig. 1. Model of meaning construction

4   Case Study: A Meaningful Cross-Cultural Interactive Music Box

The Kam's minority culture is from their community in Tongdao county in Hunan province, central south China. Their culture is unique and famous for their wooden buildings with exquisite structures, their ethnic music, instruments, their carpenter skill of wooden products, and their local customs [27]. With their unique and well preserved traditional culture, Tongdao has attracted numerous tourists from other regions of China as well as foreigners from across the world in recent years, which has greatly helped local economic development. An emerging need is a range of high quality souvenirs to enhance the souvenir product value as well as to promote the local cultural identity. Researchers have focussed on this issue since 2009 through the engagement with the Kam's minority culture [1,3,27]. In the summer of 2016, a concentrated exploration based on long-term research concerns was carried out focusing on designing a meaningful cross-cultural tourist souvenir, which is reported here.

As mentioned above, music and musical instruments are a very important factor in Kam culture. Meanwhile, the music box is a traditional western artifact - a kids toy and romantic gift often with craft patterns and physical interaction - which is now a familiar object for Chinese people as well. With the rapid development of sensors and digital sound technology, numerous interactive music boxes have been built with various interactions in various forms, both commercially and including a series tangible objects designed for collaborative group playing [23,24], and a series of performative objects for live musical performance [25,26]. Our idea in this work is to merge interactive technologies and industrial design methods to develop a new musical consumer product for domestic tourist markets and for those who seek a new and exotic souvenir.

4.1 Design Process

Cultural Exploration. The design process started with an open ended exploration of local culture to help designers to understand and study new environments, and generate inspirational data to inform the design process. Four aspects of design were asked to look at when collecting local inspirations: Culture, Interaction, Form, and Sound. It offers a general structure for designers to explore and pay attention to during this process. As the main local challenges that designers meet during design process is to gain the local knowledge [1], cultural exploration is a necessary step for designers to overcome the knowledge barriers and cultural boundaries [27]. Two designers in our group, together with five designers in the other groups, set out with cameras to local villages, took pictures of the land marking architectures such as their memorial gateway, tower bridge, and drum tower, and interviewed local people about their handicraft and articles for daily use. The basic target for this activity was to engage with the local community, gain local cultural knowledge, and to identify the unique culture factors as well as the shared culture factors.

Through two days of cultural exploration at Kam culture, we found a traditional local object, Lucky Flower, which is a blessing hung in the beams of symbolic buildings, such as the village gate, the drum tower, or the tower bridge in Kam communities. The Lucky Flower is a set of colourful patterned boxes in geometric shape organized with wire in hierarchy layers, see Fig. 2. Whenever a new building is completed, Kam people will hang several Lucky Flowers on the roof to pray for bless to the building. Usually they are made by local grandmas voluntarily with recycled cardboard and knitting wool. We found the Lucky Flower is a symbolic culture object, as well as a suitable archetype for music box with modern form and design. Therefore it is used as a design archetype to extract unique cultural meaning for our target interactive music box.

Unique Meaning Construction. In our case the unique meaning is extracted from the cultural symbolic object, the Lucky Flower, to support the identity of the product. For our target music box we constructed the unique meaning based on the form and content, see Fig. 3. The basic shape, color and pattern of Lucky Flowers are unique Kam cultural factors which we extracted as the form of our target music box. Although one set of Lucky Flower consists of several layers of geometry boxes lined with strings, the geometric shape across the layers are the same, differed in size. The hollow square pattern twined with wool thread on Lucky Flower represent good luck in Kam culture. The bright green and red color on Lucky Flowers are typical Kam colors as featured in their cloth and fabrics. Therefore, the basic geometry shape, the color and the patterns were adopted as the form for our target music box as a unique meaning component.

In terms of the content, Kam music is a famous and exquisite ethic feature that tourists find novel. Also, the stories of Kam culture as well as the stories

Fig. 2. Original Lucky Flower

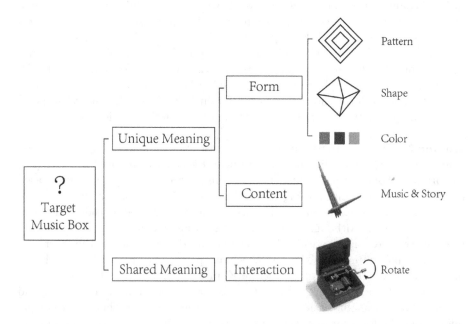

Fig. 3. Structure of meaning construction (Color figure online)

of Lucky Flower are an interesting and unusual content source for outsiders. Therefore, we adopted Kam music and Kam stories as the content of target music box - another unique meaning component.

Shared Meaning Construction. As outlined in the previous section, an important step is to construct a shared meaning, as well as a unique meaning, by examining the shared cultural factors, contexts, representations between the music in Kam culture and the target product - the music box.

For traditional music box, a typical interaction is to rotate the small handle somewhere on the box to trigger the music. For Chinese people, the rotation action of traditional music box is a familiar concept. In the Kam tourist market in Tongdao there are conventional music boxes for sale, all of them include such rotating interaction. Moreover, rotation is also a familiar behaviour in everyday life of Kam culture. For example, when the weaver preparing the thread, rotation is a repetitive action. Besides, when Lucky Flowers are hung on the roof of the tower bridge or drum tower, they rotate in the wind. Based on this shared knowledge, rotation was adopted for the basic interaction of our new music box as a component for shared meaning, with the aim of supporting understandability as well as usability, see Fig. 3.

Table 1. Comparison of two boxes

Product attributes	Story box	Music box
Interaction (Shared meaning)	Rotate to switch between stories	Tilt to switch between music & Rotate to add live sound effect
Form - shape (Unique meaning)	Lucky Flower	Lucky Flower
Form - color (Unique meaning)	Cultural color (red/green)	Normal color (pink/blue)
Content	Stories of Lucky Flower	Local music

Comparative Music Box. We decided to build two music boxes with slightly differed features to allow us to make a comparison of the effectiveness of our proposed design method. A comparison of the two boxes is given in Table 1. The first box, the *story box*, was built on a rotatory interaction, with red/green color, and with the content of stories of lucky flower.

The comparative box, the *music box*, used tilt as the primary interaction. Instead of rotating the knobs, users can tilt the box to certain angles to switch between sounds. The idea of tilt came from the shape of lucky flower. The six sides of the shape offer the affordance of tilting when holding it in a hand. However, there is no shared meaning being built here. In terms of the form, the *music box* has with the same shape as the first. However, in terms of the color, a light pink and blue, which is an unusual color for Kam culture, were chosen for comparison. Informed by the novel interactive music systems mentioned earlier [23–26], a playful feature to add real-time sound effects to the music was designed. Rotation is adopted as a secondary interaction here for this feature. Whenever users rotated the knob, the pitch of the music will be randomly changed within a certain range which creates an interesting sound effect.

4.2 Implementation

The working prototypes are shown in Fig. 4. The red/green box is the *story box* with three rotatory knobs around the perimeter to switch between stories. The pink/blue is the *music box* with tilt interaction to switch between pieces of music and one nob on top to add live sound effect by rotating.

Fig. 4. Two design of Kam Tunes (Color figure online)

The implementation involved three parts: (i) the form implementation that involves the physical model of the boxes; (ii) the interaction implementation that involves the electronic sensors and software; (iii) the content implementation that involves the stories and music. The making process is illustrated in Fig. 5.

When designing the form and content of both boxes we conducted an iterative process of co-creation with local people. We learned from local grandmas to make the shape with recycled cardboard. Together with their knowledge of cultural color and patterns, we chose the color of wool thread and learned to wrap the box in the cultural pattern. We interviewed local grandmas about the history of Kam culture and Lucky Flower. Three stories were extracted from their story telling. We also recorded local music with folk artists and collected three pieces of music.

In terms of the interaction, we built the system with sensors, material and tools in a workshop space for social innovation located in the local village [27].

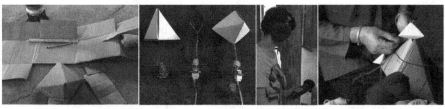

01 Make shape with cardboard   02 Encoder Sensor & Structure   03 Record music & stories   04 Wrap with wool thread

Fig. 5. Making process

For the *story box* that adopted rotatory interaction, three rotary encoder sensors were assembled with iron wire in the corner of the box so that the users could rotate the knobs to choose and switch between the stories. An Arduino board [28] is used to get the data from sensors, together with a sound board to play the sound with a micro-speaker. All of these items are embedded in main body of the *story box*.

For the *music box* that adopted tilting interaction, three tilt sensors were glued on the top inner sides of the box so that when the box is tilted to certain angle, one piece of music will be triggered. A rotary encoder sensor was assembled on top of the box to control a live sound effect of pitch changing. An Arduino board was used to process the data from sensors. The sound program was written in Processing language. To run this box, the Processing sketch needed to be run on a connected computer to play back the sound.

5 Evaluation

An agile evaluation in the local setting which collected 'in-situ' feedback for further design iterations were conducted with tourists in local tourist market and with local residents in the village. We started by introducing the two boxes, then encouraged participants to play with the two boxes for a while, followed by simple interview questions. Due to the time constraints, only a limited number of participants were involved in this process.

Two months later the two boxes were displayed at a public exhibition in London. We started by introducing the background of Kam culture and the two boxes to visitors. They were then asked to play with the two boxes for a while, followed by filling in a simple questionnaire. The questionnaire asked participants to rate statements based on their agreement on a 7-point Likert scale from 1 (strongly disagree) to 7 (strongly agree). There are 7 statements, including: (S1) I prefer the Red prototype in general; (S2) The interaction of Red prototype is more intuitive than the Pink prototype; (S3) The Red prototype is more fun than the Pink prototype; (S4) The sound of Pink prototype is more expressive than the Red prototype; (S5) I feel more engaged with the Pink prototype; (S6) I feel more creative with the Pink prototype; (S7) I like adding live sound effect on the sound. Field notes were taken by the researcher whilst participants were playing with the boxes to record their questions, judgements, attitude, as well as the researcher's observations of participants' behaviour and interaction.

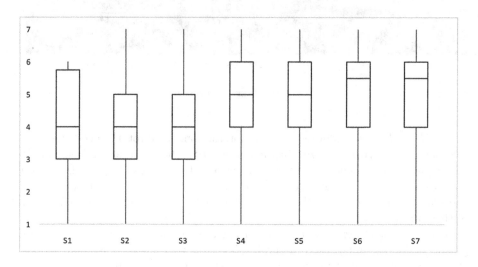

Fig. 6. Box plot of questionnaire from London exhibition

5.1   Results

In the local evaluation, five local participants (two adults and three children, all Chinese) were given the boxes to play with and interviewed afterwards, each of them interacted with the boxes for around 5 min in total. Two children and two adults liked the *music box* because they found the sound effect is more playable than the *story box* without the real-time sound effect. They also reported that the stories are not interesting because they are quite familiar with the stories. One child liked the *story box* because he thought it looks like a spaceship with the three nobs around the big shape. Three tourists (one adult and two children, all Chinese) from outside Kam culture were also interviewed, following the same procedure as the previous one. One child liked the *story box* because of its shape and colour, the others liked the *music box* because it's more playable with the real-time sound effect, and because the stories becomes boring after a while of playing.

The observational results reveals interesting behaviours of the participants. For example, majority kids (four out of five) started laughing when they heard the sound was twisted because of the real-time sound effect whiling rotating the nob on the *music box*. Two of them started rotating the nob even faster to test the effect on the sound. This behaviour showed that the real-time sound effect triggered the kids' interest to play with the sound. Moreover, two local kids were curious about the sound from the box that they examined the box all over. They asked questions such as "why is there sound coming out from the box" and "why does the sound changing". The *music box* gave them surprise with the embed interactive technology in the traditional symbolic object.

A total of 34 questionnaires were collected at the public exhibition in London (17 female and 17 male, mean age = 30, sd = 8.91, 5 Chinese). A box plot was generated from the questionnaire data as shown in Fig. 6. In general, our participants were neutral regarding their preference between the two prototypes. There is also no obvious preference in terms of the interaction. In terms of the engagement and creativity, participants preferred the *music box* with the feature of playing with live sound effect.

Review of the field notes reveals interesting behaviour by the participants with respect to the interaction and content of the boxes. For example, there are observations related to the interaction: "participant said that 'the red interaction is more intuitive, self-explanatory'", "participant feel the red prototype is easier to understand in the first place", "participant was squeezing the Pink prototype and thought it works in that way", which suggests that the rotatory interaction is easier to understand for users. Moreover, there are observations related to the content, "participant was more interested in the stories in the story prototype", "participant prefer the red prototype more because the content is more interesting", "participant played longer with Pink prototype". These statements suggest that the story content is attractive despite the significant language barrier.

There is no evidence suggesting the color of the boxes affect participants' preference between the boxes in the second evaluation. However, this is quite different compared to the opinions of local grandmas, who helped us to build and wrap the boxes. When chose the color for the second comparative box (the *music box*), all grandmas at presence (six of them) insisted using local cultural color such as bright red, green, blue, etc. For the purpose of comparison for later evaluation, we tried to avoid using the cultural color for the *music box*, which was clearly not the good choice for the grandmas, as they described our chosen color 'uggly' and kept persuading us to change to their traditional color. Although later the feedback from participants outside local culture indicated that the color made no difference, according to the grandmas' attitude, it seems that the product identity is reduced with non-traditional color from local people's perspective.

6   Further Discussion

In general, six amongst eight participants in the local evaluation liked the *music box*. However, feedback showed that there were more participants from foreign countries interested in the *story box* because of the story content. Some of the foreign participants expressed strong interest in listening to the stories even though they could not understand the language at all. They were also willing to learn the history of Kam culture while listening to the box. This preference is completely opposite compared to the participants in China, who reported the stories became boring after awhile. A possible reason for this is that narrative story telling is a common form of knowledge sharing across cultures, which might be a hidden shared meaning we as designers didn't realise in the beginning.

The shape of the box is so distinctive and exotic that it attracted foreign participants' interest instantly at first sight, according to the results from the exhibition. Most of them spoke highly on the aesthetics of the shape for both boxes. Moreover, it triggered participants' interest in the Lucky Flower itself - they were curious about the original form, its material, the process of making and its function. From this we can see that embedding culturally unique meaning in product supports the cultural identity. It is also interesting to note that the *story box* was favoured by two Chinese kids because of its form, i.e. its shape is similar to the spaceship.

In terms of the interaction, more participants figured out the rotatory interaction of the *story box* compared to the tilt interaction of the *music box*, according to the observation at the symposium. Moreover, five participants spoke highly on the rotatory interaction as it is "straightforward" and "expressive". This can be explained with the affordance theory [29], that the form of rotatory knobs gave an affordance of operation. Instead of pulling or pressing, most participants figured out the rotatory interaction without much effort. It seems that the rotatory interaction was more intuitive and made more sense to the participants. This evidence leads to the conclusion that the shared meaning in our design, the rotatory interaction in traditional western music box, helped participants to understand the interaction of the *story box*.

The above discussions of the results in relation to the music boxes' content, form and interaction, suggest that the two-layer framework of meaning and its mapping helped the prototypes to be understood by participants outside the local culture, whilst also helped to preserve the cultural identity. This two-layer meaning construction model is a complement of the MMA method [7] that only addressed the culturally determined usability problems. It addressed the problems related to cultural identity by integrating the theories and methods of cultural product design [18,19,21,22] to satisfy the culturally heterogeneous consumers. The model offered a clear idea from the beginning to guide the process on designing a cross-cultural interactive product. And also, it gave a structure to organise the evaluation, by analysing the effectiveness of the two-layer meaning as well as the design attributes.

There are limitations to these findings, however. As the target was to design a mass production tourist souvenir, one important issue is the material of product, as it is important for the traditional and urban communities to encourage social practice "from a sustainable perspective to promote traditional cultural heritage and the rational use of the environment and natural resources" [1]. Although in our case study we used the recycled cardboard following local grandma's practice, we did not take the material and mass production into account in the design model. Therefore, for future work, it would be necessary to take the material and its environmental friendliness into consideration, and expand the current model toward a more practical guidance. Moreover, the evaluations were undertaken with limited participants, especially the agile one at local. In that case, our results may not truly represent the preference of the majority of people. A larger scale and more formal evaluation needs to be conducted in future work. Besides, as we found there are diverse preference between Chinese tourist and foreigners, it would be useful to go further and study the different preference, which will be another useful guidance for designers.

7 Summary

In this paper we presented a model for designing meaningful cross-cultural interactive products through a process of two-layer meaning construction. By identifying the culturally shared and unique meanings, designers will be able to map the target meaning onto the product attributes - form, content and interaction. In this way, it is possible to design a product that is culturally identifiable and also cross-culturally acceptable.

A case study of designing a meaningful cross-cultural interactive music box for Kam culture was described. The detail of the meaning construction process, implementation and evaluation was presented. Feedback showed that the feature built on shared meaning helped the outsiders of a local community to understand the interaction, whilst the feature built on unique meaning helped the product to preserve the cultural identity, and thus trigger participants' interest in the local culture. The results also showed that participants from different culture prefer different feature of the sound, for example the story content attract participants outside Chinese culture, while Chinese participants preferred playful and interactive features of the sound. The positive results suggests that the design model presented in this paper has practical implications in terms of guiding design practice for cross-cultural products. Moreover, it also has implications for the evaluation of cross-cultural design outcomes.

Future work will continue to explore the role of material in the proposed design model from the perspective of sustainable development, and will also explore a larger scale evaluation of this design model.

Acknowledgements. This work was made possible by Prof. Ji Tie, and the DESIS Research Center at Hunan University, China. We kindly thank the grandmas in Hengling village, and the participants in our study. This work is partly supported by the China Scholarship Council, the Centre for Digital Music EPSRC Platform Grant (EP/K009559/1), the EPSRC and AHRC Centre for Doctoral Training in Media and Arts Technology (EP/L01632X/1), and the Hunan S&T International Collaboration Program (2015WK3029).

References

1. Ji, T., Yang, Q., Wang, W.: Design and social innovation. Design practice and methods based on networks and communities. In: Product-Service System Design for Sustainability, pp. 345–360 (2014)
2. Liu, L.-W.: Reflections on community empowerment: consideration of urban-rural differences, perspectives of urban development, and exploration of the bottom-up concept. J. City Plan. **35**(14), 313–338 (2008)

3. Wang, W., Ji, T., Jaafarnia, M.: Positioning designers into the craft revival of emerging markets: a case study on Chinese ethnic brocade industry. In: Proceedings of the 19th Design Management Conference (2014)
4. Wu, T.-Y., Cheng, H., Lin, R.: The study of cultural interface in Taiwan Aboriginal Twin-Cup. In: HCI International (2005)
5. Fauconnier, G., Turner, M.: The Way We Think: Conceptual Blending and the Mind's Hidden Complexities. Basic Books, New York (2002)
6. Urquijo, S.P., Scrivener, S.A.R., Palmén, H.K.: The use of breakdown analysis in synchronous CSCW system design. In: de Michelis, G., Simone, C., Schmidt, K. (eds.) Proceedings of the Third European Conference on Computer-Supported Cooperative Work 13–17 September 1993, Milan, Italy ECSCW 1993. Springer Netherlands, Dordrecht (1993)
7. Bourges-Waldegg, P., Scrivener, S.A.R.: Meaning, the central issue in cross-cultural HCI design. Interact. Comput. 9(3), 287–309 (1998)
8. Kano, N.: Developing International Software for Windows 95 and Windows NT. Microsoft Press, Redmond (1995)
9. Markussen, T., Krogh, P.G.: Mapping cultural frame shifting in interaction design with blending theory. Int. J. Des. 2(2), 5–17 (2008)
10. Rampino, L.: The innovation pyramid: a categorization of the innovation phenomenon in the product-design field. Int. J. Des. 5(1), 3–16 (2011)
11. Griffith, S.J., Skibsted, J.M.: In pursuit of the design icon. In: Proceedings of the Tsinghua International Design Management Symposium (2009)
12. Manzini, E., Susani, M. (eds.): The Solid Side, p. 175. VCK Publishing, Philips Corporate Design, Eindnoven (1995)
13. Yair, K., Tomes, A., Press, M.: Design through marking: crafts knowledge as facilitator to collaborative new product development. Des. Stud. 20(6), 495–515 (1999)
14. Lin, R.-T.: Transforming Taiwan aboriginal cultural features into modern product design: a case study of a cross-cultural product design model. Int. J. Des. 1(2), 45–53 (2007)
15. Shen, S.-T., Woolley, M., Prior, S.: Towards culture-centred design. Interact. Comput. 18(4), 820–852 (2006)
16. Tung, F.-W.: Weaving with rush: exploring craft-design collaborations in revitalizing a local craft. Int. J. Des. 6(3), 71–84 (2012)
17. Hsu, C.-H., Lin, C.-L., Lin, R.: A study of framework and process development for cultural product design. In: Rau, P.L.P. (ed.) IDGD 2011. LNCS, vol. 6775, pp. 55–64. Springer, Heidelberg (2011). doi:10.1007/978-3-642-21660-2_7
18. Leong, D., Clark, H.: Culture-based knowledge towards new design thinking and practice - a dialogue. Des. Issues 19(3), 48–58 (2003)
19. Dahl, S.: Intercultural Research: The Current State of Knowledge, 12 January 2004. Middlesex University Discussion Paper No. 26. Available at SSRN: https://ssrn.com/abstract=658202
20. Lee, K.-P.: Design methods for cross-cultural collaborative design project. In: Proceedings of Design Research Society International Conference. Futureground. Monash University, Melbourne Leedy (2004)
21. Spencer-Oatey, H. (ed.): Culturally Speaking: Managing Rapport Through Talk Across Cultures. A&C Black, London (2004)
22. Moalosi, R., Popovic, V., Hickling-Hudson, A.: Culture-orientated product design. Int. J. Technol. Des. Educ. 20(2), 175–190 (2010)
23. Weinberg, G.: The Beatbug - evolution of a musical controller. Digit. Creat. 19(1), 3–18 (2008)

24. Weinberg, G.: Interconnected musical networks: toward a theoretical framework. Comput. Music J. **29**(2), 23–39 (2005)
25. Sheridan, J.G., Bryan-Kinns, N.: Designing for performative tangible interaction. Int. J. Arts Technol. **1**(3–4), 288–308 (2008)
26. Nakanishi, Y., Matsumura, S., Arakawa, C.: BOMB – Beat Of Magic Box –: stand-alone synthesizer using wireless synchronization system for musical session and performance. Gesture **5**, 6 (2014)
27. Wang, W., Bryan-Kinns, N., Ji, T.: Using community engagement to drive co-creation in rural China (2016)
28. https://www.arduino.cc
29. Norman, D.A.: Aordance, conventions, and design. Interactions **6**(3), 38–43 (1999)

RETRACTED CHAPTER: Design for Meaningful Materials Experience: A Case Study About Designing Materials with Rice and Sea-Salt

Liang Yin[1,2(✉)], Ziyu Zhou[1], and Hang Cheng[2]

[1] Politecnico di Milano, Via Durando 38a, Milan, Italy
liang.yin@polimi.it, ziyu.zhou@mail.polimi.it
[2] Jiangnan University, No. 1800, Lihu Road, Binhu District,
Wuxi, Jiangsu Province, China
chenghangchloe@gmail.com

Abstract. Material could elicit meaningful user experiences in and beyond its utilitarian assessment. For designers, they are required to qualify the material not only for what it is, but also for what it expresses to, what it elicits from, and what it guide people to do. To find out the answer, designers need to guide the development of materials by experiential goals. In this paper, we will first introduce material experience as our theory foundation and explain the importance of meaning contribution for materials. In the design phase, we are following an innovative design practice with natural materials to create experience. The method we apply is Material Driven Design (MDD) which could facilitate designing for material experiences. In the end, we will analyze how materials experience be generated through innovative design practices.

Keywords: Materials experience · Meaning of materials · Material driven design

1 Instruction

Materials of artifacts always attract people's initial attention. In the past, we tend to discuss materials based on fabrication, application, and appreciation which dealing with the reception from users (Doordan 2003). Now we have a broader sense that corresponds with the experiences we have with the materials embodied in the artifacts around us. It refers to the mix of sensory appreciations, meanings, feelings, and thoughts that we have toward particular material (Karana et al. 2015).

Materials can not only shape products but also elicit user experiences (Karana et al. 2014) at sensorial, interpretative, affective, and performative level (Giaccardi and Karana 2015). The concept of 'materials experience' shows us that in the material driven design project, user experience could be an expected outcome. How to design for experiences with and for a particular material and how materials are expected to shape and affect the overall user experience seem to become a new research task for designers.

The erratum to this chapter is available at https://doi.org/10.1007/978-3-319-57931-3_61

In this paper, we will follow the Materials Experiences theories and Material Driven Design (MDD) Method developed by Karana to present our design process with Full-natural Sea Salt named Melach, which is developed within the course of Designing Materials Experiences aa.2016/2017 by Valentina Rognoli with Camilo Ayala and Stefano Parisi. Then we will apply MDD to design meaningful experience with these materials.

2   Materials Experience

Materials are sensorial abundant in our daily life. If we want to look at materials from an experiential perspective, it is to establish material interactions occurring through our senses. Also, research found that according to cultures, individuals and different contexts of use, the interactions between materials and users are modulated a time (Karana et al. 2015).

Although we experience materials every day, the concept of materials experience has taken a long time to be in front of us. In 20th century, Manzini (1986) emphasized that although new materials were characterized by their functionality, designers need to understand material's potential applications, performance and ultimate effects on users give rise to materials experiences. Then, Ashby and Johnson (2009) revealed the importance of the aesthetic experience of materials for a proper materials selection in product design. They added "aesthetic" attribute of materials to the material properties list for designers.

Finally, Karana (2014) defined 'Material Experience' as a phrase that acknowledges the experience people have with and through materials and it involves four levels: sensorial, interpretive, affective and performative.

2.1   Materials Experience Generation

Materials experience at sensory level has been long discussed, Zuo (2011) built up a database to find the certain relationship between physical performance of materials and emotional reaction. In recent years, the importance of people and their activities are at a premium. Giaccardi and Karana (2015) indicated the dynamic relationship between materials, people and practices, then they built up a tri-nominal logit model of material experience (see Fig. 1). In their theory, 'practices' are considered as situated 'ways of doing' that unfold and become assimilated into an ongoing set of everyday performances.

2.2   Four Levels of Materials Experience

In the original description of Karana et al. (2008), materials experience consists of three experiential components: 1. aesthetic or exactly say, sensorial experience which is like cold feeling, smooth and so on, 2. experience of meaning which more related to the semantical aspect of materials, and 3. emotional experience which elicit certain emotional reaction like surprised or happy. Giaccardi and Karana (2015) extended the original definition of 'materials experience' by adding another experiential component on a performative level. The performative materials experience is generated from sensorial perceptions, ascribed meanings and emotions which all affect us to respond differently to the embodiment of a material. The performances we establish around

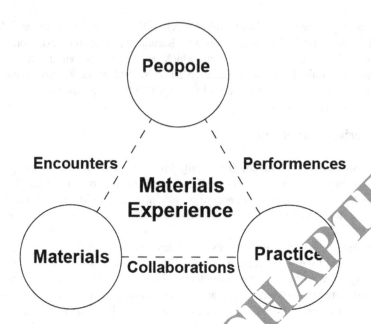

Fig. 1. The framework of material experience (Giaccardi and Karana 2015)

material objects are significantly influenced by such perceptions, meanings and affects. Furthermore, the unfolding of performance into unique and peculiar ways of doing, and their assimilation into practices, are both mediated and affected by the material character of such performances.

Karana et al. (2015) then emphasized that a comprehensive definition of 'materials experience' should acknowledge the active role of materials not only in shaping our internal dialogues with artifacts, but also in shaping ways of doing and practices. Accordingly, they defined four levels of materials experience as: sensorial, interpretative, affective, and performative.

2.3   Meaning of Materials in Materials Experience

Meaning has been taken as the relation of signs to users. The meaning of a product is constructed based on the relations between its form, function, color and all the features that compose the product (Krippendorff and Butter 1984).

Materials contain various meanings in products. Semantic functions of materials in product appraisals has been widely discussed, and the effectiveness in transferring meanings is explored, too. Karana (2009) claimed that the meanings of materials usually depends on four aspects: the type of meaning, the type of material, the product in which the material is embodied, how the product is used and user background. Designers usually attribute meanings to materials according to the characteristics of a situational whole in which certain materials are experienced. This attribution happens as an outcome of a dynamic action between the user and the material embodied in an artifact. When a user with his or her particular prior experiences comes into visual or physical contact with the material of an artifact, appraises that material–artifact combination, and attributes meaning to it.

In materials experience, in addition to certain associative descriptions from users, it usually requires retrieval from memory and past experiences which can also express particular qualities of materials, such as toy-like, human-like. These descriptions are commonly used in material appraisals and behave like expressive characteristics.

Accordingly, meanings of materials consist of semantic and expressive associative characteristics which are used for defining the qualities of materials. In conclusion, meanings of materials are what we think about materials, what kind of values we attribute after the initial sensorial input in a particular context (Karana 2009) and material meanings are highly intertwined, subjective, time- and context-dependent attributes.

3 Design Meaningful Materials Experience Through MDD

How to design for experiences with and for a particular material need to be supported by a distinguished approach which is experience-oriented perspective. Material Driven Design (Karana et al. 2015) is such a method to facilitate design processes for material experience in which materials are the main driver. It is made up by 4 main action steps (see in Fig. 2) presented in a sequential manner as: (1 understanding the material:

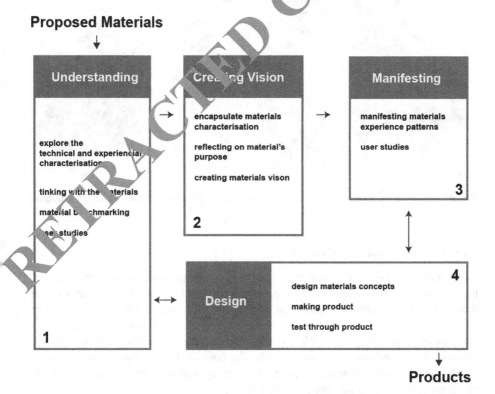

Fig. 2. The process of MDD (Karana et al. 2015)

technical and experiential characterization, (2) creating materials experience vision, (3) manifesting materials experience patterns, (4) designing material/product concepts.

We hope to design meaningful materials experience with sea-salt and rice according to this method. We choose sea-salt and rice because they are full natural resources with plastically and natural texture. On the other hand, as we use these materials on our daily life, it is easy to understand its physical and technical characters. As these materials seem hard to link to settled meanings, we need to define application areas through exploring user experiences, identities for materials, then we will have opportunities to bring new meanings to materials.

According to the material-centered interaction design theory (Wiberg 2014), we need to know which the material is approached from the perspective of the user, material properties and character and how our materials be appraised within a composition. So, we made some samples (see in Fig. 3) which allow us to make forth and back thinking about the detail of the materials. After these work, our group members had a common understanding about materials.

Fig. 3. Materials made by sea-salt and rice, made by Ziyu Zhou, Dajana Grubisic, Nastaran Nikaein

3.1   Understanding the Material

MED method consists of several steps with the first named understanding the material that includes an extensive study of the material, with an emphasis on the experience that derives from hands-on exploration. During this step, we gained an opportunity to have a deep understanding about the material and characterized it technically and experientially in order to be able to recognize its unique qualities and limitations, improve the manufacturing process, define the position of the material among other similar ones, discover potential application areas as well as to explore the meanings, emotions and reactions that the material may elicit.

This step involved three concurrent activities of equal importance: (1) tinkering with the material during and after the process of production (see in Fig. 4), (2) material benchmarking studies (see in Fig. 5), (3) user studies. With a purpose of understanding and improving the material itself as well as the manufacturing process and the relationship between the variables of the process and expressive- sensorial properties of the material, modifications were made during process. Different kinds of binders were tested (both natural and those that are not), other materials were included, salts of various colors and sizes were introduced as well as the molds in several sizes and made of different materials.

Fig. 4. Tinkering with the materials to understand the technical characterization

	Melach — DIY material, Different kinds of salt, sand, rice	Roberto Tweraser — Sea salt with a small percentage of synthetic binder	SALGHT Pro — By Think Forward, Silicom combined with resin	The Home Project — Crystallized salt	The Home Project — Rock salt (Halite)	The Salt Project — By Eric Geboers, Sea salt with algae starch	Salt rings — By Wenhui Li, Salt crystals, Fimo, Resin, Acrylic Paint
CHARACTERISTICS OF THE MATERIAL:							
Roughness	●		●	○	●	●	●
Irregularity	●	●	○	●	●	●	○
Natural colour	●	●	○	●	●	●	
Hardness	●	●	●	●	●	●	●
Resistance to compressive forces		●	●	●	●	●	●
Resistance to tensile forces	●		○	○	●	◐	○
Density	●	●	●	●	●	●	●
Flexibility		○	○		◐	◐	
Waterproofness	●	●	●	●	●	◐	●
Hygroscopicity	●	○	○	○	●	●	○
Translucency	○	●	●	○	●	●	○
Opacity	●	●	●	●	●	●	○
...bility	●	●	●	●	●	●	●
No...ness	●	○	○	●	●	●	○
Shaping	handmade and/or moulded	moulded	moulded	Crochet technique	handmade	moulded	Salt crystals were grown on media
APPLICATIONS:							
Architecture/building						●	
Product design		●	●	●	●	●	
Jewellery design							●
EMPHASIZED VALUES:							
	Handmade craftsmanship; the use of the local resources; sustainability	The use of the local resources; interpretation of typical local industries and products	authentic, engaged, sustainable material culture; value of tradition and the craftmanship	authentic, engaged, sustainable material culture; a return to the craft	The use of locally available resources; create architecture without producing waste (closed ecosystem)	Spontaneous growing process (nature creates its own original products); personalized products;	

Fig. 5. Material benchmarking for the salt-based composites made by Ziyu Zhou, Dajana Grubisic and Nastaran Nikaein (○ Low   ◐ Medium   ● High)

When the white rice was defined as appropriate binder, various ways of cooking were analyzed with the intention to determine the density and temperature that is most adequate for the process of material production. In addition, temperatures and moisture changes are also taken into consideration as the factors important for the duration of drying and the final outcome of the process.

3.2   Creating Materials Experience Vision

For the purpose of articulating design intent of materials, we tend to build up the Materials Experience Vision which expresses how designers envisions the role of materials in creating functional performance and unique user experience when embodied in a product.

We clustered our findings and then mapped them so that we could see how they complemented each other, and how together they formed new insights relevant to the application context (see Appendix A). Based on these structed findings, we got our final vision: "We appreciate the value of little things. These little things are often exactly what we appreciate most and remember the longest. That is why we desire that the user experiences a unique and long-lasting emotional bonding with the material due to the fact that it is identified and accepted as delicate and precious, in the same way our memories, emotions and relationships are."

3.3   Manifesting Materials Experience Patterns

In this stage, we tended to understand how other people experience or interact with materials. We first sought examples of the envisioned interaction from daily life, existing products and existing materials. In the following brainstorming session, we posted our feelings related to our imagination on a big map, then identified two meanings that evoke the aimed interaction as 'delicate' and 'precious' (see in Fig. 6).

In order to find patterns to evoke the aimed meanings, we adopted another supportive method named Meaning Driven Materials Selection (MDMS) which familiarizes the designers with key aspects (such as shape, user, manufacturing processes, etc.) playing an important role in attributing meanings to materials (see in Fig. 7). More important, this method supports designers in understanding other people's understanding of preferential meanings.

With MDMS, we were approached to participate in a study with the following three tasks:

(1) select a material according to your feeling (smart, sharp, modern, etc.)
(2) make an imagination of the material
(3) explain the choice and evaluate the material against a set of specially devised sensorial scales.

After analyzing the provided images and descriptions from the participants, we evaluated the result qualitatively and quantitatively.

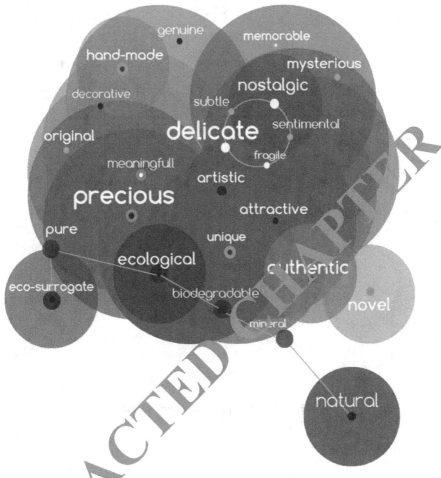

Fig. 6. Brainstorming to identify meanings

3.4 Creating Materials Concepts

In the final stage, we integrate all our findings into a concept generation phase. In the beginning, we created several material samples by incorporating the outcome of Step 3. Then, six promising samples that differed from each other with regard to technical properties and experiential qualities were selected to be used in the product concept creation.

In the following design process, we hope to design a product with the given material concept by using the given technical data sheet and materials experience patterns; thus, the ultimate product was expected to express the meanings 'precious' and 'delicate'. In order to give these meanings to materials, we generated several product concepts in the brainstorm phase then get some ideas of product design.

Then we further analyzed the ideas against their fit to the intended Materials Experience Vision; their feasibility which involving cost and production and their technical performance to make sure that the material can fulfill the required function. In

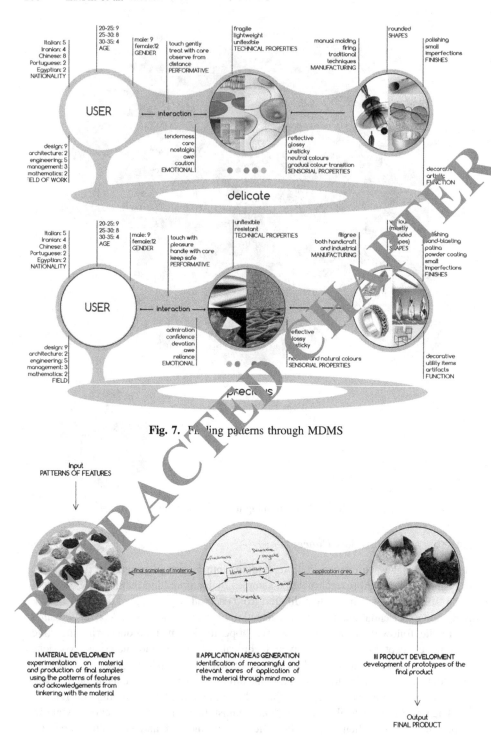

Fig. 7. Finding patterns through MDMS

Fig. 8. Designing product concept

the product design phase, we found that what has emerged through the previous steps of the MDD Method is the fact that the most widely embraced feature of the material is its ability to reflect light. In addition, it is suitable to be applied design of decorative objects and accessory, products that are appreciated their delicacy and beauty. Therefore, candle holders as a part of the home accessory (see in Fig. 8) seem to be the most adequate solution.

4 Conclusion

On the basis of this research, we know that materials experience could be designed through meaning contribution while the meaning of materials should be guided under an experience-oriented perspective. Designing meaningful materials experiences requires designers to know not only the aesthetics, functional and emotional aspects, but also to understand the effects of various design aspects, user characteristics and context of use on the resulting materials experience.

MDD works well in our project as we have a deep understanding of current situation (how the material is appraised by intended user, how it is experienced on 4 levels, etc.) and fully analyzing and interpreting our research outcomes. We also realized that in the patterns manifesting process, co-design with users could facilitate concept generation as the whole materials experience design is a forth and back thinking process which user participation is needs in both four steps.

A Appendix

LITTLE THINGS
Belief in the value and presciousness of little things in details, in undertone and in discovery. It is still possible to improve through little things. These little things often exactly what we appreciate and remember the longest.

EMPHATIC DESIGN
he definition of empathy is the ability to be are of, understanding of and sensitive other person's feelings and thoughts without having had the same experience. As human-centered designers, we consciously work to understand the experience of our clients and their customers. These insights inform and inspire our designs.

UNIQUE PRODUCTS
Recent years have seen a growing trend toward unique products that contribute to individual expression or a personal sense of authenticity. Numerous studies have shown that these products may only improve customers satisfaction.

LANGUAGE OF MATERIALS
Nonverbal communication between people is communication through sending and receiving wordless clues. In the same way materials communicate with people by providing visual cues, proxemics, haptics, chronemics or oculesics cues.

THE POWER OF PRECONSCIOUS AND UNCONSCIOUS
The preconscious contains thoughts and feelings that a person is not currently aware of, but which can easily be brought to consciousness. The preconscious is like a mental waiting room, in which thoughts remain until they 'succeed in attracting the eye of the conscious' (Freud, 1924).
Our feelings, motives and decisions are actually powerfully influenced by our past experiences, and stored in the unconscious. The unconscious mind comprises mental processes that are inaccessible to consciousness but that influence judgements, feelings, or behavior.

SYMBOLISM OF VALUABLE MINERALS
Gemstones have played various roles in the myths and legends of human cultures throughout history. Some tell a story or are believed to have special power but all of them share a commonality. Each gemstone is unique with a special color with their history. Gemstones come in every color of the rainbow and are gathered from all corners of the world, with each colored gemstone possessing a unique creation of beautiful color. Some gemstones have been treasured since before history began and others were only discovery recently.

MATERIAL DRIVEN DESIGN
The approach through which the product design intends to comfort to to to elicit long-lasting and unique user experience.

TASTE OF THE SEA
The salty taste is very distinguishable and possesses the ability to evoke memories on the sea. This kind of associations may only have the positive effect on the ultimate experience with the product due to the fact that pleasant environmental experiences are often long-lasting in subconsciousness.

SALT: INTORWOVEN INTO ALL CULTURES
As far back as 6050 BC, salt has been an important and integral part of the world's history, as it has been interwoven into countless civilizations. Undeniably, the history of salt is both broad and unique, leaving its indelible mark in cultures across the globe. Salt was of crucial importance economically but it has also played a vital part in religious ritual in many cultures, symbolizing purity. In short, the white granular substance we know today as "salt" has been essential to all life, especially with respect to its long and varied history.

SENSORY MEMORY
Like all other beings, humans are also bound to explore the world by using their senses, independently or in conjuction in order to obtain knowledge about the world that surrounds them. Since their early childhood, people collect these sensorial memories and the associations they carry strongly affect the way they interpret new things and the relationships with people or objects.

References

Ashby, M., Johnson, K.: Materials and Design. The Art and Science of Material Selection in Product Design, 2nd edn. Butterworth-Heinemann Elsevier, Oxford (2009)

Doordan, D.P.: On materials. Des. Issues **19**(4), 3–8 (2003)

Karana, E.: Meanings of materials. Ph.d. dissertation, Delft University of Technology (2009)

Giaccardi, E., Karana, E.: Foundations of materials experience: an approach for HCI. In: Proceedings of the 33rd Annual ACM Conference on Human Factors in Computing Systems, pp. 2447–2456. ACM (2015)

Karana, E., Pedgley, O., Rognoli, V.: Materials Experience: Fundamentals of Materials and Design. Butterworth-Heinemann, Oxford (2013)

Karana, E., Pedgley, O., Rognoli, V.: Materials Experience: Fundamentals of Materials and Design. Butterworth-Heinemann, Oxford (2014)

Karana, E., Pedgley, O., Rognoli, V.: On materials experience. Des. Issues **31**(3), 16–27 (2015a)

Karana, E., Hekkert, P., Kandachar, P.: Materials experience: descriptive categories in material appraisals. In: Proceedings of the Conference on Tools and Methods in Competitive Engineering, pp. 399–412. Delft University of Technology, Delft (2008)

Karana, E., Hekkert, P.: User-material-product interrelationships in attributing meanings. Int. J. Des. **4**(3), 43–52 (2010)

Karana, E., Hekkert, P., Kandachar, P.: Meanings of materials through sensorial properties and manufacturing processes. Mater. Des. **30**(7), 2778–2784 (2009)

Karana, E., Barati, B., Rognoli, V., et al.: Material driven design (MDD): a method to design for material experiences. Int. J. Des. **19**(2), 35–54 (2015b)

Krippendorff, K., Butter, R.: Product semantics: exploring the symbolic qualities of form. J. Indus. Des. Soc. Am. **3**, 4–9 (1984)

Manzini, E., Cau, P.: The Material of Invention. MIT Press, Cambridge (1989)

Rognoli, V., Bianchini, M., Maffei, S., et al.: DIY materials. Mater. Des. **86**, 692–702 (2015)

Wiberg, M.: Methodology for materiality: interaction design research through a material lens. Pers. Ubiquit. Comput. **18**(3), 625–636 (2014)

Zuo, H.F.: Sensory Perception of Materials in Product Design. The Economic Daily Press, Beijing (2011)

Research on the Design of Bicycle Service System in Colleges and Universities Based on Contact Mining

Yi-qian Zhao[✉] and Ya-jun Li

School of Design Art and Media, Nanjing University of Science and Technology,
Nanjing, Jiangsu, People's Republic of China
1355256445@qq.com

Abstract. University campus is a place where bicycles are used a lot and there are many people choosing bicycle as their vehicle, with the increase of users, the vast volume of bicycles also brings high pressure on the entire campus bicycle service system and causes many problems, the existing service system could no longer meet users' demands. This thesis targets the **university bicycle service system** as the research target, adopts the **service design theory** as the fundamental support, takes **contact** as the entry point, integrates **service design method** to develop research, and establishes service system **process chain network** (PCN) model to supplement and improve research results.

Firstly, determine the main users of service system, so as to research its demands from both qualitative and quantitative levels, qualitative level is to use Personas to extract the characteristics of main users, use the method of stakeholder to excavate other users with relevant interests with the main users, integrate the key character map method to determine the interactive relationship between the main users and other users, and extract user demands. Quantitative level is to, based on the research result on qualitative level, further determine the main demands of main users through the questionnaire survey and data statistic analysis on the demand level of main users. The demands of main users shall be concluded based on the comprehensive summarization of the two levels above.

Secondly, systematically use the interview method, situational approach and role playing method to analyze the process of main users in using the existing service system and excavate the contact. So as to conclude the problems in existing system from both qualitative and quantitative levels, qualitative level is to summarize the corresponding problems of each contact through field investigation and from contact perspective. Quantitative level is based on qualitative level, it determines the relatively prominent problems in the existing service system through questionnaire investigation and data statistic analysis on the level of prominent questions, and provides foundation for subsequent improvement and model establishment.

Finally, integrate the demands of main users and improvement of problems in exiting service system, use the process chain network (PCN) tool method to position the contact in the process chain, establish the process chain network (PCN) in university bicycle service system, further determine the interactive relationship between main users and service providers in contact.

© Springer International Publishing AG 2017
P.-L.P. Rau (Ed.): CCD 2017, LNCS 10281, pp. 269–287, 2017.
DOI: 10.1007/978-3-319-57931-3_22

Keywords: Bicycle service system · User demand · Contact mining · Excavation · Process chain network model

1   Introduction

Currently, with the development of service design, its application field becomes wider [1], in the field of campus transportation, the university bicycle service system is a set of brand-new campus bicycle service system with users as the center, service design method as the research means and with multiple functions in one formed through research and optimization of service process [2].

2   User Demand Research of University Bicycle Service System

The users of university bicycle service system can be classified into main users and other users with interest relevance, this user demand research mainly targets the main users.

Firstly, determine the main users of service system, through large volume of literature summarization and research. The university students account for 60.32% of the total users, university teachers account for 22.59% of the total users, university staff account for 11.92% of the total users, these three types of users account for majority of the users of service system. So it is determined that the main users in this research include university students, university teachers and university staff, so as to have in-depth research on the demands of main users from both qualitative and quantitative levels.

2.1   Qualitative Research of User Demand

The demands of main users shall be analyzed through three steps, including extraction of user characteristics, stakeholder analysis and research on the interactive relationship between users and stakeholders.

2.1.1   Extraction of User Characteristics

Use the personas method in service design to summarize the basic characteristics, psychological characteristics and behavioral characteristics of main users [3]. Establish personas model cards, including the three types of groups, namely university students, university teachers and university staff, in which the personas model card of university students is as follows (Table 1):

The personas model card of university teachers and university staff shall be formed in same method.

Table 1. Personas model card of university students

	University students model A	University students model B	University students model C
Basic			
Name	Li Siyuan	Wang Jia	Liu Yifan
Age	24	22	26
Gender	Male	Female	Male
Occupation	Master	Bachelor	Doctor
Psychological			
Attitude	Irritable	Quiet	Modest and gentle
Hobby	Football, riding	Shopping, sleeping	Reading, watching
Lifestyle	Taking classes+resting +reading literature +working on research programs	Taking classes +reviewing+resting +travelling	Going to teaching and research office +participating in academic meetings +working on research programs
Character	Conforming	Amiable	Modest and introverted
Behavioral habits			
Vehicles chosen by users in campus	Bicycle (they would purchase relatively high-end bicycles, and they are bicycle fans)	Walking, not good at sports, like watching K-drama and chasing stars	Bicycle (they would purchase ordinary bicycles, and mainly use them in campus as travel tools for its convenience)
Attitude of users towards the bicycle service system in university campus	The service system need improvement, especially in the aspect of bicycle deposit and pickup aspects, which need to be both convenient and safe	There could be such a system that provides option of public bicycles to replace walking	The service system, needs to adjust targeting on parking lot to facilitate parking of vehicles

2.1.2 Analysis of Stakeholders of Users

With main users as the core, use the stakeholder method to have in-depth excavation of the other users with relevant interests in the university bicycle service system, such as decision maker level(Personnel of university leadership bodies), contractor manufacturers level(Manufacturing partners), design and manufacturing level (System programmers) and operation and management level (Management and maintenance personnel).

2.1.3 Research on the Relationship Between Users and Stakeholders

Summarize and classify the other users in the service system with relevant interest with the main users [4]. Adopt the key character map method to have detailed research on the interactive relationship between main users and stakeholders, which is as follows (Fig. 1):

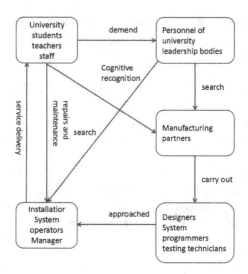

Fig. 1. Interactive relationship between users and stakeholders

Firstly, the main users have demands for establishment of campus bicycle service system, so as to interact with the decision making level (personnel of university leadership bodies), then the personnel of university leadership bodies decide to interact with contracting manufacturers (manufacturing partners) for establishment of service system, determine contracting manufacturers by integrating the brand awareness degree of manufacturer brands, after entering the design and manufacturing stage, the manufacturers would interact with the designers, system programmers, system testing technicians and installing personnel for establishment of service system. The manufacturers would interact with the operators, management and maintenance personnel. When users use the service system, the main users would have bilateral interaction with the operation and management personnel, meaning finding the related personnel for maintenance when there is any problem in the system, while the operation and management personnel provide users with service.

Through extraction of user characteristics, analysis of stakeholders and the interactive relationship between main users and stakeholders, the concluded demands of main users include: establishment of intelligent campus bicycle service system and lease service system, optimization of bicycle extraction and pickup procedure, marking of bicycle parking areas, adding of the related anti-theft and charging facilities of bicycles, improvement of bicycle parking order and management system, integration between bicycle parking areas and campus environment, timely updating and maintenance of service system, interaction and feedback with users and service providers.

2.2   Quantitative Research on User Demand

Based on the research on qualitative level, determine the main demands of main users on quantitative level through the survey and data analysis on the demand degree level of main users.

2.2.1 Research Method of User Demand

The method adopted in this part is the questionnaire survey and data processing method, the questionnaire includes 5 parts and contains 15 questions regarding user demands in service system. The first part is basic user information. The second part is the survey and analysis about users' demand in bicycle service system model. The third part is the survey and analysis on users' demand for the internal service process factors of bicycle service system. The fourth part is the survey and analysis on users' demand for the integration between the management of bicycle service system and campus ecological environment. The fifth part is the survey and analysis on users' general demand in the service system, the high-frequency words from the 6 words describing the user demands in the service system shall be extracted as the main user demands.

The level-by-level survey on the demand degree of main users in the campus bicycle service system is in order to have quantitative analysis on user demand and extract its main demands. There are 6 different demand degree levels designed for each question in the questionnaire, level 1 means the weakest demand degree, level 6 means the strongest demand degree, so on so forth.

2.2.2 Hierarchical Analysis of User Demand Degree

This questionnaire survey issued 300 questionnaires and successfully withdrew 271 questionnaires, after further sorting and researching of the questionnaires, there were 235 final valid questionnaires.

Analyzing through the survey result of the demand of bicycle service system model in second part of the questionnaire, mean value was adopted on the demand degree level of each questionnaire in this part, the biased chart of demand degree level is drawn as follows (Fig. 2):

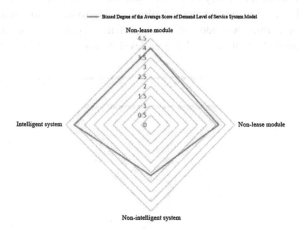

Fig. 2. Biased degree of the average score of demand level of service system model

The main users have relatively high demand for the service system that has designed and established the intelligent setting and included two modules of leased and non-leased bicycle.

Analyzing through the survey result of the demand for internal service process factors of bicycle service system model in third part of the questionnaire, mean value was adopted on the demand degree level of each questionnaire in this part, the biased chart of demand degree level is drawn as follows (Fig. 3):

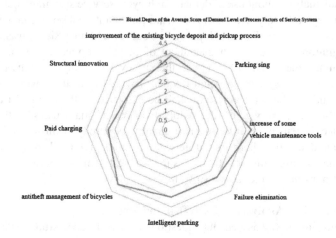

Fig. 3. Biased degree of the average score of demand level of process factors of service system

The main users have relatively higher demand for the three aspects in the process factors of system service, including improvement of the existing bicycle deposit and pickup process, proper increase of some simple vehicle maintenance tools and antitheft management of bicycles.

Analyzing through the survey of the demand for integration between management of bicycle service system and campus ecological environment in fourth part of the questionnaire, mean value was adopted on the demand degree level of each question in this part, the biased chart of demand degree level is drawn as follows (Fig. 4):

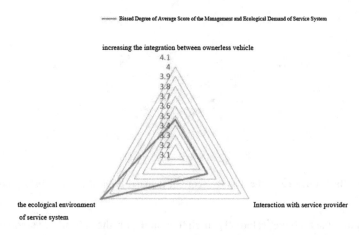

Fig. 4. Biased degree of average score of the management and ecological demand of service system

The main users have relatively high demand for increasing the integration between ownerless vehicle and the ecological environment of service system.

The main users extracted high-frequency words from the 6 words describing user demand of service system as the main user demands, the biased chart is drawn as follows based on the statistics of the quantity of selected words (Fig. 5):

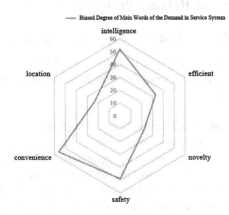

Fig. 5. Biased degree of main words of the demand in service system

The highest-frequency words describing the demands of main users in service system include convenience, intelligence and safety.

2.3   Conclusion of User Demand

List the demands of main users on qualitative level and excavate its main demands on quantitative level, which are summarized as follows (Table 2):

Table 2. Conclusion of main demands of main users in the service system

Entire system	Establishment of intelligent bicycle service system
Internal factors	The service system includes two modules of leased bicycle and non-leased bicycle
	Improvement and optimization of bicycle deposit and pickup process of system
	Adding of simple bicycle maintenance tools into the system
	Adding of bicycle antitheft facilities into the system
Management and ecology	Increase of ownerless vehicle management
	Integration between service system and campus environment
Summarization of words	High-frequency words: Convenience; Intelligence; Safety

Comprehensively and deeply excavate the demands of main users, and select its main demands, so as to provide clear direction for the establishment and innovation of subsequent system model.

3 Analysis of Contact Excavation of University Bicycle Service System and Related Problems

3.1 User Behavior Process Analysis and Contact Excavation

The service system researched this time includes manual service system and intelligent service system, and the intelligent service system includes the intelligent non-lease type and intelligent lease type.

3.1.1 Contact Excavation of Manual Service System

Manual service system is the most common form in the existing university bicycle service system, the entire service system has relatively low automation degree, which adopts manual deposit, pickup and locking of bicycles, there is no intelligent and automatic technology [5]. It is to identify the information of behavioral process of manual service system and excavate contact from it. The main users' use of manual service system has three scenarios: deposit of bicycle, pickup of bicycle and use or repairs of bicycle. Contacts are excavated as follows with the scenario of depositing bicycle as an example (Fig. 6):

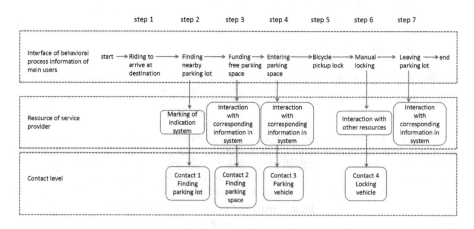

Fig. 6. Contact excavation in the bicycle depositing process of manual service system

The method and process of excavation contact of the scenario of picking up bicycles and repairing bicycles shall be done in the same manner. Finally the contacts excavated in the behavioral process information of the main users in using of the existing university bicycle manual service system are concluded as follows (Table 3):

Table 3. Contact excavation in the process of manual service system

Contact excavation in the process of existing university bicycle manual service system				
Scenario deposit of bicycle	Contact 1	Contact 2	Contact 3	Contact 4
	Finding parking lot	Finding parking space	Parking vehicle	Locking vehicle
Scenario picking up bicycles	Contact 5	Contact 6	Contact 7	Contact 8
	Entering parking lot	Finding bicycle	Opening lock	Picking up bicycle
Scenario use and repairs of bicycle	Contact 9	Contact 10	Contact 11	Contact 12
	Finding repairing point	Contact with repairing personnel	Inspection and repairs	Expense payment

3.1.2   Contact Excavation of Intelligent Service System

Compared with manual service system, the intelligent service system has higher intelligent degree and automatic degree, and mostly in the model without specific management personnel [6]. Intelligent service system can be classified into lease type and non-lease type. The main users' use of intelligent non-lease-type service system includes three scenarios: deposit of bicycle, pickup of bicycle and use or repairs of bicycle. Referring to the contact excavation method of manual service system, the contacts of intelligent non-lease-type service system are excavated as follows (Table 4):

Table 4. Contact excavation in the process of intelligent non-lease-type service system

Contact excavation in the process of existing university bicycle intelligent non-lease-type system				
Scenario deposit of bicycle	Contact 1	Contact 2	Contact 3	Contact 4
	Login system platform	Positioning	Finding parking lot	Finding chosen parking space
	Contact 5	Contact 6	Contact 7	
	Certification and identification	Parking and locking of bicycles	Receiving parking information	
Scenario picking up bicycle	Contact 8	Contact 9	Contact 10	Contact 11
	Login system platform	Inquiring parking information	Choosing parking number	Information verification
	Contact 12			
	Unlocking and picking up bicycle			
Scenario use and repairs of bicycle	Contact 13	Contact 14	Contact 15	Contact 16
	Login system platform	Inquiring repairs information	Selecting repairs point	Contacting repairs personnel
	Contact 17	Contact 18		
	Inspecting and repairing	Paying repairs fee		

The main users' use of intelligent non-lease-type service system includes three scenarios: lease of bicycle, return of bicycle and report and repairs of bicycle. Referring to the contact excavation method of manual service system, the contacts of intelligent lease-type service system are excavated as follows (Table 5):

Table 5. Contact excavation in the process of intelligent lease-type service system

Contact excavation in the process of existing university bicycle intelligent lease-type system			
Scenario lease of bicycle	Contact 1	Contact 2	Contact 3	Contact 4
	Installing system platform	Information binding	Charging	Scanning for certification
	Contact 5	Contact 6		
	Unlocking	Opening bicycle for using		
Scenario return of bicycle	Contact 7	Contact 8	Contact 9	Contact 10
	Parking	Locking bicycle	Returning bicycle on system	Fee payment
Scenario report and repairs of bicycle	Contact 11	Contact 12	Contact 13	Contact 14
	Selecting failure and report it for repairs	Parking bicycle	Locking bicycle	Returning bicycle on system
	Contact 15			
	Repairing personnel repairs bicycle			

3.2   Analysis of Problems in Existing University Bicycle Service System

The analysis of problems in existing university bicycle service system shall be developed on both qualitative and quantitative levels, qualitative level is to deeply analyze, through field survey and from contact perspective, the corresponding problems of each contact in the using process of main users of existing service system. Quantitative level is to, based on the problems summarized on qualitative level, use questionnaire survey and data analysis to analyze and determine the relatively prominent problems in the existing system. The main problems of existing service system shall be concluded and summarized based on the two above, and provide basis for the establishment of service system model.

3.2.1   Qualitative Analysis of Problems in Service System

The problems existing in the current service system shall be summarized through field investigation and from contact perspective, the objects of which include manual service system, intelligent non-lease-type service system and intelligent lease-type service system. Firstly, the problems involved in deposit of bicycle scenario of manual service system such as: lack of intelligent and automatic technology, unreasonable layout and planning, low efficiency in interaction between users and system, lack of effective signs at parking space, chaotic parking of bicycles, inconvenient deposit and pickup of bicycle, mutual occupation of parking space with motored vehicles, lack of management of ownerless bicycles, lack of falling-proof, antitheft facilities of bicycles and difficulty in identify bicycles.

The problem analysis method in the intelligent non-lease-type service system and intelligent lease-type service system shall be done in the same manner as that of manual service system.

3.2.2 Quantitative Analysis of Problems in Service System

The method adopts in this part is the questionnaire survey and data processing method, the questionnaire includes 3 parts and contains 15 problems existing in service system. The first part is mainly the basic overview information of the users participating in the survey. The second part is the survey and analysis of problems in users' use of entire bicycle service system. The third part is the survey and analysis of internal problems in users' use of bicycle service system.

The adoption of questionnaire survey and data qualitative analysis to determine the prominence hierarchy of problems in existing service system is designed to have quantitative analysis of problems in existing system and extract the main problems. Each problem in questionnaire has 6 different prominence hierarchy, level 1 means the least prominent, level 6 means the most prominent, so on so forth.

In this questionnaire survey, 500 questionnaires were released, 456 questionnaires were successfully withdrawn, after further sorting and research on the questionnaires, the quantity of final valid questionnaires was 420.

Analyzing through the survey result of the problems existing in the entire bicycle service system in second part of the questionnaire, mean value was adopted on the prominence level value of each problem in this part, the biased chart of prominence hierarchy is drawn as follows (Fig. 7):

The main users believed that the prominence hierarchy of the following problems is relatively high, including the lack of intelligent and automatic technology in existing service system, unreasonable layout and planning, and low efficiency in interaction with users and low controllability, meaning that the problems above are relatively prominent.

Analyzing through the survey result of the internal problems existing in the bicycle service system in third part of the questionnaire, mean value was adopted on the prominence level value of each problem in this part, the biased chart of prominence hierarchy is drawn as follows (Fig. 8):

The main users believed that the prominence hierarchy of the following problems is relatively high, including the lack of management of the scrapped, used and idle bicycles, chaotic parking of bicycles in parking lot, inconvenient deposit and pickup of bicycles, lack of falling-proof and antitheft facilities of bicycles and day-to-day bicycle repairing tools, meaning that the problems above are relatively prominent.

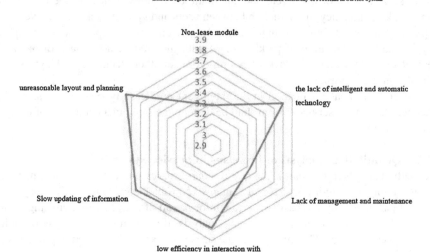

Fig. 7. Biased degree of average score of overall prominence hierarchy of problems in service system

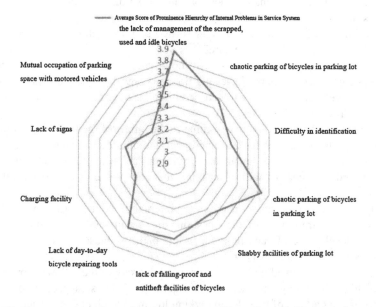

Fig. 8. Average score of prominence hierarchy of internal problems in service system

To sum up, through the research and summarization on both qualitative and quantitative levels, the relatively prominent problems existing in the current university bicycle service system are concluded as follows (Table 6):

Table 6. Conclusion of prominence hierarchy of problems in service system

Entire system	Lack of intelligent and automatic technology
	Unreasonable layout and planning
	Low efficiency in interaction between users and system
Internal factors	Management of scrapped, used and idle bicycles
	Chaotic parking of bicycles
	Inconvenient deposit and pickup of bicycles
	Lack of falling-proof and antitheft facilities of bicycles
	Lack of day-to-day bicycle repairing tools

Based on the analysis and improvement of the main problems in current service system, provide preconditions for the establishment of service system model.

4 Establishment of the Process Chain Network (PCN) Model of University Bicycle Service System

This part firstly describes the design positioning of service system, then defines the concept of process chain network (PCN) and positions contact in process chain, and finally establishes the process chain network (PCN) model of university bicycle service system.

4.1 Design Positioning of Service System

The design positioning of university bicycle service system is to improve based on the demands of main users and the main problems in the current service system. To sum up from the contents above, the main users' main demands include establishment of intelligent campus bicycle service system, contain two modules of leased and non-leased, improve and optimize the bicycle depositing and pickup process, add antitheft facilities and repairing tools of bicycles, and integrate parking lot with environment. The main problems existing in current campus bicycle service system includes lack of intelligent and automatic technology, unreasonable layout and planning of parking lot, low efficiency in the interaction between users and system, problem in the management of the scrapped, used and idle bicycles, chaotic parking of bicycles, inconvenient deposit and pickup of bicycles, lack of falling-proof and antitheft facilities in parking system and day-to-day repairing tools. Integrating the contacts of manual and intelligent service system excavated before, determine and establish the process chain network (PCN) model of university bicycle service system, including intelligent non-lease-type module, intelligent lease-type module, sales and purchase of bicycle module.

4.2 Concept of Process Chain Network (PCN)

Process chain network (PCN) is a network chain composed of multiple processes and steps based on sequence. Process and step involve the entities with effect on resources, like supply chain of product manufacturing, generally process chain would cross multiple entities and connect them together [7]. Each process entity has one process field, this is a collection of processes and steps that are initiated, guided and implemented as well as controlled to certain extent by process entity. Process chain network (PCN) is a tool and method that has strong functions and effects on research on the processes and steps (contacts) of service system [7], such method could effectively analyze and establish the process chain network (PCN) model of service system. The basic concept of process chain network is as follows (Table 7):

Table 7. Composing parts and concepts of process chain network

Composing parts of process chain network	Notes and explanation of concepts
Process chain	Sequence of steps with the same purpose
Entity	The entity that participates in certain process chain and makes decision on certain steps
Certain beneficiary	The entity that participates in process chain and uses certain ability of such process chain to satisfy its demands
General beneficiary	The entity that participates in process chain and obtains general resources (money) to satisfy its needs in other process chains
Process field	A part of process chain controlled by entity
Process area	Area of certain type of step in process field
Direct interaction	Step involving interaction between different people among entities
Agency interaction	Step involving interaction of non-human-type resources (such as technology or information) with another entity
Independent handling	Step unrelated to other entity in process chain network

In the university bicycle service system, entities include service providers and main users, all the process steps (contacts) shall be positioned in the process field of service providers and main users, in which the service providers that provide service to users to possibly obtain general resources (money) shall be defined as general beneficiary, the main users that accept service to meet its own demands shall be defined as certain beneficiary. Process steps (contacts) shall be, based on their own characteristics and properties, positioned in 5 process fields, including independent processing by service provider, agency interaction by service provider, direct interaction, agency interaction by main users, and independent processing by main users, the positioning basis and principle include scale economy benefit, cost, controllability of service process chain, complexity and divergence of process steps (contacts), process efficiency, customization, advantage of agency positioning and interaction strength.

4.3   Positioning of Contacts in Process Chain

University bicycle service system includes three modules, namely intelligent non-lease-type, intelligent-lease-type and sales and purchase of bicycle. Taking the bicycle deposit process in the intelligent non-lease-type module as an example, the process steps (contacts) in the process is positioned as follows based on the positioning principle (Table 8):

The positioning of the process steps (contacts) contained in intelligent lease-type module and sales and purchase of bicycle module in the process chain shall be done in the same manner referred to above.

Table 8. Process area positioning of contacts in bicycle deposit process of intelligent non-lease-type service system

Process steps (contacts) of main users	Judging criteria	Process area positioning
Login system platform	Demand of main users Main problems in existing system Positioning basis and principle of process steps (contacts)	Agency interaction area of main users in process field
Positioning		Agency interaction process area of service provider in process field
Finding parking lot		Agency interaction area of main users in process field
Finding chosen parking space		Agency interaction area of main users in process field
Certification and identification		Agency interaction process area of service provider in process field
Parking and locking of bicycles		Agency interaction process area of service provider in process field
Receiving parking information		Agency interaction process area of service provider in process field

4.4   Establishment of Process Chain Network (PCN) Model of Service System

The resources contained in the independent area of the process field of service provider include: establishment and university campus bicycle service system platform, design and manufacturing of the instruction signs and certification facilities in parking lot, improvement of public facilities in parking lot, marking of rational parking area, establishment of automatic locking pile or structure, provision of simple repairing tools, establishment of repairing points and arrangement of repairing personnel. Service provider shall satisfy users demands and effectively solve the problems in current service system through improvement and provision of resources.

Firstly, establish the process chain network (PCN) model of the intelligent non-lease-type module in service system, the majority of process steps (contacts) are positioned in the agency interaction area of the process field of service provider and main users, which enhances the efficiency of entire service system and degree of customization, and reduces the cost of service provider. The process steps (contacts) of interaction area includes the contact with repairing personnel and payment of repairing fee, etc., by positioning these processes and steps in direct interaction area, it enhances the user interaction strength, meanwhile, users' demands could timely feedback to service provider. So on so forth, the entire service system optimizes the bicycle deposit and pickup process, and enables the use to be more convenient, which is as follows (Fig. 9):

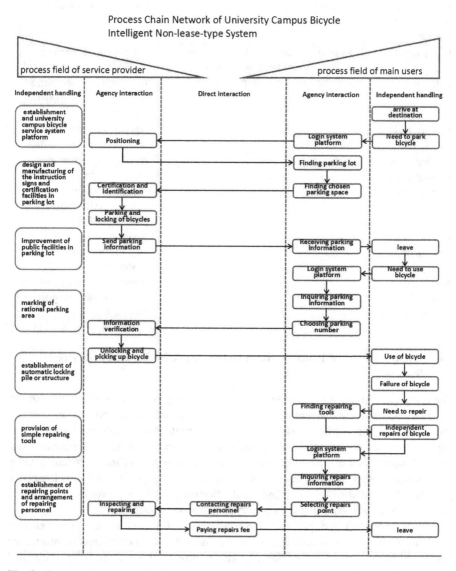

Fig. 9. Process chain network of university campus bicycle intelligent non-lease-type system

Secondly, establish the process chain network (PCN) model of intelligent lease-type module, the majority of process steps (contacts) of lease system are positioned in the agency interaction area of the process field of main users, meaning the adoption of self-help service method to enhance the efficiency of entire service system and reduce the interaction strength of users, when there is any failure in public bicycle, user could report it on the system for repairs and return the bicycle, through the interaction between system platform and service provider, service provider could contact the repairing personnel for repairs, there is no process steps (contacts) in the direct interaction area of the entire process chain, so the using efficiency would be greatly enhanced, which is as follows (Fig. 10):

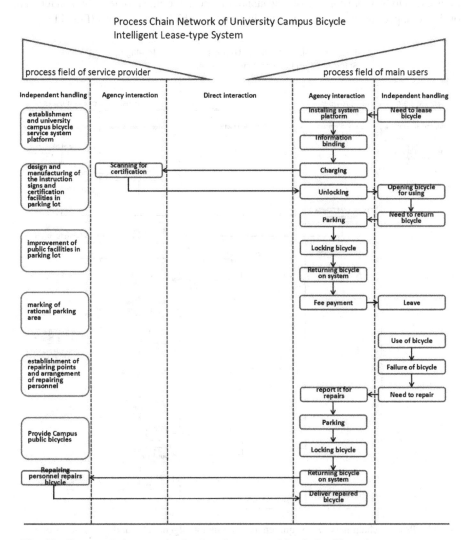

Fig. 10. Process chain network of university campus bicycle intelligent lease-type system

Finally, establish the process chain network (PCN) model of sales and purchase of bicycle module, the majority of process steps (contacts) are positioned in the agency interaction area of the process field of main users, the minority is positioned in the process steps (contacts) of direct interaction area moved to the agency interaction area in order to enhance the efficiency and reduce the user interaction strength, meaning that service provider could certify and supervise the bicycle information marked by main users, such method effectively solves the problem of false bicycle information and enables the entire trading process to be more standard. The process steps (contacts) positioned in direct interaction area include the communication between seller and buyer, meaning that it could timely and accurately obtain information through the two between direct interaction. So on so forth, the entire service system enables the campus bicycle transaction to be more convenient and standard, and solves the problems in management of the scrapped, used and idle bicycles in campus, which is as follows (Fig. 11):

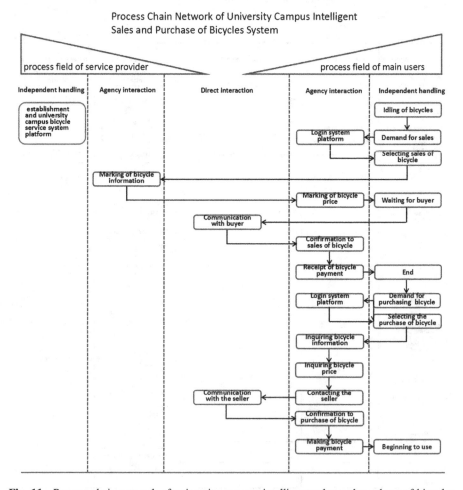

Fig. 11. Process chain network of university campus intelligent sales and purchase of bicycles system

The process chain network (PCN) model of intelligent non-lease-type module, the process chain network (PCN) model of intelligent lease-type module and the process chain network (PCN) model of the sales and purchase of bicycle module constitute a complete process chain network (PCN) module of university campus bicycle service system. This module could to certain extent satisfy the demands of main users and effectively solve the problems in current service system.

5 Conclusion of Research

The thesis explores the demands of main users in service system on both qualitative and quantitative levels, adopts systematic methods to research the process of users using the service system and excavate contacts from it, and summarizes the main problems in the existing service system from qualitative and quantitative levels. The thesis also considers the demands of main users and the improvement of the main problems in current service system as the foundation, takes the contacts as the entry point of research, adopts process chain network (PCN) tool as the method, positions process steps (contacts) in the process chain of service system, so as to establish the process chain network (PCN) model of university bicycle service system, determines the interaction method of service provider and main users in process steps (contacts), so as to better satisfy the demands of users and effectively solve the problems in current service system, enable the traffic of campus to be more orderly, and provide reference to subsequent researches.

References

1. Lin, J.R., Yang, T.H.: Strategic design of public bicycle sharing systems with service level constraints. Transp. Res. Part E Logist. Trans. Rev. **47**(2), 284–294 (2011)
2. Huang, Y., Yang, Z., Xiong, S.: The research on the control algorithm of IOT based bicycle parking system. In: IEEE, International Conference on Cloud Computing and Intelligent Systems, pp. 1221–1225. IEEE (2012)
3. Guo, A., Liu, G.: A design of bike sharing system based on GPS. In: Jin, D., Lin, S. (eds.) Advances in Mechanical and Electronic Engineering. (LNEE), vol. 176, pp. 587–592. Springer, Heidelberg (2012). doi:10.1007/978-3-642-31507-7_93
4. Nemoto, Y., Akasaka, F., Chiba, R., et al.: Establishment of a function embodiment knowledge base for supporting service design. Sci. China Inf. Sci. **55**(5), 1008–1018 (2012)
5. Milano, P.D.: The Research of Product Service System Design in "Bike-Sharing" based on European Cities, Italy
6. Chen, L.L., Huang, J.: Design and implementation of public bicycle rental system service platform based on IOCP and JSON. Adv. Mater. Res. **998–999**, 1100–1103 (2014)
7. Kazemzadeh, Y., Milton, S.K., Johnson, L.W.: A comparison of concepts in service blueprinting and process chain network (PCN). Int. J. Bus. Manag. **10**(4), 13 (2015)
8. Lin, J.R., Yang, T.H., Chang, Y.C.: A hub location inventory model for bicycle sharing system design: Formulation and solution. Comput. Ind. Eng. **65**(1), 77–86 (2013)

SDIV: Service-Defined Intelligent Vehicle Towards the 2020 Urban Mobility

Bo Zhou, Xiaohua Sun[✉], and Binhui Zhang

Tongji University, Shanghai, China
{13zhoubo,xsun}@tongji.edu.cn

Abstract. This paper explores a new approach to the design and development of the future intelligent vehicle from the aspect of service innovation, by which the mobility service and intelligent vehicle could be integrated within the same context and objective. For this purpose, contexts, stages, stakeholders, and the types of data are used as the key elements to generate the service opportunity points. A four-dimension space constructed with these elements is adopted as an effective tool, which is helpful for considering the diversity and interactivity of the elements. Thus, 136 opportunity points are produced and used as the factors to define the vehicles. A theory from the Center of Automotive Research (CAR) is referenced to build the travelling model map. It describes nine travelling modes distributed in flexible/distance coordinates, and each of the modes is represented by an intelligent vehicle. The travelling model map is divided into nine sections by a three-by-three matrix, and the opportunity points are plotted into the corresponding section. In this way, a connection is established between opportunity points and the intelligent vehicles. Based on this theory, seven intelligent vehicles are endowed with respective characteristics and defined by services with similar properties. Finally, by studying the user journey of each service-defined intelligent vehicles (SDIVs) and analyzing the use case through the touchpoints/vehicles matrix, the features of SDIVs are furthered detailed and reflected by the interface design.

Keywords: Intelligent vehicle · Smart mobility · Service design · Product-service system

1 Introduction

With the evolution of self-driving, vehicle-to-everything (V2X) technology, artificial intelligence, and other technologies, the development route of intelligent vehicles is becoming increasingly clear [1]. From 2013 to 2014, NHTSA and SAE released the automation level for vehicles. Then, automotive OEMs published their timetables of achieving autonomous vehicles. Most of these timetables are set as 2018 to 2020 [2].

Consequently, urban mobility is facing a series of innovation challenges: First, the occupancy volume of the house-holding car will be declined dramatically [3]. In addition, the transportation system will be highly flexible and self-organized. Meanwhile, on-demand service and end-to-end data sharing will be realized. Car-sharing and intelligent transportation system will significantly improve the efficiency and the user experience of urban mobility [4].

© Springer International Publishing AG 2017
P.-L.P. Rau (Ed.): CCD 2017, LNCS 10281, pp. 288–298, 2017.
DOI: 10.1007/978-3-319-57931-3_23

In this situation, vehicles no longer will be isolated but will become the key node and hybrid touchpoint [5] of new mobility services. Building new services to suit the urbanization of the future is an inevitable way to improve the quality and user experience of intelligent vehicles [6].

As new mobility services attract widespread concerns from both industry and academia. OEMs have different focusses: Volkswagen and BMW pay close attention to the consistency of different travelling scenarios. Specifically, Moia from Volkswagen offers connected commuting, ride-hailing, and moil next to meet different demands [7]. And BMW has released the new services of Drive Now, Park Now, and Charge Now [8]. In addition, Daimler and Toyota focus on smartphone-based mobility concepts. Daimler optimizes the use of existing transportation infrastructure and has developed flexible and eco-friendly mobility solutions, such as Car2go, moovel, and mytaxi [9]. Toyota launched Hamo as a solution to build an optimal connection between personal transportation modes and public transportation [10]. In addition, Ford focusses on providing more convenience for vehicle owners, and has released GoDrive as the first service to offer one-way trips with guaranteed parking [11]. Not only OEMs but also suppliers have embarked on these types of activities. For instance, SiMobility is a platform released by Siemens, which enables the incorporation of various service providers into a single-source portfolio for the user [12].

The research field has always focussed on the integration of public transportation means. In recent years, the main study direction has turned to the establishment of unified protocols and open platforms. Researchers have attempted to realize unified payment, billing, trip planning, and package subscription by mobile app. Grounded on this, many concepts are presented. First, a typical example is the Challenge of the Internet of Mobility to the Intelligent Transportation System [13]. The EU-funded project 'Mobinet' will be accomplished in July 2107. This project will build an open-service platform covering the whole of Europe, and will provide components and tools both for end users and service suppliers. Second, the so-called 'integrated mobility' concept intends to make progress from the aspect of a whole mobility life cycle. It aims to integrate information, planning, transport services, infrastructure, and traffic management as a single solution [14] (e.g., the IRMA developed by Pavia University). Similarly, seamless transportation is a concept which emphasizes the synergies and connections between different travelling types, infrastructures, and travel services [15] (e.g., the HS2 project in the UK). Furthermore, door-to-door mobility is another similar concept. It focusses on building services to improve travelling flexibility and reachability [16]. Maas is a concept that has emerged in recent years, first proposed in Finland by Sampo Hietanen [17] and promoted by Sonja Heikkila [18]. As defined by the Maas alliance, 'Maas puts users, both travelers and goods, at the core of transport services, offering them tailor made mobility solutions based on their individual needs. The first Maas solution, Whim, has been released by MaaS Global [19].

Although a consensus is being reached that service will play a vital role in urban mobility, few people are concerned about how the intelligent vehicle adapts to and supports the service. In the industry field, vehicles and services are designed independently. Few design cases treat service and vehicle as an indivisible target (Leap is an exception [20]). In the beginning of production planning, most of the vehicle concepts do not take into account the demand for mobility service, especially the human-machine interaction and in-car infotainment system. Meanwhile, most of the services are designed for current vehicles rather than the future intelligent vehicle.

Therefore, from the perspective of the service-product system, this paper attempts to provide a new approach to the design and development of the intelligent vehicle within a service orientation. Specifically, there are four steps (Fig. 1). First, a four-dimension opportunity space is built, which is used as a tool for generating the service opportunity points (SOPs). Second, SOPs are generated and evaluated after two rounds of workshops. Each of them is matched with touchpoints and sorted into 14 categories. Third, the travelling model map with seven types of intelligent vehicles is set up. The map is divided into nine sections by a three-by-three matrix. Each opportunity point is plotted in the corresponding section. In this way, the SOPs get connected with seven types of intelligent vehicles. Fourth, based on the user journey mapping, the generality and individuality of SDIVs are discovered. In addition, generality and individuality are deconstructed by the touchpoints/vehicle matrix, the design requirements of the interfaces are defined.

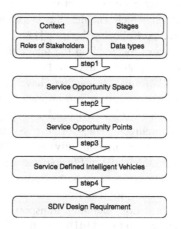

Fig. 1. The methodology of SDIV development

2 Exploring the Service Innovation Opportunities

2.1 Opportunity Space Construction

Contexts, stakeholders, and lifecycle stages are the key elements to a service [21]. In the development of automotive technology, these elements have gradually shown the properties of diversity, complexity, and interactivity.

In the near future, urban mobility will involve multiple contexts and will run through all the travelling stages based on the connected car and V2X technology. Furthermore, the stakeholders of the service will play multiple roles. Specifically, the owner of the vehicle can be the provider as well as the consumer of the service, and the consumer could choose to be a driver or a passenger on account of autonomous driving and manual driving. Moreover, with the development of the 'vehicle as a sensor' and big-data technology, data will become an input with important influence upon the service. Smart service based on data will be more intelligent and delivered more accurately.

These four elements will become the driver of new mobility development, and bring great opportunity for service innovation. For the purpose of discovering potential opportunities through service innovation, we construct a four-dimensional opportunity space (Fig. 2).

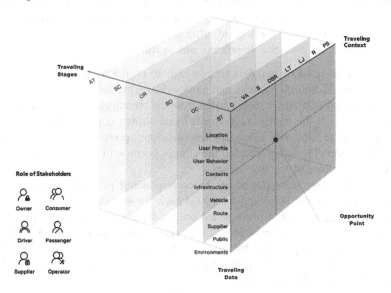

Fig. 2. Four-dimensions opportunity space

Although the specific contents of each dimension were set based on preliminary research (Table 1), the contents are variable according to the design objective and strategy.

Table 1. The contents of four dimensions

Contexts	Data types	Stages	Roles
Commuting for Work, Business or Education (C)	Location	Before the Trip (BT)	Owner
Visiting and Appointment (VA)	User Profile	Getting the Car (GC)	Consumer
Shopping(S)	User Behavior	Before the Departure (BD)	Driver
Dining, Social, and Recreation (DSR)	Contacts	On the Riding (OR)	Passenger
Leisure and Tours (LT)	Infrastructure	Stopping the Car (SC)	
Long Journey to another City (LJ)	Vehicle	After the Trip (AT)	
Returning Home (R)	Route		
Picking Up and Sending People or Goods (PS)	Supplier		
	Public		
	Environments		

2.2 Opportunity Points Generation

Based on the theory of opportunity space, two workshops were organized to generate the service opportunity points (SOPs).

In the first workshop, eight team members were separated into four groups equally, with each group playing a specific role. In representing the demands of each role, participants brainstormed opportunities for service innovation. The brainstorming comprised six rounds in total, with each round directed at a particular travelling stage, which could be from 'before the trip' to 'after the trip'.

During each round, the specific process was as follows:

(1) A matrix with contexts and data types was built on the white board.
(2) The host introduced the process and gave a demonstration.
(3) The first round of brainstorming started from the travelling stage 'before the trip'. With the help of the matrix, participants made written notes of all their ideas.
(4) When the time limit was reached, each participant presented the ideas to other team members. Then they decided the correct position of the notes and whether some notes belonged to other stages.
(5) Most of the notes were posted in the corresponding position, but some notes applied to the wrong stage and were held back for the correct stage.
(6) After all of the notes had been posted on the white board, the participants supplemented the notes with new ideas in the sparse area after evaluating what kind of service could be provided by specific data in a specific travelling context.
(7) Then the host organized the notes and took them off the board, except for those notes that applied to other stages.
(8) The remaining stages were handled according to the same process.
(9) In the end, all the notes were organized and the similar ideas were combined.

In this way, 324 SOPs were generated after six rounds of brainstorming.

Table 2. Example for SOPs

Opportunity point	Category	Rating
When a ride-sharing request has been confirmed, the real-time location would be displayed both on the driver and consumer's devices	LBS	4.5
Playing AR game with Other passengers in same route	Social	4.0
Recommending a parking space proactively when driving into the particular region	Parking	4.0
By personal schedule syncing, the driver would be reminded and asked whether want to call the relevant person when the expected time exceeded	Trip planning	4.2
People invite friends to join the car-sharing community and give them permission to use the car	Identity	3.8
People take a test and get a visible analysis for selecting the suitable service package	Analysis	4.2
...	...	...

In the second workshop, eight professionals with different backgrounds got together to vote on the results. Five indexes were provided for them as references: user
benefit, commercial benefit, innovativeness, efficiency, and irreplaceability. Each index
was weighted equally and used a scale of 0–5. The final score was subject to the
average of all items (0 = negatively abandon, 1 = unworthiness, 2 = low value,
3 = medium value, 4 = high value, and 5 = a strong advocate). The statistical result
indicated that 136 SOPs scored above the mean value 3.5, and they were divided into
14 categories: Recommendation, Local-based Service, Trip Planning, Analysis, Info-
tainments, Identity, Cockpit Ambience, Reminding, Goods Shipping, Parking, Contact,
Maintenance, Payment, and Billing. Table 2 presents partial information from the 136
cases.

3 Defining the Intelligent Vehicles by Mobility Service

3.1 Plotting the SDIV

The SOPs mentioned above are not targeted but universal to most travelling modes. By
referring to the different characteristic of travelling, they can be divided into clusters,
and each cluster would support the travel under certain conditions. Additionally, the
intelligent vehicles that support specific travelling also could be divided by the same
reference. Therefore, a tool for describing the travel modes is required, which is helpful
for exploring the connection between the SOPs and intelligent vehicles.

Thus the travelling model map is introduced based on the Center of Automotive
Research (CAR) theory. 'Which service is best for a given trip depends on trip distance
and the amount of flexibility (time, destinations, availability) that the traveler has
available for the trip' [22]. Based on coordinates by flexibility and distance, CAR [23]
describes nine types of New Mobility Service (NMS) modes in its report. This paper
makes a few adjustments:

First, the CAR's coordinates are divided by fuzzy intervals, which can provide a
better reference to define in which part the services are located. The flexible axis is
divided into three sections as 'arbitrary', 'adaptive', and 'stable'. The distance axis is
divided into three sections as 'within 5 km', 'city center', and 'urban areas'. Thus, a
3×3 matrix covers the whole coordinates section.

Second, each NMS modes are represented by corresponding specific intelligent
vehicles, and they were named as Carbot, Cario, Mycar, Minibus, UrbanTransit,
Microtransit, and Microshuttle. Each of them fits a special niche (presented by different
colours), but they also partially overlap with one another (Fig. 3).

Each of the SOPs has a particular degree of sensitiveness and tendentiousness.
Some are more sensitive to flexibility. For example, parking and route planning tend to
be available under flexible travel. In contrast, trip planning and travel reminding tend to
be applied in the inflexible modes, and route-based service is in the middle degree.

The other SOPs are more sensitive to distance. For example, in-vehicle entertainment and vehicle booking are more suitable to long distance, immediate
vehicles-finding and spot guidance are more suitable to short-distance, and parking
service is more likely for the midterm.

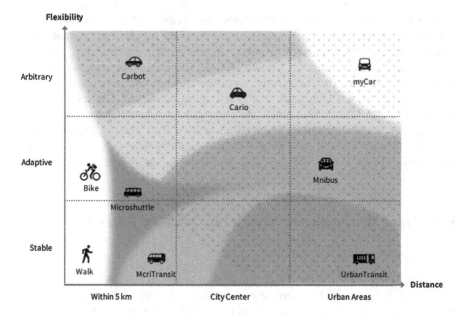

Fig. 3. Traveling model map

Based on this, the 136 SOPs were plotted on a flexibility/distance matrix (Fig. 4). To be adaptive to different parameters, some SOPs were plotted on a single grid while others were plotted in more than one grid. In addition, some universal SOPs, such as payment and evaluation, were plotted outside the region.

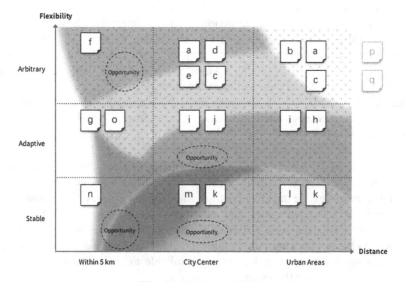

Fig. 4. Plotting the SOPs

As a result of this exercise, it is easy to find the uneven density of the SOPs on the travelling model map. Thus the empty areas (such as the lower left corner) are regarded as innovative opportunity areas, another round of brainstorming was conducted as a supplement.

Finally, SOPs establish the relationship with the intelligent vehicle in the same grid. The larger the vehicle occupy the grid, the higher the priority for the corresponding SOPs. In this way, seven types of intelligent vehicles were defined.

3.2   SDIV Design Requirements Refinement

After the SDIV was defined, the design requirement for each vehicle could be further specified and clarified.

The previous SOPs were used as the material for SDIV user stories, which are helpful for finding out particular user journeys. For example, Fig. 5 describes a private car-sharing service based on myCar.

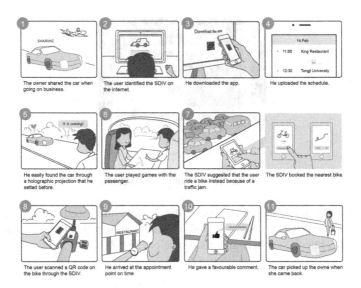

Fig. 5. Storyboard of private car sharing

The user story mapping leads to the discovery of both generality and individuality of SDIVs. In summary, there are common touchpoints as well as different user actions. In addition, although different SDIVs are intended for different travelling purposes, they could be supported by a single platform and integrated by a single product-service system. Therefore, a touchpoints/vehicle matrix was built to deconstruct the user journey and produce the use cases (Table 3).

In this way, a framework based on four interfaces is set up. It includes the universal interface (Website, Owner App, and Hailing App) which supports all SDIVs, and the proper interface (Car HMI), which varies with the different SDIVs. The functions of these are as follows:

Table 3. Touchpoint matrix for use case generation

Touchpoints / Vehicles	Web	Owner App	Hailing App	In-car Interface
Guider	Exploring the Service, Siging Up, Subscribing to a Package, Viewing the Distribution of Vehicles...	Setting Route, Monitoring,.	Booking, Check In...	Showing the Location...
MicroBus			Joining a Community...	Reminding Destinations...
myCar		Sharing Car,Check Car info...	Paying and Rating...	Contacting the Passenger...
Cabot			Finding and Unlocking...	Synchronizing User Preference...
Cabot			Hailing a Cabot...	Greeting, Setting Destination...
MicroShuttle			Planning the Daily Trip,Billing...	Showing Next Trip Schedules...
UrbanTransit			Reminding of the Departure...	Gaming, Station Reminding...

- The website is the first touchpoint for understanding the product-service system, getting related information, signing up, etc. (Figure 6).

Fig. 6. The layout of the Website

- The Hailing App is for getting access to the service and managing the travel. Before the travel, people plan, book, and hail a vehicle through this app. After the travel, people pay, rate the service, and get a receipt (Fig. 7).

Fig. 7. Mobile App UI design for consumer and vehicle owner

- The Owner App supports vehicle owners in making travel plans, managing their vehicle, and publishing the sharing service (Fig. 7).
- The In-Car HMI supports the service when the user is driving or riding, and should be designed in accordance with the specific vehicle (Fig. 8).

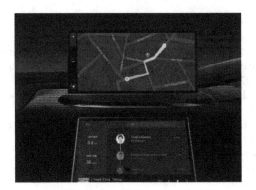

Fig. 8. In-car dashboard UI design for Microbus

4   Conclusion

The SDIV is put forward based on the new situation of the automotive industry. It is a methodology for defining the service-oriented intelligent vehicle, as well as a new approach for product planning of intelligent vehicles.

Mobility innovation could be more effective and efficient under the guidance of this theory. Specifically, researchers could integrate the processes of product planning and service design, and make the output of the two parts more suitable. In service innovation, research could take into account more factors of future intelligent vehicles instead of conventional vehicles. In vehicle innovation, research could be more targeted and structured.

In addition, the SDIV is a multiple interactive way to inspire creativity. The factors such as the opportunity space and travelling model map are variable. Researchers could modify the factors according to technology development and business strategy, and try to approach discovery from multiple angles.

Finally, the SDIV draws the service-product system thinking into vehicle planning. Compared to the conventional vehicles, the SDIVs aims to improve the utilization of resources and promote the development of sustainability mobility. In this way, it could create greater business, social, and consumer value.

Although there are both scientific deductions and practical works in this paper, more research is required. Future work will face two main challenges: first, how to define more vehicle attributes based on service, for example, body styling and the cockpit user experience; and second, how to make the SDVI's features respond rapidly to the changes in service demand. More experiments and simulation studies should be adopted to promote the SDIV in becoming an effective means of dealing with the complexity of future urban mobility.

References

1. Narla, S.R.K.: The evolution of connected vehicle technology: from smart drivers to smart cars to… self-driving cars. Inst. Transp. Eng. ITE J. **83**(7), 22 (2013)
2. Litman, T.: Autonomous vehicle implementation predictions. Vic. Transp. Policy Inst. **28** (2014)
3. Schoettle, B., Sivak, M.: Potential impact of self-driving vehicles on household vehicle demand and usage (2015)
4. Schade, W., Krail, M., Kühn, A.: New mobility concepts: myth or emerging reality. In: 5th Conference-Transport Solutions: From Research to Deployment on Transport Research Arena-TRA 2014 (2014)
5. Lo, K.P.Y.: Hybrid touchpoints for relational service in social innovation: a case study of "Eat Me!" (2014)
6. Cornet, A., Mohr, D., et al.: Mobility of the future: opportunities for automotive OEMs. In: McKinsey Advanced Industries (2012)
7. MOIA. https://www.moia.io/
8. BMW Innovation. https://www.bmwgroup.com/en/innovation/technologies-and-mobility/mobility-services.html
9. Daimler Products. https://www.daimler.com/products/services/mobility-services/
10. Toyota Innovation. http://www.toyota-global.com/innovation/intelligent_transport_systems/hamo/
11. https://media.ford.com/content/fordmedia/fna/us/en/news/2015/01/06/mobility-experiment-city-driving-on-demand-london.html
12. https://www.mobility.siemens.com/mobility/global/en/integrated-mobility/imp/pages/simobility-connect.aspx
13. Noyer, U., Schlauch, T., Wissingh, B., et al:. MOBiNET: architecture and experience from a marketplace for mobility services. In: 11th ITS European Congress (2016)
14. Motta, G., Ferrara, A., Sacco, D., et al.: Integrated mobility: a research in progress. J. Softw. Eng. Appl. **6**(3B), 97 (2013)
15. Preston, J.: Integration for seamless transport. In: International Transport Forum Discussion Papers, No. 2012/01. OECD Publishing (2012)
16. Stopka, U.: Identification of user requirements for mobile applications to support door-to-door mobility in public transport. In: Kurosu, M. (ed.) HCI 2014. LNCS, vol. 8512, pp. 513–524. Springer, Cham (2014). doi:10.1007/978-3-319-07227-2_49
17. Kamargianni, M., Li, W., Matyas, M., et al.: A critical review of new mobility services for urban transport. Transp. Res. Proc. **14**, 3294–3303 (2016)
18. Heikkilä, S.: Mobility as a service-a proposal for action for the public administration, Case Helsinki (2014)
19. MaaS Global. https://maas.global/
20. Leap. http://rideleap.com/
21. Vasantha, G.V.A., Roy, R., Lelah, A., et al.: A review of product–service systems design methodologies. J. Eng. Des. **23**(9), 635–659 (2012)
22. Kirby, R.F., Bhatt, K.V., Kemp, M.A., et al.: Paratransit: Neglected Options for Urban Mobility. Urban Institute, Washington, DC (1974)
23. Spulber, A., Dennis, E.P., et al.: The impact of new mobility services on the automotive industry. In: Center for Automotive Research (2016)

Cross-Cultural Communication

Cross-Cultural Grammar, 324

Investigating the Comprehension of Public Symbols for Wayfinding in Transit Hubs in China

Dadi An[1,2(✉)] and Edwin H.W. Chan[1]

[1] The Hong Kong Polytechnic University, Kowloon, Hong Kong, China
dadi.an@polyu.edu.hk
[2] Tongji University, Shanghai, China

Abstract. Public symbols are essential components of signage in public transit stations or terminals. Comprehensibility of public symbols directly influences the performance of wayfinding. This study investigated 107 participants with 25 public symbols to understand the effects of travel characteristics and symbol features on comprehension of public symbols. Statistical analysis results showed that travel frequency and meaningfulness of public symbols are significantly associated with comprehension scores. Designing public symbols should be balanced between regulation and localization. Public symbols those are conveying the most meaningful information for wayfinding in transit hubs require further investigation.

Keywords: Public symbols · Comprehensibility · Wayfinding

1 Introduction

Public transit hubs, connecting bus, taxi, metro, railway, and even airport, have become large multi-functional terminal buildings that they resemble a small city (Fewings 2001). Passengers within the unfamiliar environment are always particularly confused. Signage in transit hubs is like a graphical layer, or to say semiotic layer (Hamid 2014) represents the everyday organizations of public settings (Denis and Pontille 2010).

Signage with public symbols can directly convey navigation information for people with different language backgrounds to understand a particular message. Ng et al. (2013) defined public symbol as a graphical method to convey information in all locations and sectors open to public access. Some of these symbols are essential components of signage system, while others are mostly used as a dependent sign. Public symbols can effectively support passengers' wayfinding and direct them to their destinations smoothly. Therefore, the comprehensibility study of public symbols for wayfinding has become impending.

According to McDougall et al. (1999), measurement of symbols is based on the features of icons like familiarity, concreteness, simplicity, meaningfulness, and semantic distance. Ng and Chan (2007, 2008, 2010) argued that these five features have become the central concerns in sign and icon research. Researchers used these features to exam the guessability of traffic symbols (Ng and Chan 2007) or safety icons (Chan and Ng 2012).

© Springer International Publishing AG 2017
P.-L.P. Rau (Ed.): CCD 2017, LNCS 10281, pp. 301–311, 2017.
DOI: 10.1007/978-3-319-57931-3_24

In the context of public transit, Liu and Ho (2012) tested the effects of age and design features on symbol comprehension in central rail hubs in Taiwan. With regard to wayfinding in transit hubs, few relevant literatures or knowledge contributions were found.

The purpose of this study is (1) to evaluate the comprehensibility of public symbols those are widely used in transit hubs in China; (2) to understand the effects of travel characteristics and symbol features on comprehension score; and (3) providing some design strategies on public symbols to promote the performance with regard to wayfinding.

2   Methodology

2.1   Subjects

According to GB/T 10001.1-2006 (The National Standards of the People's Republic of China for public information graphical symbols for use on sign), there are totally 118 public symbols in different categories, such as universal, tourist and recreation, transportation, and medical.

In order to have an efficient investigation on public symbols in transit hubs, this study employed 25 symbols (Fig. 1) of high-frequency appearance in public transit stations or terminals (10 for transit facilities, 10 for service facilities, and 5 of warning symbols), to evaluate the features related to comprehension of symbols. These public symbols showed basic information about major facilities in transit hubs, including entrances, left luggage, check-in, lost and found, meeting point et al., to support the navigation of passengers during their mobility.

Fig. 1. Public symbols (shown to participants without text labels)

2.2   Questionnaire

A self-administrated questionnaire was created in Chinese and published on-line or sent randomly in Hongqiao terminal in Shanghai. The first part of the questionnaire asked about the participants' demographic information including gender, age, education background, occupation, and their travel characteristics. Travel characteristics were surveyed to capture the habits of participants by six aspects as following: experiences of overseas travel, commuting modes, driving license, and the frequency, transport mode choice as well as the last time of domestic travel.

The second part is to evaluate the features of symbols. Each of the 25 selected symbols is presented in a 1.5 cm × 1.5 cm squares following questions for rating. Participants were asked to subjectively rate the symbol features (familiarity, concreteness, simplicity, and meaningfulness) from 0 to100 points. In addition, we had a brief introduction of the meanings of each features. Familiarity means the frequency with which the symbol has been encountered; concreteness refers to whether the symbol is abstract or figurative; simplicity is defined in terms of the detailed contents with which the symbol contains; and meaningfulness refers to how meaningful you perceive the symbol to be. After evaluating these four features of symbols, a close-ended choice question is displayed under each symbol for choosing the meaning of the symbol to test the sematic closeness of the symbols. The process was repeated until the evaluation of all the 25 selected symbols were finished. A pre-test of the questionnaire with 8 participants showed the general time to finish all the questions cost 25–30 min.

3 Results

3.1 Comprehension Scores

There are two levels of standard for evaluating the precision rate of public symbols. International standards organization (ISO) stipulates the comprehension rate at 67%, while the American national standard institute (ANSI) requires a higher level at 85%. Our survey showed that the comprehension correct percentages vary significantly from each other, and only 12 of the 25 public symbols satisfied the ANSI standards. The most easily comprehensive five symbols were no littering (100%), meeting point (99.02%), tickets (97.06%), airline tickets (97.06%), and kiosks (96.08%). On the contrary, luggage check-in (12.75%), subway (32.35%), conductor office (47.06%), subway (32.35%), and baggage check-in (12.75%) were the most difficult five symbols to understand (Fig. 2).

Box plots can intuitively express the characteristics of data, especially outliers, by simple graphics. As shown in Fig. 3, the comprehension score for each participant was in the range from 56 to 100 (Mean value = 86.50, SD = 10.48), and most of the scores are more than 70. Remarkably, the box plot showed that most scores are gathered into a cluster, while the symbol of luggage check-in (no. 11) was assessed as an outlier below the box, indicating that this symbol is very abstruse on account of unfamiliarity or irrelevant design of this symbol.

3.2 Travel Characteristics

With respect to travel characteristics, we investigate participants' travel behaviors in terms of oversea experience, commuting mode choice, whether holds a driving license,

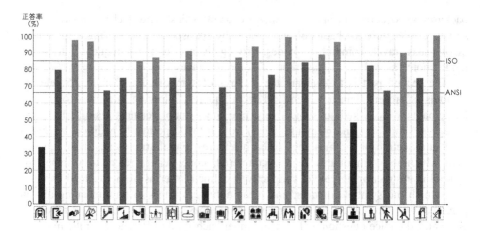

Fig. 2. Participants' comprehension percentages of selected symbols with ISO (67%) and ANSI (85%) recommended standards

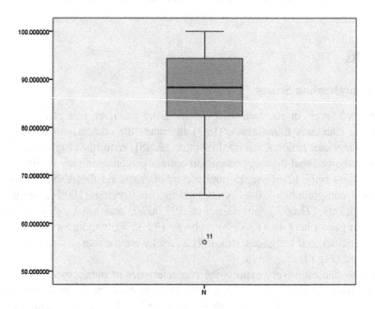

Fig. 3. Box plot of coefficients of variation on comprehension scores

domestic travel frequency, transport mode choice and the last time of domestic travel. In this investigation and statistic, there are 58.88% of them have an experience travelling abroad; over 70% of the participants chose buses or metro as daily commuting modes; about half of them are holding a driving license; a proportion of 49% have a domestic travelling every four months; about 52% of them chose to go by train or coaches, and lastly, a majority of the participants' last domestic travel was more than two months ago (Table 1).

Table 1. Travel characteristics and comprehension scores

Travel characteristics		Number (n = 107)	Comprehension score	
			Mean	SD
Experiences of overseas travel	Yes	63	87.70	6.24
	No	44	84.80	6.83
Commuting modes	Private car	20	87.10	6.63
	Taxi	3	78.00	1.41
	Bus	38	84.55	7.07
	Subway	36	87.94	5.34
	Others	10	87.90	6.49
Driving license	Yes	57	88.07	6.38
	No	50	84.72	6.48
The frequency of domestic travel	>4 per month	3	91.67	12.74
	1–4 per month	15	85.80	7.30
	<1 in two months	36	87.11	6.00
	<1 in four months	53	86.00	6.49
Transport mode choice of domestic travel	Private car	27	87.67	6.81
	Coach	30	86.67	6.18
	Train	25	86.72	5.94
	Plane	25	84.84	7.55
The last time of domestic travel	Within a week	12	87.33	5.68
	More than a week	11	85.82	6.43
	More than 2 months	56	85.34	6.98
	More than half year	28	88.75	5.97

The result of Kruskal-Wallis test showed that the effect of travel frequency, which is supposed to be the main factors, showed the result of highly significant ($x2 = 8.231$, $df = 3$, $p < 0.005$). Participants who traveled more than 4 times a month could get higher correct answer rates (87.3%) than other group of participants (75.87%, 78.09% and 77.71%). All the other travel characteristics including the overseas travel experiences, commuting modes, driving license, and the factors of domestic travel are not significantly ($p > 0.05$) correlated with the accuracy of symbol comprehension.

3.3 Features of Public Symbols

The choice of features of public symbols to be evaluated was determined by a review of a literature (McDougall et al. 1996). Generally, the features of familiarity, concreteness, complexity, meaningfulness, and semantic distance have become the central concerns for studying public symbols. However, in order to reduce the degree of difficulty for participants, we altered the feature of semantic distance to choice questions to choose the meaning of a symbol what they think is right. Each of the options in the choice questions was assigned a value depends on its relationship with the right answer. Then the average values of comprehension for each symbol were calculated by equation:

Comprehensive score = $(100 \times Na + 50 \times Nb + 25 \times Nc) \div (Na + Nb + Nc + Nd)$, where Na to Nd refers to the number of participants who choose the option. Then correlation analysis was conducted to evaluate the hypothesis that the comprehension scores are highly related to public symbols those are familiar, concrete, simple, and meaningful.

Table 2 shows some of the highest and lowest scores of the four features including familiarity, concreteness, simplicity, and meaningfulness. It is clear that the symbol of no. 25 (⚐, Do not throw rubbish) obtained the highest scores in the aspects of familiarity, simplicity, and meaningfulness with the values of 71.33, 78.56, and 80.99, while the symbol of no. 20 (⚒, Conductor office) got the lowest scores in the aspects of familiarity and simplicity. In addition, the symbol of no. 2 (⬅, Entrance) and no. 9 (⬆, Elevator) got the highest and lowest scores with respect to concreteness, with 58.32 and 41.48. Within the last three symbols of comprehension score, the symbol of no. 1 (⚑, Metro stations) and no. 11 (⚑, Checking luggage) got relative lower scores of concreteness (42.61 and 46.59), while the symbol of no. 20 (⚒, Conductor office) got a higher score of 53.16. Our intuitive analysis shows that the relationship among symbol design features and comprehension score are of abnormal distributions, implying the complex and indirection correlations among the four feature of public symbols and their comprehension scores.

Table 2. The highest and lowest scores of familiarity, concreteness, simplicity, and meaningfulness

	The highest scores				The lowest scores			
	No.	Symbol	Content	Score	No.	Symbol	Content	Score
Familiarity	25		Do Not Throw Rubbish	71.33	20		Conductor Office	38.21
Concreteness	2		Entrance	58.32	9		Elevator	41.48
Simplicity	25		Do Not Throw Rubbish	78.56	20		Conductor Office	51.66
Meaningfulness	25		Do Not Throw Rubbish	80.99	24		No Disturb	54.73

With regard to familiarity, it determines pedestrians' understanding and memorization of a public symbol. A symbol with higher familiarity can express a simple meaning without any explanation over different languages and characters of different countries. The familiarity of symbol can be strengthened by designers, by producing the users' association, cognizing, as well as resonance. In our investigation, the symbol of no. 20 (▲, Conductor office) got the lowest score of familiarity. On one hand, the necessity of this symbol is not significant for a majority of people. On the other hand, the result dues to the uncertain meanings of this symbol, people would possibly consider this symbol with ambiguities of local police stations or information desk.

Although the correlation between concreteness and comprehension score was not significant, it is still an undoubted fact that the abstraction is the most symbols features for designers. Actually, a public symbol is an output of common sense by extracting the substantive characteristics and generalities. Since most of the public symbols are displayed and used during pedestrians' mobility, it is very important to insure that people are capable to read and identify the meanings of each symbol. The analysis addressed the symbol of no. 1 (▥, Metro stations) with lower abstraction, indicating that there are too many components within the image resulting misunderstanding of tunnels or railways to some extent.

The feature of simplicity lies on familiarity. Under circumstance of similar familiarity, the simplicity of a symbol is related to form, size, lighting, color, luminosity difference, and observation distance. Remarkably, a pictogram is not direct as characters to express specific information. Thus, designers should pay more attention to simplicity compared with other features. Generally, public symbols with complex components results in lower comprehension, while some of over-simple designs also lead to information missing. One example is the symbol no. 20 (▲, Conductor office), several participants misunderstood its meaning because of the lack of necessary components.

The same as characters, each of the public symbols must contain a unique signified referring semiotics. The meaningful of a symbol refers to whether the icon is producing the right meaning. As a primary tool for designers to describe or visualize the contents of direction, location, regulation, culture, or history, the options of pictograms are closely related to the environmental and functional features. In this investigation, the symbol of no. 24 (▯, No disturb) was considered as meaningless, indicating that it is not necessary in the context of public transit hubs, where passengers are more likely to concentrate on the direction of to transfer or looking for the right entrance and platform.

The values of the four symbol features were normally distributed (one-sample Kolmogorov Smirnov test, $p < 0.05$). The Pearson correlation coefficients of the relationship between symbol features and comprehension score are shown in Table 3. Despite of the low correlation between the features of simplicity and concreteness ($r = 0.155$, $p = 0.112$), most interrelationships among the features are significant,

Table 3. Pearson correlation coefficients amongst public symbol features and comprehension scores

	Familiarity	Concreteness	Simplicity	Meaningfulness
Familiarity	1			
Concreteness	.237[*]	1		
Simplicity	.648[**]	.155	1	
Meaningfulness	.492[**]	.240[*]	.702[**]	1
Comprehension score	.007	.153	.137	.217[*]

[*]Correlation is significant at the .05 level (2-tailed).
[**]Correlation is significant at the .01 level (2-tailed).

revealing that the subjective assessments of these symbol features are closely interrelated with each other. The correlation between simplicity and familiarity is relatively high, implying that simple designed symbols are easier to get acquainted. On the contrary, the lower correlation between familiarity and concreteness emphasizes the importance of abstract for a symbol. The more abstract a symbol is designed, the easier for people to understand. With respect to comprehension score, three of four symbol features are not significant as expected, while meaningfulness correlated most highly with the comprehension score ($r = 0.217$, $n = 107$, $p < 0.05$), indicating the importance of meaning on people's comprehension of a symbol.

4   Discussion

Based on the investigations on comprehension of public symbols above, it is clear that the results revealed two main findings: travel frequency significantly influences the symbol comprehension, and that the level of symbol comprehension is closely associated with the feature of meaningfulness. Thus, discussions of the results will be carried out in aspects of travel characteristics and symbols design features.

4.1   Travel Characteristics

In this study, participants who traveled more frequently were better at comprehending public symbols, generally because they are more familiar with the transit environment and the context of signage system. The result was similar with formal study (Ng and Chan 2007) showing that the visiting experience had a significant effect. As the traffic sign regulation, signage and symbols in terminals are also regulated at national or international levels. The ISO 7001:2007 (Graphical symbols–public information symbols) was issued to increase a series of symbols to promote accessibility to public transport, tourist attractions and other public facilities. Mostly these regulations are not mandatory and designers are obsessed with modifying or developing new symbols. Usability tests are necessary during the development process (Lee et al. 2014).

In addition, designer should balance the globalization and localization and consider the basic features those are effective on comprehension. Although a variety of systems have developed public symbols applied by countries, regions ore tourist authorities, provinces, municipalities, tour operators, businesses and many other organizations (Neves et al. 2016), it is obviously to notice that, in general, the importance of the localized design integrating considerations of native cultures, religions, and customs.

On one hand, travelers are in demand of familiar public symbols during their mobility (even frequently travelers). On the other hand, people need different impressions, especially in consideration of details such as signage, in different environments. This situation generates the opportunities and challenges for pictogram designers to find a balance point between the two aspects of contradictions. Based on the standardizations, some tiny details of colors, outlines, or figure-ground relations reflecting local characteristics can be integrated during the creations of public symbols, which is a substantial derivation of the standardized ones (Fig. 4).

Fig. 4. Public symbols from China, Japan and Dubai (Source from UNIT Design, Germany)

4.2 Symbol Features

With regard to the five symbol features, preceding studies (McDougall 2001; Ou and Liu 2012) have proved that semantic closeness is the most significant factor on comprehension, followed by meaningfulness, concreteness, familiarity, and simplicity. Since the participants were asked to answer close-ended questions on semantic of symbols, this study remove semantic closeness from the model to test the interrelationships among the other four features. The result implied that passengers are better at understanding the symbols those are important to them.

Since the amount of public symbols is getting large with new requirement of high quality of design, it is necessary for graphic designers to firstly figure out symbols those are important to pedestrians. When people walk in an unfamiliar environment, they would mostly acquire wayfinding information form symbols those they are most familiar with. Chaotic symbols within wayfinding systems would reduce the efficient spatial perception. In the context of transit hubs, where most people are unfamiliar with the environment and need to get the location information as quick as they can, it is important to understand what are the most prior symbols the really need. In other words, the more meaningful symbols people regard to, the more prior for designers to emphasize in a wayfinding system. Therefore, a series of forehand field studies for pedestrians' demands are integrant.

5   Conclusion

This study selected 25 common public symbols to evaluate their comprehensibility of by correlation analysis with variables of travel characteristics and symbol features. The results identified that travel frequency and the symbol feature of meaningfulness significantly influences the symbol comprehension. This finding gives insights to provide some design strategies on public symbols to promote the performance with regard to wayfinding. Most standardized public symbols in China are generally lack of originality, dynamic, and personable. The theoretical features are actually the minimum standard for public information communication. Based on the features of meaningfulness, concreteness, familiarity, and simplicity, public symbols should be unique connected with localization. There still exist spaces for graphic designers to develop new public symbols with the combination of local cultural characteristics. Meanwhile, designer should pay attention to the balance between globalization and localization. At last, we suggest more studies of investigations on the most meaningful public symbols and their contribution to the performance of wayfinding within transit hubs for further research.

The limitations of this study lie to several aspects. First, the authenticity of participants' questionnaire needs further validation. If circumstances permitted, it's better to ask participants to answer two times that two consistent answers are considered to be real and effective questionnaires. Second, the ratings of public symbol features are subjectively based on participants' feeling, and different evaluation criterion may increase the statistical error. Third, selected participants are with relative high generality of age and education background that make this study a lack of universality.

References

Hashim, M.J., Alkaabi, M.S.K.M., Bharwani, S.: Interpretation of way-finding healthcare symbols by a multicultural population: navigation signage design for global health. Appl. Ergon. **45**(3), 503–509 (2014)

Lee, S., Dazkir, S.S., Paik, H.S., et al.: Comprehensibility of universal healthcare symbols for wayfinding in healthcare facilities. Appl. Ergon. **45**(4), 878–885 (2014)

Hamid, S.A.: Walking in the city of signs: tracking pedestrians in glasgow. Curr. Urban Stud. **2**(03), 263 (2014)

Siu, K.W.M., Wong, Y.L., Lam, M.S.: Quality of public symbol: the five principles supported by the drawings of young users. In: Toulon-Verona Conference "Excellence in Services" (2015)

Denis, J., Pontille, D.: The graphical performance of a public space. The subway signs and their scripts. Urban Plots Organ. Cities 11–22 (2010)

Fewings, R.: Wayfinding and airport terminal design. J. Navig. **54**(02), 177–184 (2001)

Neves, J., da Silva, F.M., Raposo, D., Silva, J.: Ergonomics and information design: design, standardization and uniformization of graphical symbols for public information. In: Rebelo, F., Soares, M. (eds.) Advances in Ergonomics in Design. (AISC), vol. 485, pp. 615–623. Springer, Cham (2016). doi:10.1007/978-3-319-41983-1_56

Rousek, J.B., Hallbeck, M.S.: Improving and analyzing signage within a healthcare setting. Appl. Ergon. **42**(6), 771–784 (2011)

Liu, Y.C., Ho, C.H.: The effects of age on symbol comprehension in central rail hubs in Taiwan. Appl. Ergon. **43**(6), 1016–1025 (2012)

Ng, A.W.Y., Chan, A.H.S.: The guessability of traffic signs: effects of prospective-user factors and sign design features. Accid. Anal. Prev. **39**(6), 1245–1257 (2007)

Ng, A.W.Y., Chan, A.H.S.: The effects of driver factors and sign design features on the comprehensibility of traffic signs. J. Saf. Res. **39**(3), 321–328 (2008)

Ou, Y.K., Liu, Y.C.: Effects of sign design features and training on comprehension of traffic signs in Taiwanese and Vietnamese user groups. Int. J. Ind. Ergon. **42**(1), 1–7 (2012)

Chan, A.H.S., Ng, A.W.Y.: The guessing of mine safety signs meaning: effects of user factors and cognitive sign features. Int. J. Occup. Saf. Ergon. **18**(2), 195–208 (2012)

Mcdougall, S.J.P., Curry, M.B., de Bruijn, O.: Measuring symbol and icon characteristics: Norms for concreteness, complexity, meaningfulness, familiarity, and semantic distance for 239 symbols. Behav. Res. Methods Instrum. Comput. **31**(3), 487–519 (1999)

Interpretation of Space: From Images to Vocabulary

Li-Yu Chen[1(✉)], Ya-Juan Gao[2], Wun-Cong Yen[1], and Ching-Hui Huang[1]

[1] Department of Interior Design, Chung Yuan Christian University,
Chung-Li/Taoyuan City, Taiwan
chenly99@gmail.com, wcyan1990@gmail.com, b3017987@ms22.hinet.net
[2] Graduate School of Creative Industry Design, National Taiwan University of Arts,
Ban Ciao/New Taipei City, Taiwan
78343821@qq.com

Abstract. Interior design can be executed in various stages, during which designers (the sender) deliver their ideas to client s (the receiver) via communication channels (the medium) in the form of language, words, images, and drawings. The question is whether the sender and receiver have a mutual understanding and interpretation of the message or not determines if the design is able to satisfy the client's needs. In order to understand the different backgrounds of receivers (professionals and non-professionals), it is important to note if they have different spatial perceptions when interpreting the same spatial image and if they use different spatial vocabulary to describe how they feel. Images and vocabulary are used as research materials. With spatial images and vocabulary as research instruments, professionals (designers with more than five years of work experience) and non-professionals (college freshmen) are asked to complete questionnaires to analyze the different spatial vocabulary used by professionals and non-professionals for the same spatial image as well as the two groups of participants' different interpretations towards spatial vocabulary based of their written descriptions. Research findings show that: (1) spatial vocabularies that describe an interior space need to be able to clearly identify the characters, ambience, and style of the space; (2) if a space has obvious differences in style, color, and material, vocabularies become more consistent; (3) the abundance and complexity of furniture play an important role; for example, less furniture or simple furnishings tend to be interpreted as simple or basic.

Keywords: Communication · Interpretation · Vocabulary · Spatial perception

1 Introduction

In an existing building, an interior space can be divided into segments with elements such as ceilings, walls, and floors and its spatial ambience is created with style, colors, and materials to satisfy the user's psychological perception and needs. Interior design is the creative process of interior space composition. The job can be divided into design (drawing) and decoration (construction), each requiring different participants to complete the job. During the design process, the owner of the space expresses his or her needs and preferences in spoken words, written words, or pictures to the designer. After

© Springer International Publishing AG 2017
P.-L.P. Rau (Ed.): CCD 2017, LNCS 10281, pp. 312–323, 2017.
DOI: 10.1007/978-3-319-57931-3_25

receiving the message, the designer will convey the ideas verbally, in words, or on drawing or animations. A design project is formed through the concept, development, and implementation stages. The cognitive ability of drawings and ability to describe using text and speech are important factors that affect the understanding of space. Therefore, during communication, the designer and owner could interpret the messages differently. In this case, communication and mutual understanding is a vital part of conveying ideas effectively and achieving your dream design.

Chiu and Yan (1996) showed that a designer usually communicates with the consumer using words, text, or pictures. Messages delivered between the sender and the receiver may be obstructed or distorted due to misinterpretation during the process of coding and recalling [1]. Vocabulary is the rational logical thinking and symbols accumulated through visual experience. Specific of text code must be made through convention in order to achieve communication [2].

Kaplan (1981) argued that spatial cognition is a process during which humans store, perceive, and reconstruct environmental stimulus. Spatial cognition can be considered as the process where people modify and organize information after being stimulated by the environment or space and then convey their understanding through words or images [3].

Previous studies have shown that media such as vocabulary, images, and pictures are mostly used to explore the user's preference and perception towards an interior space through 2D or 3D simulation and perform a differential analysis. Wang (2004) employed PC-MDS to analyze the spatial cognition framework of interior designers and consumers from "spacious and splendid" to "simple and plain" and from "daring and innovative" to "traditional and antique [4]. Chuang (2010) aimed to understand the relationship between the physical features of built environment and the human aesthetic responses, they undertook this study to explore different instruments and methods for empirical aesthetic evaluation and used pictures of interior design house furnished as the investigation instrument, and conducted two investigations. A total of 1176 effective samples were collected in this research [5]. Hsu (2011) used the theory of color harmony to explore people's perception towards different color combinations and performed an analysis on the vocabulary and color harmony of a living space [6]. Cheng (2014) created a spatial sample with computer simulation to evaluate psychological response using the semantic differential technique and explored the emotional responses, scenario perception, spatial perception, and preference of participants towards different interior styles and color harmonies [7]. Hong (2009) employed explorative factor analysis to investigate consumers' cognitive levels towards interior designers and the elements affecting their choice of interior designer and design style. Hong also explored the differences in cognitive levels, factors influencing their choice of interior designer and design style between consumers with different backgrounds [8].

Spatial perception is a person's cognitive level, ability to control, user preference, and affective response of the surrounding environment and the reaction towards various components of space [9].

Spatial descriptive ability refers to the perceptions produced from personal preferences and subjective opinions of the observed space. The shape, material, and ambiance of the interior space are then conveyed through text, words, pictures, and images. Liang

(2006) indicate that in the thinking process, hand drawings, design drawings, images and pictures, and text are used to communicate design ideas. In terms of drawings, the designer uses drawings based on personal preference and experience to communicate. Thus, the designer's values have an effect on the use and judgement of drawings [10].

On the other hand, photos are mainly used to record and capture images through photography, transforming complex spatial sequence into simple still images and recreating space through perspective drawings [11].

Vocabulary refers to a collection of words and is used as a tool for communication and knowledge acquisition. It changes with time, age, and background. Different vocabulary can be used to describe the same object. Chu (2006) views vocabulary as a type of symbol or sign that carries correct information. Therefore, the functions and style of design projects are signs reflecting the designer's intuitive interpretation and cognition [12]. Chen and Yan (2016) indicate Spatial vocabulary refers to nouns and adjectives that are used to describe spatial feelings or perceptions and to acquire knowledge. Chi (2014) applied Kansei Engineering to explore the relationship between affective vocabulary and living room environment components and established a parameter-based bi-prediction model [13].

During various stages, designers (the sender) deliver their ideas to clients (the receiver) via communication channels (the medium) in the form of language, words, images, and drawings. The question is whether the sender and receiver have a mutual understanding and interpretation of the message or not determines if the design is able to satisfy the client's needs. This study aims to understand the different backgrounds of receivers (professionals and non-professionals) by exploring the different spatial perceptions they have when interpreting the same spatial image and if they use different spatial vocabulary to describe how they feel.

2   Research Framework

Sun et al. (2009) performed an experiment on participants from different grades in university where they were asked to read a text of words and convert what they interpreted into a drawing. The research found that, whether or not they took storyboarding training, in terms of the cognition of images, the results were different. Moreover, participants showed limitless imagination in the surreal scenario image [3].

Therefore, this study tested the hypothesis that professionals and non-professionals have different spatial perceptions of the same interior space and use different spatial vocabulary when describing their feelings based on their work experience, communication tools, and preference of expression.

This study is divided into three stages. The first stage involves the screening of spatial images and vocabulary, during which text and pictures are extracted from design projects. In the second stage, participants pick vocabulary for every image and specify the reason for choosing them. The purpose is to analyze the difference between cognitive levels and communication skills of professionals and non-professionals. The third stage is where the second questionnaire survey was conducted. Based on the previous survey results, we came to the conclusion that the selection of spatial vocabulary and images should be redefined to prevent similar pictures or words with similar meanings from affecting participants. For the second questionnaire survey, participants choose spatial images and vocabulary again based on spatial features and ambience with the aim to explore the effect of seniority, communication tools, and communication methods on communication ability Table 1.

Table 1. Framework for interpreting images to vocabularies

Spatial images and spatial vocabulary screening		Spatial vocabulary survey (first)	Spatial vocabulary survey (second)
Purpose	Collect spatial vocabulary and images to describe projects	Investigate the difference of spatial vocabulary used by participants with different backgrounds	Explore the effect of seniority, communication tools, and communication methods on communication skills of participants with different backgrounds
Subject	Text and pictures from projects featured in 12 issues of Taiwan interior design magazine from 2014 to 2015	Professionals (designers with over five years of experience) and non-professionals (college freshmen)	Professionals (designers with over five years of experience) and non-professionals (college freshmen)
Method	Extract 134 nouns and adjectives from Taiwan interior design and select 46 spatial vocabularies	Provide 46 vocabulary choices for each spatial image for on-site and online questionnaire survey	Screen spatial vocabulary and images based on spatial characters and ambience and modify the questionnaire for a second survey

3   Spatial Vocabulary and Spatial Images

Taiwan Interior Design is the only professional and official magazine published by the National Association of Interior Design in Taiwan. Therefore, this study chooses to use pictures and text taken from this publication.

3.1   Screening of Spatial Vocabulary

Spatial vocabulary used in this study is taken from articles about design projects featured in 12 issues of Taiwan Interior Design bimonthly from 2014 to 2015. According to similarities and frequency of appearance, 134 nouns and adjectives are selected and categorized into spatial element, spatial scale, style and characteristics, color, material, spatial ambience, spatial style. The vocabularies are then screened based on univocal words and synonyms. Univocal vocabulary include pure (27), harmony (5), monotonous (3), complete (2), extend (17), flow (9), repressed (9), smooth and shiny (2), round (2), long and slim (1), bright (28), saturated (6), colorful (3), elegant (4), soft (15), plain (13), light (8), rigid (7), decorative (4), texture (3), solid (2), transparent (2), aesthetic (78), simple (54), romantic (12), lavish (38), and mix-and-match (7). Synonyms (19 groups) include varied (8), open-spaced (39), penetrating (33), warm (47), comfortable (113), relaxing (34), unique (87), abundant (52), fun (46), sweet (18), private (11), graceful (45), joyful (4), modern (74), fashionable (24), basic (51), luxurious (44), classical (7), and retro (14). A total of 46 spatial vocabularies are selected for this study Table 2.

Table 2. Spatial vocabulary (first screening)

Attribute	Item	Univocal	Synonym
Interior space definition	Spatial elements	Pure, harmony, monotonous, complete	Varied
	Spatial scale	Extend, flow, repressed	Open-spaced, penetrating
Interior space components	Style and characteristics	Smooth and shiny, round, long and slim	
	Color	Bright, saturated, colorful, elegant	
	Material	Soft, plain, light, rigid, decorative, texture, solid, transparent	Warm
Interior space properties	Spatial ambience	Aesthetic, simple, romantic	Comfortable, relaxing, unique, abundant, fun, sweet, private, graceful, joyful
	Spatial style	Lavish, mix-and-match	Modern, fashionable, basic, luxurious, retro, classical

3.2   Screening of Spatial Images

A total of six interior design projects in the housing category honored by the 4th annual Golden Creativity Award organized by the National Association of Interior Design featured in Taiwan Interior Design are used as subjects. Projects include one gold, silver, and bronze winner each in category A (below 50 ping) and category B (over 50 ping). As the magazine only features distinguishing characteristics of design projects, it lacks a complete and detailed description of space. Therefore, the following criteria is followed during the screening process: (1) the main visual photo of projects reported in the magazine; (2) living rooms and dining rooms are primary choices as they present a more complete spatial composition (e.g., ceiling, floor, wall, furniture) so bathrooms, toilets, cloakrooms, or walk-in closets are not considered (Table 3).

Table 3. Spatial images (first screening)

Fig 1-1	Fig 1-2	Fig 1-3
Fig 1-4	Fig1- 5	Fig 1-6

4   Spatial Vocabulary for Interpreting Images

4.1   First Questionnaire Survey

The 46 spatial vocabulary and six spatial images are used to perform a six-question test. Each question is presented on an A4 paper on which a spatial image is attached with 46 spatial vocabularies to choose from and a blank space beneath. The images are arranged in the order of award levels (gold, silver, and bronze). Participants are asked to fill out questionnaires on site or online. The former involves a written questionnaire and projected images that are displayed from numbers one to six with each image playing for three minutes. For the latter, a website linking to the online questionnaire is given to participants to complete.

To allow the images to be more realistic, the spatial images are first scanned and converted into PDF files with a resolution of 300 × 300 dpi. However, due to different scanners, the colors in spatial images and magazine pictures may vary slightly.

Participants include professionals and non-professionals. Professionals are designers with more than five years of experience in interior design. Considering that the participants come from different places and cannot all be interviewed in person, online questionnaires are created for their convenience. Thirty valid questionnaires returned. Non-professionals refer to college freshmen majoring in interior design at Chung Yuan Christian University (CYCU). At a requested time and place, they are given 20 min to choose suitable words to describe their feelings towards a spatial image and write down the reason why. Out of the 57 questionnaires distributed, 30 valid ones returned.

4.2   Survey Results and Discussion

The frequency of the spatial vocabularies chosen for the spatial images is tested. From the highest to lowest number of times, the result is decorative (25), texture (20), extend (17), plain (16), and elegant (16).

According to Table 4, the word that appears the most times in Fig. 1 and Fig. 1-6 is "decorative". The two images both contain a variety of furniture to create a "decorative" spatial ambience. In Fig. 1-2 and Fig. 1-4, "texture" is used the most times to describe participants' feelings. The two images both feature marble and wooden furnishings.

Table 4. Analysis of spatial vocabulary (first questionnaire survey)

Fig 1-1		Fig 1-2		Fig 1-3		Fig 1-4		Fig 1-5		Fig 1-6	
Professionals	Non-professionals	Professionals	Non-professionals	Professionals	Non-professionals	Professionals	Non-professionals	Professionals	Non-professionals	Professionals	Non-professionals
Decorative (10)	Decorative (10)	Texture (14)	Texture (20)	Simple (12)	Plain (16)	Texture (12)	Texture (14)	Extend (17)	Texture (13)	Decorative (25)	Decorative (18)
Colorful (8)	Texture (9)	Decorative (10)	Rigid (12)	Spacious (7)	Simple (13)	Harmony (9)	Spacious (12)	Texture (17)	Simple (9)	Texture (7)	Varied (5)
Varied (7)	Complete (8)	Rigid (10)	Decorative (10)	Decorative (7)	Spacious (7)	Penetrating (7)	Penetrating (10)	Elegant (16)	Complete (7)	Saturated (7)	Texture (5)
Spacious (5)	Colorful (8)	Complete (4)	Complete (7)	Complete (7)	Extend (5)	Spacious (5)	Harmony (9)	Simple (13)	Harmony (7)	Varied (6)	Solid (5)
Harmony (5)	Varied (7)	Simple (4)	Harmony (7)	Long and slim (5)	Long and slim (5)	Long and slim (5)	Elegant (8)	Harmony (10)	Elegant (7)	Solid (6)	Saturated (5)

Based on the five spatial vocabularies with the highest frequency rate and the reasons participants gave, four vocabularies including decorative, texture, extend, plain, and elegant were all chosen by non-professionals, indicating that college freshmen tend to use the same words and have the same feelings towards an image due to their similar learning environment and courses. Professionals, on the other hand, come from different backgrounds and therefore tend to have different feelings and use of words.

The main findings of this survey are as follows:

(1) Confusing vocabularies: Some of the spatial vocabularies selected from the first screening process are unable to clearly describe an interior space. For example, extend, round, long and slim, saturated, and soft may confuse participants.
(2) Similar images: Some of the spatial images are too similar, making it difficult for participants to choose suitable words for them.
(3) Differences in cognitive levels: According to the frequency test, non-professionals typically show the same cognitive levels for an image due to the fact that they learn from same educational environments, while professionals have different back-grounds and therefore tend to show more differences in their cognitive levels. Based on the reasons participants provided, despite both choosing the word "decorative" for Fig. 1, professionals and non-professionals have different reasons. Professionals think that detailed with molding and complex chandelier are decorative, while non-professionals think that variety of furniture enhance a living space.
(4) Differences in communication skills: Nine questionnaires indicate that non-profes-sionals are unable to clearly describe their spatial perceptions with words, which may be because of their lack of professional training in interior design since they are only taking beginner courses in freshman year. Professionals have more expe-rience in the interior design sector and therefore are equipped with better commu-nication skills.

4.3   Second Questionnaire Survey

The results of the first survey show a significant difference in using words to describe spatial perceptions between professionals and non-professionals. In terms of choosing spatial vocabulary, non-professionals use more or less of the same words while profes-sionals show more of a variety in choosing vocabularies. However, images that are too similar or words that have similar meanings easily confuse participants and affect their choices. Therefore, it is important to choose more specific spatial vocabulary and spatial images based on the characteristics, ambience, and style of a spatial composition. Design communication questions are also added to investigate whether communication tools and methods professionals and non-professionals adopt affect their choices.

Regarding spatial vocabulary screening, words that are unable to clearly describe a space are eliminated, namely pure, harmony, monotonous, complete, extend, flow, round, long and slim, bright, saturated, colorful, elegant, soft, plain, rigid, decorative, transparent, penetrating, warm, relaxing, unique, fun, and joyful. The remaining 23 vocabularies are then divided into three categories: (1) spatial characters: open-spaced, private, solid, smooth and shiny, varied, repressed, light, texture; (2) spatial ambience:

abundant, simple, comfortable, sweet, romantic, aesthetic, graceful; (3) spatial style: fashionable, luxurious, lavish, mix and match, retro, basic, classical, and modern (Table 5).

Table 5. Spatial vocabulary (second screening)

Spatial character	Spatial ambience	Spatial style
Open-spaced	Abundant	Fashionable
Private	Simple	Luxurious
Solid	Comfortable	Lavish
Smooth and shiny	Sweet	Mix and match
Varied	Romantic	Basic
Repressed	Aesthetic	Classical
Light	Graceful	Retro
Texture		Modern

To prevent participants from having difficulty choosing suitable spatial vocabulary because some spatial images are too similar, this time 12 images are chosen from the magazine based on spatial definition elements (ceiling, floor, area, furniture) for participants to give subjective opinions on each image according to the main items of spatial perception (style, color, material). Then, four images with the biggest difference in each item are chosen; that is, images with different spatial perceptions as shown Table 6.

Table 6. Spatial images (second screening)

Fig 2-1	Fig 2-2	Fig 2-3	Fig 2-4

In the second questionnaire, questions are redesigned for four spatial images and 23 spatial vocabularies. New questions about design communication tools and design communication methods are added to explore the differences between professionals (designers) and non-professionals (college freshmen).

4.4   Survey Results and Discussion

According to Table 7, the results show: (1) the tools designers and owners use to communicate are design drawings, verbal communication, written words, and actual models; (2) the tools designers and construction workers use to communicate are design drawings, verbal communication, actual models, and written words; (3) the tools students and teachers use to communicate are verbal communication, design drawing, and actual models.

Table 7. Design communication methods

Subjects		Written words	Verbal communication	Design drawings	Actual models
Professionals	Designers to client	7.1%	28.6%	71.6%	3.6%
	Designers to workers	3.6%	17.9%	82.1%	8.7%
Non-professionals	Students to teachers	0%	43.8%	40.6%	15.6%

As shown in Table 8, in terms of means of communication, professionals (designers) believe that proper transmission of information, knowledge and skills, reaching a consensus, and excellent communication skills are most important. On the other hand, non-professionals (college freshmen) consider proper transmission of information, excellent communication skills, reaching a consensus, and knowledge and skills as priorities. This shows that professionals think knowledge and skills and reaching a consensus are far more important than excellent communication skills.

Table 8. Effective communication methods

Subjects	Proper transmission of information	Excellent communication skills	Reaching a consensus	Knowledge and skills
Professionals	46.4%	10.7%	17.9%	25%
Non-professionals	62.5%	18.8%	9.4%	9.4%

In Fig. 2-1, which mainly features the color white, non-professionals use open-spaced, simple, and basic the most while professionals use open-spaced, comfortable, and basic more.

In Fig. 2-2, which has a richer variety of colors, non-professionals and professionals use varied, abundant, and mix and match.

In Fig. 2-3, which contains classical furnishings, non-professionals use texture, graceful, and basic while professionals use texture, graceful, and classical.

In Fig. 2-4, which is more simple and open-spaced, non-professionals use open-spaced, simple, and basic while professionals use texture, simple, and modern (Table 9).

Compared to the results of the first questionnaire survey, the second questionnaire produced more distinctive results; participants did not have difficulty answering the questions. Therefore, professionals and non-professionals all use the same words for Figs. 2-1, 2-2, and 2-3 (open-spaced, varied, and texture, respectively) and their second choice of words is also the same for Figs. 2-2, 2-3, and 2-4 (abundant, graceful, and simple, respectively).

Table 9. Selection of spatial vocabulary (second questionnaire)

	Fig 2-1	Fig 2-2	Fig 2-3	Fig 2-4
Image				
Professionals	Open-spaced, comfortable, basic	Varied, abundant, mix and match	Texture, graceful, classical	Texture, simple, modern
Non-professionals	Open-spaced, simple, basic	Varied, abundant, mix and match	Texture, graceful, basic	Open-spaced, simple, basic

5   Conclusion

Spatial cognition refers to the acquisition, organization, and classification of information obtained from spatial environments. Communication is required to reach a consensus between information and cognition. Interior design is the communication process that presents a design idea by means of words, text, drawings, and animation. In other words, communication media is the key to making the information sent by the sender and information received by the receiver consistent. This study provides different spatial images for professionals and non-professionals to interpret and spatial vocabulary for them to choose. After two questionnaire surveys, the main findings of this study are as follows: (1) spatial vocabularies that describe an interior space need to be able to clearly identify the characters, ambience, and style of the space; (2) if a space has obvious difference in style, color, and material, vocabularies become more consistent; (3) the abundance and complexity of furniture play an important role; for example, less furniture or simple furnishings tend to be interpreted as simple or basic.

References

1. Chiu, M.L., Yen, S.J.: Design representations and visual communication phenomena in the architectural design process. J. Des. **3**(2), 87–110 (1998)
2. Sun, C.W., Chen, C.H., Chiang, S.B.: The differences in visual interpretation of scene framing incurred during converting situational descriptions into visual images. J. Des. **14**(4), 1–22 (2009)
3. Li, H.C.: A study on the influence of illuminance and color temperature of artificial lighting on visual perception and survey of lighting models-using living room as an example. Unpublished master thesis, Department of interior design, Chung Yuan Christian University, Chung-li (2002)
4. Wang, T.H.: A study of residential interiors' spatial images. Unpublished master thesis, Department of interior design, Chung Yuan Christian University, Chung-li (2004)
5. Chuang, H.T., Liu, S.Y., Chen, J.H., Wu, M.H.: The aesthetic evaluation of furnished interior space. J. Architect. **74**, 155–174 (2010)
6. Hsu, H.Y.: A study on the visual image of home space applied to color harmony theory. Unpublished master thesis, Department of Visual Communication Design, National Yunlin University of Science and Technology, Yunlin (2011)

7. Cheng, Y.R.: An investigation on the preferences of subjects for different interior style and tone, Unpublished master thesis, Department of Architecture and urban design, Chao Yang University of Technology, Taichung (2014)
8. Hong, J.K.: The residential interior design style and space consumer demand. Unpublished master thesis, Department of Mathematic, Chung Hua University, Shin-Chu (2009)
9. Jan, H.T.: Urban People: The Sense, Symbol and Explanation of Urban Space. Commonwealth Publishing Company, Taipei (1996)
10. Liang, C.Y.: The thinking and presentation in drawings -a study from the book, why architects draw. Unpublished master thesis, Department of Architecture, National Taiwan University of Science Technology, Taipei (2006)
11. Chen, L.Y., Yen, W.C.: Discussion on the cognition and expression of interior design from the perspective of communication. In: The 12th Conference of CIIAD, Yunlin (2016)
12. Chu, S.T., Lee, C.F.: A study on the form phrase of switch movement with semantics perspective for 3C products. J. Des. Res. **6**, 210–218 (2006)
13. Chi, T.Y.: The element and structure of house living room research by Kansei engineering. Unpublished master thesis, Department of interior design, Chung Yuan Christian University, Chung-li (2004)

A Study on Signage Design and Synesthesia in Senior Residences

Miao-Hsien Chuang[1](✉), Tong-Fang Ni[2], and Jui-Ping Ma[3]

[1] Department of Visual Communication Design, Ming Chi University of Technology,
New Taipei City, Taiwan
joyceblog@gmail.com
[2] Department of Public Affairs Relations, Chang Gung Medical Foundation, Taipei City, Taiwan
sophia@cgmh.org.tw
[3] Department of Property Management, Chien Hsin University of Science and Technology,
Taoyuan City, Taiwan
artma2010@gmail.com

Abstract. Aging and aged societies have gained widespread attention across the world in recent years. In Taiwan, senior citizens will soon account for over 14% of the population, officially designating Taiwan as an "aged society". Consequently, aspects of senior care such as senior housing and residential facilities are becoming issues of note. This study applied theory developed by Norman (2004) to the Chang Gung Health And Culture Village (hereafter referred to as the Village). We examined this case study of the first senior residence in Taiwan using Norman's three levels of emotional design: visceral, behavioral, and reflective. We conducted case analysis, experimental design, and semi-structured interviews to explore and validate research results. Initial observations revealed the following underlying problems: poor pedestrian orientation resulting in pedestrians frequently getting lost; a sense of rational efficiency in the overall design; and signage that is difficult to recognize and remember. The present paper evaluates the visual effects of signage in the Village and then makes recommendations for improvement. These include the addition of curves and floral patterns to the signage system so as to cause higher levels of synesthesia. We also discovered that (1) the elderly do not have difficulty appreciating the beauty of western design; (2) figures, patterns, and numbers with additional verbal explanations can increase the likelihood of seniors receiving and remembering the messages of signage. These research findings contribute to improved signage design for the Village and other senior residences in Taiwan, as well as those in other countries influenced by Chinese culture.

Keywords: Signage design · Senior residences · Synesthesia

1 Introduction

It is predicted by the WHO that by 2020, those over 65 will account for 10–20% of the population in the majority of countries; in some countries, the number will be even higher. Taiwan is no exception to this global trend. It is predicted that the demographic

© Springer International Publishing AG 2017
P.-L.P. Rau (Ed.): CCD 2017, LNCS 10281, pp. 324–333, 2017.
DOI: 10.1007/978-3-319-57931-3_26

"death cross" will become a reality in Taiwan in 2017, when the senior population will account for more than 14% of the total population, definitively designating Taiwan as an "aged society". The Long-term Care Services Act was passed in 2016 in Taiwan, legalizing the government's obligation to provide disabled people with improved care and facilities. This has placed the issue of senior citizens' well-being and residence at the top of the priority list in Taiwan.

Many Taiwanese seniors choose to live with their adult children (57.97%); even those who do not actually live with their offspring wish to (61.22%). However, nearly 40% of senior citizens consider themselves "a burden to their family or society". Statistics show that 10% of those over 65 in European countries and the US, and 5% of the seniors in Japan either live in senior residences or use assisted facilities. In Taiwan, however, only a few senior residences funded by the private sector can be found for the elderly. This gap in the market has been acknowledged by the recent promotion of house-for-pension schemes to build high-quality senior residences for 50–65 year-olds who have a high level of education, are financially independent and forward-planning. This new market makes the quality of senior living facilities and provision of care a topical issue in research.

Seniors are apt to feel frustrated when they experience a decline in vision, hearing, sense of balance, and muscular strength. This can be exacerbated by the onset of chronic disease. Therefore, in addition to increased physical assistance, seniors also need avenues to generate emotional attachments to their communities, which encompass both people and surroundings. Hence it is vital that senior homes employ well-designed signage to create a sense of familiarity and cordiality in their residences, allowing the elderly to feel comfortable calling these places "home".

2 Literature Review

2.1 Older Adults' Vision and Emotions

Senior people tend to become visually impaired and are likely to develop other problems such as senile macular degeneration, cataract, diabetic retinopathy, open angle glaucoma, and angle-closure glaucoma. Older adults take longer to adapt to changes in light, and cannot endure blue light for as long as younger people. They often fail to quickly recognize the movement of objects (Liu 1991). Eifler (2011) pointed out that the elderly require light levels three times stronger to recognize familiar objects, while they are extremely sensitive to light rays. Therefore the guidelines regarding visual design for the elderly are as follows: (1) Avoid too bright or yellow-colored graphics. (2) Use contrasting colors in interior design: for example, the color of a chair should be highly contrastive to that of the floor, so an elderly person can avoid accidentally bumping into it. (3) Use colors such as soft blues or light shades of purple, which elicit a sense of safety and warmth in viewers. Floral patterns are also highly recommended to evoke happy memories or to remind viewers of peaceful pastoral scenery.

Liu (1991) drew on Erikson's theory of life stages as a cycle in his suggestion that old age is a stage when one learns to cope with disappointment and calmly accept one's changed reality and identity. Psychological factors that affect aging are heredity and gender, physiological health, ecological environment, and cultural and educational backgrounds. Senior people often feel dismayed by a sense of loss and deterioration when they approach advanced age. Nostalgia is a common coping strategy associated with this stage; older adults therefore tend to develop strong emotional attachments to people, things, and their environment.

2.2 Signage Design

When people find themselves in an unfamiliar environment, they use spatial cues in their wayfinding behavior, which involves a recursive process in which information is processed and decisions are made (Tseng 2005). Factors that affect wayfinding behaviors can be categorized into three types: (1) Personal attributes: the ability to find the right path varies from individual to individual. (2) Spatial attributes: the clues embedded in an environment, whether it be too many or too few, are likely to make users feel uncertain about formulating judgments. (3) The features of the signage system: both software components (words, graphics, arrows or combination of colors) and hardware components (material, form, or size) are used to render explicit, concrete descriptions. The location and design of the signage system as well as the amount of signboards in a venue also are crucial factors affecting wayfinding behavior. Easterby (1978) stated that "readability," "legibility," and "visibility" are three evaluative indicators of signage design.

According to Guidelines regarding the Design of Common Public Signs formulated by the Research, Development and Evaluation Commission, Executive Yuan (2005), public signs can be classified into the following five types: (1) Identification: these signs indicate the functions of a facility, place or object; (2) Direction: these signs are used as spatial cues to help direct people to their desired location or goal; (3) Orientation: a floor plan or map is used to illustrate the locations and relative positions of each and every feature of a facility or environment; (4) Explanation: these signs are used to inform people of the properties and functions of an object and how to use it; (5) Regulatory: regulatory signs can be used for prohibition or warning, and most often rely on graphics or symbols to convey their core message.

Public signs are a series of standardized signs that are recognized and used across the globe. Whether users of different nationalities have their own cultural preferences with regard to signage has long been a topic of debate. Lin (1998) studied three groups of participants with different educational backgrounds to conclude that both cultural differences and the quality of design (clarity of messages) have a huge impact on users' cognition of the signage.

2.3 Synesthesia

Rodaway (1994) pointed out that "perception" depends on both sensation and cognitive abilities. Sensation is generated from the five senses: sight, hearing, smell, taste, and touch, with which humans receive messages from and communicate with the world. Human cognition refers to the mental activities involved in compiling messages and forming judgments. In short, the perceptual process starts from receiving a multitude of stimuli from the environment, which is later transmitted as signals by the nervous system to our consciousness so we can create a knowledge structure through life experience.

Chen and Yang (2000) suggested that the five senses, which are produced through sense organs, not only respond to certain stimuli, but also engender "synesthesia". The word "synesthesia" has its origin in the Greek roots, as "syn" means "union" and "aisthēsis" means "sensation". Synesthesia is a secondary perceptual process—a condition in which one sense is simultaneously perceived as if by other senses. According to Hsu (2001), this process bears some relation to the concept of ruthlessness (無情) stressed by the renowned Chinese philosopher, Zhuangzi, in which one attempts to relinquish mundane desires and achieve a sublime state of mind, which involves forming a deep connection with the natural world, synesthesia, an emotional state emphasized by the art world.

2.4 Summary

The impact of age-related vision loss can be minimized by the use of contrasting colors. In addition, floral patterns help to bring a peaceful atmosphere and evoke memories of happiness. It is vital to pay particular attention to the signage design of senior residences, especially in the respects of legibility and visibility. Cultural differences and the quality of design (clarity of messages) have a significant impact on users' cognition of the signage. After a viewer processes the forms and colors of an object, and her/his spirit has achieved a sublime state of mind, it is possible to experience synesthesia. The above literature is of great value to our subsequent study of signage design and verification of our hypotheses.

3 Methodology

This study considers the case of the Chang Gung Health and Culture Village, funded by Formosa Plastics Group (hereafter referred to as FPG). In this case study, we employed

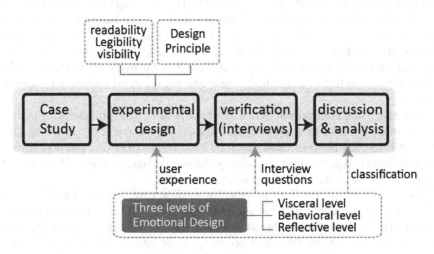

Fig. 1. Research process

observation, experiments, and semi-structured interviews to explore user experience of the signage design. The steps of this research process are shown in Fig. 1.

Norman (2004) analyzed the following three levels of design using a teapot as a case study: visceral (appearance-based), behavioral (user-friendliness and satisfaction), and reflective (rationalization of the product, its narrative and its link to self-image). This study applied Norman's theory in the design of experiments and interviews as well as in subsequent discussions on emotional design. These three levels of emotional design and their roles in the experiment are shown in Table 1.

Table 1. Three levels of emotional design and their roles in the experiment

Three levels of emotional design	Visceral	Behavioral	Reflective
Purpose	Exterior design (exterior, tactile, feeling)	User experience (functions, efficacy, and applicability) Inner satisfaction	(self-image, satisfaction level, and memory)
Design concerns	Sensation (vision impairment)	Cognition	Synesthesia
Guidelines and verification	1. Color: discrimination and memory 2. Line: thickness, rigid/organic 3. Font: decoration 4. Layout: grouping and hierarchy	1. Legibility 2. Direction 3. Memorable	1. A sense of belonging and identification 2. Experiences of friendliness and cordiality

3.1   Case Study

The Chang Gung Health and Culture Village is part of the Chang Gung medical network, which is funded by FPG. This medical network has long been known for its prominent leadership in Taiwan's medical system, and its aim is to provide comprehensive medical care to citizens at all phases of life. Wang Yung-Ching, the founder of the Village, declared that the Village was built to provide a comfortable living environment for older adults so they can live in a dignified manner and engage in the multitude of activities on offer.

Since the Village officially launched its service in 2005, it has provided a high-quality service of care for senior people within the supportive network of the Chang Gung Memorial Hospital. However, under the rigid management of FPG, a traditional plastic-manufacturing company with a long history, the interior signage of the Village conveys a sense of aloofness and rational efficiency.

Aside from the provision of professional medical care services, the Village also offers a variety of cultural activities for senior people. Noted for its green architecture, open-plan hallways, and accessible design, the 17-hectare Village provides ample space and a cordial atmosphere for senior people to freely interact with other inhabitants.

However, the complex design of the buildings in the Village has caused older residents to experience much difficulty in finding their way. For example, Building A is constructed in the form of the letter G, while Building C is built in the form of a capital B and P (shown in Table 2).

Table 2. Floor plan of Buildings A & C (Source: http://www.yunzhan365.com/basic/87997642.html)

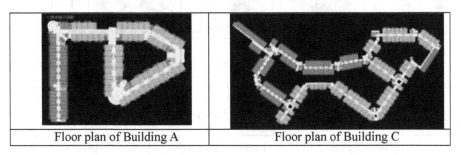

| Floor plan of Building A | Floor plan of Building C |

As the complexity of building design often leads to the confusion of senior residents and young staff of the Village, the role of signboards within the Village cannot be over-emphasized. The current signboards are ineffective partly because the font family, style and size of these signs are hardly to recognize. In addition, the scarcity and location of these signboards result in poor traffic flow. Observation and interviews revealed the following problems related to signage design:

1. Pedestrian orientation is not well thought-out, which results in pedestrians often getting lost.
2. The design is standardized, which conveys a sense of aloofness and rationality and lacks a friendly touch.
3. Too much variation in color and too many room numbers make the information difficult to remember.
4. Where an attempt at elegance has been made (for example the Microsoft Standard Kai Font), the shadow effect produced from the "hollowing out" of characters decreases legibility.

3.2 Design of Experiments

We presented three experimental designs, which are in accordance with the three selected evaluative indicators: Identification, Direction, Orientation (designs shown in Tables 3, 4 and 5).

Table 3. Experimental design: #Identification

Current design	Experimental design			Ongoing design work
				* Simplicity * Floral pattern *Telling stories about how to live longer and better.
	Figure A	Figure B	Figure C	

Table 4. Experimental design: #Direction

Current design	Experimental design	Ongoing design work
		*Gestalt psychology * Legibility *Night-time illumina-tion
Figure D	Figure E	

Table 5. Experimental design: #Orientation

Orientation (example#1)			Orientation (example#2)		
Current design	Experimental design	Ongoing design work	Current design	Experimental design	Ongoing design work
		*Organic lines *Contrasting colors *Simplifying expressions with numbers			*Color: discrimination *Color: contrast *Mapping (to find geographic positions)
Figure F	Figure G		Figure H	Figure I	

3.3 Semi-structured Interviews

We conducted semi-structured interviews among the 32 residents of the Village. The sex ratio was 50:50, and the age ranges from 65–92. Of these surveyed inhabitants, 3 persons were aged 65–69, 8 persons aged 70–79, 14 persons aged 80–89, and 7 persons aged 90–92. The average age was 81.1, which was approximate to the Villagers' average age of 81.4. The proportion of the respondents who have received no education at all was low (only 3). Two persons had attended compulsory education, while 2 and 7 persons achieved lower and higher secondary education, respectively. Fourteen persons had received their bachelor's degrees, 6 persons master's degrees and 1 person a doctoral degree. 47% of the residents had lived abroad for many years. 30% of these respondents stated they got lost when they first moved in the community.

4 Results and Discussion

4.1 Visceral Level

With regard to clarity and eligibility, 94% of the respondents preferred Fig. E over Fig. D, although some of them suggested bigger fonts. A minority of respondents appreciated the classical fonts in Fig. D, yet they suggested decorative fonts for a lively touch. 90% of the respondents were satisfied with the night-time lamination of signboards. As to the floor plan's visual effect, Fig. G was generally believed to be far clearer than Fig. F. When it comes to the disorder arranged arrows of Fig. D, only 12% of the respondents found them distracting. Respondents unanimously agreed that the arrow's size and clarity were the most important factors.

4.2 Behavioral Level

Most respondents agreed that the 5-digit room numbers after additional verbal explanations were easy to remember. They have got used to these 5-digits numbers and would be reluctant to see them changed. Yet 30% of the respondents were uncomfortable with the representation of English words replacing the numerical digits. When it comes to reading a map, only 40% of those surveyed did not like too much variation in color in Fig. H, yet they generally agreed that the black-grey-white colors, albeit very recognizable, are boring.

4.3 Reflective Level

We hypothesized that adding curves and floral patterns would elicit higher synesthesia from people. To achieve this effect, we made three types of signage for the rhythm center. Fig. A shows only an icon and Chinese characters, Fig. B includes some simple lines and diamond-shaped ornamentations, whereas Fig. C presents highly decorative floral patterns. Not a single person chose Fig. A, 16% of the respondents picked Fig. B, and the remaining 84% of these respondents liked Fig. C the most. 97% of the respondents were satisfied with dark crimson as the background color, and would choose dark blue if there was a second option. As to the floor plan, 67% of the respondents regarded the floral circles of Fig. G acceptable, 8% of them were ambivalent, and 14% of them thought that floral circles did not render meaning to the floor plan.

78% of the respondents held a positive attitude toward the warm background colors of Figs. B and C, and floral designs of Figs. B, C, E & G. Some participants took a strong liking to the decorative patterns and expressed gratitude toward designers for their effort to render a cozy and friendly atmosphere to the surroundings. 19% of the respondents were only attracted to one or two of the designs of Figs. B, C, E, & G.

We first took preference variables (preferences towards Chinese traditional paintings vs. western paintings) and synesthesia effect variables (on a Likert's 3-point scale: (1) totally agree, (2) partially agree, (3) disagree) into consideration, and then carried out a Pearson's chi-square test. Statistical results showed that Chi-square value X2 = 5.6, df = 6. This suggests that the null hypothesis cannot be proven false. In other words, "preference variables" and "synesthesia effect variables" exist independently from each other. Then we carried out a Pearson's chi-square test taking experience living abroad and synesthesia effect variables into consideration. Statistics results revealed that Chi-square value X2 = 0.5706, df = 2. This suggests that the null hypothesis cannot be proven false too.

5   Conclusions and Suggestions

The results from this case study analysis indicate that "legibility" can be increased when the signage design is improved in accordance with the evaluative indicators for signage systems and guidelines regarding visual design. Results of the interviews suggest that night-time lighting, bigger and clearer fonts, and sprightly colors with high contrasts further help to improve legibility. Curves or floral patterns are believed to elicit synesthesia from viewers toward their environment. However, cultural background (experiences abroad or preference for Chinese traditional paintings or western artworks) does not influence evaluation of the designs. Explanations for graphics (such as plants that contribute to longer and better life) and meanings for the numbers (representing "building," "neighborhood," "floor," or "room") help enhance the seniors' reception and memory, irrespective of their educational backgrounds or life experience. These research results serve as reference for interior and signage design applied in the Village and other senior residences in Taiwan, as well as those in countries influenced by Chinese culture.

References

Anon: 2016 The 17th China Hospital Construction Conference Ricky Liu & Associates ppt preview (n.d.). http://www.yunzhan365.com/basic/87997642.html. Accessed 15 Jan 2017

Chen, C.H., Yang, T.M.: Introduction to Visual Communication Design. Chuan Hwa Book Co., Taipei (2000)

Easterby, R.S.: Tasks, processes and display design. In: Information Design: The Design and Evaluation of Signs and Printed Material. Wiley, New York (1978)

Eifler, E.: The Effects of Aging on Color Vision (2011). http://blog.colourstudio.com/2011/11/effects-of-aging-on-color-vision.html. Accessed 15 Jan 2017

Hsu, F.K.: Chinese Art Spirit. East China Normal University, Shanghai (2001)

Lin, R.: Cultural differences in icon recognition. J. Des. **3**(2), 13–30 (1998)

Liu, S.C.: Gerontology. Hochi, Taipei (1991)

Norman, D.A.: Emotional Design: Why We Love (or Hate) Everyday Things. Basic Books, New York (2004)

Research, Development and Evaluation Commission, Executive Yuan: The Guidelines Regarding the Design of Common Public Signs. Research, Development and Evaluation Commission, Executive Yuan, Taipei (2005)

Rodaway, P.: Sensuous Geography: Body, Dense, and Place. Routledge, London (1994)

Tseng, J.H.: The effects of spatial ability, viewpoint and emotional factors for the player's cognitive resource distribution during wayfinding in 3D computer game. Unpublished master's thesis, Institute of Communication Studies, National Chiao Tung University (2005)

Chinese Migrant Food Business in Italy and Design Researches for Intercultural Dialogue

Shushu He[✉]

Department of Design, Politecnico di Milano, Milan, Italy
shushu.he@polimi.it

Abstract. In the age of globalization, different ethnic cultures spread in the migratory flows, and coexist with local cultures, sometimes producing cultural conflicts which are looming with the increasing numbers of migrants that call for the intercultural dialogue. Food for its communicational and cultural attributes can be regard as a point-cut that intercultural dialogue can be fostered basing on the cultural seminaries and differences. The overseas Chinese community in Milan has reached a considerable population, and the migrants have adapted to the local economy while maintaining forms of social separation that is regarded as a cultural enclave.

This paper takes the Chinese migrant food business as the breakthrough since it is one of the most common migratory activities in Milan, and Italian people relatively wider accept Chinese food. This paper adopts two digital methods, OpenStreetMaps (OSM) and Web crawler, to capture the context of Chinese migrant food business in Milan and to explore Italian customers' viewpoints about it. The result shows the need of improving Chinese migrants' public image and enriching Italian hosts' knowledge of migrants. The paper proposes four design goals: information sharing; participatory knowledge production; co-create value; and scale out from individuals to communities. The investigation can benefit to intercultural dialogue, and it provides a reference to improving the cross-cultural communication towards to sustainable pluralistic society.

Keywords: Cultural conflict · Intercultural dialogue · Chinese migrant food business · Design research

1 Introduction

1.1 Globalization, Migration Flow and Culture Conflict

The global is replacing the bounded nation-state, and the creation of migratory communities is one of the consequences of globalization (Olaniyan 2003). Different ethnic cultures spread in the global migratory flows. Globalization and migratory flows feed the cultural difference. Meanwhile, the cultural conflicts embed in the territorial and group cultures. Huntington argues that in the age of globalization will result in conflict and that its primary source will be cultural, which exists beyond not only individual or group identity but as a part of a broader category of group membership (Huntington 1997). The interaction between different cultural groups inevitably leads to

© Springer International Publishing AG 2017
P.-L.P. Rau (Ed.): CCD 2017, LNCS 10281, pp. 334–344, 2017.
DOI: 10.1007/978-3-319-57931-3_27

insurmountable differences, which can escalate to violent conflicts. The interaction mentioned above also can be seen as a combination of beliefs about the nature of human nature, of identity, and of human interaction (Montuori 1989; Bernstein 2005; Eisler 2012). On the other hand, the collaboration of the ethnic community members leads to the tribalism. Manzini manifests that the tribalism shows in which people cooperate against someone else in the name of their particular identity (Manzini and Coad 2015). Cultural conflict becomes a societal issue in the age of globalization. Misunderstandings, migratory enclaves, discriminations, and violence, can be seen as some of the forms of cultural conflicts. Thus, cross-cultural communication is needed to deal with the societal challenge.

1.2 Intercultural Dialogue Is Necessary to Ease the Conflict

Intercultural dialogue can ease the cultural conflicts and strengthen the mutual understanding. According to the definition given by the Council of Europe, intercultural dialogue is a process that includes an open and respectful exchange or interactions between individuals, groups and organizations with different cultural backgrounds or world-views. From this aspect, intercultural dialogue plays a key role as it allows people to prevent ethnic, religious, linguistic and cultural divides. An intercultural dialogue can also enable individuals to move forward together, to deal with different identities constructively and democratically by shared universal values (Europe, B.C.O. 2010). In short, intercultural dialogue can contribute to a sustainable pluralistic society, understand the cultural diversity and create the co-values. Samovar regards the intercultural communication as an interactive process, which a person from one culture sends a message to be handled by one from another culture (Samovar et al. 2011). To foster the intercultural dialogue, therefore, identifying a point-cut is necessary.

This article discusses feasibility to improve intercultural dialogue through design. In the following paragraphs, the paper elaborates the possibilities to foster intercultural dialogue based on food and food culture. The OpenStreetMaps and Web crawler are adopted to investigate Chinese migrant food business in Milan and comes out with design goals to foster intercultural dialogue in such a context.

2 Food as a Point-Cut of Intercultural Dialogue

2.1 Food Provides Intercultural Dialogue a Better Mutual Understanding Precondition

This article takes food as a point-cut for intercultural dialogue as it plays an irreplaceable cultural role. Food is described as a manifestation of a nation's culture (Lannon 1986; Anderson 2005; Montanari 2006; Rozin 2006). Kluckhohn states what people eat are partly regulated by culture. (Kroeber and Kluckhohn 1952). The act of eating is used to establish an identity and to define a certain group, class, or person (Fonseca 2008). The prominent role of food is noticeable as an important expression form used for the purpose of communicating something (Valli and Traill 2005). Food as a cultural symbol, which contains cultural identities, traditions, and customs can bring more communication opportunities basing on the cultural seminaries and differences.

People's elemental needs for food made us regard food irresistible and likable, as Fox says, "we have to eat; we like to eat; eating makes us feel good" (Fox 2003). Delicacies are easy to be welcomed by people, whichever they come from. Besides, eating can be regarded as an experience that contains physical senses and mental factors, since food is always associated with emotions that embody in gustatory memories, such as nostalgia, childhood memories (Holtzman 2006; Sutton 2010; Zampollo 2013). Food also is given a social meaning that provides people a chance to sit face-to-face, conversing, smiling and communicating (Jones 2007). On the other hand, the diversity of food and food cultures could bring more opportunities for intercultural dialogue. Food represents our identities to set us apart from others by what we will (or will not) eat (Fox 2003; Brulotte 2016). The dissimilarities in food and food culture illustrate the cultural distance and difference between ethnic groups, classes, territories and countries (Jonathan 1999), and it can also bring more cross-cultural discussions so to create more occasions for communicating and share ideas (Kittler et al. 2011). Thus, taking food as a point-cut can provide intercultural dialogue a better mutual understanding precondition basing on common senses, also, it enables discussions of dissimilarities and shares different values.

2.2 Food Culture and Sustainability as a Design Issue

Food is always something that connects people together and which has the potential to inspire and engage individuals in new and exciting experience (Spence and Piqueras-Fiszman 2013). To understand the complexity and diversity of the relationship between people and food, designers and scholars start to investigate from multiple aspects, such as technology, sustainability, experience, cultural diversity, etc. Choi explores the role of Human- Computer Interaction (HCI) design in encouraging individual users to participate in creating sustainable food cultures with five core constituents: the perspective of transdisciplinary; the domains of interest of people, place, and technology; and the perspective of design (Choi and Blevis 2010). The human-food interaction design takes food as a point from which to understand people and design technology, which requests designers and researchers to pay more attention to people and the ways in which they engage with food than efficiencies and novelties new technologies may provide (Comber et al. 2014). The CHI 2012 workshop aims to 'attend the practical and theoretical difficulties in designing for human-food interactions in everyday life' identifying four thematic areas of food practices: health and wellbeing; sustainability; food experiences; and alternative food cultures. Similarly, exhibition 'Food Culture: Eating by Design' shows the links between design, food, the origins of what we eat and propose people's complex relationship with food. Kerr, Tan, and Chua present a discussion of the methodological complexities of understanding and designing for food practices, particularly in diverse cultural contexts (Kerr et al. 2014).

To sum up, the present studies point to the methodological, disciplinary, and design complexities involved in balancing the technical with sociocultural to improve the sustainability of food for today and tomorrow that requires concerted efforts across a diverse group of stakeholders including researchers, practitioners, governments, industries, and communities within the given socio-technical context. Food as a cross-cultural communication point-cut seeks to draw attention to the questions and foster further discussions and design research.

3 Foster Intercultural Dialogue for Chinese Migrant Food Business in Milan

3.1 Overseas Chinese Community in Milan: A Cultural Enclave

Italy was not a popular immigrant country for Chinese migrants until 1990s. There were only about ten overseas Chinese in Italy before the World War I, and in the 1960s, the population increased to 800, then reached 1,000 in 1980s (Zhu 1996). At the beginning of the 1990s, the number of Chinese migrants living in Italy kept on climbing, reaching about 20,000 (Fu and Chen 2003).

Chart 1 shows the growth of the Chinese immigrant population in Italy from the year 2002 to 2015. Up to now, Chinese immigrant community is the fourth biggest community in Italy after Albania, Morocco, and Romania. 80% Chinese migrants in Italy share the same ancestral home – Zhejiang Province (which locates on the east coast of China), especially from Wenzhou city, that leads the migrants to live together for better cooperation and to ease the nostalgia. The migrants' social network ties up people in a fixed and closed community that excludes outsiders. The migrant community tends to keep the original habit rather than cater to the native lifestyle (Smyth and French Eds. 2009; Gao 2009). The language, additionally, is another barrier that hampered migrants to communicate with Italian people (Scibetta 2013). Besides, Wenzhounese people have a strong tradition of trade that made them pay more attention to their own business, but not enough on other aspects (Fig. 1).

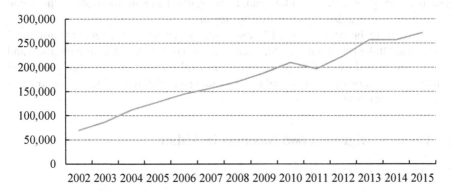

Chart 1. The population of overseas Chinese in Italy from 2002 to 2015 (Demo.istat.it 2016)

To sum up, Chinese migrants in Italy has formed a huge but closed community due to language barriers, business cooperation, and the same ancestral home, which is considered by natives as a 'secret' 'quiet' and 'exclusive' community that calls for more

Fig. 1. Photos of Via Paolo Sarpi took in the 1950s and now (picture from Google)

openness and mutual understandings. Moreover, the overseas Chinese community has adapted to the Italian economy. However, the cultural adaptation still needs to be improved. Also, the increasing population of Chinese migrants and the expanding migratory enclave lead to rapid change in the local environment, while the native residents cannot accept, and the lack of communication escalated the cultural conflict. Hence, intercultural dialogue is desiderated to improve between Chinese migrants and the host society.

3.2   The Breakthrough Point: Chinese Restaurants in Milan

This article takes Chinese food business in Milan, especially migratory restaurants, as the point-cut for improving intercultural dialogue as it provides across-cultural context that Chinese migrants and Italian customers interact in. Besides, running restaurants is one of the most traditional and important Chinese migratory businesses. In this context, stereotypes are embodied in vividly, for instance, Chinese restaurants are widely considered as cheap, poor quality and low-end, additionally, there are food taboos that some Chinese food is regarded as non-edible by Italians.

Dealing with the stereotypes of Chinese restaurants can not only benefit to migrants' business and Italian customers' experiences but also contribute to Chinese migrants and Italians understand each other better basing on food culture. On the other hand, food enables a foundation of better mutual understanding and different value sharing towards to transform stereotypes.

4   Chinese Migrant Food Business in Milan

4.1   Mapping the Context

The research adopts two digital methods to map the context of Chinese migrant food business in Milan. The OpenStreetMaps (OMS) took place in the first phase. According to the user rating and information provided by Google, TripAdvisor, and Huarenjie.com, the map pinned 274 restaurants which are owned by Chinese. As shown in Fig. 2, there are eight colors of pins sorted by the user ratings online and the type of restaurant, which are: Chinese restaurant with grade lower than 3.5; Chinese restaurant with grade between 3.6~4.5; Chinese restaurant with grade higher than 4.6; Japanese restaurant with grade lower than 3.5; Japanese restaurant with grade between 3.6~4.5; Japanese restaurant with grade higher than 4.6; Italian restaurant; and restaurant does not have grade online. It can be seen that the amount of the Japanese restaurant overweighs the number of Chinese restaurants. Besides, many Chinese restaurants which lack customer feedback are spread centrally in Chinatown. Besides, there are only 11 restaurants that offer traditional Chinese cuisine and have won good ratings. Overseas Chinese's restaurant business has reached a considerable scale in Milan. However, it does not represent authentic Chinese cuisine and Chinese food culture.

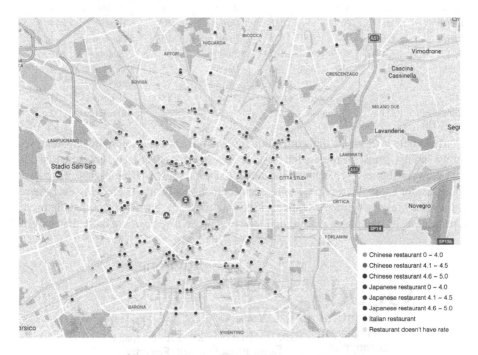

Fig. 2. Restaurants owned by Chinese in Milan City

4.2 Extracting Keywords

To understand what do customers, especially Italian customers think about these restaurants, the Web crawler took place in the second phase and extracted 6,332 feedbacks from above mentioned websites. Table 1 lists 60 high-frequency keywords (which have been translated into English in this article) generated through the web crawler, and the most frequently mentioned words are: Chinese, tasty, good, price, and service.

Table 1. Extracted keywords and the frequencies

Keyword		Keyword		Keyword		Keyword	
Chinese	1438	Fish	331	Friendly	139	Happy	82
Tasty	1372	Environment	328	Satisfy	134	Poor quality	81
Good	1170	Authentic	325	Owner	130	Expensive	71
Price	875	Clean	324	Home	128	Vegetable	68
Service	868	Waiter	257	Noodles	128	Experience	63
Quality	854	Fresh	242	Warm	122	Thai	60
Sushi	694	Beautiful	238	Atmosphere	111	So-so	60
Dinner	560	Like	225	Recommend	111	Slow	55
Japanese	556	Bad	224	Asian	110	Traditional	54
Lunch	535	Pizza	218	Dumplings	107	Terrible	44
Italian	476	Wine	185	Comfortable	103	Convenient	44
Fast	474	Meat	184	Shrimp	99	Cantonese	38
Polite	455	Rice	180	Desert	93	Vegetarian & vegan	33
Milan	345	Economical	169	Wait	85	Sichuanese	32
Come again	337	Disappoint	145	Spicy	84	Romantic	32

The article also adopts the word cloud tools to present the result more apparent. As shown in Fig 3, most customers left positive comments, such as tasty, good, and fast. It also shows customers' preferences like dinner, fish, and spicy, and highlights customers' concerns, for example, service, quality, environment, and atmosphere. However, there are several words which are irrelative with Chinese cuisine, but also be frequently used: Japanese, sushi, and pizza. According to the first phase investigation, more than half of

Fig. 3. The word cloud of high-frequency keywords

restaurants owned by Chinese in Milan are not the typical Chinese restaurant, and the food these restaurants offered are mixed, such as Japanese dishes, Asian fusion, and Italian pizza. Also, there are also some negative feedbacks like 'bad', 'disappoint', 'terrible' and 'poor quality', which expresses there are some aspects are not satisfying.

To sum up, the food business of Chinese migrants has reached a considerable scale in Milan from both quantitative and acceptable viewpoints, meanwhile, there are some unsatisfying aspects due to the lack of cross-cultural communication, for instance, there is a gap between the service and product quality provided by Chinese restaurateurs and perceived by Italian customers. Also, some misunderstandings and stereotypes lead to dissatisfaction, such as the comment 'typical Chinese style' usually connects with 'cheap' which is similar to the cliché of Chinese products: cheap but have poor quality. On the other hand, Chinese restaurateurs have not realized the value of their culture. The number of non-Chinese restaurants is much more than typical Chinese restaurants, as the restaurateurs pay more attention to gaining profit by selling low-cost food, but not attaching cultural value in their business. Another reason is Chinese food business was pummeled by people's scare during SARS. Thus, many Chinese restaurateurs had to cut off their business with Chinese identity (Eleonora 2009). Hence, overseas Chinese food business is an appropriate point-cut of intercultural dialogue, not only because of the prerequisites that it is relatively accepted by Italian but also because there are demands of cross-cultural communication.

5 Design Goals

Aiming at fostering intercultural dialogue between Chinese migrants and local citizens in Milan, the design should first take place in dealing with the Chinese migratory community's problem, such as language barrier, quality improving, the closeness of the social network, so to improve the community's public image. Meanwhile, the design also can be helpful to enrich Italian people's knowledge about Chinese migrants and Chinese culture, towards to dispose of misunderstandings and stereotypes. In the light of investigation mentioned above, there are four aspects that design can intervene in:

(a) **Information sharing:** since communication is an interactive process that creates shared meaning by sending, transmitting, or giving information to others (Carey 2002; Stajcic 2013), design can bring more interactions and more ways of interaction in the process of communication. Besides, design can help to overcome the communication barriers by taking food as the non-verbal language between Chinese migrant restauranteurs and Italian customers. Thus, through design for information sharing, Chinese restauranteurs will better meet customers 'needs and Italian customers' will perceive product and service quality better.

(b) **Participatory knowledge production:** design can foster the participatory knowledge production based on food in which Chinese migrants, Italian customers, and other actors can dialogue, cooperate, conflict, and compromise equally. The participatory process endows actors with changeful roles, for instance, the Chinese restauranteur is not only a provider who offers product and service, but also a listener of his customers, a speaker of his identity, a learner of the host culture, an innovator of migratory food business, a contributor of the intercultural dialogue, etc. The new knowledge produced in such a participatory process can help Chinese migrants to cater their business to Italian customers, on the other hand, it can also enrich Italian people's knowledge about Chinese migrants and Chinese culture, so to deal with negative stereotypes in the cross-cultural context.

(c) **Co-create value:** food culture is not static nor isolated, but keeps changing and evolving with the environment. Specifically, Chinese food in Milan needs to keep pace with the local customers' demands and adapt to the culture of the host society. Design can enable Chinese migrants and Italian hosts to the co-create value of Chinese cuisine in the context of Milan. The empathy coincides with the co-create value so that the Chinese migrant community and Italian host society can be bridged.

(d) **Scale out from individuals to communities:** the innovation of Chinese migrant food business can contribute to Chinese migrants' public image, and help them to gain more business opportunities. The innovation can first take place in the Chinese food business, and influence to other migratory aspects, such as retailing, wholesale, manufactory, import-export, etc., then scale out to the overseas Chinese communities and towards to a broader intercultural dialogue.

6   Conclusion

In summary, intercultural dialogue is significant to cope with culture conflicts in the age of globalization. Food for its communicational and cultural attributes can be regard as a point-cut for fostering intercultural dialogue. This paper focuses on the cross-cultural context of Milan and two digital methods are conducted to capture Chinese migrants' food business in Milan and to extract meanings from customers' online feedbacks so to explore customers' viewpoints and stereotypes in this context. The result shows that the Chinese food business has achieved a considerable scale in Milan and the food provided by Chinese restaurants are widely accepted. However, the restauranteurs are not aware enough the cultural value of Chinese food and there are some stereotypes impeded the cross-cultural communication, thus, it calls for the efforts from both migrants and Italian hosts. The paper proposes four design goals according to the investigation. In the light of design goals, the further design practices can take place in the three aspects:service design supporting information sharing; participatory design for knowledge co-production and co-create value; and design for social innovation.

This paper provides a reference to improve migrant community's public image and enrich the knowledge of the host society so to bridge the cultural gap towards to the sustainable pluralistic society. Hence it provides a base for design activities aimed at a better reciprocal knowledge and appreciation between native and migrant communities sharing the same territory. It also shows the possibility to enable individuals to move forward together, to deal with different identities, to share values basing on intercultural dialogue as a potential of cultural, social and economic growth in urban environments.

References

Olaniyan, T.: African writers, exile, and the politics of a global diaspora. In: West Africa Review (2003)

Huntington, S.P.: The Clash of Civilizations and the Remaking of World Order. Penguin Books India, Kolkata (1997)

Montuori, A.A.: Evolutionary Competence: Creating the Future. Brill Academic Pub., Leiden (1989)

Bernstein, R.J.: The abuse of evil: the corruption of politics and religion since 9/11. Polity (2005)

Eisler, R.T.: The chalice and the blade: our history, our future. Contemp. Sociol. **25**(4), 85–86 (2012)

Manzini, E., Coad, R.: Design, When Everybody Designs: An Introduction to Design for Social Innovation. MIT Press, Cambridge (2015)

Europe, B.C.O. White paper on intercultural dialogue: 'living together as equals in dignity (2010)

Samovar, L.A., Porter, R.E., McDaniel, E.R.: Intercultural Communication: A Reader. Wadsworth Publishing Company, Boston (2011)

Lannon, J.: How people choose food: the role of advertising and packaging. In: Ritson, C., Gofton, L., McKenzie, J. (eds.) The Food Consumer. Wiley, Chichester (1986)

Anderson, Eugene N.: Everyone Eats: Understanding Food and Culture. New York University Press, New York (2005)

Rozin, P.: The integration of biological, social, cultural and psychological influences on food choice. In: Shepherd, R., Raats, M. (eds.) The Psychology of Food Choice, CABI Pub., Wallingford, UK, Association with the Nutrition Society (2006)

Montanari, M.: Food Is Culture. Columbia University Press, New York (2006)

Kroeber, A.L., Kluckhohn, C.: Culture: a critical review of concepts and definitions. In: Papers. Peabody Museum of Archaeology and Ethnology, Harvard University (1952)

Fonseca, M.: Understanding consumer culture: the role of "Food" as an important cultural category. In: LA-Latin American Advances in Consumer Research, vol. 2 (2008)

Valli, C., Traill, W.B.: Culture and food: a model of yoghurt consumption in the EU. Food Qual. Prefer. **16**(4), 291–304 (2005)

Fox, R.: Food and Eating: An Anthropological Perspective. Social Issues Research Center, Oxford (2003)

Holtzman, J.D.: Food and memory. Annu. Rev. Anthropol. **35**, 361–378 (2006)

Sutton, D.E.: Food and the Senses. Annu. Rev. Anthropol. **39**, 209–223 (2010)

Zampollo, F.: Food and design: space, place and experience. Hosp. Soc. **3**(3), 181–187 (2013)

Spence, C., Piqueras-Fiszman, B.: Technology at the dining table. Flavour **2**(1), 16 (2013). doi: 10.1186/2044-7248-2-16

Choi, J.H.J., Blevis, E.: HCI and sustainable food culture: a design framework for engagement. In: Proceedings of the 6th Nordic Conference on Human-Computer Interaction: Extending Boundaries, pp. 112–117. ACM (2010)

Comber, R., Choi, H.J., Hoonhout, J., O'Hara, K.: Designing for human–food interaction: an introduction to the special issue on 'food and interaction design'. Int. J. Hum Comput Stud. **72**(2), 181–184 (2014)

Kerr, S.J., Tan, O., Chua, J.C.: Cooking personas: goal-directed design requirements in the kitchen. Int. J. Hum. Comput. Stud. **72**(2), 255–274 (2014)

Zhu, L.: Wencheng County. Zhonghua Book Company, Beijing (1996)

Fu, X., Chen, P.: Inseparable from China - Italy overseas Chinese impression, p. 10. People's Daily (2003)

Demo.istat.it.: Statistiche demografiche ISTAT (2016). http://demo.istat.it/str2015/index_e.html. Accessed 13 Dec 2016

Jones, M.: Feast: Why Humans Share Food. Oxford University Press, Oxford (2007)

Fox, R.: Food and eating: an anthropological perspective, pp. 1–22. Social Issues Research Center (2003). http://sirc.org/publik/foxfood.pdf

Brulotte, R.L.: Edible Identities: Food As Cultural Heritage. Routledge, Abingdon (2016)

Kittler, P.G., Sucher, K.P., Nelms, M.: Food and Culture. Cengage Learning, Boston (2011)

Eleonora, C.: Migrants and consumption: an analysis from the supply perspective (2009). http://www.sociol.unimi.en/documents/files.CASTAGNONE_Migrantieconsumo.pdf

Stajcic, N.: Understanding culture: food as a means of communication. Hemispheres **28**, 5–14 (2013)

Carey, J.: A cultural approach to communication. In: McQuail's reader in Mass Communication Theory, pp. 36–45 (2002)

Swift, J.S.: Cultural closeness as a facet of cultural affinity: A contribution to the theory of psychic distance. Int. Mark. Rev. **16**(3), 182–201 (1999)

Collaborative Service for Cross-Geographical Design Context: The Case of Sino-Italian Digital Platform

Chenhan Jiang[(✉)] and Yongqi Lou

Tongji University, Shanghai, China
chenhan0713@126.com, Lou.yongqi@tongji.edu.cn

Abstract. Recently, cross-geographical cooperation with multi-stakeholders is frequently involved in design exploration process. Problems and limitations have also cropped up following this trend, such as temporal and geographical boundaries, transportation of different formats, project management effectiveness, and the time-consuming multinational communication. To response such new challenges, a set of services for digital collaborative work arise at the moment. However, design strategies or paradigms for facilitating cross-geographical design collaboration context are still not clear. To make the user experience more smooth and friendly, designers also have some confusion to clarify a more efficient service approach. This study aims to give a strategic guidance for collaborative service design. With the methodology of case study, research results can be drawn through five stages: (1) Literature review on elements and mechanism of user experience, collaborative service and CSCW. (2) Inquire and insights for collaboration work features under the real design context. (3) User experience integrity (accessibility, tolerance and restriction) clarifying through case study on typical collaborative service products (i.e. Teambition, BIM and ZOOM). As the research findings, a dynamic strategy model combined with three key attributes (Relationship construction, interaction capacity, and experience extension) is put forward. The specific case of Sino-Italian Digital Platform is introduced to present a contextual design paradigm to response the strategy mentioned above. Such hypotheses and findings of this study as recommendations explore a tentative approach for designers who are interested in innovating service systems. This study also provides practice supports and theoretical extension for both service design and user experience.

Keywords: Collaborative service · Cross-geographical design · User experience · CSCW · Design strategy

1 Introduction

In this systematic, complex, and fast iterative design era, the importance of enabling designers to create human-centered solutions with distributed resources is greater than

This research is supported by Key Program for International S&T Cooperation Projects of China (Grant No. 2012DFG10280).

© Springer International Publishing AG 2017
P.-L.P. Rau (Ed.): CCD 2017, LNCS 10281, pp. 345–355, 2017.
DOI: 10.1007/978-3-319-57931-3_28

ever. To respond such real problems, cross-geographical collaboration is increasingly involved in design development activities currently. About collaborative service and the design transformation, many scholars and practitioners had clarified the definition, features and key elements. As a holistic and systematic solution, collaborative service is able to optimize to the maximum of participants' contribution and activism, it uses peer-to-peer involvement mechanism to solve complex problems. Computer Supported Cooperative Work (CSCW) is a practice application under the collaborative service theory. Compared with traditional designers who work in a geographically distributed environment, some emerging CSCW services have provided flexible participation forms for users. With the tech-supports like immediate communication, data calculation, synchronous conference management and documents compatibility CSCW could match various collaboration needs of stakeholders. However, the uniqueness of design and creating activities requires all participants to contribute their knowledge and thoughts. Design collaboration should focus on multi-actors' active involvement like ideas sharing, concepts co-creation and collaborative exploration according to individual ability.

Such emerging features bring both practical and theoretical paradox in this specific context. On one hand, traditional interaction design or service design guidance could not specifically satisfy such user needs or solve problems. Service developers and designers are lack of effective action strategy or paradigm to develop systematic solutions for cross-geographical design. On the other, user experience or collaborative service researches also need to be explored in this real working context. Such imbalance between demands and current situation becomes the new conflict and the research orientation for researchers and practitioners. Therefore, this study tries to clarify a strategic guidance with several key attributes based on contextual features of collaborative design. The practical case of Sino-Italian digital platform as a design paradigm is selected to provide a tentative exploration for applying such strategy in authentic situation.

2   Literature Review

2.1   User Experience

As the user-centered solutions, user experience is the essential element and contextual basis for collaborative services. A common definition of user experience is "users' cognitive impression and response to the products, system or services in use or to be used" (Kuniavsky 2009). It could also be understood as the multiple feelings such as emotion, preference or satisfaction during the interaction between users and products or services. User experience requires synchronous interaction produced among users, environment and other people. Several worldwide forefront scholars have articulated the features of user experience and its measuring criteria respectively. For example, James Garrett has introduced a five-levels user experience, including surface, skeleton, structure, scope and strategy (Garrett 2006). Norman has put forward three ways of better user experience that takes time as the dimension of interaction, and they are instinct, behavior and reflection that designers should take into consideration (Norman 2004). Furthermore, 5E principle as the guidance gives a summary on how to measure and perceive user experience in the process of interaction completely. It includes Effective,

Easy to learn, Engaging, Error tolerant, and Efficient (Quesenbery 2003). Because the driven factors affecting user experience is mainly influenced by subjective feelings to the usability of interactive models. Thus, a honeycomb model built by Peter Morville divides such factors into 6 aspects, which are useful, desirable, accessible, credible, findable, usable and valuable (Morville 2004). As for tangible interactions, designers should pay specific attention to ergonomic platform, handheld terminals, input and output devices and operating experience (Liu and Lou 2014).

2.2 Collaborative Services

The core of collaborative service is the peer-to-peer pattern and it focus on the identity equivalence between different roles of participants (Manzini and Meroni 2007). The boundary between service providers and receivers in traditional way has been ambiguous and individual abilities are accessible for all the stakeholders in a typical collaboration service system (Jégou and Manzini 2008). It could also be understood as an economic and cultural mode characterized by "me + we" pattern which is an interdependent consumption form and lifestyle (Belk 2014). Group participants as the key driving force for collaborative system, provides group dynamics introduced by Kurt Lewin, the psychologist who defines group collaboration is a dynamic system where participants complement each other and improve personal abilities. In the real context of collaborative design, new concepts are developed under a proper cooperative mechanism with the application of group intelligence (Lou 2008). Traditionally, cross-graphic design work is decentralized, and designers tend to be separate from other members in a developing team. However, participants' collective intelligence is accessible currently thanks to the collaborative interaction platform, and contributions from group stakeholders are much greater than those from individuals. With this trend, the emerging role of design is becoming quite different, as an integrated and holistic strategy, it is an overall process of an innovation chain as well as an industry chain ranging from financing, production, management, service to promotion (Lou 2015).

2.3 Computer Supported Cooperative Work (CSCW)

Computer Supported Cooperative Work (CSCW) originated from the technology integration of communication, computer and network (Greif and Cashman 1988). It includes the research of group work style, support technology and application development. The collaboration environment contributes to the improvement of communication and efficiency, and also helps to eliminate or reduce time and space barriers. Over the years, researchers have identified a number of elements of collaborative work including:

- Interaction progression: intense interaction, instant communication and perception in the shared workspace and informative space;
- Participant features: users dynamics, uncertainty and mobility;
- Work forms: flexible collaboration model such as session model, conference model, process model and creation model to ensure the work quality (Zhang and Liu 2007);
- Design approaches: visualization of communication and information exchanges to enable learning and greater efficiencies (Hutchins 1995).

3   Context Understanding

In this study, five cases of typical design areas covering architectural design, urban planning, product design, fashion design and media design are selected to inquire what happened under the real cross-geographical design context. Through a set of methods such as participatory observation and interview, some basic insights of collaboration intervention points, collaboration behaviors and features in design process could be clarified (Fig. 1). As is shown in following figure, main procedures in the design collaboration process include: early and preparation stage, concept discussion and brainstorming, concept generation (sketch, modeling, rendering), presentation and early evaluation, prototype generation, user test and iteration, concept implementation and discussion, material and equipment preparation, design delivery and construction. The roles of participants show on the vertical axis include: foreign designers, first party, Chinese designers, technical teams, project managers, engineers, suppliers, construction teams and other teams.

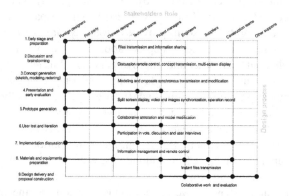

Fig. 1. Collaboration needs insight in cross-geographical design context

From such cases analysis, current collaborative design work forms can be classified into following four modes:

- Face to face interaction: several collaborative participants join the discussion and communication at the same time and on different locations, this form is usually supported by online conference services.
- Asynchronous interaction: several participants conduct collaborative design at flexible times and on the same location, this form is usually supported by data and documents sharing services.
- Asynchronous distributed interaction: several participants conduct collaborative design at different time and on different locations, this form is usually supported by distributed database project management interaction platforms.
- Synchronous distributed interaction: several participants conduct co-creation and cooperation at the same time and on different locations. Such services should match the

needs of knowledge sharing, concepts co-generation and project co-management, thus it brings more complex challenges for interaction carriers.

4 Methodology: Case Study

As another part of methodology of this study, several typical collaborative service cases including Teambition, BIM and ZOOM are selected to get a basic knowledge of collaboration work features and key elements. These three cases represent the different work types identified above. Through comparison of the service content, interaction carrier, participation feature, involved with collaboration form and user experience integrity, some systematic aspects can be clarified as Table 1. Case of Teambition which is an integrated service for enterprises project collaboration. It provides users several easy-to-learn options such as schedule management, immediate meeting arrangement, documents and material sharing to ensure high-quality co-working experience. It also connects all participants to enable them to innovate their own co-working style, which includes collaborative annotation, upstream and downstream communication and project progression management. BIM (Building Information Modeling), an important tool for architectural engineering modeling, allows participants to carry out simulation analysis and data assortment for the process prediction and design evaluation. The service content proposals visualization, coordination and simulation promote collaboration efficiency, quality and implementation. ZOOM is a wide-use online communication and presentation service product. As a distributed terminal application, it offers flexible and easy to use accesses for users. From these selected cases, we can conclude four main aspects as follows:

Table 1. The case study on four typical collaborative services

Cases	Interaction carrier	Participation feature	Collaboration work form	User experience integrity
Teambition	Websites and applications	Multi stakeholders; flat collaboration	Asynchronous and synchronous distributed interaction	Strong
BIM	Modeling software	Participators with certain roles; collaboration based on individual abilities	Asynchronous interaction	Middle
ZOOM	Terminal applications	User-defined participations	Face to face interaction	Weak

Based on above-mentioned case studies, the user experience integrity of these collaborative services can be clarified into following attributes:

Accessibility. Accessibility, as the fundamental element of user experience, indicates that service carriers should be available and easy to learn to all participants. It also reflects an effective transformation between solutions and demands. The user-friendly interface and habit-based interaction gestures should be taken into consideration to promote a smooth experience. For example, with the movable interconnection technology development, collaboration interaction forms have turned more flexible and user-centered. Compared with the collaboration under specific space, mobile collaboration platforms like applications, websites or other channels have integrated users' fragmented time efficiently. This accessibility guarantees user-defined co-work styles, and also diversifies collaboration design content, approach and carrier interactions under both physical and virtual space.

Tolerance. Tolerance is mainly reflected on the collaboration scale, scope and networks. Firstly, the scale and form of participation is tolerable. For example, from above indicated cases, the number of participants, forms of participation and time schedule for instant conferences could be adjusted according to real conditions. Secondly, the scope of collaboration is interactive and tolerable. When sharing information and resources under work context, users are also contributing service contents to the system, which produces the maximum values within a reasonable scope to some extent. Thirdly, collaboration network is tolerable. Emerging collaboration applications rely on digital data in storage for constructing service network, the complex systems require the proper touch points to tolerate different comprehension abilities and operating habits.

Restriction. Collaborative design belongs to the knowledge developing activity. Thus, on the basis of improving meaningful user experience, protection to intellectual property and restriction to access mechanism is required to be carried out. A mutual-trust relationship is fundamental to develop a good collaborative atmosphere. Like the case of Teambition, it set different access level and entrance for multi actors, such as authentication to users' qualification and identity, systematic monitoring mechanism and data security are applied to guarantee the order and safeness of collaborative relationship.

The performance evaluation of above-mentioned four cases in accessibility, tolerance and restriction is demonstrated in analysis diagram as the following picture indicated (Fig. 2), and some interesting points and features can be found.

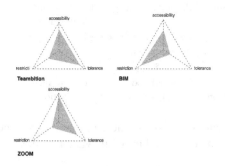

Fig. 2. Evaluation of the user experience integrity

5   Findings

According to the comparison and analysis from above-mentioned cases, a dynamic model as a strategic guide for collaborative services can be put forward (Fig. 3). It describes several key attributes that service developers and designers should take into consideration. Meanwhile, as the response for difficulties of user experience and inter-action quality existing in cross-geographic design context, this model provides a recommended strategy for design approaches. As we can see from the figure horizontally, with experience development line, collaborative services involve multi-actors to create values. From the vertical perspective, collaboration degree includes three systematic evolutionary steps: relationship creation, interaction capacity and experience extension. Such key attributes are treated as an effective mechanism can affect the experience quality and integrity.

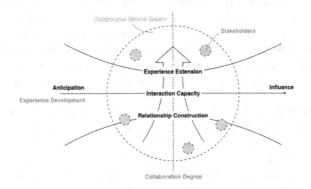

Fig. 3. Dynamic strategy model for collaborative service design

5.1   Relationship Construction

Individual Role. This relationship type means individuals are able to independently select collaborative partners and cooperate with them according to their own roles. For example, users by applying collaborative conference and data sharing service, select specific partners with known roles and knowledge contributions to conduct co-operation.

Role-to-System. Role to System relationship means participants assisted by the system going through certain conditions, select their collaborative partners. System as the supervisor provides a platform helps different roles to carry out effective design approaches. This type of relationship also indicates a circulative process from decen-tralization to centralization and then to decentralization again.

System-to-Community. It indicates the innovative communities who have reached consensus on collaboration habits and co-creation sense. These empowering communities use the system to conduct collaborative design and cultivate meaningful and useful work style. For example, like Teambition service, users are able to have a quick match in the networks to manage cooperation details like instant group discussion, collaborative annotation or work process tracking. The connecting between upstream and downstream sectors becomes more easily because the construction of efficient community.

5.2 Interaction Capacity

Less Cognitive Burden. Facing new services or interactive behaviors, users often feel so confused and find it hard to learn. Getting used to new interactive functions take more cognitive burden. Therefore, simplification for interaction learning is an important factor to engage users actively. As for touchpoints design, it is supposed to integrate distributed functions into basic modules. Meanwhile, current interaction habits and preference should also be properly applied in design outputs. For example, design approaches with modularized interface or visualized linear management could be much user-friendly for novices. Like Teambition, the function "agenda" helps users arrange daily work schedule and conference agendas with normal subscription on smart phones. Users will be informed once there is any development or change on the programs they have managed online. This simple interaction progression based on the cognitive and operating habits user already have been familiar with, so it promotes the collaboration efficiency greatly and satisfies the demand for immediate and valuable user experience.

Optimal Interaction Path. Interfaces of a complex or integrated collaborative platform have structural inter-action logic and multiple functions. It brings confused feeling for users when they try to find the earliest access just for simple needs like sharing files or discussions. It indicates the simplified design language should be used in optimal interaction path. For example, the hot-key function of ZOOM create quick accesses to new programs on the computer, and use flat interaction operation to support quick presentation with multi-terminal screens. Shortest interaction path helps to promote ideas sharing and feedbacks instantly.

From Information to Thinking and Progression Visualization. For collaboration design context, approaches should rely on thinking and progression visualization instead of simple information visualization. Designers should involve participants' thoughts and thinking contribution to the system with an accessible and visual interaction to ensure everyone could touch invisible resource. Compared with the traditional information management, and this context also focus on decision co-making and models co-generating. In other words, the value of co-creation process is much greater than the result delivery. Like the service content of BIM, besides the design sketches presentation, the collaboration interaction like simulations of project process and output are also available. With visualization of process, designers, construction teams and project managers could have common knowledge and agreement in advance to the design proposals. And it can boost the high-efficiency collaboration work.

5.3 Experience Continuity

Modularized Services. On future developing iterative pattern and commercial pattern, the scale of collaborative service is required to be customizable. Users could construct and select collaborative patterns which can match particular situations. That means suitable customized and modularized service sectors are flexible for users. Different personalized sections can help users define the scale, the scope and the level of participation. Besides, collaborative interaction platform should involve distributed resources to support cross-geographical design.

Co-creative Behaviors Reconstruction. The other attribute of experience continuity refers to the co-creation work style and the cultivation of users' approval sense for co-creation value. Like BIM, Teambition or other similar CSCW platforms promote users forming efficient collaboration habits, and also contribute to intellectual property protection and optimal use for participators' knowledge resources. This influence should also include the interaction carrier design. That means interaction gestures and forms should according to users habits. Like operation step tracing and intellectual property protection, and the link between technical development and marketing to support design proposals realization.

6 Practical Case: The Sino-Italian Digital Collaboration Platform

The Sino-Italian digital platform is developed based on the authentic context of collaborative design between Chinese and Italian designers. This platform as an exploratory practice introduced in this study aims to provide a design paradigm with the strategy model reference. The Sino-Italian digital platform integrates VR, instant messaging, synchronous and asynchronous technologies, and provides a holistic collaborative solution to cross-geographic design challenges. The physical space like Fig. 4 shown supports co-design and co-exploration through CSCW technology. The innovation point of this practice is the connection between design proposals and prototypes generating, like hardware integration of several useful equipment like three-dimensional printer and laser cutting machine are involved into collaboration system. As for the interfaces design, according to features held by synchronous and asynchronous collaboration, it ensures the easy-to-learn experience quality. For example, the electronic white broad as an interactive platform, is put forward to support online instant concepts creation and group discussion. Such interaction gestures form natural behaviors in design activities offline, can reduce the participators' learning load. The tracing function can inspire the common scenes and actions from multi-participators. The interaction structure, working space and interaction progression are indicated as the following figures (Figs. 4 and 5).

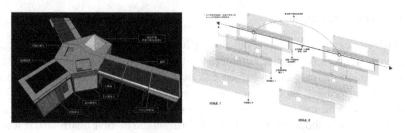

Fig. 4. The physical workplace and interfaces structure of Sino-Italian digital collaboration platform (Source: the Sino-Italian digital collaboration platform project)

Classification and sorting with multiple indexes.	Reviewing and tracking according to time order.	Collaboratively annotating and cconcepts generating on the main white board.
Collaborative 3D modelling.	Post-it online and instant modification; Concepts discussion and synchronous brainstorming.	Integration for multiple documents.

Fig. 5. The interaction gestures and progression for core functions (Source: the Sino-Italian digital collaboration platform project)

7   Conclusion

This study based on the methodology of case study and facing to the difficulties between cross-geographic context and relative theory, it has provided a comprehensive design strategy for experience improvement. The dynamic strategy as main result responds the research hypothesis. The case of the Sino-Italian Digital Collaborative Platform provides the design guidance for both operation level and strategic level. Such research finding also brings a new angle of view to look at the value of collaborative service. By clarifying these strategic attributes could enable more active designers and researchers to facilitate ideal proposals in the future, the extension for service design and user experience research also provides some reflection in the real design context.

Acknowledgement. We would like to thank all the participants who are dedicated for the Sino-Italian Digital Platforms design and implementation. We also express gratitude for the users and researchers who are involved in the research process.

References

Kuniavsky, M.: User Experience and HCI (2009)

Garrett, J.J.: Customer loyalty and the elements of user experience. Design Manag. Rev. **17**(1), 35–39 (2006). Diller, S., Shedroff, N., Rhea, D.: Making Meaning: How Successful Businesses Deliver Meaningful Customer Experiences. New Riders Publishing (2005)

Norman, D.A.: Why We Love (Or Hate) Everyday Things. Atlanta (2004)

Quesenbery, W.: Dimensions of Usability: Defining the Conversation, Driving the Process (2003)

Jégou, F., Manzini, E.: Collaborative services – social innovation and design for sustainability. Theory (2008)

Belk, R.: You are what you can access: sharing and collaborative consumption online. J. Bus. Res. **67**(8), 1595–1600 (2014). Manzini, E.: Design, When Everybody Designs: An Introduction to Design for Social Innovation

Sangiorgi, D., Meroni, A.: Design for Services. Brunel University, Uxbridge (2011)

Zhang, D.C., Liu, H.: Research on multi-hierarchy cooperation model in CSCW. Appl. Res. Comput. **24**(3), 59–61 (2007)

Morville, P.: User Experience Design. Semantic Studios LLC, Ann Arbor (2004)

Greif, I., Cashman, P.: CSCW: A Book of Readings. Morgan Kaufmann, San Mateo (1988)

Hutchins, E.: Cognition in the Wild. MIT Press, Cambridge (1995)

Manzini, E., Meroni, A.: Emerging user demands for sustainable solutions, EMUDE. In: Michel, R. (ed.) Design Research Now, pp. 157–179. Birkhäuser Basel, Basel (2007)

Liu, W., Lou, Y.: The Sino-Italian collaborative design platform: designing and developing an innovative product service system. In: Rau, P.L.P. (ed.) CCD 2014. LNCS, vol. 8528, pp. 766–774. Springer, Cham (2014). doi:10.1007/978-3-319-07308-8_73

Lou, Y.: Calling for 'She Ji': rethinking and changing the changes in China. In: Cipolla, C., Peruccio, P. (eds.) Proceedings from International Design Research Conference Changing the Change: Design, Visions, Proposals and Tools, pp. 85–90. Allemandi Conference Press, Turino (2008)

Lou, Y.: Opening keynote–crossing: HCI, design and sustainability. In: Proceedings of the 33rd Annual ACM Conference Extended Abstracts on Human Factors in Computing Systems, pp. 805–806. ACM (2015)

A Pilot Study of Communication Matrix
for Evaluating Artworks

Rungtai Lin[1(✉)], Fengde Qian[2], Jun Wu[3], Wen-Ting Fang[1], and Yige Jin[4]

[1] Graduate School of Creative Industry Design, National Taiwan University of Arts,
New Taipei City, Taiwan
rtlin@mail.ntua.edu.tw, f_wenting@163.com
[2] College of Art and Design, Nanjing Tech University, Nanjing, People's Republic of China
363986551@qq.com
[3] Department of Animation, School of Journalism and Communication,
Anhui Normal University, Wuhu, People's Republic of China
junwu2006@hotmail.com
[4] School of Fashion and Craft, Shanghai Art and Design Academy,
Shanghai, People's Republic of China
yigeqll@sina.com

Abstract. The use of information technology in multimedia is becoming common and accessible to users. Artistically literate citizens apply a variety of artistic media, symbols and metaphors to independently create and perform work that expresses their own ideas and communicates their life experience. The arts are the media which provide powerful and essential means of communication. Thinking about art as a process of social interaction, how the artist's performances are conceived, developed, delivered and received, and how the viewer is attracted, accurately understanding the artwork, and affected by the artwork need to be studied. Therefore, the purpose of this study is intended to derive and validate the cognitive factors that affect artworks, and to propose a communication matrix for evaluating artworks. The results suggested that the communication matrix approach will be validated in more testing and evaluating of artworks in further study.

Keywords: Communication matrix · Evaluating artworks · Micro film · Cognitive engineering

1 Introduction

Social networking is a relatively new term that has emerged over the last decade. It may appear to be a new concept that is a regrouping of the previously known concepts of social interaction, communication and language. Social networking has received increased attention in the academic and business communities over the past decade (Lenhart and Madden 2007). Both academics and practitioners emphasized that the role of social networking in relationship development relates not only to the human community, but also to aspects such as business, management, arts, and even in different fields of therapy (Dwyer et al. 2007; Livingstone 2008; Pempek et al. 2009; Trusov et al. 2009). The arts are the media which provide powerful and

© Springer International Publishing AG 2017
P.-L.P. Rau (Ed.): CCD 2017, LNCS 10281, pp. 356–368, 2017.
DOI: 10.1007/978-3-319-57931-3_29

essential means of communication (Trivedi 2004). However, we now live in a small world with social networking. Social communication has been a recent shift from traditional ways to a technological approach based on discovering new opportunities in social networks. Companies are now more focused on adapting new technologies and combining them in ways that create new experiences and value for customers. With the development of industrial tendencies, most companies gradually realize that the keys to "word of mouth" communication are not only market and technology aspects but also service innovation design (Trusov et al. 2009).

The use of information technology in multimedia is becoming common and accessible to users. Artistically literate citizens apply a variety of artistic media, symbols and metaphors to independently create and perform work that expresses their own ideas and communicates their life experience. Thinking about art as a process of social communication, this article intends to study how the relationship between the artist and the audience is potentially altered in social networking (Peterson 2004; Pratt 2012; Shelley 2002). Previous studies have indicated that the communication studies were effective in evaluating comprehension of human behavior. However, the capability of tradition evaluating tools depends on whether the underlying rating factors have been chosen properly, as for example, communication style inventory (De Vries et al. 2011; Gameren and Vlug 2009), communication matrix (Rowland 2011), and cognitive style (Allinson and Hayes 1996; Cools and Van den Broeck 2007).

In the social networking era, connections between artist and audience have become increasingly close. For the artworks to be effective in communication, they need to be meaningful, understandable, memorable, etc., (Porter et al. 2011). In order to evaluate artworks, it is necessary to find out the cognitive factors affecting them. These factors can then be used as the basis for evaluating artworks during the creation stage. Most of the studies are focused on the evaluation after the artworks is completed. Very few have ever mentioned the approaches of artworks evaluation at the creation stage to ensure the artworks for communication (Trivedi 2004). The importance of communication studies is shown repeatedly in several studies of evaluating artworks. Despite the recognized importance of social interaction between artist and audience, they lack a systematic approach to explore it. (Peterson 2004; Pratt 2012; Shelley 2002; Trivedi 2004). Therefore, the purpose of this paper is to study factors affecting the evaluation of artworks. Then, these factors are analyzed and discussed in order to establish a communication matrix to understand the perceptions of artist and audience.

2   Research Framework

For the evaluation of artworks, we need a better understanding of artist-audience communication not just for taking part in the social context, but also for developing the interactive experience between artist and audience (Goldman 2004; Trivedi 2004). Lin et al. (2009) proposed a framework for examining the way designers interact across cultures and the interactive experience of users in the design process. Furthermore, Chen et al. (2014, 2015) devised a research framework to investigate the cognition of emotional responses and visual scenes when turning poetry into painting. In addition, the research framework seems to be a better way to provide a possible solution for exploring the feeling of turning poetry into painting that is clearly worthy of further research (Gao et al. 2016). For the communication study, three levels of problems are identified in the study of communication: technical, semantic, and effectiveness. The technical level requires getting the viewer's attraction for the recognition through his/her senses. The semantic level requires letting the viewer accurately realize the meaning of the message through his/her realization. The effectiveness level concerns the ways in which the viewer is made to take the right reflection through his/her affecting (Craig 1999; Fiske 2010; Jakobson 1987).

Jakobson (1987) proposed six constitutive factors with six functions in a communication model. The six constitutive factors are as follows: addresser, addressee, context, message, contact, and code. Each of these factors determines a different function in each act of communication: emotive, conative, referential, poetic, phatic, and metalingual. (Fiske 2010; Jakobson 1987). Norman (2013) proposed a conceptual model that includes three parts: design model, user's model, and system image. When a designer designs a product for a user, the designer expects that the user will understand and use it in the desired way, meaning that the user's model is identical to the design model. For emotional design, Norman (2005) proposed three levels of design processing—visceral, behavioral, and reflective design that represents three kinds of user's experience that is aesthetic, meaningful, and emotional experience. Based on previous studies (Fiske 2010; Jakobson 1987; Lin et al. 2009, 2015, 2016), a research framework combining communication theory with communication and mental models was proposed to explore the issue of communication matrix as shown in Fig. 1.

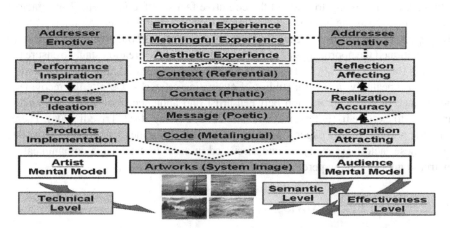

Fig. 1. A framework for communication research

For evaluating artworks, the artist involves three key stages to express significance through his or her artworks: performance (inspiration), process (ideation), and product (implementation). Performance is the inspiration to produce a kind of significance that the artist's intentions can be expressed through the artwork. Process represents the artist's ideation that through the artwork, the artist's imagination, thoughts, and feelings can be reproduced. Product is the implementation of signification and expression which can then be transmitted to the viewer while the artist's and the viewer's thoughts are identical (Lin et al. 2009, 2015, 2016). For the viewer, there are three key steps to understanding the meaning of an artwork: recognition (attracting), realization (accuracy), and reflection (affecting). Recognition requires letting the viewer receive a message through perception, such as seeing, hearing, touching, or even feeling as the ways in which the viewer can accurately receive a message through the artwork. Realization requires letting the viewers understand the meaning of the message without misinterpreting, misunderstanding, or not understanding at all. The degree of realizations measures how accurately the transmitted message expresses the desired meaning. Reflection concerns the ways in which the viewer is made to take the right actions showing how effectively the message affects conduct in the expected way (Chen et al. 2014, 2015).

This study was designed to take into account the changing nature of social communication issue, resistance to artworks evaluation and the context for evaluation and impact assessment. It involved literature reviews, derivation of the matrix, and validation on artworks as the following steps:

(a) A review of current claims for artistically literate citizens in relation to impact and arts practice and a mapping of good practice.
(b) Exploration of the purpose and nature of evaluation and impact assessment.
(c) Development of an evaluation framework and tools for assessing the impact of artworks.
(d) Recommendations for development of the framework and evaluation of communication matrix.
(e) Validation of the communication matrix for evaluating artworks.

3 Study I: Derivation of the Communication Matrix

3.1 The Method

Study I involved using questionnaire interviews to derive the cognitive factors that affect evaluating microfilm as shown in the Fig. 2. Fifteen art-related professional designers were equally assigned to groups A, B and C. Another 15 subjects from the Graduate School of Creative Industry Design were assigned to group D. This study consisted of three different sessions. Each session was separated by at least one week.

Session 1: Subjects in group A were asked to describe in their own words any item that would influence the microfilm about technical problems, and group B and C would describe any item that affects the microfilm about semantic and effective problems respectively. The descriptions of the three subject groups were analyzed and summarized.

Session 2: A questionnaire consisting of the summarized items derived from subject group A and B were given to the subjects group D. The subjects were requested to rate each item by its importance to the audience on a rating scale from 1 to 7. Based on these importance ratings, subjects were asked to rank these items. The rating and ranking data were used to determine the statistically important attributes for evaluating microfilm.

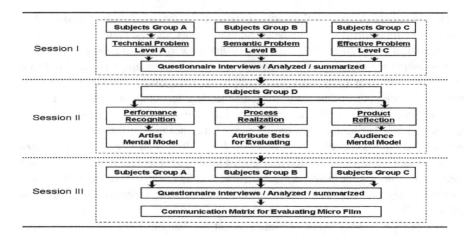

Fig. 2. Procedures for derivation of the communication matrix

Session 3: The attribute sets derived from session 2 were listed on another questionnaire. Then, Group A, B, and C were requested to rank items according to their importance for evaluating micro film. The ranking data of the three subject groups were analyzed and summarized in a communication matrix.

3.2   The Results

Session 1 and session 2 employed two subject groups to cross-test important items for icon recognition and design. In session 1, subject groups A, B and C listed 32, 28 and 26 items respectively that were thought to have an influence on microfilm. These items were summarized into 12 items each for tree level, technical, semantic and effective, respectively. In session 3, through the ranking data of the 12 items of each group, items that had an estimated median significantly smaller than the median of 12 were classified as "Important" items. There were 9 important items selected for each group as shown in Table 1.

Table 1. The attribute sets for evaluating microfilm

Group A	Group B	Group C
A1 Appropriately captured	B1 Curiosity raising	C1 Topic and acknowledgement
A2 Creative and clever	B2 Desire exploring	C2 Going beyond reality
A3 Video effects	B3 Emotion stirring	C3 Affluence in life
A4 Well-paced	B4 Moving stories	C4 Thought provoking
A5 Touching plot	B5 Mood changing	C5 Deep planting
A6 Sensitive settings	B6 Atmosphere bulging	C6 Immersion
A7 Well defined personalities	B7 Richly culturally-loaded	C7 Emotional resonance
A8 Skillful and appealing	B8 Realistic characteristics	C8 Authentic experience
A9 Warm touching	B9 Role identity	C9 Mental simpatico

3.3 The Communication Matrix

Based on Table 1, the subjects groups A, B and C were discussed and integrated into the three dimensions for evaluating microfilm as shown in Table 2. In contrast with existing evaluation tools, this communication matrix is a multi-dimensional evaluating tool that places the artist and artistically literate citizen's values at the core of the matrix. Its first dimension facilitates the identification of the core values involved in any artworks, including performance, processes and products. Its second dimension facilitates identification of the related theory that may need to be taken into account in assessing outcome and impact. These include communication theory, mental model and information processing. The third dimension is flexibility, as the matrix can be adapted to the needs and priorities of the different context of the artist, viewer and artworks. It allows relevant measures and indicators of quality and impact to be identified.

Table 2. The communication matrix for evaluating microfilm

	Artist (Coding)			
	Performance Inspiration	Processes Ideation	Products Implementation	
Level C	C7-1: Topic and Acknowledgement	C8-1: Thought provoking	C9-1: Emotional resonance	Reflection Affecting
	C7-2: Going beyond Reality	CE-2: Deep planting	C9-2: Authentic experience	
	C7-3: Affluence in life	C8-3: Immersion	C9-3: Mental simpatico	
Level B	B4-1: Curiosity raising	B5-1: Moving stories	B6-1: Richly culturally-loaded	Realization Accuracy
	B4-2: Desire exploring	B5-2: Mood changing	B6-2: Realistic characteristics	
	B4-3: Emotion stirring	B5-3: Atmosphere bulging	B6-3: Role identity	
Level A	A1-1: Appropriately captured	A2-1: Weil-Paced	A3-1: Well defined personalities	Recognition Attraction
	A1-2: Creative and clever	A2-2: Touching plot	A3-2: Skillful and appealing	
	A1-3: Video effects	A2-3: Sensitive settings	A3-3: Warm touching	
	Aesthetic experience	Meaningful experience	Emotional experience	
	Audience (Decoding)			

4   Study II: Validation on Microfilm

4.1   The Method

Study II was conducted to validate the communication matrix for evaluating microfilm in which 9 attributes of three cognitive factors 27 were used. A microfilm for promoting amature artists served as the stimulus. The research was designed to take into account the communication matrix to evaluate the content and impact assessment between artist and audience. It involved the following five steps.

(a) Exploration of the purpose and nature of the communication matrix for evaluating the microfilm.
(b) Development of an evaluation framework and questionnaires for assessing the microfilm.
(c) Conducting a microfilm of promoting amature artists for artistically literate citizens
(d) Validation of the communication matrix for evaluating the microfilm.
(e) Recommendations for development of the framework and evaluation of the communication matrix.

4.2   The Nature of the Communication Matrix

Based on the communication matrix, an effective approach to assessing the impact of the microfilm must address the following three questions:

- What are the key factors and which need most attention: technical, semantic or effective level?
- What are the different values that are important to artist and audience?
- What are the key stages in the process of an art project and where do the evaluation and assessment processes need to play a part?

Based on the framework shown in Fig. 1, how the artist's performances are conceived, developed, delivered and received, and how the viewer is attracted, accurately understands the artwork, and is affected by the artwork need to be studied. In Table 2, both the artist's coding of the artwork and the viewer's subsequent decoding need to be studied in the evaluation of artworks. Combining the key factors in the communication matrix, nine questioners was developed for evaluating the total image of the microfilm as follows:

- A-1. The scenes of the film are appropriately-captured, and the video effects are creative and clever which provide the audience with unique video effects.
- A-2. The story of the film is well-paced and has a touching plot exhibiting moving sensitive settings.
- A-3. The characters in the film have well-defined personalities, and the performances of the actors are skillful and appealing presenting a deeply moving experience.
- B-4. The film arouses people's curiosity and stimulates the desire to explore the film which has an effect of stirring emotions.

- B-5. The film has a touching story, transforming the audience's mentality and reaching the state of atmosphere bulging.
- B-6. The characters in the film are richly culturally-loaded and realistically drawn to serve the purpose of role identity.
- C-7. The film has a clear topic and acknowledgement, and its creativity goes beyond reality contributing to an experience of an affluent life.
- C-8. The plot of the film is thought-provoking and plants its moral deeply in the minds of people leading to an immersive cinematographic experience.
- C-9. The film has emotional resonance and creates an authentic experience in order to achieve mental simpatico.

In addition, communication study involves the three key levels: Level A, B and C for the audience, and three key factors: performance, process and product for the artist. Performance is the expressive production of artworks to produce artworks. Process is the understanding and use of art elements to effectively convey messages for a variety of interactions within a variety of contexts and with a variety of audiences. Product refers to the use of non-verbal and verbal communication combined to express and respond to the expression of artworks. To study the communication issue, another nine questions were used to rate the key factors of total performance as followings:

- A1-1. Please rate the fitness of "Appropriately Captured" for the film.
- A1-2. Please rate the fitness of "Creative and Clever" for the film.
- A1-3. Please rate the fitness of "Video Effects" for the film.
- B4-1. Please rate the fitness of "Curiosity Raising" for the film.
- B4-2. Please rate the fitness of "Desire Exploring" for the film.
- B4-3. Please rate the fitness of "Emotion Stirring" for the film.
- C7-1. Please rate the fitness of "Topic and Acknowledgement" for the film.
- C7-2. Please rate the fitness of "Going beyond Reality" for the film.
- C7-3. Please rate the fitness of "Affluence in Life" for the film.

4.3   Conducting a Micro Film for Evaluating

Recently, artistically literate citizens apply a variety of artistic media, symbols and metaphors to independently create and perform work that expresses their own ideas and communicate their life experience. In order to promote the concept, a microfilm entitled – Amateur Artists Enrich the Retired Life" was conducted and used as the stimulus to be evaluated. The microfilm together with the questionnaire was established on the website:

https://www.youtube.com/watch?v=8mYh5uf2hNc, Questionnaire website:

https://docs.google.com/forms/d/e/1FAIpQLSczDpZh2YvY_iJnXfAS1gMVtH_vCUVrhDevoQ40t2OA3lruMQ/viewform

This study was conducted on the internet. Social network groups (e.g., Face Book, Line, WeChat) were invited to participate as subjects and who agreed to follow the experimental procedure. On the website, the purpose of the experiment was explained to the subjects and the microfilm was presented. The subjects were then asked to rate the total image of the microfilm and then rate its key factors. Generally, the subject completed the experiment within 15 min.

4.4   The Results and Discussions

All subjects were volunteers from Taiwan and mainland China. Of a total of 206 subjects: 106 were from Taiwan and 100 from mainland China. For the Taiwan subjects group: 57 were males and 49 females. 14.2% were under 30 and 85.8% over 31 years of age. The majority (89.6%) of the subjects were from non-art professions while 10.4% of the remaining subjects held professional backgrounds in art-related fields.

For the China subjects group: 42 males and 58 females the ages of under 30 (45%) and between 31–50 (55%) participated in the study. The majority (77%) of the subjects were from non-art professions while 23% of the remaining subjects held professional backgrounds of art-related fields.

Table 3 summarizes the rating of the total image of the microfilm and key factors of the performance of the two groups. The comparison of the two groups is also listed in the same table. The column of "total image of microfilm" indicates the rating of the two groups and their comparison. For Question A1, the average rating of "Total Image of Microfilm" was 81.44% for the China group and 75.94% for the Taiwan group. The paired t-test results show that the average matching rate of 81.44% for the China subjects group is significantly higher than that for the Taiwan subjects group at 75.94% ($t = 2.48$, $p < .05$). The column of "Key Factors of Performance" indicates the rating of two groups and their comparison. For Question A1-1, the average rating of "key factors of performance" was 82.19% for the China group and 76.69% for the Taiwan group. The paired t-test results show that the average matching rate of 82.19% for the

Table 3. Summary of rating data and comparison with two groups

Subjects	N	Total image of microfilm				Key factors of performance			
		Q.	Mean	sd	t value	Q	Mean	sd	t value
Taiwan	105	A1	75.94	16.50	2.48*	A1-1	76.69	14.84	2.79**
China	100		81.44	15.15			82.19	13.38	
Taiwan	105	A2	78.02	14.20	2.57*	A1-2	74.19	15.85	1.95
China	100		82.85	12.60			78.42	15.25	
Taiwan	105	A3	74.79	16.22	3.16**	A1-3	78.82	13.93	2.84**
China	100		81.53	14.32			83.97	11.94	
Taiwan	105	B4	78.08	14.44	2.97**	B4-1	79.83	13.30	2.89**
China	100		83.46	11.24			84.68	10.65	
Taiwan	105	B5	76.39	15.84	3.57***	B4-2	80.06	12.70	3.05**
China	100		83.18	11.06			85.06	10.72	
Taiwan	105	B6	77.45	15.43	3.17**	B4-3	77.50	13.38	3.68***
China	100		83.62	12.21			83.86	11.25	
Taiwan	105	C7	76.90	15.60	2.06*	C7-1	75.42	16.83	3.35***
China	100		81.34	15.19			82.35	12.37	
Taiwan	105	C8	75.50	14.62	3.18**	C7-2	78.71	12.31	3.78***
China	100		81.99	14.62			84.81	10.71	
Taiwan	105	C9	76.68	15.00	2.98**	C7-3	78.32	15.00	3.36***
China	100		82.61	13.52			84.32	10.22	

*P < .05,**P < .01,***P < .001

China subjects group is significantly higher than that for the Taiwan subjects group at 76.69% (t = 2.79, p < .01).

For communication style, previous studies have indicated that it was effective in evaluating comprehension of human communication behavior (De Vries et al. 2010, 2011). But the capability of communication depends on whether the underlying rating dimensions have been chosen properly. De Vries et al. (2010) proposed the following six main dimensions of communication styles: verbal aggressiveness, expressiveness, preciseness, assuredness, supportiveness, and argumentativeness. Furthermore, a six-dimensional model of communication styles, each consisting of four facet-level scales, was proposed by De Vries et al. (2011) and operationalized using as the Communication Styles Inventory (CSI). Based on the concept of CSI, the results from Table 3 could be re-arranged in Table 4 using the communication matrix to explore the relationship between the artist and audience. Further studies are needed.

Table 4. The relationship between artist and audience in communication matrix

	Artist (Coding)			
	Performance Inspiration	Processes Ideation	Products Implementation	
Level C	C7	C8	C9	Reflection Affecting
	T:76.90(15.60)*	T: 75.50(14.62)**	T: 76.68(15.00)**	
	C:81.34(15.19)*	C: 81.99(14.62)**	C: 82.61(13.52)**	
Level B	B4	B5	B6	Realization Accuracy
	T: 78.08(14.44)**	T: 76.39(15.84)***	T: 77.45(15.43)**	
	C: 83.46(11.24)**	C: 83.18(11.06)***	C: 83.62(12.21)**	
Level A	A1	A2	A3	Recognition Attraction
	T:75.94(16.50)*	T:78.02(14.20)*	T: 74.79(16.22)**	
	C:81.44(15.15)*	C:82.85(12.60)*	C: 81.53(14.32)**	
	Aesthetic experience	Meaningful experience	Emotional experience	
	Audience (Decoding)			

The rating data focusing on the key factors of performance were re-arranged in the communication matrix as shown in Table 5 because it seems to be a better way to explore the relationships between artist and audience.

Table 5. The key factors of performance between artist and audience

	Artist (Coding)			
	Performance Inspiration			
Level C	C7-1	C7-2	C7-3	Reflection Affecting
	T:75.42(16.83)***	T: 78.71(12.31)***	78.32(15.00)***	
	C:82.35(12.37)***	C: 84.81(10.71)***	84.32(10.22)***	
Level B	B4-1	B4-2	B4-3	Realization Accuracy
	T:79.83(13.30)**	T: 80.06(12.70)**	T: 77.50(13.38)***	
	C:84.68(10.65)**	C: 85.06(10.72)**	C: 83.86(11.25)***	
Level A	A1-1	A1-2	A1-3	Recognition Attraction
	T:76.69(14.84) **	T:74.19(15.85)	T: 78.82(13.93)**	
	C:82.19(13.38) **	C:78.42(15.25)	C: 83.97(11.94)**	
	Aesthetic experience			
	Audience (Decoding)			

5   Conclusion

In evaluating artworks (e.g., microfilm), understanding how an audience evaluates an artwork is as complex as understanding the artworks perception itself. Because the cognitive factors that affect the appreciation of artwork have not been properly analyzed, the evaluation of artworks is typically ill-defined. For example, Shelley (2002) argued for the two key factors of character and role of principles in the evaluation of art. Sullivan (2006) argued that art practice can be conceptualized as a form of research that can be directed towards a range of personal and public ends. This study used communication matrix as a technique for evaluating microfilm. It is suggested that the communication matrix approach will be validated in more testing and evaluating of artworks in further study.

In the present study, two pilot studies were conducted to explore the communication matrix as an approach for evaluating micro film. Study I obtained the key factors which were used to establish a communication matrix for evaluating microfilm. Then, the communication matrix was validated in study II using a microfilm. The results showed that a communication matrix could be applied for evaluating the micro film effectively and could provide artists with an idea of how to concentrate their efforts at the creation stage in order to communication easily with the audience. The communication matrix approach appears to have an advantage over the subjective interpretation of artworks. Although the idea of using a communication matrix to explore the evaluation of artworks is quite simple, this study is only the first step in testing the utility of communication matrix as an approach for understanding the creation and recognition of artworks and is clearly worthy of more in-depth study.

For example, why there was a significant difference between Chinese and Taiwanese responses or what that difference implies for analyzing art works. There must be some important reasons for such significant differences?

References

Allinson, C.W., Hayes, J.: The cognitive style index: a measure of intuition-analysis for organizational research. J. Manage. Stud. **33**(1), 119–135 (1996)

Craig, R.T.: Communication theory as a field. Commun. Theor. **9**(2), 119–161 (1999)

Cools, E., Van den Broeck, H.: Development and validation of the cognitive style indicator. J. Psychol. **141**(4), 359–387 (2007)

Chen, S.J., Lin, C.L., Lin, R.: The study of match degree evaluation between poetry and paint. In: Proceedings of the 5th Asian Conference on the Arts and Humanities (ACAH 2014), Osaka, Japan (2014)

Chen, S.J., Lin, C.L., Lin, R.: A cognition study of turning poetry into abstract painting. In: The Fifth Asian Conference on Cultural Studies (ACCS 2015), Kobe, Japan (2015)

De Vries, R.E., Bakker-Pieper, A., Oostenveld, W.: Leadership=communication? The relations of leaders' communication styles with leadership styles, knowledge sharing and leadership outcomes. J. Bus. Psychol. **25**(3), 367–380 (2010)

De Vries, R.E., Bakker-Pieper, A., Konings, F.E., Schouten, B.: The communication styles inventory (CSI): a six-dimensional behavioral model of communication styles and its relation with personality. Commun. Res. **40**, 506–532 (2011). 10.1177/0093650211413571

Dwyer, C., Hiltz, S., Passerini, K.: Trust and privacy concern within social networking sites: a comparison of Facebook and MySpace. In: AMCIS 2007 Proceedings, p. 339 (2007)

Fiske, J.: Introduction to Communication Studies. Routledge, London (2010)

Gameren, K., Vlug, M.: The content and dimensionality of communication styles. Commun. Res. **36**, 178–206 (2009)

Gao, Y.-J., Lin, Y., Chen, L.-Y., Dai, D.C.H.: From "Idyllic" to "Living Space"—turning "Art Work" into "Interior Design". In: Rau, P.-L.P. (ed.) CCD 2016. LNCS, vol. 9741, pp. 345–354. Springer, Cham (2016). doi:10.1007/978-3-319-40093-8_35

Goldman, A.: Evaluating art. In: The Blackwell Guide to Aesthetics, pp. 93–108 (2004)

Griswold, W., Mangione, G., McDonnell, T.E.: Objects, words, and bodies in space: bringing materiality into cultural analysis. Qual. Sociol. **36**(4), 343–364 (2013)

Jakobson, R.: Language in literature. The Belknap Press of Harvard University Press, Cambridge (1987)

Livingstone, S.: Taking risky opportunities in youthful content creation: teenagers' use of social networking sites for intimacy, privacy and self-expression. New Media Soc. **10**(3), 393–411 (2008)

Lin, R., Lin, P.-H., Shiao, W.-S., Lin, S.-H.: Cultural Aspect of Interaction Design beyond Human-Computer Interaction. In: Aykin, N. (ed.) IDGD 2009. LNCS, vol. 5623, pp. 49–58. Springer, Heidelberg (2009). doi:10.1007/978-3-642-02767-3_6

Lin, C.L., Chen, J.L., Chen, S.J., Lin, R.: The cognition of turning poetry into painting. J. US-China Educ. Rev. B **5**(8), 471–487 (2015)

Lin, R., Hsieh, H.-Y., Sun, M.-X., Gao, Y.-J.: From ideality to reality- a case study of Mondrian style. In: Rau, P.-L.P. (ed.) CCD 2016. LNCS, vol. 9741, pp. 365–376. Springer, Cham (2016). doi:10.1007/978-3-319-40093-8_37

Lenhart, A., Madden, M.: Social networking websites and teens: an overview, pp. 1–7. Pew/ Internet (2007)

Norman, D.A.: Emotional Design: Why We Love (Or Hate) Everyday Things. Basic books, New York (2005)

Norman, D.A.: The Design of Everyday Things: Revised and Expanded Edition. Basic books, New York (2013)

Pempek, T.A., Yermolayeva, Y.A., Calvert, S.L.: College students' social networking experiences on Facebook. J. Appl. Dev. Psychol. 30(3), 227–238 (2009)

Peterson, R.A.: Sociology of the arts exploring fine and popular forms. Contemp. Sociol. J. Rev. 33(4), 454–455 (2004)

Porter, A., McMaken, J., Hwang, J., Yang, R.: Common core standards the new US intended curriculum. Educ. Res. 40(3), 103–116 (2011)

Pratt, H.J.: Categories and comparisons of artworks. Br. J. Aesth. 52(1), 45–59 (2012)

Rowland, C.: Using the communication matrix to assess expressive skills in early communicators. Commun. Disord. Q. 32, 190–201 (2011). 1525740110394651

Shelley, J.: The character and role of principles in the evaluation of art. Br. J. Aesth. 42(1), 37–51 (2002)

Sullivan, G.: Research acts in art practice. Stud. Art Educ. 48(1), 19–35 (2006)

Trivedi, S.: Artist-audience communication: Tolstoy reclaimed. J. Aesth. Educ. 38(2), 38–52 (2004)

Trusov, M., Bucklin, R.E., Pauwels, K.: Effects of word-of-mouth versus traditional marketing: findings from an internet social networking site. J. Mark. 73(5), 90–102 (2009)

Family, Friends, and Cultural Connectedness: A Comparison Between WeChat and Facebook User Motivation, Experience and NPS Among Chinese People Living Overseas

Chunhui Xie[(⊠)], Jagannadha Sri Harsha Putrevu, and Chelsea Linder

Department of Product-User Experience, Angie's List,
1030 E. Washington Street, Indianapolis, IN 46202, USA
{victoria.xie,sri.putrevu,chelsea.c}@angieslist.com,
victoriaxie886@gmail.com

Abstract. This empirical study compared the user experience of WeChat—the most popular mobile application and social networking platform in China, and Facebook—one of the most popular social networking sites in the world through the lenses of NPS and user motivation among Chinese people living overseas. An online survey with 423 responses measured user engagement, user experience, and user motivation of both applications. 10 follow-up interviews were conducted based on the survey responses. This study also explored the Net Promoter Score (NPS) for both WeChat and Facebook among the same group of Chinese users, and concluded that WeChat has a more positive word-of-mouth than Facebook in this particular group of users. This study found positive correlations between NPS and user engagement and user experience. The authors hope to further understand user experience in social and cultural context.

Keywords: WeChat · Facebook · User motivation · User experience · NPS · Cultural context

1 Introduction

Social networking sites such as Facebook have attracted millions of users worldwide, and more than 80% of teens and young adults in the U.S. (Duggan and Brenner 2013). Facebook released its 2016 full year operational highlights in its fourth quarter earnings call, and reported 1.86 billion monthly active users (MAUs) as of December 31, 2016, an increase of 17% year-over-year (Facebook 2016). Since its founding in 2004, people have used Facebook to stay connected with family and friends, and to discover what's going on in the world.

As is known to many, Facebook has been blocked in mainland China since 2009 due to political reasons, leaving the opportunity for alternative local social networking sites to grow their user base. One of these alternatives is WeChat (called Weixin in Chinese), a free, cross-platform and mobile text and voice messaging communication service and social media platform developed by Tencent, a Chinese technological company. Tencent is one of the largest Internet companies as well as the largest gaming

© Springer International Publishing AG 2017
P.-L.P. Rau (Ed.): CCD 2017, LNCS 10281, pp. 369–382, 2017.
DOI: 10.1007/978-3-319-57931-3_30

company in the world (Newzoo 2016). Since its first release in January 2011, WeChat has grown rapidly both inside and outside of China. As of December 2015, WeChat had more than one billion created accounts, and 70 million of its 697 million users were located outside of China (Business Insider 2016). The active WeChat users in Malaysia grew by 1,187% from quarter one of 2013 to quarter three of 2014 with 80% of the user base belonging to the young demographic, aged between 16 and 34. WeChat also boasts a 95% smartphone penetration rate (Bakar 2016). According to Tencent's 2016 third quarter earnings call, WeChat had 846.1 million monthly active user (MAUs) accounts as of WeChat September 2016 WeChat (2016), a 21% increase from the fourth quarter of 2015's reported monthly active user of 697 million. The tech giant surveyed a group of 40,443 netizens in China and reported that 94% of WeChat users are daily active users, and half of them used it more than an hour every day (AllChinaTech 2016).

Compared to WeChat's rapid growth and stable daily user engagement, 61% of Facebook users say that one time or another in the past, they have voluntarily taken a break from using Facebook for a period of several weeks or more (Madden et al. 2013). Based on this data along with the authors' initial participatory observation, this paper will compare the user experience of WeChat and Facebook using the same group of users who own accounts for both platforms, to see whether there is a preference in the user participation between these two social media applications.

One of the most popular functions within WeChat is called Hongbao, or digital Red Packet/Lucky Money in English. WeChat Red Packet allows the sender to send a certain amount of money through either a 1:1 chat window, or a group chat setting by controlling the amount, the number of Red Packets available, and the way of receiving. The sender can default an identical amount of money to everyone or a random amount to individuals in the group. 70% of WeChat users spend more than 100 Chinese Yuan (15.4 US dollars) on Red Packet every month (AllChinaTech 2016). From New Year's Eve to the fifth day of the first month in Chinese Lunar calendar in 2015, WeChat Red Packets were sent 32.7 billion times. Culturally, in demand and popular, it's since ancient times, and still practiced today, the Red Packet ritual clearly illustrates a process that is rich with symbolism and meaning in the Chinese society (Liu et al. 2015; Park 2016). Chinese people love the color red, and regard red as the symbol of energy, happiness and good luck. Sending red envelopes is a way to send love, luck, and good wishes. This paper explored the social and cultural aspects of WeChat usage among Chinese people to understand its popularity both in and outside China.

2 Literature Review

As the world becomes a global marketplace where technological products and services are being sold and utilized worldwide throughout different cultures, it has become increasingly critical to understand how culture affects the user acceptance and user experience of mobile services through globalization.

2.1   Usability and User Experience

User experience (UX) has been used in several ways in the HCI literature. On one hand, it is used to denote the design and use of user interfaces, in effect working as a synonym for interaction, usability, or even user-centered design. It was referred as "an umbrella phrase for new ways of understanding and studying the quality-in-use of interactive products" (Bargas-Avila and Hornbaek 2011). As Walsh et al. (2010) pointed out, usability focuses on how the user interacts with the product or whether the user finds a product useful in task completion. Global users, however, expect more from products and services than utility and usability: they are looking for experiences—human experiences that that fulfil users' stimulation, identity needs, and values.

For many researchers, the emphasis on positive aspects of UX leads to a focus on human values and needs, which include symbolic and aesthetic value. They ultimately determine why users react positively to something (Van Schaik and Ling 2009). This paper will measure UX through emotional, symbolic and cultural perspectives.

2.2   Emotional Experience

The HCI community has been showing a great deal of interest in refining the concepts of "user-centered design". Researchers and professionals in HCI increasingly moved the emphasis from efficiency and usability to a broader holistic context of human behavior. This holistic and behavioral context tries to understand human-computer interaction by studying the meanings, experiences, and values relevant to personal or cultural contexts (Norman 2006). This research direction has opened up deeper investigations of the meaning of affect, emotion, and experience (Lim et al. 2008).

Emotion was defined as "a resource for understanding and communicating what we experience" (Forlizzi and Battarbee, 2004, p. 264) and "a significant channel for expressing experience" (Lim et al. 2008, p. 4). The framework used in this paper to categorize and organize the different emotional responses users have was adopted from Jordan's (2002) definition of pleasurable experience. This includes physical pleasures, evoked by textures, sizes, temperatures, or colors; physiological pleasures, related to a behavioral control for a short period of time; and ideological and social pleasures, the reflective level, also the highest level of intellectual or cultural reaction.

2.3   Cultural Factors in UX Design

UX design should take into account users' socio-cultural context, because in designing UX there is greater focus on content, brand, and emotions, rather than a focus on designing merely for usability (Marcus 2006). Companies that succeed in their efforts usually understand the importance of culture of their target audience and how cultural inheritance plays a vital role in user-centered design. Much literature shows that cultures impact the process of information selection, receiving, and cognition. As early as 1993, Ockman (1993) proposed that good designs rely on users' cultures, including tastes, habits, and lifestyles, and cultural images could be divided into both implicit and explicit directions. Similarly, Taiwanese scholars Chen et al. (2009) found that culture reflected on interaction design in three levels: surface layer (visual and material), middle layer (behavior and habits), and inner layer (thoughts and spirit).

Lei and Wei (2013) analyzed the task flows of 20 Android mobile applications that integrated the ink-rhyme effect of Chinese calligraphy culture into interactive feedback, to form gradient modality, and concluded that the integration of cultural factors enhanced user experience, especially emotional experience of excitement, fun, and deep impression.

2.4 Chinese Red Packet Culture

In Chinese traditional culture, the senior members of society give some money to the unwed juniors during Chinese New Year. The senior members of the society may also give newlyweds some money in a red envelope when they meet for the first time. This unique type of monetary gift-giving culture has grown from Chinese New Year (Spring Festival) greetings to many other social occasions such as new births, weddings, graduation ceremonies, and even birthdays. The red envelopes/packets represent love, wealth, abundance, and good fortune.

Red Packets are still associated with traditional meanings in Chinese culture. Besides luck and wishes for special occasions, they also represent a social code that indicates a hierarchal bestowal from senior to junior parties (Chan et al. 2003). Further, the Red Packet ritual symbolically manifests the traditional values of social harmony and respect to hierarchy, evoking traditional collectivist Chinese culture (Park 2016).

Given the popularity of Facebook and WeChat, and the fact that no research has been done to measure and compare WeChat and Facebook user experience through the lens of Net Promoter Score (NPS) and cultural context, this paper tries to fill the research gap in the HIC community, and explores the relationship between user motivation, user experience and NPS, and how cultural factors affect them.

3 Method

3.1 Instruments

A triangulation research approach was utilized with an online survey and follow-up interviews for this study. The online survey (Cronbach's Alpha = .94) was created based on expert interviews with the authors' colleagues, including user experience researchers and strategists, and initial online panel discussions with 12 users.

There are three sections in the survey. The first section captured basic usage metrics of both applications, including frequency of use, daily length of use, total count of "friends", and length of ownership of the accounts.

The second section measured user motivations while using both Facebook and WeChat. Lien and Cao (2014) examined the effects of psychological motivations (entertainment, sociality, and information) on WeChat users' attitudes. The researchers drafted a questionnaire categorizing statements of "WeChat is fun/entertaining/ pleasing to use" as "Entertainment", "I can meet new friends/find old friends/keep in touch with my family and friends through WeChat" as "Sociality", and "WeChat is a convenient/good/timely source of information" as "Information". This paper adopted a similar question design, and drafted statements for both WeChat and Facebook to measure user motivation and attitudes.

The third section measured the users' emotional experience through satisfaction ratings regarding the overall experience, and other aspects of WeChat and Facebook that provide physical/visual pleasures, physiological pleasures, and ideological and social pleasures (Jordan 2002). This included "look and feel", "security", "positive attitude", and "cultural connectedness" aspects of both applications. In addition, a Net Promoter Score (NPS) question was asked to measure user loyalty.

Reichheld (2003) introduced the idea of a Net Promoter Score (NPS). He claimed that this single summary number is a sufficient basis for profitably measuring and managing customer loyalty. On a 0-to-10 scale, users answer the question "How likely is it that you would recommend [company X] to a friend or colleague?" Users who rate the company 0–6 are labeled as "detractors", 7 or 8 are "passives", and 9 or 10 are "promoters". The Net Promoter Score (NPS) is the percent of "promoters" minus the percent "detractors." According to Reichheld (2003), this single number has more relationship to company financial performance than all others he tested. As part of the survey, a Net Promoter Score (NPS) question was asked to both WeChat and Facebook users to measure their level of positive word-of-mouth and user loyalty.

The questionnaire was reviewed and pre-tested by the authors' colleagues—a group of user experience researchers, and was piloted with a small group of WeChat and Facebook users. It resulted in 423 responses after the full-launch and the data was analyzed using SPSS.

10 interviews to follow up with the survey responses were conducted after the survey was closed. Each interview was half an hour in length, and was conducted remotely.

3.2 Participants

Chinese people who are currently living outside China were recruited by snowball sampling from all over the world. Survey respondents were screened to be both WeChat and Facebook users. A total of 423 users participated in the study (233 females, 190 males). Participants were aged from 14 to 60, with an average age of 27.99 (SD = 8.18). Participants reported 9 countries of residence (Australia, Canada, France, New Zealand, Singapore, Malawi, UK, South Korea and United States) in 5 continents (Australia, North America, Asia, Europe, and Africa) as their current residency. Remote follow-up interviews were conducted with 10 participants who currently reside in the United States and Australia.

3.3 Procedures

The survey was created online and the web link was sent by WeChat and Facebook platforms. The survey was closed after the number of responses reached a statistically valid sample size (over 384) at a 95% confidence level.

After data was collected, Pearson's Correlation was run to test the correlation between NPS and users' satisfaction level, user engagement level, and other metrics.

One-way T-test was run to see whether the two groups (WeChat and Facebook) have any significant difference in terms of NPS, and overall user satisfaction. Textual analysis was conducted by coding all the open-ended comments from the survey and the interview transcriptions.

4 Analysis

4.1 Quantitative Results

WeChat Has a Significantly Higher Level of User Engagement than Facebook
Frequency: 89% of users reported they use WeChat at least twice a day, which is significantly higher than Facebook's 12% in the same category (p < .005).

Daily time spent: More than 60% of WeChat users reported they spend at least one hour per day on the platform, with a peak of almost 30% of users stating more than 3 h spent on WeChat on a daily basis (see Table 1). Only 12% of users reported using Facebook at least one hour per day with a peak of 45% users reporting less than 30 min per day, which is significantly lower than WeChat (p < .005, sig.).

Table 1. WeChat, daily time spent on platform

		Frequency	Percent	Valid percent	Cumulative percent
Valid	Less than 30 min	52	15.1	15.1	15.1
	30–60 min	104	24.7	24.7	39.8
	1–2 h	80	19.1	19.1	58.9
	2–3 h	56	13.3	13.3	72.2
	3 h+	121	27.8	27.8	100
	Total	423	100.0	100.0	
Missing	System	0	0		
Total		423	100.0		

Account ownership length: 32% of users reported they have used Facebook for more than 5 years, while 15% of users reported WeChat usage for more than 5 years.

WeChat Has a Significantly Higher NPS than Facebook Among the Chinese Users
When asked to rate the 11-point scale of "How likely is it that you would recommend WeChat to a friend or colleague?" 66% rated 9 or 10, 21% rated 0 to 6, which makes WeChat's NPS 46 among the Chinese users overseas. 46 is a very high score based on industry best practices. On the other hand, Facebook's NPS among the same group of users is −21, which is significantly lower than WeChat's NPS (p < .005, sig.).

WeChat Has Better User Experience than Facebook Among the Chinese Users
Overall experience: 87% of users reported being "satisfied" or "very satisfied" with WeChat, which is significantly higher than Facebook's favorable ratings of 42% (p < .005, sig.). More Chinese users feel indifferent about Facebook (43%) than WeChat (11%) (p < .005, sig.).

Significant difference was also found between WeChat and Facebook ratings for all the other user experience metrics, such as "look and feel", "ease of use", "navigation", "security", "reliability", "usefulness", and "intuitiveness".

User Motivation: WeChat Provides more Sociality, Entertainment and Information than Facebook to the Chinese Users

When comparing WeChat and Facebook, ratings on WeChat in terms of all three categories of user motivation (entertainment, sociality, and information) are significantly higher than Facebook. T-test results showed significant difference between the means of WeChat and Facebook's user motivation ratings. The statements being rated were "WeChat/Facebook is fun/entertaining/pleasing to use", "I can meet new friends/find old friends/keep in touch with my family and friends through WeChat/Facebook", and "WeChat/Facebook is a good/timely/convenient source of information".

Comparing the ratings of the three layers of user motivation within each platform, WeChat provides more entertainment and sociality than information, while Facebook provides more information than entertainment and sociality for Chinese users.

NPS Is Positively Correlated with User Satisfaction and User Experience

NPS is positively correlated with user satisfaction and positive user experience: "overall experience" (r = .851, n = 423, p = .000), "frequency of use" (r = .663, n = 423, p = .000), and "daily time spent on the platform" (r = .666, n = 423, p = .000) Tables (2, 3, 4, 5, 6, 7, and 8).

Table 2. Correlations between WeChat NPS & overall experience satisfaction

		WeChat, NPS	WeChat, overall satisfaction
WeChat, NPS	Pearson Correlation	1	.851**
	Sig. (2-tailed)		.000
	N	423	423
WeChat, overall satisfaction	Pearson Correlation	.851**	1
	Sig. (2-tailed)	.000	
	N	423	423

**Correlation is significant at the 0.01 level (2-tailed).

Table 3. Correlations between WeChat NPS & frequency of use

		WeChat frequency of use	WeChat, NPS
WeChat frequency of use	Pearson Correlation	1	.663**
	Sig. (2-tailed)		.000
	N	423	423
WeChat, NPS	Pearson Correlation	.663**	1
	Sig. (2-tailed)	.000	
	N	423	423

**Correlation is significant at the 0.01 level (2-tailed).

Table 4. Correlations between WeChat NPS & daily time spent on platform

		WeChat, NPS	WeChat, daily time spent
WeChat, NPS	Pearson Correlation	1	.666[**]
	Sig. (2-tailed)		.000
	N	423	423
WeChat, daily time spent	Pearson Correlation	.666[**]	1
	Sig. (2-tailed)	.000	
	N	423	423

**Correlation is significant at the 0.01 level (2-tailed).

Table 5. Correlations between WeChat positive attitude & sociality

		WeChat, positive attitude	Most of my family friends use WeChat
WeChat, positive attitude	Pearson Correlation	1	.687[**]
	Sig. (2-tailed)		.000
	N	423	423
Most of my family friends use WeChat	Pearson Correlation	.687[**]	1
	Sig. (2-tailed)	.000	
	N	423	423

**Correlation is significant at the 0.01 level (2-tailed).

Table 6. Correlations between positive attitude towards WeChat and cultural connectedness

		WeChat, positive attitude	WeChat, cultural connectedness
WeChat, positive attitude	Pearson Correlation	1	.523[**]
	Sig. (2-tailed)		.000
	N	423	423
WeChat, cultural connectedness	Pearson Correlation	.523[**]	1
	Sig. (2-tailed)	.000	
	N	423	423

**Correlation is significant at the 0.01 level (2-tailed).

Table 7. Correlations between positive attitude towards WeChat and information

		WeChat, positive attitude	WeChat, good source of information
WeChat, positive attitude	Pearson Correlation	1	.518**
	Sig. (2-tailed)		.000
	N	423	423
WeChat, good source of information	Pearson Correlation	.518**	1
	Sig. (2-tailed)	.000	
	N	423	423

**Correlation is significant at the 0.01 level (2-tailed).

Table 8. Correlations between positive attitude towards WeChat and entertainment

		WeChat, positive attitude	WeChat, entertaining
WeChat, positive attitude	Pearson Correlation	1	.440**
	Sig. (2-tailed)		.000
	N	423	423
WeChat, entertaining	Pearson Correlation	.440**	1
	Sig. (2-tailed)	.000	
	N	423	423

**Correlation is significant at the 0.01 level (2-tailed).

Sociality Has the Strongest Correlation with Users' Positive Attitude Towards WeChat, Followed by Cultural Connectedness, Entertainment and Information

Pearson Correlation results showed that positive attitude towards WeChat is positively correlated with sociality ($r = .687$, $n = 423$, $p = .000$), cultural connectedness ($r = .523$, $n = 423$, $p = .000$), entertainment ($r = .518$, $n = 423$, $p = .000$), and information ($r = .440$, $n = 423$, $p = .000$). Among all these factors, sociality has the strongest correlation with positive attitude towards WeChat.

The majority of Chinese users installed WeChat in its Chinese version (75%), instead of the English version (12%), and another 13% switch the language option between Chinese and English from time to time. Additionally, 97% of users responded they have used and 95% of them like the Red Packet feature on WeChat.

4.2   Textual Analysis

After coding all the comments and interview transcriptions, a few themes emerged:

Sociality. In addition to the quantitative results shown above, participants also stated, "it is very convenient to talk to my family and friends using WeChat"[1] and "I like using WeChat to keep in touch with my family and friends"[2] during interview sessions.

WeChat has a feature of selecting up to five contacts on top as the users' favorites in the contact book. When asked who these favorites are and why, most users put: "because they are important people in my life and we talk almost every day"[3]. According to Venkatesh et al. (2003), social influence is defined as the extent to which individual perceived that people who are important to him or her think he or she should use the system. Given the popularity of WeChat in mainland China, social influence definitely plays a role for its Chinese users overseas.

Cultural Connectedness: Traditional and New. A participant who lives in the United States stated the following in her interview:

> "WeChat is a way of communication, but also a way of life. Everyone in my family uses WeChat, including my parents who barely know how to send an email. WeChat is free compared to expensive international texting or data plans my mobile carrier offers. Also, I enjoy following my family and friends' Moments postings…it feels like I am not too far away from home."[4]

Regarding the reasons why Chinese users like the Red Packets feature, most respondents reported that it's a way to show love and send wishes, especially during the Chinese New Year season. "It's like you are celebrating the Spring Festival even when you are just going through your normal daily routines"[5]. A new element surfaced besides the traditional cultural aspect of the Red Packets, which is using it as a new way of saying "hello". Most Chinese users surveyed reported that sending a Red Packet now serves as an ice-breaker and usually the Red Packet greetings are reciprocal.

5   Discussion

WeChat versus Facebook. The Chinese users dominantly reported they prefer WeChat versus Facebook in terms of the frequency of use, daily time spent on the platform, and almost all other user participation and engagement metrics. The social context that Facebook is not publicly accessible in mainland China leaves WeChat the advantage of building user base in China. Once it spreads within China, the sociality

---

[1] Interview participants 3, 5, 7, 8, 9 and 10.

[2] Interview participants 1, 2, 3, 5, 6, 7, 8 and 10.

[3] Interview participants 2, 3, 4, 5, 6, 7, and 9.

[4] Interview participant 3.

[5] Interview participant 5.

and cultural context helps WeChat reach the users overseas who share the same language and cultural background.

Information versus Communication and Connectedness. The survey respondents reported that they use Facebook more for information, and rated Facebook favorably regarding its availability of timely information. In comparison, WeChat users mainly focused on the social aspect of using WeChat as a communication tool to stay connected with family, friends, and their home culture. The Chinese government has long kept tight reins on both traditional and new media to avoid potential subversion of its authority. Its tactics often entail strict media controls using monitoring systems and firewalls, which shutter publications or websites by keyword search (Xu 2014). This particular study didn't further explore the media censorship and whether it contributed to the amount of information available, or what type of information Chinese users are seeking. Most participants (7 out of 10) reported in the follow-up interviews that they enjoyed checking Facebook for its updates and news, but not necessarily initiating posts and sharing them.

Cultural Context: Filial Piety and Online Collectivism. Chinese Filial Piety, which is a virtue of respect for one's parents, elders, and ancestors in Confucian philosophy, was demonstrated in WeChat. WeChat enables Chinese people overseas to pay respect to their parents and elders by daily communication and sending monetary gifts very conveniently. The respondents reported that WeChat makes them feel less guilty for "leaving parents at home and living abroad"[6], especially for empty nesters. The linking of their bank cards to WeChat reduced the physical distance with family and allowed families to share the experience and culture of Red Packets virtually (Yangtze Evening Post 2014).

Cultures are defined as collectivist if the society holds a consistent world view, where adherence is given to interpersonal relationships, reciprocity, and social norms (Hempel et al. 2009; Oyserman et al. 2002). 95% of the respondents in this study use the Moments feature of WeChat (Social networking profile) and post something there on an average of once a week. Interestingly, users repost and share family and friends' moments more on WeChat than on Facebook, especially the ones that were seeking help, either in a commercial way or non-commercial way. Noronha (2002) stated that collectivist cultures have been observed to have a tendency toward social group inclusion and support, and a general value is placed on social obligations and commitments. The reciprocal relationship of Red Packet sending and receiving almost instantly manifests the collectivist culture as well.

6 Limitations and Future Research

This study used snowball sampling and an unknown amount of respondents are friends and family members of the authors'. This convenient sampling methodology might have been biased by the "like-minded" social group as the authors are in. Also, 83% of

---

[6] Interview participant 2, 3, 4, 5, 7, 9 and 10.

the respondents are millennials (aged under 34), and 84% of them have a bachelor's degree and above, which makes the sample possibly biased with first-generation Chinese immigrants, such as international students and young professionals who have not been living abroad for too long, and still have strong ties in China. It will be interesting to explore the popularity of WeChat among the second or third generation of Chinese users, who might not share as much strong connection as their parents or grandparents do.

Another limitation of the study would be that the definition of emotional experience was not very clear, and is hard to measure or quantify to begin with. More in-depth qualitative research, or usability testing sessions could help determine the emotional aspect of the user experience and usability of WeChat. Additionally, although NPS is widely adopted in the industry, and used by companies such as Apple, Southwest, and Best Buy, to track customer satisfaction and loyalty, it also has some critical concerns regarding its validity from scholars and practitioners (Grisaffe 2007).

Lastly, despite the popularity of both Facebook and WeChat worldwide, and the fact that they share a great amount of similar features and functionalities, they are not the same. Additionally, Facebook is blocked in China. Further research could include experiments with Chinese participants from mainland China who use Virtual Private Network (VPN) to access Facebook, and measure their user experience in comparison with their usage of WeChat.

7   Conclusion

This study examined users' perceived user experience of WeChat and Facebook. A triangulation research approach was utilized, including a survey with 423 Chinese users of both WeChat and Facebook, and textual analysis of the open-ended comments and follow-up interviews. It concluded that Chinese users who live outside China, prefer using WeChat over Facebook. WeChat has a much higher NPS, overall satisfaction, and user engagement compared with Facebook among this group. Social context and cultural factors were included to better understand the findings. The quick adoption and popularity of WeChat among Chinese people overseas, especially the digital Red Packets feature, and the way users post on Moments, are deeply rooted in the traditional Red Packets, filial piety, and the collectivist nature of the Chinese culture.

Acknowledgement. We would like to gratefully acknowledge the supervision of Dr. Anand Tharanathan, Ph.D. in this study. We would not have been able to complete this study without his candid feedback and suggestions. Also, we want to express our gratitude to Dr. Shad Gross, Ph.D. for his assistance with the overall organization and methodology of this paper. We also thank our colleagues, including visual and interaction designers and user experience researchers and strategists Nicholas True, Stacia Lowery, and Derek Payne from the Department of Product-User Experience at Angie's list who provided insight and expertise that greatly assisted the research. Additionally, we appreciate the respondents who participated in the survey and interviews of this study.

References

AllChinaTech: Tencent Survey: 94% of WeChat users open the app daily (2016). http://www.allchinatech.com/tencent-survey-94-of-wechat-users-open-the-app-daily/

Bakar, M.S.A.: Continuance Usage Intention of WeChat By Users in Malaysia (2016)

Bargas-Avila, J.A., Hornbæk, K.: Old wine in new bottles or novel challenges: a critical analysis of empirical studies of user experience. In: Proceedings of the SIGCHI Conference on Human Factors in Computing Systems, pp. 2689–2698. ACM, May 2011

Business Insider: WeChat breaks 700 million monthly active users (2016). http://www.businessinsider.com/wechat-breaks-700-million-monthly-active-users-2016-4

Chan, A.K., Denton, L., Tsang, A.S.: The art of gift giving in China. Bus. Horiz. **46**(4), 47–52 (2003)

Chen, C.-H., Chen, B.-C., Jan, C.-D.: A study of innovation design on Taiwan culture creative product – a case study of the facial mask of Ba Ja Jang. In: Aykin, N. (ed.) IDGD 2009. LNCS, vol. 5623, pp. 337–346. Springer, Heidelberg (2009). doi:10.1007/978-3-642-02767-3_38

Duggan, M., Brenner, J.: The Demographics of Social Media Users, 2012, vol. 14. Pew Research Center's Internet & American Life Project, Washington, DC (2013)

Facebook (2016). http://seekingalpha.com/article/4041792-facebook-fb-q4-2016-results-earnings-call-transcript

Forlizzi, J., Battarbee, K.: Understanding experience in interactive systems. In: Proceedings of the 5th Conference on Designing Interactive Systems: Processes, Practices, Methods, and Techniques, pp. 261–268. ACM, August 2004

Grisaffe, D.B.: Questions about the ultimate question: conceptual considerations in evaluating Reichheld's net promoter score (NPS). J. Consum. Satisf. Dissatisfaction Complain. Behav. **20**, 36 (2007)

Hempel, P.S., Zhang, Z.X., Tjosvold, D.: Conflict management between and within teams for trusting relationships and performance in China. J. Organ. Behav. **30**(1), 41–65 (2009)

Jordan, P.W.: Designing Pleasurable Products: An Introduction to the New Human Factors. CRC Press, Boca Raton (2002)

Lei, T., Wei, S.: An Exploration of Relationships between Culture Images and User Experience of Gesture Interaction (2013)

Lien, C.H., Cao, Y.: Examining WeChat users' motivations, trust, attitudes, and positive word-of-mouth: Evidence from China. Comput. Hum. Behav. **41**, 104–111 (2014)

Lim, Y., Donaldson, J., Jung, H., Kunz, B., Royer, D., Ramalingam, S., Thirumaran, S., Stolterman, E.: Emotional experience and interaction design. In: Peter, C., Beale, R. (eds.) Affect and Emotion in Human-Computer Interaction. LNCS, vol. 4868, pp. 116–129. Springer, Heidelberg (2008). doi:10.1007/978-3-540-85099-1_10

Liu, W., He, X., Zhang, P.: Application of red envelopes–new weapon of WeChat payment. In: 2015 International Conference on Education, Management, Information and Medicine. Atlantis Press, April 2015

Madden, M., Lenhart, A., Cortesi, S., Gasser, U., Duggan, M., Smith, A., Beaton, M.: Teens, social media, and privacy. Pew Res. Center **21**, 2–86 (2013)

Marcus, A.: Cross-cultural user-experience design. In: Barker-Plummer, D., Cox, R., Swoboda, N. (eds.) Diagrams 2006. LNCS (LNAI), vol. 4045, pp. 16–24. Springer, Heidelberg (2006). doi:10.1007/11783183_4

Newzoo: Top 25 companies by game revenues (2016). https://newzoo.com/insights/rankings/top-25-companies-game-revenues/

Norman, D.A.: Words matter. Talk about people: not customers, not consumers, not users. Interactions **13**(5), 49–63 (2006)

Noronha, C.: Chinese cultural values and total quality climate. Manag. Serv. Qual.: Int. J. **12**(4), 210–223 (2002)

Ockman, J.: Architecture Culture. Rizzoli, New York (1993)

Oyserman, D., Kemmelmeier, M., Coon, H.M.: Cultural psychology, a new look: reply to Bond (2002), Fiske (2002), Kitayama (2002), and Miller (2002) (2002)

Park, L.: WeChat Red Bags: How International Students from China Use Social Media While Attending a Public University in California. UCLA: Education 0249 (2016). http://escholarship.org/uc/item/55v3195g

Reichheld, F.F.: The one number you need to grow. Harv. Bus. Rev. **81**(12), 46–55 (2003)

Van Schaik, P., Ling, J.: The role of context in perceptions of the aesthetics of web pages over time. Int. J. Hum.-Comput. Stud. **67**(1), 79–89 (2009)

Venkatesh, V., Morris, M.G., Davis, G.B., Davis, F.D.: User acceptance of information technology: toward a unified view. MIS Q. **27**(3), 425–478 (2003)

Walsh, T., Nurkka, P., Walsh, R.: Cultural differences in smartphone user experience evaluation. In: Proceedings of the 9th International Conference on Mobile and Ubiquitous Multimedia, p. 24. ACM, December 2010

WeChat: Tencent Holding Ltd. ADR 2016 Q3 Results – Earnings Call (2016). http://seekingalpha.com/article/4023988-tencent-holding-ltd-adr-2016-q3-results-earnings-call-slides

Xu, B.: Media censorship in China. Counc. Foreign Relat. **25**, 1–6 (2014)

Yangtze Evening Post, February 2014. Chun Jie Qiang Fa Wei Xin Hong Bao Chuan Qin Qing. http://news.jschina.com.cn/yzwb.html

Design for Social Development

Design for Neighborhood Amateur Cultural Club – A Community Regeneration Practice in Qinglong Hutong

Zhiyong Fu[✉] and Xue He

Tsinghua University, Beijing 100084, China
fuzhiyong@tsinghua.edu.cn, hexue1991@foxmail.com

Abstract. This paper investigates the role of cultural amateur clubs of residents' community in the traditional neighborhood, and focuses on involving design in community activities to explore the new opportunities and possibilities of community regeneration. With the development of urbanization in China, traditional communities' environment has changed a lot. The mixture of new and old buildings not only broke the traditional residential environment integrity, but also changed the neighborhood relationship in communities. Under the macro-context of social background, understanding the existing problems and situation that residents who live in the modern communities may face when participating in daily cultural activities in the public space, has great practical significance in improving interpersonal relationship's situation, further promoting the development of the social harmonious. Using the Living Lab participatory design method and ethnographic study, we visited and interviewed the residents who live in Qinglong Hutong, Dongcheng District, Beijing, China. First of all, we describe the background, purpose and methods of this research, and then study the current situation of how the residents in Qinglong Community participate in the daily cultural activities. By identifying the persona, sampling investigating and researching on the residents, we create the model on social interaction and network establishment of the amateur cultural activities in the community. The final outcomes of this paper include participatory workshops on Beijing Opera, the applet based on the WeChat, and initiative on cultural regeneration during the Beijing Design Week. The model and sustainable mechanism developed in this paper will be used to support the further community regeneration project.

Keywords: Social innovation · Amateur cultural club · Social interaction · Neighborhood relationship · Community regeneration

1 Introduction

Burley argued that city is highest embodiment and important crystallization of the human culture, and the development of a city depends on both economic and cultural strength. The relationship among the culture, economy and city has been redefined: It is not the city shaping the culture, but the culture that makes the city better; the inputs of culture can be transformed into the outputs of economic and society [1].

© Springer International Publishing AG 2017
P.-L.P. Rau (Ed.): CCD 2017, LNCS 10281, pp. 385–398, 2017.
DOI: 10.1007/978-3-319-57931-3_31

However, with the changes of society in big cities, because of the social mobility of residents and the development of migration which reduced the possibility of communication among neighbors, the traditional neighborhood relationship suffered unprecedented the challenge, the cultural life in the big city becomes increasingly barren. Louis Wirth, who is the leading figure in Chicago School Sociology, describes the city as a "Substitution of secondary for primary contacts, the weakening of bonds of kinship, the declining social significance of the family, the disappearance of neighborhood and the undermining of traditional basis of social solidarity" [2].

To the late 1970s and early 1980s, culture is considered as the one of the driving forces for the regeneration of the old city in a number of cities in North America and Western Europe, which set off the upsurge of using the culture to promote the regeneration of the old cities. The cultural capital helped a host of decline areas in developed countries readjust the position and gradually revive in the post-industrial age and new economic environment [3]. Adjusting and improving the function of the old city, enhancing and even rebuilding the vitality and environmental quality of the historic city is the important part of "Urban Revitalization" work [4]. Cultural orientated regeneration of the old city means we should regard the culture as the catalyst and the engine for the regeneration [5]. In order to maintain the sustainable benefits of the regeneration, we should pay attention to develop the "culture based production system" [6].

With the deepening of the process of urbanization, the reconstruction of community culture has become the driving force of the urban regeneration. Amateur cultural clubs turn into the DNA of community culture and an important carrier to fulfill the civic cultural needs. It plays an important role in enhancing residents' ownership and the centripetal force, creating a friendly cultural environment, improving the cultural quality and the tastes of the residents, fulfilling the demand of the urban culture construction and other aspects [7].

2 Research Methods

2.1 Method and Process

According to the research goals of this paper, we carried out the in-depth field researches and user interviews in Qinglong community many times to find the pain points and residents' needs.

Discovery of pain points – Using the living lab participatory approach to conduct the research. Living Lab provides the open innovation methods in real life settings. User-driven innovation is also fully integrated in the co-creative process of new services, products and societal infrastructures [8].

Clarifying the needs – Using the ethnographic methods to conduct the qualitative research. Ethnographic investigation is a method which mixed the in-depth observation with the guided interviews, using the participant observation and unstructured interviews to collect the data [9].

Considering that most users are unable to assess their own behavior accurately. We use the qualitative research methods like interviewing stakeholders, interviewing subject-matter expert (SME), user observation, ethnographic field studies, literature research and so on [10], to clarify the requirement by collecting the first-hand data, and determine the design direction.

2.2 Field Survey

Beijing Dongcheng Qinglong Hutong, formerly known as Qinglong Temple, Copper Factory. Qinglong Hutong is the office location of a multitude of design and cultural innovation companies, but also the home of original inhabitants. It is located in Dongcheng District, which insists on "Strong culture area" strategy raised by the government.

According to the open data, which shows the culture index of 16 districts and counties in Beijing in 2014, we found that Dongcheng District only has 2 public libraries, 7 museums within the Cultural Relics Bureau System, 1 archives, 6 professional art troupes, 18 art venues, 17 street cultural activity centers and more than and 200 community cultural activity rooms [15]. Compared with other districts, the cultural basis of Dongcheng is relatively deeper, but the related supporting services are not well provided.

2.3 Target Group

We did many researches to explore the different aspects of Qinglong community, Dongcheng District. This paper will mainly focus on the Beijing Opera Club, one of grass-roots amateur clubs in Qinglong community.

Our interviewees are mainly 40–80 years old Beijing Opera Club members. The mainly research methods are personal interviews and focus group [10]. We interviewed around 20 common members and 3 key members. For the key members, we did in-depth interview to dig more details. The research lasted about two months and was mainly founded by the Service Design Institute of Tsinghua University.

This research was one of projects in a joint course on the urban sustainable development, which has been carried out for three years, between Tsinghua University and Stanford University. We tried to use interdisciplinary research and tele-cooperation methods to enhance quality of life in urban environments. With the help of Gehua Design Service Center (DSC), we apply a set of activity design method on Qinglong Hutong, which is close by the Gehua Building, to promote the integration of the neighborhood relationship, build a smart and harmonious community at the same time. The whole project was shown in the end of this program in December 7, 2016 at Stanford University, California, USA. We received plenty of precious advices and encouraging words from audiences.

3 Findings

3.1 User Investigation

During the joint class, a sociology student made a community autonomy presentation, which inspired us to start the research from the community activist, who is the key person to mobilize the enthusiasm of residents to participate in activities. After the deep investigation in community, we found that community activists and leaders exist in some amateur cultural clubs. In the end, we successfully got in touch with the head of Beijing Opera Club in Qinglong Hutong, and conducted the face-to-face interviews with him as well as other members of the club.

3.1.1   Interviews

Mr. Wang, who is the head of Beijing Opera Club, said, *"We'll make an appointment in advance. Usually, we'll practice together from 8:50am to 11:00am here (Qinglong Hutong) from Tuesday to Friday, but on Monday we'll gather at the basement in Bei Guan Ting No. 8. There is no activity at weekend, because their children will visit them at that time. The members volunteer participating the daily activity, even some of them who live far away will take the subway to get here despite of the bad weather. Others may ride a bike or just walk... If there is a temporary change, I'll call them. Because most of them are retirees, they may not that familiar with the application in the smart phone..."*

He continued to say, *"I'm younger than most of them and totally enamored of Beijing Opera, and then I set up this club to let us practice together. Nowadays, young men have less interest in the traditional culture, so I hope we can make a little contribution to the protection of the Intangible Culture Heritage..."*

Mr. Chen, who is the tutor of the club, said, *"Although they are not that professional, but their enthusiasm touched me deeply, after the performance, I will come here to participate in activities from time to time..."*

Mr. Zhang, who has just retired, said, *"One day, the weather was not that bad, I went to the park, and saw them performing the Beijing Opera. At first, I just sat down and listened to them. After two months, they invited me to sing a few words, and I wasn't very confidence at the beginning, because I didn't sing very well..."*

Mr. Liu, who is an 80-year-old retired artillery, said, *"Now, this house is going to be torn down, after that, it's hard to find such a place for us to practice Beijing Opera..."*

Mr. Li, who plays the drum, said, *"I think we must do something to keep the Beijing Opera alive, and I truly hope there can be more young people in our club..."*

We found that most of the members of the community are retirees, they got the belonging, dignity, and self-fulfillment in club, but this kind of grass-roots cultural amateur clubs still faces a multitude of challenges and problems.

3.1.2   Workshop

With the help of Gehua Design Service Center (DSC), we obtained the permission that we can conduct the activity on 13th floor in Gehua Buiding for whole morning. After that, we inform Mr. Wang, who is the head of Beijing Opera Club, the specific time and place of this activity. At the same time, we published the activity information online. In November 28, 2016, it turned out to be successful according to the feedback and the statics.

3.2 Character Analysis

The permanent members are backbone of the club and they tend to be participants, cultural communicators in daily activities, as well as the strongest driving force in sustainable development of the club.

Most of members in grass-roots cultural amateur clubs of the Qinglong community are retired workers, whose average age is about 60 years old. They are exceedingly willing to communicate with other residents and find a meaningful thing to spend their leisure time.

Key stakeholders (club leaders) are responsible for the organization of the clubs and interaction with the outside world. Their age is relatively smaller than others. Leaders are invariably enthusiastic about the public affairs of club and community, at the same time, their leadership and expertise enable them influence or mobilize other residents. They are always recommended by the leaders of neighborhood offices or neighborhood committees, or you can find them during the research and activities of community [11].

The ordinary residents (bystanders) in club are potential members of clubs, and they are the hidden power of sustainable development to clubs. They don't have much interest in Beijing Opera, but they want to find something to kill time after retirement, so they won't feel that lonely and frustrated. After joining clubs, they can get to know what happened in community, find something meaningful to enrich retirement life and receive the comfort and care from clubs.

3.3 Main Findings and Solutions

Through the follow-up investigation, we found that there are certain patterns in organizing these grass-roots amateur cultural clubs.

3.3.1 Main Findings

Problems and Challenges. Because lacking of support from local government, it's hard to find activities venues due to the soaring city land price. Most members are retired, because other age groups don't have enough time and energy to participate in daily activities of clubs, consequently the clubs may lack vitality and their activities lack appeal and influence to the strangers. So, there is very limited resource for leaders to maintain operation of the club.

Club Management Form. Residents who live in the same community may not know others, and a few members will form a small club though the opinion leader (core figure), permanent members will organize a number of activities now and then to attract new members and enhance relationship with others. During that time, they can find and develop shared interests, begin to socialize with others. With the support from various organizations, the club will have sustainable development. And these policies which strive to protect the interests of the public are often achieved after the agreement between commercial institutions and the government [12] (Fig. 1).

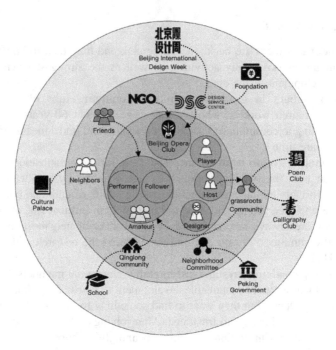

Fig. 1. The amateur cultural clubs' social connection network

The Participant Roles. The participation is the key to the community engagement. Therefore, there are different promotion ways and skills of community participation to different groups.

For club activists, we give them opportunities to provide the plan and make a multitude of decisions and create the chances of connecting the outside with other groups as well as enhance their leadership satisfaction, and improve residents' engagement and external support.

For club bystanders: design the activities to expand their ways of participating and make them become the volunteers and contacts to link the interpersonal resources in community.

For club strangers: Provide them the ways of open participation and invite them to come. Capture their attention, as well as provide them detailed information and introduction of the clubs. Understand their concerns and needs through the interaction.

Learning Method. The members learn Beijing Opera still mainly by word of mouth, which lacks systematic and repeatable teaching methods. A host of beginners feel embarrassed to perform in public. Especially they are elders, which can be a huge barrier to them. Most of them are disabled in moving and acting, few elders even have vision and hearing impairment.

Social Engagement. Because of the frequent communication of daily activities, the relationship among members of the club, especially those permanent members, get increasingly close, and they begin to take care of each other in daily life. Similar age, interests and experience makes them become familiar with others quickly.

Activities Promotion. During this activity, we use the Internet as a platform for interaction and promotion. We connect with the members offline and edit and publish the activity online, users can search, collect and enroll the activities they are interested in. Finally, characters can broadcast or share the pictures, videos and their thoughts in WeChat or other applications. Internet makes the influence of activity far wider than before.

3.3.2   Potential Solutions

Designers can help the club activities to be organized more effectively through the integrating, allocating and utilizing the external resources, and designing the flexible plans depends on the specific situation.

Design Space. According to the Fu Si yard community cultural activity center, or the Chaoyang Cultural Center, we hope to find the permanent space to the clubs through acquiring the support from local government [13], or semi-permanent space, like steel structure pavilion during Beijing Design Week in Qinglong Hutong. We can design the space to fit the performance needs.

Activity Organization. With the joint help of the community organizations (neighborhood committees), which are established by the government, as well as the residents' voluntary organization (Beijing Opera Club, Poetry Club, Calligraphy Club), even some commercial organizations, the club activities will be more rich.

Cultural Heritage. WeChat, a very popular social communication tools in China, can play an important role in cultural promotion. How to attract the young people to be participants can be meaningful to be discussed, for example, we can organize the open workshop to facilitate them attend as volunteers, cultivate the spirit of public spirit and the interest to traditional culture as well.

Community Construction. Amateur cultural groups can help to build more strong local network and elderly residents can quickly find a sense of belonging in these interest groups. Through the living lab approach [8], we are able to gather the data from elderly resident, explore the efficient methods to organize the activities and build community autonomy system gradually, after that, we can extend influence of clubs by corporation with various external resources and get the consistent support from local government.

4   Activity Planning

4.1   Activity Overall Planning

Through this activity as well as the follow-up researches, we summarized some top-level activity design, and by means of multilateral cooperation, it enables follow-up activity organization to develop sustainably in a spiral line (Fig. 2).

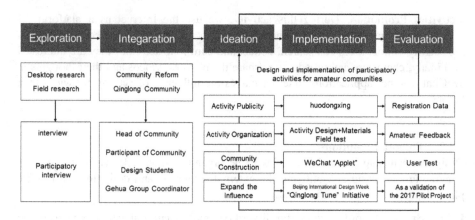

Fig. 2. Using the living lab model to design sustainable activities of amateur clubs

4.2   Execution of Activity

Topic: Qinglong tune
Time: 9:30am–11:00am, November 28, 2016
Location: 13th floor, Gehua Building, Dongcheng District, Beijing
Agenda:

9:30am	Activity starts and the host addresses to the audience
09:30am–10:00am	Beijing Opera performance (single performance, consists three people)
10:00am–11:30am	Storytelling: the legends behind the lines in Beijing Opera; The memories among the members in this club; Question and Answer
11:30am–12:00am	End of the speech; Taking the group photos; Giving the gifts

Goals: To promote the interaction among neighborhoods in the community by organizing a cultural workshop, and welcome the new members to this club as well.

4.2.1   How to Organize the Activities

By the combination of online and offline tools, it makes the promotion and dissemination of the activities get wider, faster and more convenient (Fig. 3).

The Final Results of This Activity Online. The online release date is November 24th, and just in three days after releasing, the enrollment reached to 10 people, and the access number has grown to over 500 people, 52 of them collected this activity. At the end of the activity, there are 3 new members who join this club, which shows that the Internet tool can be more efficient and flexible than offline methods (Fig. 4).

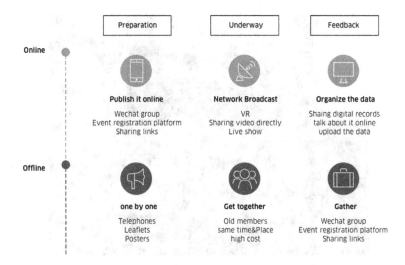

Fig. 3. Online and offline tools for activity promotion

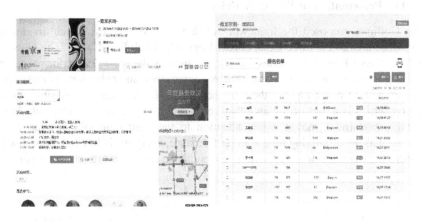

Fig. 4. Online promotion website and statistics about the enrollment

Feedback. Many members in the club said that it was not easy for everyone to get together, because the previous temporary room was not big enough to accommodate all the members. Since the 13th floor of Gehua Building is spacious, all the members were able to attend the activity at the same time thanks to it. Because the activity attracted a lot attention from outside, Gehua Building got more attention than before at the same time, accordingly the clubs in community can have the chance to use the floor space, and the provider is able to receive more exposure.

The new member, Ms. Li, said, *"I don't know how to find this kind of groups before, as soon as I saw the activity which was published online, I signed up and came here to attend it, at the end of the activity, I added him (the club organizer) in WeChat, I hope I can be involved in the follow-up activities..."* (Fig. 5).

Fig. 5. Posters and group photos of the "Qinglong Tune"

4.3   The Presentation of Self in Activity

Erving Goffman proposed the framework of dramaturgical theory, which divides the performance area to the three parts, "Front Region", "Back Stage" and "The Outside" [14]. The "Front Region" includes the setting, such as the stage for performance and personal appearance, which includes personal appearance and behaviors. For example, the actors will sit down or read the lines here. The "Back Stage" is invisible for the audience, which is a part of the area that keeps the audience and outsider out. At the backstage, performers may not pay attention to the limitations of appearance and image, such as the discussing time after performance, everyone is free to talk or discuss with others. "The Outside" may include the audience and other organizations (Fig. 6).

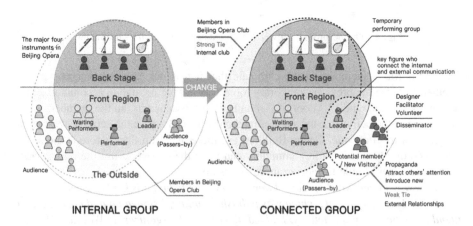

Fig. 6. The role map during the activity

Before Activity. The leader gave us a warm-up performance at first, quite a few members whispered to sing along or just beat time softly following the rhythm. Others drifted in during that time.

During Activity. The members performed one by one, the leader will encourage members who itched to perform on stage, he gave them some suggestions about the performed works, at the same time he would adjust the schedule of the activity.

After Activity. Under the guidance of the host, members of the club began to chat with others about the earlier performance and told us about their own stories, for example, Mr. Li thanked others who cared for him during his illness. In the end, the leader summarized the experience of this activity, proposed the next plan and made, if not most, work arrangement.

5 Outcomes and Discussion

5.1 Outcomes

Use New Technology to Organize Activities. Because it is not easy for local residents to get the information of community activities, which results the lack of

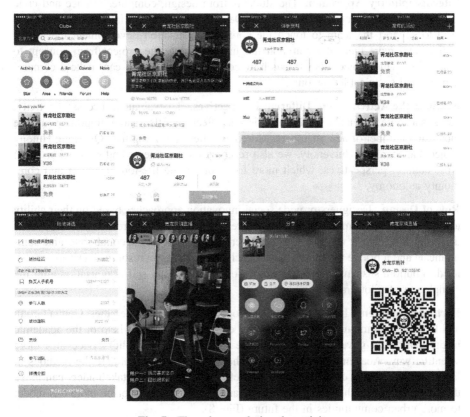

Fig. 7. The role map during the activity

community participation, So one of the outcome of this research is Club+, which is an applet in WeChat, a very popular app in Chinese, even in the elderly. We designed an applet called Club+ in WeChat based on the Html 5 to facilitate the management and organization of activities and clubs for different stakeholders. It can help the residents find or post the activities based on their interest and location. As for beginners, they can learn more about the clubs before attending the activities. Through put a reward button on WeChat article, people who are interested in the activity can fund little money to support the daily operation of the club. The leader of club can also initiate the crowdfunding to find the suitable activity space (Fig. 7).

New Media Promotion to Connect Audiences. For promoting the activity, we passed out the booklets with QR code to encourage residents, audiences, especially the young people to scan the code, so they can subscribe the WeChat Official Accounts, which will introduce Beijing Opera and the basic information of this club, then encourage them to participate in the follow-up experiencing activities and even the volunteer work.

5.2   Discussion

Interdisciplinary Approach. The students from design, computer science and civic engineering work together in this project. Design thinking on social innovation tools is used to support the team to touch the core of urbanization development the urbanization, and gave them the common language to move the project from concept to production. This project also shows how collective intelligence can make a comprehensive and sustainable outcome.

Evaluate the Activity from Different Perspectives. To evaluate a successful activity, the sustainable influence and transmission effect are the same important as the increasing number of new members. Moreover, after presenting the "Qinglong Hutong project" at Stanford University, we also received the comments and suggestions from cross-cultural perspectives, which more focus on online life-long learning and community autonomy.

Role of Design. Designers provide social innovation approaches based on their ability to collaborate and communicate with different stakeholders and resources. The role of design is to create a way among the different stakeholders to collaborate and communicate and a bridge to connect the local club with different resources. Designers also need to build a sustainable mechanism to foster community self-organization after the completion of pilot project.

Partner Ecosystem. In this project, the cooperation among universities, Gehua Group and Qinglong Community create a partner ecosystem. With the help of the academic institutions, local government can manage the community public service in a more scientific way. Academic institutions also have the chance to validate the methods in laboratory in the real context. These joint efforts from various stakeholders can make the community more habitable, innovative and lively. We look for promote this model to more urban communities in the future (Fig. 8).

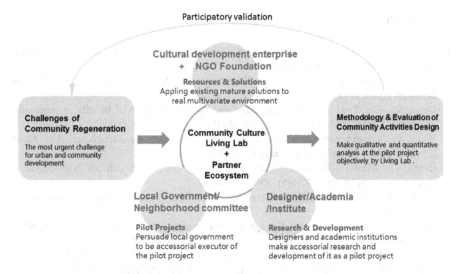

Fig. 8. The cooperation model among different stakeholders

6 Conclusion

This paper investigates the Beijing Opera clubs in QinglongHuton and explores participatory methods to promote community engagement. Amateur cultural club activate the community from the bottom, increase neighborhood participation, and improve the neighborhood's ability to resolve public affairs through community involvement and empowerment. The final outcomes of this paper include participatory workshops on Beijing Opera, the applet based on the WeChat, and initiative on cultural regeneration during the Beijing Design Week. Through promoting the cultural activities, we also generate the new mindset and solution in implementing culturally supporting the aged in community. With the help of the culture organizations, like Gehua Group and local community committee, it is possible to expand influence through a variety of channels. For example, we can help the local government to implement the pilot project on traditional culture during Design Beijing Week, which is popular event for young people and encourage them to participate in traditional culture regeneration. Amateur cultural club will become the carrier of urban culture. Maintaining the sustainable development of the amateur clubs in community is very important to reshape the urban culture DNA and facilitate the urban regeneration better. The model and sustainable mechanism developed in this paper will be used to support the further project on community regeneration as well.

Acknowledgments. Many thanks to Deland Chan and Kevin Hsu at Stanford University and Lan Li at Tsinghua University co-conduct the class, and the project related students including Xue He, Dan Yao, Yihao Shen, Jiahui Zhu, Ziye Huang, Bowen liu, Weili Wang, John Zhao, Zay Smith, Terence Zhao, Jen Han, Jia Lin. We express the sincere thanks to their contributions.

References

1. Miles, S., Paddison, R.: Introduction: the rise and rise of culture-led urban regeneration. Urban Stud. **42**(5), 833–839 (2005)
2. Wirth, L.: Urbanism As a Way of Life (Reprint Series in Sociology). University of Chicago Press, Irvington (1991)
3. Miles, S.: 'Our Tyne': iconic regeneration and the revitalisation of identity in newcastle-gateshead. Urban Stud. **42**(5/6), 913–926 (2005)
4. Wang, J.: "Urban regeneration" and urban design. Urbanism and Architecture (Urb Arch), (2) (2009). Heilongjiang Science and Technology Press
5. Evans, G.: Measure for measure: evaluating the evidence of cultures contribution to regeneration. Urban Stud. **42**(5/6), 959–983 (2005)
6. Lu, R.: Thoughts on innovation management of amateur cultural groups. Dazhong Wenyi (14) (2016)
7. Sasaki, M.: Urban regeneration through cultural creativity and social inclusion: rethinking creative city theory through a Japanese case study. Cities **27**, S3–S9 (2010)
8. Füzi, A.: Quadruple Helix and its types as user-driven innovation models (2013)
9. Brewer, J.D.: Ethnography, p. 10. Open University Press, Philadelphia (2000)
10. Cooper, A., Reimann, R., Cronin, D.: About Face 3: The Essentials of Interaction Design. Wiley, Hoboken (2007)
11. The Institute of Sustainable Communities (ISC), Guangzhou Participation Community and Participation Service Center: Participatory methods for urban community-based sustainable development
12. Grodach, C., Loukaitou-Sideris, A.: Cultural development strategies and urban revitaliztion: a survey of US cities. Int. J. Cult. Policy **13**(4), 349–370 (2007)
13. Xiao, D., Wei, X.: Chaoyang District cultural center's exploration of community democratic self-government organization. Renwen Tianxia **1**, 25–28 (2015)
14. Goffman, E.: The Presentation of Self in Everyday Life. Random House, New York (1959). Anchor
15. Wang, Q., Xu, L.: Urban Culture Development Index of China. People's University Publication House, p. 154 (2016)

Design to Improve Medication Adherence for the Elderly in China

Long Liu[1], Chu Wang[1], Qian Zhou[2], and Ziying Yao[3(✉)]

[1] College of Design and Innovation, Tongji University, Shanghai 200092, China
liulong@tongji.edu.cn
[2] Designaffairs Business Consulting (Shanghai) Co., Ltd, Shanghai, China
qian.zhou@designaffairs.com
[3] College of Mechanical Engineering, Donghua University,
Shanghai 201620, China
ziyingyao@dhu.edu.cn

Abstract. Elderly people are likely to suffer from different chronic diseases which need to be treated for long time. By now, medication is still one of the most widely accepted and adopted ways of treatments but how to promote the medication adherence for elderly is a global challenge. Statistics show that generally only 50% of the patients are adherent to prescriptions. In China, with the increase amount of elderly population, medication adherence is becoming an important issue in healthcare industry. This paper described a study to find out the medication adherence situation for elderly patients in China based on questionnaire and interview. The key findings both in cognitive and behavioral aspects are presented, and a design strategy with service design to promote medication adherence in China is proposed.

Keywords: Medication adherence · Elderly patient · Healthcare design

1 Introduction

For elderly people with chronic diseases, medication is one of the most widely accepted and adopted ways of treatment. Previous researches and reports showed that both physiological and psychological factors have influence on medication adherence. In physiological aspects, elderly patients are more likely to experience hearing loss, impaired vision, memory deterioration, cognitive decline, emotional instability, and other disorders, while in psychological aspects more on anxiety feeling, intense fear, and depression when they experience diseases. The complex and diverse experience of the elderly patients as well as their knowledge background, family status, financial situation, etc. make their behavior difficult to study and to change.

How to promote medication adherence for elderly is a global challenge. Non-adherence will ultimately increase the likelihood of treatment failure [1], and it may lead to disease complications, increase unnecessary medical expenses and expenditures, cause disability and even premature death too [2]. In all patient age groups, the elderly population earns the largest benefit from medication but they are also the most dangerous group when medicine adherence is not ensured [3].

© Springer International Publishing AG 2017
P.-L.P. Rau (Ed.): CCD 2017, LNCS 10281, pp. 399–411, 2017.
DOI: 10.1007/978-3-319-57931-3_32

In developed countries, about 50% patients are adherent to prescriptions [4, 5]. This figure is much lower in developing countries where healthcare resources are limited and healthcare services are relatively poor. In China, the general medication adherence is around 43% [2]. As the world's most populated country with elderly people, China accounts for 1/5 of the global total elderly population [6]. In 2010 during the sixth National Census, a total of 17,658,702 elderly aged over 60 carried out a self-assessment of their health status. Unhealthy elderly accounted for 16.85% of that group [7].

With the increase of elderly population in China, medication adherence is becoming an important issue in healthcare industry. It is necessary to cope with this issue with some design solutions developed to support patient's behaviors. Therefore, in the College of Design and Innovation (D&I) of Tongji University, researchers have conducted a study with the following goals:

- To understand the current situation of medication adherence for elderly in China;
- To summarize key findings in both cognitive and behavioral aspects;
- To propose potential design solutions based on the key findings.

2   Research

2.1   Methods and Process

Questionnaire
The purpose of the questionnaire is to collect overall information of elderly patients' medication adherence, to provide data for targeted selection of in-depth interviews and to support the follow-up interview design. The questionnaire for elderly patients is composed of four parts: medication adherence, disease and therapy, healthcare and physician-patient relations, and other relevant and basic information [8]. In the medication adherence part, a self-report questionnaire, the eight-item Morisky Medication Adherence Scale (MMAS-8) is applied [9]. All items are translated into Chinese. Collected data are presented in Fig. 1.

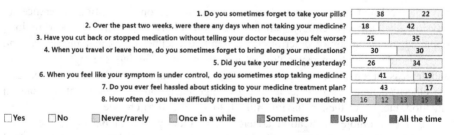

Fig. 1. Questions and results of the MMAS-8

The questionnaire was mainly carried out through the network and paper. The network part was created by a network platform named 'Wenjuanxing' and then the links were forwarded to participants. The paper part was carried out directly to distribute questionnaire to participants. In total 60 elderly patients were recruited from Shanghai, Hangzhou, and Zhuji city in China. The following standards were considered in choosing the participants:

- Over 45 years old, outpatient
- At least one year medication-taking experience
- At least once per day of medication-taking
- At least with one chronic disease
- Having hospital experience within 6 months

Interview

The purpose of interview is to verify the findings or speculations in the questionnaire results and to collect future expectations in the healthcare domain. The interview is conducted in a semi-structural way with both elderly patients and care providers. For elderly patients it is conducted with the same four parts as in the questionnaire, but more freely. For care providers it is planned to collect the following information:

- Brief introduction of the job content and workload
- The whole process of treating a patient
- Experience of the elder patient with chronic disease
- Experience of the medication adherence issue
- Attitude and standpoint towards physician-patient relations
- Expectation of the future healthcare domain

Five elderly questionnaire respondents are chosen to interview. Another five care providers are contacted for one-to-one interview (Table 1).

Table 1. Basic information of interviewees

No.	Age	Gender	Living situation	Medication adherence level	No.	Age	Gender	Job
1	58	Female	Retied	High	1	52	Male	Specialist
2	83	Male	Retied	Low	2	48	Male	Doctor
3	55	Male	Employee	Low	3	45	Female	Pharmacist
4	69	Female	Retied	Medium	4	35	Female	Nurse
5	79	Male	Retied	Medium	5	32	Female	Nurse
Elderly patients					Care providers			

2.2 Result Analysis

Basic Situation

The questionnaire is conducted with 25 male patients and 35 female patients. Their mean age is 61 years old. Among them, 29 (48.3%) patients have more than three diseases, and all participants over 80 years old have at least three diseases. In general, the medication adherence level is low. From the data in Fig. 1, it can be seen that 46

(76.7%) are in low medication adherence category, 13 (21.6%) the medium category and only 1 (1.7%) the high category. Basic information in the ways of communication shows that mobile phones are popular among them, 29 (48.3%) use smart phone app and 25 (41.7%) use cellphone calls.

Cognitive Aspect

As Fig. 1 shows, 43 (71.7%) participants feel hassled about sticking to medicine treatment plan. It is very common that patients reduce or stop taking medicine without telling doctors. 25 (41.7%) participants have done it because of adverse drug effect; 41 (68.3%) stop medicine taking as they believe that the symptoms are under control. In respect of physician-patient relations, 38 (63.3%) participants consider that the physician-patient communication is a hierarchical relationship, while 17 (28.3%) consider it as partner or friend. And, the latter has better medication adherence than the former. According to the interview, most of the elderly are also eager to gather health relevant information rather than to take medication according to prescription.

Behavioral Aspect

According to Fig. 1, 38 (63.3%) participants respond that they forget to take medication sometimes. Most of them read drug instructions. As shown in Fig. 2, when using drug instructions, 52 out of 60 patients concern time and dose, 31 pay attention to side effects and expiry time. Regarding the ways of collecting health information, 39 participants collect it from doctors, beside the ways of TV-program, Internet, newspaper and magazine. According to the interview, some patients involve in prescription in some ways. But they don't much involve in developing treatment plan of their doctors.

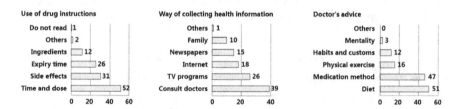

Fig. 2. Some results of the questionnaire

Healthcare Aspect

As shown in Fig. 2, doctors are more likely to provide diets and medication information, than to give physical exercise and lifestyle advice. The information on psychological aspects is still less. Furthermore, different care providers with different functions have different understanding on medication adherence. There are no unified methods to follow to improve adherence. In fact, the patients are facing with information with contradictions in practice.

2.3   Key Findings

Key findings are summarized in the aspects of cognitive, behavioral and healthcare relevant, as following:

Cognitive Aspect

- Neglect the importance of adherence
- Lack medication relevant knowledge
- Pay attention to health, but have a negative attitude towards medication
- Good physician-patient relationship is beneficial to improve adherence
- Lack understanding the situation of treatment

Behavioral Aspect

- Often forget to take medicine
- Most of them read drug instructions
- Pay attention to the medication time, usage and dosage, followed by side effects
- Methods of collecting health information are various
- The elderly involve in medicine treatment decisions

Healthcare Aspect

- Doctors' advice is not comprehensive
- Different care providers have different impact on medication adherence

3   Design Proposal

3.1   The Transtheoretical Model

The transtheoretical model (TTM) is a model of intentional behavior change which has applied to a wide range of health behaviors, including medication adherence [10]. It uses a temporal dimension, the stages of change, to integrate processes and principles of change from different theories of intervention. Six stages of change and ten processes of change have been identified as Fig. 3 [11].

3.2   Design Strategies Proposal

As shown in Table 2, the first two columns are stage of changes and process of changes from the TTM. The research finding column is corresponding insights which should be solved and which will guide the design strategy. The techniques of intervention column include techniques provided by the TTM in order to design measures. And data is referenced, which had an experiment to estimate overall mean effect sizes (ESs) for medication adherence of various interventions through meta-analysis [12]. ES_0 and ES_1 denote the value of ES before and after the intervention. The higher the ES value, the larger the impact of intervention behavior. Integrating the guidance of the TTM, research findings and referenced intervention characteristics, corresponding design strategies are presented at the sixth column of Table 2. A service system design is proposed according to design strategies.

| Stage of change | Process of change | Techniques of intervention |

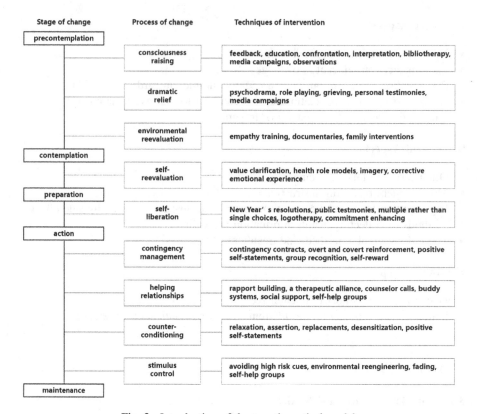

Fig. 3. Introduction of the transtheoretical model

3.3   Medication Management System Proposal

The design of medication management system pays attention to the process and experience of medication treatment. As a service solution, it includes designing the using process of the service platform, the interactive logic of an App, and the low fidelity interface and product design. Main functions of the system and implementation methods are presented by integrating design strategies in Table 2.

Various Accesses to Health Information

Health information is promoted and subscribed with the App. In order to improve the awareness, information is presented to emphasize the importance of medication adherence. Other functions such as popularizing the knowledge and disease, presenting positive and negative examples are also included. The patients can also consult the doctors directly via the App. A community communication platform is established for the elderly to share experience with each other.

Emphasis of the Time, Usage and Dosage in the Instructions

When buying the drugs, succinct written instructions with enlarged font are pasted onto pill bottles by staff to make it clear for the elderly. Design a drug packaging as a special container that indicates the time and dose. The same instructions are presented within the App to understand their medicine information.

Table 2. Proposing of design strategies

Stage of change	Process of change	Research finding	Technique of intervention	Referenced intervention characteristic ($ES_0 \rightarrow ES_1$)	Design strategy
Precontemplation					
	Consciousness raising	Neglect the importance, lack related knowledge	Media campaigns	Integration of provider care (0.24 → 0.37)	Stress the importance, popularize the knowledge, inform the effect of non-adherence
	Dramatic relief	Negative attitude towards medication	Personal testimonies	Disease symptoms self-monitoring (0.30 → 1.18)	Show positive and negative examples
	Environmental reevaluation	Good physician-patient relationship is beneficial	Empathy training	Disease symptoms self-monitoring (0.30 → 1.18)	Compare effects of compliance and non-compliance, evaluate the impact on families and doctors
Contemplation					
	Self-reevaluation	Lack understanding the situation of treatment	Corrective emotional experience	Disease symptoms self-monitoring (0.30 → 1.18)	Record the situation of medication and health, provide integrated feedback of the information
Preparation					
	Self-liberation	The elderly involvement in treatment decisions	Multiple rather than single choices	Disease symptoms self-monitoring (0.30 → 1.18)	Share medication feelings and disease symptoms with doctors and friends
Action					
	Contingency management	Often forget to take medicine	Overt and covert reinforcement	Stimulus every time (0.30 → 1.06)	Increase reminders, with various ways to remind medication
	Helping relationships	Various methods of collecting information	Counselor calls, buddy systems	Integration of provider care (0.24 → 0.37)	Provide consulting service, establish community communication platform
	Counter-conditioning	Most of them read drug instructions	Replacement	Packaging (0.30 → 0.67)	Stress instructions, provide special containers that indicate the time and dose
	Stimulus control	Pay attention to time, usage and dosage	Environmental reengineering	Succinct written instructions (0.29 → 0.61)	Add tips on time and dose with enlarged font
Maintenance					

Remind Taking Medicine

When it's time to take medicine, the smart bracelet will remind taking medicine by sound and vibration like an alarm clock, which can be stopped by the patients before they take medicine. A second reminder will be initiated by the smart bracelet after short time to ensure medication taking.

Record and Monitor the Situation, and Provide Feedback

As the bracelet remind again, if having taken medicine, press the button again, the interface of smart phone will light up to record the medication in concern. Meanwhile, the smart bracelet can monitor pulse, movement and sleep. The App can then provide feedback and advice on health situation of the patients, which makes them understand their physical and treatment condition, assess their situation before and after medication, etc. Furthermore, if the elderly is monitored with a dangerous situation, the system will give immediate feedback to doctors for an emergency.

4   Design Solution

4.1   Design of the Service Usage Process

Figure 4 is the service blueprint showing the service process for the elderly with four stages: aware, join, use, and develop. The service evidence, stage, user behavior, front service, back service and backstage process are presented in column. The user behavior row presents a series of actions and interrelations between them. The front service and back service rows present service actions which are visible and not visible to users respectively. The backstage process row shows the support process of service. The service touch points mean service encounters for the elderly. The service evidences are listed on the top, indicating tangible evidence exposed through the whole experience process.

The Aware Stage

The aware stage is a cultivating cognition stage. Various medication and health related information is available to the elderly, so that they can well accept the adherence knowledge then start to develop a habit based on their consciousness.

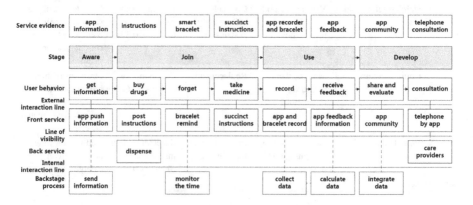

Fig. 4. The service blueprint

The Join Stage

The join stage is a guiding stage, in which user behaviors like buying drugs, taking medicine are well supported. Succinct written instructions add tips and reconstruct the medication environment when buying and taking medicine. Bracelet reminding provides stimulus and improves adherence from the behavioral aspect.

The Use Stage

During the use stage, the service becomes an assistant for the elderly. They can record medication situation and monitor pulse, movement and sleep. Moreover, the recorded data can give them health suggestions after integrating. Disease symptom self-monitoring enhances their confidence and understanding of themselves.

The Develop Stage

During the develop stage, the service becomes a friend of the elderly. It is possible for the elderly to share experience, evaluate impacts before and after medication, which provides them convenience and makes them more independent.

In short, the functions of the service are constantly changing, from cultivating cognition, to guiding, assisting, and becoming a friend of the elderly. Forming a habit is a long process, which means that the positioning of the service and the relationship between the users and the service are dynamic.

4.2   Design of the Service System

The service system is designed to operate in the way shown in the service map in Fig. 5. When the elderly buy drugs from pharmacies, they can get succinct instructions, which are provided by the service platform. The smart bracelet can provide reminding and monitoring service under the support of service platform. After calculating the recorded data, the service platform gives medicine and health related feedback to the elderly and the doctor. The elderly can know themselves better, and the doctor can adjust prescriptions according to the feedback.

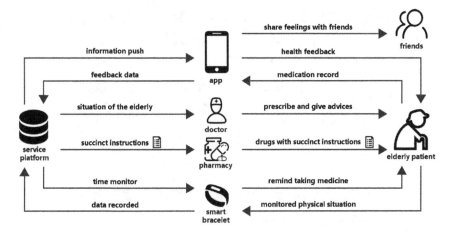

Fig. 5. The service system map

4.3   Design of the App Interactive Logic

The logic map shows the framework of App in Fig. 6. There are four tabs in total, namely Homepage, Record, Consultation and Mine. The Homepage displays the current time as a clock and subscribed health and medication information. In the Record tab, the elderly can understand their medication, pulse, movement and sleep

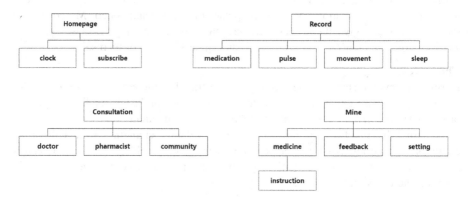

Fig. 6. The logic map

Fig. 7. The low fidelity interface design

situation. The elderly can consult doctors and pharmacists directly via the Consultation page, as well as share feelings in the community. As for the Mine tab, the elderly are able to check their medicine list, read the feedback and set their personal information. The low fidelity interface design is shown in Fig. 7.

4.4   Design of Ancillary Products

The instruction design is shown in Fig. 8. The left side contains time, dosage and side effects, making it clear for the elderly. The right side contains the medicine name and a QR code. The instructions are provided by the service platform and posted onto the medicine package by the staff in pharmacies. When the elderly buying drugs, the QR code is scanned by the staff and information of patients and drugs are recorded correspondingly into the service platform. Then the elderly can check their medicine lists with App.

succinct instruction   instruction on the bottle   instruction on the pill box

Fig. 8. Instruction on packaging

The smart bracelet design is shown as Fig. 9. With a small screen on the bracelet, it shows the current time. When it's time for medicine, it reminds the elderly taking medicine through sound and vibration. Then a button can be pressed to indicate the confirmation and to stop the reminding. Sensors within the smart bracelet monitor the pulse, movement and sleep. The recorded information will be sent to the service platform and integrated into health feedback to the elderly and the doctor.

Fig. 9. Smart bracelet

5 Discussion

In China, aging and the healthcare for elderly are induce issues which should be well considered. This paper presents a study on investigating the current situation of medication adherence for the elderly in China. Key findings are concluded as follows: in cognitive aspects, the consciousness on medication is not strong; in behavioral aspects, forgetting is the most common situation.

Proposal of design strategies is made by integrating the transtheoretical model, the study findings and referenced experiment data. The way of techniques of intervention are chosen based on the design strategies, which provides good way for propose a final design solution, hereby in form of a service system design. There might be other effective design strategies. The way to select design strategies should be further studied. The value and feasibility of different design strategies should be evaluated with a set of criteria. The priority of design strategies should also be well studied to connect it to the results of the investigation on current adherence situations in China.

With the change of cognition and behavior of the elderly, the relation between users and service is changing; therefore, the service experience is dynamic and holistic. It is necessary to evaluate and improve the design constantly when needed. In addition, improving the medication adherence is a change of group behavior, which involves diverse factors in social development. Multifarious effort is required for improving adherence, including hospital medication regulations, service provision through a platform, and cooperation among hospitals, pharmacies, community, and the users, etc.

As many elderly use smart phone as a communication way, the service provision could be well implemented based on an App with necessary functions to promote adherence such as provide medication and healthcare knowledge, emphasize importance of adherence to increase consciousness, assist patient well manage medication information and medicine taking process, monitor health status to feedback the effect of medication, etc. Ancillary products such as instruction label with written information and QR code, smart bracelet, etc. can be designed to connect the elderly well with the service platform.

There are several limitations to the study. Only elderly patients from three cities in the Yangtze River Delta, which is a developed region in China, are investigated. The impact of urban differences has not been considered. The influencing factors such as level of income, social classes and living style, etc. are not included in the study. These factors will be considered in the future studies.

References

1. Murray, C.J.L., Lopez, A.: The Global Burden of Disease. World Health Organization, Geneva (1996)
2. World Health Organization: Adherence to Long-term Therapies: Evidence for Action (2003)
3. American Society on Aging: Adult Medication: Improving Medication Adherence in Older Adults. American Society of Consultant Pharmacists Foundation (2006)

4. Haynes, R.B.: Interventions for helping patients to follow prescriptions for medications. In: Cochrane Database of Systematic Reviews, vol. 2001, no. 1 (2001)
5. Sackett, D., et al.: Patient compliance with antihypertensive regimens. Patient Couns. Heal. Educ. **1**(1), 18–21 (1978)
6. Report and Predication of the Trend of Aging in China. Chin. Women's Mov. **2007**(2), 17–20 (2007). (in Chinese)
7. Population Census Office of the State Council: Population Census of China 2010. China Statistics Press (2012). (in Chinese)
8. Zhou, Q., Liu, L., Zheng, Q., Li, J.: Improving medication adherence for the elderly in China-an user study in design. In: Rebelo, F., Soares, M. (eds.) Advances in Ergonomics in Design: Advances in Intelligent Systems and Computing, pp. 515–526. Springer, Cham (2016)
9. Pedersini, R., Isherwood, G., Vietri, J.: Harmonizing Measurement of Adherence Across the 4-Item and 8-Item Morisky Medication Adherence Scale Using Cross-Sectional Data from Patients Treated for Irritable Bowel Syndrome. Value Heal. **16**(7), A604 (2013)
10. Redding, C.A., Joseph, P., Rossi, S., et al.: Health behavior models. Int. Electron. J. Heal. Educ. **3**(3), 13–26 (2000)
11. Prochaska, J.O., Velicer, W.F.: The transtheoretical model of health behavior change. Am. J. Heal. Promot. **12**(1), 38 (1997)
12. Conn, V.S., Hafdahl, A.R., Cooper, P.S., et al.: Interventions to improve medication adherence among older adults: meta-analysis of adherence outcomes among randomized controlled trials. The Gerontologist **49**(4), 447–462 (2009)

Open Your Space: A Design Activism Initiative in Chinese Urban Community

Minqing Ni[✉]

College of Design and Innovation, Tongji University, Shanghai, China
niminqing@tongji.edu.cn

Abstract. This paper presents a recent design activism initiative named *Open Your Space* in Chinese urban context. The project aims to help the urban community acquire a better sense of sustainability, comfortability, and accessibility to public space. It draws on the relationship between design factors and socially motivated ideas as well as to explore and practice how design activism shapes the public realm to maximize shared value and catalysis in the built environment. The practice investigates the definitions of public space across disciplines and tools, tactics and consequences of reclaiming. *Open Your Space* project focuses on moving beyond design activism as a curiosity, to make a conscious effort to work toward a social and culture stance, to develop solutions through incremental steps. Design activism as main factor of DesignX approach is needed in social change, is a response to cultural conditions, policymaking, economic practices, social engagement and environmental challenges.

Keywords: DesignX · Design activism · Placemaking · Design intervention · Public space · Leftover space · Social innovation

1 Introduction

In the fall of 2015, College of Design of Innovation Tongji University hosted the DesignX workshop to discuss about the future of design and design education in Shanghai. Many of world's leading design educators participated and contributed their thoughts in the meeting. The workshop was followed the framework of DesignX, a position paper written in 2014, which introduced the design challenges of complex sociotechnical systems such as healthcare, transportation, governmental policy, and environmental protection [1]. DesignX, described by Norman and Stappers, it called 'X'—as in the algebraic variable traditionally used to represent an unknown value. DesignX is a new, evidence-based approach for addressing many of the complex and serious problems facing the world today. It adds to and augments today's design methods, reformulating the role that design can play [2]. How the designers attempted to combine their professional skills toward social change? The themes behind the DesignX initiative was stated, the designers must play an active role in implementation, and develop solutions through small, incremental steps [1].

It was relevant to explore the different approaches that designers are adopting to engage in social and political issues, especially from the perspective of a creative actor to an enabler [3]. Design activism is the one of them encompasses a wide range of

© Springer International Publishing AG 2017
P.-L.P. Rau (Ed.): CCD 2017, LNCS 10281, pp. 412–431, 2017.
DOI: 10.1007/978-3-319-57931-3_33

socially and environmentally responsible actions in design. As Lou Yongqi argued that design requires a new, more proactive approach to economic and social change. Design must shift from passive to active [4]. There is more and more evidence that a range of worthwhile initiatives have been undertaken by design professionals who choose to pursue socially responsible practices, and by practitioners who are shifting away from a focus on pure aesthetics and market-driven practices. Design activism has emerged in recent years as a term to denote creative practices that invoke social and political issues. The case introduced by this paper may further discussion on the topic of design activism as well as the DesignX problem.

2 Background and Context: Siping Story

As a part of long-term community based design intervention project, an ongoing research project entitled "Open Your Space (OYS)" was launched in 2015. And followed the design practice in Siping community, Shanghai China. The community locates in the Midwest of Yangpu district of Shanghai (Fig. 1), it is 2.75 km^2 in area and has a population of over a hundred thousand. In Chinese language, the connotation of "community" refers to "neighborhood committee area", which is the smallest administrative area in city management. Tongji University is located within the community, which is one of the main characteristics of Siping, and it took almost one third of the population (Fig. 2).

Fig. 1. Illustration map of Siping community

The community includes one of Shanghai's first workers Village called Anshan village. It was built in the 50's of last century and become one of the largest villages in Shanghai at that time. After continuous expansion, it now includes 8 villages (Fig. 3). For example, Sujiatun road, one of the well-known roads in Siping community with

Fig. 2. Entrance of College of Design and Innovation Tongji University, open campus between college and Siping community

Fig. 3. Worker village in Siping community

elegant environment that is enriched by trees that change during different seasons and create harmonious urban atmosphere (Fig. 4). In the street, there are various types of public space and facilities for daily leisure and exercises, also the place for the annual community folk culture festival. It is not only a "star street" praised by the residences, but also selected as one of ten landscape streets in Shanghai.

In Siping community, two thirds of the buildings were built in the 70s through the 80s in the past century and it is recognized as an old community due to deterioration of architectural conditions, outdated infrastructure, and lacking of quality in public space, the environment for socializing, relaxing, sharing. And in the same time, there are lots

Fig. 4. Daily view in Sujiatun road

of leftover space and hidden space have not been used very well. Due to these issues, it become essential to upgrade both the space and service for public life to satisfy the changing needs and re-envisioning the community life.

What can design add and what can the designers contribute while enhancing problem-finding and observational skills? How design could address the complex issues in the built environment? After the observation and preliminary research, the team of OYS project proactively submitted a proposal to local government, which presents the studies of the residual public space as well as how to improve the public life of the Siping community, by involving the administrative office, local residents and students, designers and artists. Fortunately, the project gained full support from the government smoothly, because it coincidences with the political vision to develop Siping community into an active place through spatial interventions.

3   The Core Idea: Open Your Space

Open your space (OYS) as a research and design project under the scheme of regional innovation strategy explores an urban community that contains physical spaces with social and cultural significance. It draws on the relationship between design factors and socially motivated ideas in Chinese urban context, as well as to explore and practice how design intervention collectively shapes the public realm to maximize shared value and catalysis in the built environment. In Siping context, it helps the local communities acquire better sense of sustainability, openness and participation to the built environment. "Open Your Space" strive to be a sociocultural framework that represents a special design attitude for collective space and public activities. "Open" as a keyword of the project due to its numerous meanings, such as: physical, cultural, emotional, inclusive, sustainable, connected, shared and interactive. The term "open", together with the term "space" involves co-creation, this is an emerging paradigm that advocates new procedures in imagining the public space. Like the Design Harvests project, OYS adapted the similar acupunctural design approach, a series of small but connected design intervention, to generate systemic changes [5].

"Open Your Space: Design intervention in Siping community" as a pilot project, it started from October 2015 and opened to the public on 19 December 2015. The project was the collateral exhibition of 2015 Bi-City Biennale of Urbanism\Architecture. This initiative brought along with a case exhibition, site-specific projects and micro design interventions as well as a community creative festival and several cultural activities. Ten site-specific projects and more than thirty micro design interventions have been spread across outdoor public space within the center of Siping community, by providing perspectives on how design activism and placemaking approach inspires people to create and improve their public places. OYS project follows three main design strategies: empower multiple-stakeholders to drive local change, encourage creativity and new appropriation, and enhance the diversity of the community environment (Fig. 5).

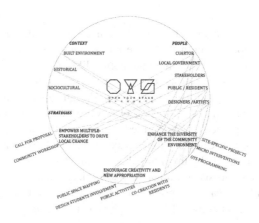

Fig. 5. "Open your space" Project concept map

Engage Multiple-stakeholders to Drive Local Change. OYS proposes a pragmatic curatorial approach, when dealing with local context, community space, designers and social consequence. In order to explore multipartite participation for the role of design, the team defined "open" as a core principle and value. The concept of "open" is not only embodied in the open gesture and rich imagination of the local government by providing deep degree flexibility to the design team; but also reflected in the highly open design process of multidimensional contribution and participation of students, designers, architects, artists and local residents. At the beginning of October 2015, the project started to call for design proposal to the public. There are plenty of creative proposals has been received and many people who want to contribute their ideas come to visit the community in that time (Fig. 6).

Fig. 6. The designers and artists were visiting Siping community

At the beginning of the project, two community workshops with local residents have been held, as a warm-up session also was a chance to collect local opinions. During the workshops, residents shared their concerns about how public spaces were used in the community, pointed out the positive and negative space and built ideal models in plasticine of the public spaces they would like to see. The young generations also have been invited into the workshop, they were exciting about those activities and same time they contributed their imagination of the future public space in community (Fig. 7).

Fig. 7. Residents were pointing the positive/negative space during the community workshop

The roles of different participants (Public Sector-Professional Organizations-People) in the project are as following:

- Public sector represented by the Siping sub-district office in OYS project, which plays a powerful role in financial and policy decision. Three departments have been involved in the project: department of party and government affairs, department of culture, and department of administrative.
- Professional organizations along with over forty design students from College of Design and Innovation in Tongji University, and more than ten design professional studios. Their design ability and rich innovation are the key to the quality of interventions.

- The individual residence living in Siping community, they are the users of public space. In the project, they were encouraged to express their memories, life stories and wishes related to local community.

Encourage Creativity and New Appropriation. In order to encourage more creativity, different approaches have been applied during the development of the project.

- *Public space mapping.* The mapping of the public space in the center area of Siping community helps to understand the daily life of the community and how the public space has been using (Fig. 8). Despite the fact that buildings and streets constitute the boundaries of the everyday public space, there is an ambiguous in between space between them. At Siping community, this in-between space becomes a place where residents' spontaneous behaviors take place. It could be shops, greenery, and the pavement. In this ambiguous space, residents could have rest, play cards, read newspapers and even dry out their clothes. Those microelements - street furniture, signs and paving that constitute the public space various activities, but also it shows there is less public space which people could use, and the experience in the built environment need to improve for everyday life.

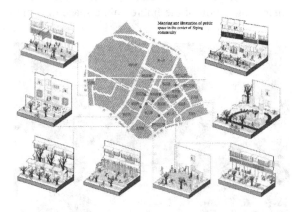

Fig. 8. Mapping and illustration of public space in the center of Siping community

- *Design students involvement.* Over thirty students from BA fourth year and twelve MA students have contributed their ideas in OYS project (Fig. 9). The students did research on the inactive public space and also observed the problem on it, then developed potential intervention strategies through issue mapping and placemaking approach. The study involved both physical spaces, as well as the types of urban community in terms of social studies and cultural significances. Finally, more than thirty micro design interventions in the public space have been realized, which maximize the impact of design interventions achieved in social scenarios, in order to improve community physical setting attributes as well as spatial experience. They brought direct and positive change to the community, promoted the local residents and social resources to participate in co-creation, as well as transformed the public spaces in Siping area into both fun and functional, combined old and new resources

Fig. 9. Students were presenting their design concept.

for the community. The students' involvement specificity gives a peculiar character –they are encounters with actors (the students) who, by the nature of their position, are transient. The shared idea was that this kind of encounter can play a positive role in communities; they can help permanent residents better understand how fresh creative idea could regenerate their daily environment, thus helping them to become more open.

- *Co-creation.* In a co-creation effort, multiple stakeholders come together to develop new idea that traditionally would have emerged only from a top-down process. OYS bag as the souvenir in the project, which co-created by the curatorial team and a local tailor Mrs. He. The team provided fabric and design module to her, and she decided the pattern and location for each bag. Finally, one hundred bags were produced which demonstrated the interaction between designers and local residents (Fig. 10). In doing so, co-creation as a design tool to involves the residents fully in the process and helps boost the chances of engagement by pulling the residents further into the fold.

Fig. 10. Local residents with OYS bags at the project opening in December 2015

- *Public activities.* In order to enlarge the project, more public engagement was considered as an effective way to amplify the creativity. The open call of design proposal, the film documentary about the community craftsman, the exhibition of worldwide design intervention for urban public space, the OYS opening ceremony, the forum themed on creative placemaking, the public movie night, the creative market in the opening day and the artist research exhibition in the community gallery. All the public involvements attracted more than two thousand visitors to participate, and they have been organized in different phases to scale up the social impact as well as receive the user engagement and feedback. The activities are inseparable from the community volunteers, especially on the exhibition daily management. They come everyday to the gallery to mange all the equipment and take the notes of every visitor. They all happy and proud that more and more people come to the community to see the changes happen.

Enhance the Diversity of Community Environment. Following the curatorial approach, design interventions that have taken place in the public spaces of the Siping community through three types of engagements: site-specific projects, micro-interventions and public activities. The design interventions have been drawn attention to the leftover spaces, hidden spaces, and interstitial spaces.

Fig. 11. SPace gallery before and after comparison

Site-Specific Projects. The ten site-specific projects have been commissioned to architects, urban planners and product designers. The designers followed the instruction from the curator, and curator discussed the proposals between designers and local government in order to obtain the community consensus on the proposed projects. Here lists 5 projects to show the changes after the intervention.

Space. The first leftover space the team has found was the four vacant shops. The team takes the result of the workshop that lots of the residents want to have a gallery in the community. Italian architect Tiziano Cattaneo commissioned for the renovation project with low cost requirement. The four shops were transformed into a temporary community gallery by using minimal design approach. The new place named "SPace", it is the combination with the initials of Siping and the word "space". The newly renovated space with its simple form, it becomes a place which community people could gather together as well as a window to show the community cultural life (Fig. 11).

Home Courtyard. One hidden space located at Sujiatun Road has been reused for a community garden. It made with plants and wood steps in order to create more seating space for the road. The garden, which design by urban planner Feng Fan, created a peaceful environment for the people could temporary stop by for rest and enjoy the sunshine in the sunny day, also become a new meeting point. It promoted a collective identity of home, a home that turns street space into active community space (Fig. 12).

before

after

Fig. 12. The residents were playing Chinese chess at the new garden

Ring Island. Another useless public space located at Fushun Road has been regenerated. As few bicycles park there and huge space was wasted, also in the community there is no open playground for children. Architect Liu Yang proposes a project named Ring Island by transforming the abandoned bicycle racks into the colorful and playful facility as well as the sand pool. The new place becomes the most popular playground in the community and reactivated available open space for its member to play, gather, share and communicate (Fig. 13).

Fig. 13. Kids and parents enjoy staying in the new playground

An Interval Connection. Due to lots of activities happen in Sujiatun road and lack of seating, this installation has been chose to set in the empty open space. The project designed by Canadian artist Nestor Kruger, based on a common six-piece interlocking puzzle known historically by various names including Lu Ban Locks.[1] The solution to the puzzle is to combine all six pieces into a double cross that contains no internal voids. Working with these puzzles does require but can also develop a stronger understanding of complex spatial relationships and while the pieces in this public

---

[1] Lu Ban Locks is a traditional Chinese folk educational toy allegedly being invented by ZhugeKongming with Chinese carpenter Lu Ban's techniques. http://wiki.china.org.cn/wiki/index.php/Luban_Lock, accessed February 14, 2017.

sculpture are too heavy to manipulate with the hands, visually imagining how they might be assembled to discover a solution might provide a stimulating companion activity to the state of rest that the current scale of the sculpture invites (Fig. 14).

Fig. 14. The installation can be modified by the residents due to the activities take place in the open space

Micro Interventions. The micro interventions have not been commissioned but they were self-discovered by the designers, artists and students instead, whom have followed their own on site observation and research. Here are presented a short selection of those micro-interventions.

Siping Face. In Chinese community, there are always have propaganda slogans and posts on the wall, no one to pay attention on it. It was completely changed the spirit of local community after a series of photos were replaced with the smiling faces of Siping residents. The residents present themselves vividly and proud of be part of the community. It is the transformation of community cohesion (Fig. 15).

Jump Jump. The student Xiaoyu discovered a garbage station face by the entrance space of the elementary school. This micro design intervention utilized the open space in front of the garbage shed and stages a revised hopscotch in color. The revised hopscotch incorporates basic information of how to sort garbage into its game logic.

Fig. 15. The comparison of the street view

Fig. 16. The kids learn from garbage sorting through walking experience

It is not only to improve the environment around the garbage shed, but also to provide a unique walking experience to the students from nearby school (Fig. 16).

Tree Crystal Ball. The running track on Sujiatun Road is the destination for local residents to enjoy walking and jogging. The designers Yin Shun and Yao Weiwei found out that the track was quite dark during the night. How to improve the experience when there is a lack of proper lighting? The micro intervention created a translucent ball that could hang on the tree, along with interactive experience responding to the number of pedestrians around it. The ball has been attacked the movement under the tree as well as created a medium for communication (Fig. 17).

Welcome. Brazilian photographer Leticia Lampert proposed to photograph the moments of local residents opening their doors. Walls divide the living spaces of the community and border different domestic units. At the same time, it measures the distances between individuals. Through free roaming, the photographer knocks on strangers' doors with simplest motivation and form, the community residents all kindly open up their door and welcome her (Fig. 18).

Fig. 17. The day and night view of lighting installation

Fig. 18. The moments of local residents opening their doors

Mario. The design of the installation is derived from video game Super Mario. It attempts to construct fun experience both virtual and physical in community public space through the scene from the video game, in order to engage the young generation living in the community. Four mobile pavilions with wheels consist the installation, it can be arranged freely into different shapes and spatial forms. The units are perfect for kids to play with: sit, stand, crawl through and climb on, while the parents can rest on them and wait.

OYS Programming. The team firmly believe that the success of public spaces can largely be attributed to the activities, events, recreational uses and social gatherings that take place there, whether planned or spontaneous, ongoing or temporary. Beside the design interventions, the OYS public program including the case study exhibition, forums, movie night and creative market festival.

The case exhibition named "Worldwide design intervention in urban public space" presents the selective creative interventions cases in public space of the world, which exhibited in the newly renovated community gallery space. The exhibition aims to show different strategies that deal with open space in the context of urbanization in the world. The exhibition attracted by the scholars, students and local residents in three months. In particular, the local residents had the chance to see the global movement of the public space, to understand how to improve the qualities of public space through urban regeneration and design, thus to bring vitality to urban life (Fig. 19).

Fig. 19. The visitors enjoy the community gallery

The framework of the exhibition has been built starting from the conceptions of publicness, cultural diversity, resource integration, and the value of social engagement. The exhibition has been designed in order to collect and critically analyze the realized projects worldwide, which foster the regeneration of urban leftover spaces, hidden spaces, interstitial spaces, and the spaces between public and private. Based on a qualitative research approach, the projects' anthology has been realized. To complete this compendium, over ten international academic institutions and organizations were invited to contribute to the projects' collection.[2] Case studies are from cities including

---

[2] Academic institutions and organizations are including: DESIS Network, Human Cities, Tongji DESIS Lab, European Prize for Public Space, The Helen Hamlyn Centre for Design Royal College of Art, Politecnico di Milano, Central Saint Martins University of Art London, China Lab for Architecture and Urban Studies University of Pavia, School of Architecture the Chinese University of Hong Kong, Department of Urban Studies and planning MIT, 100In1Day, ARUP Associates, Parsons DESIS Lab Parsons School of Design The New School, University of Sheffield, University of Huddersfield.

Milan, Shanghai, Seattle, New York, Graz, Gdynia, Saint-Etienne, Hong Kong, Bilbao, London, Bogota, Torino, Bristol, Leeds, Lisbon, Blackburn, and Zaragoza that demonstrate how to improve the qualities of public spaces through different design intervention strategies.

Through analysis of collected projects it was possible to identify common patterns and contradictions in the design of public space and analyze them to achieve the research objectives defining four intervention strategies: playful city, citizen initiatives, guerilla urbanism, and smart community. Those four strategies describe that design-driven initiatives strategically link communities with people to improve quality of life, create a sense of place, and revitalize local economies in order to increase long-term sustainability and the quality of the built environment. It is necessary to build a connection between the site and its users. How to protect and return to the perception of local history, experience, and the emotion of a site, and to help them develop the sustainable public space that can strengthen the social cohesion of a community by replacing new space with the approach of re-articulating existing site.

"Open your space: Design Interventions in Siping Community" project was officially launched at SPace gallery plaza in 19 December 2015 (Fig. 20). The leaders from Yangpu district of Shanghai, director of Siping Road Sub-district Office, leaders of Tongji University all attended the opening ceremony and gave the speeches. OYS Creative Market bring together with the designers, students, local craftsmen as well as residents from community. This activity goes beyond mere financial profits, it represents the spirit of the community and creative platform for culture and idea exchange.

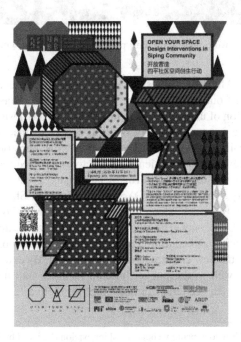

Fig. 20. Project poster

On the movie night, SPace hosted a screening of "Be a Changemaker".[3] The team hopes to bring these positive senses of power into the community in order to influence more people to be a change maker. Two forums were held in the following day of opening. Designers and artist who has participated in OYS project carried out the presentation on the design process, discussed how to improve the quality of public space through design intervention approach along with the local residents and community mangers (Fig. 21).

Fig. 21. The designer were presenting their project and discussing with the local residents

OYS Duplicability. After the successful social impact, the second phase of OYS has continually carried out in 2016. In the new season, the project aims to not only explore the combination of urban public environment with art, design and creativity but also how strength the innovation ability of local region so that a sustainable development could be realized. More community street was transformed by public art which providing a new visual experience to reactive the streetscape. After one-year self-operation, *SPace* will retrofit into Tongji University Creative Jewelry and Glass Innovation Laboratory. Thanks to the OYS's social impact, Shanghai glass museum will set up a community branch, along with the jewelry lab of College of Design and Innovation of Tongji University. The laboratory will integrate cultural, artistic, design, aesthetic lifestyle, training and education programs and coffee shop, in order to create a shared experience for the new concept of cultural platform. By extending the university to the community as well as the public museum facilities into the community environment, the space will be transformed into an active creative learning and

---

[3] "Be A Change Maker" is a documentary about social innovation produced by Kenny Choi, a Chinese young designer who is keen to promote social change in China. He was travelling around the world interviewing social entrepreneurs and innovators.

communication center. Another space about to regenerate is the street waste recycling station. The plan is to transform it into the first Living Lab in Shanghai rely on the real environment to establish new solutions for sustainable community life.[4] All the actions rather than give the form but more beneficial content for the community. It is a social constructive process of citizen engagement through design activism and community participation.

Outcomes and Findings. The radical shifts are needed to allow any form of activism to evolve. OYS project start with problem finding by the designers and consistently works toward developing innovative solutions to benefit the community. During the entire process, the project team has gone through substantial negotiation with the local government that could be absorbed in the historical and cultural context of the community space. The team members have worked closely with the local residents as well as the designers and artists to ensure the proposed plans attend the efficiency, accessibility, diversity of function, and viability of the proposed sites. The negotiations, mediations, compromises, collaborations, and conflicts have left a meaningful footprint of the project. The design interventions have helped engage local residents and other social assets in the process of local development, transformed the public spaces in Siping area into both fun and functional, an organic community with a good balance of old and new resources. Thanks to the power of public media including newspaper and social media such as Wechat,[5] the project has been reported in a larger scope that attracts more interests from other communities in Shanghai. They not only come to visit and learn, but also would like to apply the mode into their own communities which could make positive influences.

The major difficulties were in implementation with complex social issues [2]. In OYS project, the team has to deal with government, designers and residents, the process involve complex human and social elements, some of them lack of understanding of limitations of in design. The design solution requires collaboration and agreement of multiple social entities and political actors. These eventually constraints require compromises. But fortunately, the concept of "open" is embodied in the open motion and open the wide version of the local government by providing complete flexibility to the design team, also it is reflected in the highly open design process: multidimensional contribution and participation of students, designers, architects, artists, and local residents. The project collectively redefines ideas of public space and its multiple functions. It has convened scholars, artists, architects, and planners to engage contemporary critical discourses and practices on urban space. The practice investigated the definitions of public space across disciplines and the tools, tactics and consequences of reclaiming.

---

[4] A living lab is a research concept. A living lab is a user-centred, open-innovation ecosystem, often operating in a territorial context, integrating concurrent research and innovation processes within a public-private-people partnership. http://openlivinglabs.eu, accessed February 14, 2017.

[5] WeChat is a cross-platform instant messaging service developed by Tencent in China, first released in January 2011. It is one of the largest standalone messaging apps by monthly active users. As of May 2016, WeChat has over a billion created accounts, 700 million active users, with more than 70 million outside of China. Available at: https://en.wikipedia.org/wiki/WeChat, accessed February 14, 2017.

The OYS project intends to initiate the public sector innovation to build an urban community in Shanghai with better sense of sustainability and friendly to adapt urban transformation. It enhanced the quality of public space and forged more identity to local place, and has been achieved a positive impact to the local community environment. Placemaking, incorporates the role as agent contributing in an original way to social building of places [6]. OYS dedicated to helping people create and sustain public spaces that build stronger communities and also try to help citizens transform their public spaces into vital places that highlight local assets, spur rejuvenation and serve common needs. As part of the curatorial team, I feel extremely gratified at witnessing how these new additions to the community have been gradually integrated into the local public life, and have been accepted and used by most of the local residents. Ultimately, the project proposes to introduce creative lifestyles to the community and to increase their aesthetic awareness. OYS in Siping community is a first example of integrating community assets and university intelligence in Shanghai. It starts with space, but hopes to, in the context of local reality, introduce the community with more innovations, created by rebuilding places and connected communities to emerge SLOC (small, local, open, connected) scenario and creative concepts to drive its entrepreneurship, enhance the energy levels, and inject a renewed vitality into the community [6].

Design as thought and action for solving problems and imagining new futures [7]. The OYS project focuses on the influence of art and design for public space and deals with quality that shift the discussion on public space toward discourse on the built environment by unpacking, reevaluating, and recombining the social innovation. But on other hand, the problem appeared though the design process, such as public awareness, facilities maintenance and "public" and the "private" social understanding. The improvement of public space in China needs strong commitment, responsibility and effort from everybody: from the government to the citizens, from educational system to the research centers, from entrepreneurs to institutions [8]. Recognizing the value of places goes hand-to-hand with the emergence of new idea of a sustainable well-being. China's undergoing transition, the social, political, cultural, and economic relations are negotiated amidst rapidly changing urban space. The composition of public space itself is a contested and contextualized category [9]. Stimulated by the changing waves of urbanization, the new production and practices of public spaces are currently experiencing and generating a new dynamism, which cannot be profitable only for real-estate speculation but might create resilient urban communities.

4 Conclusion

OYS focuses on moving beyond design activism as a curiosity, to make a conscious effort to work toward a social and culture stance. The active intervention on public space is a part of social innovation strategy, while we need to aware of the fact that OYS it is not an arrival point but it is a starting point.

The design workshop and proposals was embracing the principles of activism. The evolement of the design students was also a challenge to let them to rethink as the activist designers. Design plays an active role to connect public sector and people in order to trigger more participation. Rooted in community-based participation, OYS explores the possibility of design thinking for innovative problem solving and generating new vision. Design activism principle help produce design interventions, events and services that are capable of generating meaningful encounters and resilience, sustainable ways of being and doing. Design activism as main factor of DesignX approach is needed in social change, is a response to cultural conditions, policymaking, economic practices, social engagement and environmental challenges.

References

1. Norman, D.A., Stappers, P.J.: DesignX: complex sociotechnical systems. SheJi **2**, 83–94 (2015)
2. Friedman, K., Lou, Y., Norman, D.A., Stappers, P.J., Voûte, E., Whitney, P.: DesignX: A Future Path for Design (2014). http://www.jnd.org/dn.mss/designx_a_future_pa.html. Accessed 14 Feb 2017
3. Lou, Y.: Enabling society: new design processes in China the case of Chongming. J. Des. Strateg. **4**(1), 22–28 (2010)
4. Lou, Y.: Design activism in an era of transformation. Art Des. **7**, 17–19 (2015). (In Chinese)
5. Lou, Y., Valsecchi, F., Diaz, C.: Design Harvests: An Acupunctural Design Approach Towards Sustainability. Mistra Urban Futures, Gothenburg (2013)
6. Manzini, E.: Design, When Everybody Designs: An Introduction to Design for Social Innovation, p. 189. The MIT press, Cambridge (2015)
7. Bont, K.D.: Frame Innovation: Create New Thinking by Design (Design Thinking, Design Theory), p. X. The MIT Press, Cambridge (2015)
8. Cattaneo, T., Giorgi, E., Ni, M., Manzoni, G.D.: Sustainable development of rural areas in the EU and China: a common strategy for architectural design research practice and decision-making. Buildings **6**(4), 42 (2016). doi:10.3390/buildings6040042
9. Gaubatz, P.: New public space in urban China. In: China Perspectives (2008). http://chinaperspectives.revues.org/4743. Since 01 Dec 2011, Accessed 14 Feb 2017

Designing Architectural Space Using Service System Design Approach

Jintian Shi and Xiaohua Sun[✉]

College of Design and Innovation, Tongji University, No. 281 Fuxin Road, Shanghai, China
shijintian1017@126.com, xsun@tongji.edu.cn

Abstract. Some problems may exist in traditional architecture design process, such as lack of coherence between different phrases, design scenarios cannot satisfy practical needs, and design methods not in a systematic structure. While the design thinking and some methods of service system could address these issues effectively. Firstly, this paper would introduce the service system design approach; Secondly, give analysis of "these issues" from the perspective of architecture design; And then as a usable approach, the application of service system design in these issues would be elaborated; Finally, the new design approaches also brought about new aspects to architecture design and its procedure, such some new virtual flows, and new evaluation criteria for architecture design.

Keywords: Architectural space design · Design approaches · Service system

1 Introduction

Architecture design is a complicated procedure integrating with various aspects. In this procedure, architects are always confronted with multiple problems: such as lack of coherence of different designing phrases in the whole process, design scenarios cannot satisfy many needs in real context, low efficiency in the holistic design process and so on. And these three problems are the main aspects for this paper to discuss.

Therefore, considering the "complexity" lying in architecture design, it is obvious that divergent problems could be caused by different reasons, and solutions could be found from multiple perspectives. For the above three issues, the main reasons basically are: the traditional one-directional architecture design path, lack of correlation between design phrases, ambiguity in designing starting point (or designing center), design approaches not in a systematic network and so on. And service system design approaches, which feature in being user-centered, co-creative, evidencing and holistic [1], could give us a lot of inspirations for addressing these issues. Because in the logic of service system design, architecture is supposed to be defined as an aggregation of various resources.

2 Service System Approach in Designing Architectural Space

Service science may require methods and theories from other disciplines including operations, industrial engineering, marketing, computer science, psychology, information

P.-L.P. Rau (Ed.): CCD 2017, LNCS 10281, pp. 432–440, 2017.
DOI: 10.1007/978-3-319-57931-3_34

systems, design, and more [2]. And for service system design, the key point doesn't lie in the detailed service designing, but lies in the system construction of all services. Because of the systematicness of service system design, it focuses on the reciprocal integration of all logical sub-systems. Service system design thinking was proposed to regard architectural space as a complex of certain kind of functional services in specific environment. This approach is highly capable of helping effectively organize and coherently sort out related services of a specific environment [3]. And after sorting all services into different sub-systems, the holistic macro-level structure was built up.

Comparing with the one-way route of traditional architecture design, service system-oriented architectural space design procedure behaved to be more iterative, and the main points of different phrases are emphasized to be more concrete. So, it's more explicit to discover problems or defects in every phrase.

Meanwhile, many designing tools or methods of service system design are categorized into different clusters per certain subjects, which makes these approaches be more specific and targeted aiming at varied phrases and goals.

One of the reasons for some issues existing in architecture design is that the design activities get used to only focusing on some certain elements, such as function, form, material of architecture, but ignoring that the aims of design activities are the services offered and conceptions conveyed by the environment, and eventually transferred these services and conceptions to people as final users. Using the design thinking of service system for architectural space designing, it will underline the whole system rather than single elements, and mark the final need of architectural space as serving people from multiple degrees.

The characteristics of service system design give the reasons why service system design approaches could resolve some issues in traditional architecture design.

3   Application of the Service System Design Approach

After the basic introduction of service system design approach, this paper would be elaborated on how to apply the method into some aspects in traditional architecture design in the following paragraphs.

3.1   Different Design Phrases

Generally, architecture-designing procedure is staged and always developed one-directionally: the designing usually gets started from the master plan or site plan; and then based on the requirements in design briefs, to settle down the architecture form in responsive of functions; next step is to check whether the form coincide with all kinds of physical limitations… During the whole process, every single phrase is conduct centering on one certain element [4]. Just as Kevin Lynch wrote in *Urban Planning & Design*, during the procedure for architecture designing, the four aspects (form, clients, design brief and site) are always conducted in order [5]. This kind of both one-directional also staged designing approach divides the consistent route, as it should be, but into separated fragments. However, the essence of architecture designing is how to integrate various entangled elements into a holistic system, and obviously, it is not enough to merely consider only based on one certain element. Therefore, architecture designing acquires to be iterated from multiple-phrase and multiple-dimensionally.

As shown in Fig. 1, service design has followed the full-link working principle of 4D: Discover, Define, Develop, Deliver [6]. Different with architecture design, the process of service design emphasizes the integration among various elements and coherence in multiple phrases. Once the designing procedure got started, it also commenced iteration. The 4D principle is helpful to control the designing path and organize a consistent route into a closed loop.

If we apply the service-system mindset to designing environment, on one hand it could establish a systematic connection between different phrases overall; on the other hand, it could help the reciprocal causations among four phrases, or even among various elements in each phrase or different phrase, become more explicit. A more traceable relationship between elements with results could largely improve the design accuracy.

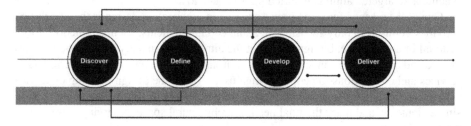

Fig. 1. 4D full-link procedure of service system design

3.2 Design Scenarios

One of the main tasks of architecture-design is, through designing the environment, to help people sense the architecture and acquire specific services. The architectural space itself is more like the physical media assisting people to sense surroundings. In traditional architecture design procedure, as Lynch's opinions, it always gets started with form, clients, design brief and site orderly. We often pay too much attention to the function and form of the architecture, rather than the final users of the architecture. Even in some real using contexts, people must adjust to the architectural space. This is one of the main reasons why design scenarios always cannot satisfy many practical needs.

To get a more reasonable and holistic design scenario for architectural space, the core of design should be reconsidered by service system thinking.

The design thinking of service system acquires that, as the center of design, all potential stakeholders who are concerned with services occurring in the architectural space should be taken into consideration at beginning; or even together with offerings map, they should be regarded as two important starting points to develop the following procedure. From perspective of services, these stakeholders could be categorized into service recipients and service providers, and both could be elaborated into multiple parties further. From perspective of the involvement and importance, stakeholders could be categorized into primary and secondary ones. There are also many other classifications besides these, and no matter in which kind of category, it could structure all potential stakeholders related to services in the space into a comprehensive, prospective and systematic network.

How to construct a stakeholder network more systematically? One of the methods to build up stakeholders hierarchy could be deployed as following (Fig. 2): (1) be comprehensive: to specify all the existing activities, needs and services; (2) be prospective: based on the step (1), to associate current services with potential and promising trends; (3) be responsive: associate the services with related stakeholders; (4) be systematic: by generating stakeholder hierarchy (main, secondary, tertiary ...), then to help settle down environmental space layout correspond to the hierarchy. What worthy to figure out is that we couldn't settle down service hierarchy merely by the frequency or participant number of certain activities, the contribution to improving service consistency and efficiency are more reasonable factors.

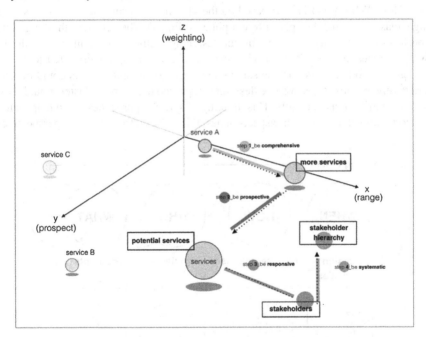

Fig. 2. Four orders of classification for stakeholders

After the above four orders, a service-oriented stakeholder hierarchy has been built up. Correspondingly, the hierarchy could generate services and flows (physical and virtual) related to stakeholders, which is called system map in service logic. The system map contains vital factors like services, stakeholders and flows, and it could be applied into architectural space planning and designing more holistically. This kind of result-driven design procedure can correspond services to related architectural spaces.

In this way, inconformity between design scenarios with practical using contexts could be easily addressed. Agreeing with the notion that people are the final users of architecture, service system design thinking proposes final users to the early stages of architectural designing. This way could be functioned as a proper benchmark to coincide design scenarios with practical needs.

3.3   The Whole Design Procedure

As the above paragraph saying, the current architectural-designing approaches are mutually independent and remain to be correlated. The lack of this connection to some extent speed down the designing process and decrease the designing quality.

Using the design logic of ESSD, various design approaches would be clustered per different categories. This kind of "Cluster" could make different methods both to be more specific to targeted contexts, and more integral to the whole system. For example, as Fig. 3, many designing approaches of service system design could be classified as design activities, representations, recipients and contents altogether four categories by When, How, Who, What [7]. Or based on the 4D full-link principle of service system design, classify approaches per different phrases (Fig. 4). The "cluster" thinking could be performed to classify not only current designing methods of architecture, but also new approaches emerged from service system. It can sort up uncorrelated tools into different "method clusters". In the same one project, divergent clusters could be used alternatively, because the same one designing approach in different clusters could make different contributions to results. This thinking of sorting approaches could help us find more correlation among various aspects of designing object, from different perspectives.

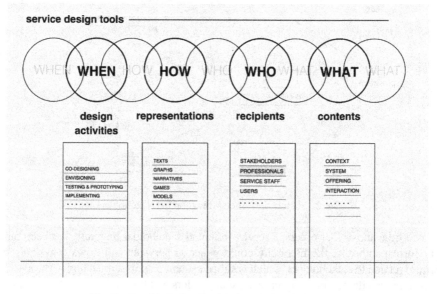

Fig. 3.   One kind of collection for service design tools

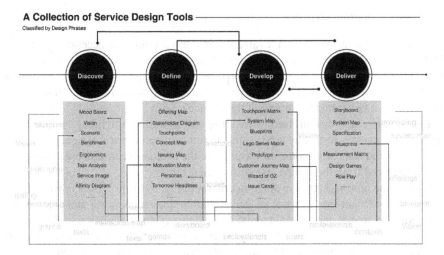

Fig. 4. Display of service design tools on different phrase

Throughout the existing multiple architecture design tools, what lack of are not design methods and single centered-on element in one certain phrase, but what lack of is an iterative path and systematic process containing various design approaches. This path could not only extract a single element out, but also return it back to the whole system, which is the real representation of architecture design procedure. The design thinking of ESSD could meet these needs well.

4   New Aspects Brought by the Service System Approach

Due to some new approaches from ESSD applied in architectural space design, on one hand the three issues could be effectively addressed: Lack of coherence between different phrases, Practical needs always beyond design scenarios, Low efficiency of design procedure; and on the other hand, some new aspects have been created for architectural design.

4.1   New Virtual Flows

In normal architectural design process, referring to flow analysis, it always means the site-nearby people flow, traffic flow, wind direction flow and another physical indicator for analyzing. However, these physical flows are only considered from perspectives of physical condition, but not based on the real operation scenario of services occurred in the architecture. Some intangible flows, such as the current and possible personnel movements in the system, the information exchange channel among divergent phrases, and the financial relationships produced by different stakeholders and so on, also should be generated and defined respectively into staff flow, information flow and financial flow. These Virtual flows are more helpful in representing the scenario of the proposed architecture, by all kinds of "Flows" regarding different aspects.

4.2 New Evaluation Criteria

In traditional architecture design, evaluation is normally not one necessary part of it. While in the 4D-Link of service system design procedure, simulation and evaluation are also inevitable aspects in the "Deliver" phrase. With related stakeholders and some assistive tools, to create an evaluation environment approximate to the real context could help us to get a better understanding of the service quality.

Like architectural design itself, measuring and assessing a building is quite a big topic, which involves too many aspects. In addition to meeting various rigid rules of the design brief and standards, some new aspects of the evaluation criteria are also significant, if analyzed from the perspective of service design.

Among the new aspects of evaluation criteria in Fig. 5, the first layer is whether the service has been put into practice in one certain architectural space and whether the corresponding spatial design could assist in the delivery and circulation of the service. The second layer is whether the efficiency of personnel structure and operational network within the service system is maximized. Good service system design can help the stakeholders to carry out efficient interaction and coordination, and the spatial design based on ESSD should take full account of the multi-run relationships within it, providing required physical environment space for the existing and possible activities and personnel. The third layer is whether all the parties involved have got the sense of self-identity [8], which is also one of the highest criterions for evaluating service system design. This standard can help the service-system-based architectural space designing to set up a building space with more social value from a broader humanistic point of view, no matter in functions or in forms.

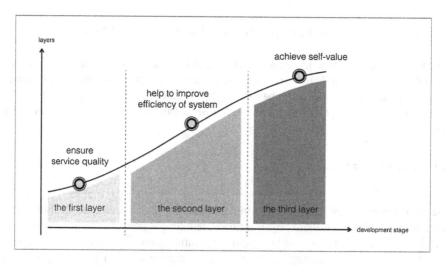

Fig. 5. New aspects of evaluation criteria for service-oriented architecture design

4.3   New Kinds of Design

Yarmo Suominen, service architect and professor from Aalto University, deemed that, architecture would become a service platform. If we regard building as a service, the architectural space itself is an integration with many open resources, and many people could co-create values together in it. Therefore, when designing architecture, we should also take consider the design of user experience to improve environment affordances, the design of interaction between people-surroundings and people-people to strengthen social ties, the design of services to connect activities and mobility, the design of business to boost open-source economy, the design of management to optimize the operation route. Just as illustrated in Fig. 6, all these different kinds of design are also necessary components in the service logic and should be considered in architectural space designing, which needs architects to build up a multi-disciplinary design mindset and arm with more design skills [9].

Applying service system design thinking into architecture design, all existing components in architectural space, together with these new kinds of design, require to be construct in a systematic structure. And how to integrate various designs into a whole architectural space design in the service system logic, need to find more working principles aiming at different context in the next step of research.

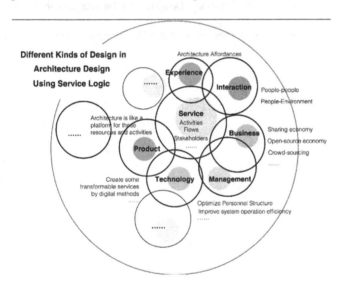

Fig. 6. Different kinds of design in architecture design using service logic

5   Summary

This paper discussed some problems existing in current architecture design: lack of coherence between different phrases, practical needs beyond design expectations and design methods being under systematic; and how to use some designing approaches from service system to address the issues to some extent. Through this paper, we aim at providing architecture design with a new design thinking from the point of view of service logic, taking supplements on approaches of architecture design multi-semantically and multi-disciplinarily. And the other goal of our research is exploring relevant characteristics and methods for service system design thinking applied in different contexts, such specific-environment based, specific-time based and so on.

References

1. Stickdorn, M.: This Is Service Design Thinking (2011)
2. Maglio, P.P., Spohrer, J.: Fundamentals of service science. J. Acad. Mark. Sci. **36**(1), 18–20 (2008)
3. Sun, X., Shi, J.: Environment-specific smart service system design. In: Rau, P.-L.P. (ed.) CCD 2016. LNCS, vol. 9741, pp. 592–599. Springer, Cham (2016). doi: 10.1007/978-3-319-40093-8_58
4. Daqing, G.: Space, tectonics and design. Architect **1**, 13–21 (2006)
5. Lynch, K.: Site Planning, 2nd edn. Urban Planning & Design, pp. 35–57 (1971)
6. Design Council: The Design Process, March 2011. http://www.designcouncil.org.uk/designprocess/
7. Service Design Tools. http://Servicedesigntool.org
8. Manzini, E.: Design, When Everybody Designs: An Introduction to Design for Social Innovation
9. Knappers, C.: Using the Unused: Spaces for Aalto University's Creative Community (2013)

Web Content Analysis on Power Distance Cultural Presence in E-Government Portal Design

Wan Adilah Wan Adnan[(✉)], Nor Laila Md Noor, Fauzi Mohd Saman,
and Farez Mahmood

Universiti Teknologi MARA, Shah Alam, Malaysia
{adilah,norlaila,fauzi}@tmsk.uitm.edu.my,
farez@gmail.com

Abstract. Governments worldwide have recognized and made e-government implementation as their top priority for a better service delivery to their citizens. Besides emphasizing the use of emergent technology, culture considerations in the e-government portal design and development has been claimed as critical strategy to promote greater citizen engagement, participation and empowerment. This paper aims to explore the presence of cultural values in e-government portals design and its impact. The selection of e-government portals is based on the 2016 Waseda-IAC International e-Government ranking which emphasize on citizen centric. The cultural values examined in this paper focuses on Power Distance cultural dimension from Hofstede's model. Web content analysis method was employed to explore the Power Distance cultural presence in the selected e-government portals. In addition, statistical analysis was performed to examine possible relationship between Hofstede's Power Distance Index and citizen centric e-government development. The cultural markers for the web content analysis focuses on visual design elements suggested in the web design guidelines on Power Distance culture. The results of this study show that the e-government portal design conform to Hofstede's Power Distance cultural dimension. In addition, statistical analysis shows a significant positive relationship between Power Distance cultural presence and Hofstede's Power Distance Index, and a negative relationship between Power Distance cultural presence and Waseda e-Government Ranking. Findings from this study provide better understanding of Power Distance cultural presence in the e-government website design as well as supporting the notion that Power Distance cultural dimension is correlated to citizen centric e-government development.

Keywords: E-government portal design · Cultural design · Power Distance cultural dimension · Hofstede's cultural model · Citizen centric e-government · Waseda e-Government development ranking

1 Introduction

Governments worldwide have recognized and made e-Government implementation as their top priority for a better service delivery to their citizens. Besides emphasizing the use of emergent technology, culture consideration in the e-Government portal design

© Springer International Publishing AG 2017
P.-L.P. Rau (Ed.): CCD 2017, LNCS 10281, pp. 441–450, 2017.
DOI: 10.1007/978-3-319-57931-3_35

and development has been claimed as critical strategy to provide greater citizens engagement, participation and empowerment [1]. However, cultural studies in the context of e-Government development and implementation is still lacking [2]. Furthermore, most of the e-Government studies concentrated on a few individual countries or regions and not on a global scope [1].

The primary aim of this study is to explore the presence of cultural values in the e-government portal designs. This study employed web content analysis method and used two secondary sources, which are Hofstede's Power Distance Index [3] and 2016 Waseda-IAC International e-Government ranking [4]. Both secondary sources are well established and frequently cited in the area of cultural and e-Government development studies respectively [5, 6]. Furthermore, this study is using the latest available data sets of Waseda e-Government ranking that would provide a better understanding of the current global state of e-Government development.

Web content analysis was conducted to evaluate the extent to which homepage design of an e-government portal conforms to the Hofstede's Power Distance cultural dimension. In addition, this study examined the possible relationship between the Power Distance cultural dimension based on Hofstede's Power Distance Index and citizen centric e-Government development approach based on Waseda e-Government ranking for year 2016. The cultural markers for the web content analysis focused on visual design elements suggested in the Web design guidelines on Power Distance culture [7, 8].

2   Literature Review

2.1   Hofstede's Cultural Model

Hofstede definition of culture emphasizes on aspect of thinking pattern, feeling and acting, which is aligned to what has been highlighted by Marcus and Gould [8] about culture in the context of web design. Literature has acknowledged the important role of culture in the success and failure of a project or system including the e-government project [9]. One of the most popular and well accepted cultural model is the model that proposed by Hofstede [3]. In his model, Hofstede classified 6 national cultural dimensions namely: Power Distance, Individualism vs. Collectivism, Masculinity vs. Femininity, Uncertainty Avoidance, Long-Term Orientation, and Indulgence vs. Restraint. Hofstede argued that each country has and dominant culture, and thus through his comprehensive study, he quantifies each of these national cultural dimensions for each country.

Hofstede's cultural model is well acknowledged and is the most widely used in studies examining the culture differences in various context [1, 5] including in e-Government [2, 5]. Therefore, Hofstede's cultural model will be employed in this research as the foundation to examine the influence of culture on e-government development and homepage design.

Among these six cultural dimensions, the current research has recognized that Power Distance is one of the strongest influential cultural dimension and has strongly recommend to include Power Distance in any cross-cultural studies [10–12]. For this reason, in this study, Power Distance is chosen to be explored in determining the presence of cultural values in the homepage of e-Government on a global scope.

Hofstede defines Power Distance as "the extent to which the less powerful members of institutions and organizations within a country expect and accept that power is distributed unequally". In other words, it relates to the degree of equality among people in the country's society. Thus, countries that rank high in the Power Distance Index, tend to accept that inequality in power is a norm. Based on Hofstede calculations, a high index has a score of more than 50 and a low is for index score below 50 [3]. A country with high Power Distance has greater emphasize on power and authority compared to a country with low Power Distance.

2.2 Important of Culture Consideration in E-Government Development

Prior study by Zhao [13] in examining the correlation between e-Government development index based on UN e-Government survey 2010, and cultural dimensions index defined by Hofstede, has found that Power Distance is one of the three cultural dimensions that has a significant correlation. In addition, a study by [14] also found that cultural dimension from the Hofstede's Power Distance Index has a significant impact on e-government readiness that was measured by UN survey index.

Another study by Aykut [15] on 26 Euro countries has shown that culture influence the e-government adoption level. The study has found that countries with higher Power Distance culture tend to have lower e-government adoption. Study conducted by [9] on 197 Jordanian citizens, has found similar result that Power Distance has significant impact on citizens' adoption of e-government with emphasize on the important role of website design.

Cultural Elements in Web Design

Key components of web design that reveal the cultural values in a government portal design includes language, page layout, symbols, color, visual images and sound/music [16]. Prior studies have shown that Power Distance cultural dimension is one of the national culture that has been recognized to affect the web design, particularly the e-government portal [7–9, 17, 18]. Marcus and Gould [8], has identified the design elements that reflect Power Distance culture which include prominent authority figure, official stamps, logos, certification and color. Ahmad et al. [7] in his web design guidelines for Power Distance, has proposed a similar model to Marcus and Gould suggestions. Hierarchy structure represented by displaying the organization chart and information on prominent figures of the hierarchy together with its titles and positions is emphasized in the high Power Distance culture. A high Power Distance culture also focuses on experts, official certifications, awards and logos that are viewed as symbols of universal recognitions. Besides, [8] has highlighted that in web design, interfaces with high Power Distance has greater emphasis on social models such as nationalism and has restricted information access, and vice versa for low Power Distance.

2.3 Waseda-IAC International E-Government Development

Japan Waseda University Institute of e-government, a non-profit center at academic institution, has produced an annual survey report on overall e-government development of a country since 2005. Waseda-IAC International e-Government Development ranking survey has been recognized as a well-established international annual benchmarking studies that measure best practices of e-government development with emphasize on citizen centric approach [4, 19].

The 2016 Waseda-IAC International e-Government ranking survey had covered 65 countries, an additional of 2 countries compared to year 2015. The 2016 survey was based on 10 indicators, with an additional of one new indicator on "the use of emerging ICT technologies", focusing towards citizen centric e-government development approach. The 12th Waseda-IAC international e-Government Rankings Survey 2016 Report has highlighted the need to pay special attention in adopting a comprehensive citizen centric approach in e-government development to encourage for greater citizens' participation, engagement and empowerment.

In other word, a country with high Waseda e-Government ranking can be considered as having greater adoption of citizen centric e-government development approach compared to a country with low Waseda e-Government ranking. Thus, in this study possible relationship between Hofstede's Power Distance cultural dimension and the Waseda e-Government ranking will be further examined.

2.4 Citizen Centric E-Government Development Approach

For a successful implementation of e-government, citizen centric approach need to be recognized and adopted in the e-government design and development [20]. This means citizens' needs and expectations for a quality delivery of information and e-government services need to be responded to ensure for citizen satisfaction and quality experience [21]. As highlighted in the 2016 Waseda e-Government ranking, a new indicator, the use of emerging technology has been added in its assessment to ensure quality and responsive services to citizens can be efficiently and effectively delivered for citizens' needs and satisfactions [4].

The adoption of citizen centric approach in e-government development is to support for greater citizens' participation which encourage for a greater level of citizens' engagement in decision making processes and would result in better citizens' empowerment. One of the crucial criteria that need to be emphasized in implementing a citizen centric e-government is designing a user-centered e-government portal/website [22], which has been considered as one of the key indicators in the Waseda e-Government survey. A poor web design that is complex and difficult to use would reflects a lack of citizen centricity in e-government implementation which in return may affect the e-government adoption [22].

3   Method

This study employed web content analysis and used two well established secondary sources: Hofstede's Power Distance Index and 2016 Waseda e-Government Ranking representing the global perspective of national culture and citizen centric e-government development indices respectively. The objective of the web content analysis was to examine the extent to which the homepage design of e-government portal conforms to the Hofstede's Power Distance cultural dimensions, and the possible relation to Waseda e-Government ranking. The selection of the e-government portals was based on Waseda e-Government Ranking and Hofstede's Power Distance Index. A total of 30 e-government portals were selected representing the highest fifteen scores and the lowest fifteen scores from 2016 Waseda Ranking, in which they must also appeared in the Hofstede's Power Distance Index listing. Table 1 shows the listing of selected countries based on the top 15 and lowest 15 scores of 2016 Waseda e-Government ranking. The Power Distance Index is accessed from official Hofstede website at www. geert-Hofstede.com and the most recent result of Waseda e-Government ranking from its official website at https://www.waseda.jp. The content analysis on the selected e-government homepage was conducted in September 2016.

Table 1. Countries with Waseda ranking score and power disctance index.

Top 15 Waseda score			Lowest 15 Waseda score		
Country	Waseda score	Power Distance Index (PDI)	Country	Waseda score	Power Distance Index (PDI)
Singapore	91	74	China	50.3	80
USA	90.2	40	Saudi Arabia	49.4	80
Denmark	88.8	18	Argentina	46.2	49
Korea	85.7	60	Peru	44.5	64
Japan	83.2	54	South Africa	44.1	49
Estonia	81.8	40	Columbia	42.0	67
Canada	79.9	39	Venezuela	41.9	81
Australia	76.4	36	Uruguay	41.1	61
New Zealand	74.1	22	Costa Rica	40.9	35
United Kingdom	72.7	35	Morocco	40.7	70
Taiwan	72.7	58	Kenya	40.4	64
Norway	70	31	Pakistan	39.7	55
Austria	69.6	11	Fiji	38.3	78
Sweden	68	31	Egypt	36.8	80
Finland	67.6	33	Nigeria	35.0	77

Based on literature review that has been discussed, three hypotheses have been identified to examine the extent to which cultural presence in the e-government portal conform to Hofstede's Power Distance Index as well as possible relationship with the Waseda e-Government development ranking. The hypothesis H1 is developed based on the expectation that countries with high presence of high Power Distance cultural identity in its e-government portal homepage, tend to have a high Power Distance Index. In other word, it is anticipated that the degree of Power Distance cultural presence is positively related to Hofstede's Power Distance Index. For next hypothesis H2, it is anticipated that countries with high presence of high Power Distance identity in its homepage design tend to have a low level of citizen centric e-government development. In other word, the degree of Power Distance cultural presence is negatively related to 2016 Waseda e-Government development ranking. Similarly, for the third hypothesis H3 it is anticipated that countries with high Power Distance Index tend to have a low level of citizen centric e-government development. The hypotheses to be statistically tested in this study are as followings:

H1   There is significant relationship between the degree of Power Distance presence and Hofstede's Power Distance Index

H2   There is significant negative relationship between degree Power Distance presence and citizen centric e-government development

H3   There is significant negative relationship between Hofstede's Power Distance Index and citizen centric e-government development

The web content analysis was performed to examine the degree of Power Distance cultural presence by identifying the cultural markers representing Power Distance cultural dimension as suggested by Ahmed et al. [7]. Based on their proposed model, five visual web design elements that reflect the Power Distance cultural identity had been chosen as cultural markers for the web content analysis checklist. These cultural markers are: 1. official logo, 2. national flag, 3. prominent authority figures, 4. image of signature building, and 5. color representing national flag or logo. These cultural markers represent the national symbols that reflect high power centricity, and are indicators for high Power Distance cultural identity. From the checklist, the total number of cultural markers adopted in the homepage was calculated to signify the degree of Power Distance cultural presence. The degree of Power Distance cultural presence is considered high for a homepage design that has greater number of cultural markers compared to a homepage that has less number of cultural markers. High degree of Power Distance cultural presence indicates that a lack of citizen centricity is emphasized in the visual design of e-government portal homepage.

In order to examine the extent to which the homepage design of an e-government portal conform to Hofstede's Power Distance Index, a correlation analysis was conducted to analyze relationship between the degree of Power Distance cultural presence and Hofstede's Power Distance Index represented by hypothesis H1.

This study also examined the possible relationship between the degree of Power Distance cultural presence with the citizen centric e-government development based on 2016 Waseda e-Government ranking, which is represented by hypothesis H2. Correlation analysis between these two data sets was also conducted to provide a better understanding on the relationship between the national cultural values of Power Distance and the citizen centric approach of e-Government development, represented by hypothesis H3.

4   Analysis and Results

4.1   Web Content Analysis on Power Distance Cultural Presence

A total of 30 e-government portals have been examined using five cultural markers that reflect the identity of high Power Distance cultural presence. These cultural markers are:

1. official logo, 2. national flag, 3. prominent authority figures, 4. image of signature building, and 5. color representing national flag or logo. These cultural markers represent the national cultural symbols, are indicators for high Power Distance cultural identity. From the checklist, the total number of cultural markers adopted in the homepage was calculated which signify the degree of Power Distance cultural presence. Table 2 shows the degree of Power Distance cultural presence for each of selected countries.

Table 2. Results from web content analysis

Country	Degree of power distance cultural presence	Country	Degree of power distance cultural presence
Singapore	1	China	3
USA	1	Saudi Arabia	2
Denmark	1	Argentina	2
Korea	2	Peru	2
Japan	2	South Africa	3
Estonia	2	Columbia	3
Canada	2	Venezuela	5
Australia	2	Uruguay	3
New Zealand	1	Costa Rica	4
United Kingdom	1	Morocco	4
Taiwan	2	Kenya	2
Norway	0	Pakistan	5
Austria	2	Fiji	2
Sweden	2	Egypt	3
Finland	3	Nigeria	3

The degree of Power Distance cultural presence is considered high for a homepage design that has greater number of cultural markers compared to a homepage that has less number of cultural markers. Table 2 shows that the e-government homepage of Pakistan and Venezuela have adopted all the five selected cultural markers representing the high Power Distance cultural identity. Therefore, these two countries are considered to have higher degree of Power Distance cultural presence compared to other selected countries. High degree of Power Distance cultural presence may indicate that a lack of citizen centricity is emphasized in the visual design of e-government portal homepage. On the other hand, the result shows that the homepage of Norway e-government does not adopt any of the five selected cultural markers. Hence Norway has the lowest degree of Power Distance cultural presence among the selected countries.

In order to examine the extent to which the homepage design of an e-government portal conform to Hofstede's Power Distance Index, a correlation analysis was conducted to analyze relationship between the Power Distance cultural presence and Hofstede's Power Distance Index. Spearman rank correlation was used to analysis the relationship between the degree of Power Distance cultural presence and the Power Distance Index as well as Waseda e-Government ranking.

Spearman rank correlation analysis has shown a significant positive relationship between Hofstede's Power Distance Index and the degree of Power Distance cultural presence with coefficient value of 0.454 and significant value of 0.006. The positive coefficient indicates that a country with high Power Distance Index is associated with high level of Power Distance cultural presence in website design. In other words, country with high Power Distance Index is more likely to adopt greater number of high Power Distance cultural identity design elements in its homepage portal. This finding provides evidence that the presence of Power Distance cultural identity in the web design conform to Hofstede's Power Distance Index score. Hence, H1 is supported.

The results from the Table 2 shows that majority of the country that were in top 2016 Waseda e-Government ranking has smaller number of Power Distance cultural markers compared to the country that are in the bottom ranking. This indicates that there is possible relationship between the Power Distance cultural presence and the Waseda e-Government ranking. Spearman analysis was conducted to examine the relationship and the result has shown a significant negative association between them with coefficient value of −0.714 and significant value of 0.001. The negative coefficient indicates that a country with high Waseda e-Government ranking is associated with low presence of high Power Distance cultural identity in its web design. In other words, web design for country with a high citizen centric e-government development adopts less number of design element representing the high Power Distance cultural identity. Therefore, H2 is supported.

4.2   Relationship Between Hofstede's Power Distance and Waseda E-Government Development Ranking

For examining the relationship between Waseda e-Government ranking and Power Distance Index, the hypothesis H3, a Pearson correlation analysis was perform as both data sets are normally distributed. The result has shown that a significant relationship between them with coefficient value of −0.557 and significant value of 0.001. The

Table 3. Hypothesis testing result

Hypothesis		Correlation coefficient	Significant value	Result
H1	There is a significant positive relationship between the degree of Power Distance cultural presence and Hofstede's Power Distance Index	0.454	0.006	Supported
H2	There is a significant negative relationship between degree Power Distance cultural presence and citizen centric e-government development	−0.714	0.001	Supported
H3	There is a significant negative relationship between Hofstede's Power Distance Index and citizen centric e-government development	−0.557	0.001	Supported

negative coefficient indicates that a country with a high Waseda e-Government development ranking is associated with low Power Distance Index and vice versa. This result is aligned to prior findings by Zhao [13]. This results indicates that a country with high citizen centric e-government development approach is associated with Low Power Distance Index. Hence, H3 is supported. The summary of result from the statistical hypothesis testing is shown in Table 3.

5 Conclusion

This study investigated the presence of Power Distance cultural dimension in thirty e-government portals by conducting web content analysis using five cultural markers that signify national cultural identity and prominent authority symbols and image. This study used secondary data sets consisting of Hofstede's Power Distance Index and 2016 Waseda e-Government development ranking to examine possible relationship between these indices. The results show that the e-government portal design conform to Hofstede's Power Distance cultural dimension as well as has a significant relationship between Power Distance Index and the Waseda e-Government Ranking. Findings from this study provide better understanding of Power Distance cultural presence in the e-government website design as well as supporting the notion that Power Distance cultural dimension is correlated with the citizen centric approach of e-government development. Further research will be extended to examine the effect of cultural design elements that reflects the Power Distance cultural identity on citizens' emotion and experience which would provide empirical evidence on the impact of cultural presence in e-government portal design.

Acknowledgment. The authors would like to record our sincere thanks to the Research Management Institute (RMI) and Ministry of Higher Education Malaysia for the financial support. This research is conducted under the support and funding of Fundamental Research Grant Scheme (FRGS) no: FRGS/2/2014/ICT01/UITM/01/1.

References

1. Nguyen, A.: A cross-cultural study on e-government services delivery. Electron. J. Inf. Syst. Eval. **19**(2), 121–134 (2016). http://www.ejise.com
2. Zhao, F., Shen, K.N., Collier, A.: Effects of national culture on e-government diffusion: a global study of 55 countries. Inf. Manag. **51**, 1005–1016 (2014)
3. Hofstede, G.: www.geert-hofstede.com
4. The 12th Waseda-IAC International e-Government Rankings Survey 2016 Report, Tokyo, Japan. International e-Government, Waseda University and International Academy of CIO, July 2016. https://www.waseda.jp/top/en-news/43676
5. Allaya, A., Mellouli, M.: National culture and e-government services adoption Tunisian case. In: Recent Advances in Communications, pp 287–290 (2015)
6. Máchová, R., Lněnička, M.: Reframing e-government development indices with respect to new trends in ICT. Rev. Econ. Perspect. **15**(4), 383–411 (2015). doi:10.1515/revecp-2015-0027

7. Ahmed, T., Mouratidis, H., Preston, D.: Website design guidelines: high power distance and high-context culture. Int. J. Cyber Soc. Educ. **2**(1), 47–60 (2009)
8. Marcus, A., Gould, E.M.: Crosscurrents: cultural dimensions and global web user-interface design. Interactions **7**(4), 32–46 (2000). doi:10.1145/345190.345238
9. Al-Hujran, O., Al-dalahmeh, M., Aloudat, A.: The role of national culture on citizen adoption of e-government services: an empirical study. Electron. J. e-Gov. **9**(2), 93–106 (2011)
10. Thomas, D.: The moderating effects of power distance and collectivism on empowering leadership and psychological empowerment and self-leadership in international development organizations. Faculty Publications - School of Business, 80. Ph.D. dissertation. http://digitalcommons.georgefox.edu/gfsb/80
11. Lee, K., Scandura, T.A., Sharif, M.M.: Cultures have consequences: a configural approach to leadership across two cultures. Leadersh. Q. **25**(4), 692–710 (2014). doi:10.1016/j.leaqua.2014.03.003
12. Kirkman, B.L., Lowe, K.B., Gibson, C.B.: A quarter century of cultures consequences: a review of empirical research incorporating Hofstede's cultural values framework. J. Int. Bus. Stud. **37**(3), 285–320 (2006). doi:10.1057/palgrave.jibs.8400202
13. Zhao, F.: Impact of national culture on e-government development: a global study. Internet Res. **21**(3), 362–380 (2011). doi:10.1108/10662241111139354
14. Kovačić, Z.: The impact of national culture on worldwide e-government readiness. Inf. Sci. J. **8**, 143–158 (2005)
15. Aykut, A.: Cross-cultural analysis of European e-government adoption. World Appl. Sci. J. **7**(9), 1124–1130 (2009)
16. Goyal, N., Miner, W., Nawathe, N.: Cultural differences across governmental website design. In: Proceedings of the 4th International Conference on Intercultural Collaboration, pp. 149–152 (2012)
17. Moura, T., Singh, N., Chun, W.: The influence of culture in website design and users' perceptions. J. Electron. Commer. Res. **17**(4), 312–339 (2016)
18. Van Dam, N., Evers, V., Arts, F.A.: Cultural user experience issues in e-government: designing for a multi-cultural society. In: Besselaar, P., Koizumi, S. (eds.) Digital Cities 2003. LNCS, vol. 3081, pp. 310–324. Springer, Heidelberg (2005). doi:10.1007/11407546_18
19. Máchová, R.: The assessment of e-government readiness in the globalization process. In: 16th International Scientific Conference Globalization and Its Socio-Economic Consequences (2016)
20. Sorn-in, K., Tuamsuk, K., Chaopanon, W.: Factors affecting the development of e-government using a citizen-centric approach. J. Sci. Technol. Policy Manag. **6**(3), 206–222 (2015). doi:10.1108/jstpm-05-2014-0027
21. Md Noor, N.L., Harun, A.F., Wan Adnan, W.A., Mohd Saman, F.: Towards the conceptualization of citizen user experience: citizen's preference for emotional design in E-Government portal. In: Proceedings of 4th International User Science and Engineering Conference (2016)
22. Alomari, M., Woods, P., Sandhu, K.: Predictors for e-government adoption in Jordan: deployment of an empirical evaluation based on a citizen-centric approach. Inf. Technol. People **25**(2), 207–234 (2012). doi:10.1108/09593841211232712

Designing to Support Community Gardens by Going Beyond Community Gardens

Xiaolan Wang[1(✉)] and Ron Wakkary[1,2]

[1] Simon Fraser University, Surrey, BC, Canada
{xiaolanw,rwakkary}@sfu.ca
[2] Eindhoven University of Technology, Eindhoven, Netherlands

Abstract. Community gardens connect to many organizations in order to receive and offer resources and services. The complex sociotechnical systems in which community gardens inhabit bring both opportunities and challenges for designers who endeavor to support them. In this study, we investigated three community gardens to explore the organizational connections that support them. Our aim is to articulate an expanded understanding of a community garden as an end-user that includes a diverse connection of stakeholders. By revealing the multiple connections they make, our results show that the community gardens in our study have established three paths to connections with diverse organizations. The reasons for these connections include community inclusion, assistance, peer-support and administration. In these connections, the roles community gardens play are also distinct. In addition, a community garden's role is fluid rather than fixed. Based on these findings, we propose design implications to support community gardens beyond the gardens themselves and three scenarios to illustrate opportunities for design. We thus suggest researchers to broaden the existing limited focus on gardeners and their practices in gardens. Our work reveals a new space that design and HCI could support to promote urban agriculture and civic engagement. By providing practical design scenarios as illustrations to support community garden that are actively embedded in complex sociotechnical systems, this work responds to the theme of the session *DesignX: Acting to Complexity* which calls for designers to "play an active role in implementation, and develop solutions through small, incremental steps."

Keywords: Community garden · Urban agriculture · Communities · Organizational relationship · Civic engagement

1 Introduction

A community garden is physically a green farmland in an urban environment managed by a non-profit neighborhood community [16]. In community gardens, people self-organize, explore, and use resources around them. They collaboratively overcome problems, maintain and develop the community [18]. There is usually a coordinating committee who are elected by community gardeners. Coordinators lead gardeners to develop community garden policies and guidelines, prepare site infrastructure and promote gardening workshops. Over the past few years, HCI and interaction design

© Springer International Publishing AG 2017
P.-L.P. Rau (Ed.): CCD 2017, LNCS 10281, pp. 451–468, 2017.
DOI: 10.1007/978-3-319-57931-3_36

communities have explored a range of technologies to support gardeners' interactions with gardens and tools [18, 19].

However, community gardens are not isolated entities. They connect widely with a larger set of organizations aiming to receive and give help. This situation suggests that designs for community gardens are not merely about the gardens themselves, but also relate to the complex sociotechnical systems they inhabit in. Designing to support community gardens is a situation of DesignX, which is articulated by Norman and Stappers [13]. We argue it is necessary to examine the connections that community gardens have in order to better understand their impacts in a broader view, thereby revealing larger design spaces for promoting urban agriculture. In HCI, however, little research has explored the community connections that support and interact with community gardens. In this paper, we aim at articulating an expanded understanding of a community garden as an end-user to include a diverse connection of stakeholders. Also, this research is driven by the personal interest of the lead author of this paper. The author has been a community gardener over years. Through conducting gardening practices, the author found a community garden was involved in plenty of connections that were hidden from the design researchers' eyes. We recognize that for design and HCI, we need to reframe the focus of our design from the community garden and gardener to explore beyond to include the diverse stakeholders that connect to a community garden. We believe this work serves as a concrete example of DesignX situation. More significantly, it provides practical steps for designers who are acting to the complexity in the context of community gardens.

In this paper, we articulate how rich the connections of community garden are. In our study, we conducted interviews with five community garden coordinators from three different community gardens. Our findings show that community gardens have built connections with diverse organizations through a variety of ways. Driven by different reasons, a community garden plays different roles in those connections. More interestingly, a community garden's role is changing with its development: at first, it is a receiver, then it becomes a matcher and at last it grows to be a giver. Based on our findings, we proposed design implications and three scenarios to illustrate the opportunities for design and HCI to support community gardens by going beyond them.

In the following sections, we outline the related work on community gardens as well as communities, non-profit organizations and inter-organizational networks. We then describe our methodology, study, and findings. We conclude with design implications and three scenarios.

2   Related Work

Urban agriculture enables people to have easier access to fresh food in the city [27]. Prior work on urban agricultures largely focuses on "food production". Community gardening, as an increasingly popular local food producing practice, has drawn researcher interests in HCI and interaction design [10, 18, 19]. For example, Pearce *et al.* [19] introduced an internet-based application that helps gardeners analyze water amounts in their gardens. Similarly, Angelopoulos *et al.* [1] developed a system that is able to automatically adjust to environmental conditions and supply specific amount of water for different kinds of plants. Besides focusing on production, Hirsch [12] has a wider view on urban agriculture. He illustrated that urban agriculture practices also include distributing and consuming food in cities. This understanding broadens the focus of urban agriculture as a collective project of diverse organizations, urban systems and resources, and stakeholders from different communities.

Research in HCI often focuses on working together with communities to tackle social problems and create appropriate solutions. Researchers engage different individuals and public organizations (e.g. non-profit organizations, government and companies) in the co-design or co-operative process. For example, in his project called "Neighborhood Network" [7], DiSalvo and his colleagues held a series of participatory design work-shops with residents to reflect on the utilization of technologies in their everyday life. In addition, they held co-designed programs with local residents to enable them to design their own products to solve community problems [6]. Le Dantec et al. also pointed out that researchers should start to think about how technologies can "empower people to self-organize" in their communities [14].

To better facilitate civic engagement, HCI and interaction design researchers have also studied relationships of organizations. In the context of organizations and the public, Voida et al. [28] described the role of volunteer coordinators in the bridging of organizations with the public. In their research, they conducted interviews with volunteer coordinators from non-profit organizations about their work. They also summarized how social computing can be a useful tool to support them. Moreover, Voida et al. [29] found that volunteer coordinators created a unique database to manage their everyday information, such as the information of their large number of volunteers and related stakeholders.

Significant research has been conducted on inter-organizational networks [5, 11, 20–22]. Nardi et al. [17] addressed the significance of individual's social network in organizational context. Inter-organizational network is defined as "a collection of organizations that pursue sustained relations of exchange with one another and, at the same time, lack a legitimate organizational authority" [20]. In other literature about inter-organization, Goecks et al. [9] conducted research on collaborative computing in non-profit fundraising. They proposed a model of independent relationships among donors, non-donors, beneficiary and third parties in this practice. Stroll et al. [25] investigated the reasons why some connections between organizations do not exist. They addressed the importance of awareness in the collaboration among organizations. Furthermore, they proposed four factors that hinder the collective action of organizations. The factors are "inside competitiveness due to funding pressure", "asymmetry in ICT access", "reliance on volunteer workforce" and "hinging on personal motivations and trust among individuals". Besides the formal collective action, Stroll et al. [25] also did research on informal coordination. They found two features of informal interactions, the first is "common goal as primary basis for interactions", and the second one is "avoidance of formal commitments". Their work complements the work of [4, 23] which identified informal interaction as non-hierarchical structure and lack of formally characterized roles in the process.

Our research views community garden not only as an urban agriculture practice, but also as a non-profit grassroots, which has plentiful inter-organizational interactions for reaching its goal of civic engagement. By exploring its connections with corporations, institutions, groups and other organizations, we aim to reveal broader space for researchers and designers to support community gardens and even other non-profit organizations.

3   Study Design and Methodology

In our study of connections of community gardens, we sought to answer the following research questions: What organizations are connected to community gardens? How and why do they connect with each other? What are the roles of community gardens in these connections?

The fieldwork for this research consisted of three community gardens in Vancouver. By visiting the sites, talking with the garden coordinators and reviewing websites, we understood that the goal of Community Garden 1 (G1) is to help meet the increasing demands for urban agriculture and the need to grow communities through community groups. Community Garden 2 (G2) aims to develop an inclusive community and a spirit of openness and cooperation among its members and the promotion of organic gardening methods. Community Garden 3 (G3) belongs to a local business improvement association (BIA). The mission of this BIA is to make the local area a safe and lively community through various creative programs like community gardening. The goal of G3 is to provide local people more opportunities to access green space within a mixed residential and industrial neighborhood.

3.1   Semi-structured Interview

Our interviews are selective. There are many people involved in community gardens, however we chose to interview the coordinators. Our reasoning is that the coordinators of community gardens know about and take responsibility for the connections of the gardens. We recruited 5 coordinators from the previously mentioned three gardens. P1 and P4 are from G1. P1 is the membership coordinator. P4 is the coordinator who is responsible for public relations. P2 is the G2's coordinator who maintains most of the connections with other organizations. Both P3 and P5 are from G3. P3 is a member of the BIA and responsible for the local resource park process. P5 is the executive director of BIA. We knew P1, P2, and P3 from previous research that we conducted on community gardens. P4 and P5 were suggested by P1 and P3 for this study.

Interviews were between 30 and 60 min. Prior to the interviews, each participant was given an outline with background information about our research and was told that data would remain confidential and anonymous. Participants were asked about the organizations related to the community garden and about the qualities of those connections. Specific questions included: *"What organizations are connected to your garden?"*, *"How and why does your garden connect with that organization? Is it through an individual or another organization?"*, *"What do you support it or get support?"* We also asked participants to tell us how the connection serves the goal of their organizations.

3.2 Garden Site Visits

After each interview, we visited the sites of all three gardens with coordinators. The coordinator showed us different plots in the garden and described the organizations that own the plots. Coordinators gave more details on the organizations during the visit. We took notes and photographs. We were also invited to observe and participate in one of garden's anniversary party.

3.3 Volunteering in the Anniversary Event (Fig. 1)

We volunteered in and observed an anniversary event for G3. During the event, people from other related organizations came to visit. For example, a small urban homesteading shop facilitated two garden workshops. On site, there was a demonstration of a truck farm. There were also local pocket farmers' who marketed fresh fruits and vegetables at the event. We talked with people from different organizations and asked questions about why they participated in the event, how they knew the garden, and how they support each other and developed the relationship.

Fig. 1. Volunteering in the anniversary event

3.4 Data Analysis

We transcribed audio recordings and notes and then performed a thematic analysis on the transcribed data. This involved coding data into themes based on our interpretation of the data. The themes include: (1) types of organizations; (2) paths and reasons for building connections; (3) community garden's roles in these connection. In the following sections, we describe the main findings from our study.

4 Findings

4.1 Diverse Organizations Get Connected

We found community gardens connect with various kinds of organizations (Fig. 2). Below we present a brief description of the organizations related to each community garden.

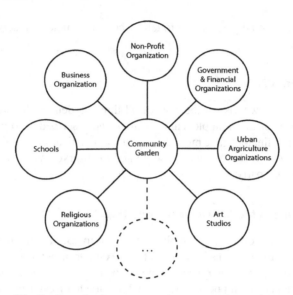

Fig. 2. Organizations connected to community gardens

Business Organizations. For anonymity reasons, we use O1x to represent the organization related to community garden G1, O2x for G2 and O3x for G3.

In Table 1, we present the business organizations that related to three community gardens. As we can see in the table, there are business groups involved from local level to municipal level. There are also national and international business organizations that are related to community garden with various supporting (we will give more details in the following sections).

Table 1. Business organizations

Organization	Sub-type	Description
O16	Local small business	A local coffee shop
O115	Local small business	A local microbrewery
O22	National landscape industry	Provides progressive landscape maintenance programs, along with contemporary designs, installations, and ecologically conscious plant health care
O23	International forest company	A forest products company specializing in the manufacture of high quality cedar lumber products
O32	Local small business	Provides Vancouver residents with a convenient, one-stop shop where they can find know-how and supplies for a wide range of do-it-yourself urban homesteading projects
O38	Municipal gardening business	Provides plant material, such as trees, shrubs, annuals, perennials, vines, fruits & vegetables

Non-profit Organizations. Community gardens relate to many non-profit organizations (see Table 2). According to our data, we found gardens to be connected to local neighborhood houses, community centers and other municipal or national levels of non-profit organizations that support community building and their development.

Table 2. Non-profit organizations

Organization	Sub-type	Description
O11	Local neighborhood house	A member of the Association of Neighborhood Houses of British Columbia. Their goal is to make their neighborhood a better place to live
O12	Municipal society	The umbrella organization for all community gardens in Vancouver
O15	Local BIA	A BIA to create an enhanced business environment and to assist their members with any related individual concerns
O17	Provincial NPO	An industry-led, not-for-profit organization working to foster growth and innovation across British Columbia's agriculture and agri-food industry
O18	Local NPO	A volunteer group dedicated to sharing the unique voices of Vancouver's East of Main community
O112	Local neighborhood house	A nearby restaurant and gallery neighborhood house
O21	Municipal NPO	A not for profit community living service provider, initiative tackles the challenge of social isolation through gardening
O11	Local neighborhood house	A member of the Association of Neighborhood Houses of British Columbia. Their goal is to make their neighborhood a better place to live
O25	National NPO	A multilingual non-profit organization dedicated to addressing issues that affect immigrants and refugees in the course of their settlement and integration into Canadian society

Government and Financial Organizations. Community gardens are related to the government because they are situated in the city and follow municipality rules or guidelines. In addition, based on our research, we found that community gardens receive funding from some financial organizations (see Table 3).

Urban Agriculture Organizations. Community gardens build connection with other gardens and urban agriculture organizations, such as an urban farm or community garden society (see Table 3).

Table 3. Government, financial, urban agriculture and other organization

Organization	Sub-type	Description
O116	City government	City's park board
O113	Provincial bank	The tenth largest credit union in BC
O114	Local urban farm	An urban farm that enables community-engaged learning through urban agriculture
O111	School	A nearby elementary school
O34	International religious organization	An international Christian church that provides housing, food and community services
O36	Local art studio	Supports artists from diverse traditions working with ecologists to explore the creative repurposing of green waste

Other Organizations. We also found that community gardens have connections to local schools, tool libraries, religious organization (e.g. Christian church) and art studios (see Table 3). Not only the types of organizations are diverse, but also the paths or ways gardens take to connect them are various.

4.2   Paths for Building Connections

According to our interviews, we generated three paths community gardens tread to connect to other organizations. The first one is what we called *organization-individual(s)-organization*. This means community garden establish connections with other organizations through its own member(s). The second type is *organization-organization-organization*, which we found that community garden could build a new connection with another organization through one organization they already know. The third type of connection is what we labeled as *organization-internet-organization*. With this type of connection, community gardens search on the Internet to look for the organization that could offer them certain help.

Organization-Individual(s)-Organization. There are two modes in this type of connection. The first one is two organizations are connected by one person who works for both organizations. This individual becomes a bridge between the garden and the organization.

> *"Our BIA connected to that school (O39) because we want the students to teach people who are from the neighborhood house (O33) to cook healthier food using cheap and simple vegetables* (most vegetables are from G3). *By doing this, students from O39 could offer their time and expertise to help the poor people to live a healthier way. We knew O39 through a member of our sustainable committee. This member is also working in O39 and she got this idea."* – P5

The other mode is that a member of a community garden knows a person in another organization. Based on this relation, two organizations are then connected.

> *"My coworker runs it (O18). They had an event and she asked me whether the garden could be a guest speaker in that event."* – P4

This way of connecting is often vulnerable to the problem that if any of those individuals left that organization, the connection gets lost and the relationship ends. According to our interviews, community gardens have a hard time to rebuild lost connections.

Organization-Organization-Organization. Organizations can also be an effective bridge to help community garden connect with another organization, which it needs help from. For example, one of our participants told us they became connected to another organization through the introduction of the city government. According to our data, compared with connections built through an individual, we found that a connection through an organization is more stable.

Organization-Internet-Organization. Another common connection between community gardens and organizations is through the Internet. When community gardeners need help they can't get from the organizations they are connected with already, they search online to look for organizations that could offer support. Some community gardens also use Twitter in similar ways.

> *"We find O37 through Internet searching. We found they had technically supported many communities in the past, so we tried to call them and they agreed to help us... Yeah, it is hard to look for an organization that could give us special help we need on the Internet." – P5*

Finding a special support from an unknown organization by searching online is a big challenge for gardeners. Besides, building connection with other organizations is especially difficult before the garden is build.

> *"Initially we made a conscious effort to develop relationships. It was part of getting approval from the park board. We had the relationships before we built the garden. This is part of what makes the garden a community organization, not just a garden." – P4*

In summary, community gardens make invest substantial effort to access and to reach other groups or institutions. In an ad hoc manner they receive recommendations from other organizations or individuals or they find help from the Internet. These paths are unstable, uncertain or easily fail.

4.3   Reasons for Connection

Community gardens connect with above various organizations for different reasons. In this section, we list three main ones that emerge from our data. Uncovering these invisible rationales helps us clearly categorize the roles that community gardens play in the connection and what community gardens provide to or take from other groups.

Connecting for Community Inclusion. As we mentioned in the introduction section, there are different kinds of community gardens. A common goal of community gardens is to facilitate *community inclusion*.

To realize this goal, a popular approach that community gardens use is to include organizations by giving or renting them plots in the garden. Those organizations usually are ones who help and provide housing and job support to vulnerable people (e.g., local community center). The following quote represents the fact that the community garden G2 sets special plots for people from those organizations.

"We want to include vulnerable people that are isolated in our society. So we created our garden to save 10% of our beds to either people who have disability or youth. They are from the program that supports youth refugees of O25 and disabilities of O26." – P2

Besides plots, community gardens donate parts of their harvest to these organizations, as another way for building a more inclusive community.

Connecting for Getting Assistance. Community gardens ask assistance from other organizations during their development. This assistance for example includes helping building garden infrastructure and executing events. One of our participants from G3 told us,, in getting help to build the community garden G3, they made connected with a non-profit organization that provides assistance from building professionals.

"It is very technical and a lot of new vocabularies. O37 made a lot of drawings and put them on a piece of paper. They helped us a lot to pass the zoning bylaws." – P5

Connecting for Peer Support. Besides connecting for community inclusion and getting assistance, community gardens team up with other community organizations for supporting each other. For example, G1 along with other local community gardens set up an association O12. The following is a peer-supporting instance told by our participant.

"We were able to sign a popular gardener to come to do a workshop for us from California. So we were able to partner with a few other gardening organizations to market the event, like other community gardens market the event to their email lists, and other community organizations that focus on healthy living." – P1

Connecting Because of Being Administrated. Most community gardens are built on municipal land. This means the garden must meet municipal policies and land-use codes, as well as accept being administrated in part by city staff. One of our participants from G1 explained the many specific rules to follow since their garden is in a park:

"There are a lot of regulations, you know? You have to be far away from the street. You have to have water available. There are a lot of small guidelines, so sometimes the Parks Board come to the garden once a year just to see if everything is been used correctly, or anything needs to be changed." – P1

Gardens not only need to follow the city policies, but also local guidelines.

"We contact the elementary school (O111) near us when we are doing a project that might affect them, for example making a bee hive." – P4

Different from previous reasons driven by which community garden could create flexible, varied and unstable connections with diverse organizations, the connections built because of being supervised are rigid, uniform and stable.

4.4 Three Roles of Community Gardens

As we articulated, community gardens connected to diverse organizations because of different reasons. When we read closer to our data, we found that community gardens play different roles in those connections. In some cases, community gardens contribute to other organizations. There are also connections in which community gardens take advantages of other organizations. And sometimes, they try their best to preserve an equal balance of giving and getting. In this section, we illustrate these roles and present their respective characteristics.

Community Garden as a Giver. As a giver, based on our data, community gardens offer resources to other groups. The giving is usually plots and harvests from the garden as well as gardening knowledge. For example, in previous sections, we have mentioned that gardens usually contribute gardening beds and part of their food to special non-profit organizations which have vulnerable people, for making them less isolated in the society. There might be more types of resources that community gardens provide to the society, but based on our study, compared to the assistance they receive from other organizations, what community gardens have to offer is very limited.

The limits on these resources impact the garden's development. As one of our participants said:

> *"We connect with the library as needed. They have allowed us to use their display case to make a display. We gave them a list of books to purchase, and they took our advice! They let us use their meeting room before we had built the garden. Now, we try not to ask for too much because they usually do things for us, and we can't do too much in return."* – P4

Community Garden as a Receiver. In contrast to a garden's limits as a giver, community gardens receive plentiful and varied support from other organizations. Below, we present four specific advantages community garden receive from other organizations.

Garden Materials. Community gardens get support of materials especially when they are starting and have to build structures. They need wood, compost and tools. Therefore, a lot of organizations give help on the building day of the garden.

> *"On the building day, we got wood and wood chips donations from O23. ... We also got soil for free for building the plots."* – P2

Labor. Organizations also send volunteers to community gardens to help them on the building day. Community gardens also get help from gardeners from other gardens.

> *"O12 is the umbrella organization for all community gardens in Van. They helped us get started."* – P4

> *"We got a lot of help from O27. They brought many volunteers to help build the garden."* – P2

Technical Expertise. Building a garden is not easy work. It requires landscape design, architecture and irrigation. Community gardens need technical expertise support to meet these requirements.

Funding. Community gardens in our study often apply and receive grants for building new facilities or holding events. Usually, in this relationship model, community gardens need to report to the organizations that give grants about how the money is used.

> *"They gave us $500. We try to keep in touch to tell them how we use their money. For O112 we had to contact them a lot to get the money from the fundraiser. Now we are finished working with them." – P4*

Community Garden as a Matcher. In some connections, gardens both provide for and recieve support from other organizations. There usually exists an "exchange", in which community gardens often use their plots, harvests or gardening abilities to "trade" with other groups to obtain what they want. Following is an example that community garden utilize their gardening beds to trade with a local business.

> *"O32 has technical expertise to take care of the garden and also teach people gardening knowledge. As a for-profit local store, O32 uses the garden to give workshops and let itself known by people. And for us, there are other people take care of the garden rather than ourselves." – P5*

In addition, the "exchange" can be intangible. For example, community gardens publicize each other on social network platforms.

> *"We've stayed in touch with O114 and repost each others' Facebook posts, random things like that...O18 had an event on "local food" and one of our gardeners gave a speech on permaculture for them. Then they retweet our tweets." – P4*

Above we have discussed diverse types of organizations community gardens connect to, the reasons for connecting to them and community garden's different roles in these connections. For a clearer understanding of the relationship between the connection reason and community garden's role, we create a table and make a summary here.

From Table 4, we can find that for receiving support and funding, a garden mainly plays a role of receiver in the connections. When gardens build connections for peer support, they become matchers that exchange or swap resources. Moreover, for making a more inclusive community, community garden aim to or become a giver within the connection. The results we present here seems static, however, both the connections and the roles of gardens are gradually changing during the development of a community garden.

Table 4. Roles in each type of connections

Reason for connection	Community garden's role
Getting assistance	Receiver
Being administrated	
Peer support	Matcher
Community inclusion	Giver

Role Transformation of Community Garden. With the development of the community garden, its connections are strengthened, change to another type or become broken sometimes. We found the roles of community garden in these connections are not always the same or stable. They are fluid.

> *"Relationships have changed over time - at first it was to get expertise and money, but also symbolic support. Now it's about peers like O114 and O14, people with whom we can have ongoing relationships." – P4*

We found at the beginning of a community garden, it builds more connections for getting assistance (the role of a *receiver*). Later, when the community garden becomes more mature, it develops peer-support connections, which consist of new connections and those transferred from old connections that were built on getting assistance. According to the community gardens' goal of *community inclusion*, we assume that a potential future step of community garden is to develop more connections to the point a community garden becomes a *giver*.

Furthermore, through comparisons of these three gardens, we found that G1 is more a "matcher" than G2 and G3 who can be viewed as "receivers". By exploring their activities, we also found that G1 has more variety of activities than G2 and G3, which makes G1 more involved with the neighborhood and connected to a wider group of stakeholders. To reach the goal of community inclusion, community gardens are gradually transforming their role from a receiver to a matcher, and then to a giver.

5   Design Implications and Discussion

This study has explored diverse connections that community gardens have. During their growth, community gardens invest efforts to establish relations with diverse organizations for different reasons. In this process, they constantly change their role from a *receiver* to a *matcher,* and to a *giver.* By understanding this, how should we, as designers, support community gardens and prompt their role transformation and development? In this section, we outline a range of implications based on our findings.

5.1   Visible and Traceable Resources and Services

As we discussed previously, gardening materials, tools, and technical building professionals are commonly needed by community gardens, especially those newly created. However, it is not always an easy task for gardeners to find the organizations that can give them support. Even if there are some possible organizations recommended by individuals or another organization, it is not certain that they can provide the specific services the gardens need. Therefore, we see the benefits in visualizing the varied resources and services that could be provided to community gardens. Besides making these visible, the assistances should be traceable. Community garden could clearly know where the assistances they have already gotten come from. By this way, community garden can manage the support they receive and make choices of providers in the future. For example, instead of creating a manual database to manage volunteers as described by the participants in Voida's study [28], they can clearly see where their volunteers come from and easily find and recruit more if needed. Making resources and supports visible and traceable would also be important in the case of the individuals who built the connection and later left the community garden. Moreover, visible and traceable resources and services could also be beneficial to other community groups who are currently at the stage as a "receiver". For example, an elementary school that is looking for support to build an educational garden in their playground could also take advantage of these visible resources and services.

5.2 Awareness of Both Organizational and Individual Connections

Community gardens receive assistance from other organizations to further develop. During this process, community gardens constantly build abilities and accumulate assets. When they become more mature, they are not only "receivers" who receive help. More significantly, they start to become "matchers" who make transactions with other groups.

With awareness of both organizational and individual connections, community gardens could find more opportunities to exchange or trade resources or knowledge with other organizations. This will be very beneficial to gardens at the "matcher" stage. Technologies developed for knowledge bartering or resource exchange for individuals have become popular nowadays, for example, *Shared Earth* [24], *Zilok* [30] and *Trade School* [26]. People can exchange or swap knowledge and resources in these platforms. However, there is dearth of systems that have been developed for organizations to make transactions, especially for non-profit organizations. Systems could be designed and developed to fill this gap. The issues for organizational transaction we think designers should consider about are how to make the transitions fair, trackable, and exceptions detectable.

In addition, we learned that community gardens donate local food to other organizations, such as local community centers and neighborhood houses. This creates the opportunity to see how urban agriculture impacts is as much about food distribution and consumption as it is about production. It would be beneficial to see where and how the local food is distributed and consumed through the network. Thus, there are design opportunities to track the food over time and geographically. Consistent with Hirsch's opinion [12], this would be helpful to clarify the "green flow" of urban agriculture enabling researchers to understand the "production-distribution-consumption" cycle better.

5.3 Promote Civic Engagement

A significant goal of community gardens is creating an inclusive community. We envision community garden in the future could serve the society as a "giver" when it evolves to be more mature. As a "giver", a community garden would be willing to make their resources public and accessible to other groups. They thus get ready to share and offer what they have to new community gardens or other groups to promote their development. This complements Le Dantec's idea of "empower people to self-organize" [15]. Designers could support this process by helping community gardens that are at the "giver" stage to public their resources and services. Moreover, technologies could be developed to recruit new community groups who can be the receivers of those public resources. Clearly, if this could be realized, the issue of "receiver" community garden is not an issue any more. Therefore, when the system supports community gardens well, it can attract and involve more new organizations. This will create a virtuous cycle. The local food movement could be also promoted in the process.

In conclusion, a community garden can be seen as a seed in our societal environment. It absorbs various nutrients from the earth at the beginning. When it gets stronger, they fit with other species and benefit each other. Bees come to it for making honey and pollination. When it becomes mature, it returns its fruit to the society and nourishes the soil for more new seedlings to grow.

6 Design Scenarios

In this section, we propose three design scenarios to better illustrate how designers can support community gardens of different stages. The scenarios successively feature an online system that support community garden at "receiver", "matcher" and "giver".

6.1 Scenario 1

Mike and many of his neighbors received approval from the city to build their community garden at the corner of their neighborhood park. They have wood and soil provided by the City Park Board but they still need tools for people to use on the building day. Mike was introduced to the website "Find Your Local Resources" to find the tools for his group to use. He registered in the system with the address of their garden. By searching the keyword "tool", the system presents all the nearby organizations with the tools and related services they are providing. Mike was excited and surprised since he never knew there were so many available tools nearby. After comparing the price for lending and the distances to these organizations, Mike finally chose the community public tool library and "Building Home" which is a landscape association that supports landscape maintenance programs. Mike borrowed many building tools from the tool library. He also bought common gardening tools from "Building Home" for the members to use in daily gardening. Mike and his group were happy since their garden was successfully built at a low-cost.

6.2 Scenario 2

Time flies fast. It has been three years since the start of Mike's community garden. That last year was a good year. The garden harvested an abundance of honey, fruit and vegetables. Gardeners' faces were full of smiles. However, Mike also received complaints from gardeners that many of their tools were too old to use and some of them were broken. This problem became more serious in the busy harvest season when all members frequently required tools. Mike went back to "Find Your Local Resources" again. Their old friend "Building Home" was still providing tools. Different from last time, Mike talked to "Building Home" not about buying new tools but asking whether they could exchange tools for fresh local honey and vegetables. "Building Home" was interested in this exchange because the business would have a party and they needed vegetables and honey. Both Mike's community garden and "Building Home" thought it was a good deal. Mike thus negotiated with "Building Home" through the system a fair exchange between the quality of the tools and the amount of honey and vegetables. The system also scheduled the best times for the exchange since the party was not for some time and Building Home wanted fresh produce. Once all the conditions were agreed upon through the system, both were satisfied.

6.3   Scenario 3

Two more years have passed. Mike's community garden has made numerous transactions with new and old connected organizations by exchanging tangible and intangible resources in the system. Many organizations and individuals in the city have come to know about Mike's community garden. Instead of looking for resources and help from other organizations in the system, the garden now frequently posts what it offers in the system. It offers gardening knowledge, garden building assistance service, local honey, fresh fruits and vegetables as well as gardening tools that are visible and available in the system for trade and purchase. The garden also wants to provide what they have to newly created community gardens and other groups. On a Sunday, Mike received a new message in the system. Not very far from their neighborhood, Lucy and her team members would build a garden in the school playground. They needed tools and garden building professionals. Mike and his garden members gladly offered help. It was seen as a step in realizing their goal of community inclusion. Mike's community garden, beautiful and mature, is playing an increasingly important role in promoting civic engagement.

7   Conclusion

By investigating three community gardens in Vancouver to explore their related organizations, this paper has articulated an expanded understanding of a community garden as an end-user to include a diverse connection of stakeholders. Our results show that community gardens have built a variety of connections with diverse organizations during their development process. Based on the findings, we proposed design implications and three design scenarios to illustrate the possibilities that design and HCI can support community gardens during different stages. Admittedly, our study has its limitations. For example, there are many different kinds of community gardens that may have more types of connections in around the world. This research only explored cases of community gardens in Vancouver. The results might be limited by the unique politics and connections of our city related to urban agriculture. However, our work broadens the existing limited focus on community garden practitioners. It reveals a new space that design and HCI could support to promote urban agriculture and civic engagement. By providing small but practical design scenarios as illustrations to support community gardeners who are actively embedded in complex sociotechnical systems, this work responds to *DesignX: Acting to Complexity* which suggests that "designers cannot stop at the design stage: they must play an active role in implementation, and develop solutions through small, incremental steps to reduce political, social, and cultural disruptions" [13].

Acknowledgments. We thank all our participants. We also thank Chinese Scholarship Council (CSC) for financial support of this study.

References

1. Angelopoulos, C.M., Nikoletseas, S., Theofanopoulos, G.C.: A smart system for garden watering using wireless sensor networks. In: MobiWac 2011, pp. 167–170. ACM (2011)
2. Bender, T.: Community and Social Change in America (1982)
3. Buechley, L., Rosner, D.K., Paulos, E., Williams, A.: DIY for CHI: methods, communities, and values of reuse and customization. In: CHI EA 2009, pp. 4823–4826. ACM (2009)
4. Chisholm, D.: Coordination Without Hierarchy: Informal Structures in Multiorganizational Systems. University of California Press, Berkeley (1989)
5. Coburn, C.E., Russell, J.L.: District policy and teachers' social networks. Educ. Eval. Policy Anal. **30**(3), 203–235 (2008)
6. DiSalvo, C., Louw, M., Coupland, J., Steiner, M.: Local issues, local uses: tools for robotics and sensing in community contexts. In: C&C 2009, pp. 245–254. ACM (2009)
7. DiSalvo, C., Nourbakhsh, I., Holstius, D., Akin, A., Louw, M.: The neighborhood networks project: a case study of critical engagement and creative expression through participatory design. In: PDC 2008, pp. 41–50 (2008)
8. Tanenbaum, J.G., Williams, A.M., Desjardins, A., Tanenbaum, K.: Democratizing technology: pleasure, utility and expressiveness in DIY and maker practice. In: CHI 2013, pp. 2603–2612. ACM (2013)
9. Goecks, J., Voida, A., Voida, S., Mynatt, E.: Charitable technologies: opportunities for collaborative computing in nonprofit fundraising. In: CSCW 2008, pp. 689–698. ACM (2008)
10. Goodman, E., Rosner, D.: From garments to gardens: negotiating material relationships online and 'by hand'. In: CHI 2011, pp. 2257–2266. ACM (2011)
11. Hermann, F., Rummel, N., Spada, H.: Solving the case together: the challenge of net-based interdisciplinary collaboration. In: Dillenbourg, P., Eurelings, A., Hakkarainen, K. (eds.) Proceedings of the First European Conference on Computer-Supported Collaborative Learning, pp. 293–300. McLuhan Institute, Maastricht (2001)
12. Hirsch, T.: Beyond gardening: a new approach for HCI and urban agriculture. In: Choi, J., Foth, M., Hearn, G. (eds.) Eat, Grow, Cook: Mixing Human-Food and Human-Computer Interactions, pp. 227–242. MIT Press, Cambridge (2014)
13. Norman, D.A., Stappers, P.J.: DesignX: complex sociotechnical systems. She Ji: J. Des. Econ. Innov. **1**(2), 83–106 (2016)
14. Stoll, J., Edwards, W.K., Mynatt, E.D.: Interorganizational coordination and awareness in a nonprofit ecosystem. In: Proceedings of the 2010 ACM Conference on Computer Supported Cooperative Work, pp. 51–60. ACM, February 2010
15. Le Dantec, C.: Considering the rights (and wrongs) of community technology. Interactions **19**(4), 24–27 (2012)
16. Lee, V.N.: Community Gardens (2010)

17. Nardi, B.A., Whittaker, S., Schwarz, H.: NetWORKers and their activity in intensional networks. CSCW **11**(1–2), 205–242 (2002)
18. Odom, W.: Mate, we don't need a chip to tell us the soil's dry: opportunities for designing interactive systems to support urban food production. In: Proceedings of the CHI 2010, pp. 232–235. ACM (2010)
19. Pearce, J., Murphy, J., Smith, W.: Supporting gardeners to plan domestic watering: a case study of designing an 'everyday simulation'. In: Proceedings of the OZCHI 2008, pp. 227–230. ACM Press (2008)
20. Peter, S.W.: Collective capabilities: building a theory of coordinated collective action in a networked improvement community. In: CSCW 2012, pp. 355–358. ACM (2012)
21. Powell, W.W., White, D.R., Koput, K.W., OwenSmith, J.: Network dynamics and field evolution: the growth of interorganizational collaboration in the life sciences. Am. J. Sociol. **110**(4), 1132–1206 (2005)
22. Provan, K.G., Fish, A., Sydow, J.: Interorganizational networks at the network level: a review of the empirical literature on whole networks. J. Manag. **33**(3), 479–516 (2007)
23. Rank, O.: Formal structures and informal networks: structural analysis in organizations. Scand. J. Manag. **24**, 145–161 (2008)
24. Shared Earth. http://sharedearth.com/
25. Stoll, J., Edwards, W., Mynatt, E.D.: Informal interactions in nonprofit networks. In: CHI 2010, pp. 533–536. ACM (2010)
26. Trade School. http://tradeschool.coop/
27. Viljoen, A., Howe, J. (eds.): Continuous Productive Urban Landscapes. Routledge, Abingdon (2012)
28. Voida, A., Harmon, E., Al-Ani, B.: Bridging between organizations and the public: volunteer coordinators' uneasy relationship with social computing. In: Proceedings of the CHI 2012, pp. 1967–1976. ACM Press (2012)
29. Voida, A., Harmon, E., Al-Ani, B.: Homebrew databases: complexities of everyday information management in nonprofit organizations. In: CHI 2011, pp. 915–924. ACM (2011)
30. Zilok. http://us.zilok.com

Sewing for Life: The Development of Sewing Machine in the Tune of Women Life Experience in Taiwan

Ju-Joan Wong[✉] and Hsiao-Hua Chen

Department and Graduate School of Industrial Design,
National Yunlin University of Science and Technology,
Douliou 64002, Yunlin, Taiwan, R.O.C.
wongjj@yuntech.edu.tw, catpollen@gmail.com

Abstract. This study attempts to explore the female life history embedded in the sewing machines. This study examines the experience of women in Taiwan of different periods to use sewing machines through the historical studies and qualitative research, which can be used as historical supplement of women users and relevant products that have long been neglected in design, but also reflect numerous mysteries in modern design through their experience.

Keywords: Sewing machine · Science · Technology and society (STS) · Design history · Feminism

1 Introduction

The chain-stitch single-thread sewing machine manufactured by Thomas Saint in 1790 was generally considered to be the earliest sewing machine prototype (Lewton 1930), but this machine was not put into mass production. Subsequently, other investors such as Barthelemy Thimonnier, Walter Hunt, Elias Howe, Allen B. Wilson, Isaac Merrit Singer and James EA Gibbs gradually improved the lockstitching ways, driving devices and appearance of the sewing machines, and mass produced such machines as merchandises. However, the early sewing machines were expensive, so only the tailor-made tailoring shops and clothing factories would buy them, while the housewives still insisted on handstitching.

In the mid-19th century, manufacturers in the Western society began to innovate sewing machines, and promoted the machines to ordinary families, so the sewing machines were promoted earlier than washing machines and television sets. Singer Corporation started to sell sewing machines to housewives in installments in 1856 for the first time in the United State where tons of sewing machine manufacturers competed fiercely. In order to remove the stereotype of the general public that women were not good at operating machines, the manufacturers specially arranged skilled women to demonstrate the ways to use the machines in the display window (Fig. 1). Besides, in order to distinguish the sew machines from the production equipment used in the workplace, merchants began to add fine engravings and decorations to the surface of the machines, which eliminated the link between sewing machines and labor

© Springer International Publishing AG 2017
P.-L. P. Rau (Ed.): CCD 2017, LNCS 10281, pp. 469–481, 2017.
DOI: 10.1007/978-3-319-57931-3_37

Fig. 1. A woman operating the sewing machine (Source: http://quilting.about.com/od/vintagesewing machines/ig/Sewing-in-Women-s-History/Sewing-on-Singer-Machine–1860.htm)

oppression and successfully promoted household sewing machines in the U.S. market (Forty 1986).

Singer Corporation originally adopted the same technique to market sewing machines all over the world, and promoted that this technology was suitable for women through the patterns showing women worldwide operated the sewing machines. The early trademark of Singer's sewing machines is presented in Fig. 2. Behind the bright red letter 'S' was a lady operating a sewing machine, which clearly indicated the relationship between the sewing machine and women and meant that this product was given a specific gender implication. Nonetheless, this conflicted with the phenomenon where most of the tailors were men in China back then. For the ordinary people, it surprised them to learn from women about how to operate a machine, which forced Singer to withdraw from the Chinese market (Yuan 2009). In the India's sales experience, since the local traditional women's clothing hardly needed sewing, the initial consumer market targeted at the colonial British women. It was not until the modern fashion were introduced into India that people started to wear suits and the sewing machines were gradually used (Arnold 2013).

Fig. 2. The trademark of Singer's sewing machine in the 19th century. (Color figure online) (Source: https://sites.google.com/site/singerhomesewingmachine/)

Until 1914, sewing machines had always been the first durable goods for mass production and consumption and were widely distributed around the world (Godley 2001). Even if manufacturers did not deliberately promote the sale of Western-style clothing by selling sewing machines, suits and dresses still swept the world with modern symbols (Ferguson 2011). At the beginning of the 20th century, affected by the Japanese colonial government's promotion of modernization and Westernization, Taiwan elites increased their needs for suits in order to change the Qing Dynasty styles, and the use of sewing machines and teaching of foreign tailoring started to be introduced (Chen 2009). Yet, most of the sewing machines were imported at that time, and the majority of people could not afford them. It was until the Recovery of Taiwan, the sewing machines began gaining popularity.

Sewing has long been considered as domestic labour and has often been the most experience in women's life history. Sewing machines were included in the life history of women in Taiwan, coupled with family modernization. Most of sewing-related technology and cultural transmission were classified as women's fields. Therefore, along with the gender stereotype, the sewing machine was given a particular social significance. For example, the sewing machines used to be one of the essential items for women's dowry in Taiwan. Additionally, the sewing machine also found its way into household thanks to the national policy of advancing economic development.

In the 1960s and 1970s, the garment industry in Taiwan saw a rapid growth, with many rural girls joining the read-to-wear production lines. By the 1980s, read-to-wear clothing had been very popular in the domestic market and the sewing clothes were no longer necessary housework. Moreover, in 1987, the garment industry gradually declined (Cheng 2010). Also, the read-to-wear sub-contract manufacturing was no longer a common family economic production activity, so the sewing machine had lost its status of essential household supplies. In the 1990s, in response to the changes in consumer trends, the sewing machine manufacturers integrated the sewing peripheral products and talent teaching, and introduced the leisure use modes from Japan, Europe and the United States, reinvigorating the domestic sewing machine market (Economic Daily News 1994). As a result, the sewing machine was given a specific cultural significance with the role of women in society. The sewing machine was originally created as a utensil to emancipate women from heavy manual sewing, but the experience of women in Taiwan in using the sewing machine unfolded a history that they were given different social roles in different stages by the country and based on specific goals. If the evolution of products originates from people's material desire and imagination, will such imagination lead them to foster new progressive values in the changing times? In fact, the existing social structure is not challenged, but are the patriarchal system's expectations and imprisonment of gender role repeatedly reproduced? Moreover, what is the role of designers in the historical process of role evolution in struggles of different ideologies?

In view of these, this study reviewed the form evolution of sewing machines in different periods and the meaning of sewing machines in Taiwan women's life history. Apart from using as the historical supplement to the female users and their related products that are long been ignored in the design history, this study also reflected on a host of mysteries in the contemporary design through their experience in using the sewing machines.

2   Design History Filled with Gender Mysteries

Feminist design historians have noted that the existing writing of design history was suppressed by the patriarchal society and intentionally or unintentionally ruled out the contribution of women or considered their activities unimportant. The design historian Attfield (1990) thought that in terms of the problems studied by the mainstream design history, for one thing, one is the methodological paranoia — The recording and selection generally focused on men, while women were the observed objects only. For another, this gender stereotype was derived from the concept of rigid binary opposi-tions, resulting in every confidence in the structure that "male-culture-exchange value" was superior to "female-nature-use value".

The design historian Buckley (1986) pointed out by dismantling the framework of patriarchy and capitalism that the traditional design history was often accompanied by the viewpoints of Western white male elites and concentrated on science and tech-nology, industrial mass production and modernist aesthetics and activities. By contrast, hand-made products, handicrafts or decorations were classified as pre-modern activities and were belittled. The craft was thereby expelled from the design history, and women engaging the craft design were concealed in the design history. Besides, when women were educated, they were often thought to be more suitable for development in the latter field, so they were rejected from the industrial system, leading them to be con-stant in a non-mainstream position, which is the representation of social ideology suggested by Goodall (1990). Since women could not enter in the corridors of power, it was difficult for them to address the unequal treatment in the design activities. Con-sequently, the seemingly objective and neutral design history is in fact rooted in the society's established stereotypes and rationalizes people's behavior. These deep-rooted constraints also affect the design studies on which topics are worth exploring and how they are conducted.

Aside from the asymmetry of research methods and objects, Julier, the scholar of design culture studies also pointed out the limitations of design (2013). In order to effectively mark the design as a kind of lifework, most of the design history writings adopt the linear history theory established by Nikolaus Pevsner, the founding father of design history, and coupled with particular products and changes in styles, create the so-called "canon of design" in order to justify the professional form of design. When the modernist aesthetic paradigm demonstrates its orthodox status with specific items, chairs also become necessary works which today's designers use to be remembered. Compared with other products, chairs were more easily referred to as "design classics", so design history was also often regarded as the history of a series of lofty chairs (Sudjic 2009). Those that are closely related to daily life such as sewing machines were rarely found in the writings of design history. Besides, the periodic international fur-niture exhibitions, as well as labels of star designers also drove such design discussions to stagnation. Also, objects were packaged as empty symbols to meet the specific values, separated from the real society and hence lost wild vitality (Attfield 2000).

The above-mentioned discussions not only point out the unconscious "sex blind-ness" of the design history and give rise to increasingly restricted subject matters of writing, but also expose the research dilemma from the female point of view: First, due to the disregard of mainstream studies, the activities concerning women are less documented. Second, since material culture, physical experience or other information is less adopted, women's unique culture and experience are often marginalized. Buckley (1998) used oral history and family albums to review the history of women's clothing in this family and found that women were able to redefine themselves and build self-identity through designing clothes. Unlike the official government records or statistics, video and audio data offer dynamic information, not only allow us to have a new understanding of women's experience, but to reflect on and probe into the existing research.

The design scholar Whiteley (1993) published *Design for society* and sorted out relevant theories and movements criticizing consumerism. Among them, the feminist point of view revealed the problem of consumption dominance: Besides conveying the meaning of products by constantly objectifying women, the presence of female users was long neglected. Such male-centered design consciousness often lacked the female unique socialization knowledge system, so that design was considered as a means of consumerism and the social need was undervalued.

Design theory re-established a link with the society through exchanges with different ideas. Some design historians also attempted to get rid of the discussions that specific works and designers' individual will were centered on by mainstream design historian, which could rather be the elements of change of time (Forty 1986). No more do they create legends by dazzling design under the spotlight, but placing the design in daily life and thus see the magnificent era of waves. This not only removes the limitations of research into the previous design history, and also enables the marginalized issues to be noted.

In respect of sewing machines, there are newly arising issues: the major sewing technology innovations are not made in Taiwan, but what is the significance of such a technological object when used in Taiwan society after the manufacturers' technology transfer and agent selling? How did this modern technology developed in the advanced industrial countries enter Taiwan? Sewing machines, as a production tool, are used in paid work, unpaid domestic work, and even self-creation, but are placed in home which is not regarded as a "production site". How does it find its way into home? How do the sewing machines interact and connect with Taiwan women's life experience? Moreover, how are the gender consciousness hidden behind the scientific and technical materials connected to the special historical context of Taiwan society?

3 Sewing Machines Embedded in Local Context

3.1 Sewing Machines as a Mechanism for Transformation of Traditional Women's Virtues into Modern Values

By inspecting the historical accounts of traditional Chinese culture, all handicrafts such as sewing, embroidery, weaving, spinning and knitting were included in needlework (Chang 1998). Needlework not only reflected the gender labor under the social division of labor that "men do farm work and women weave", but can be used as a standard for women's virtues. According to the four virtues specified in the *Lessons for Women*, apart from expecting women to speak and act cautiously and to maintain their appearance, needlework was even used to judge the women's talent and morality and the housekeeping ability (Mann 1997).

The education for women during the Japanese Occupation Period also exerted a significant influence. Under the influence of Westernization, the Japanese colonial government realized the importance of education to the prosperity of a country, and women's education was fundamental to promoting education. Therefore, through a series of courses about becoming a good wife and loving mother, women were trained to play the roles of assisting their husband, doing housework and educating young children. In 1897, the Japanese government opened the Women's Faculty Affiliated to the Mandarin Language School for Taiwanese women between the ages of 8 and 30. The tailoring courses were run for women only (Fig. 3) and helped them to gain a place among the tailoring masters dominated by men. This measure was closely related to the fact that more women than men engaged in foreign tailoring in Taiwan afterwards and that women would learn tailoring in the tailor masters' or tutoring classes before marriage (Chen 2009).

Fig. 3. Tailoring classes at Daitotei Women's School (Source: Special exhibition entitled her history in Taiwan)

3.2   Logistics Women Soldiers for Anti-communism and Restoration

At the beginning of Recovery, in order to meet the overall strategic objectives of the country — counterattack on mainland China and recovery of lost territory, women were mobilized as wartime reserves. Women's federations were set up across the country and encouraged women to make use of their skills and make their due contribution, such as sewing military uniforms, laundry, relief, writing letters, consoling soldiers and their families in order to boost morale and achieve the overall objectives of anti-communism and resistance against Russia (United Daily News 1952a).

Besides, in order to help settle down the military dependents who came to Taiwan with the Koumintang Government and lacked the means to earn a living and related equipment, shelters nationwide gradually run sewing workshops and establish sewing factories (Fig. 4). The military dependents could sew military uniforms and get enough food in the shelters, and could receive ideological education at work (United Daily News 1952b). In addition, in order to improve the economic levels of people in Taiwan, local governments and farmers' associations also gradually granted loans

Fig. 4. Madame Chiang visited the sewing factory for military dependents (Source: http://www.igotmail.com.tw/home/33935)

for purchasing sewing machines and encouraged farmers to engage in family side job (United Daily News 1953). Besides, the shelters took in unfortunate adopted daughters or prostitutes and taught them sewing techniques so that they could be self-sufficient, or prepare them for a normal marriage (United Daily News 1955). Promoting women's operation of sewing machines, apart from increasing personal or household income, could also enhance the overall national recovery strength. Due to the active guidance of the Koumintang Government, the effects of promoting sewing to women were remarkable.

3.3   Invisible Driver of Economic Boom — Women in Garment Factories

The 1960s and 1970s witnessed booming development of Taiwan's garment industry, and many rural girls left farm work behind and worked in factories and engaged in the sewing garment industry (Fig. 5). This boom could be observed from the recruitment notices in the news-paper and numerous sewing work-shops (Cheng 2010). Women passively or actively threw themselves into the production lines. In addition to earning more money compared with working in rural areas, this also reflected that women at that time started to have opportunities to walk away from family and into the workplace used to be regarded as "men's exclusive domain".

Fig. 5. Early garment factory in Taiwan (Source: http://favorlang.blogspot.tw/2012/08/blog-post_246.html)

In addition, the government pulled out all the stops to mobilize housewives who could not work outside and included their surplus labor into national economy. In 1972, Tung-min Hsieh, chairman of Taiwan Province, put forward the slogan that "living room as factory", established "family production" and appealed to housewives to make full use of idle time at home to engage in family side job in a bid to boost family income and national productivity. Sewing garments with sewing machines was often one of the options for home sub-contract manufacturing. (Economic Daily News 1972; Central News Agency 1972)

In 1975, Chairman Hsieh was against the custom of extravagant weddings and proposed a new dowry idea of "one machine and two boxes". The so-called "one machine" referred to the sewing machine (United Daily News 1975), which demonstrated the significance of economic production tool. This also means that the sewing technology of women in this period was linked to the global labor market from unpaid domestic work. Even if women gained the opportunity to be economically independent due to sewing, they became the cheap labor required by the provision of transnational capital for the purpose of national economic development without any policy protection.

Quality yet inexpensive products of the domestic read-to-wear clothing was favored by the global market and the export peaked in 1987. Subsequently, since 1985, the NT exchange rate continued to increase, producing an adverse impact on export. Because of wage increases and labor fluctuations, coupled with sluggish read-to-wear market in America in 1988, the garment industry in Taiwan gradually declined. The labor which had long depended on the traditional industries started to separate itself from the manufacturing sector, and then flew to the service industry or financial investment. The garment industry became the victim of this wave of industrial transformation. The sharp decrease in Read-to-wear sub-contract manufacturing orders also changed the usage pattern of the home sewing machines.

3.4   From Labor to Leisure

Now, sewing machines are no longer the first choice when daughters get married, and most housewives no longer need to earn extra money with the sewing machines. Instead, women can step out of the house and devote themselves to various workplaces. In the end of the 1980s, thanks to the improvements in the overall domestic economic level, the sewing machines started to be included in the recreational tools "do-it-yourself" (DIY). Such transition could be seen from the 1986 "First DIY Exhibition of the Republic of China" (Economic Daily News 1986). The sewing machine manufacturers allowed consumers to learn and use the machines through product distribution stores, materials, tools, reference books and courses and other services. In this way, the consumers did not need to travel to shops, cloth stores and classrooms, thereby enhancing the interest in learning (Economic Daily News 1994). The sewing skills which were bound to lose reemerged in leisure activities. However, when the sewing changed from the basic needs of daily life to creative or leisure activities, women were often troubled by assuming family responsibility and pursuing personal interest. They needed to live up to the expectations of family members but also fought with such expectations. Moreover, this scene was 20 years later than the scene first described by manufacturers' advertising.

Singer Corporation in Taiwan once used American-style promotion techniques of offering teaching in case of a sewing machine in the 1970s magazine advertising (Fig. 6). Nonetheless, in contrast to the real situations in which women used sewing machines at the time, most women sew other people's clothes, read-to-wear sub-contract manufacturing, at home (Fig. 7). Even the real models used by them were not the household sewing machines produced by Taiwan sewing machine manufacturers, but were a kind of industrial sewing machines called lockstitch machines. The development of Taiwan's sewing machine industry breaks away from people's daily life experience precisely reveals the invisible beauty and sorrow behind the reputation of Taiwan as the king of sewing machines.

Fig. 6. Singer sewing machine advertisement (Source: The Woman, November 1971)

Fig. 7. "Living room as factory" — Read-to-wear processing at home (Source: *Century-old life in Taiwan*)

4   Conclusion and Suggestion

4.1   Constantly Changing Social Significance of Sewing Machines in Use

In the early days, sewing machines were used as Taiwan's post-war strategic products and found their way into family, which mainly resulted from the living needs and the national mobilization policy at that time. The mutually beneficial relationship between the users and the industry was established thereby. Such a relationship worsened in the 1960s when the policy was shifted to be export-oriented. With the foreign technical guidance, the household sewing machines expected the users to have such product appeals as advanced countries' lifestyles, lightweight, convenient storage and multi-functional. This differed from the expectations of the ordinary sub-contract manufacturing users in Taiwan at that time. Therefore, the single-function, fast and durable industrial sewing machines entered into families.

With the transformation of economic structure and improvement in national living standards, no longer are sewing activities women's necessary daily tasks, and they do not need to diligently pedal the sew machines in order to support the family. Yet, women's sewing is often considered to pass the time, and is not an artistic leisure activity.

Since the domestic market demand is not heavy, there is a gap between production and consumption. In order to expand business, manufacturers drew on the sales experience of Japan, Europe and the United States and changed the sew machines from production tools to leisure facilities so that the demand for household sewing machines increased in the local market. Even so, the sales of sewing machines in the domestic market rebounded slightly, but the domestic need cannot exceed 5%, as shown in Table 1.

Table 1. Characteristics of Taiwan female users and sewing machines in different times

Time	1930s to 1950s	1960s to 1980s	1990s to present
Women's employment types	Agriculture, forestry, fishery and husbandry	Manufacturing	Services
User characteristics	Basic skills of women	Home sub-contract manufacturing mothers	Leisure hobby creators
Work contents	Make clothes for friends and family, earn extra money and sew military uniforms	Read-to-wear sub-contract manufacturing, or manufacturing of other processed products such as: backpacks and dolls	Personal leisure creation
Work demands	Meet the basic needs of life	Able to cope with large orders for delivery, durable and fast products	Select sewing machines based on personal needs
Common tool types	Foot-type household sewing machines	Industrial sewing machines: Lockstitch machines, overlock machines and embroidery machines	Electric, electronic or computer-type household sewing machines and industrial sewing machines
Tools are regarded as	Daily necessities	Production tools	Creative tools

4.2 Invisible Labor/Value

Household sewing machines started to have a specific form in the 1860s in order to distinguish from the equipment used by workers and integrate into home decorations. In this regard, Forty (1986) believed that after the industrial revolution, work was gradually separated from family activities to factories and that home was simply for rest. This way of change separated production and males to the workplace, while the homeplace became the place for women's consumption and providing reproduction. Techniques associated with women like cooking, knitting, embroidery or sewing are generally regarded as the gifts that naturally came to women or the products of family duties but without value.

Wajcman (1996) criticized the patriarchy-dominated science and technology opinions, and held that the knowledge associated with science and technology was still mastered by men. Even if women worked in the workplaces which were initially monopolized by men, they were still assigned to the most basic, labor-based jobs. The study of Collins (2002) further revealed that the value system associated with technology was actually declared with the society's evaluation of gender. In other words, there was gender difference in the standards of capitalist market economy for labor value.

This sewing production line in Taiwan also extends from factories to families, and includes housewives. When the country strove to mobilize surplus labor to pursue economic growth, families became invisible factories in the informal economy and women in the family became the engaged but invisible labor.

The female labor in the family is certainly does not have 'the exchange value' in the capitalist operation but is given social functions. When implementing the policy that "living room as factory", Tung-min Hsieh further explained that encouraging women to engage in home sub-contract manufacturing was not designed to earn money but to develop their hard-working habits. Apart from calling on women in the family to become workers, this strategy also conveyed the instruction that "business is virtuous but idleness is evil" in order to hone housewives' ability to manage the household industriously and thriftily. The government mobilized housewives to engage in economic production activities, and also advocated mothers to maintain social and family virtues.

4.3 Recommendations for Follow-up Study — Study on Local User Experience of Sewing Machines

This study not only shows the influence of sewing machines on the social role shift of women in Taiwan, but also demonstrates there is still gender inequality in the topics of science and technology. The development process as a backward industrial country and the fixed sub-contract manufacturing role of domestic household sewing machine industry cause the needs of local users not to be the main reference subjects of industrial design. This suggests that women in backward industrialized countries are still at a disadvantage in the topics of capitalism and science and technology.

Sewing machines, as a pioneer of family modernization, also profoundly changed the world's clothing habits, besides changing the contents of female housework. When women generally no longer have to make clothes, sewing techniques are no longer passed down as in the old days. The knowledge system associated with sewing activities is gradually collapsing. This activity internalized as physical practice may eventually be "deskilled". When people enjoy the convenience of scientific and technological progress, they, nevertheless, also forgot their own cultural characteristics and values. The scientific and technological development without integrating the local use experience will render the originally diverse and creative activities homogeneous, unified and lifeless.

Acknowledgement. This research is part of Ministry of Science and Technology, Republic of China and National Yunlin University of Science and Technology granted project. (MOST 103-2410-H-224-036).

References

Arnold, D.: Everyday Technology: Machines and the Making of India's Modernity. The University of California Press, Chicago (2013)

Attfield, J.: Form/female follows function/male: feminist critiques of design. In: Walker, J.A. (ed.) Design History and the History of Design, pp. 199–225. Pluto press, Massachusetts (1990)

Attfield, J.: Wild Things: The Material Culture of Everyday Life. Berg, Oxford (2000)

Buckley, C.: Made in patriarchy: toward a feminist analysis of women and design. Des. Issues 3(2), 3–14 (1986)

Buckley, C.: On the margins: theorizing the history and significance of making and designing clothes at home. Des. Hist. 11(2), 157–171 (1998)

Central News Agency: Living room as factory, Tung-min Hsieh called housewives to engage in side job to increase income, August 1972

Chang, D.Y.: Chinese Needlework: The Art of Mothers. Han Sheng, Taipei (1998)

Chen, P.T.: Transforming traditional Taiwanese costumes into modern western costumes (1985-1970). Unpublished master's thesis, Feng Chia University, Taichung (2009)

Cheng, H.S.: The Mother's Six-Decade Career in yōsai (Dressmaking). Ink., New Taipei (2010)

Collins, J.L.: Mapping a global labor market: gender and skill in the globalizing garment industry. Gend. Soc. 16(6), 921–940 (2002)

Economic Daily News: Living room as factory, Tung-min Hsieh called housewives to engage in side job to increase income, August 1972

Economic Daily News: The first DIY exhibition opened yesterday and draw a large crowd, October 1986

Economic Daily News: A rigorous marketing campaign of the sewing machines rejuvenated this business, May 1994

Ferguson, N.: Civilization: The West and the Rest. Penguin, New York (2011)

Forty, A.: Objects of Desire: Design and Society Since 1750. Thames and Hudson, New York (1986)

Godley, A.: Selling the sewing machine around the world: Singer's international marketing strategies, 1850–1914. Res. Econ. Hist. 20, 1–45 (2001)

Goodall, P.: Design and gender: where is the heart of the home? Built Environ. **16**(4), 269–278 (1990)

Julier, G.: The Culture of Design, 3rd edn. Sage, Los Angeles (2013)

Lewton, F.L.: The Servant in the House— A Brief History of the Sewing Machine. Smithsonian Institution, Washington (1930)

Mann, S.: Precious Records: Women in China's Long Eighteenth Century. Stanford University Press, Stanford (1997)

Sudjic, N.: The Language of Things. Penguin, London (2009)

United Daily News: On the female mobilization from the viewpoint of defense — to celebrate the Forty-Third International Woman's Day, March 1952a

United Daily News: The two years of the branch of National Women's League of the R.O.C. in General Political Department, May 1952b

United Daily News: To buy her a sewing machine to celebrate Woman's Day; Penghu County will hand out sewing machines, March 1953

United Daily News: Help prostitutes and child brides regain their freedom through skill training, job placement, or matchmaking, May 1955

United Daily News: Chairman Hsieh promoted the new concept about dowry; changing the '4 gold' to '2 boxes' to fulfill the duty of good wife and mother, May 1975

Yuan, R.: The sewing machines and the social transformation of contemporary Shanghai (1858–1949). Unpublished doctoral dissertation, Fudan University, Shanghai (2009)

Wajcman, J.: The technology of production: making a job of gender. In: Wajcman, J. (ed.) Feminism Confronts Technology, pp. 27–53. The Pennsylvania State University Press, Pennsylvania (1996)

Whiteley, N.: Design for Society. Reaktion Books, London (1993)

The Design Thinking Leading to Different Levels of Change: Example of the Togo Village in Southern Taiwan

Cecile Ching-yi Wu[✉]

Department of Adult and Continuing Education,
National Taiwan Normal University, Taipei City, Taiwan
Muse2015@gmail.com

Abstract. This article explores the design thinking of a design team that forges social innovation for a rural community through the in-depth case study of the Togo village in Southern Taiwan. The research method is based on the analysis of interviews, field observation notes and documents. In this article, I first review the shift of design thinking focus, the search for innovation in rural areas and Brown's perspective of design thinking. Then, from the perspective of Scharmer's Theory U, I describe the transformative process of Togo in terms of four levels of design thinking and change. Their design thinking involves a personal and collective inquiry from the outer world to the inner world, tapping into the source of their purposes and crystallizing their vision in the prototype. The study reveals the importance of exploring inwardly the source of purpose and the highest potential instead of focusing on the surface of the problems, proposing strategies or methods to foster creative solutions.

Keywords: Design thinking · Theory U · Co-design · Co-creation · Social innovation

1 Role of Design in a Complex Changing World

1.1 Shift of Design Thinking Focus

Many aspects of design thinking (psychology, neuroscience, aesthetic, methodology, management) are studied and anchored in a long history of social science research. Design thinking has been evolving from the perspective of "design for optimization" in 1970s to that of "design for possibility" in 1990s, from problem solving orientation to problem restructuring orientation (Li 2002). Simon (1969) represents the optimized perspective which probes comprehensive understanding of the problem and rational analytical process before designing solutions while the design for possibility is in the same vein of D. Schon's reflection-in-action which emphasizes the dialogue with the situation and early solution finding. Contrast to design for optimization, the possibility design perspective is hermeneutic and open to possibility exploration which encompasses more uncertainty and conflict (Li 2002).

In the modernist world, the fragmentation and segmentation of knowledge keep the us from thinking in an integral way (Wilber 1998). Brown (2009) contends the

© Springer International Publishing AG 2017
P.-L.P. Rau (Ed.): CCD 2017, LNCS 10281, pp. 482–494, 2017.
DOI: 10.1007/978-3-319-57931-3_38

designers are in general not invoked until the planning decision is made rather than from the beginning of a plan. Designers are used to serve to make up a product. However, today the world changes rapidly and complicatedly, the challenges demand the designers to react with integral and multi-disciplined perspectives. Designers' roles cannot be confined in the expertise of product, industrial or architectural design but imply a whole and integral concern about the context of design and cross-disciplinary links. Furthermore, it is futile to only depend on design experts to develop solutions for us (Banathy 1996). More and more cases have witnessed the successful co-creation between the design experts and stakeholders in a co-design or co-creative way. Scharmer (2009) proposes, in order to solicit profound change and innovation, the design team and people need to redirect their attention toward the inner knowing, exploring the source of the deeper purposes and collective vision as well as to crystalize their will for the realization of change.

1.2 In Search of Rural Innovation

Today, many problems intertwined in the rural communities demand the re-design of the system. Since the economic boom in Taiwan in 1970s, the uneven structure between agricultural production and selling, and the inclination for industrial development have resulted in young labor outflow and aging that leave abandoned houses and lack of vitality in the villages. Consequently, the rural areas stay far from changes.

Taiwan government has been implementing several policies such as the Community-Building Policy for two decades or Rural Regeneration Policy from 2010 in order to reinvigorate the villages. However, two major difficulties are eminent. Firstly, the financial and human resources supported by the government have been reducing. Secondly, the communication between the elitist designers and the villagers is ineffective (Li 2007). The community-building policy notably favored architectural and landscape professionals to design for the local organizations without really empowering the people. In most of the community-building cases in Taiwan, the designers are paid to do the design for the local people. They may conduct some discussions with the people or design with them. Then the designers hang over a final project or drawings that the residents unnecessarily follow. But, it happens repeatedly when the designers finish the work for the community, the residents are not capable to continue to develop. Especially in the rural context, the residents are not credited with design literacy and capacity to talking about design with the experts to the extent that the residents become indifferent to the design that concerns their future. The absence of the participation of the users who are affected by the design is due to the fact they are not encouraged and guided to express their opinions and to cultivate their literacy and capacity of design (Banathy 1996). Since the transformation of a community takes time and requires long-term engagement, few are the designers who keep engaged and deepen its change.

Nevertheless, nowadays some designers all over the world involve themselves in searching alternative solutions for rural reinvigoration, to the extent they also inspire the general public to join the action. The case presented here is one of these instances: a group of young designers devote themselves in transforming a declining rural village into an cultural and ecologically sustainable village in Southern Taiwan.

I intend to analyze the Togo design team's design thinking that leads to changes and innovation in different levels, and reflect on the design thinking linking to social innovation. In line with the perspective of Scharmer's Theory U, I describe the process of the transformation of the village, how the design team coped with the residents and explored the alternatives leading to the emerging future.

In the following discussion, firstly, I conduct a critical review on Brown's design thinking discourse, then I discuss design thinking from the perspective of Scharmer's Theory U. In the Sect. 4, I analyze the Togo design team's design thinking leading to different levels of change and the kernel of design thinking leading to innovation.

2   In Search of Design Thinking Leading to Innovation

2.1   Tim Brown's View of Design Thinking

The twentieth century witnessed the stalemate of the problem-solving mode based on logical analysis and scientific rationality. Many attempts of design thinkers have been dedicated to free from the domination of the scientific rationality analytic mode of thinking. They advocate the value and uniqueness of "designerly" way of thinking or design thinking, such as Cross in the 1990s and Brown in 2009 among the others. Brown (2008) argues that design can transform problems into opportunities. So designers should exert their particular way of thinking by participating in the process of product innovation from the beginning. He regards design thinking as human-centered, and the generation of design thinking as an interaction among three spaces: Inspiration, Ideation and Implementation. Brown (2009) also emphasizes to make creative idea into prototype as early as possible and to evolve the idea to be more desirable, feasible, and viable, instead of pursuing fully analysis and description of the problems before taking any action.

Brown's design thinking emphasizes users' needs by exploring the social context of users (2009). However, needs come from the unsatisfied desire and often negative emotions driven by terror, hate, rupture or fright. The design that satisfies the needs of people is to fulfill the unsatisfied desires is far from really changing the existing state. Brown suggests learning from the extremes so as to stretch designers' thinking beyond assumptions and to get bolder ideas. Nevertheless, as one's observation and thinking mode are framed by his belief and judgement that guide his knowing, a designer can hardly truly understand the users without being aware of that impact. Whereas Brown's approach proposes mainly a methodology or strategies rather than questions the patterns of thinking that allow designers and users to go beyond old thinking, his design thinking methodology is probably hindered in dealing with social system changes which involve more mindset and behavior transformation.

Senge's (1994) iceberg metaphor of mental functioning shows that we often focus on finding common signs or structures of events or phenomena, and then re-structure and redesign activities and details while ignoring that the assumptions and taken for granted beliefs that frame our reasoning and action are the very key to solve problems.

Therefore, the real and profound innovation relies not on the modification or redesign in work process or methods, but on the transformation of the mindsets, assumptions, beliefs and values. Creative thinking is to re-frame the problem and to see the world in a new light (Li 2002).

Then, how do the designers who intend to be creative and innovative transform their thinking? How do they touch the source of collective action linking to the emerging future?

2.2   The Different Levels of Change of Scharmer's Theory U

Scharmer interviewed in a MIT project with 150 prominent entrepreneurs, scholars and NGO leaders their empirical experiences about innovation and collective transformation for organization, he discovers that the real and profound change comes basically from the individual and collective internal awareness and inquiry to the deep source of self which links to an emerging future. The evolution of the internal process is symbolized in the U-shaped movements. The key to innovation is not novelty in strategy or process, but the intrinsic qualities of the leader and designer (their purpose, beliefs, and values), and where his attention is focused. According to the different focus of attention and inner awareness that leaders have, they will lead their actions into changes of four levels, from external to internal:

1. **Focus: surfacing on the current reality.** Facing the challenges, one focuses on what he perceives or the surface of the facts that he sees. His diagnosis of the problem comes from his knowledge, taken-for-granted thought and values. Thus, the change is to adjust the structure and mode of operation, resulting in the re-structuring of the system.
2. **Broadening: perceiving other perceptions.** When one "opens his mind" and exchange views with others, he extends his personal point of view. "Open mind" means to rationally analyze other thoughts and broaden one's sensing perspective. As long as one suspend his judgement and knowledge, he'll release inner space to let new perception enter in, so to perceive different perspectives.
3. **Deepening: dialogue and surfacing deep assumptions.** Like Brown, Scharmer also emphasizes on empathy in observation and listening in the field, but Scharmer highlights above all the awareness of our downloading way of thinking that shapes our knowledge and judgement. The complexity of problems arises from the wrestling of different points of views. Only when people temporarily suspend their views and see from others' eyes, they get aware of the assumptions and values behind their own knowledge and judgement. After this reflection, people may escape from the original thinking frame and find new possibilities. "Open heart" helps us to redirect our attention, to shift our attention from personal self to the field of bigger Self, and makes us feel connected with each other as a whole. Deep and empathetic understanding is possible through numerous rounds of open and equal dialogues among the different stakeholders. Deep dialogue leads to re-frame the problems and thus generate new ideas. This echoes the "design dialogue" concepts that Jenlink and Banathy (2008) posit for changing social systems.

4. **Purpose: exploring the source of our commitment and creativity.** One redirects his attention "from the 'exterior' to the 'interior' by turning the attention toward the source of the mental process rather than the object (Scharmer 2009)".

When the attention turns internally, one probably experiences some period of reflective retreat, letting go the old and unessential things. He will feel integrated into the whole and link with his deepest source by asking himself "Who am I?" and "Why do I do it?". Scharmer calls this experience "presencing" which is a threshold of letting go old thinking and accepting new ideas, linking to one's highest potential. Here, "open will" helps to clarify and crystalize one's purpose and vision. Then, one will commit to embody the vision and creative ideas in action by making rapid prototype in the real world to test, evaluate, modify iteratively. It needs the integration of brain, heart and will. The realization keeps evolving with the change of the environment.

2.3   Research Questions

Following Scharmer's line of thought, this study intends, through the case study of Togo village, to explore the design team's design thinking throughout their transformative process. I focus on the following questions:

- What have been the challenges that the Togo design team encountered? What kind of design thinking has the design team responded to these challenges and what are the results?
- What are the different levels of design thinking and changes that lead to the social innovation in Togo Village?

3   Research Methods and Introduction to the Case Togo

3.1   Qualitative Research and Case Study Approach

This study explores the experiences of the design team in the transformation of Togo village and reflects on their design thinking. This study follows the principles of qualitative research by means of the case study approach through field observation, in-depth interviews and document analysis from January 2015 to January 2016. I chose to perform case study of Togo village for several reasons. A case study approach helps to draw the boundaries of inquiry precisely around the system of action performed by Togo design team and the residents, and to look at it as a whole. This approach also highlights in-depth investigation in a real-life, natural context, and the interaction between the agents and the social historical context, affording external validity for the findings (Yin 2008). Moreover, Togo's transformation of more than a decade offers rich historical and current information about the challenges that rural communities face when they conduct a change. Finally, Togo is still evolving so that some of the insights from this study may provide them with follow-up development reference, incorporated into their future design thinking.

3.2 Data Collection and Analysis

For primary data collection the technique of in-depth interviews with semi-structured script was adopted. Documents encompassed news reports, government documents, dissertations written by the designers, the Facebooks and websites of Togo Rural Village Art Museum and of the "Elegant Farmer" companies. The data of multiple sources, field notes, the transcription of interview recordings were examined and analyzed. The data analysis consist of coding that transforms data into concepts and categories, and then integrating the categories into a logical structure, forming the propositions or themes on the research phenomenon through continuing comparison between the concepts, categories and the existing theories. Case studies rely on a variety of sources, so the different data must converge and reach the same conclusion under triangulation (Yin 2008).

3.3 Introduction to the Togo Village

Togo is located in the northeast corner of the Houbi District of Tainan City in Southern Taiwan, which is the most important rice agricultural area in Taiwan. There are only 366 people per square kilometer (compared to Taipei City per square kilometer population of 9,918 people).

Since 2002, a handful of local middle-aged have initiated the community building by self-reliance building. From 2003 to 2010, successive young graduate school students of architectural arts proceeded their action researches in the Togo village under the principles of co-design. In the long process of communication and interaction between the designers and the villagers, they've established mutual trust and affection and evolved the mindsets through design participation and artistic involvement. Consequently, they not only revitalized the deserted village with collective artistic creation, but also triggered the vision and action to build a well-being community integrating creativity, arts, ecology and technology. After accomplishing their graduate degrees, the young designers returned to Togo village and run social enterprises and were elected as the core cadre of local association. Since 2012, the designers and residents have co-created the Togo Rural Village Art Museum which aims to explore the alternative way of living in the rural areas.

4   Research Findings and Discussion: Design Thinking Leading to Different Levels of Change

I present in the Fig. 1 the different levels of design thinking and changes of the design team along the transformative process of Togo village in terms of Scharmer's three tools for enhancing the capacities for exploring the source of the purpose and the highest potential, named "presencing", that is, from "open mind", "open heart" to "open will". On top of the three tools, I add the "open sense" that corresponds to the level1.

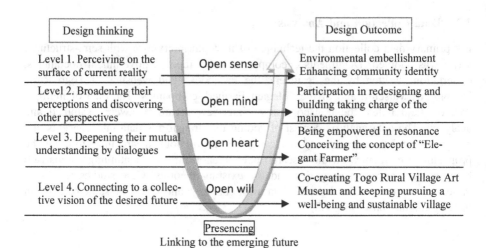

Fig. 1. The different levels of design thinking and outcome

4.1 "Open Sense" Perceiving on the Surface of the Current Reality

In 2002, the problems that the initiators of Togo local association faced encompassed the increasingly aging and solitude, abandoned houses, deserted dirty spots, discarded old farming tools, abandoned train tracks to be eradicated, resulting in the wipeout of local memory. The initiators of Togo village started up with cleaning and rearranging their neighborhood environment, such as planting trees along the main road, fixing the old discarded oxcarts and turning them to display agricultural products. At the beginning, indifference and cynicism from the neighbors here and there contrasted the volunteering action of the initiators and their families. However, their practice contributed to significant and visible changes in the environment, witnessed by the residents who waited and saw. Gradually, more and more residents recognized and joined the action. Even so, it was not easy to motivate the people to participate in public affairs. It often took several months to communicate and persuade a landlord to lend his land for free design and build.

In the past, due to the environmental pollution of their homeland, the residents felt shameful, now the tangible changes in the neighborhood made them feel hopeful and enhanced their community identity.

4.2 "Open Mind" Broadening Their Perceptions and Discovering Other Perspectives

(a) Collective Learning and Broadening the Perceptions

The design team organized several "learning journeys" aimed to broaden their perceptions and perspectives. They brought with them in-depth and purposeful inquiries through the visit of relevant but different community-building cases both in Taiwan and

Japan. The learning journey also offered opportunities for the residents to dialogue and imagine together about their community. The learning journey not only enhanced their knowledge about design communities, but also broadened their perspectives about agriculture, ecology and culture. For instance, a farmer of the design team gave up the conventional farming and learned organic farming because he connected to the right persons and resources, and witnessed the benefit of natural farming through the learning journeys.

The design team was mindful in guiding the farmers to observe and perceive what appealed to them as design. For example, the team offered each participant a polaroid camera asking them to shoot what they liked and found beautiful. After one week, when they met, each farmer were invited to share his pictures and the reasons why he chose to shoot. In this way, the designers gained insights about the farmers' preference of design.

(b) Introducing External Energy to Stimulate Imagination

The design team invited artists to work *in situ* and interacted with the residents in the attempt to broaden the residents' perceptions. They used buffalo as metaphor of the hard-working perseverance of elder farmers who adhered to the land and dedicated their lives to the cultivation. This spirit was embodied in the buffalo stone sculpture created by artist Jia-fu Hou, who worked in a park just along the primary road of Togo village that attracted the residents' curious observation and questions. These dialogues and interactions made the artist more aware of the interests of the residents. The insights he got about the farmers' childhood memory and their desire of transmission from a generation to the next generation were finally represented on the sculpture in the image of a child climbing on the back of the buffalo. However, each collaboration with artists didn't achieve the synergy between the artists and the villagers. Contrast to artist Hou, an iron sculptor insisted in completing the work in his private studio without communication with the villagers. When his sculpture was installed in the park, the residents could hardly tell the story about the artwork.

The interaction and dialogue between the artist and the residents not only extends the perception and perspectives of the residents, but also stimulates the artists to reflect on the relationship between artistic creation, men and the society.

(c) The Reflection-in-Action of the Young Design Team

Since 2004, successive graduate school students had joined in the design team, mainly adopting the approach of co-design. When entering in the field, they perceived very soon the gap between their expertise and the tangible practice preference in the rural world. Having perceived the decline of the traditional rural values, the young designers tried to evoke the public's attention through the action called "Building a House for the Buffalo". They called on young people to build a house for the last buffalo in Togo village. In this event, the young designers, despite the co-design concept, neglected to integrate the villagers into performing, leaving them to watch, nothing to do by the side. The young designers finally reflected on their multiple roles in the field, one of which was to guide and encourage the residents to contribute their knowledge and participation.

(d) **Translate Language and Images as Tools for Facilitating Mutual Understanding**

Following the co-design principles, the designers spent a lot of efforts in communicating with the residents and guiding the design. The designers must transform their expertise language into farmers' language, or used their own language to articulate things that interested the others (Young 2007). The three-dimensional sketches and rough scale models served as the most useful tools for the communication of the design concepts. However, unexpected misunderstanding and taboos made some construction unacceptable by the residents so that the designers redid it.

4.3   "Open Heart" Deepening Their Mutual Understanding by Dialogues

(a) **Suspend the Judgement and Redirect the Attention toward the Field**

The young designers couldn't really understand the villagers until they suspended their expertise and assumptions. They moved to live inside the village and interacted with the farmers during four years. Rather than analysis and reasoning, they observed and felt the whole rural context including the environment, the weather, the people, the culture, the colors, the smells, the sounds that orchestrated the particular atmosphere of the village. They also spent much time chatting with the elderly and building relationships based on trust and friendship to the extent they redirected their attention toward what the residents really cared. The old farmers and young designers dialogued and understood each other by "opening heart", that is, redirecting their attention to listen mindfully to the others.

(b) **Guiding Users to Become Designers through Company and Co-creation**

Artists and designers are required to incorporate elements familiar to local people into their artistic creation, such as red bricks, wood, stone as well as images of dragonflies, pigs and buffaloes. For example, when transforming the pig house into a cultural activity room, the design team succeeded in encouraging the seventy-year-old farmer, who had never taken a painting brush, to draw images of his familiar countryside. Through the expression of familiar local elements, the design team tried to guide the residents to appreciate the aesthetic value of rural objects, reestablishing their confidence and identity to their homeland. Furthermore, the playful and creative part of artistic work overturned the farmers' habitual ways of seeing and making, pushing them to step out boundary of habitual experience. Another example was the old cement artisan's self-transformation who engaged himself in searching for the fittest way to realize the design, letting go his habitual thinking on efficiency, and empathizing the designer's intention. They finally co-created an unconventional work. Besides, the working process of artist was accompanied and assisted by the residents, leading to the fusion of perspectives of the artists and the residents.

On the one hand, the designers and artists were ready to explain to the residents the reasons and stories, inviting them to open up heart to feel and accept new things, also enabling them to re-frame their local knowledge. On the other hand, these artists proposed to redefine the meaning of artistic creation. They accentuated the interaction and meaning-making between the art and people, social context rather than the conventional monologue mode of artists who sought the recognition of elite museums.

(c) The Bridge Between the Designers and the Farmers

The core members of the local association have played an essential role of bridge between the designers and the farmers in the co-designing and co-creating. They have been esteemed in the neighborhood for their altruistic action resulting in tangible changes for several years. In every event, they conducted a dialogue with the designers where everybody was equal, welcome and open to contribute his opinion. Then they decided in a collective way before mobilizing the other residents and implementation. Most importantly, the cross-generational team backed up each other when facing the farmers' refutation and supported mutually in organizing activities. In addition, since the designers lived within the village, the farmers frequently invited them to have lunch or dinner, taking care of them as if they had been their own family.

Contrast to general relationship between the designers and users, the young designers and the residents of Togo establish more profound relationship and friendship which serve as the key condition of the incubator environment that encourages and supports the free dialogue and creative idea to generate.

4.4 "Open Will" Connecting to a Collective Vision of the Emerging Future

(a) Exploring the Source of Their Purposes and Highest Potential

The young design team understood empathetically the happiness and sorrows of the farmers and the structural problems of agriculture because they interacted deeply with the residents and almost became a member of the community. Accordingly, they were motivated to change it, as the young designer Michael said "while proceeding small projects together, we have actually nurtured a bigger dream." In 2008, as sculptor Hou decided to immigrate into Togo, the young designers designed and built an alternative house for him. They named it "Togo Artist Hut" through which realized their dream of "residents become artists whereas artists become residents" embodied in the image of "elegant farmer". This idea resulted from the long process of intense interaction and trusty connection between the artists, designers and local people in the village of Togo. This "atmosphere" or "field" in the sense of Nonaka and Katsumi (2004/2006) provided the environment and opportunities that encouraged people's "inner knowing" to enact, so as to draw together the picture of their desired future.

Therefore, they fostered the purpose to transform the poor farmers into "elegant farmers" by means of new knowledge, technology and creativity. The new identity of "elegant farmer" involves the integral rural development in terms of cultural creative industries, agriculture and ecology. The vision is emerged from the design team's deep intention to create a new way of life in rural context, beyond personal interest, but looking for the possibility for a desired community as a whole.

(b) Retreat and Crystallization of Their Intention

In 2010, the young designers left Togo for fulfilling the citizen military service. This period meant a stage of retreat and reflection which kept them detached from the familiar environment, asking themselves "who am I?" and what they really desired to do in the future. Through this period of solitude and distance, they delved into the source of their purposes, the highest potential and unique competencies. As soon as they finished the one-year military service, they settled in Togo village and started five companies which provided service on landscape design, community building, environmental education and music creation at the same time they continued to realize the vision of the "elegant farmer".

(c) Rapidly Prototype Realization

In 2012, the design team proposed the idea of "Togo Rural Village Art Museum" and was supported by the local association. Despite lacking experiences and funds, they still did their best to carry out the project. Under the declaration "The village is an art museum; the art museum is the village; the houses display the exhibition whereas the rice field is the canvas; the farmer is the artist while the agricultural product is the art" (Togo Rural Culture Association 2013), the exhibits of the museum consisted of all the corners and pocket parks that they created during the past decade spreading in the village, the pastoral landscape and some artists' artwork. This "museum" challenged people's conception of arts, triggering them to sense the beauty of rural environment and the spirit of the farmers through chatting with them. As a result, this five month festive event surprisingly attracted thousands of visitors, numerous positive media reports and they finally made a profit for the first time.

(d) Evoking and Connecting to the Inspired People

The design team spreads their social innovative concepts and actions through social media, mainly their website and the Facebook. In 2011, the design team called on youth "to return to rural areas" and" to create an elegant farmer's homeland with art" by incorporating the youth's knowledge and creativity (Togo Rural Culture Association 2013). In the attempt to raise funds for the second year of the "Museum", they organized a "Farmer's Feast" party, including a concert, contemporary art exhibitions, hand-made bazaars, farmer markets, and "pastoral art planting" project which encouraged young artists to settle in the village. The banquet material came from small organic farmers throughout Taiwan whom the design team interviewed on site. They reported every farmer's story through the Facebook site. They finished by successfully drew the public's support and raised funds.

Since 2014, a young pottery artist and a painter, a senior natural dye artist have settled in Togo village. At the same time, some native youth of Togo have returned to run a cafe, a pizzeria and two natural farms, as well as two retired couples immigrating into Togo. Moreover, the design team continues to tackle the issues of accompanying the elderly and the young entrepreneurs who settle and develop in Togo. Since then, an art teacher has volunteered to teach the elderly, named "the Pastoral Studio".

(e) Iteration and Evolution

These young entrepreneurs adopt the social enterprise model rather than the non-profit local association model which relies mainly on governmental resources. Nowadays the designers try to make business by combining the artistic creation with local farmers, cultural creative workers, natural garden lovers, environmental educators in the attempt to develop Togo village with sustainable management. They also help the farmers to promote local product through their design and marketing technology. With a determined purpose, the entrepreneurs take out a loan of 161 thousands US dollars in order to transform a decayed house and garden into "Elegant Farmer's Artist Park" that provides the public with creative activities in a rural context.

5 Conclusion

I explore in this study how the design team engaged themselves in the transformation of Togo village. Their design thinking involved a personal and collective inquiry from the outer world to the inner world, and then delved into the source of their purposes and crystallized their vision in the prototype "Togo Rural Village Art Museum". Scharmer's perspective helps to interpret the design thinking in the transformative experience of Togo because it sheds light on the importance of exploring inwardly the source of purpose and the highest potential instead of focusing on the phenomenon of problems or proposing strategies or methods to foster creative solutions.

As conclusion, if we desire to make fundamental changes occur in today's complex world, product-oriented strategic design thinking is not sufficient to cope with it. We need to deepen the individual's inner strength and forge collective consensus and vision. Scharmer affirms in the Theory U that the inner transformative process leading to innovation requires three tools of opening, from open mind, open heart to open will and the exploration of the source of our deeper purposes and vision linking to the future. His distinction in the four levels of change in organization is worth noting that represents critical perspective in reflecting design thinking, which is not prominent in the earlier writings of design theorists. For the future studies, it is suggested to depict the principles of design thinking leading to social innovation and the roles of designer in terms of the different levels of design thinking.

References

Banathy, B.H.: Designing Social Systems in a Changing World. Plenum Press, New York (1996)

Brown, T.: Design thinking. Harv. Bus. Rev. **86**(6), 84–92 (2008)

Brown, T.: Changed by Design: How Design Thinking Transforms Organizations and Inspires Innovation. HarperCollins, New York (2009)

Cross, N.: The nature and nurture of design ability. Des. Stud. **11**(3), 127–140 (1990)

Jenlink, P.M., Banathy, B.H.: Dialogue as a Collective Means of Design Conversation. Springer, New York (2008)

Li, D.Z.: Preface. In: Young, H.R. (ed.) How do the Communities Move?, pp. 1–4. La Rive Gauche, Taipei (2007). (in Chinese)

Li, M.F.: Fostering design culture through cultivating the SSER-designers' design thinking and systems thinking. Syst. Pract. Action Res. **15**(5), 385–410 (2002)

Nonaka, I., Katsumi, A.: The Essence of Innovation (Li, Y.K., Hong, P.H. Trans.). Gaobao, Taipei (2004/2006). (in Chinese)

Scharmer, C.O.: Theory U: Leading from the Futures as it Emerges: the Social Technology of Presencing. Berrett-Koehler Publishers, San Francisco (2009)

Senge, P.M.: The Fifth Discipline: The Art and Practice of the Learning Organization. Doubleday/Currency, New York (1994)

Simon, H.A.: The Sciences of the Artificial, 3rd edn. MIT Press, Cambridge (1969)

Togo Rural Culture Association Togo Rural Village Art Museum. Togo Rural Culture Association, Tainan (2013). (in Chinese)

Wilber, K.: The Marriage of Sense and Soul. Random House, New York (1998)

Yin, R.K.: Case Study Research: Design and methods, 4th edn. Sage, Thousand Oaks (2008)

Young, H.R.: How do the Communities Move?. La Rive Gauche, Taipei (2007). (in Chinese)

Discussion on the Dynamic Construction of Urban Public Space with Interactive Public Art

Ping Zhou[1] and Zhiyong Fu[2(✉)]

[1] School of Architecture and Art, Central South University, 41000 Hunan,
People's Republic of China
zhouping_322@126.com
[2] Academy of Art and Design, Tsinghua University, Beijing, China
fuzhiyong@tsinghua.edu.cn

Abstract. Interactive public art focus on the topic, participatory, interactive, experiential appeal, the introduction of urban public space to create a viable feasibility study, it has become an important issue for public art researchers. In this paper, theoretical analysis and case studies are combined in order to find the contemporary urban public space to create a dynamic law, special requirements and methods. Thinking about the integration of "urban public space design" and "interactive public art" in the future. To explore the performance of interactive public art. For the city residents to provide a more experiential, participatory, dynamic spatial form, to enrich the vitality of urban public space to create innovative ideas.

Keywords: Interaction · Public art · Urban public spaces · Vitality · Evaluation

1 Introduction

It has been thirty years since China's reform and opening up, the national economy, living standards have undergone tremendous changes, and people enjoy the pursuit of spiritual life very much along with the growing material and cultural life. The construction of city public space is a kind of social behavior includes the spiritual civilization, in order to meet the people's pursuit of material form and the urban population in the spiritual needs, create a rich emotional public space. With the rapid development of information technology network, it not only pour new space elements into the city space design, but also weaken the vitality, the lively scenes of the traditional city public space has all gone: mobile phone online shopping allows some shopping malls neglected; the development of social networks makes part of the city square, public gardens, streets lack of the scene that few People are hurrying to and fro; all kinds of movie theater, entertainment programs on the Internet take us from the corner of the city party, chat, chatted to the screen; urbanites are now more accustomed to communicating with people through the screen, but they are not willing to meet new friends in real life...today we live in a network information and large data world, our work, study and life can't do without them, how to improve people's communicative

P.-L.P. Rau (Ed.): CCD 2017, LNCS 10281, pp. 495–506, 2017.
DOI: 10.1007/978-3-319-57931-3_39

behavior, create a dynamic atmosphere of urban space, evaluate the vitality of urban space and stimulate the vitality of the city through the existing urban public space is the content of this paper, this paper attempts to start from the interaction of public art, use case analysis to explore the strategies and methods of city public space construction.

2   Selection of Research Methods and Theoretical Model Design

2.1   The Relationship Between Interactive Public Art and Urban Public Space

City public space is an important place for people to live in the city, it provides places for people to communicate with nature; people are the main body of space activities, the relationship between people and people, people and nature, people and objects constitute the city public space; city public space is the carrier of social life, and social life is the content of city public space. People, as the main body of social activity, can use "artificial space, space plastic people" to express the relationship between people and city public space, so people can't do without the public space of city if they want to live in the city, flexible and diverse urban public space, to a certain extent, promote social life develop towards in a more innovative and abundant direction. In addition, the urban public space, including the history, culture, aesthetics and so on, which is closely related to people's spiritual life, at the same time, it is an important part of the image of the city. The development of urban public space has become one of the basic forms of social life.

Public Art as a cultural concept of contemporary art appeared in the United States in 1960s, it is different from the traditional concept of environmental sculpture, but it has a close relationship with the development of the city. The social division of labor and the intensive living environment, the evolution of commodity exchange makes the city continue to develop. The development of the city has laid a solid foundation for the production of public art. [1] for the relationship between public art and city public space, contemporary public artist Mr. Yuan Yunfu thought: "Public art is a kind of special large-scale art form, which is a kind of artistic language that is coordinated with the external form and style of the artist and the environment, it is the public art, which is designed and made for the public building, environment and mass activity place and facilities, including paintings, sculpture, landscape, city landscape and integrated design etc." [2] Urban public art is an important part of the urban landscape, and it is the organic composition of the city, it represents a city's appearance and characteristics and it is the card displayed by the city outward the world.

At present, the city is densely populated, and the city public space is the most direct contact with the public, which is closely related to people's activities. This requires the design of urban public space emphasizes humanization. Accordingly, the works of art contained in urban public space should also be based on human nature, meet the aesthetic needs of people and in line with the needs of social development. Only in this way can we ensure that the public space of the city is utilized effectively. Therefore, it is necessary to set up the public works of the public space, which are public, open, artistic and interactive.

Interactive public art is built on the basis of public art, with multiple qualities includes "interactivity", "interactivity", "perceptibility" and "artistic", "publicity" and "aesthetic". Traditional public art, for example, murals, sculpture has its own public art characteristics for viewing and dissemination but it hasn't the "interactive" feature, interaction is based on people's feelings and interactive experience, it emphasizes the sense of participation. There are some interactive public art creation are completed by artists and the public joint participation, public participation gives public art multi meaning, interactive public art adopts sound and light, information technology, network technology and other technical means to achieve the interaction effect between people and it. At present, the development of digital technology brings deep communication and interaction with the audience for city public art, art is no longer just for the audience, but it integrates into the daily life of the audience, interactivity, and even participates in the process of creation, feel beauty and happiness brought by the works of art. People involved in the city and formed positive interaction effect with all kinds of social activities, change the city act fine style, communication, and display all kinds of city culture and art spirit.

The relationship between interactive public art and urban public space in the information age:

(1) *The background of the development of information technology provides a lot of creative content and rich technical means for the creation of interactive public art and the design of urban public space.*

(2) *Interactive public art needs to rely on urban public space as a place to display, and the content of urban public space needs interactive public art.*

(3) *Interactive public art from the static state of communication into a dynamic, from unitary to multiple for the urban public space.*

Interactive urban public space enhances the participation of the masses, promote the development of multi culture and boost urban life aesthetics (Fig. 1).

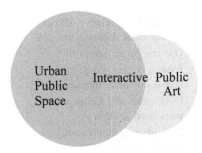

Fig. 1. The relationship between interactive public art and urban public space

2.2   Brief Introduction of Research Methods

The influence factors of urban public space are the basis of evaluation of vitality. The relevant evaluation criteria are: public space quality evaluation standard (Jan Gail, the new city space, 2003), open public space quality tools (Broomhall 2005), environmental assessment of public entertainment space (Saelens), green space of urban neighborhood (Dillen), vitality design guidelines (Bloomberg), vitality evaluation of city public space (Jiang Difei) and others analyzes the dynamic factors of urban public space from different angles, they put forward that space, aesthetic, safety facilities, roads, accessibility, the surrounding environment and may aspects can affect the vitality of city public space [3]. However, there is a lack of analysis and comparison of the interaction between public art and urban public space. Therefore, this paper puts forward the evaluation model of interactive public art to the vitality creation of urban public space. The evaluation model of interactive public art to the construction of urban public space vitality should include four aspects: safety factors, interactive factors, entertainment factors, aesthetic factors.

The quantitative method of experience as the center is obtained through the comprehensive calculation of satisfaction, emotional reflection and aesthetic response in the process of experience, and it is the degree of experience. The method is based on the user's subjective factors to quantify the user experience. It is necessary to complete by the method of questionnaire. The satisfaction was recorded as C, the emotional reaction was recorded as F, the aesthetic response was recorded as A, and the experience was recorded as E, E = C+F+A. There are four factors that can't be observed directly in the evaluation model of interactive urban public space, such as comfort and ornamental, it must take appropriate observable variables to reflect, therefore, combining the quantitative method with experience as the center, quantitative four parts including safety, interaction, entertainment, beauty, create description and parameters.

Table 1. Index system of urban public space vitality construction

Comment content	Main indicators	Description	Parameter	Indicator dimension
Safety factors	Protection	Participants can gain better protective measures when touch it	P1	3. Better
				2. General
				1. Unqualified
	Accessibility	The degree of relative difficulties among space distance, time, etc	P2	Ibid.
Interactive factors	Participation	One can participate in it	P3	Ibid.
	Interactivity	It has a certain degree of human-computer interaction	P4	Ibid.
Entertainment factors	Comfort	Participants will feel comfortable when participate in it	P5	Ibid.
	Pleasure	Participants gain pleasant psychologically	P6	Ibid.
	Convenience	To facilitate the participants in the process of participation	P7	Ibid.
Aesthetic factors	Color	It equips with good theme color	P8	Ibid.
	Diversity	It is in line with the rule of aesthetics of form	P9	Ibid.
	Ornamental	Its aesthetics can be viewed	P10	Ibid.

2.3 Model Design

Discussion on the combination of literature research, finally, the paper comes to the 10 evaluation indexes of urban public space vitality: protection, accessibility, participation, interactivity, comfort, pleasure, convenience, color, diversity, ornamental. These indicators and their respective descriptions are shown in Table 1.

According to the above study, the initial establishment of evaluation model of urban public space vitality shown in Fig. 2.

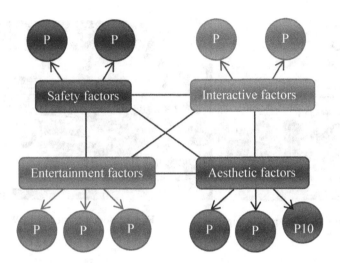

Fig. 2. Evaluation model of urban public space vitality

3   A Case Study on the Construction of Urban Public Space Vitality

Through the case study method, the following four aspects summarized the method of interactive public art to urban public space vitality. On the basis of the above parameters, this paper makes an analysis and evaluation of the interactive public art to the dynamic factors of urban public space vitality, which makes it has a certain intuitive.

3.1   By Means of Science and Technology

Digital technology provides strong technical support for the realization of new functions of public art, and the changes of the aesthetic mode and psychological cognition of modern people have also put forward new requirements for public art. The diversification of media and a full range of senses makes digital public art become a public feast.

The music steps developed by the German Volkswagen and first implanted in subway station in Stockholm, Sweden (Fig. 3), we can also see it in China's Hongkong, Shanghai, Qingdao and other urban public space. The music step designed the stairs as a huge piano keyboard, and every step on the floor will produce a corresponding note. It consists of four parts: infrared, signal acquisition, signal processing and music synthesizer, when people go up and down stairs, infrared sensors will be sent to the signal acquisition device, collector will control audio playback. It advocates a positive and healthy attitude towards life, it not only can exercise, but also can save resources and reduce carbon emissions. In this case, the interaction factors and entertainment factors in the evaluation model of vitality are stronger, followed by the safety factors and aesthetic factors.

Fig. 3. *"Music steps"* in a shopping mall in Shanghai   **Fig. 4.** SoundRobot BIGPOW

"Audio robot BIGPOW" of Taipei "Art Park" also has a strong interactive factors and entertainment factors as well as aesthetic factors, it is an interactive installation art works designed by Taiwan artist Li Mingdao. It is mainly composed of sound media and video media. It is composed of three robots which are lively and lovely and have bright color, stylish appearance, these robots have headphones on their chests, people can put their own mobile phone jack, MP3 and other music player connect the robot body, they will play the corresponding song, so we can share the beautiful music (Fig. 4) [4]. Since this group of robots were placed in the park, the deserted places has now become the crowds, mobilize people to participate in the enthusiasm of the city green space.

3.2   Express with the Aid of Language

In recent years, more and more new materials are used in public art, and new materials provide a new means of expression for the public art. It spreads the way of public art.

Beautiful island station is only now Taiwan's circular underground station, it also the Kaohsiung MRT station with the largest volume and area, Narcissus Quagliata Designer integrated the humanistic spirit of Kaohsiung into the "Kaohsiung sketch and life story" with a special combination of glass, painting and lighting, sketch the "Kaohsiung people and the story of life" to create art masterpiece "The Dome of Light".

It created a romantic atmosphere of art and life harmony in public space with the characteristics of materials with a huge glass dome breathtaking. Its diameter is 30 m, covering a floor space more than 660 m², with a total of 1,152 glass windows. The creative idea Is that convey the value of human life, the relationship between people and people, environment and all things through the work, a realm, and some people hate to lose in the struggle. The dome is a special combination including glass, painting and lighting, the production of materials, including high-temperature hot melt glass, traditional mosaic glass, hand blown glass and Venice classic crystal disk [5]. Figure 5 is about The Dome of Light. This piece of public art in the maximum limit to bring people the shock of beauty in the city public space, people can feel the deep meaning of color and graphic communication in appreciating their color and variety of forms, but it also can bring joy to people's entertainment, interactive participation factors.

Fig. 5. The Dome of Light (Color figure online)

3.3 The Combination of Narrative Techniques and Environment

"*Nine Walls*" series of works drawn from the local historical fragments, consider the demolition behavior, evoke a good memory, combined with a variety of sculpture means to highlight the public art pieces and tourists, the interaction of the public. Figure 6 is about "*Nine Walls*".

Fig. 6. "*Nine Walls*" series works   **Fig. 7.** "*Beijing ·Memory*"

"*Beijing Memory*" sealed representative old objects of Beijing with glass, set in the subway station with much characteristics of Beijing, the entire process fermented as a cultural and artistic event through various media means. Figure 7 is about "*Beijing Memory*".

These two pieces of public art have done better in the aspect of participation and appreciation, which can bring the audience into the situation through the narrative techniques, and make them resonate and recall. The combination of historical narrative and the surrounding environment gave the audience a stronger sense of the situation, which is more and more able to arouse the audience's emotional interaction.

3.4   Relying on the Surrounding Space

Campanula palace theater of "*See Mount Wutai Again*" also does good in participation and ornamental, the theater echoes the theme of architectural design and Drama, in order to reflect the Buddhist culture, designers reject duplicate or reproduce the traditional architectural style of Mount Wutai Temple, the shape of the Theatre was designed as the "folded Buddhist" shape, the theater and its surrounding space design have a perfect fusion with mountain, landscape and play in the process of creation, and use architectural language express the accuracy of the drama theme, it can fully reflect the People's understanding and feeling of Buddhist culture, which is delivered by Campanula palace through this way, it will bring a new experience to the viewer. Figure 8 is about "*See Mount Wutai Again*".

Fig. 8. Campanula palace theater of "*See Mount Wutai Again*"

Fig. 9. "The old music and new picture"

"*The old music and new picture*" video device works made the 490 m high floor of the Hong Kong World Trade Plaza as the exhibition space, projection content awakened young people's memories, dreams, reflect the rapid change of social reality, the fresh and nostalgic mood let the venue suddenly become sensitive and sentimental. Figure 9 is about "*The old music and new picture*". Figure 10 is a comparison with the indicators mentioned above.

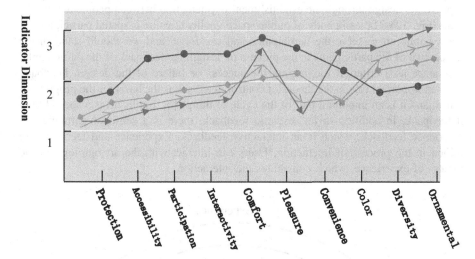

Fig. 10. Comparison diagram of interactive public art to urban public space vitality

4 Questions and Discussions

In the future, more and more interactive public art will appear in the urban space of our life, and inject new vitality into the urban public space. In the face of creative design of interactive public art, art aesthetic, humanized design and technology integration relationship is that we should concern and think, how to make the art and technology elements integrate with city public space better. Through the above analysis of the establishment of model and the case, we known the relationship between the evaluation of urban public space vitality and the creation of public art, as shown in Fig. 11.

- safety factors
- interactive factors
- entertainment factors
- aesthetic factors

- By means of science and technology
- Express with the aid of language
- The combination of narrative techniques and environment
- Relying on the surrounding space

Fig. 11. The thickness of the line represents the relationship more closely

With the development of new media, public artists combine with new media means and new materials, the narrative techniques to create a rich sense of art, technology and experience of public art, the realization way and the interactive method for public art interactive activities to city public space vitality creation are mainly reflected in the:

4.1 Establishment of Interactive Relationship

The establishment of interactive relationship is the basis of realizing the interaction between audience and art, audience and artist, audience and environment, among them, the audience's experience is the core factor. We can obtain user's feedback and improve the design through the establishment of interaction between people and works of art (Fig. 12). The main body of public space vitality creation is spatial participants, it needs public art to serve the participants and use for it, and we should stand in the perspective of the participants in the process of design, the feedback of the participants' experience as a criterion for judging the success or failure of the design. Feedback plays an important role in the theory of control, feedback is the basis for the progress of things, and it is an important part of the cycle of things [6]. Public art is a special kind of feedback, in addition to its aesthetic feedback, there is a sense of participation, experience feedback, which is an interactive feedback. Experience and feedback are unified in the process of interaction. Users can interact with the art ontology in the process of experience, which constitutes the interaction.

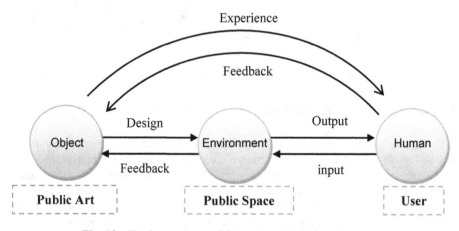

Fig. 12. The interaction model between man and environment

4.2 Interactive

Interactive public art is based on the traditional public art, which is influenced by the development of computer science and psychology, and it has a close relationship with human computer interaction technology. In the interactive input system, the input signal can be input through the camera, sensor, lens on the image, action, sound, body temperature. Output system can be a display, the building facades, the art itself, show images, video and other information. In the interactive public art, human-computer interaction plays an important role, and the relationship between human-computer interaction similar to focus on people, machine and environment of the three, with the development of digital technology, human-computer interaction started towards the development of computer and information technology, human-computer interaction is essential content in the public art interaction, it direct influenced the realization of interactive public art.

4.3   Interactive Method of Interactive Public Art

The combination of the interactive public art in urban public space and citizen culture has become an "event" in urban life and a trend of urban life in the future. The interactive process between the public art and the audience is the process of the public participation in the story, and the audience is also creating their own stories, which is more enlightening and dynamic. The interactive process of interactive public art is not to see the behavior of the audience as an isolated existence, but integrate their actions and behaviors. The interactive way of interactive public art can be divided into: viewing interaction, experiential interaction, participatory interaction, virtual interaction. There is a certain difference between the four forms of interaction, but the boundaries are not very clear, there are a number of interactive works can be classified into several kinds.

The admiration is a passive appreciation a single party, but it is not completely passive here, in fact all interactive public art can't do without watching, watching is the first step to happen "events" with the works of art, visual observation provides up 60% of the information for us, so here we call interactive viewing. Interactive experience is to let the audience into the work, feel the fun of art, experience the meaning of interactive public art. Participatory interaction is that the audience participates in public art creation, a part of the public art is completed by audience participation, experience and feedback have been shown here, the effect of the works and the content is not controlled by the artist, it is random and not preset, and it is completed by the audience. Virtual interaction should rely on multimedia, digital technology, etc., achieve the interaction between the works and the audience, it refers to the interaction between the audience in the behavior and virtual space objects, the interaction between the visual and the image.

5   Conclusion

It is a cross disciplinary field to study the dynamic construction of urban public space with the interaction of public art, which is an interdisciplinary subject, such as interactive design, urban design, architectural planning, design research, computer science and so on. With the development of the new technology and its application, the future urban public space structure will more involve in the participation of the people, the public is not only the audience but also the participants in the space design. In the traditional public art, the new media, Internet technology and new technology will further expand the performance of public art, and more man-machine interaction will produce more interactive content. Under the condition of new technology, installation art, video art, photoelectric art, new material art have greatly expanded the field of public art creation, enrich the traditional visual style to the artists, provide space to express infinite, so that they can express their views through the use of a lot of science and technology, make people's vision, hearing, touch are me, the new media has become a new form of rich vitality and creativity in the field of public art. In the future, the construction of urban public space vitality will become a new topic of public space design, interactive public art will become more and more popular, and their combination will collide with more updated spark.

References

1. Fu, X.: Marking urban culture - on the design culture of urban public art. J. Sci. Technol. Forum 175–176 (2007)
2. Yuan, Y.: Chinese Contemporary Decorative Art. Shanxi People's Publishing House, Shanxi
3. Chen, F., Lin, J., Zhu, X.: The difference study on landscape activity evaluation between winter and summer of public space in cold city. Landsc. Gard. 118–125 (2015)
4. https://yukiblog.tw/zh-cn/read-1686.html
5. Zhao, S., Ruan, R.: To enhance the public art theme of subway through station design - a case study of beautiful island station and central park station in Kaohsiung MRT, Taiwan. Res Urban Rail Transit. 6–10 (2012)
6. Wang, F.: The Research on the Interactive Design of City Public Art under the Background of Digital Age (2010)
7. Florida, R.: The Rise of the Creative Class: And How It's Transforming Work, Leisure, Community and Everyday Life. Perseus Books Group, New York (2002)
8. Zhang, X.: The Application and Development of New Media Art in Public Art (2010)
9. Liu, L.: Dissertation Submitted to Zhejiang University of Technology for the Degree of Master (2010)
10. Weng, J.: Urban Public Art. Southeast University Press, Nanjing (2004)
11. Sun, Z.: Public Art Age. Jiangsu Fine Arts Publishing House, Jiangsu (2003)
12. Zhou, M.: Public Art Design. Intellectual Property Press, Beijing (2004)
13. Wang, H., Jiang, D.: Evaluation system research on vitality of urban public space. J. Railw. Sci. Eng. 56–60 (2012)
14. Liu, L.: Evaluation index of residents' satisfaction in urban public space. Urban Probl. 65–72 (2012)
15. Li, D.: The research of livable communities evaluation in Chinese city. Dalian University of Technology, Dalian (2009)

Cross-Cultural Design for Learning

DanMOOC: Enhancing Content and Social Interaction in MOOCs with Synchronized Commenting

Yue Chen[✉], Qin Gao, and Quan Yuan

Department of Industrial Engineering, Tsinghua University, Beijing, China
{chenyue14,yuan-q15}@mails.tsinghua.edu.cn,
gaoqin@tsinghua.edu.cn

Abstract. To enhance interactions between learners, instructors, and content for MOOC courses, this study purposes a new video lecturing interface that embeds synchronized discussions and notes anchored to the video timeline. The design concept was evaluated with 4 MOOC instructors, 8 teaching assistants, and 7 learners using a prototype. Most participants agreed that the design would enhance learner-content, learner-learner, and learner-instructor interactions, and may further improve learning performance, satisfactions, and may decrease dropout rate. However, the form of presenting discussions and possibly unrelated content may distract learners, and the design requires further improvement.

Keywords: E-learning · MOOC · Online video interface · Synchronized commenting

1 Introduction

Massive open online courses (MOOCs) developed fast and became popular in the past few years. The features of MOOCs, such as openness, diversity, autonomy, interactivity and connectedness attracts people to join in [1]. However, very few learners can keep on learning and complete a course. One of the reasons is the insufficient interactions in MOOCs among learners, between learners and instructors, and between learners and content.

Researchers have revealed the importance of these interactions in a successful learning process. Higher learner-instructor interaction during class [2], more participation in forum discussion [3, 4], and more cooperation among learners [5] have been found leading to better learning performance. Discussions among learners and instructors increase course completion rate [6, 7]. Learning activities through social network services also improve learning performance, satisfaction and motivation level [8]. Higher interaction level is related to higher learners' satisfaction to the course and the MOOC system [9, 10].

However, these interactions in MOOCs are still unsatisfying. On the one hand, according to a survey study of MOOCs [7], learners complained about the chaos of discussion forum, the lack of interaction with instructors, and the lack of help. On the other hand, although instructors wanted to interact with learners as much as possible,

P.-L.P. Rau (Ed.): CCD 2017, LNCS 10281, pp. 509–520, 2017.
DOI: 10.1007/978-3-319-57931-3_40

the large scale of MOOC participants makes it impossible to communicate as much as in the face-to-face classes. Compared with face-to-face courses in school, the class in MOOCs is lack of students' responses and feedback to instructors, and discussions among students [11]. This lack of interactions also leads to a lower sense of belonging to a class and less satisfying learning experiences, which may further lead to high dropout rates. To improve the interactions between learners, instructors, and content for MOOC courses, this study purposes a new video lecturing interface that embeds synchronized discussions and notes anchored to the video timeline. The design concept was evaluated with 4 MOOC instructors, 8 teaching assistants, and 7 learners using a prototype.

2   Related Work of Designs for Lecture Videos in MOOCs

To enhance interaction of MOOCs, researchers designed innovative video interaction techniques for lecture videos. For example, Kim et al. designed LectureSpace [12], a video system with an interactive timeline based on edX. A 2D rollercoaster timeline shows the amount of navigation activities, such as pause, resume, or jump, and the peaks of the amount are marked. When the cursor is around peaks, the friction to move the cursor increases. The interview for usability evaluation showed that by using this system, learners perceived higher level of interaction with video content and other learners than that when using the original edX platform.

To stimulate during class discussions, Yousef et al. designed L2P-bMOOC [13] for blended MOOC, a lecture video system in which learners can make annotations such as suggestions and questions on the timeline. These annotations are public to all other learners and learners can comment or like annotations. The annotations can enhance interaction in the blended MOOCs, in which a relatively small scale of learners take part. In xMOOCs or cMOOCs with thousands of learners, the enormous annotations are hard to directly present on the video timeline.

Another approach to present during viewing discussion is to overlay comments anchored to the video timeline in the form of moving subtitles on the video screen, which is called Danmaku commenting. Comments from previous viewers at specific time points of a video are presented to all the other viewers who watch the same video latter. Danmaku commenting originated in Niconico Douga, which is one of the most popular video sites in Japan. It is now popular in China and most video sites in China (such as Bilibili, Tudou, and Youku) support Danmaku commenting. Danmaku commenting can satisfy viewers' needs for video-related information and facilitate information seeking activities [14]. By applying Danmaku commenting in MOOCs, learners can see discussions about particular sections of the video as soon as they see the video contents. Therefore, Danmaku commenting may improve interaction in MOOCs.

Lee et al. studied the effect from Danmaku commenting on the experience of learning MOOC lecture videos [15]. They conducted laboratorial experiments and found that Danmaku commenting can increase learner's perceived engagement and engage them into the discussions. Compared with the static list of comments, these dynamicallyflying comments increase perceived social interaction. Comments about the lecture content increase learning outcomes, meanwhile comments for social interaction do not decrease learning outcomes.

However, these comments are short and cannot be replied, therefore cannot support deeper during class discussions. To improve interaction and performance of MOOC lecture learning, we try to adopt features of Danmaku commenting and design Dan-MOOC, a video lecture interface to enhance both content-learnerand social interaction in MOOCs.

3 User Needs Gathering

We investigated the current situation of interaction in MOOCs from both literatures and interviews with five participants. They were two students, two teaching assistants, and an engineer in XuetangX (one of the most popular MOOC platforms in China), aged from 22 to 30. Their experience with MOOCs ranged from 6 months to 2 years. Their experience with Danmaku commenting ranged from 6 months to 7 years. We interviewed them about the interaction among learners, instructors, and content under different situations (i.e., face-to-face classes or MOOCs). The two students were asked why they joined in MOOCs. The five participants were also asked their opinions about applying Danmaku commenting in the MOOC videos.

Both literatures and results of interviews suggested various motivations to join in MOOCs. Learners with different motivations to join in MOOCs have different needs for interaction. Some of the MOOC learners want the certification and they may treat MOOCs as important as offline courses and learn MOOCs according to the time table. These learners may need more interaction during lecture learning and timely helps like in the face-to-face class. Some learners want to make friends or learning with others by MOOCs. They need interaction with other learners and collaborative learning. Some learners take MOOCs to complement their offline learning, and treat MOOCs as supplementary resources or learning materials. They do not care about whether complete the whole course. For these learners, the system is required to provide the most relevant knowledge and effective and efficient ways of information retrieval. Some learners browse MOOC videos for entertainment and satisfying the curiosity. For example, they may view MOOC lecture videos about art or history during eating the breakfast, and may not want to complete any assignment. To attract these learners and increase retention rate, the course and system need to be lively and entertaining.

Participants said Danmaku commenting had the potential to improve interaction, but some of them worried that the Danmaku commenting distracted learning. If too many comments overlays on the screen, these comments may distract viewers and bring visual clutter, increase cognitive load, and further reduce learning performance. In videos for learning, this problem is more severe than that in the most online videos for entertainment. In addition, one of the two students suggested that some of the Danmaku comments may supplement the current content in the lecture video, and he had the need to clip these comments to his notes or take notes anchored on the video timeline.

To satisfy these needs, we aim to design an interface with the following goals:

1. Enhance interaction, i.e., facilitate discussion specific to video content, and enhance the sense of learning with the accompany of a class
2. Facilitate discussion for different learning needs or motivations
3. Reduce visual clutter and cognitive load caused by discussion
4. Enhance the connection of notes and video content.

4 DanMOOC: MOOC Videos with Synchronized Commenting

To achieve these goals, we proposed an interface of MOOC lecture videos called DanMOOC. We introduce three interaction features: (1) comments and threads on timeline, (2) filter of comments and threads, and (3) notes anchored to the timeline.

4.1 Comments and Threads on Timeline

We adopt Danmaku commenting, i.e., the commenting technique that overlays comments synchronized with the video timeline in the form of moving subtitles on the video screen. In our design, both comments and threads are overlaid on the screen and scrolling on the right sidebar list synchronized with the video timeline (see Figs. 1, 2, and 3). Comments enhance co-viewing experience and the sense of learning with the accompany of other learners (goal 1). Threads connect long and deep discussions with video content (goal 1). To avoid visual clutter (goal 3), the title of each thread is shown in the Danmaku commenting and sidebar list. To see detailed content and following comments of a thread, viewers need to click it and skip to the area D in the Fig. 1, which shows both threads to the whole video and the threads anchored to the timeline. Users can expand a thread to see detailed content and the replies of it. Unlike the anonymous Danmaku commenting in the most video sites such as Bilibili and Niconico Douga, in this design the author's social information, such as the username, avatar, the type of the user (e.g., teacher, TA, or active user), is shown in the sidebar list (goal 1).

4.2 Filter of Comments and Threads

To avoid visual clutter and reduce distraction, viewers can choose to see only a part of the comments and threads by types (comments/threads) in the setting panel in the sidebar (goal 2 and 3, see Fig. 3). They can also choose to only see the comments and threads from active learners or reviewed by the instructor. Viewers can set the maximum amount of comments and threads on the screen at one time point, and then system will only show comments and threads with high quality or priority, which is calculated by, e.g., the number of likes and comments and whether reviewed and accepted by instructors (goal 3). Viewers can also adjust the transparency of comments on the video or hide all comments and threads (goal 3).

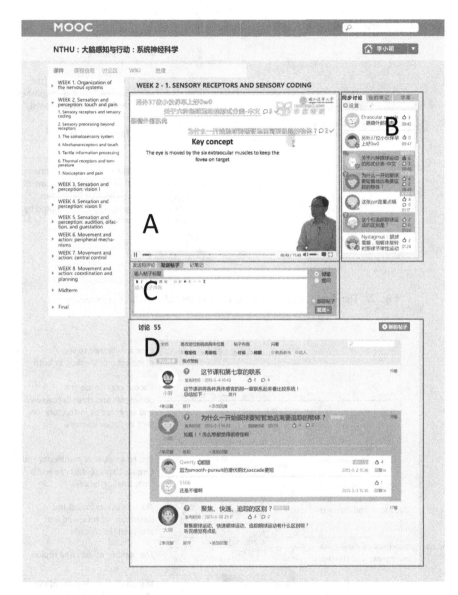

Fig. 1. Overview of DanMOOC. (A) The video with flying overlaid comments and titles of threads. (B) The sidebar that shows all comments and titles of threads. (C) The area for sending comments and threads. (D) The area for both threads to the whole video and the threads anchored to the timeline. Users can expand a thread to see detailed content and the replies of it.

4.3   Notes Anchored to the Timeline

Learners can take notes anchored to the video timeline when learning the video (goal 4). His/her notes are shown in the order of the video playback time in the sidebar, in a

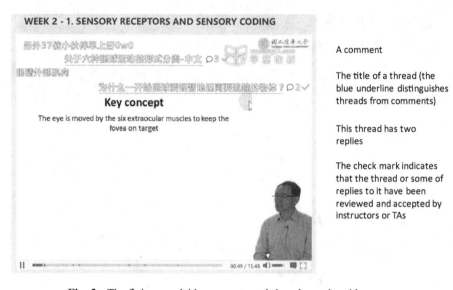

Fig. 2. The flying overlaid comments and threads on the video area

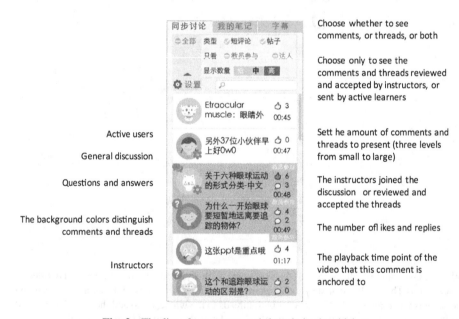

Fig. 3. The list of comments and threads in the sidebar

form of vertical timeline (see Fig. 4). At each note point, both screenshot and learner's notes are listed. In addition, each note point is marked as red points in the video timeline.

Go to the page of the
learner's notes of this course

The playback time point that
this note is anchored to

Thes creenshot of the video
at the time point that this
note is anchored to

The note

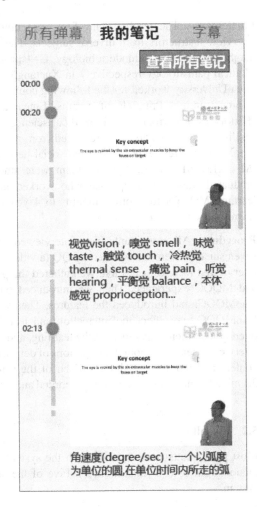

Fig. 4. Notes of the video in the sidebar

5   Evaluation

5.1   Method

We made a static prototype (see Fig. 1) based on the lecture interface of XuetangX, which is one of the most popular MOOC platforms in China. We illustrated the interface in the following scenarios: (1) when the user enters the interface, (2) when the user posts a comment or thread, or takes a note, (3) when the user modifies the filter settings, (4) when the user goes see the detailed content of a thread, and (5) when the user switches the sidebar tabs to see his/her notes. To initially evaluate the design, explore how it can enhance interaction, and improve the design, we interviewed 4 teachers, 8 teaching assistants, and 7 learners.

Participants. The teachers and TAs were invited through XuetangX. We tried to interview instructors from diverse subjects. The 4 teachers from Tsinghua University taught Introduction to modern biology, C++ programming, Principle of Marxism, and Medical parasitology respectively in XuetangX. The 8 teaching assistants from Tsinghua University worked for the following courses in XuetangX: Financial analysis, C++ programming, Principle of circuits, Linear algebra, Great art, Zi Zhi Tong Jian (History as a Mirror). This is medical science, and Listening and speaking of daily English. The 7 learners were recruited from a WeChat group of active users of XuetangX and the researchers' personal social networks. Their age ranged from 18 to 28 (M = 21.6, SD = 3.3). Most of them were students (from high school students to graduated students) except one who worked in a HR department. They had been learning MOOCs for from 2 months to 4 years. All of them had the experience of learning MOOCs on XuetangX.

Procedure. All participants were interviewed in the quiet environments. Six of the seven students were interviewed by QQ (a video chatting tool). Other participants were interviewed face to face. First, we gathered the participant's demographic information and MOOC experience. Then we introduced our purpose, showed the prototype of DanMOOC, and introduced the features. Then we interviewed him/her about (1) how DanMOOC may affect the interaction and learning performance, (2) how the flying overlaid comments may distract the learning, and (3) the effectiveness of notes. We also interviewed learners about their opinions of design details (e.g., how to present expanded content and replies of a thread). Each of the semi-structured interviews lasted about 30 min. All interviews were audio-recorded and transcribed into text for further analysis.

5.2 Results

Most participants were satisfied with the system and they reported the score of satisfaction from 5 to 6 (maximum 7). Five of the seven students would like to try this system.

Interaction of Commenting System. Most participants agreed that the connection of discussion and content at different video time points may enhance learner-content interaction, promote understanding, and increase learning efficiency. First, the connection may stimulate discussion. Two TAs said that students may miss many instant thoughts, questions or comments if they discuss after finishing viewing the lecture video. A teacher said the synchronized overlaid comments may create an atmosphere of discussion and attract more learners to join in. Second, the connection may make it convenient to discuss or ask questions about content at certain time points in the lecture video. TAs said this feature may reduce their work load of searching students' questions in the lecture video. Interviewed learners said that these comments and threads provided helps and summaries of questions immediately when they learnt the concept, and therefore the repeatedly asked questions would be reduced. Third, the connection may enrich the lecture content. As TAs said, this synchronized commenting system may provide an entrance from the video to user generated content, expand the lecture content, and promote collaborative learning.

The commenting system may enhance learner-learner interaction. TAs said students may get to know others' feelings, such as perceived difficulty. Some learners said they could share inspirations with others and the sense of accompany could be enhanced. They could even make new friends and further develop a sense of belonging to the class. Teachers said the overlaid flying comments can create a lively atmosphere similar to the face-to-face class. For example, the teacher of Medical parasitology said the learners would not be scared of the parasites with the company of comments. These merits may increase the completion rate. However, the TA of Linear algebra said that few learners needed to discuss in the Math class and it was hard to type formula immediately during class. Therefore, he thought it was hard to enhance learner-learner interaction.

The commenting system may enhance learner-instructor interaction. Teachers and TAs said that by the amount of comments and threads, they may figure out which parts of the video attracted or confused learners. The system could also help learners correct the mistakes of videos, and make it easier to ask or answer questions located in specific time points. Although the commenting system may provide an approach of learner-instructor communication, the major of participants said that instructors needed effective and efficient ways to learn students' feedbacks from a potentially large scale of comments and threads. Useful information required to be abstracted and presented in a clear form.

Although the commenting system may enhance interaction, a few participants said that the interaction brought more harms than benefits. Some learners worried that the during class discussion would distract them from focusing on the video content. One teacher and one student said that although the connection of video content and discussion was helpful, the overlaid flying comments were distracting and they preferred other forms such as the list in sidebar. Some participants said the enhanced student-student interaction may increase useless information and therefore decrease the learning efficiency.

Distractions. Most participants said too many comments overlaid on the screen would distract learning, therefore they appreciated the functions of filter, transparency setting, and hiding.

However, they still concerned about the quality of comments and the visual clutter. First, the commenting system may increase discussions both related and unrelated to the course. Most participants said content-related comments could benefit learning, but they had different opinions about other comments, such as comments for social interaction. Some of them said social comments could attract learners and create an active atmosphere, whereas others said social comments may provide useless and chaotic information for learning. Second, learners of MOOCs usually have different levels of knowledge and skills. Some interviewed learners worried that they were forced to see comments and threads that may be too easy or boring to them, even if the comments were related to the content. Third, in addition to the individual learning habits and knowledge levels, the form of the video also influenced the perceived distraction. Most students and TAs said if there were slides with dense texts in the video, the overlaid comments would be more distractive than that when a teacher was present and speaking in the video.

Notes. Only one of the seven learners used Evernote when learning MOOCs. Other learners took notes on paper notebooks when learning MOOCs. Therefore, although most participants said the notes may be convenient, they may not want to use it. The teacher of Medical parasitology also said paper was more suitable for notes of Medical parasitology. The Evernote user in the seven learners and some teachers and TAs said learners may try to take notes in DanMOOC system if they could export their notes organized in a clear layout from the DanMOOC system, for reviewing after class.

Teachers and TAs said that notes may reflect learners' learning process. For example, playback time points with many notes may indicate that the content there was difficult to many learners. Teachers could find out unexpected difficult points of the lecture and adjust his/her teaching.

Design Details. In the prototype, the detailed content and following replies of each thread were shown in the area D in Fig. 1. Most participants said that this skip from the view of video to the bottom of the page would interrupt the learning ofthe lecture. In

Back to the list of comments and threads

The title of the thread

The playback time point of the video that this thread is anchored to

The date and time when the thread was posted

Content of the thread

Reviewed and accepted by instructors

Replies to the thread

The input field for new replies

Fig. 5. Detailed content and replies of a thread is showed on the sidebar in the improved design

addition, in the most current MOOCs, forum is independent from the lecture videos. Few courses provided the function of discussing a specific video. Therefore, we removed the area for threads to the whole video, and presented the detailed content and following repliesof threads anchored to the timeline directly in the sidebar (see Fig. 5).

6   Discussion and Conclusion

To enhance interaction in MOOCs, this study purposes DanMOOC, a video lecture interface for lectures of MOOCs that shows synchronized discussions and notes anchored to the video timeline. The design was evaluated by interviews of 4 teachers, 8 teaching assistants, and 7 learners of MOOCs.

On the one hand, most participants agreed that the design would enhance learner-content, learner-learner, and learner-instructor interactions. The connection of discussion and lecture content can stimulate thinking and collaborative learning, facilitate Q&A between learners and instructors, help learners to develop a sense of accompany, and create a lively atmosphere that attract learners. These merits may further improve learning performance and decrease dropout rates.

On the other hand, the form of overlaid flying comments and the unrelated content may distract learners. Previous research suggests that some unrelated comments (e.g., for social interactions) anchored to the video timeline do not decrease learning outcomes [15]. However, in our study, some participants concerned that, if they are forced to see all discussions, unrelated comments and discussions that are too easy for them may distract their learning and reduce learning efficiency. Therefore, future research may focus on how to present adaptive and personalized comments and threads on the video for different learners.

This study has the following limitations. First, we only designed the interface for learners. Instructors require information such as which parts of the lecture triggers a large number of comments and threads and what are the most asked questions. The current interface cannot provide this information. Future research may investigate the needs of instructors and designed interface for instructors. Second, the interviews were based on pictorial prototypes and descriptions of the researchers. The prototype may be less clear to present the interactive features and discuss the impacts than a real system. Future research may develop an operable system, and conduct experiments to evaluate the real interaction, learning performance, and satisfactions of learners when they are learning MOOCs from this system.

Acknowledgments. This study was supported by the Online Education Research Foundation of the Online Education Research Center, Ministry of Education, P. R. China (教育部在线教育研究中心在线教育研究基金(全通教育), Project No. 2016ZD303) and the National Natural Science Foundation of China (Project no. 71401087).

References

1. Downes, S.: Half an Hour: Connectivist Dynamics in Communities. Half Hour (2009)
2. He, W.: Examining students' online interaction in a live video streaming environment using data mining and text mining. Comput. Hum. Behav. **29**, 90–102 (2013). doi:10.1016/j.chb.2012.07.020
3. Finnegan, C., Morris, L.V., Lee, K.: Differences by course discipline on student behavior, persistence, and achievement in online courses of undergraduate general education. J. Coll. Stud. Retent. Res. Theory Pract. **10**, 39–54 (2009). doi:10.2190/CS.10.1.d
4. Gillani, N., Eynon, R.: Communication patterns in massively open online courses. Internet High Educ. **23**, 18–26 (2014)
5. Borokhovski, E., Bernard, R.M., Tamim, R.M., et al.: Technology-supported student interaction in post-secondary education: a meta-analysis of designed versus contextual treatments. Comput. Educ. **96**, 15–28 (2016)
6. Adamopoulos, P.: What makes a great MOOC? An interdisciplinary analysis of student retention in online courses, pp. 4720–4740 (2013)
7. Khalil, H., Ebner, M., Herrington, J.: How satisfied are you with your MOOC? - A research study on interaction in huge online courses. In: Actas AACE World Conference Educational Multimedia Hypermedia Telecommunications, Victoria, pp. 830–839 (2013)
8. Castaño, C., Maiz, I., Garay, U.: Design, motivation and performance in a cooperative MOOC course. Online Submiss. **22**, 19–26 (2015)
9. Kuo, Y.C., Walker, A.E., Belland, B.R., Schroder, K.E.E.: A predictive study of student satisfaction in online education programs. Int. Rev. Res. Open Distance Learn **14**, 107–127 (2013)
10. Ke, F., Kwak, D.: Online learning across ethnicity and age: a study on learning interaction participation, perception, and learning satisfaction. Comput. Educ. **61**, 43–51 (2013)
11. Hew, K.F., Cheung, W.S.: Students' and instructors' use of massive open online courses (MOOCs): motivations and challenges. Educ. Res. Rev. **12**, 45–58 (2014)
12. Kim, J., Guo, P.J., Cai, C.J., et al.: Data-driven interaction techniques for improving navigation of educational videos. In: Proceedings of the 27th Annual ACM Symposium on User Interface Software and Technology, pp. 563–572. ACM, New York (2014)
13. Yousef, A.M.F., Chatti, M.A., Schroeder, U., Wosnitza, M.: A usability evaluation of a blended MOOC environment: an experimental case study. Int. Rev. Res. Open Distrib. Learn. **16** (2015)
14. Chen, Y., Gao, Q., Rau, P.-L.P.: Watching a movie alone yet together: understanding reasons for watching Danmaku videos. Int. J. Hum.–Comput. Interact. (2017)
15. Lee, Y.-C., Lin, W.-C., Cherng, F.-Y., et al. Using time-anchored peer comments to enhance social interaction in online educational videos. In: Proceedings of the 33rd Annual ACM Conference on Human Factors in Computing Systems, pp. 689–698. ACM, New York (2015)

Exploring Factors Influencing Knowledge Sharing of International Students at Chinese University

Zhe Chen, Shunong Deng, Adila Mamtimin, Jiaxin Chang, Feng Liu,
and Lin Ma[✉]

School of Economics and Management, Beihang University, Beijing, China
09818@buaa.edu.cn

Abstract. Knowledge sharing is an effective and efficient way for students to obtain knowledge in universities. Students share knowledge with their colleagues to improve the learning performance and at the same time to strengthen their social networks. Knowledge sharing of international students may be different from local students due to various reasons.

Previous studies indicated many factors which had influences on knowledge sharing for international students in other countries, for example, language barriers, cultural differences, lack of feedback, sharing channels, personal obstacles and etc. These factors included two types, internal reasons, and external reasons. Internal reasons referred to the characteristics of students. External reasons referred to the environment.

Chinese culture has its uniqueness from other cultures, for example, Chinese culture respect collectivism. International students in China might be influenced by the Chinese culture when they share knowledge. This study aims to investigate the factors influencing knowledge sharing of international students at Chinese University.

After a literature review, an interview and a scenario-based experiment were conducted at Beihang University in this study. In the interview, nine international students were invited to participate. The results of the interview indicated the motivators and hinders of knowledge sharing of international students in the Chinese university. The motivators focus on enhancing social networking skills. The hinders included language barriers and cultural differences. In the experiment, participants were first asked to read a knowledge-sharing scenario and then asked to fill a questionnaire based on the scenario. The questionnaire was designed to test the motivators and hinders of knowledge sharing. Twenty-one participants were invited to the experiment. The results indicated that international students were willing to share knowledge with other students for two main reasons, which were strengthening their knowledge quality and making friends. For the hinders, language barriers and cultural difference are still the main reasons which have negative effects on knowledge sharing of international students.

Keywords: Education · Knowledge sharing

© Springer International Publishing AG 2017
P.-L.P. Rau (Ed.): CCD 2017, LNCS 10281, pp. 521–530, 2017.
DOI: 10.1007/978-3-319-57931-3_41

1 Introduction

Knowledge sharing between international students requires more investigation. In China, there are many foreign students in Chinese universities now. For example, the number of international students has increased from 382 to 1704 from 2001 to 2014 in Beihang University, a university in Beijing of China. Not only is the number of international students increasing, but also the Chinese government and universities are paying higher and higher attention to the international exchange of education. Take Beihang University for example, there are various international studying programs and for international students such as bachelor program, master program, doctoral program, and exchanging program. Most schools of Beihang Universities are accepting international students. A school, called international school, are established to mainly served for the international students. International education plays an important role in Chinese higher education.

The national distribution of international students studying in Beihang by 2015 shows that international students comes from countries in North America, Europe, South America, Africa, Asia and Oceania. It indicates that the current international students at Beihang University have a strong national diversity. It's inevitable that such large background diversity may leads to the exchange and integration of culture. During the studying period in China, foreign students also have adopted the unique culture of China and the students. Using them as the medium of cultural and cultural exchange is important to efficient communicate. Therefore, the quality of international education is not only related to the overall level of China's higher education quality but also related to China's international academic and cultural exchanges.

The study of knowledge sharing will help improve the quality of international education. Through the study of the knowledge sharing behavior of international students, this study can summarize their preferences and characteristics, motivations and obstacles in knowledge sharing behavior, so as to discuss the most appropriate way which students use in the whole process of knowledge acquisition, collation, absorption, feedback, and sharing. Exerting the international education accordingly and scientifically, the students can learn more efficiently and reduce the unnecessary time waste and meaningless formal steps in the learning process. This will fully increase the humanity and scientificity of Chinese international education, and thus improve the overall quality of higher education level.

The main factor that affects the knowledge sharing behavior is cultural background. Affected by different cultures, people from different countries will form different characters and habits, so that the behavior in the knowledge sharing varies a lot. The reason why China is chosen to conduct this survey is that China, as a representative of oriental culture, has a relatively unique culture than any other countries. Taking foreign students studying in China as subjects, using Chinese culture as the researching background, the research clearly reflects the impact of cultural differences on knowledge-sharing behavior.

Therefore, researching the knowledge sharing behavior of international students in China will not only provide a positive and helpful reference to the improvement of the international education system of Chinese universities, the daily teaching skill and the communication between international students, but also make contribution to the international academic and cultural communication among young people at home and abroad.

2 Methodology

This study includes two parts: follow-up interview filling out questionnaires and single questionnaire.

2.1 Follow-up Interview and Questionnaires

In this part, this study chose some international students in Beijing University of Aeronautics and Astronautics randomly as our participants. The participants would be interviewed and then asked to complete a questionnaire. The Demographical information of the participants was shown in Table 1.

Table 1. Demographical information of participants in the interview

Age	Gender	Program	Studying length in Beihang (month)	Studying length in China (month)	Major
24	Male	Master	3	3	Economics
30	Male	Ph.D.	60	60	Mechanical Design & Theory
42	Male	Ph.D.	3	3	Management Science
26	Male	Ph.D.	4	4	Fluid Machinery
26	Male	Master	3	3	Space Technology Applications
25	Female	Ph.D.	3	3	Management Science
23	Female	Master	72	60	Economics
25	Male	Master	60	60	Management Science
40	Male	Master	12	12	Management Science

The concludes some demographical information, like age, gender, program, staying in China period in months, studying in China period in months and major. Next, there are some common forms of knowledge sharing among international students, concluding class discussions, student presentations, chatting or discussing through social network, group projects, small group discussions, academic lectures, answering questions to other, making or taking recommendations about studying and using online knowledge repositories (such as Wikipedia and Answer.com), these participants will

the among these activities according to the frequency of their participation in daily life. At last, participants will be asked about the motivations and hinders influencing their participation in knowledge sharing activities.

2.2 Questionnaire

Using scenario-based experiment, this study set a circumstance about knowledge sharing to participants, then let them complete the questionnaire. The scenario-based experiment is widely used in sociology and psychology's experimental investigation. In the field of knowledge sharing, the scenario-based experiment is always used to control different social and situation variables. Twenty-one participants were invited to the experiment. Their demographical information was shown in Table 2.

Table 2. Demographical information of participants in the experiment

Basic information		Number	Percentage
Age	16–20	5	25.00%
	21–25	11	55.00%
	26–30	4	20.00%
Gender	Male	16	80.00%
	Female	3	15.00%
Education	Doctor	0	0.00%
	Master	7	35.00%
	Undergraduate	12	60.00%
	Others	0	0.00%
Staying period (months)	0–6	5	25.00%
	7–12	2	10.00%
	13–24	7	35.00%
	25–36	4	20.00%
	>36	2	10.00%
Studying period (months)	0–6	4	20.00%
	7–12	1	5.00%
	12–24	7	35.00%
	24–36	4	20.00%
	>36	2	10.00%
Major	Mechanical Engineering	7	35.00%
	International Economic Trade	6	30.00%
	Civil Engineering	1	5.00%
	Electronic Engineering	1	5.00%
	Aeronautical Engineering	2	10.00%
	MBA	1	5.00%
	Chinese Culture	1	5.00%
	Environment Engineering	1	5.00%

This questionnaire has four parts: basic information, approaches, sharing obstacles and sharing motivation, 26 questions in all, and each part's questions are placed alternately to increase the credibility of the result. Participants were asked to choose each question one corresponding point from five-points Likert scale, from "1: strongly disagree" to "5: strongly agree".

3 Results and Analysis

3.1 The Results of Follow-up Interview Filling Out Questionnaires

The basic information of each participant as follow:

Through the interview, It's drawn that the main motivation is helping others, improving own social skills and acquiring knowledge at the same time.

The main obstacle is language barriers, cultural difference and time tightness.

The language barrier and cultural difference lead to the loss of educational efficiency. As international students, seeking knowledge in the foreign country, encountering cross-cultural communication is unavoidable. Except for cultural collisions like the behavioral pattern and custom concept. "Culture learning" has also become an important factor which affects the effect of learning. "Culture learning," referring to the act of the teaching and learning, principles, a set of values, beliefs, and expectations, has its cultural origin and has been held for the foreign students participating in teaching activities.

3.2 The Results of Questionnaire

Questionnaire distribution Site: Building 10 (student apartment), Day noun Village.

Time: From 22:00 to 23:00

Number: 20 questionnaires, 19 of them valid basic information of participants.

The age group of the subjects is concentrated in the 21–25 years old. Most of them are under graduate. The duration of them being in China and studying in China is the same, 13–24 months mostly. The number of students majoring in mechanical engineering, international trade and aviation engineering is more than others.

Hinders

- The question 24 gets the highest mean, which indicates that the biggest obstacle that discourages foreign students from knowledge sharing is language barriers.
- From the score of question 11, it is concluded that lack of proper channels is also a critical hinder.
- Question 2 with a relatively higher average score implies that lack of understanding also hints students from communicating with each other.
- Question 22, with an average score of 2.8 and a high standard deviation of 1.322, shows a great controversy of foreign students in this item.
- Another question not mentioned above isn't relatively critical factors when it comes to knowledge sharing (Tables 3 and 4).

Table 3. Barriers in knowledge sharing

Barrier	Mean	N	Std
24. Language barriers does harm to knowledge sharing	3.2	20	1.152
11. I lack avenues to share information or to communicate with others	3.1	20	1.071
2. I do not know the other person well	2.95	20	1.099
22. Culture difference does harm to knowledge sharing	2.8	20	1.322
14. I lack understanding as to what to share and with whom to share	2.75	20	1.02
20. I lack confidence to share knowledge with others	2.75	20	1.293
13. I fear that I would provide wrong information	2.7	20	1.129
1. I lack time to do the former activities	2.65	20	0.933
16. I fear that a clash of opinion may spoil relationship	2.65	20	1.089
26. The loneliness because of living in foreign land does harm to knowledge sharing	2.55	20	1.099
9. I lack motivation or rewards in sharing knowledge	2.45	20	1.395
4. I fear that I would be perceived as a "show-off" person	2.4	20	1.046
18. I fear that others may outperform me in studies	2.2	20	1.152
6. I don't trust others to share my knowledge	1.9	20	0.968

Table 4. Motivators in knowledge sharing

Motivators	Mean	N	Std
7. I want to make more friends	4.3	20	0.865
12. I am eager to help others or share	4.3	20	0.801
19. It helps me to innovate ideas or other knowledge	4.25	20	0.55
3. I want to keep connection with others	3.95	20	0.826
15. I want to keep the discussion or activity moving on	3.95	20	0.759
8. I will feel belonging to and fit within the group	3.75	20	0.967
10. I further my own understanding of concepts learned in the class through sharing ideas with other students	3.7	20	0.865
23. I am eager to study	3.7	20	1.031
21. It will enhance cooperative ability	3.6	20	1.142
5. It will enhance self-learning ability	3.45	20	1.234
17. I want to gain recognition	2.85	20	1.268
25. I want to get reward (money, other's return)	2.6	20	1.188

Motives

- The charts above shows that question 7, question 12, question 19, question 3, question 15, question 10, and question 8 get a higher average score and standard deviation, which indicates that students' knowledge sharing motivation are mostly for reach their indirect and direct needs.
- Among them, indirect need, namely social networking need is seemed to be much more urgent than the direct need of knowledge sharing. Indirect needs, listed in the chart, shows that they strongly want to communicate and relate more with people

through knowledge sharing and keep contact with each other so that they can find a sense of belonging in a totally strange country. Direct need, namely the need for knowledge, as the main aim of knowledge sharing activities, is their hope to acquire new knowledge, creative ideas and different understanding through knowledge sharing.

- In the subject with a low score, the standard deviation of the two questions is high, indicating that most of the students gave lower scores to the question, especially questions 5 and 17, indicating that students don't make too much consideration about their utilitarian in the knowledge sharing, most of the foreign students share knowledge not for improving their ability or getting recognition.

4 Discussion

The aim of this study is to explore the motivations and hinders of knowledge sharing among foreign students in Chinese universities.

As to motivations, they were classified into two parts: direct needs and indirect needs. It were obvious and proved in this study that direct needs such as getting new knowledge are important factors influencing knowledge sharing among foreign students. This finding is accordance with the previous study which highlights the complementary knowledge sharing as the main theme in the experiences of nursing students participating in an educational exchange program between Madagascar and Norway. It's apparent that, as the fundamental and also vital function of knowledge sharing, acquiring new knowledge is always the principle motivation.

Interestingly, when it comes to indirect needs, namely social networking needs, displayed as the most intense motivations in our study, there is few previous study ever focusing on this critical factor.

As to hinders, this study shows that the biggest obstacles discouraging foreign students from knowledge sharing are no doubt language barriers and lack of appropriate channels, which are both consistent with the perception of knowledge sharing among nursing students participating in an educational exchange. Since language is key to communication, and without an available channel can not be done a knowledge sharing, the language, and channel means a lot to a successful knowledge sharing activity. Besides, listed as one of "the most difficult languages in the world", Chinese keep many foreign students from participating a knowledge sharing activity. To make matters worse, the same language problem also bother Chinese students who are not an excellent foreign language speaker.

Another obstacle stopping a knowledge sharing is the lack of understanding between students. This factor is also revealed in the previous study reporting knowledge sharing is affected by partner characteristics. As for Chinese students and foreign students, deeply influenced by Confucianism, Chinese people are implicit and conservative, which sometimes leave an impression of unwillingness on foreign students' and thus impede the knowledge sharing.

5 Conclusion

According to the questionnaire analysis, this study concludes that the main motives of students' knowledge sharing are social networking motivations, desire to communicate with others, and desire to make friends. The main obstacles are language barriers, lack of channels and lack of understanding.

Regarding language issues, this study believe that firstly the universities can increase the requirements on foreign students' Chinese level, which not only encourages students to pay attention to Chinese learning but also a direct increase in students' Chinese language level at first and lay a good basis for the study and life after school. Second, for those students with poor Chinese, colleges, and universities can arrange training and regular assessment, and make their Chinese level be linked to their results and scholarships, encouraging students to continuously learn and improve their Chinese.

Regarding the channels of knowledge sharing, colleges and universities can make full use of campus network resources, set up relative online classes and discussion forum to facilitate the communication between teachers and students. They can also encourage students to set up their student learning union or interest groups, which can lead students to learn and communicate with each other.

Every can establish a formal student union or various associations, giving these organizations the rights and obligations so that students can acquire a sense of belonging and autonomy. These institutes can also organize other activities characterizing prominent national theme just like international days or national exchange for months, in which way they can enhance mutual understanding between students and also lead to more concern about the foreign students in the campus.

6 Limitations

The first limitation is that our questionnaire focuses on only one school. It is difficult to generalize from one to all with a single-sample box study. Another limitation is the small size.

This study ignores the nationalities of these twenty foreign students. Setting China, a country with typical and unique oriental culture, as the big background, there are not so many differences among these foreign students.

Acknowledgement. This study was funded by a Development Foundation for Graduate Education of Beihang University grant 4302026 and a National Natural Science Foundation China grant 73038101.

Appendix

Questions in questionnaire:

1. I lack time to do the former activities.
2. I do not know the other person well.
3. I want to keep the connection with others.

4. I fear that I would be perceived as a "show-off" person.
5. It will enhance self-learning ability.
6. I don't trust others to share my knowledge.
7. I want to make more friends.
8. I will feel belonging to and fit within the group.
9. I lack motivation or rewards in sharing knowledge.
10. I further my understanding of concepts learned in the class through sharing ideas with other students.
11. I lack avenues to share information or to communicate with others.
12. I am eager to help others or share.
13. I fear that I would provide wrong information.
14. I lack understanding as to what to share and with whom to share.
15. I want to keep the discussion or activity moving on.
16. I fear that a clash of opinion may spoil a relationship.
17. I want to gain recognition.
18. I fear that others may outperform me in studies.
19. It helps me to innovate ideas or other knowledge.
20. I lack the confidence to share knowledge with others.
21. It will enhance cooperative ability.
22. Culture difference does harm to knowledge sharing.
23. I am eager to study.
24. Language barriers do harm to knowledge sharing.
25. I want to get a reward (money, other's return).
26. The loneliness because of living in a foreign land does harm to knowledge sharing.

References

1. http://is.buaa.edu.cn/index.php/About/info/id/17.html
2. Tjoflåt, I., Razaonandrianina, J., Karlsen, B., Hansen, B.S.: Complementary knowledge sharing: experiences of nursing students participating in an educational exchange program between Madagascar and Norway. Nurse Educ. Today **49**, 33–38 (2017)
3. Li, X., Roberts, J., Yan, Y., Tan, H.: Knowledge sharing in China–UK higher education alliances. Int. Bus. Rev. **23**(2), 343–355 (2014)
4. Ambos, T.C., Ambos, B., Eich, K.J., Puck, J.: Imbalance and isolation: how team configurations affect global knowledge sharing. J. Int. Manag. **22**(4), 316–332 (2016)
5. Rachel Zhou, Y., Knoke, D., Sakamoto, I.: Rethinking silence in the classroom: Chinese students' experiences of sharing indigenous knowledge. Int. J. Incl. Educ. **9**(3), 287–311 (2005)
6. Rowley, J.: Is higher education ready for knowledge management? Int. J. Educ. Manag. **14**(7), 325–333 (2000)
7. Ardichvili, A., Maurer, M., Li, W., Wentling, T., Stuedemann, R.: Cultural influences on knowledge sharing through online communities of practice. J. Knowl. Manag. **10**(1), 94–107 (2006)
8. Cañas, A.J., Hill, G., Carff, R., Suri, N., Lott, J., Eskridge, T., Carvajal, R.: CmapTools: A knowledge modeling and sharing environment. In: Concept Maps: Theory, Methodology, Technology. Proceedings of the First International Conference on Concept Mapping, vol. 1, pp. 125–133, September (2004)

9. Ardichvili, A., Maurer, M., Li, W., Wentling, T., Stuedemann, R.: Cultural influences on knowledge sharing through online communities of practice. J. Knowl. Manag. **10**(1), 94–107 (2006)

10. Carroll, J., Ryan, J. (eds.): Teaching International Students: Improving Learning for All. Routledge, New York (2007)

11. Wang, S., Noe, R.A.: Knowledge sharing: a review and directions for future research. Hum. Res. Manag. Rev. **20**(2), 115–131 (2010)

12. Andrade, M.S.: International students in english-speaking universities: adjustment factors. J. Res. Int. Educ. **5**(2), 131–154 (2006)

13. Guruz, K.: Higher Education and International Student Mobility in The Global Knowledge Economy: Revised and Updated, 2nd edn. SUNY Press, Albany (2011)

14. Lu, L., Leung, K., Koch, P.T.: Managerial knowledge sharing: The role of individual, interpersonal, and organizational factors. Manag. Organ. Rev. **2**(1), 15–41 (2006)

15. Yaghi, K., Barakat, S., Alfawaer, Z.M., Shkokani, M., Nassuora, A.: Knowledge sharing degree among the undergraduate students: a case study at applied science private university. Int. J. Acad. Res. **3**(1), 20–24 (2011)

16. Huang, Y., Basu, C., Hsu, M.K.: Exploring motivations of travel knowledge sharing on social network sites: an empirical investigation of US college students. J. Hosp. Mark. Manag. **19**(7), 717–734 (2010)

17. Yang, S.J., Chen, I.Y.: A social network-based system for supporting interactive collaboration in knowledge sharing over peer-to-peer network. Int. J. Hum. Comput. Stud. **66**(1), 36–50 (2008)

18. Pemberton, L., Winter, M., Fallahkhair, S.: Collaborative mobile knowledge sharing for language learners. J. Res. Center Educ. Technol. **6**(1), 144–148 (2010)

19. Jer Yuen, T., Shaheen Majid, M.: Knowledge-sharing patterns of undergraduate students in Singapore. Libr. Rev. **56**(6), 485–494 (2007)

20. Xue, Y., Bradley, J., Liang, H.: Team climate, empowering leadership, and knowledge sharing. J. Knowl. Manag. **15**(2), 299–312 (2011)

21. Chen, Z., Gao, Q., Yang, Y.: Cultural difference on the usage pattern of tagging system for knowledge sharing. In: Rau, P.L.P. (ed.) CCD 2014. LNCS, vol. 8528, pp. 534–545. Springer, Cham (2014). doi:10.1007/978-3-319-07308-8_51

Breakout: Design and Evaluation of a Serious Game for Health Employing Intel RealSense

Jimmy Chhor[1,2], Yun Gong[2], and Pei-Luen Patrick Rau[2(✉)]

[1] RWTH Aachen University, Aachen, Germany
jimmy.chhor@rwth-aachen.de
[2] Department of Industrial Engineering, Tsinghua University, Beijing, China
gong-yl4@mails.tsinghua.edu.cn,
rpl@mail.tsinghua.edu.cn

Abstract. The motion capture system Intel RealSense enables fine-motoric gesture recognition and its small form factor allows for pre-integration into notebooks and tablets, substituting conventional cameras. This setup enables new methods of therapy in the form of serious games which are engaging, low-cost and easy to set up. By developing and evaluating a serious game prototype for rehabilitation employing Intel RealSense (called "Breakout") based on commercial game framework, immersive gaming experience is promoted. The domain of critical interaction design issues including operational range perception, spatial mapping, difficulty design and forms of interaction is highlighted and feasible solutions proposed. The findings indicate a potential to an enhancement of serious games for health, albeit further examinations are required.

Keywords: Serious game · Intel RealSense · Rehabilitation · Gameplay

1 Introduction

Clinical evaluations in recent years depict a major potential of the employment of motion tracking technologies coupled with other media in healthcare application. Benefits include the enhancement to clinical scores of partly disabled patients, a broader community integration associated with a more positive attitude and more independence in scheduling the therapy are registered as benefits [1]. Among the means of implementation, serious games for health attracts the most attention. Owed to its game characteristics uniform to commercial games, it allows for more immersion into the game and a secondary focus on entertainment, thus securing motivation for long term engagement and more success if employed as means of an accompanying rehabilitation method [2]. Most recent approaches to serious games in rehabilitation are based on Microsoft Kinect, a depth-camera featuring motion-tracking, which is chosen for its convenience in handling, affordability and reasonable pricing. Fewer clinical studies employ other sensors or customized motion tracking systems [3].

The objective of this research is to depict critical interaction design aspects encountered in employing the motion capture system Intel RealSense, to design a serious game prototype for upper body rehabilitation with focus on game design. The

© Springer International Publishing AG 2017
P.-L.P. Rau (Ed.): CCD 2017, LNCS 10281, pp. 531–545, 2017.
DOI: 10.1007/978-3-319-57931-3_42

fundamentals are based on commercial game design intertwined with serious games characteristics, enabling a more immersive gameplay than comparable serious games for health developed with Microsoft Kinect. The differences in design requirements compared to Microsoft Kinect originate in the implemented 3D virtual world and close-range interaction with the motion capture system.

The following Sect. 2 will point out distinctions between Intel RealSense and Microsoft Kinect motion capture system and refer to related research in the thematic field of serious games for upper body rehabilitation. Subsequently, in Sect. 3 the concept for the serious game is introduced: gameplay settings and interaction design including control and feedback are addressed. The successive Sect. 4 presents the evaluation method carried out in this study. The second last Sect. 5 aggregates the evaluation findings and discusses issues encountered in the game design. Concluding with Sect. 6, a short summary about the research is given and prospective future work is proposed.

2 Related Work

In the first Sect. 2.1, attributes and application area of motion capture system Microsoft Kinect V2 and front-facing Intel RealSense cameras are introduced. Sequentially, in Sect. 2.2 the concept of serious games is addressed and exemplary implementation in form of serious games for health is presented.

2.1 Motion Capture System

The employed depth-camera with specifications like Microsoft Kinect is optimized for close range interaction and allows for more accurate tracking of motoric movements in direct comparison to Microsoft Kinect. Table 1 depicts core attributes of each system.

Table 1. Specifications of Microsoft Kinect and Intel RealSense [4–6]

Attribute	Motion capture system		
	Kinect V2	Intel RealSense F200	Intel RealSense SR300
Technology	Time-of-flight	Projected structured light	Projected structured light
Weight	1.360 g	n/a	n/a (9.4 g chip)
Dimensions	249 × 66 × 67 mm	110 × 12.6 × 4.1 mm	110 × 12.6 × 4.1 mm
Range	0.5–4.5 m	0.2–1.2 m	0.2–1.2 m
Field of view	60° V, 70° H	n/a	55° V, 71.5° H, 88° D
Depth camera (pixel)	512 × 424 (30 FPS)	640 × 480 (60 FPS)	640 × 480 (60 FPS)
RGB camera (pixel)	1920 × 1080 (30FPS)	1920 × 1080 (30 FPS)	1920 × 1080 (30 FPS), 1280 × 720 (60 FPS)

Intel RealSense is available either bundled in a developer kit or can be purchased as an integrated unit substituting the ubiquitous camera unit in notebooks and tablets. The precise camera specifications depend on whether it is employed as a front- or rear-facing camera, albeit here only the former ones are reviewed. This condition reflects the advantage of Intel RealSense's small size and weight, allowing for ex works integration and eliminates the necessity of adapters as seen with Microsoft's Kinect V2 [4]. The most recent (front-facing) version is the SR300, succeeding the F200 version employed in this research and offers novel features to the system such as a new tracking mode labeled "Cursor Mode" for accurate point tracking, person tracking, increased range and tracking speed [5].

Microsoft Kinect deploys a Time-of-Flight sensor to measure the distance between an object and the sensor, while Intel RealSense generates the depth map via triangulation of a projected infrared grid. Another distinct difference is found in the field of application, also reflected in the respective working distances. Microsoft Kinect is used for far-range applications and allows full body tracking of up to six persons simultaneously with 25 skeleton joints. Further on, simple gesture detection as thumbs up, closed and open hand can also be recognized. Intel RealSense however, is focused on near-field application and enables subtler identification of features: hand gesture recognition with single joints and face tracking with up to 78 landmarks allow to detect precise motor movements. This is reflected in the accompanying Intel SKD featuring a multitude of predefined gestures like two fingers pinch, full pinch and victory sign [4, 5].

2.2   Serious Game Design and Implementation

Serious games follow the idea of guiding the user, also known as the player, with inherent game mechanics to a predetermined objective distinct from entertainment purposes such as transfer of knowledge or skills. The gamification nature hereby supports motivation [2].

The penultimate goal of the implemented serious game is the improvement of mobility for upper body, both in the sense of rehabilitation as well as exercising. Therefore, a principal aspect in game design is an easy and intuitive interaction which is adoptable to an individual's needs and scalable to the progress over the course of playing the game. This also poses high requirements to the hardware which is preferably low-cost, customizable and easy to install and use. Next generation depth-cameras, initially seeing a widely-spread use in gaming consoles like Xbox 360, offer great opportunities and synergy in the context of serious games for health: as a means of easily accessible motion capture technology, it facilitates recording training sessions and analysis of data [3].

This idea has been picked up in research and many approaches to combine Microsoft Kinect and serious games for health can be enumerated. Thematic fields range from rehabilitation and restoration of mobility after contracting diseases to the enhancement of process monitoring for distinct exercises and improving fitness by exercising.

Around 2012, low-cost serious game frameworks for rehabilitation covering essential aspects such as high configurability to adapt to patients' requirements and a dynamic adaption of game difficulty in relation to their progress have surfaced [7]. Exemplary implementations of serious games for upper body rehabilitation using low-cost motion capture systems such as Intel RealSense or Microsoft Kinect are presented below. Most approaches develop the serious game using basic motion sequences as starting points and can be categorized as matching games in a 2D virtual environment.

In "Post office trouble" the player grabs packages with a grasping gesture and matches them to boxes with predetermined topics. Game framework parameters such package size and distance to boxes are adoptable to players' motion capabilities. An initial small study with 8 healthy people aged between 52 and 79 indicates good engagement, while usability is restricted due to unnatural movements. This is owned to setup restrictions with Intel RealSense, such as the requirement for the palm to face forwards [8]. A motion-wise similar game is a jigsaw puzzle, implemented with Microsoft Kinect: matching color blocks must be identified and moved to their corresponding position in the jigsaw puzzle, whereas the reach distance to grab the puzzle pieces is adjustable. The player's movement during the game can be recorded using inbuilt software functions, but requires further development for analysis. The game has been tested under supervision of a physiotherapist with a patient suffering from post-stroke impaired hand movement. Results point towards some acclimatization time but underline the general playability, although a capability of balancing one's extremities has been identified as a requirement to operate the game [9]. In "Physio-Mate", the players are first taught motion sequences called routines in a preliminary imitation game, which awards points for mimicking predetermined motions devised by a physiotherapist. These movements are then performed in the principal game: a matching game, where appearing objects are to be moved to the designate waste container. The required motion sequence reflects the pre-taught routines. Data regarding game progress is recorded and can be accessed by the physiotherapist [10].

An approach to more immersive gameplay with Microsoft Kinect has been presented with the serious game "The Sorcerer's Apprentice" in a 3D game environment. The game is targeted at patients suffering from one-sided Shoulder Impingement Syndrome and intends to improve overall mobility through exercises. Specific gestures, performed with impaired arm, trigger actions in the game required to advance in a level while the healthy arm assumes all other motions. The implementation of meaningful play through a story differs from predominant implementations of serious games for health and enables more immersive gameplay, while further evaluation towards usability and engagement are needed [11].

In view of general functionality and capability of motion capture systems as a means of objectively assessing aspects of movement, a comparative analysis from 2016 of published papers reviewing Microsoft Kinect points towards a sufficient precision, especially for gross spatial movement [12]. The data basis is published papers, which employ additional motion capture devices or sensors to validate the data collected with Microsoft Kinect. With a view to stroke rehabilitation applications, a maximum average normalized root mean squared error of 1.74 cm in comparison to the research-grade motion capture system OptiTrack has been measured, verifying the camera's potential as low-cost progress tracking system [13]. Since camera specifications for Microsoft Kinect and Intel RealSense are largely comparable, the findings are to some extend valid for the latter motion capture system as well.

Research groups also attempt to increase the accuracy by altering existing algorithms for image analysis: for instance, the accuracy of Kinect skeletal joint coordinates has been improved by implementing constraints on recognized body segment lengths and orientation in the existing code, thus reducing body segment variance by up to 72% [14].

To garner knowledge on critical interaction design issues for near-field applications using motion capture technology in healthcare sector and to highlight potential assets and drawbacks, a serious game for rehabilitation using Intel RealSense F200 is developed and presented in this paper. The game design is inspired by commercial game design while integrating core aspects of serious game design [3, 15–17]: intuitive user-centered game design, extensive configurability and control feedback, an adequate challenge, and balancing a meaningful play while keeping the objective of health improvement. Based on these aspects, the game concept will be briefly introduced focusing on core elements and is followed by an evaluation performed in the context of user testing.

3 Concept and Implementation

The game was developed in Unity 5, a cross-platform engine with support for Intel SDK, and a developer version of Intel RealSense F200. The assets applied in game design, namely models, animations, music and fonts, are taken from openly accessible sources in the Unity asset store, i.e. Unity essential packages, and from Intel SDK with the intention of speeding up prototyping phase.

The prototype "Breakout" follows the archetype of a survival game, in which players need to protect a given objective from enemy attacks and hereby accumulate points for their achievements tracked in a high score. The game design is based on commercial game structure adapted to serious games for health, especially with regard to meaningful play through an immersive story and environment. In the following sub sections, the game concept as well as multiple game characteristics are explained in detail.

3.1 Gameplay Design

The gameplay is the compound framework of rules for setting the game's environment. It describes the player's range of actions and covers essentials such as a concept scheme, in which the previously described story line is fitted. In the following Fig. 1, a sketch of the game concept can be found.

"A" represents the game area and "C" the fixed position of an object, the player must guard. Over the course of time, enemies, represented by figures "1" and "2", randomly spawn on the map and move per their programmed AI to destination "C" while the player must prevent their advance. This is achieved by controlling an ingame

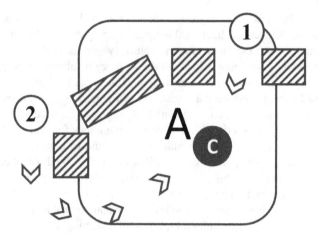

Fig. 1. Concept scheme for game play

hand object "H": by touching enemies, damage is inflicted to them and they vanish when a damage threshold is exceeded. Disabling enemies generates a score equal to their difficulty setting, whereas distinct enemy types are distinguishable through their appearance (overview in Fig. 2).

Fig. 2. Concept for ingame objects including enemies

The current iteration of the game is situated in a non-time-limited game mode. A game session is terminated, when the player cannot prevent the enemies from approaching the objective, thus deducting life points from the player's health bar until its reduction to zero. The present accumulated score is then saved to a high score chart and is visible in the main game menu.

The rough game interface is represented in Fig. 3. In the lower right corner, the health bar for the object to be protected is displayed. When damage is sustained, the bar is reduced and the screen briefly flashes to support visual feedback. The current game score is tracked in the upper middle part of the screen. The remaining two UI elements support the control via visual feedback: the upper left symbol represents a hint when the motion capture system cannot detect the player's hands during a game session and the lower right rectangular box transmits the player's live stream as recorded by the camera.

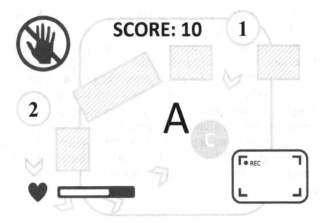

Fig. 3. Concept for game interface

3.2   Game Control Design

The game can be controlled contact-free without the necessity of further peripheral devices like a mouse and keyboard to facilitate intuitive and immersive control. The ingame camera view is set as perspective due to the size of the terrain in the virtual environment to better convey the depth aspect of the map. It is in a fixed position and located in third person aerial view to allow a better overview over the entire field of action.

Within a game session, the player takes control of hand shaped objects. Their behavior precisely reflects the player's own hands in the 3D environment in real-time and are operated contact-free as seen in Fig. 4: the ingame hand object imitates the

Fig. 4. Gameplay demonstration

player's full-pinch gesture. It is possible to use either one or both hands to play the game, while this decision should be reflected in the game settings to adapt the game difficulty. Touching enemies can be done in any manner, while specific gestures trigger predetermined actions. For instance, the game menu is invoked by signaling a thumbs-up gesture or alternatively by pressing the Esc-button on the keyboard.

The menu on the other hand can be operated with either mouse, keyboard or handsfree, although it is recommended to adopt game settings manually due to the multilayered menu structure. To choose a menu option, a separately superimposed cursor is hovered above the menu item. After a short time-interval, the item is selected. An example is demonstrated in Fig. 5 where the ingame menu is invoked. Control is possible with either the left or right hand, or in case of two-handed usage with the hand closer to the camera.

Fig. 5. Invoked game menu during a game session

3.3 Feedback Design

The game's natural control by using hands in a 3D game environment requires supplementary feedback to both convey the depth aspect of the map as well as give insight to operational range limitations.

Visual control feedback is conveyed via a live camera feed of the depth map in the lower right corner of the screen (see Fig. 5). The stream is intentionally chosen to represent a mirror-inverted view, since this is the most natural way of self-monitoring. Further on, visual hints are superimposed in the upper left corner to enhance the feedback in certain events, for instance if no hand is detected by the camera during a game session (see Fig. 3). To support the game flow while preventing excessive abuse of this function, the game speed is slightly slowed down if this event is flagged.

In case of enemy contact to the object to be protected, the screen briefly flashes red to indicate loss of health points. On the other hand, a short, subtle audio clip is replayed every time the player touches an enemy to support the perception of enemy contact.

3.4 Design of Challenge

The game's challenge is situated in personal reflexes, agility and reaction time required to ward off enemies as well as implicit challenges as the selection of which enemies to engage in the right order. This is owed to distinct enemy types identified via their appearance: one type of enemy may be slower and more resilient while others are quick but easy to disable. The types of enemy spawn as well as their spawning location are randomized. Predetermined, feasible locations differ in distance from the center of the map to introduce a factor of randomness in gameplay.

As already touched upon in Sect. 3.1, currently only one game mode with three difficulty settings ("easy", "normal" and "hard") is implemented, affecting count of enemy spawn in a set time frame and both their damage threshold and the damage they can deal. During game progression, the difficulty is dynamically scaled dependent on three different factors: elapsed time, current player health and score. As a thumb of rule the more time elapses, the more frequent enemy spawn instantiation is observed until the point is reached, where the player is overwhelmed.

3.5 Configurability of Gameplay

In terms of configurability there are three further settings apart from difficulty to customize the gameplay per the player's requirements: game speed, hand focus and object scaling. They are locally saved to the hard drive and the game boots with the last settings by default.

Game speed setting affects the overall speed of the game and is not to be confused with difficulty setting. While an increase in game difficulty equals to a higher count of enemy instantiations at the same time, a high game speed also accelerates their movement speed and attack rate. Therefore, it is possible to have a high number of slow moving enemies on the map. The threshold for speed setting is currently set to 70%, 100% and 130% (each in accordance with "slow", "normal" and "fast").

The Hand focus setting allows to choose with which hand the game is played. The options "left hand", "right hand" and "both hands" affect the principal spawn location of enemies during a game session. Generally spoken, enemy spawning is possible from predetermined locations distributed over the map with variable distances to the center of the map. For instance, "left hand" option enables a dominant instantiation of enemies on the left side of the map.

Object scaling changes the size of spawned enemies: the bigger an object is, the easier it is to spot and to touch since the collision box scales with object size. It is possible to scale objects in 50% intervals from 100% up to 200% size. Special monster spawns are excluded from this option, otherwise their size will be too large. The underlying reason is found in the implemented game physics: if enemies become too large, they will be stuck in between narrow building complexes and impede game experience.

4   Evaluation

A user testing is conducted after developing a functional prototype version of the game to gather user feedback on game design, means of control and usability in context of improving upper body movements.

4.1   Test User Profile

For the preliminary test, a total of 10 users, respectively 5 German and 5 Chinese students, are asked to participate and compensated for their expenses. The students' background is in engineering with different specializations. Students with a HCI background can give pointers towards improving user-centered design, especially with a view to game control and control feedback. Further benefit is drawn from two students' experience in designing serious games for health with Microsoft Kinect, and additional two students' expertise in depth cameras. One student is in possession of a trainer license and several years of training experience, and can give first insight to the game's potential in upper body exercising and rehabilitation. The remaining students without prior knowledge in game design or technology, assist in providing feedback from a layman's point of view.

4.2   Evaluation Procedure

The testing procedure is equal for all test users independent of potential prior knowledge and is estimated to take about 45 min per person. After a brief introduction to the Intel RealSense camera and the game framework, the participants are distributed a leaflet covering all orally relayed information. The participants are free to test the prototype game in whatever manner they see fit for a duration of about 15 min and are

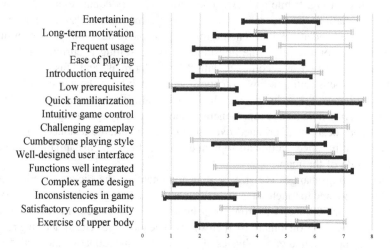

Fig. 6. Survey results, depicted with standard deviation (Chinese: grey, German: black)

free to inquire simple questions. Meanwhile, observations regarding gameplay and associated challenges are noted by an observer.

A subsequent survey and brief interview investigate vital criteria as entertainment factor, gameplay, degree of challenge, perspective of long-term motivation, user-centered design and feedback on the new non-physical user-computer-interaction via the motion capture system. The survey results are depicted in Fig. 6.

5   Results and Discussion

Evaluation findings from different sources – observation, survey and interview – are pooled together and address different facets of the game.

5.1   General Feedback

Many participants enjoyed the game and exceeded the given time frame for testing. Generally, the prototype game is better received by Chinese in view of entertainment, long-term motivation and possible frequency of playing the game in comparison to the German students.

Both groups rate the ease of play in medium difficulty, nevertheless a prior introduction to the game and control is recommended due to its unfamiliarity. The game concept is simple and the manner of control is perceived as intuitive but sometimes cumbersome. In some instances, ingame control did not properly follow the input action or hands were not correctly recognized, which is touched upon in the next sections. The gameplay experience however is discerned to be challenging.

5.2   Operational Range Perception

A major issue is observed with many subjects: the continuous tracking did not work flawlessly and the virtual hand object kept disappearing after initial fail of tracking. It is evident in case the participant's hands are outside the camera's operational boundary, which admittedly is difficult to assess as a layman. The range is exemplary illustrated in Fig. 7, resembling a distorted cuboid volume when considering minimum working distance of the motion capture system.

Still, the absence was sometimes observed even though the hand was within operational range. This was especially true for female participants with smaller hands wearing bracelets, wrist watches or rings, seemingly interfering with the camera's tracking capability. The depth map, the fundamental basis to all employed algorithms, is based on the analysis of the distortions when projecting an infrared light grid on an object's surface. Most likely, an issue arises in conjunction with polished surfaces, affecting the projected grid and thereby the calculation of the depth map.

As a means of improvement to facilitate the perception of boundaries, it is suggested to implement smart devices indicating the operational limit via vibrations as seen in Fig. 7. Thus, it is possible to mimic tactile feedback as is given with legacy peripheral devices like a keyboard. Another proposal addresses a perception enhancement of the

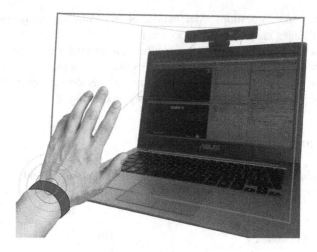

Fig. 7. Potential improvement to operational range perception via haptic feedback

operational range with a tutorial: the user traces a predefined path along the borders of operational reach to raise the sensitivity for both the visual boundary of control inside the game and the real operational boundary set by the hardware.

5.3   Spatial Mapping

Issues regarding spatial perception based on a mismatch of 3D input for control and the game display with a conventional (2D) screen are monitored. In the perspective view, moving one's hand forward and upwards seems to imply a similar movement (see Fig. 8 for ingame hand object coordinate system), although the change in object size and the

Fig. 8. Issue in spatial mapping when moving the hands

relative position to the environment indicate a disparity in illustration. The hand object does not directly interact with the environment and can slip through all environmental objects: it can both sink through the ground if the hand is moved to low or be partly obstructed by buildings.

It is observed, that participants sometimes show confusion about the inability to touch the enemies, even though in fact they were hovering the hand above the enemies instead of moving forward. Initially this phenomenon is perceived as a design error, but surprisingly the participants are eager to figure out the mechanism behind the disparity of perception and regard it as an additional challenge. After a period of acclimatization though, the participants experienced a more satisfying gameplay and displayed a steep learning curve in performance.

5.4 Difficulty Design and Configurability

There are more distinct requirements to gameplay design, especially in view of interaction and control for a serious game in upper body rehabilitation in e.g. post-stroke treatment in comparison to healthcare fields as exergaming. In this case, the principal issue is the limitation on limb control due to part palsy as an after-effect of stroke, whereas individual patients display different grades of severity. Therefore, special accommodation to their needs can be achieved by modifying game mechanics as described in Sect. 3.5: independent from the chosen difficulty level which regulates the enemy spawn and the dynamical scaling over time, the game speed can be increased or decreased to cope with personal handicaps. Further, changes regarding enemy object size scaling and the focus which hand is mainly used for control can be set. This overall process should be supervised by healthcare experts. Physical therapists can estimate the load on the patients and recommend movement patterns to support with the rehabilitation prior to conducting clinical studies. This approach can be adopted to fine-tune game mechanics as well. For instance, monster may require additional conditions like both a special gesture and a direct contact to be disabled.

5.5 Support of Natural Interaction

The interaction between player and enemies gives insight to the favored means of interaction. At first, participants attempt to push the enemies away with a palm strike and some instinctively tried picking them up with a pinch-like movement, but failed in this approach due to the game mechanics not supporting the underlying physics. Therefore, the request to a more realistic physics engine was voiced to go along with the natural control which is otherwise well perceived.

6 Conclusion and Future Work

This paper describes the experiences in designing and evaluating a prototype for a serious game in upper body rehabilitation and exercising employing Intel RealSense and concentrates on critical interaction design issues. The game itself is employed with special consideration to meaningful gameplay in conjunction with a natural user interaction and high adaptability to the player's physical capabilities. The findings garnered from early trial runs with healthy people support an additional value as a serious game for health, especially in the aspects of immersive gameplay and natural interaction. Further on, the evaluation process highlights critical game design elements affecting the usability, for instance the requirement of extensive user feedback to support spatial perception and estimation of operational range.

The present game design allows a natural control by tracking the player's hands and projecting them to the 3D virtual game environment, while gameplay does not require specific upper extremity movements. The player is free to interact with ingame elements in a feasible and desired manner. Still, to check the suitability of the game for patients with impaired upper body movement and to improve the fine-tuning of game configurability, a cooperation with a physiotherapist is desired. Apart from implemented customization options such as game speed and ingame object size, more game elements can be modified. For instance, the game environment and camera settings can be changed to exclusively coerce sideways movement of upper extremity, if that is the recommended motion sequence for the patient without changing the fundamental game structure. In a subsequent step, clinical studies under the supervision of physiotherapists with patients suffering from impaired upper body movement, can be conducted to gather meaningful data about the impact of a serious games to support in upper body rehabilitation.

Acknowledgments. The research was supported by Intel and National Natural Science Foundation China grant NSC71661167006.

References

1. Mousavi Hondori, H., Khademi, M.: A review on technical and clinical impact of Microsoft Kinect on physical therapy and rehabilitation. J. Med. Eng. **2014**, 1–16 (2014). Hindawi Publishing Corporation, New York
2. Stapleton, A.: Serious games: serious opportunities. In: Australian Game Developers' Conference (AGDC), pp. 1–6, Academic Summit, Melbourne (2004)
3. Burke, J.W., McNeill, M., Charles, D., Morrow, P., Crosbie, J., McDonough, S.: Serious games for upper limb rehabilitation following stroke. In: Proceedings of the 2009 Conference in Games and Virtual Worlds for Serious Applications (VS-GAMES 2009), pp. 103–110. IEEE (2009)
4. Microsoft: Kinect Hardware (2017). https://developer.microsoft.com/en-us/windows/kinect/hardware. Accessed 10 Jan 2017
5. Le, N.: A Comparison of Intel® RealSense™ Front-Facing Camera SR300 and F200 (2016). https://software.intel.com/en-us/articles/a-comparison-of-intel-realsensetm-front-facing-camera-sr300-and-f200. Accessed 10 Jan 2017
6. Intel: Intel® RealSense™ Camera SR300: Embedded Coded Light 3D Imaging System with Full High Definition Color Camera (2017). https://software.intel.com/sites/default/files/managed/0c/ec/realsense-sr300-product-datasheet-rev-1-0.pdf. Accessed 10 Jan 2017
7. Saini, S., Rambli, D.R.A., Sulaiman, S., Zakaria, M.N., Shukri, S.R.M.: A low-cost game framework for a home-based stroke rehabilitation system. In: Proceedings of the 2012 International Conference on Computer & Information Science (ICCIS), pp. 55–60. IEEE (2012)

8. Dezentje, P., Cidota, M.A., Clifford, R.M.S., Lukosch, S.G., Bank, P.J.M., Lukosch, H.K.: Designing for engagement in augmented reality games to assess upper extremity motor dysfunctions. In: Proceedings of the 2015 IEEE International Symposium on Mixed and Augmented Reality - Media, Art, Social Science, Humanities and Design (ISMAR-MASH'D), pp. 57–58. IEEE (2015)

9. Bamrungthai, P., Pleehachinda, W.: Development of a game-based system to support stroke rehabilitation using Kinect device. In: Proceedings of the 2015 International Conference on Science and Technology (TICST), pp. 323–326. IEEE (2015)

10. Madeira, R.M., Costa, L., Postolache, O.: PhysioMate - pervasive physical rehabilitation based on NUI and gamification. In: Proceedings of the 2014 International Conference and Exposition on Electrical and Power Engineering (EPE), pp. 612–616. IEEE (2014)

11. Fikar, P., Schoenauer, C., Kaufmann, H.: The Sorcerer's apprentice: a serious game aiding rehabilitation in the context of subacromial impingement syndrome. In: Proceedings of the 2013 7th International Conference on Pervasive Computing Technologies for Healthcare and Workshops (PervasiveHealth), pp. 327–330. IEEE (2013)

12. Breedon, P., Byrom, B., Siena, L., Muehlhausen, W.: Enhancing the measurement of clinical outcomes using Microsoft Kinect. In: Proceedings of the 2016 International Conference on Interactive Technologies and Games (iTAG), pp. 61–69. IEEE (2016)

13. Webster, D., Celik, O.: Experimental evaluation of Microsoft Kinect's accuracy and capture rate for stroke rehabilitation applications. In: Proceedings of the 2014 IEEE Haptics Symposium (HAPTICS), pp. 455–460. IEEE (2014)

14. Sinha, S., Bhowmick, B., Chakravarty, K., Sinha, A., Das, A.: Accurate upper body rehabilitation system using Kinect. In: Proceedings of the 2016 IEEE 38th Annual International Conference of the Engineering in Medicine and Biology Society (EMBC), pp. 4605–4609. IEEE (2016)

15. Ushaw, G., Davison, R., Eyre, J., Morgan, G.: Adopting best practices from the games industry in development of serious games for health. In: Proceedings of the 5th International Conference on Digital Health 2015, pp. 1–8. ACM, New York (2015)

16. Marin, J.G., Navarro, K.F., Lawrence, E.: Serious games to improve the physical health of the elderly: a categorization scheme. In: Proceedings of the Fourth International Conference on Advances in Human-Oriented and Personalized Mechanisms, Technologies, and Services (CENTRIC 2011), pp. 64–71. IARIA, New York (2014)

17. Wattanasoontorn, V., Boada, I., García, R., Sbert, M.: Serious games for health. Entertain. Comput. 4(4), 231–247 (2013). Elsevier

Instructional Design and Teaching Effectiveness of SPOCs in Chinese Higher Education

Ka-Hin Lai, Lili Dong, and Pei-Luen Patrick Rau[✉]

Department of Industrial Engineering, Tsinghua University, Beijing, China
li-jx15@mails.tsinghua.edu.cn,
{dongli2012,rpl}@mail.tsinghua.edu.cn

Abstract. This study aims to explore the current instructional design and teaching effectiveness of blended learning in the Chinese higher education system from both the student and instructor's perspective. The instructional design and teaching effectiveness of five SPOCs (Small Private Online Courses) offered in the 2016–2017 Spring Semester by Tsinghua University were investigated. Methods employed to collect data included handing out the Chinese adapted SEEQ questionnaires to students and interviewing 1 teacher and 4 teaching assistants. Results revealed that (1) for all courses, the final grades consisted of online participation and performance, face-to-face learning and performance, assignment and examination. However, different courses weighted each part differently: examination scores were weighted more heavily for science courses than arts or history courses. (2) Courses with shorter offline discussions sessions resulted in higher participation in online discussions; students were more satisfied when instructors actively participated in discussions. (3) In general, students experienced high satisfaction in learning value, instructor enthusiasm and organization and breadth of coverage.

Keywords: SPOCs · Blended learning mode · Instructional design · Teaching effectiveness

1 Introduction

Blended learning, a new mode of learning based on Information and Communications Technology (ICT) has received great interested the past years in China. Blended learning combines the advantages [1] of traditional face-to-face learning with e-learning. It allows the instructor to lead, inspire and control the teaching process and also enables students to be proactive, enthusiastic and creative in the learning process [2]. In blended learning, the instructor has a variety of instructional design and teaching methods that can be employed and these methods can be flexible depending on which aspect the instructor wishes the student to focus on: lessons help develop the students' basic abilities (memorization and understanding) while group discussion and workshops facilitate a students' advanced abilities (application, evaluation, analysis, creation) [3].

Currently, there are multiple studies on the teaching effectiveness of blended learning. Dziuban et al. [4] did a comparison study on the course completion

© Springer International Publishing AG 2017
P.-L.P. Rau (Ed.): CCD 2017, LNCS 10281, pp. 546–553, 2017.
DOI: 10.1007/978-3-319-57931-3_43

percentage of students in e-learning, face-to-face learning and blended learning courses. Absalom et al. [5] investigated the teaching effectiveness of e-learning where the test group used e-learning and control group used blended learning. They found that the latter achieved better grades. Furthermore, Cosgrove, B.S. & Olitsky et al. [6], Liu [7], Francis et al. [8], Kirwin et al. [9], Zhang et al. [10] investigated the effects of blended learning on one specific course through experiments and questionnaires. However, there is little research on how to implement blended learning in various disciplines and the effects of different teaching methods in blended learning.

SPOCs are the version of MOOCs used locally with on-campus students. However, China had a late start in MOOCs and SPOCs give little guidance in how to allocate the learning time between e-learning and offline sessions. Only few Chinese Universities such as Tsinghua University (THU) utilize the blended learning technique through existing MOOC resources in several courses. Moreover, how to organize the instructional design of offline learning sessions and whether this kind of diverse teaching method affects teaching effectiveness still requires further investigation. This paper explores the applications of SPOCs in Tsinghua University (THU) and attempts to provide a blueprint for the future SPOCs implementations in China.

This paper examines currently existing SPOCs in THU and poses the following two questions:

1. What are the different ways that SPOCs are implemented in THU and how are the offline sessions organized?
2. Do these different implementations in THU have an effect on the teaching effectiveness?

2 Method

In order to investigated the instructional design and teaching effectiveness of SPOCs in Tsinghua University, this study chose the following 5 classes from the 25 SPOCs offered at THU's 2016 Spring Semester: *an art class on eastern and western art* (arts course), *a history course on contemporary Chinese history* (history course), *an introductory computer science course* (CS course), *an introductory physics course* (physics course) and *an introductory ergonomics course* (ergonomics course). Arts, history, CS and physics courses are undergraduate courses and these courses were selected based on class size(More than 100 students enrolled in these arts course and history course respectively while less than 50 students enrolled in these CS course and physics course respectively). In addition, this study chose a graduate ergonomics course to compare with other courses. Two phases were conducted in the study.

2.1 Phase One: Interview

The first phase of the interview aimed to explore the different instructional design of each respective course from instructor's perspective. The current section introduces the methodology and results of the interview.

Interview Question. The interviews question were mainly about basic class information, online learning information, offline learning information and the suggestion of SPOCs. Main questions were: (1) How many credits in this course? (2) What is the form of offline sessions or online sessions? (3) How to allocate the discussion time? (4) What is the grading policy? (5) How to encourage students to take part in the discussion?

Participant and Procedure. A physic course instructor and 4 teaching assistants of remaining courses were interviewed. The whole interviews were conducted face-to-face in Shunde Building in Tsinghua University. The interview time for each participant was from 28 to 35 min.

Data Analysis. The interview data were analyzed to compare offline learning forms, discussion time allocation and grading policy in these 5 courses. More details will be approached in the interview result.

2.2   Phase Two: Survey

This study designed a questionnaire and surveyed students from these 5 courses. The objective was to explore the teaching effectiveness from a learner's perspective.

Questionnaire Construction. There were three parts in questionnaire: first, the basic personal information includes students' majors and grades. Main questions were: (1) What is your major? (2) What grade are you in?

In the second part, 29 items were designed based on the Chinese version SEEQ (Students' Evaluations of Educational Quality) questionnaire, a survey developed by March [11] and later revised by Meng and Liu [12] to adapt to Chinese students. In this study, the survey questions were consisted of six dimensions: learning/value, instructor enthusiasm and organization, group interaction, individual rapport, breadth of coverage, examinations/grading and assignments/readings and we amended some words to adapt to this survey. For the "group interaction" dimension, for example, an instance of item was "I think the instructor or TA encourages students to participate in the discussion." The 5-point Likert scales were used to measure different levels of agreement to the items in this part from "1 = totally disagree" to "5 = totally agree".

For the third section, students were asked to answer the question about discussion. The discussion satisfaction following three 5-point Likert scales questions: (1) The discussion (both online and offline) allowed you to gain a deeper under-standing of the class content. (2) You were able to freely express your opinion or ask questions during discussions (both online and offline). (3) The teacher or TA were helpful during the group discussions. We also asked the frequency of online discussion post.

Participants and Procedure. Questionnaires were given out to the five chosen classes via Internet. In order to keep the validity of each questionnaire, the teaching assistants of five courses forwarded the questionnaires to the students respectively. After filling the survey, each participant received 5 RMB as a reward and the teaching assistants received 40 RMB as a reward.

Data Analysis. The questionnaire data were analyzed to compare six dimensions of Chinese version SEEQ and the discussion satisfaction in these 5 courses. More details will be approached in the survey result.

3 Result

3.1 Interview Result

Summarizing the in-depth interviews from the teachers and TAs' from the five courses, several patterns of SPOCs were discovered.

Instructional Design of Offline Learning Sessions. The interviews revealed that different types of classes differed in the content and form of offline sessions, as shown in Table 1. Physics, CS and arts course only held discussions during offline sessions while history course and ergonomic course combined lessons with discussions. In addition, history course conducted offline learning sessions in the form of lectures where experts were invited from relevant fields to share their viewpoints. For discussions, the five courses had two forms of discussions: the discussions for the physics course consisted of student discussions on the solution for a specific question from the course homework, followed by time to complete individual work while in the other four courses, the TA would lead the discussion with a predetermined topic, followed by presentations from each group and a discussion of the presentation content.

Table 1. Offline session type, session length, grading policy, group number and group size of the five classes in 2016

Class Type	History	Arts	CS	Physics	Ergonomics
Offline session type					
Lessons	√				√
Discussion	√	√	√	√	√
Lecture	√				
Session length (periods)	2	2	2	3	2
Grading policy					
Online video	40%	40%	0%	20%	0%
Offline participation	30%	30%	45%	10%	20%
Project	30%	30%	40%	0%	60%
Exam	0%	0%	15%	70%	20%
Number of groups	4–5	4	4	6–7	5
Group size	3–5	5	4–5	4–5	3–4

Discussion Time Allocation and Group Size. For history, arts and CS courses, discussions lasted two periods (approximately 90 min), physics course discussions lasted 3 periods (approximately 135 min) and ergonomic course discussions consisted of one period of lesson and one period of discussion. To ensure participation in discussions, the group size for all courses were consistently around 4–6 students which conforms to the findings of Kanchanachaya [13].

Grading Policies. Traditionally, course grades are based on the students score on a midterm or final exam/paper, but research revealed that in some SPOCs, the e-learning progress of each student is also included in the final grade. However, the percentage varied across the different courses, as in shown in Table 1, the final grade consisted 70% of the final exam and 30% of class participation in physics course. The teacher from the physic course states, *"If there are no final exams, the group discussions will not be in-depth and for such an introductory courses, only exams can show if a student has really learned the material"*; In CS course, the programming assignments made up 40% of the final grade (4 assignments, each of which makes up 10%), pop-up quizzes, final exam and participation made up of 30%, 15% and 15% of the final grade respectively; In ergonomics course, the final grade was consisted of 20% reading assignments and homework, 30% midterm project, 30% final project and 20% final exam while video e-learnings were not a part of the final grade; For arts course and history course, both final grades consisted of 40% video e-learning, 30% offline discussion participation and 30% project. The TA for history course believes that *"Students from non-history majors are usually not interested in history courses, hence it is important to use grades as a motivation for each aspect of the course to ensure student participation."*

Participation Level. In SPOCs, offline discussions are usually led by teachers or TA and results in a higher participation level and the "online + offline" teaching method further motivates the students to take the initiative to learn. The participation for online learning varied: Courses with relatively less offline discussion periods such as arts course, history course and ergonomics course had a higher participation in online discussion. The arts course in particular had a highly active student body due to special online sessions where the two teachers and nine TAs would engage in real-time online discussions, resulting in high participation. On the other hand, courses with weekly offline discussions (physics and CS course) had a relatively lower participation in online discussions.

The discussion type, length, grading policy, group number and group size for the five courses are as shown in Table 1.

3.2   Survey Result

Subject Information. Questionnaires were given out to the five chosen classes and 100 surveys in total were collected from the five courses, 71 of which came from history course (630 enrolled students), 12 from ergonomics course (17 enrolled students), 8 from Physics course (40 enrolled students), 5 from CS course (19 enrolled students), and 4 from Arts course.

Questionnaire Analysis. Cronbach's alpha was used to analyze the questionnaire's reliability. The internal consistency α was 0.961, which suggests the results were reliable and suitable for data analysis.

Table 2. Mean and standard deviation in SEEQ and discussion satisfaction

	History	Arts	CS	Physics	Ergonomics	Overall
(1) Learning/value	4.4 ± 0.5	3.6 ± 1.4	4.2 ± 0.9	4.2 ± 0.4	4.3 ± 0.5	4.3 ± 0.6
(2) Enthusiasm and organization	4.4 ± 0.5	3.7 ± 1.1	4.1 ± 0.9	4.3 ± 0.5	4.2 ± 0.4	4.3 ± 0.6
(3) Group interaction	4.2 ± 0.6	3.6 ± 0.9	3.9 ± 1.0	4.3 ± 0.5	4.1 ± 0.9	4.2 ± 0.7
(4) Individual rapport	4.2 ± 0.5	3.7 ± 0.8	3.9 ± 1.1	4.1 ± 0.7	4.1 ± 0.8	4.2 ± 0.6
(5) Breadth of coverage	4.5 ± 0.5	3.9 ± 0.8	3.9 ± 1.0	4.2 ± 0.5	4.2 ± 0.7	4.4 ± 0.6
(6) Grading and assignment	4.2 ± 0.5	3.5 ± 1.1	4.1 ± 1.1	4.1 ± 0.5	3.9 ± 0.8	4.1 ± 0.6
(7) Discussion satisfaction	4.2 ± 0.7	3.9 ± 0.8	4.0 ± 1.2	4.1 ± 0.3	3.9 ± 0.8	4.1 ± 0.7
N	71	4	5	8	12	100

As shown in Table 2, the general satisfaction for all five courses are relatively high, each dimension with an average higher than 4.1 points. History course had the highest score in "Breadth of Coverage" (4.5 ± 0.5) with little fluctuations between "Group Interaction" (4.2 ± 0.6), "Individual Rapport" (4.2 ± 0.6) and "Examinations/Grading and Assignments/Readings" (4.2 ± 0.5). Arts course had an even score across all six dimensions. The CS course and ergonomic course had the higher "Learning/Value" score (4.2 ± 0.9 and 4.3 ± 0.5 respectively) while physics course scored higher in "Group Interaction" (4.3 ± 0.5) and "Instructor Enthusiasm and Organization" (4.3 ± 0.5).

As shown in Table 3, during online discussions, students in the arts course posted 11–15 times because of intermittent offline classes and the real-time online discussion sessions; History course had a larger class size and had more total replies; for the physics course which had weekly offline discussions, the online discussion was relatively inactive; lastly, the ergonomics class's online discussion functioned more as a homework submission and project presentation area, with around 6–10 posts per student. The TA from CS course said that due to the weekly offline discussions, the online forum had a relatively lower participation in online discussions. However, 4 students in CS course are active on the online discussion forum (more than 6 times to posted), that is different from what the teaching assistant said. This demonstrates that the posting frequency is related to the course's general organization and function of the discussion area.

Table 3. Frequency of online discussion post

Frequency	History	Arts	CS	Physics	Ergonomics
0–5 times	60	0	1	7	0
6–10 times	9	1	1	1	11
11–15 times	1	2	1	0	1
16–20 times	1	1	1	0	0
21 times or more	0	0	1	0	0
Total	71	4	5	8	12

4   Conclusion

With respect to student evaluations of each course, the history course had "online learning + offline discussion + lecture" teaching model and scored the highest in the "Breadth of Content" dimension (an average of 4.5 points). The students thought the varied form of classes enabled them to broaden their knowledge. In comparison, the ergonomics course followed a strict "1 + 1" teaching model (1 period of lesson and 1 period of discussion) scored relatively high in "Breadth of Content", "Learning/Value" and "Instructors Enthusiasm and Organization" (4.2, 4.3, 4.2 points respectively). The physics course scored higher in "Instructors Enthusiasm and Organization" and "Group Interaction" (4.3, 4.3 points respectively), possibly because the teacher participated into every offline discussion, encouraged students to voice their opinions and responded in time to students.

Hence, for arts or history course, discussion should be allocated more time and percentage in the final grade, which will also allow more interaction between the teacher and students to ensure full understanding of the course content. For introductory science courses, courses with offline discussions but no exam requirements might result in less comprehensive understandings of the course content so that it may be plausible to include offline lectures to reinforce the online lessons. Lastly, while considering a form of discussion (no offline lectures), exam scores may need to allocate a higher percentage in the final grade to warrant active participation and teaching effeteness.

5   Limitation and Future Research

This study is an elementary exploration of Instructional design and teaching effectiveness of SPOCs in China so that there are several limitations to the study. First, the sample size of questionnaires is insufficient. As shown in phase two, we only collected four questionnaires in art course and 5 questionnaires in CS course. The number of such questionnaires cannot explained that the instructional design of these SPOCs whether meet the students' expectation of blended learning. Secondly, we only chose five small private online courses and the number of courses is not enough to reveal the instructional design of each fields (such as history fields and engineering fields). In addition, four of these five courses are undergraduate courses, we know less about the instructional design of graduate SPOCs. Lastly, the frequency of online discussion post could not be explained in the CS course. On the basis of teaching assistant of CS course, the online forum in this course is not widely used so that the situation that one student posted more than 20 times is ridiculous.

Given the limitations of this study, future research should increase the number of samples size, in order to obtain more subjective data on the scope of classes, along with selecting more graduate SPOCs to understand the instructional design of graduate courses. And the in-depth interviews with students taking different courses and observations of the offline classes are necessary becausenot only have we wanted to know the quantitative teaching effectiveness of students, but also want to understand the qualitative subjective perception of the course learner. That we can to understand which way to organize the instructional design of offline learning sessions and whether this kind of diverse teaching method is Suitable for different courses' students in blended learning. We attempt to provide a blueprint for the future SPOCs implementations in China.

References

1. Thorne, K.: Blended Learning: How to Integrate Online and Traditional Learning. Kogan Page, Limited, London (2003)
2. Ke kang, H.: Development of education technology theory based on blending learning. J. Natl. Acad. Educ. Adm. **4**, 5–10 (2004). (in Chinese)
3. Anderson, L.W., Krathwohl, D.R.: A taxonomy for learning, teaching and assessing: a revision of bloom's taxonomy of educational objectives. Beitr. Zur Gerichtl. Med. **42**(100), 329–337 (2001)
4. Dziuban, C.D., Hartman, J., Juge, F., Moskal, P., Sorg, S.: Blended learning enters the mainstream. In: Bonk, C.J., Graham, C.R. (eds.) Handbook of Blended Learning: Global Perspectives, Local Designs, pp. 195–208. Pfeiffer Publishing, San Francisco (2005)
5. O'Toole, J.M., Absalom, D.J.: The impact of blended learning on student outcomes: is there room on the horse for two? Learn. Media Technol. **28**(2–3), 179–190 (2003)
6. Olitsky, N.H., Cosgrove, S.B.: The effect of blended courses on student learning: evidence from introductory economics courses. Int. Rev. Econ. Educ. **15**, 17–31 (2014)
7. Liu, M.: Blended learning in a university EFL writing course: description and evaluation. J. Lang. Teach. Res. **4**(2), 301–309 (2013)
8. Francis, R., Shannon, S.J.: Engaging with blended learning to improve students' learning outcomes. Eur. J. Eng. Educ. **38**(4), 359–369 (2013)
9. Kirwin, S., Swan, J., Breakwell, N.: Comparing online learning with blended learning in a teacher training program. J. Res. Cent. Educ. Technol. 5(2) (2009)
10. Wen Ping, Z., Bo Lan, L., Nian Lan, M., Shui, X.X.: Effect evaluation of blended teaching based network in medical microbiology teaching. Inst. Microbiol. **35**(10), 1641–1644 (2008). (in Chinese)
11. Marsh, H.W.: SEEQ: a reliable, valid, and useful instrument for collecting students' evaluations of university teaching. Br. J. Educ. Psychol. **52**(1), 77–95 (1982)
12. Meng, Q., Liu, H.: A study of the dimensional structure and influencing factors of evaluations of college teachers' teaching. Psychol. Sci. (2003) (in Chinese)
13. Kanchanachaya, N., Nitjarunkul, K.: How do design blended learning base on authentic learning theory to enhance pre-service teachers' ability in professional practices of the pre-service teacher and instructor point of view. In: Kantola, J.I., Barath, T., Nazir, S., Andre, T. (eds.) Advances in Human Factors, Business Management, Training and Education. AISC, vol. 498, pp. 771–777. Springer, Cham (2017). doi:10.1007/978-3-319-42070-7_71

Exploration on Education Practice Based on Employment and Entrepreneurship in Higher Institutes of China

Jing Li, Lin Ma[⊠], Xin Wu, and Zhe Chen

Beihang University, Beijing, People's Republic of China
545033356@qq.com, malin2014@buaa.edu.cn

Abstract. Promoting education for college students based on entrepreneurship is not only the objective requirement of the development of higher institutes themselves, but also the urgent demand of China's economic and social development. At present, however, it is necessary to redesign the curriculum system and update the way of teaching due to the problems of unpractical educational theories and backward educational contents in higher institutes. In this thesis, studies are made using questionnaires based on information processing theory and model of the combination of work and learning. 344 effective questionnaires are collected. Besides, by comparison with the successful cases of Stanford, three major factors limiting the development of education based on entrepreneurship in Chinese higher institutes are discovered, namely, lack of practice for social practice, great learning and academic pressure of students and unpractical teaching contents. Therefore, trans-level learning model is put forward and is divided into three levels of theory, practice and innovation, so that students can receive information from various perspectives. Through targeted education on employment and entrepreneurship, as well as target-based learning plans, students' awareness of employment and entrepreneurship are adopted so that the information acquired can be integrated to improve students' core competitiveness.

Keywords: Employment and entrepreneurship orientation · Curriculum reform · Talent cultivation

1 Introduction

Employment and entrepreneurship-oriented education (EEOE) is an education idea and practice formed in order to meet the needs of socio-economic development and education development. From the perspective of the form of socio-economic development, the rise of knowledge-based economy has increasingly presented a country's core competitiveness as cultivation, allocation and regulation of human resources and knowledge achievements. Knowledge cannot promote the development of economy unless high-quality innovative and entrepreneurial talents serve as a basis. In this context, China has laid increasing emphasis on the cultivation of innovative and entrepreneurial talents. In April 2002, the Chinese Ministry of Education started an entrepreneurship education experiment in 9 universities including Tsinghua University,

© Springer International Publishing AG 2017
P.-L.P. Rau (Ed.): CCD 2017, LNCS 10281, pp. 554–564, 2017.
DOI: 10.1007/978-3-319-57931-3_44

Beihang University, Renmin University of China, Shanghai Jiao Tong University, Xi'an Jiaotong University, Heilongjiang University, Nanjing University of Finance and Economics and Northwestern Polytechnical University. *An Opinion on Vigorously advancing Innovation and Entrepreneurship Education in Higher Learning Institutions and College Students' Self-employment* issued in 2010 requires developing innovation and entrepreneurship education in colleges and universities. Innovation and entrepreneurship education is developed in order to provide strong talent and intellectual support for implementing the strategy of "improving independent innovation ability to make China an innovative nation", "expanding employment by starting a business", and "accelerating the transformation of economic growth pattern" put forth by the Party Central Committee.

From the perspective of the trend of higher education reform and development, the sustainable development of higher education includes both scale development and quality improvement, and the major task of higher education development will be to improve quality in the future. China has listed innovation and entrepreneurship education on the *Outline of National Medium- and Long-term Program for Education Reform and Development*, and integrated it into the whole process of talent cultivation. Its core is to cultivate college students' innovation spirit and entrepreneurial competence, reform the talent cultivation pattern and education context, and combine talent cultivation, scientific research and social work together closely to gradually set knowledge orientation before competence and quality orientation to improve the quality of talent cultivation.

2 Theoretical Basis

Due to the difference in history of education between various countries, they have distinct talent education and cultivation patterns. But they also have something in common since they are in the process of development in the same historical period. Talent cultivation is combined with business, course learning is combined with future career, employment and entrepreneurship serve as orientation, full use is made of different on- and off-campus educational environments and resources, and classroom teaching-based school education is combined organically with off-campus work that can help directly gain hands-on experience in the whole process of student cultivation to train real professional and entrepreneurial talents in practice in a bid to advance the combination of working with learning in German which implements "the dual system", Britain which advocates "the alternation of working and learning", and America which develops "the cooperative education". This reflects the essence of EEOE.

Based on the extension and development of information processing theory and work-integrated learning model, we proposed an inter-hierarchy learning model (see Fig. 1), which consists of three hierarchies: theory hierarchy, practice hierarchy and innovation hierarchy. The theory hierarchy consists of specialized course learning, theoretical knowledge accumulation and scientific research exploration; the practice hierarchy involves co-cultivation by enterprises and society, exercise of students' ability to solve problems using knowledge for their career, creative study and application, and mastery through a comprehensive study. The fusion of theory hierarchy

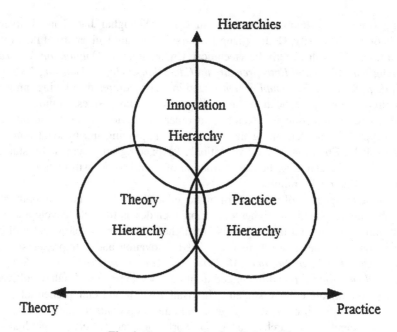

Fig. 1. Inter-hierarchy learning model

with practice hierarchy helps promote students to transform their learning of low-level theories and practice in work into high-level innovations, aimed at imparting knowledge to students from various angles, teaching them for a concrete target through specific employment and entrepreneurship education, and developing their consciousness of employment and entrepreneurship, so that they could integrate the information acquired together, and achieve a thorough mastery of the information, to have their core competence enhanced, so as to the realize the goal of EEOE.

The concept of entrepreneurship education was proposed by the UNESCO at the "International Conference of Education for the 21st Century" held in Beijing in 1989. The "third passport of learning" was proposed in the "Educational Philosophy of the 21st Century" in the conference report, which is known as entrepreneurial ability passport demanding to raise the status of entrepreneurial ability-oriented education passport to equate it with the current academic and vocational education passport (Wang and Liu 2009). Actually, the practice of entrepreneurship education has developed for decades in developed countries in Europe and America. In 1947, entrepreneurship course was offered at Harvard Business School. In 1953, "entrepreneurship and innovation" course was offered by Drucker at New York University, seeing the rise of entrepreneurial education aimed at developing students' self-employment ability in America. In 1968, the first entrepreneurship major was created for undergraduates at Babson College. In 1971, the first MBA entrepreneurship major was created at University of Southern California, raising college entrepreneurship education to a new level (Liu 2010). In the 1980s, entrepreneurship education began to break the boundaries of business school and be offered to the students majoring in all subjects, becoming one of the academic sectors developing the most rapidly at the stage of higher education in America.

As a selective course of general education offered to the students majoring in all subjects, and an important part of comprehensive quality education at higher learning institutions, public elective curriculum shoulders the heavy task of improving students' comprehensive qualities, widening the scope of their knowledge, optimizing the structure of their knowledge, promoting their personality development, and training innovative talents. All higher learning institutions at home and abroad make the most of public elective curriculum teaching. In the early 20th century, Harvard, Yale and other relevant well-known foreign universities started to explore interdisciplinary public elective curriculum education for postgraduates by combining theory with practice. Our university has gradually strengthened the efforts to offer public elective curriculum in recent years. Our university gives full play to its superiority as a comprehensive university to offer public elective curriculum to all students, particularly postgraduates for whom the courses in various fields such as natural sciences, humanities and social sciences have been provided. Also, it has been stipulated that every postgraduate must earn a certain amount of credits before graduation. From the perspective of the current implementation effect, the public elective curriculum offered has fully tapped the potential of the teachers and students, promoted the students' personality development, improved their humanistic qualities, scientific qualities, physical and psychological qualities, and driven the deepening of quality education. But at present, lots of problems have arisen in the implementation of public elective curriculum in our university, such as unitary teaching pattern, serious absence of students, doing coursework or fiddling with mobile phone in class, some teachers' inadequate attention to the teaching quality, the low depth and breadth of public elective curriculum content, and lack of practical guidance on employment and entrepreneurship. On that basis, this study conducted a questionnaire survey in Beihang University, one of the 9 pilot universities for entrepreneurship education, aimed at understanding the development status of EEOE at home, and exploring the issues restricting the development of EEOE, to provide suggestions and references for future EEOE.

3   Method

To study the current status of EEOE at colleges and universities, we employed questionnaire analysis and case comparison analysis.

On the basis of research literature, this paper designed a "questionnaire for surveys on the current status of EEOE at colleges and universities". The main content of the questionnaire consists of 2 parts: Part 1 presents basic information, including students' gender, specialty and grade. Part 2 presents surveys on the current status of EEOE, specifically including three aspects: first, undergraduates' awareness of EEOE; second, the implementation status of EEOE in colleges and universities; third, undergraduates' demand for EEOE. After the preliminary design of the questionnaire, we randomly selected 30 undergraduates for a pilot survey, and then modified the questionnaire in accordance with the pilot survey result based on experts' comments, finalizing a questionnaire. 400 questionnaires were distributed, and 371 were collected, 344 of which were valid questionnaires, with a valid collecting rate of 86%. 33.14% of the respondents were female students, and 66.86% were male students.

4 Data Analysis

4.1 Undergraduates' Awareness of EEOE

The undergraduates have high awareness of EEOE, high attention to it and high enthusiasm for it. Undergraduates' understanding and cognition of EEOE is a subjective factor influencing EEOE, thus only when undergraduates have a strong identification with EEOE and correct views on its values will it be able to be implemented effectively. This paper designed two items as points of observation of undergraduates' awareness of EEOE: the first is that attention is paid to EEOE. The vast majority of the students thought that EEOE was very important for them. 64.83% students selected "high importance", 31.1% selected "importance", and only 0.58% selected "unimportance" or "extremely unimportance", showing that the vast majority of the students think much of employment and entrepreneurship-oriented courses (EEOCs), and have a correct awareness of EEOEs. The second is whether they take an active part in EEOCs. 84.3% students expressed their willingness to select EEOC, and 12.5% said they might consider selecting EEOCs according to specific conditions, indicating that the undergraduates have a great demand for EEOCs, and regard them as important to their career development. But meanwhile, we have found that there are not many EEOEs offered in the university that just cover limited fields, most of which are nothing more than introduction or science popularization courses, such as Introduction to Entrepreneurship, A General Theory of Entrepreneurship, Guidance on Entrepreneurship and Employment, Career Planning and Human Resource Management, while only a few courses involve students' concrete needs contain key points, such as Robot Innovation and Entrepreneurship, Speech and Eloquence, and Lecture on Medical Equipment Creation.

4.2 The Implementation Status of EEOE in Colleges and Universities

There are major barriers to the development of EEOE in colleges and universities. For instance, EEOE is unvalued and inferior to professional education, there is a lack of social practice platforms, students are under great pressure from learning and scientific research, and teaching content is disconnected from students' actual needs. The attention from colleges and universities is prerequisite to the implementation of EEOE. According to the survey of "the university's emphasis on EEOE", despite the constant advancement of EEOE in recent years, the university's emphasis on EEOCs has significantly increased. 62.2% students selected "high emphasis" and "emphasis". Yet a considerable number of students (32.85%) thought that the university did not lay much emphasis on EEOE. So, the university should still place more emphasis on EEOE by carrying out more work. To "the result of EEOC learning", the students made extreme reactions. 58.14% of them said they had learned a lot, while 41.86% thought they just gained a little or nothing. This shows that there is still big room for improvement of the

EEOCs, so it is imperative to further classify the courses in line with different students' needs, and promote objective-oriented teaching. Considering the extreme effects of EEOE in higher learning institutions, we further researched the "factors influencing the effects of EEOE". See below for the first three factors: lack of social practice platforms (58.43%), great pressure on students from learning and scientific research (52.33%), and teaching content's disconnection from student's actual needs (47.97%). It is also proposed in *A Third Evaluation Report on Higher Education* to strengthen the construction of practice bases for college students, and deepen the reform of the credit management system, to give students a more flexible, larger free space, and educate them in accordance with their actual needs, so that they could achieve personalized development.

4.3 Undergraduates' Demand for EEOE

Undergraduates have diverse needs for EEOE, thus goal-oriented personalized education that meets students' actual needs is more popular. Undergraduates' demand for EEOE is a basis for higher learning institutions to design EEOE patterns and schemes, and only the EEOE pattern that meets student demand may be popular with students, avoid becoming a mere formality, and realize the implementation of EEOE. In terms of "development form of EEOE", the related courses account for 75.87%, much higher than other options, and individualized guidance on employment and entrepreneurship ranks the second, account for 59.3%, suggesting that setting of EEOCs based on a clear goal for individualized guidance on employment and entrepreneurship is an ideal way for universities to develop employment and entrepreneurship education. We further surveyed the "content of EEOCs". The options in the order of demand are interview skills (88.95%), social manners (66.86%), speech and eloquence (66.57%), and entrepreneurial orientation selection (63.08%). As can be seen, undergraduates' demand for EEOE has shown a trend of diversification, but the contents meeting their demand are rarely mentioned in the current EEOE. So, higher learning institutions should offer goal-oriented courses in line with student demand to give guidance on employment and entrepreneurship.

5 Case Comparison

EEOE reached maturity in the higher learning institutions abroad, each of which has formed a distinct system, achieving good education achievements. Taking Stanford University for example, it offers representative EEOE. The following is an analysis on Stanford's "industry-university-research integration-based" education pattern based on the three major issues in EEOE in Chinese universities.

5.1 Lack of Social Practice Platforms for EEOE in Chinese Universities

The Silicon Valley has to be referred to since Stanford University is mentioned. Stanford University promoted the birth of the Silicon Valley model in the early days, so it is honored as the "cradle" of the Silicon Valley. They not only support each other in technology and personnel, but also cooperate with each other and help each other forward in the field of culture and education. The development of Stanford University promoted the birth of the Silicon Valley, and since then the Silicon Valley has given a boost to the prosperity of Stanford University. Stanford University provides the Silicon Valley with educational and technical support. In return, the prosperous Silicon Valley provides a good platform for Stanford University. Both of them interact with each other benignly (Lenoir et al. 2004).

Stanford University founded Stanford Research Park on a piece of idle land in 1951, setting a precedent for university-based hi-tech development in America. It is the embryo of the Silicon Valley. For instance, HP founders William Hewlett and David Packard are graduates of Stanford, and the first entrepreneurs in the Silicon Valley. Such enterprises born of Stanford have served as chief cornerstones of the Silicon Valley in the past few decades. The development of Stanford University is closely associated with that of hi-tech companies, and the technologies from the former can be transformed into products quickly in the latter. The demand and development of the Silicon Valley also promotes the development of Stanford University greatly.

It is due to lots of human, technological and information resources from Stanford University that the high-tech enterprises in the Silicon Valley have made persistent innovations, having their quality constantly improved. When making use of these resources for its own development, the Silicon Valley provides a platform for the teachers and students of Stanford University to do practice. The teachers and students keep taking part in practice on this platform, where they apply their theoretical knowledge to practice to further improve the teaching level. Both sides cooperate with each other and benefit together, creating a "win-win" situation (Nelson and Byers 2005).

5.2   Great Pressure on Chinese Undergraduates from Specialized Course Learning and Scientific Research

The courses are set in order to develop students' entrepreneurial competence in an all-round way. Stanford University allows the students to select other specialized courses according to their own interest beyond the boundary between liberal arts and sciences. Stanford University focuses particularly on teaching the students basic courses by regarding basic education as important as specialized education. That's why entrepreneurship education, which comes under the category of specialized education, permeates basic education. While receiving basic education, the students can receive entrepreneurship education. In this way, the students have their awareness of entrepreneurship education enhanced unknowingly, and theoretical foundation consolidated. Entrepreneurship education focuses more on improving students' practical abilities in Stanford University. The university simulates the founding of a company, where all students can learn all courses in company founding and operation freely, such as business planning, resource integration, and business proposal. This, on the one hand, meets the students' demand for entrepreneurship education, and on the other hand, enhances their practical abilities.

The curriculum system is relatively perfect. The courses offered at Stanford University have to do with curriculum education and non-curriculum education. The Center for Entrepreneurial Study established at the business school is responsible for entrepreneurship education throughout the university. Various types of courses are offered in the well-established system, among which *Entrepreneurship Management, Entrepreneurship and Venture Investment,* and *Investment Management and Entrepreneurial Finance* are popular with the students. These courses have greatly raised the students' enthusiasm, and significantly improved their practical abilities and independent thinking capacities since teacher-student interaction prevails over cramming teaching in class. Non-curriculum education has been an effective supplement to curriculum education. With credits as a standard, Stanford University requires the students to attend a lecture on entrepreneurship education weekly to earn credits, so as to broaden their entrepreneurial knowledge. It encourages the students to participate in various scientific research projects, and does all it can do to help them participate in scientific research and off-campus collaborative projects, to promote them to do practice and develop their practical abilities.

5.3   Disconnection of EEOCs from Students' Actual Needs in Chinese Colleges and Universities

All-inclusive entrepreneurship courses are offered and lessons are given flexibly at Stanford University. The traditional text teaching does not prevail alone, while case analysis, project teaching and practical learning are adopted in class to help the students thoroughly understand entrepreneurship education, arouse their interest in entrepreneurship education, and improve their comprehensive ability. There is highly practical content in the entrepreneurship courses. For instance, *Entrepreneurship and Social Development, Entrepreneurial Opportunity Assessment, Strategic Management of Technological Innovation,* and *Entrepreneurial Spirit and Venture Investment* focus on helping students gain practical managerial experience. For another example, *Private Securities Investment, Financial Problems in Venture Investment, Environmental Entrepreneurial Spirit, IPO Management: Control System,* and *Financial Intermediation and Fund Market* focus on the study and research of economic, financial and market operation theories.

Besides, Stanford University's curriculum system is highly stratified. Stanford hi-tech entrepreneurship program is offered in the College of Engineering to promote hi-tech entrepreneurship education to enhance the entrepreneurial skills of all undergraduate and postgraduate majors. The entrepreneurship education courses offered to undergraduates, including some introductory courses such as *Introduction to Entrepreneurship* and *Management of Hi-tech Venture Enterprises,* are aimed at developing their awareness of entrepreneurship. The university offers different courses to different student groups. In detail, it offers basic courses such as *Lecture on Enterprise Ideology Leadership* to the undergraduates, profound courses such as *Global Entrepreneurial Marketing* to the postgraduates, and entrepreneurship seminar courses to the doctoral students.

Besides, Stanford University gives lectures on "Enterprise Ideology Leadership" concerning the entrepreneurial technology program weekly, at which successful entrepreneurs, hi-tech company leaders and venture capitalists are invited to teach a lesson based on their own experience, and interact with the students. Those listening to the lectures will earn credits. The founders of cloud storage service provider Dropbox, streaming media service provider Spotify and other relevant rising hi-tech companies were invited to communicate with the students.

In Stanford University, most students have many opportunities to practice after accomplishing routine learning tasks. Both professors and students can do a part-time job in the company they founded or another company, so as to transform their research achievements into a product more quickly to achieve a practical effect. All these measures give the students a more flexible, larger free space, and make education more fit for the students' needs by carrying out education pointedly to help them achieve personalized development. This "industry-university-research" integration-based education pattern has formed a benign cycle between enterprises, teachers and students, with the three parts helping each other forward, finally promoting the development of the society.

6   Discussion and Conclusions

6.1   Strengthening University-Industry Cooperation, and Building a Practice Platform for EEOE

EEOE features the combination of theory with practice and highlights practicability. Creative thinking, creative spirit and entrepreneurial awareness cannot promote innovation and entrepreneurship unless in practical activities. Therefore, EEOE should be developed in practical activities in many forms such as offering EEOCs, giving individualized guidance on employment and entrepreneurship, implementing project practice, and holding entrepreneurial competitions. For the implementation of EEOE in higher learning institutions, the industrial community should offer support and take a part. Taking America for example, the industrial community has provided great talent support, practice sites and internship positions for EEOE. In return, the EEOE offered at universities has given birth to a great number of world-renowned enterprises, such as HP, Google, Yahoo, Cisco and other relevant hi-tech companies founded in the entrepreneurial atmosphere at Stanford. These innovative hi-tech enterprises have brought vitality into the development of "the Silicon Valley", seeing a sound interaction between entrepreneurship education and industrial development in America. Chinese colleges and universities should energetically explore an industry-university integration-based EEOE pattern by reference to the successful experience of other countries, build a practice platform for employment and entrepreneurship, and establish a mechanism of interaction between government, universities and high-tech industry parks to promote the construction of practice bases for employment and entrepreneurship, as well as the bases for business incubation. By practicing in high-tech industry parks, students can study a lot of entrepreneurial cases in person, and receive more direct operational guidance from business people, to have their horizon broadened, mind widened and interest in entrepreneurship aroused. Entrepreneurial support, including equipment, capital and site, can be offered to students in the bases for business incubation. Besides, professional consulting services can be offered, so that employment and entrepreneurship-oriented education could be well implemented.

6.2 Designing a Scientific, Rational EEOC System

EEOE involves the fusion of multi disciplines, so a curriculum system needs to be designed from an interdisciplinary perspective. To design a curriculum system for EEOE, we should first consider how to effectively integrate the idea of employment and entrepreneurship into the professional teaching system to make innovative spirit and entrepreneurial competence one of the directions of professional teaching. In terms of specific implementation, importance should be attached to the complementarity of disciplines and the characteristics of course teaching, and emphasis should be laid on the organic combination of theoretical courses with practical courses to set up a highly specific, operable, multifarious EEOE curriculum system. Compared with the European and American universities, Chinese universities do not have a rational employment and entrepreneurship-oriented education curriculum system, but one beset with problems such as single curriculum form, insufficient number of curriculum, and broad curriculum classification. Compared with Stanford University and California University at Berkeley (21 and 23 entrepreneurship courses offered respectively), Chinese colleges and universities offer EEOE courses that have defects, such as broad curriculum classification (10 courses at most), and insufficient support for training for different types and levels of students (Li and Li 2013). Teaching methods, means and textbooks are important parts of the EEOE curriculum system.

6.3 Promoting EEOE to Be Efficiently Combined with the Specialized Education System

At present, EEOE is being marginalized in Chinese higher learning, and most higher learning institutions have put it under the category of technical economic disciplines or business management disciplines, while many others just position entrepreneurship education ambiguously. EEOE is commonly separated from specialized education in the colleges and universities. Even though a lot of colleges and universities have begun to think much of entrepreneurship education, particularly some have integrated the content of entrepreneurship education into talent cultivation and used it to motivate teachers and students, employment and entrepreneurship education hasn't been included in the discipline construction planning and quality evaluation system yet.

The marginalization of employment and entrepreneurship education has led to a difference in the implementation standard for EEOE between various universities, and this is inimical to the development of EEOE. Therefore, the educational administrative department should actively promote EEOE disciplines and courses to be offered, to define the status of EEOE. Meanwhile, EEOE thoughts and knowledge should be gradually integrated into specialized education. Teacher team reconstruction, curriculum setting and student cultivation should be carried out under the unified employment and entrepreneurship-oriented educational framework. EEOE should be able to develop students' innovative spirit, entrepreneurial competence, and comprehensive quality throughout educational administration to meet their actual needs and serve their future career development, so that they could benefit from it.

It is an arduous task to conduct EEOE for students to cultivate their consciousness of employment and entrepreneurship and fashion them into comprehensive talents with solid professional knowledge, employability and entrepreneurial spirit. So, this cultivation program is a complex systematic project, for which not only teaching forces but also social support is required, and a well-established system may be able to ensure a good entrepreneurial environment and encourage college students to do pioneering work bravely. Especially, the higher learning institutions must advance with times, change their backward educational concept, reform their talent cultivation pattern, and conduct goal-based EEOE for students, so that EEOE could be more in line with students' actual demand and development needs.

Acknowledgments. This work has been supported by grants from the National Natural Science Foundation of China (71502009), China Scholarship Council and the Development Foundation for Graduate Education of Beihang University (4302025).

References

Lenoir, T., Rosenberg, N., Rowen, H., et al.: Inventing the entrepreneurial university. Stanf. Co-Evol. Silicon Val. **15**(03) (2009). http://siepr.stanford.edu/programs/SST_Seminars/Lenoir.pdf. Accessed 2004

Nelson, A., Byers, T.: Organizational modularity and intra-university relationships between entrepreneurship education and technology transfer, vol. 16, no. 285, pp. 275–311 (2005)

Li, W., Li, C.: Ten-year entrepreneurship education in Chinese Universities: evolution, problems and system construction. Educ. Res. (06), 42–51 (2013)

Liu, B.: Establishment of an innovation and entrepreneurship education idea for raising innovative spirits and practical abilities. China High. Educ. (12), 12–15 (2010)

Wang, G., Liu, Q.: A new education idea in higher learning institutions—review of report on the development of the innovation and entrepreneurship education in Chinese Universities. China High. Educ. Res. (09), 56–57 (2009)

Design for Learning Through Play.
An Exploratory Study on Chinese Perspective

Maria Luce Lupetti[1(✉)], Yuan Yao[2], Jing Gao[2], Haipeng Mi[2],
and Claudio Germak[1]

[1] Department of Architecture and Design, Politecnico di Torino, Turin, Italy
{maria.lupetti,claudio.germak}@polito.it
[2] X-Studio, Department of Art and Design, Tsinghua University, Beijing, China
yao-yl5@mails.tsinghua.edu.cn,
gaojingviola@gmail.com, mhp@tsinghua.edu.cn

Abstract. This work focuses on the role of design for novel edutainment robots for children. The theme is addressed by adopting a holistic approach, aimed at framing the complexity of a phenomenon that is changing the children educational and play habits. The main aspects of this phenomenon were further investigated through a preliminary study carried out in Beijing, China. The study consisted in a questionnaire and forms about children's habits submitted to parents, and in hands-on activities supported by probes for children. The results of the questionnaire provided information that help to get a better understanding of the relation between education and play in children's life that can be used as basis for developing new design scenarios. The activities with children, instead, allowed to collect inspirational data and to identify design principles that could be adopted as drivers in the development of novel robotic products for children.

Keywords: Design in complexity · Edutainment robots · User study · Children

1 Introduction

Designing edutainment robots for children encompass a variety of issues and responsibilities. Human-robot interaction (HRI) studies highlight the importance of understanding not only technical, but rather psychological, social and cultural implications of a project [1]. In fact, in order to understand what makes a robot acceptable it is necessary to address various aspects of human perception, such as perceived usefulness, ease of use, affordance, attractiveness, moral issues [2] etc. However, in the case of robotic toys it is, firstly, necessary to understand the whole scenario of children play and how these products are changing it.

As a matter of fact, edutainment robots are experiencing a great adoption and, especially in educational contexts, such as schools, where there is a growing demand for programming and educational robotics courses [3, 4]. This large adoption is probably due to their clear potential. They have proven to be effective tools for teaching not only mere coding, but also science, technology, engineering and math (STEM) [5] in a playful way. For the same reason, despite their primary educational aim, these products are experiencing a growing adoption also in private context for entertainment,

© Springer International Publishing AG 2017
P.-L.P. Rau (Ed.): CCD 2017, LNCS 10281, pp. 565–581, 2017.
DOI: 10.1007/978-3-319-57931-3_45

answering to the parents' desire of providing more and more learning opportunities for their children. The ability to support crucial aspects of children's life, education and play, gives to these artifacts a double identity. In the private contexts they can be seen as educative toys, while in contexts like schools they assume the role of playful educational tools. As a results, the boundaries between education and play are gradually blurring, resulting in a hybrid space. Rather than separated dimensions of children's life, in fact, these two aspects can be seen as the two extremes of an axis that define not only products but also children's daily habits.

Designing novel robotic toys for children, that requires a deep understanding of the relation between learning and play [6], represents also a way to investigate the current state of a changing society that is affecting the educational and recreational habits of children. In this regard, China represents an emblematic case study. Thanks to its continuous growth, this country is facing great social, economical and cultural transformations. In particular, in the last 30 years China devoted great efforts to heal the cultural unbalance of children across the country and to reform their educational curriculums [7]. So, today this country is making great strides from the educational point of view. But, *how this affects children's leisure time and play? How learning and play relate to each other in this context? And then, what implications comes when designing for learning through play in China?*

These questions highlight the need for investigating the children's play scenario not only focusing on the relationship between play and education, but also addressing all the elements and factors that can affect both the spread of edutainment robotics and a change in children's habits. To this end, framing [8] the phenomenon of edutainment robots helps to highlight these key elements and factors, as well as to identify new design opportunities.

1.1 Framing the Edutainment Robot Phenomenon

By adopting a holistic approach, it is possible to identify four main interrelated systems that affect or are affected by the spread of edutainment robot. As shown by Fig. 1, these products are located in a hybrid space between education and play. This space represents the intersection of the public educational system and the personal play system. The educational system includes both school education and extra curricula courses, and it is characterized by the role of educators and the presence of peers (children of the same age). The private play system, instead, refer mostly to the free time that children can dedicate to play, and it is characterized by the relationship with parents as well as the individual dimension. These two systems are the ones in which the interaction with the edutainment products take place. These two systems require not only children's engagement, but also parent's and educator's acceptance and adaptation. In this regard, psychological factors like perceived usefulness and attractiveness plays a crucial role.

A third system is represented by product/service providers. This system appears independent from the first two, but still connected through the products. This system differs from the previous for the different motivations and scopes from which it is ruled. However, all the three systems are under the influence of the same regulatory system. This last, drove by political and economical factors, can have a great influence on the

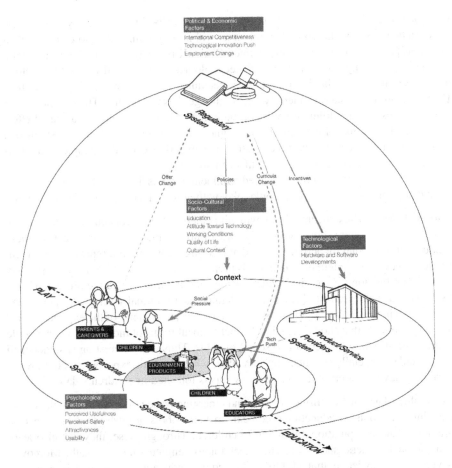

Fig. 1. Conceptual schema of the edutainment products scenario.

spread of edutainment robots by promoting incentives for the product/service providers and promoting curricula change for schools. For instance, the need for technological innovation and international competitiveness, as well as the need for adaptation to the employment change brought by technology, are leading governments to introduce programming classes from primary school [9].

In addition, the regulatory system, through its policies, determines the socio-cultural factors of a context, influencing the people perception, acceptability and adoption of these new products. These socio-cultural factors are crucial for understanding how children's play and education habits are changing.

In this panorama, edutainment robots can be seen as a sub-system that intersects and depends from higher systems. From these, it inherits the influence of technological, economical and political, socio-cultural, and psychological factors that determines its acceptability, adoption and diffusion.

The framing action described above is meant as a strategy for pointing out crucial factors and critical points of the system. It is aimed ad finding those non-linear, multifaceted problems that results impossible to describe in their totality, but can be better understood by showing their relations within a system. These so called wicked problems [10], or more specifically defined DesignX problems [11] in the design field, are characterized by the co-presence of technological, human and contextual factors, and determines the behavior of the socio-technical systems in which are ascribed. Designers are then asked to identify and challenge these problems. The complexity of these systems and the different nature of the influencing factors requires a shared effort among multiple disciplines. In this, designers can contribute through established human-centered practices by investigating the experience of the people and highlighting how the factors of a system affect them [11].

Accordingly, in the specific case of edutainment robotics, it is possible to identify two main emerging issues that affect people: play with aim, and technology driven learning.

Play with Aim. The concept of play with aim emerges from a reflection on the specific nature of edutainment robots. Both in the case of private play or public education, these products propose playful activities aimed at learning. This does not represent a problem per se, however, the extent of which this is preferred and chose instead of "aimless" play requires a reflection. In fact, it is widely recognized the importance the process of play itself without achievements [12]. Play is defined as a minimally-scripted, open-ended exploration in which the participant is absorbed in the spontaneity of the experience [13] and it is a concept that should remains distinct from all forms of thought in which people express the structure of mental and social life [14]. Thus, it is interesting to understand how people, especially parents, consider play, which kind of expectations and preference they have for their children, and how this is reflected in children's daily life.

Technology Driven Learning. The second emerging issue concerns mainly the use of edutainment robots in educational context. In fact, robots are used for teaching programming and computational thinking to children. Through these, they can also learn conventional matters, such as science, technology, engineering and math. Moreover, beyond the knowledge that children can acquire, educational robotics is part of a broader educational revolution [15], in which objectives and methodologies are changing. Already in 1990, Seymour Papert highlighted how computers and technologies sharpen existing cleavages in educational theories were on one hand education is meant for acquiring skills and learning facts, while on the other hand it is meant for personal development [16]. Referring to the LEGO/Logo project, he also suggested how technology is a powerful tool to reframe the process of learning: from a transfer of knowledge to a construction of knowledge [16]. Thus, as Papert claims, using technology in education is not about what it would make to children but rather what children would make with it.

Accordingly, educational program that introduce programming classes and educational robotics are today widely promoted, also at a national level, such as in the case of Queensland, Australia [9]. However, there is a large body of activities that, before the introduction of technology, were already adopted in educational contexts with the same aim: empowering children in their knowledge construction process. These activities are meant to support processes of active learning [17] by allowing children to act on object, people, ideas and events to build their knowledge. These includes activities oriented to deal with aspects like music, motor abilities, language, social relations, classification and others. Therefore, *how these activities will be affected by the spread of technology-based activities? Can these two approaches inspire each other, or, even converge?*

Understanding the two issues emerged from the framing of the edutainment robot's phenomenon requires further investigation. In particular, it is important to focus on the daily life experiences of children and their families, to produce qualitative, inspirational knowledge that cannot be found in datasets and statistical reports. Accordingly, an exploratory study was carried out by involving children and parents. In Sect. 2 is described the methodology adopted in the study, with a focus on the study materials produced for both parent and children. Section 3 shows the results of the activities carried out, consisting mostly in a questionnaire-based study in the case of parents, and in three activities with different kind of probes in the case of children. Finally, Sect. 4 consists of the discussion and conclusions of the study, in which some design opportunities and guidelines are highlighted.

2   Exploratory Study

The study was carried out involving children and parents for answering the preliminary research questions, mentioned in the previous paragraph, about play and education, how are changing children's habits, and to find new design opportunities. Moreover, conducting activities with children allows to observe how they approach play activities, how they self express and how they might interpret specific elements of play, such as sensory associations. On the other hand, parents can provide detailed information about their child habits and daily activities, and moreover, they can provide opinions and suggestions about toys and activities for children. Thus, parents were engaged to investigate mainly the concept of play with aim, considering it as a result of change in habits and socio-cultural factors, while the activities with children were more aimed at exploring the issue of technology driven learning, through non-technological activities. In particular, these were structured referring to existing activities for active learning, aimed at understanding how children perceive concepts like color, sounds, emotions and their associations. The intention is then to use this knowledge as source of inspiration to apply computational thinking [18] in innovative ways.

The activities, were carried out by providing to participants a set of cultural probes [19], based on existing activities about senses and storytelling. Parents and children received a big paper folder at their arrival. The bags were containing the materials prepared for the study: a set of forms for parents, and a toolkit for children. At the end of the activities, children were allowed to keep the toolkit materials as compensation, while parents received a monetary compensation. In fact, as reported by several studies [20, 21], a monetary compensation can be useful to obtain compliance, retention and good quality of data.

2.1   Forms and Questionnaire

The set of forms was composed by a *consent* and *recording release form*, a *questionnaire*, a *child one-day agenda form*, a *child one-week agenda form*, and a form were parents were invited to describe briefly their children.

The questionnaire was aimed to get a better understanding of Chinese children's play and spare time habits. To this end, parents were asked to answer 34 questions regarding general personal info, time dedicated to play by their children, play typologies, recreational activities of children with parents, and open questions about parent's opinion regarding toys, technology and children's education.

The *agendas* consisted of forms were parents were asked to mark down the daily and weekly activities of their children, from school to sports, and spare time. These two forms were aimed to get information about how busy Chinese children are and how much of their time is dedicated to educative activities and how much to play.

2.2   Children's Activities

The toolkit for children was composed by three smaller paper bags, each of which contained the materials for the activities of the study. The three activities consisted of: acting and guessing emotions; drawing soundscapes; associating sounds, objects and colors. Accordingly, in the first bag was placed a small white board, a marker, and two emotions cards. The second bag contained five white sheets of paper and a pack of colored markers. In the last bag was placed a colored board and a set of 15 objects cards. The expected outcome of this approach was getting inspirational data [19] rather than specific knowledge about given assumptions. To do so, a playful atmosphere was created by giving to children the toolkit as a sort of gift. At the end of the activities, in fact, they were allowed to take it home.

Referring to related works, the three activities were organized as sort of games paying attention to children's peculiarities. In fact, several studies show how cultural probes were in some cases redesigned as games [22], in other cases adapted specifically for children [23]. The adaptation of cultural probes as games can increase engagement of participants, as well as the amount of material produced [22]. The adaptation in terms of participant's peculiarities, namely children, is instead necessary for the effectiveness of the study. In particular, addressing the suggestion of Wyeth and Diercke [24], the number of activities was limited to three for avoiding low completion rate and loss of engagement. The level of abstraction required by the activities needed also to be addressed. In fact, as reported by Gielen [23], children's language skills and their ability di deal with abstract concepts is still under development. For this reason, the success of a study can be greatly influenced by the guiding role that researchers may assume, by the presence of figurative alternatives to verbalizations, and by promoting direct experience rather than recalling memories and latent knowledge. Thus, the materials produced for the study was designed taking account these considerations. Every playful activity was supported by materials for creating direct experiences, that were introduced by one researcher and supplemented by illustrations of the activities, showed on a screen.

Activity 1. The first activity consisted on acting and guessing emotions. Every child had two cards, each with the name of one emotion. One at the time, they were asked to perform gestures and facial expressions to describe those emotions. At the same time, the other children were asked to observe and guess which emotion was performed, and

Fig. 2. On top, left, the first activity's materials: a white board, a marker and two emotion cards with both Chinese characters and pinyin version. On top, right, the second activity's materials: colors and white paper sheets. On the bottom, the third activity's materials: a colored board with object cards for children, and a set of real objects hidden in a box for the research team. (Color figure online)

to write it down on the white board. The cards contained 18 different emotions, from simple to perform like happy, scared or angry, to more complex emotions, such as embarrassed and hurt. The children who were guessing were allowed to discuss.

This activity refers to existing practices meant for making children familiarize with emotions [25].

Activity 2. For the second activity the children were asked to listen five different soundtracks, one at the time, and to draw the scenario that these evoked to them. The soundtracks described different contexts and activities: a school bell, a city traffic, some cooking sounds in kitchen, nature with birds and water, and a luna park. After drawing all the scenarios, children were invited to stand up and describe their drawings.

Drawing, in fact, is widely used in studies with children for bringing out ideas, such as in the work by Gielen [23], were it was used as brainstorming tool, or in the work by Wyeth and Diercke [24], were it was used as a way to describe project hypothesis.

Activity 3. The last activity consisted on associating sounds, objects and colors. The team had a set of real objects hidden in a wooden box. The sounds were produced by "playing" the objects in different modalities, such as beating, squeezing or shaking. Every child had a set of cards were all the objects were represented. With these, they were asked to recognize which object was played every time and then to associate its sound to a color. This association was made by placing each object card in one of the colored areas of the board that they received with the object cards. Also in this case, the children were allowed to discuss together.

This activity was inspired by the Sound Boxes [26], a Montessori material used to promote auditory sense knowledge. These materials consist of a set of six cylinders that, if shaken, make different sounds, from loud to soft. Children can be asked to align the boxes according to similarity, grades or contrast.

2.3 Participants

The study was carried out by involving a group of 9 Chinese children and, at least, one parent for each child. The participants already knew each other, since the children attend the same school class, in Beijing. The group was composed by 4 girls and 5 boys, aged between 7 and 8 years. All the children, except one, were single child. The parents who filled the forms and questionnaire, 4 mothers and 5 fathers, were aged between 32 and 46 years.

3 Results

The results of this study consists of both quantitative and qualitative data. In particular, the questionnaire for parents allowed to collect quantitative data about children's habits, such as how much time they dedicate to education and play every day, and qualitative data about parents' considerations about toys and technology, through open questions.

The activities with children, instead, were meant to collect only qualitative data. To this end, the materials elaborated by children during the activities, such as drawings, were photographed, the whole experience was video recorded and main observations were written down at the end of the activity.

3.1 Questionnaire

The questionnaire was meant to get a better understanding of the current scenario of children play and their daily habits. Accordingly, the data collected from the parent's answers refer to four main aspects: children daily life, children play habits, parents engagement in children's spare time, and expectations and preferences of parents for children's toys and play.

A first significant finding is that the children in China dedicate many hours of their days to educative activities, including both schools and extracurricular courses. During the week, in fact, they spend at least 10 h a day for these activities. In the weekend they have more free time and they attend on average 12 h on courses in two days. However, there are cases in which the children are busy as much as during the week.

Regarding the rest of their time, less than 2 h per day is dedicated to play and they usually do free play or educative games on smartphone. Rarely they play with role playing games (dolls, cars, etc.) or traditional games (board games, chess, playing cards). Moreover, they usually play alone, since almost all of them is a single child and parents rarely have time to play together. Parents, in fact, spend between 2 and 4 h per day with their children, but this time is usually dedicated to normal daily life activities, such as cooking and eating together.

Thus, most of daily life of these children is dedicated to educational activities. Nevertheless, among the extracurricular courses they attend almost every day interesting courses like musical instrument classes, art classes and, especially, robot programming classes. These are particularly important both for the subjects of the classes and for the interaction style that proposes. In fact, these classes engage children playfully and promoting collaboration, imagination, problem solving and creativity. In particular, programming classes with LEGO are specifically designed to support active learning through hands-on activities. This approach, called playful learning [27], is in between free play and guided play.

The fact that these children regularly attend these courses affects strongly the parent's perception and expectations about toys. In the first open answer question, for instance, parents were asked to mention which characteristics should have a good toy for children. They answered this question by naming characteristics like hand-on skills, simplicity, modularity, limitlessness, interactivity, promotion of creativity, and promotion of science concepts that can all be traced to the characteristics of robot programming classes. Even more explicit were the answer to a following question on how technology should be used for children's toys. In this case they mentioned that toys should be interactive, intelligent and able to help children to understand concepts of space, math, physics, chemistry and logic.

These results show how the phenomenon of play with aim is related to both a curricula change in the education system and to people perceptions and expectations. In fact, despite children are more and more engaged in educational activities, most of parents want toys and games to be educational or to stimulate children's creativity, thinking ability and hand-on skills. In this regard it is interesting to notice that they consider the interesting courses, such as painting class and robot programming classes, as playtime and that they prefer their children to attend these courses over playing classical games. This, in fact, emerged from the question in which parents were asked to select the type of play that they prefer for they children, from a list including traditional games, role playing games, sport games, free play, interactive games and interesting courses. All of them selected interesting courses.

The answers of the parents also showed how being familiar with "technology driven learning" allows to go beyond the common concerns of parents regarding technology. In this sense, this sample of parents is particularly interesting. Since they are all familiar with robot programming classes, for instance, none of them raised concerns about the use of technology for children. Instead, most of them mentioned that technology should provide interactive abilities to toys for responding to children's actions.

3.2 Children's Activities

Activity 1. In the first activity one child at the time was asked to stand up and act to show the emotions written in the cards while the others had to guess the emotion. The children were firstly embarrassed to act and some of them were to shy to do it. Despite this, observing them allowed to understand that they were enjoying the activities, but they were also afraid of making mistakes. In fact, after that everyone performed, some of them wanted to perform again and one explained that he wanted to perform again because he saw that the other children wrote the wrong word when he was performing.

Another interesting aspect is that they performed the emotions as static poses, rather that gestures and movements.

In the end, this activity, that also was chosen as ice-breaking, appeared to be the most challenging. Children found difficulties at different levels: incomprehension of the word wrote on the cards, not knowing how to act an emotion, and difficulties in recognizing the emotion acted by the others. Simple emotions like happiness, anger and fear resulted to be easy to perform as well as to understand, while others were more difficult, such as concern, nervousness and embarrassment.

Despite the observed difficulties, the words written on the white boards are correct in for the vast majority. This is due to the fact that children were discussing all together and in many cases they told to the others what was written in their cards. However, in those case where an emotion resulted complex and the child did not share the word, the children gave more creative answers. In particular, a boy, who didn't know the correct word for some of the emotions, adopted a descriptive approach. Instead of writing another emotion, as a tentative, he used small descriptions of the expressions of the performing child, such as "What happened?" for worried, "frowning" for embarrassed, and "cannot bear it" for scared (Fig. 3).

Fig. 3. First activity: acting and guessing emotions. On the left, a child is performing an emotion. On the right, another child shows its annotations about the emotions observed.

Activity 2. In this activity children were free to chose the colors to use for drawing, and they were not asked to give a reason for that. However, some of them spontaneously gave a reason for their choice and observing their drawing it is possible to identify similarities. For instance, the drawing for the second soundtrack, urban traffic, are mainly black with parts of light blue due to the presence of rain, explained by some children. One child, while describing his drawing, said that the choice of black is because "traffic has no color, so I used black because it includes all colors". This statement is very interesting as it introduces two incongruities: on one hand, he sais traffic has no colors and then he chooses "all colors" to describe it, on the other hand his belief that black includes all color is actually incorrect, from the physics point of view.

Also in the case of the third soundtrack, children used mainly dark colors: black, brown and purple. This is probably due to the negative feeling that the soundtrack evoked to them. In fact, instead of perceiving someone cooking in the kitchen, some of them imagined a factory where workers were making things fall down. Another child imagined someone hitting a nail with a hammer and also one, that recognized a pot, described it negatively, saying "some dirty things in a pot".

The fourth soundtrack, instead, was easy to understand for all of them. They all recognized the natural setting with birds and, accordingly, they all used nature-related colors, such as light blue, blue, green and yellow.

Soundtracks:	Children								
	1 (4th)	2 (7th)	3 (1st)	4 (5th)	5 (8th)	6 (3rd)	7 (9th)	8 (2nd)	9 (6th)
School Bell	Clock	Bell	Seems a bell, but he says army horn	Seems a bell, but she says clock	Seems a cockade	Bell	Bell	Clock	Clock to wake up kids for school
Urban traffic	Car traffic with rain	Car traffic	Car traffic	Car traffic	Car traffic	Car traffic with rain	Boat in the water with rain	Car traffic with rain	Car traffic with rain
Cooking	Someone hits a drum	Someone hitting a nail with a hammer	Someone making trouble. Something falls	Some dirty things in a pot	Work tools	Factory. Workers hitting and welding	Pots	Iron factory. A worker hitting iron make other things fall	A pot falls down in the kitchen
Waterfront	Birds singing	Fishes and seabirds	Dolphins, seabirds and sea	Birds singing	Duck	Birds singing	Tree with a bird singing	Sea, birds and fishes	Sea, birds and fishes
Luna park	Kids playing	Roller Coaster	Luna Park	Roller Coaster	Roller Coaster	Roller Coaster, fire and people screaming	Party	Roller Coaster	Roller Coaster

Fig. 4. Results of the second activity. The table shows the colors chosen by children to draw after each soundtrack and the main objects/subjects represented. (Color figure online)

The last and the first soundtracks are more various in terms of colors used. However, in both cases there is presence of red associated with alert. In particular, one child motivated his use of red in the luna park soundtrack because he imagined that there was fire and scared people (Fig. 4).

This introduces a crucial aspect emerged from this activity: children go beyond what they hear. They spontaneously imagined situations with multiple subjects/objects and events. As an example, the waterfront soundtrack was easy to understand because of the clear sounds of birds and water. However, all of them added some other elements that actually have no sound that can be recognized in the soundtrack, like dolphins, fishes and a tree.

The children's imagination was even more encouraged by the ambiguous soundtracks, namely the third (cooking) and the fifth (luna park). In the third soundtrack, some drew pots, but none mentioned someone cooking in a kitchen. On the contrary, some children imagined a factory. According to one child, the context is an iron factory and a worker was hitting a piece of iron, with a hammer that weights 100 kg. At one point the worker hit the piece too strongly and make other things fall from the table. In the fifth soundtrack, instead, most of children understood that it was a luna park. However, most of them mentioned people scared and a couple of them said that it was "horrible". In particular, one said that there were two parts in the soundtrack: first the situation is normal, people are on the roller coaster, then, a fire breaks out scaring all the people, so this is why they scream. He also highlighted that, because of the fire, he used red (Fig. 5).

Fig. 5. One of the children is telling to the group what he drew. He stresses that in the last soundtrack there was fire, so he chose to use the red color. (Color figure online)

A last interesting aspect, emerged from this activity, is that most of children were enthusiastic and impatient to describe their drawing. However, two girls (5 and 7 in Fig. 2) didn't want to do it. They were the last two children left, since the speaking order was random and children were asking by themselves to stand up and tell their story. While others were speaking, they were carefully listening, but when their turn came, they appeared too shy to do it. However, looking at their drawings, it is possible to observe that both described at least 2 soundtracks differently from the rest of the group. In particular, one of the two girl draw a boat under the rain instead of urban traffic and a party instead of the luna park. Thus, it is possible to hypothesize that, after listening all the other descriptions, she felt like her drawings were wrong. However, in this activity the point was not to guess and draw the correct thing, but rather the express impressions and situations evoked by the soundtrack. Her interpretations were probably more focused on the impressions rather than on understanding the exact elements of the soundtrack. For instance, she perceived the luna park soundtrack as a cheerful situation and described it by drawing a party. If she had described her drawing, she would have probably introduced a different point of view, enriching the whole experience.

Activity 3. In the third activity, children were specifically asked to think about the association of the objects to sounds, and of sounds to colors and to give a motivation for their choices. During most of the activity, all the children were discussing together to which object belonged the various sounds, giving motivations and examples to explain to each others. For instance, to motivate the association of a sound to a plastic bottle, two children replicated that sound with their plastic bottles. In more than one case they did not agree on the association of sounds to objects, as in the case of the book: a girl was convinced that it was a hair drier and she said that the others were wrong, so, all of them wanted to listen again the sound. Many sounds, instead, were very clear to everybody.

Regarding the association of the sounds to the colors, instead, many differences can be noticed. First of all, there were objects, such as the plastic bag, that for all of them cannot be associated with a specific sound. However, they all choose light colors, like light blue, orange and yellow, to describe these objects (plastic bag, plastic bottle and glass bottle). Metal objects, such as keys, pot and cutlery, also resulted to be not easy to associate to a specific color. Differently from plastic and glass objects, these do not even share common characteristics like light colors. In fact, in these were associated to at least four colors each, from light to dark. However, referring to the cutlery, a boy motivated his association to yellow because, he says, the sound is "more pure".

Some interesting similarities, instead, can be identified in water, scissors, and paper box and clap. Water was associated by everyone to the light blue color. This is probably due to the archetypal representation of water, familiar to everyone. Scissors, instead, were associated by most of children to red. Differently from water, this object is not usually represented with a specific color, however it probably invokes concepts like anger and alert, that are culturally represented with red. Similarly, some children associated also the scotch tape, the paper, the keys and the pot to red, with the motivation that the sound of these objects is strong, noisy and one said specifically that red is for noisy sounds because it is extreme.

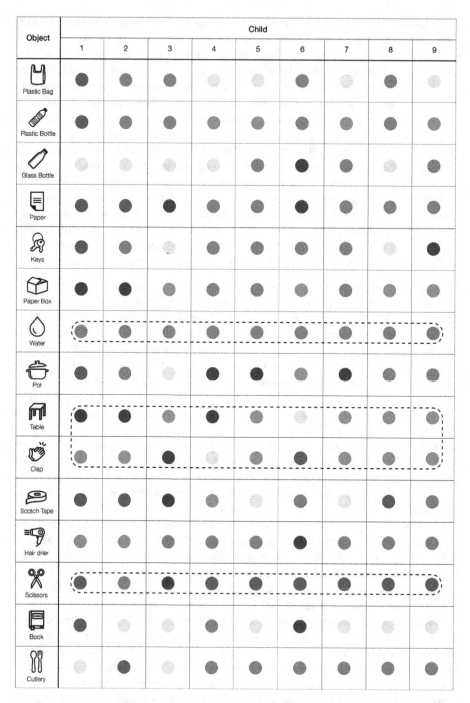

Fig. 6. Results of the third activity. The table shows the colors associated by children to the objects and relative sounds. The dotted lines show three interesting findings. (Color figure online)

Scissors and water represents also two opposite approaches in the color sound association adopted by children during this activity. Some of them, in fact, chose the colors on the basis of the colors that the material of an object usually has. Others, instead, associated sound characteristics, such as loudness, to colors.

In this regard, in fact, the table and the clap are interesting. These were mostly represented with purple and orange. Maybe orange was largely used because was the one, of the colors present on the board, more similar to brown and skin color. However, some chose purple, which is completely in contrast with the color of the materials, but was explained by a girl with the following statement: "the table is normal, so it is purple because purple is for normal things". Then, she explained that her choice of colors was driven by a self determined "rule" in which red is for strong sounds, purple is for normal sounds, and light blue and green are for pure and light sounds. She actually didn't mention yellow, even if she used it. However, it is interesting the process of categorization and self imposed rules that she adopted.

Overall, the activity resulted engaging and enjoyable for the children who were constantly discussing cheerfully and changing their choices of the colors on the basis of the discussion. At the end, they were also very curious of looking behind the box and making sounds with the real objects (Fig. 6).

4 Discussion and Conclusion

The results of the questionnaire contribute to get deeper understanding of a changing scenario in which societal changes are reflected in the daily life of children and in the specific context of China, this phenomenon is particularly evident. Chinese children are extremely busy during the whole week, attending school and extracurricular activities of various nature. Their free time for play appear to be very limited as well as the types of games that they do. Nevertheless, many of the extra curricular activities feature playful interaction styles and are often meant to promote non notional knowledge, such as creativity, imagination and collaboration. Thus, play is changing its role in children's everyday life, from a personal purposeless activity to a structured activity. On the basis of this consideration and on the information about the habits of children, a new design space emerges.

A further reflection on peculiar aspects such as attitude toward technologies, preferred game aims and play habits, it would be possible to define the main purpose of new design scenarios [28] in which the potential of computational thinking and technology can be exploited to go beyond current educational programs.

For instance, new design scenarios might focus on themes like child-parents play, reinterpretation of traditional game modalities, and on the role of extracurricular courses that could be seen as educative games or playful lessons.

In this regard, the activity with children highlighted how simple actions, such as drawing and associating sounds to colors, can rise meaningful discussions and promote children's thinking and reasoning.

During the three activities, in fact, children spontaneously gone beyond the task that were asked to them by discussing together, reasoning their choices and negotiating with the others. In the second activity they explained ambiguous soundtrack by creating their own story and giving a reason to the sound that they were unable to recognize. They also created self imposed rules to associate sounds with colors, by reflecting on sound proprieties, such as loudness. Thus, through their explanations they introduced key concepts, such as sound and color proprieties, that could be used as incipit for a knowledge construction that could start and be driven by children.

Therefore, applying the sense-react principle, introduced by interactive technologies, to concepts traditionally explored for active learning, such as color, sound, emotions and many more, can enable meaningful play. This meaningfulness, however, is not the results of a mere application of technology to traditional activities, but rather a careful design action that encompasses at least three main principles: follow children reasoning, promote imagination, encourage diversity and self expression. During the study, these principles emerged especially in the case of *ambiguity* and *absence of strict rules*, two aspects that can be adopted as design drivers. In fact, when children were missing a word to define an emotion, they made their own description for that. When they didn't recognize the context of a soundtrack they created their own stories to explain the sounds. Finally, when they were asked to associate sounds with colors, for which there is no right or wrong way to do it, they created their own rules.

To sum up, this study wishes to contribute to the understanding of what means to design edutainment products for children, by providing key principles and concepts that can be adopted as design drivers for developing, not only acceptable, but also meaningful play scenarios.

Acknowledgments. This research project is supported by Jol CRAB lab, by TIM.

References

1. Šabanović, S., Bennett, C.C., Lee, H.R.: Towards culturally robust robots: a critical social perspective on robotics and culture. In: Proceedings of HRI Workshop on Culture-Aware Robotics (2014)
2. Beer, J.M., Prakash, A., Mitzner, T.L., Rogers, W.A.: Understanding robot acceptance, pp. 1–45. Georgia Institute of Technology (2011)
3. Ye, R.: How robotics is impacting education. Robotics Trends (2015). http://www.roboticstrends.com/article/how_robotics_is_impacting_education
4. Gardiner, B.: Adding coding to the curriculum. The New York Times (2014). https://www.nytimes.com/2014/03/24/world/europe/adding-coding-to-the-curriculum.html
5. Benitti, F.B.V.: Exploring the educational potential of robotics in schools: a systematic review. Comput. Educ. **58**(3), 978–988 (2012)
6. Arnseth, H. C.: Learning to play or playing to learn-a critical account of the models of communication informing educational research on computer gameplay. Game Stud. **6**(1) (2006). http://gamestudies.org/0601/articles/arnseth
7. Zhu, J.: Early childhood education and relative policies in China. Int. J. Child Care Educ. Policy **3**(1), 51–60 (2009)
8. Forlizzi, J.: The product service ecology: using a systems approach in design. In: Proceedings of the 2nd Conference on Relating Systems Thinking and Design (RSD2), Oslo, Norway (2012)

9. Hamilton-Smith, L.: Learning curve: coding classes to become mandatory in Queensland schools (2016). www.abc.net.au, http://www.abc.net.au/news/2016-11-17/coding-classes-in-queensland-schools-mandatory-from-2017/8018178

10. Rittel, H.W., Webber, M.M.: 2.3 planning problems are wicked. Polity **4**, 155–169 (1973)

11. Norman, D.A., Stappers, P.J.: DesignX: complex sociotechnical systems. She Ji: J. Des. Econ. Innov. **1**(2), 83–106 (2016)

12. Gielen, M.A.: Essential concepts in toy design education: aimlessness, empathy and play value. Int. J. Arts Technol. **3**(1), 4–16 (2009)

13. Ortlieb, E.T.: The pursuit of play within the curriculum. J. Instr. Psychol. **37**(3), 241–246 (2010)

14. Huizinga, J., Eco, U., van Schendel, C.: Homo ludens. Edizione CDE (su licenza della Giulio Einaudi editore) (1985)

15. Collins, A., Halverson, R.: The second educational revolution: rethinking education in the age of technology. J. Comput. Assist. Learn. **26**(1), 18–27 (2010)

16. Papert, S.: A critique of technocentrism in thinking about the school of the future, E&L Memo, No. 2, pp. 248–258 (1990)

17. Hohmann, M., Weikart, D.P., Epstein, A.S.: Educating Young Children: Active Learning Practices for Preschool and Child Care Programs. High/Scope Press, Ypsilanti (1995)

18. Serafini, G.: Teaching programming at primary schools: visions, experiences, and long-term research prospects. In: Kalaš, I., Mittermeir, R.T. (eds.) ISSEP 2011. LNCS, vol. 7013, pp. 143–154. Springer, Heidelberg (2011). doi:10.1007/978-3-642-24722-4_13

19. Gaver, B., Dunne, T., Pacenti, E.: Design: cultural probes. Interactions **6**(1), 21–29 (1999)

20. Musthag, M., Raij, A., Ganesan, D., Kumar, S., Shiffman, S.: Exploring micro-incentive strategies for participant compensation in high-burden studies. In: Proceedings of the 13th International Conference on Ubiquitous Computing, pp. 435–444. ACM, September 2011

21. Church, A.H.: Estimating the effect of incentives on mail survey response rates: a meta-analysis. Publ. Opin. Q. **57**(1), 62–79 (1993)

22. Bernhaupt, R., Weiss, A., Obrist, M., Tscheligi, M.: Playful probing: making probing more fun. In: Baranauskas, C., Palanque, P., Abascal, J., Barbosa, S.D.J. (eds.) INTERACT 2007. LNCS, vol. 4662, pp. 606–619. Springer, Heidelberg (2007). doi:10.1007/978-3-540-74796-3_60

23. Gielen, M.: Mapping children's experiences: adapting contextmapping tools to child participants. Nordes **1**(5), 23–31 (2013)

24. Wyeth, P., Diercke, C.: Designing cultural probes for children. In: Proceedings of the 18th Australia Conference on Computer-Human Interaction: Design: Activities, Artefacts and Environments, pp. 385–388. ACM, November 2006

25. Fox, L., Lentini, R.H.: Teaching children a vocabulary for emotions. Beyond J., 1–3 (2006)

26. Montessori, M.: The Discovery of the Child. Aakar Books, New Delhi (2004)

27. Lillard, A.S.: Playful learning and Montessori education. Am. J. Play **5**(2), 157 (2013)

28. Rosson, M.B., Carroll, J.M.: Scenario based design. In: Human-Computer Interaction, Boca Raton, FL, pp. 145–162 (2009)

Teaching Older Adults to Use Gerontechnology Applications Through Instruction Videos: Human-Element Considerations

Pei-Lee Teh[1], Chee Wei Phang[2], Pervaiz K. Ahmed[1],
Soon-Nyean Cheong[3], Wen-Jiun Yap[3],
Qi Ma[4(✉)], and Alan H.S. Chan[4]

[1] School of Business, Monash University,
Bandar Sunway, Selangor Darul Ehsan, Malaysia
{teh.pei.lee,pervaiz.ahmed}@monash.edu
[2] School of Management, Fudan University, Shanghai, China
phangcw@fudan.edu.cn
[3] Faculty of Engineering, Multimedia University, Cyberjaya, Malaysia
{sncheong,wjyap}@mmu.edu.my
[4] Department of Systems Engineering and Engineering Management,
City University of Hong Kong, Kowloon, Hong Kong
qima22-c@my.cityu.edu.hk, alan.chan@cityu.edu.hk

Abstract. This paper aims to investigate the effect of human narrator (vis-à-vis an artificially-created cartoon narrator) in designing instruction videos to teach older adults to use gerontechnology applications. Additionally, we assess whether there is a difference if the human narrator is a child, a young adult, or an older adult. A sample of 124 older adults was collected to test the research hypotheses. Our findings suggest that in general instruction videos with human narrators are preferred by the older adults over the one without (i.e., cartoon character). More interestingly, the older adults prefer child as the human narrator (to young adult and older adult), as reflected in the highest perceived effectiveness and social presence of the video garnered among all the video versions. These insights have important implications on teaching and promoting older adults' use of gerontechnology applications via instruction videos. We conclude this paper with a discussion on the research implications, limitations and future research.

Keywords: Gerontechnology · Training · Instruction videos · Human narrator · Older adults · Child

1 Introduction

Today many countries are experiencing an aging population, and this phenomenon is bound to persist in years to come [16]. A recent report by the United Nations estimates that a quarter of the world's population will consist of older adults by 2050 [31]. With this issue also come the challenges to ensure a satisfactory living quality for the older population, given the thinning young workforce and the decreasing social resources to

© Springer International Publishing AG 2017
P.-L.P. Rau (Ed.): CCD 2017, LNCS 10281, pp. 582–591, 2017.
DOI: 10.1007/978-3-319-57931-3_46

provide the needed support. As it is unrealistic to rely solely on human aids for this purpose, the role of technologies becomes increasingly salient [17, 21]. One such technology is gerontechnology [5, 30, 32].

Gerontechnology applications refers to the use of technologies that are developed to support older adults for a better life [6, 27]. It combines technology and gerontology that concerns the study of the social, psychological, cognitive, and biological aspects of aging. One important area of gerontechnology applications is in supporting the home living of the older people, through providing them with convenience, safety, and independence in their everyday activities [23, 29, 32]. For instance, smart technologies are developed for controlling home lighting and heating through simple devices or mobile phones that can help address older adults' limitations in physical functions [12]. These technologies may help older people to live a better life alone at home when human care is beyond their immediate access.

However, it is also well recognized that older people belong to the typical group of digital immigrants, who are not born into the digital world and learn to use information technologies (ITs) only at a later stage in their lives [25]. Persuading and getting this group of people to use technologies voluntarily and effectively present a non-trivial challenge. Ideally, one-to-one hands-on guidance can be provided to teach older adults to use gerontechnology applications, but this is neither practical nor scalable given the growing older population. Especially in the developing countries, lack of resources is likely to prevent this to be achieved at a large-scale. Against this backdrop, teaching older adults through instruction videos may be a viable option [3, 18, 28]. These videos record the instructions on how to achieve a task or to learn a new skill (e.g., using a gerontechnology application), and can be used repeatedly to reach a mass audience.

Yet, most of the extant studies on the use of instruction videos have focused on the younger populations, such as children [28], young people [10] and adults [4]. When presenting instruction videos to the older adults, different considerations may be needed. Among the limited literature addressing the use of instruction videos for older adults, the emphasis has been on the cognitive aspects of teaching this group of people, such as designing videos that can compensate for their relatively limited processing resources, lack of inhibition, cognitive slowing, and sensory deficits [9, 15, 19]. Less attention has been paid to the psychological aspects of teaching older adults to use ITs, despite gerontology research clearly indicates their psychological differences from the younger people [2, 11].

In this study, building on relevant gerontology theory and literature, we posit that in order to promote the receptiveness of older adults to the instruction video and the gerontology technology concerned, it is important to incorporate a sense of human into the videos. Specifically, this can be achieved by having a human narrator (vis-à-vis artificially-created character) to provide step-by-step instructions (i.e., guided actions) on how to use a gerontechnology application. Furthermore, it also matters whether the human narrator is a child, a young adult, or an older adult. To test our propositions, we are conducting experiments (ongoing) to assess older adults' perceived effectiveness of four versions of instruction videos, with: (1) a cartoon character to provide the narrations; (2) a female child as human narrator; (3) a female young adult as human narrator; (4) a female older adult as human narrator. All the videos are the same (with exact content of the guided actions and instructions) except for how the narrations were provided (per the four versions). We invited older adults aged 50 and above to participate in the experiment; each was randomly assigned to view one of the video versions. They would then use the focal gerontechnology application that allows them to remotely operate the TV (switching on, off, and between TV programs), lighting (switching on and off), and fan (switching on and off), after which they were asked to fill in a short survey. In the survey we assessed their perceived effectiveness of the instruction video, intention to adopt the gerontechnology application, and perceived social presence.

Our initial findings suggest that in general instruction videos with human narrators are preferred by the older adults over the one without (i.e., cartoon character). Furthermore, the older adults prefer child as the human narrator (to young adult and older adult), as reflected in the highest perceived effectiveness and social presence of the video garnered among all the video versions. The initial results suggest older adults' preference for human presence in the instruction videos targeted at them, which may be understood through the continuity perspective [1]. That is, older adults prefer something that gives a sense of human they are similar with, compared to something "technological" that appears remote or "cold" to them. Moreover, probably arising from a desire to protect their dignity [34], older adults prefer child to teach them to use gerontechnology applications compared to young adults and their peers. These insights have important implications on teaching and promoting older adults' use of gerontechnology applications via instruction videos. We conclude this paper with a discussion on the plans for our future research.

2   Literature Review and Research Hypotheses

We build primarily on the gerontology literature, in particular the continuity theory [1] and the studies about older adults' dignity [34], to develop our research hypotheses. Overall we propose that older adults would prefer instruction videos with human narrators than without, in that the former are perceived as more effective than the latter. In addition, having a child as a human narrator would be perceived as more effective than having a young or an older adult in delivering the instruction video.

Continuity theory suggests that older adults make adaptive choices in an effort to preserve ties with their past experiences to reduce environmental uncertainty [2]. This often manifests in the form of habits that people develop as they grow old, which persistently influences preferences in their daily lives. Being typical digital immigrants [25], older adults grew up in an environment whereby IT use was not yet prevalent. Thus, it can be expected that older adults are more used to having human contacts [24] in attaining a purpose, e.g., to learn a new skill. Consequently, older adults may prefer seeing human narrator in an instruction video compared to seeing an artificially-created character. The latter is likely to give a "cold" feeling to older adults, since the artificially-created characters are not the familiar ways through which they learn something (i.e., being taught by a person). In contrast, having a human narrator is likely to elicit a higher social presence feeling that leads to their more favorable perception about the video, in terms of its effectiveness to teach them how to use the gerontechnology application. This should also enhance their intention to adopt the application. The preceding discussions led us to hypothesize:

H1: Instruction videos with human narrator would be perceived by the older adults as having higher effectiveness compared to one without human narrator (i.e., cartoon character).

H2: Instruction videos with human narrator would lead to a higher intention of the older adults to adopt the gerontechnology application concerned compared to one without human narrator (i.e., cartoon character).

Furthermore, we believe that having a child, a young adult, or an older adult as the human narrator would make a difference to how older adults perceive the effectiveness of the video, and also their intention to adopt the gerontechnology application taught in the video.

Previous research suggests that preserving dignity is a salient concern for the older adults [7, 34]. With rich life experiences accumulated, older adults are likely to feel that they know more than their younger counterparts. Also due to this desire to preserve their dignity, they are rather sensitive to receiving advices from others. For instance, Yardley et al. [35] note that older adults might reject an advice on fall prevention if it hints at them being unfit or incapable. Thus, care is needed in providing advices to them such that they do not feel their dignity is being threatened [35]. In a similar vein, we expect the same to apply for delivering instruction videos to older adults to teach them to use a gerontechnology application.

Among the human narrators (who provide voice instructions together with the guided actions in the video), we expect that child would be perceived more favorably by the older adults compared to young adult and another older adult. In particular, older adults are more likely to resist instructions given by young adults. Being older in age, they may feel that having to be taught by a younger adult is a threat to their dignity. As the saying goes, "wise men don't need advice", not to mention them may pride themselves as the "old wise men." Indeed, it is typically the older adults who try to impose their views and knowledge on the young adults, not the other way round [33].

By contrast, older adults may be relatively more receptive to being taught by other older adults. Seeing them as peers who also possess rich life experiences, it may be deemed more acceptable to receive instructions or advices from other older adults. Previous research indicates that it is common for older adults to receive helps, advices and supports from each other, e.g., through online networks [14]. Yet, being peers also means that there could be a comparison tendency among the older adults (e.g., "What? He/She knows this thing more than I do?") [8], this may discount the receptiveness of the older adults to receiving video instructions from their peers to some extents.

Children, on the other hand, do not instill this peer comparison tendency, and at the same time pose minimal threat to older adults' dignity. Research on advertising suggests that the presence of children in an advertisement is effective in inducing purchases, due to their innocence that confers feelings of credibility [20]. In addition, older adults may feel a sense of affinity and affection towards children appearing in the video, linking them to their own grandchildren [22]. This should also in turn promotes perceived social presence of the instruction video, which refers to a feeling or sense of warmth and sociability with a medium [13].

Collectively, based on the rationales above, we hypothesize the following:

H3: Among child, young adult, and older adult as narrator, instruction video with child as the narrator will (a) be perceived as most effective; (b) lead to highest adoption intention; (c) elicit highest sense of social presence.

3 Research Methodology

3.1 Research Method

We employ an experiment method to test our research hypotheses. All research procedures are being performed in accordance with university research ethics approval. We recruit older adults aged 50 and above to participate in the experiment (ongoing). Participation is voluntary and all participants are assured of anonymity. Each participant is given a cash voucher of USD2.5 as a token of appreciation for their participation. Participants are randomly assigned to one of the four treatments (Treatment 1: Video A with cartoon character as narrator; Treatment 2: Video B with child as narrator; Treatment 3: Video C with young adult as narrator; Treatment 4: Video D with older adult as narrator). We carefully prepared the instruction videos using cartoon and human characters. We chose normal-looking individuals for the human narrators. In particular, we obtained informed consent of the individuals and selected those with normal appearance (i.e., neither too attractive nor too unattractive) and who look similar (including hair style). For the cartoon character, we created an original cartoon character to avoid feelings of familiarity (e.g., famous cartoon character).

The smartphone home application is an in-house developed assistive technology that provides a portable and convenient home experience for older adults. We leveraged on the Near Field Communication (NFC)-enabled technology and Bluetooth-Low-Energy (BLE)-enabled Raspberry-PI to develop the smartphone home application. The application does not require an Internet connection which are regarded as costly and inconvenient to older adults. The application enables a "tap-to-connect" interaction between the physical world and virtual world with the use of NFC smartphone and photo interface. For example, user taps his/her smartphone on a photo interface (embedded with NFC tags) to operate the home appliances such as turning on/off TV, switching on/off lights, etc.

3.2 Sample

A total of 124 older adults have participated in this study when this paper is written. The breakdown of age group is as follows: 18 participants between 50–54 years old, 57 participants between 55–64 years old, 38 participants between 65–74 years old, 9 participants between 75–84 years old, and 2 participants above 85 years old.

Before the experiment, the participants were briefed on the research objective, the experimental tasks and informed consent was obtained. During the experiment, the participants were required to view the instruction video before they were asked to operate the smartphone home application. After the product-trial session, each participant was required to answer a survey questionnaire, followed by a face-to-face interview.

In the survey, we measured three variables, i.e., perceived video effectiveness, adoption intention, and social presence. All of the variables were measured on a seven-point Likert scale where 1 = strongly disagree and 7 = strongly agree. A pretest of the instrument was conducted with three information systems experts and five older adults to check the content validity, following which minor re-wording was made. We also conducted a pilot study with thirty older adults ($n = 30$) before the main data collection.

4 Results

4.1 Reliability, Validity and Factor Analyses

We first assess the psychometric properties of the survey items. All variables are reliable as the values of Cronbach's Alpha and Composite Reliability are greater than 0.80. Convergent and discriminant validity are assessed using Average Variance Extracted (AVE). Convergent validity was established as AVE of all constructs are greater than 0.50. Discriminant validity is examined through the comparison of square roots of the AVE of variables pairs to the correlation between variables pairs. All the square roots of AVE values are greater than the off-diagonal coefficients in the correlation table, indicating that discriminant validity is acceptable (refer to Table 1).

Table 1. Results of reliability and validity

	Perceived effectiveness	Social presence	Adoption intention
Perceived effectiveness	0.883[a]		
Social presence	0.258**	0.937	
Adoption intention	0.462**	0.713**	0.943
Average variance extracted	0.780	0.878	0.925
Composite reliability	0.914	0.956	0.974
Cronbach's alpha	0.838	0.929	0.959

[a] The italicized values in the diagonal row of correlation matrix are square roots of the corresponding AVE. ** $p < 0.01$.

Based on the initial set of data collected, we then conducted a between-subjects MANOVA to assess if there are differences in how the older adults perceive the video across the different video versions. The results indicate that there are significant perception differences for the focal variables (i.e., perceived effectiveness of the instruction video, social presence, adoption intention) across the different video versions (Wilks' lambda = 0.794, $F(8,176) = 2.695$, $p = 0.008$). This provides partial support for the hypotheses; however, to understand how the perceptions differ across the video versions, follow-up ANOVAs were conducted (see Table 2 below).

Table 2. Mean differences of focal perceptions across video versions

	Perceived effectiveness	Social presence	Adoption intention
Child	6.448 (0.721)	5.948 (1.522)	6.323 (1.004)
Young adult	6.323 (1.004)	5.033 (1.349)	6.022 (0.792)
Older adult	6.219 (0.701)	4.208 (1.996)	6.208 (1.106)
Cartoon character	5.811 (0.604)	4.800 (1.613)	5.378 (0.942)
F-value	4.116**	6.187**	5.782**

Note: The values above represent the mean (standard deviation). ** $p < 0.01$.

As can be seen from Table 2, instruction videos with human narrators (child, young adult, and older adult) were generally perceived as more effective than the one with a cartoon character as the narrator. Also we compare the means of the human narrator group with that of the cartoon character; the difference is significant with $F = 7.936**$. This provides initial support for H1. In addition, instruction videos with human narrators also prompted higher adoption intention of the gerontechnology application compared to one with a cartoon character. Again we compare the means of the human narrator group with that of the cartoon character on this measure; the difference is significant with $F = 15.904***$. This provides initial support for H2.

Across the human narrators, the mean values show that the child narrator elicits the highest perceived video effectiveness, social presence, and adoption intention (Table 2). However, based on the initial data collected, test of significance shows that it is only between child and young adult that the difference is close to being significant for perceived video effectiveness ($p = 0.067$). Thus, H2 (a) is only supported to some extents. No significant difference is found for adoption intention, which renders H2 (b) being not supported based on the initial data set. With regard to perceived social presence, significant difference is found across the three groups ($F = 8.889***$), which provides initial support for H2 (c). Furthermore, we tried regressing social presence on perceived video effectiveness and adoption intention, and found the effects to be significant ($t = 2.941**$ and $3.408**$). This could mean that the difference between child, young adult, and older adult may operate via how they elicit a sense of social presence from the older adult, which we will further explore in subsequent studies.

5 Discussion and Conclusion

The objective of this paper is to investigate the psychological aspects of designing instruction videos to teach older adults to use gerontechnology applications. Specifically, we assess whether it matters to use a human narrator (vis-à-vis an artificially-created cartoon narrator), and if so, whether there is a difference if the human narrator is a child, a young adult, or an older adult. Our initial results show that the difference is non-trivial for older adults, they seem to prefer human narrators in general, and child as the narrator in particular. Furthermore, we find that the sense of social presence elicited could potentially explain the difference.

We believe this paper has important implications to both research and practice. To research, we fill in an important void of designing instruction videos for the older adults. Previous research has mostly addressed the issue for the younger people [4, 10, 28], or if they do for older adults, focused on its cognitive aspects such as designing videos that can compensate for their relatively limited processing resources, lack of inhibition, cognitive slowing, and sensory deficits [9, 15, 19]. The psychological aspects of designing instruction videos for this group of users have not received the deserved level of attention, considering that older adults are likely to have different needs such as maintaining their preferences and habits and to preserve their dignity [1, 7, 34, 35].

To practice, the findings of this study may contribute towards promoting older adults to use gerontechnology applications (such as smart home) for a better independent home living. Previous research has indicated that training older adults to use information technologies could be beneficial to their welfare. For instance, Shapira et al. [26] show that older people who used the Internet felt less depressed and lonely, and were more pleased with their current quality of life than did people who were engaged in other activities for the same period of time. Yet, a pre-condition is to overcome the resistance of older adults, who are the most typical digital immigrants, to using information technologies. Our paper helps provide a better understanding of how to design instruction videos for this group of users, which can teach them to use gerontechnology applications at a large-scale. This has broad implications, given the burden of caring for an increasing numbers of older people with limited societal resources.

This paper currently has some limitations that will be addressed in subsequent research. First, the sample size remains small, which may hinder the making of highly confident conclusions. Nonetheless, the trends and patterns of the results look promising. We will continue to collect more data to obtain more robust results. Second, more work is still needed to obtain more comprehensive insights. For instance, while we make all the narrators to be female to avoid possible gender bias, we plan to subsequently develop more video versions with male narrators to assess how older adults perceive the two genders in giving video instructions to them. In addition, we can examine if male and female older adults evaluate the videos differently, which is more practical with a larger data set collected. Furthermore, we plan to evaluate the effectiveness of the instruction video in a more objective manner, by observing the actual actions when older adults operate the gerontechnology application after watching the video, e.g., speed of achieving designated tasks and errors committed.

Acknowledgements. This research was supported by Ministry of Science, Technology and Innovation (MOSTI), Government of Malaysia, and Monash University Malaysia campus under grant ES-1-14/06-02-10-SF0211 and 2015-CRC-Geron. The authors wish to express their appreciation for the volunteers who participated in the study. Special thanks are due to Saramma Joseph, Stephanie, Jeffery, Hadi, Raveena, Jonathan, Wai Luen, Venise, Kaixiang, Mei Kuan, Andria, Guang Hong and Jia Wei for their help in data collection.

References

1. Atchley, R.C.: Retirement. The Gerontologist. **12**(4), 436–440 (1972)
2. Atchley, R.C.: A continuity theory of normal aging. Gerontologist **29**(2), 183–190 (1989)
3. Bennett-Levy, J., Perry, H.: The promise of online cognitive behavioural therapy training for rural and remote mental health professionals. Australas. Psychiatry **17**(1), 121–124 (2009)
4. Bidwell, M.A., Rehfeldt, R.A.: Using video modeling to teach a domestic skill with an embedded social skill to adults with severe mental retardation. Behav. Interv. **19**(4), 263–274 (2004)
5. Bouma, H., Fozard, J.L., van Bronswijk, J.E.M.H.: Gerontechnology as a Field of Endeavour. Gerontechnology J **8**(2), 68–75 (2009)
6. Bronswijk, J.E.M.H., Bouma, H., Fozard, J.L., Kearns, W.D., Davison, G.C., Tuan, P.C.: Defining Gerontechnology for R&D purpose. Gerontechnology J. **8**(1), 3–10 (2009)
7. Calnan, M., Badcott, D., Woolhead, G.: Dignity under Threat? a study of the experiences of older people in the united kingdom. Int. J. Health Serv. **36**(2), 355–375 (2006)
8. Cockerham, W.C., Sharp, K., Wilcox, J.A.: Aging and perceived health status. J. Gerontology. **38**(3), 349–355 (1983)
9. Czaja, S.J., Lee, C.C.: The impact of aging on access to technology. Univ. Access Inf. Soc. **5**, 341–349 (2007)
10. Embregts, P.J.C.M.: Effects of video feedback on social behaviour of young people with mild intellectual disability and staff responses. Int. J. Disabil. Dev. Educ. **49**(1), 105–116 (2002)
11. Erikson, E.H., Erikson, J.M., Kivnick, H.: Vital Involvement in Old Age: The Experience of Old Age in Our Time. Norton, New York (1986)
12. Fozard, J.L., Rietsema, J., Bouma, H., Graafmans, J.A.M.: Gerontechnology: creating enabling environments for the challenges and opportunities of aging. Educ. Gerontology. **26** (4), 331–344 (2000)
13. Gefen, D., Straub, D.W.: Managing User Trust in B2C E-services. E-service J. **2**(2), 7–24 (2003)
14. Godfrey, M., Johnson, O.: Digital circles of support: meeting the information needs of older people. Comput. Human Behav. **25**, 633–642 (2009)
15. Jones, B.D., Bayen, U.J.: Teaching older adults to use computers: recommendations based on cognitive aging research. Educ. Gerontology **24**(7), 675–689 (1998)
16. Joseph, S., Teh, P.L., Chan, A.H.S., Ahmed, P.K., Cheong, S.N., Yap, W.J.: Gerontechnology usage and acceptance model (GUAM): a qualitative study of Chinese older adults in Malaysia. Gerontechnology J. **14**(4), 224–238 (2016)
17. Ma, Q., Chan, A.H., Chen, K.: Personal and other factors affecting acceptance of smartphone technology by older Chinese adults. Appl. Ergon. **54**, 62–71 (2016)
18. McCulloch, E.B., Noonan, M.J.: Impact of online training videos on the implementation of mand training by three elementary school paraprofessionals. Educ. Training Autism Dev. Disabil. **48**(1), 132–141 (2013)
19. Naumanen, M., Tukiainen, M.: Guiding the elderly into the use of computers and internet – lessons taught and learnt. In: Proceedings of the IADIS International Conference on Cognition and Exploratory Learning in Digital Age, pp. 19–27 (2007)
20. North, E., Millard, S.: Children and race in south african magazine advertising. Ecquid Novi. **24**(1), 37–54 (2003)
21. Osman, Z., Poulson, D., Nicolle, C.: Introducing computers and the internet to older users: findings from the care online project. Univ. Access Inf. Soc. **4**(1), 16–23 (2005)

22. Parida, B.: Presence of Children in Advertisements and its Impact on Consumers' Purchase Behaviour. IIM, Ahmedabad (2013)
23. Peek, S.T.M., Luijkx, K.G., Rijnaard, M.D., Nieboer, M.E., van der Voort, C.S., Aarts, S., van Hoof, J., Vrijhoef, H.J.M., Wouters, E.J.M.: Older adults' reasons for using technology while aging in place. Gerontology 62(2), 226–237 (2016)
24. Phang, C.W., Kankanhalli, A., Sabherwal, R.: Usability and sociability in electronic communities: a comparative study of knowledge seekers and contributors. J. AIS 10(10), 721–747 (2009)
25. Vodanovich, S., Sundaram, D., Myers, M.: Research commentary—digital natives and Ubiquitous information systems. Inf. Syst. Res. 21(4), 711–723 (2010)
26. Shapira, N., Barak, A., Gal, I.: Promoting older adults' well-being through internet training and use. Aging Ment. Health 11(5), 477–484 (2007)
27. Siriaraya, P., Ang, C.S., Bobrowicz, A.: Exploring the potential of virtual worlds in engaging older people and supporting healthy aging. Behav. Inf. Technol. 33(3), 283–294 (2014)
28. Shukla-Mehta, S., Miller, T., Callahan, K.J.: Evaluating the effectiveness of video instruction on social and communication skills training for children with autism spectrum disorders: a review of the literature. Focus Autism Other Dev. Disabil. 25(1), 23–36 (2010)
29. Teh, P.L., Ahmed, P.K., Cheong, S.N., Yap, W.J.: Age-group differences in near field communication smartphone. Industr. Manag. Data Syst. 114(3), 484–502 (2014)
30. Teh, P.L., Lim, W.M., Ahmed, P.K., Chan, A.H., Loo, J.M., Cheong, S.N., Yap, W.J.: Does power posing affect gerontechnology adoption among older adults? Behav. Inf. Technol. 36(1), 33–42 (2017)
31. United Nations: World Population Prospects: The 2015 Revision, Key Findings and Advance Tables. Department of Economic and Social Affairs, Population Division. Working Paper No. ESA/P/WP.241 (2015)
32. Van Bronswijk, J.E.M.H., Bouma, H., Fozard, J.L.: Technology for quality of life an enriched taxonomy. Gerontechnology J. 2(2), 169–172 (2002)
33. Williams, A., Giles, H.: Intergenerational conversations young adults' retrospective accounts. Human Commun. Res. 23(2), 220–250 (1996)
34. Woolhead, G., Calnan, M., Dieppe, P., Tadd, W.: Dignity in older age: what do older people in the united kingdom think? Age Ageing 33(2), 165–170 (2004)
35. Yardley, L., Donovan-Hall, M., Francis, K., Todd, C.: Older people's views of advice about falls prevention: a qualitative study. Health Educ. Res. 21(4), 508–517 (2006)

A Preliminary Study on the Learning Assessment in Massive Open Online Courses

Quan Yuan[✉], Qin Gao, and Yue Chen

Department of Industrial Engineering,
Tsinghua University, Beijing 100084, China
{yuan-ql5, chenyuel4}@mails.tsinghua.edu.cn,
gaoqin@tsinghua.edu.cn

Abstract. Massive Open Online Course (MOOC) is a new online education form. MOOC aims to provide the advance systematic educations to the public and share the access to the best high educations to Internet users. Although the MOOC platform contained many video lessons of high-quality courses from famous universities around the world, the assessment of students' learning, including testing methods, grading methods and feedback to student, was unsatisfactory according to XuetangX, an xMOOC websites leading by Tsinghua University in China. Setting effective and satisfactory assessment methods to test and grade students' learning performance in MOOC has significant values for all stakeholders including instructors, students and the MOOC platform. An interview study was conducted to understanding the current situation of assessments and the opinions towards different types of assessment methods from both instructors and students. We interviewed five teachers, eight course assistants of different categories of MOOCs in XuetangX, and six students from different MOOC platforms. Some conclusions and suggestions about the assessment on students' learning performance in different categories of MOOCs were drawn in the study. The findings in the study can be referred as guidelines for instructors to design great assessment methods in different MOOCs.

Keywords: MOOC · Learning assessment · Test method · Grading

1 Introduction

Massive Open Online Course (MOOC) is a new online education form [5]. MOOC aims to provide the advance systematic educations to the public and share the access to the best high educations to Internet users. Online users can take University courses on MOOC for free mainly by watching class videos, interacting with teachers and other students, doing homework, taking examinations and some other ways. MOOC is arousing global interest and leading to a new revolution in the education. Till today, hundreds of Universities have joined, thousands of courses have been provided, and millions of learners around the world have participated in varieties of MOOC platforms [4].

Currently MOOC is not very popular among people, and the high drop rate is a serious problem existing in the MOOC [10, 19]. The key characteristics of MOOC are openness, diversity, autonomy, connectedness and interactivity [7], and these arouse

© Springer International Publishing AG 2017
P.-L.P. Rau (Ed.): CCD 2017, LNCS 10281, pp. 592–602, 2017.
DOI: 10.1007/978-3-319-57931-3_47

many students joining in MOOC courses. The characteristics however bring three severe problems to MOOCs at the same time, particularly in student assessment [21]. Although the website contained many video lessons of high-quality courses from famous universities around the world, the assessment of students' learning, including testing methods, grading methods and feedback to student, was unsatisfactory according to XuetangX, an xMOOC [11] website lead by Tsinghua University in China. Because of the limitation of massive and open online education, a MOOC often had various students with different objectives and uneven knowledge level, and some of them had low level of knowledge and low learning skill but high study expectations [2]. It was hard for instructors to set appropriate courses and test for all students and for students to have motivations to learn the courses [18]. Consequently, teacher could not perfectly test students' ability and achievement as they did in real class.

Setting good assessment to test and grade students' learning performance in MOOC has significant values for stakeholders. For students, good assessments help them know the degree of knowledge acquisition, adjust their learning state, increase the sense of presence [1], improve learning motivations, and reduce the possibility of dropping out of the course [9]. For instructors, including teachers and course assistants, effective assessments can test students' ability, which can be a reference for instructors to adjust what they teach in time. For MOOC platforms, successful assessments can earn students' positive opinions of the course quality, and get the higher public acceptance to the course certification in MOOC platform. Thus, the ability to assessing learning performance of students is a necessary and important issue for the success of MOOCs.

This study attempted to: (1) investigate the current situation and requirements of assessment in MOOCs; (2) collect good example cases of assessment methods, summarize some suggestions about designing the test, grading and feedback; and (3) prepare for future work about proposing guidelines of how to design assessments for a MOOC. Firstly, we conducted interviews to instructors and students of different course types in XuetangX, to explore the applications of the different types of assessment methods to different courses, and the effects of those methods for evaluating students' performance. Secondly, we analyzed the data from interviews and concluded the effectiveness and satisfaction of the different assessment methods with varieties of courses in instructors' opinions.

2   Literature Review

2.1   Types of Tests in MOOCs

Assessment methods in MOOCs included objective questions, such as true-false, multiple-choice, filling in the blanks and matching, and subjective questions such as essay and product design. Group work and student engagement are separately special assessment method for offline course and online course.

Objective questions are the common assessment methods of students' performance both in traditional classes and in MOOCs. Objective questions test what extent the students remember and understand the knowledge [16]. It contains several common question types such as true-false, multiple-choice, filling in the blanks and matching, suiting for examining closed-ended response and detailed knowledge [24]. Therefore, automatic judgment by computer can be conveniently done to objective questions, which are the benefit for MOOCs. Assessment consist only of objective questions for a MOOC has amounts of problems. Firstly, objective questions cannot test students about open-ended problems and their skills [12], and secondly, the test distinguishing degree of the questions was not good [3]. In addition, students can easily cheat in online objective question test. Besides objective questions, there should be other types of assessment methods used to judge students' performance in MOOCs.

Subjective questions are another common assessment methods. Those questions have no exact answer, usually asking students about their opinions to an open-ended item or designing a product such as painting, program and article. Subjective questions are used to test students' levels of understanding and using knowledge, and examine students' abilities of analyzing, summarizing and evaluating a problem and expressing their opinions [24]. Subjective questions are widely used in traditional education courses, but bring heavy checking burdens to instructors. As MOOCs are openness and generally arouse thousands of students to take the class, several instructors in one MOOC cannot check the subjective answers from such many students one by one.

Group work is a special type of subjective questions generally used in course assessment. Several students form a group to finish one assessment task, write one answer and hand it to instructors as their common assignment. Students in a group need high communications to finish one task. There were many restrictions in the group work. Firstly, students having different learning targets and attitudes are hard to come to an agreement about to what extent the assignment answer quality is. Secondly, a group member had dropped out from the course influence the process of the group work. Thirdly, students in a group can be difficult to gather together to discuss how to finish the work because of the time and place conflicts. In addition, a member's different consideration of the same work may be ignored by others in a group, letting that member giving up joining the group to work together with others [6]. Those problems stop the application of group work, particularly in MOOCs.

Student engagement is also a usual assessment in a course. In some traditional course, instructors frequently let students register their attendance at lessons, and take the attendance into consideration to grade students' final score. In MOOCs, the engagement of students is mostly measured by discussion. More discussions with higher quality bring better score to MOOC students. The engagement partly refers that how serious a student take part in the course, and is related to the students' performance, but some instructors thought the engagement makes no sense to students' knowledge level.

2.2   Grading Methods in MOOCs

The assignments are usually scored by instructors in traditional class. It is an effective grading method for courses which had small class size. Instructors have no enough time and energy to grading all assignments from a large number of students in MOOCs [22]. Even though they graded all the assignment by themselves, they had no time to give appropriate feedback to every student in time.

Auto-grading is used widely around MOOC platforms. The objective questions are effectively graded by auto-grading in XuetangX. But for subjective questions and other complex problems, it is often difficult to design machine grading systems which are accurate [20].

Peer review was a wide-used way of grading in MOOCs. It is a way to reduce instructors' checking burdens, and at the same time strengthen students' autonomy. It means a student's assignment is grading by his or her classmates. It has been used in Coursera, one of the most popular MOOC platforms. The knowledge gap among students in MOOCs may cause the problem of reliability and validity in peer review [13].

2.3 The Criterions of a Valid Assessment

The validity of an assessment includes both the effectiveness and satisfaction to the assessment, and the two items can come from both instructors' expert evaluation and students' judgment.

The effectiveness of an assessment includes [6, 15, 23]:

- if the assessment can examine the teaching knowledge of the course
- if the assessment can examine students' abilities of integrating knowledge and applying knowledge to analyze and solve a problem
- if the assessment can reflect the learning improvement of students

The satisfaction of an assessment is related to the following factors [13, 25]:

- if the assessment can motivate students for harder and better studying
- if the instructors offer helpful assessment feedback in time in studying process
- if the assessment is clear and fair

3 Interview

The objectives of interview research were to understand the overall assessment status and requirements of the MOOCs, and concluded some useful design guidelines for better assessment of MOOCs.

There are some factors that are related to the effectiveness and satisfaction of an assessment, and need to be figured out in the interview. Xia and Jiang [24] stated that education evaluation should consist of cognition, skills and affection, where the general method to measure cognition and skills was test. Firstly, at the student angle, the motivation to take a MOOC class will influence the completion of the course [17], and the foundation knowledge level of students about a specific course affects learning outcomes and further affects assessing and grading. Secondly, the assessment of a course and the feedback of the assessment can change students' learning motivation [9, 14]. Moreover, the types of course and teaching objectives influence the design of assessment methods and contents, and then affect the validity of the assessment.

3.1   Interview Process

Course Classification. Different types of assessment method fit for different courses, and similar types of assessment method usually fit for same categories of courses. As the instructors often used different assessment methods according to different types of courses, the first step preparing for an all-sided interview was classifying courses into different categories at XuetangX.com. Referring to national standard classification of disciplines, and considering the current categories of XuetangX at the same time, we divided MOOCs into eight categories: (1) science, (2) medical science, (3) computer science of engineering, (4) other engineering, (5) business and economics, (6) art and design, (7) language, (8) other liberal arts.

Participants. 13 instructors and 6 students of MOOCs in XuetangX.com were interviewed in the research. The instructors included five teachers who set up at least one courses of different categories on XuetangX, and eight assistants of MOOCs in eight different categories. Table 1 showed the interviewing instructors' courses and categories information. C++ Program Design and English Listening & Speaking were two courses of which we interviewed both teacher and assistant. As the table showed, we encoded the instructors with different categories 1−8 and whether he or she was I. teacher or II. assistant. For example, 3-I referred a teacher for computer science. The students were all XuetangX users from different place in China. All of them had study or were studying one or more MOOCs belonging to different categories. Some of students had experiences on studying on other MOOC platforms such as Coursera and edX.

Table 1. The courses of interviewing instructors

Category	I. Teachers	II. Assistants
1. Science	*Modern Biology*	*Linear Algebra*
2. Medical science	*Medical Parasitology*	*Introduction to Medical*
3. Computer science	*C ++ Program Design*	*C ++ Program Design*
4. Other engineering	None	*Circuit Theory*
5. Business and economics	None	*Financial Valuation Analysis*
6. Art and design	None	*Art of Eternity*
7. Language	*English Listening& Speaking*	*English Listening & Speaking*
8. Other liberal art course	*Basic Principle of Marxism*	*History As A Mirror*

Interview Questions. We interviewed teachers, assistants and students with different open questions. The teachers were interviewed about their teaching objectives, course content, student information, current assessment methods and their opinions about all kinds of assessment in their MOOCs. We asked assistants about the course content, assistant tasks, details about students, current assessment methods, opinions about all kinds of assessment and grading methods. Students expressed their objectives they wished to get from the MOOC, the current situations about course teaching and assessment of different MOOCs, the opinions whether a specific assessment methods fit for those MOOCs, and the suggestions that they thought the course assessment should be.

Procedure. All interviews for instructors were conducted face to face. All interviews for students were conducted through online phones. The interview time for each participant was about 20 min.

4 Results

4.1 Instructors

Current Situation Analysis. Table 2 showed the teaching objective, teaching content and student information in different MOOCs according to instructors. The left column of the table contained several descriptions related to the course, and other columns referred different courses and their true and false about each description. The course is coded as we mentioned above, 1–8 for categories and I/II for the identities of participants. Y referred that the description was true in the course, and N referred that the description was false in the course, and the white piece referred that the description was not mentioned by instructors.

Table 2. Current situations in different MOOCs

Descriptions	1-I	1-II	2-I	2-II	3-I	4-II	5-II	6-II	7-I	8-I	8-II
Low teaching objectives	Y	Y		Y	Y	Y	Y		Y		Y
Simple study content	Y		N		N				Y		
Simple assesment	Y		Y		Y			Y	Y	Y	Y
No course improvement	Y	Y		Y	Y				Y		
Big gap of students'basic level	Y	Y	Y	Y	Y	Y	Y		Y		Y

We got the following course features:

- The MOOCs were simpler than off-line classes in both teaching contents and ways to assessment, and were not improved during the semesters changing
- Instructors generally knew less about students' learning status, including large amounts of students and the big gap of students' basic knowledge level
- Students were not active during course
- The MOOCs were regarded as a resource but not an online class

Current Assessment Method. Table 3 showed current assessment methods in different MOOCs. The structure and coding of the table was similar with Table 2, with the descriptions, courses and true/false information from instructors.

We got the following assessment features:

- All of the courses whose instructors were interviewed used only objective questions to test students' performance whatever the course categories were, and the objective questions used included true-false, multiple-choice and filling in the blanks, with

Table 3. Current assessment in different MOOCs

Descriptions	1-I	1-II	2-I	2-II	3-I	4-II	5-II	6-II	7-I	8-I	8-II
Homework	Y	Y	Y	Y	Y	Y	Y	Y	Y	Y	Y
Final exam	Y	Y	Y	Y	Y	Y	Y	Y	Y	N	Y
Discussion bonus	N	N	Y	N	N	Y	Y	N	N	Y	N

automatic check and without feedback from the instructors to students. No subjective questions be applied by the courses

- Half of instructors considered that students' bonus on discussion were helpful to measure students' active level and speech quality, but were not applied by instructors because of the suggestion from XuetangX that the scores were too subjective to be used in the MOOCs. There were three courses had cut the discussion bonus they had set up before. Instructors expressed their dissatisfaction about the decision made by XuetangX

Opinions About Different Assessment. We introduced opinions to different assessment method separately.

Opinions about Objective Questions.

- Majority of the instructors agreed that the most important role the objective questions played was examining whether a student had watched the uploaded teaching video in a MOOC
- Most art and design and liberal art subjects cannot validly test students' performance only with the objective questions, while science and engineering courses' instructors thought the objective questions were enough for them to test students' actual learning level, according to the instructors of *Linear Algebra, Circuit Theory, Financial Valuation Analysis, Modern Biology* and *Introduction to Medical*
- The objective questions mostly fit for students' basic knowledge level, according to the instructors of *English Listening and Speaking* and *Medical Parasitology*
- Students were able to cheat easily when answering the objective questions
- All the assistants thought helpful feedback in questions could reduce the workload of instructors from answer questions, and improve students' learning outcomes

Opinions about Subjective Questions.

- All the instructors affirmed the instructive and positive effect of subjective questions.
- The most important role the subjective questions played was examining a students' true learning status, skills and abilities the course taught in most liberal art subjects in a MOOC, such as *Basic Principle of Marxism, History As A Mirror* and *Art of Eternity*
- In most science and engineering courses, such as programming and proof problems, subjective questions can test the knowledge and skills, but they were too hard for all the students to complete it as an assignment

- XuetangX thought the discussion bonus was violated the object evaluation of the students' learning status, and did not support it
- The subjective questions would bring heavy burden to instructors as they always need to grade all assignments, and the number of students in one MOOC was always a large amount

Opinions about Discussion Bonus.

- Majority of the instructors considered that the most important roles the discussion bonus played were examining whether a student made an effort to learning the course, and provided an active atmosphere in MOOCs
- Most art and design, liberal art and biology courses need test students' performance only with the discussion, while the engineering courses' instructors thought the discussion cannot test students' actual learning level
- XuetangX thought the discussion bonus was violated the object evaluation of the students' learning status, and did not support it. There actually existed the course that needed students to discuss. The discussion bonus should not be completely eradicated
- The discussion bonus was hard for instructors to grading. MOOC platforms should add a function supporting to collect students' discussions for instructors

Opinions about Group Work and Peer Review. Group work was anxiously needed by the courses that focused on opinion changing, communication and discussion, including language, art and design and social sciences subjects. But the group work was the advantages brought by small size class teaching in traditional education. Instructors were worried about the difficulties during the implementation and application of group work in large-scale teaching such as MOOCs. With less instructors' leading and more students and groups, group work might cause little attention to one specific student, which did worse than normal assessment. And group work would bring a large heavy burden to instructors, especially to assistants. Moreover, there were no successful precedent of group work used in MOOCs, so instructors were dare to use it.

Half of the instructors gave positive attitudes towards the peer review's effects on solving the grade process to judge subjective questions, and reducing the burden of assistant to check all the answers students submitted. The implementation of the peer review was ever hard. The instructors thought there must exists students that had no enough knowledge to assess other students' assignment, and students refused to grade other works and even give the score at random, which let the score finally need to be graded again by instructors. There were successful cases in *English Listening and Speaking* and *Art of Eternity* for peer review. Detailed grading criterions and good punitive measures should exist for peer review. The punishment to a student who scored other works at random should be established. An assignment should be distributed to several students, verifying there were at least a serious score given to the assignment.

4.2 Students

Learning Objectives. There were two main ideas about why the six students began studying a MOOC: (1) They were interested in the topics of the course; (2) They wanted to get useful knowledge or skills in the MOOC so that they can use what they had learned in future. The students who had different objectives chose different categories of MOOCs and had large different expectations for what they can get from the course. Those who studied for interest preferred (a) art and design and (b) liberal art courses, such as *News Photography* and *Introduction to Psychology*. Engineering, business and economics and language categories were more likely chosen for studying useful knowledge, for example, programing courses and English courses.

Opinions about Current Assessment. There almost existed no subjective questions in all courses the six students studied in XuetangX. For those studying for useful knowledge, they thought that objective questions were simple in most cases, and could not test their true grade and brought no positive effects on promoting their motivations to study. But in some science and engineering course, objective assignments could be hard to do. Some particular cases were mentioned that subjective questions were used. The good examples are photos in *News Photography* and story discussing in *Introduction to Psychology*. The good subjective questions aroused students' interest and sense of participation during studying. One of them suggested that the subjective questions and answers could be provided as materials but not assignments, so that students who need more exercises used it, and teachers had no need to grade the questions. For liberal art courses, course forums and online instant chat services were considered to be good places to discuss the subjective topics.

Opinions about Other Assessment. All of students had positive attitudes towards group work and peer review. They thought both could increase the communications with students, and improve the sense of participation and motivations to study. Appropriate laws should be set at the same time to better assessment. Valid test and acceptable work burden could be achieved for both instructors and students. One students said it would be better to test different questions with different difficulty for different students, and students could choose assessment according to their own needs.

5 Conclusion

Some findings about the assessment on students' learning performance in MOOCs were prompted in the study:

Firstly, there actually existed some types of courses as follows whose assessment needs can be met to test students' performance:

- The courses that primary problems are solved by analytic methods and having only one correct answer, including (a) parts of science, (b) engineering and economics subjects
- The courses focusing on examining fixed knowledge point in details which need to remember by students, including (c) some science and (d) medical science subjects

The subjective questions can also be used in MOOCs we referred above to get better evaluation.

Secondly, the subjective questions were necessary in the following courses:

- The courses need students' expression about their opinions to topics and submitting their products, including (a) social sciences, (b) art and design subjects
- The courses requiring students to improve themselves through communication with others or group work to complete a task, including (c) language and (d) some medical science subjects

Subjective questions in most courses were difficult for most students to finish. Instructors can offer the subjective questions to students as reference materials. The completeness of those questions were not the criterions to students' final scores.

Thirdly, Students' discussion played a key role to activating course atmosphere and promoting students' expression and communication. It was able to work on most of liberal arts courses. Course forum and online instant chat services were the way to discuss.

Fourthly, feedback for some difficult test and discussions was necessary, including different arguments about a topic on liberal art courses and common mistakes on science and engineering courses.

Fifthly, group work and peer review were useful for most categories of courses but hard to use. Peer review could strengthen students' autonomy. Grouping and burden problem should be solved in future. Detailed grading criterions and good punitive measures were the current ways to better peer review.

In addition, designing different degree of test difficulties might be the solution for the diversities of students' learning objectives and knowledge levels.

The findings in the study were guidelines on how to designing better assessment methods of MOOCs. More details about building valid assessments in a specific MOOC need to be intensively studied according to the interview. A handbook including guidelines and attentions about how to design the assessment in MOOCs should be proposed and verified in future work.

Acknowledgement. This study was supported by the Online Education Research Foundation of the Online Education Research Center, Ministry of Education, P.R. China (Project No. 2016ZD103) and the National Natural Science Foundation of China (Project No. 71401087).

References

1. Anderson, T., Dron, J.: Three generations of distance education pedagogy. Int. Rev. Res. Open Distrib. Learn. **12**(3), 80–97 (2010)
2. Belanger, Y., Thornton, J.: Bioelectricity: A quantitative approach Duke University's first MOOC (2013)
3. Chen, X., Dai, S., Zhao, X., Bai, Z., Liu, Q., Zhi, S.: Efficiency analysis of different question types in a medical imaging examination (in Chinese). Chin. J. Med. Educ. Res. **11**(11), 1160–1163 (2012)

4. Christensen, G., Steinmetz, A., Alcorn, B., Bennett, A., Woods, D., Emanuel, E.J.: The MOOC phenomenon: who takes massive open online courses and why? (2013). SSRN 2350964

5. Cormier, D.: The CCK08 MOOC–Connectivism course, 1/4 way (2008)

6. Cross, S.: Evaluation of the OLDS MOOC curriculum design course: participant perspectives, expectations and experiences (2013). http://oro.open.ac.uk/37836/

7. Downes, S.: Connectivism: A theory of personal learning (2008). http://www.slide-share.net/ Downes/connectivism-a-theory-of-personal-learning. Accessed on July 14, 2014

8. Harmon, O.R., Lambrinos, J.: Are online exams an invitation to cheat? J. Econ. Educ. **39**(2), 116–125 (2008)

9. Hsia, L.H., Huang, I., Hwang, G.J.: Effects of different online peer-feedback approaches on students' performance skills, motivation and self-efficacy in a dance course. Comput. Educ. **96**, 55–71 (2016)

10. Kolowich, S.: Coursera takes a nuanced view of MOOC dropout rates. The chronicle of higher education (2013)

11. Kop, R.: The challenges to connectivist learning on open online networks: learning experiences during a massive open online course. Int. Rev. Res. Open Distrib. Learn. **12**(3), 19–38 (2011)

12. Krathwohl, D.R.: A revision of Bloom's taxonomy: an overview. Theory Pract. **41**(4), 212–218 (2002)

13. Luo, H., Robinson, A.C., Park, J.-Y.: Peer grading in a MOOC: reliability, validity, and perceived effects. J. Asynchronous Learn. Netw. **18**(2), n2 (2014)

14. Maier, U., Wolf, N., Randler, C.: Effects of a computer-assisted formative assessment intervention based on multiple-tier diagnostic items and different feedback types. Comput. Educ. **95**, 85–98 (2016)

15. Manalo, J.M.A.: An Evaluation of Participants' Levels of Satisfaction and Perceived Learning Regarding the MOOC in@ RAL Platform. Malays. J. Distance Educ. **16**(1), 101–121 (2014)

16. Miranda, S., Mangione, G.R., Orciuoli, F., Gaeta, M., Loia, V.: Automatic generation of assessment objects and remedial works for MOOCs. In: 2013 International Conference on Information Technology Based Higher Education and Training (ITHET), pp. 1–8. IEEE (2013). http://ieeexplore.ieee.org/xpls/abs_all.jsp?arnumber=6671018

17. Nikola, S.: Effects of motivation on performance of students in MOOC. In: International Scientific Conference of IT and Business-Related Research-SINTEZA, pp. 418–422. Singidunum University (2014)

18. Onah, D.F., Sinclair, J., Boyatt, R.: Dropout rates of massive open online courses: behavioural patterns. Proceedings on EDULEARN14, pp. 5825–5834 (2014)

19. Parr, C.: MOOC completion rates 'below 7%'. Times Higher Education, 9 (2013)

20. Readers, H.: Professionals against machine scoring of student essays in high-stakes assessment. Human Readers (2013)

21. Sandeen, C.: Assessment's place in the new MOOC world. Res. Pract. Assess. **8**, 5–12 (2013)

22. Shah, N.B., Bradley, J., Balakrishnan, S., Parekh, A., Ramchandran, K., Wainwright, M.J.: Some scaling laws for MOOC assessments. In: KDD Workshop on Data Mining for Educational Assessment and Feedback (ASSESS 2014) (2014)

23. Suskie, L.: Assessing student learning: A common sense guide. Wiley, Hoboken (2010)

24. Xia, H., Jiang, S.: Educational Psychology. Tsinghua University Press (2015). (in Chinese)

25. Yousef, A.M.F., Chatti, M.A., Schroeder, U., Wosnitza, M.: What drives a successful MOOC? an empirical examination of criteria to assure design quality of MOOCs. In: 2014 IEEE 14th International Conference on Advanced Learning Technologies (ICALT), pp. 44–48. IEEE (2014)

Culture and User Experience

Busting the Myth of Older Adults and Technology: An In-depth Examination of Three Outliers

Robert Beringer[(✉)]

Royal Roads University, Victoria, Canada
myresearchrms@mac.com

Abstract. Background: A myth persists that seniors do not use the Internet, are ambivalent toward information and communication technologies (ICT's), and that a technological divide exists between older and younger generations. **Aims**: To explore the role of ICT's in the lives of seniors, in particular, those outliers who are thriving and fully engaged in the use of these technologies. **Method(s)**: This study employed a quasi-ethnographic methodology. In-depth semi-structured interviews were held with research participants in an effort to capture their context-dependent *lived experience* and deeply explore the role of these technologies in their lives. **Results**: Four themes emerged from the analysis of the data: social connectivity; face-to-face contact remains; positive addiction; and back to the future. **Conclusion**: This research is an exploratory study and provides a glimpse into the level to which some older adults are engaged with ICT's, in particular social media such as Facebook and video-conferencing technologies such as Facetime. The research findings are contrary to the persistent myth that seniors do not use these technologies.

Keywords: Gerontechnology · Older adults · Aging · Social networks · Internet

1 Introduction

The use of information and communication technologies (ICT's) and the concomitant increase in Internet use has been rather dramatic in older adult populations in Canada and the U.S. where 59% of adults aged 65+ used the Internet in 2013, compared to just 22% in 2004 [1, 2]. Even seniors over 80 years of age, 37% of them, are now going online regularly. Older adults use the Internet for a variety of tasks, including but not limited to, communicating with friends and family, social activities (dating), and seeking health information [3–5]. Internet usage has been associated with a number of reported beneficial effects including decreased loneliness [6] and increased sense of community [7]. Gatto and Tak [8] have further indicated that older adults have experienced a sense of connectedness and satisfaction when going online for communication. In spite of these findings there persists a myth that seniors do not use the Internet, are ambivalent toward ICT's, and that a technological divide exists between older and younger generations [9, 10]. The bulk of the research in regard to seniors and the Internet is geared toward quantitative surveys and little research exists exploring the

© Springer International Publishing AG 2017
P.-L.P. Rau (Ed.): CCD 2017, LNCS 10281, pp. 605–613, 2017.
DOI: 10.1007/978-3-319-57931-3_48

experiential dimension of ICT use in this population. The purpose of this study was to explore the role of ICT's in the lives of seniors, in particular, those outliers who are thriving and fully engaged in the use of these technologies.

2   Methods

This study employed a quasi-ethnographic methodology. The boundaries of an ethnographic methodology are often unclear [11] and I have incorporated two traditional ethnographic methods in this study, namely, semi-structured interviews and participant observation. Given these blurred boundaries I feel most comfortable referring to this work as quasi-ethnographic. The approach was well suited to explore the *meaning-making* activities (ICT use) in the lives of these *social actors* (my research participants) [12–15]. In-depth semi-structured interviews were held with research participants in an effort to capture their context-dependent *lived experience* [16] and deeply explore the role of these technologies in their lives. Observation of the participants online activities validated the themes that emerged from the interviews.

2.1   Recruitment and Data Collection

Attesting to the intrinsic and exploratory nature of this research [17] a small sample (n = 3) was purposefully selected [18] to ensure participants were active ICT and Internet users. An interview guide was developed and used to structure the interviews; however, a flexible approach was maintained stemming from the idea that excessive structure may inhibit one's ability to access participant worldviews [19]. Interviews took place at a location convenient to the participant (two at my home, the other at the home of the participant), consent was obtained and the interviews were audio recorded. Pseudonyms were used to maintain confidentiality of participants. Participant observation was employed to triangulate and validate the data [18, 20].

2.2   Sample

The participants in this research project all live on Salt Spring Island, B.C. The first participant Jean, is widowed, 88 years of age, and has had a computer since 1995. She uses a variety of devices including iPhone (smartphone), Skype, Facetime, Lifeline (an emergency call alarm system), Internet, and social media such as Facebook and Pinetrest. She actively uses email, and plays a variety of online games against both friends and strangers. She has created accounts at Linkedin and Twitter but rarely uses these platforms.

Paula is separated, 71 years of age and could not pinpoint the exact date she started using computers. She mentioned she used them in the workplace and had an interest in technology dating back to the 1970's. Similarly, she could not recall the exact date when she began to use the Internet, but was able to approximate that it was "long ago". Paula has an iPhone, iPad, laptop and desktop computers. She actively uses email, Facebook, Apple TV, and plays a variety of online games but only against friends. She has also created accounts at Linkedin and Twitter but does not often use these.

Bill is a married gay man, 82 years of age and he started using computers in the early 1990's and the Internet around 2005. He has had a desktop computer and now uses a laptop exclusively, he does not have any other devices. Bill uses email, Facebook, Skype and plays online games with friends.

3 Data Analysis

In place of *naïve reading* [21] the recorded interviews were listened to repeatedly in order to gain an overall understanding of the data. Key passages from the recordings [22] were then transcribed verbatim into a Word document. The transcript was examined line-by-line and coded for themes that were emerging from the data [18, 20]. The purpose of this deep analysis was to ensure that the lived experience of the participants would surface from this process.

3.1 Ethical Considerations

This research was conducted under the guidelines provided by the Royal Roads University Research Ethics Policy [23]. The participants in this research project were volunteers, they provided written consent, and were informed that they could leave the study at any time.

4 Results

Four themes emerged from the analysis of the data: (1) social connectivity; (2) face-to-face contact remains; (3) positive addiction; and (4) back to the future.

4.1 Social Connectivity

When asked about the role that the Internet and social media played in their lives, all participants provided rich and very personal descriptions, evidenced in the following quotations:

Jean: "a huge one, um, I now have over 800 friends on Facebook… so this is where we gather a lot of friends that we didn't know before… and it's all very interesting to get all these different viewpoints."

Paula: "They keep me connected, I love Facetime, because um, if my daughter's walking through Central Park and it's dark, I'm there with her (laughing) and keeping an eye out making sure she's not, you know, in any trouble, because quite often she gets to the park and she calls me and we do the walk together so I feel as if I'm in New York, I feel connected to her little puppy and I feel she uses it to keep tabs on an elderly mother."

Bill: "It's a good form of communicating, especially with old friends, and it is also a form of entertainment and information. It keeps your mind going because it kind of stimulates your thoughts and you have a chance to react, it keeps you engaged with what's going on in the world and in your circle of friends. It keeps you from being isolated, in fact, after losing my partner of 42 years, I met my new partner online 7 years ago (at the age of 75) and that would have never happened without the Internet, I would still be by myself."

The theme of social connectivity was present throughout all of the transcripts. Had the entire conversations been transcribed verbatim a content analysis would have revealed plentiful usage of the terms *connected* and *connectivity*. Paula's comment on walking with her daughter in New York, suggests her lived experience includes a sense of virtual embodiment at a transcendental level. Not mentioned in the above quote, Bill also reminded me that he moved to Canada from the U.S to be with his new partner, attesting to connective power of the Internet, and also breaking another stereotype we have about aging – that of sexuality.

4.2   Face-to-Face Contact Remains

One concern regarding the use of and reliance on technology, particularly in regard to older adults, revolves around the idea that it may replace in-person contact and social connection. Interestingly, all participants in this study asserted that the majority of contact with local friends was in-person – "the people I know here, I engage with personally" (Jean), and Paula elaborated further:

"I prefer in my home here to be outdoors, to play tennis with my friends, to hike on the trails with my friends, um, to get that physical exercise that you need that you don't get when you're just sitting at a computer."

Bill noted:

"The Internet helps with face-to-face contact, for example, if I need to find a partner for a bridge game at the senior center I can easily contact friends online, it's a real plus."

All participants were quite adamant in highlighting the importance of maintaining frequent contact with local friends *offline* and *in-person* and these assertions factored into my decision to label the next theme positive addiction versus addiction.

4.3   Positive Addiction

On one hand, addiction may be described as an uncontrolled behavior that harms both the user and those family, friends, and potential strangers that surround them. Positive addiction on the other hand, refers to a behavior that provides a positive force in one's life and provides a sense of empowerment [24]. The interviews revealed tendencies toward somewhat excessive use of ICT's; however, in light of the connectivity provided by these technologies and the participant's maintenance of in-person contact with friends and family, I felt the commentary could be classified as positive addiction:

Jean:

"Yeah, Compuserve was the email thing then and um, so we were communicating with my son and family, and um gradually other people who got computers (laughing) and then the world wide web arrived on the scene and so we were in on the beginning of that almost and I don't know, I just got hooked (laughing)."

Paula:

> *"I think I'm compulsive and sometimes I want to get something done and three hours can be gone by before I know it, you know, and I'm still on my computer and I don't think that's healthy ... early on I think there was a time when I um became a little antisocial and spent too much time on my devices, uh I'm now trying to put everything in perspective and I'm trying to spend less time and more time with real people, that's important to me."*

Bill:

> *"There's a tendency to use it (Internet) a little too much, especially on rainy days, and there is the potential for it to make you a little more lazy...it's a little bit addictive because you come to depend on it sometimes."*

Paula's comment appears to have some qualities of addiction, but her awareness of her own compulsiveness and the interview taken as a whole do not suggest any negative outcomes as a result of her ICT use. Having said that, we both found some humour in the following:

Paula:

> *"I think you have to pace yourself and realize when you're too addicted to certain aspects of your life (her phone rings) ... that might be my daughter (she feels compelled to check, I smile, and we share some laughter)."*

4.4   Back to the Future

This theme revolves around the participants tapping deep into their memories and sharing some insightful and in the case of Jean (reflecting on memories of her father, now passed away) touching commentary.

Paula:

> *"I remember in the 50's our teachers used to talk about robots and the future and I couldn't envision it and it's here...and I never used to think that was possible but we're getting a glimpse of that....you could really become introverted and I don't think that's a good thing, I think it's really important to have that connection with people and to still meet people...so I'm hoping that technology doesn't take over completely, because I think it would be a sad world if it did."*

Jean:

> *"I have a memory...my father used to write a letter (when Jean and her mother were away from her father due to his work and traveling around the world)...and I remember still he said wouldn't it be lovely, and I'm talking 1935, if we had a short wave radio that we could talk to each other with and see each other with while we're apart.....so now we have."*

Bill:

> *"The miracle of technology is that you can talk to people and see them at the same time, this is a miracle that we never envisioned...for instance I can talk to friends and relatives overseas that I would not otherwise have the opportunity to be in contact with on this personal and direct level, it used to take two weeks for a letter to get there!"*

The lived experience is reflected in all of the themes. Here it is revealing to see how in reflecting upon past thoughts about technology they are in a sense marveling and expressing thanks for having lived their lives in this period of dynamic and what is perceived to be positive change. Interestingly, Paula remains aware and warns of the potential for this seemingly positive state of affairs to descend into a dystopian future.

5 Participant Observation

All participants are on my friends list on Facebook. In the week prior to and following the interviews, I checked their usage regularly and noted they use social media daily, often appearing online every 2–3 h. The following screenshots were taken to confirm the participants engagement on Facebook. From Jean's page (confirming her number of friends):

 Friends · 856 (10 Mutual)

From Paula's page:

Louie and Buddy having an early morning chat on FaceTime. Louie is pooped from having spent an hour in Central Park. He found the biggest stick ever and insisted on carrying it all the way home. It is a dog's life.

From Bill's page, confirmation of his engagement with online gaming:

Playing since Dec. 8, 2012

| Victory Percentage | 41 % |
| 372 Wins 511 Losses 4 Draws | |

| Best Word Score | 140 pts |
| "BETONIES" | |

| Best Game Score: | 548 pts |

| Bingos | 618 |

| ELO Rating | 1767 |

Jean's 856 friends is comparable to the level of engagement one might expect from a person in their 20's or 30's. Even more illuminating is Paula's post that provides us with confirmation of the Facetime call to her daughter and evidence of the virtual *walk* in Central Park that was described in her interview commentary.

6 Discussion

The findings in this study provide contrary evidence to the myth that older people don't use technology and are not online. While we know from quantitative data that seniors are in fact using the Internet [1, 2] this research provides a glimpse into the depth to which some seniors are engaged online. All participants in this study may be viewed in terms of what Rogers [25] categorized as *early adopters* of technology.

While one theme displayed a tendency toward categorizing one's behavior online as addictive, it appears that such addiction was of the positive variety. The positive health benefits associated with social connectivity [6–8] as evidenced in the discourse of these three participants appear to outweigh any negative consequences. The embodiment theme outlined in the passages from participant Paula in regard to videoconferencing (on Facetime), and the sense of *being there* replicate the findings of Beringer & Sixsmith [26].

It was interesting to note that these participants found technologies such as social media provided them with another layer of social engagement and that it did not lead to the social disengagement and replacement of human contact that has been theorized in numerous studies [27–29].

7 Conclusion

This research is an exploratory study and provides a glimpse into the level to which some older adults are engaged with ICT's, in particular social media such as Facebook and videoconferencing technologies such as Facetime. The research is contrary to the persistent myth that seniors do not use these technologies. Interestingly, this in-depth examination of three outliers suggests future research may be directed toward developing a better understanding in regard to the level of *engagement* older adults are in fact having with these various technologies. Further, contrary to the tendency of existing literature to focus on the negative aspects of technology, this research provides insight into the potential for these technologies to help seniors thrive as they move through their later years.

References

1. Allen, M.K.: Consumption of Culture by Older Canadians on the Internet. Statistics Canada, Ottawa (2013). http://www.statcan.gc.ca/pub/75-006-x/2013001/article/11768-eng.pdf
2. Zickuhr, K., Madden, M.: Older adults and Internet use. The Pew Internet Project and American Life (2012). http://www.pewinternetorg/Reports/2012/Older—adults—and—internet—use.aspx
3. Hilt, M.L., Lipschultz, J.H.: Elderly Americans and the Internet: email, TV news, information and entertainment websites. Educ. Gerontol. **30**, 57–72 (2004)
4. Rosenthal, R.L.: Older computer-literate women: their motivations, obstacles, and paths to success. Educ. Gerontol. **34**, 610–626 (2008)
5. Wagner, N., Hassanein, K., Head, M.: Computer use by older adults: a multi- disciplinary review. Comput. Hum. Behav. **26**, 870–882 (2010)
6. Sum, S., Mathews, R.M., Hughes, I., Campbell, A.: Internet use and loneliness in older adults. Cyberpsychol. Behav. **11**, 208–211 (2008)
7. Sum, S., Mathews, R., Hughes, I.: Internet use as a predictor of sense of community in older people. Cyberpsychol. Behav. **12**, 235–239 (2009)
8. Gatto, S.L., Tak, S.H.: Computer, Internet, email use among older adults: benefits and barriers. Educ. Gerontol. **34**, 800–811 (2008)
9. Ferrara, M.: On boomers, seniors and technology myths. Blog Post (2011). http://www.matthewferrara.com/rssfeed/tech_myths/
10. Beringer, R., Gutman, G., de Vries, B.: Fostering end-of-life planning among older LGBT adults the development of the British Columbia LGBT end-of-life resource inventory. Canadian Virtual Hospice, The Exchange (2016). http://virtualhospice.ca/
11. Hammersely, M., Atkinson, P.: Ethnography: Principles in Practice, 2nd edn. Routledge, New York (1995)
12. Noblit, G., Hare, R.W.: A meta-ethnographic approach and the Freeman refutation of mead. In: Atkinson, P., Delamont, S. (eds.) SAGE Benchmarks in Social Research Methods: SAGE Qualitative Research Methods, vol 1–4, pp. 338–354 (2011). http://dx.doi.org/10.4135/9781446263334
13. Levers, M.D.: Philosophical paradigms, grounded theory, and perspectives on emergence. SAGE Open 1–6 (2013). http://sgo.sagepub.com/content/spsgo/3/4/2158244013517243.full.pdf

14. Scotland, J.: Exploring the philosophical underpinnings of research: relating ontology and epistemology to methodology and methods of the scientific, interpretive, and critical research paradigms. Engl. Lang. Teach. **5**(9), 9–16 (2012)
15. Sefotho, M.M.: A researcher's dilemma: philosophy in crafting dissertations and theses. J. Soc. Sci. 42 (1, 2), 22–36 (2015). http://www.krepublishers.com/02-Journals/JSS/JSS-42-0-000-15-Web/JSS-42-1-2-15-Abst-PDF/JSS-42-12-023-15-1760-Sefotho-M-M/JSS-42-12-023-15-1760-Sefotho-M-M-Tx[3].pdf
16. Eberle, T.: Phenomenology as a research method. In: Flick, U. (ed.) The SAGE Handbook of Qualitative Data Analysis, pp. 184–203. Sage Publications, London (2014)
17. Baxter, P., Jack, S.: Qualitative case study methodology: study design and implementation for novice researchers. Qual. Rep. **13**(4), 544–59 (2008). http://www.nova.edu/ssss/QR/QR13-4/baxter.pdf
18. Creswell, J.W.: Research Design: Qualitative, Quantitative, and Mixed-Methods Approaches, 2nd edn. Sage Publications, Thousand Oaks (2003)
19. Sixsmith, J.: The meaning of home: an exploratory study of environmental experience. J. Environ. Psychol. **6**, 281–98 (1986)
20. Bryman, A., Teevan, J.: Social Research Methods, Canadian edn. Oxford University Press, Don Mills (2005)
21. Flood, A.: Understanding phenomenology: Anne Flood looks at the theory and methods involved in phenomenological research. Nurse Res. **17**(2), 7–15 (2010)
22. Pulla, S.: SOSC 730 Class discussion. Royal Roads University, Victoria (2016). 29 February–10 March
23. Royal Roads University Academic Council. Royal Roads University Research Ethics Policy (2011). http://research.royalroads.ca/sites/default/files/web_files/RRU_EthicsPolicy_16Feb2011r.pdf
24. Achor, S.: The Happiness Advantage: Seven Principles of Positive Psychology that Fuel Success and Performance at Work. Crown Publishing, New York (2010)
25. Rogers, E.: Diffusion of Innovations. Macmillan Publishing, New York (1962)
26. Beringer, R., Sixsmith, A.: Videoconferencing and social engagement for older adults. In: Sixsmith, A., Gutman, G. (eds.) Technologies for Active Aging, pp. 189–200. Springer Publishing, New York (2013)
27. Demiris, G., Rantz, M., Aud, M., Marek, M., Tyers, H., Skubic, M., et al.: Older adults' attitudes towards and perceptions of smart home technologies a pilot study. Med. Inf. **29**(2), 87–94 (2004)
28. Mortenson, B., Sixsmith, A., Beringer, R.: No place like home? Surveillance technologies and the meaning of home among older adults. Can. J. Aging **35**(1), 103–14 (2016)
29. Percival, J., Hanson, J.: Big brother or brave new world? Telecare and its implications for older people's independence and social inclusion. Crit. Soc. Policy **26**(4), 888–909 (2006)

Evaluating the Use of LINE Software to Support Interaction During an American Travel Course in Japan

Dave Berque[1(✉)] and Hiroko Chiba[2]

[1] Computer Science Department, DePauw University, Greencastle, USA
dberque@depauw.edu
[2] Modern Languages Department (Japanese) and Asian Studies Program,
DePauw University, Greencastle, USA
hchiba@depauw.edu

Abstract. This paper describes our use of the LINE social media software system to promote interaction, convey mood and emotion, and teach students about *Kawaii* culture during an international travel course that exposes undergraduate students at an American liberal arts college to Japanese culture, technology and design. The LINE user experience incorporates the important Japanese pop-culture principle of *Kawaii* (cuteness in the context of Japanese culture) and Japanese users enjoy interacting with LINE's *Kawaii* interface. We report on our method of integrating LINE software into an international travel course and our evaluation of how students compare LINE's *Kawaii* interface with the communication tools and social media tools that they are more familiar with. We also report on the extent to which the students believe that using LINE helped them understand *Kawaii* design. We also report on opportunities and barriers associated with cross-cultural adoption of social media platforms.

Keywords: LINE · *Kawaii* · Japanese design · Japanese culture · HCI education · Social media

1 Introduction

1.1 *Kawaii* Culture

Japanese cuteness described as *Kawaii* has been ingrained in Japanese contemporary society in many forms. The word *Kawaii* stemmed from the word *kawayushi* that appeared in the book *Makura no Sōshi* (The Pillow Book) in classical Japanese literature, in which it meant pitiful, shameful, or too sad to see [5]. During the course of Japanese history, the meaning of the word started describing the small, weak, and someone or something that intrigues the feeling of "wanting to protect" [5]. The meaning has been extended to the concept of "Japanese cuteness" in contemporary society. The notion of "*Kawaii*" (cuteness in the context of Japanese culture) is pervasive in Japan and ranges from Hello Kitty products to road signs to posters created by the Japanese government, just to name a few examples. Japanese products are consciously tailored to accommodate widely preferred "cuteness." In other words, "*Kawaii*" is an important concept for

© Springer International Publishing AG 2017
P.-L.P. Rau (Ed.): CCD 2017, LNCS 10281, pp. 614–623, 2017.
DOI: 10.1007/978-3-319-57931-3_49

making products. The visual representations of *Kawaii* are also manifested in social media. Emoji (literally, "picture letters" in Japanese) and cute stickers (or stamps) are widely used as forms of emotive communication.

1.2   The LINE Social Media Tool

Social media and communication systems such as FaceBook, WhatsApp, Skype and text messages are ubiquitous among college students in the United States. However, most American college students are unfamiliar with LINE [4] which was first released in 2011 and then became very popular among Japanese college students [1]. LINE is currently the most popular messaging and social media system in Japan [3].

LINE's feature-set offers comprehensive interaction tools including one-on-one chat, group chat, voice communication optionally including video, timeline organization, newsfeeds, language translation services, games, music and cute stickers [2].

The stickers are often characters such as a bunny, frog, bear, and other adorable creatures that convey the user's message or emotion. The use of these stickers is one of the key features of LINE and allows users to personalize their messages to help them communicate emotion and mood. LINE stickers embody *Kawaii* design and Japanese users enjoy interacting with LINE's *Kawaii* interface.

Figures 1 and 2 compare a typical text message exchange using the built-in iPhone Messages App to a typical message exchange using LINE.

Fig. 1. Typical message exchange using the iPhone Messages App

Fig. 2. Typical message exchange using the LINE App

1.3 Course Context

The authors regularly teach a three-week Winter Term course that exposes undergraduate students at an American liberal arts college to key concepts related to Japanese culture, technology and design, as previously described in [2]. This course has been offered three times, with a combined enrollment of approximately seventy-five students. In our most recent offering, we modified the course by using LINE software on smartphones to enhance interaction during the course. This also provided us with the opportunity to give our students hands-on experience with the concept of *Kawaii* as it is manifested in the LINE interface and to evaluate their perception of this immersive experience.

The first phase of the three-phase course takes place on-campus in a traditional classroom and provides students with background related to design principles, robotics, Japanese culture and pop-culture, Japanese history and geography, Japanese aesthetics, and Japanese language prior to departing for Japan. During this part of the course, we presented *Kawaii* as one of several key Japanese design principles. Students also installed, and became familiar with the LINE software system in preparation for using it during our travels. This gave us the opportunity to use LINE as an example to help students gain hands-on experience with the Japanese pop-culture principle of *Kawaii*, even before we left campus.

The second phase of the course took place in Japan and lasted two weeks. This portion of the course included a three-day homestay in a small town to experience Japanese design in daily-living, a five-day Tokyo stay to study the design of modern technology, a visit to Nagoya to learn about industrial development, a four-day stay in Kyoto to study traditional Japanese craftsmanship, and a one day-trip to Hiroshima to learn about the potential negative consequences of design and technology.

During our stay in Japan, students were encouraged to immerse themselves in Japanese design principles. Most relevant to this paper, they experienced the *Kawaii* design principle in part by using LINE software as our electronic communication and social media tool. Uses of LINE ranged from one-on-one and group chats with other course participants, keeping in touch with home-stay hosts and Japanese students who we met at the university we visited in Tokyo, exchanging information about daily schedules and sharing information about historical sites we visited as a group. When appropriate, students were encouraged to use stickers to communicate mood and emotion. Specific uses of LINE are described in more detail in Sect. 2 of this paper.

The third phase of the course took place after returning to campus. During this phase, students completed a survey that included quantitative and qualitative questions that captured student opinions about LINE as compared to their opinions about more familiar communication and social media tools. The results of this assessment are reported in Sect. 3 of this paper.

2   Integrating LINE and *Kawaii* Culture into Course Activities

2.1   Pre-departure Uses of LINE

At the start of our January 2017 offering of the course, we confirmed that each of the twenty-five course participants owned an American smartphone. We used the course budget to allocate $60 to each student at the start of the course. Each student was required to use these funds to purchase an international data plan from his/her carrier.

Prior to leaving for Japan, the class used LINE in a variety of ways. Some uses were intentionally initiated by the instructors, while other uses were initiated by the students. Examples of the more typical uses are described below:

- The instructors invited the students to install LINE and to join a group that was set up for the course.
- The instructors asked students to express their feelings using stickers when they joined the group.
- When the instructors taught the *Kawaii* aesthetic as a Japanese design principle, they used LINE as one of several examples of the principle. Since students had already experienced the LINE interface, it gave them a concrete example of *Kawaii*.
- When the instructors taught the difference between usability and user-experience, they compared the iPhone Messages App to LINE (see Figs. 1 and 2). This gave us a concrete way to explain that the two apps offered similar functionality (similar usability) but very different user-experiences.

- The instructors regularly communicated with the group about class materials and logistics such as meeting times, citation formats.
- Student groups were required to research sites we would visit in Japan. In addition to giving presentations about those sites, they were required to post notes about the sites on LINE for their classmates to read.
- Students sometimes posted stickers to express their random emotions and reactions, even without prompting from the instructors.
- Students asked questions about class material.
- Students asked and answered specific questions about the trip, such as time and place to meet as a group.
- Students asked and answered questions of each other, such as communicating about their whereabouts at the airport.

We were pleased to see the students using LINE spontaneously, almost immediately after introducing the tool to the class.

2.2 Uses of LINE While in Japan

During our fourteen days in Japan, LINE was once again used in a variety of ways. Again, some of these uses were initiated by the instructor and others were initiated by students. Over time we observed that students were more likely to use stickers to convey their messages and express their mood. Examples of the more typical uses are described below:

- Instructors sent a "welcome to Japan" message to the group.
- Instructors posted urgent matters such as changes in meeting time or location.
- Instructors posted information about daily logistics.
- Students posted messages about their first morning in Japan.
- Students asked instructors about logistics such as the daily schedule, questions about how to access to Japanese phone network, etc.
- Students posted photos in real time and they reacted to the photos using both text and stickers.
- Instructors asked students to indicate how they felt about leaving Japan and students spontaneously expressed their feelings through stickers.

3 Evaluation

After returning from Japan, and with approval from the DePauw University Institutional Review Board, we invited all 25 undergraduate students enrolled in the course to complete an online anonymous survey regarding their experiences using LINE software.

The survey included demographic questions, a sequence of yes/no questions, a sequence of questions that students responded to using a five point Likert scale as well as open-ended questions. Each of the 25 students responded to the survey. Of the 25 respondents, 15 (60%) reported as male and 10 (40%) reported as female. Overall, only 2 (8%) of the respondents reported that they had used LINE prior to this course.

One set of objective questions focused on determining the ways in which students used LINE during the course. These responses are summarized below.

- 96% of students used LINE to send stickers even when they were not asked to do so by the instructors.
- 96% of students posted a photo on LINE.
- 84% of students used LINE to communicate with their host families and/or other people they met in Japan.
- 64% of students used LINE to make voice calls.
- 48% of students used LINE to communicate with family or friends from home who were not part of the course.
- 44% of students posted a video on LINE.
- 24% of students used LINE to share their location.
- 8% of students used LINE to make video calls.

When students were asked if they expected to use LINE after the course ended, 76% of students responded affirmatively. Several students indicated that they planned to use the system to keep in touch with people from Japan but that they would not use the system to communicate with American friends. For example, students wrote:

- "I plan on using it to keep in touch with friends I made in Japan."
- "I will probably only use it to keep in touch with people I met from Japan, because not many people in the US have line."
- "I doubt I will use it much to stay in contact with anybody from the course, as I'll probably revert back to other apps like Facebook and GroupMe. But I will use it to continue to keep in contact with my host mother, and possibly also with some students from the Chiba Institute of Technology."

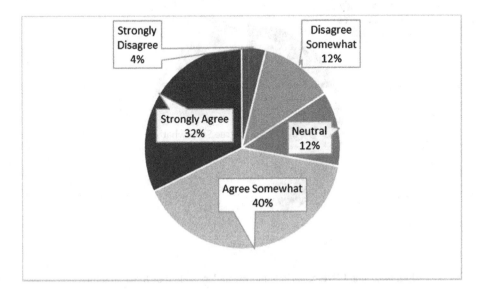

Fig. 3. I understood the concept of *Kawaii* culture prior to enrolling in this course.

Given the importance of *Kawaii* culture to the course goals, an important set of Likert scale questions focused on measuring the student's impression of the their change in understanding of *Kawaii* culture as well as the value of LINE in helping them with this learning. These questions, along with the associated responses, appear below in Fig. 3 through Fig. 6. All percentages are rounded (Fig. 3 through Fig. 6).

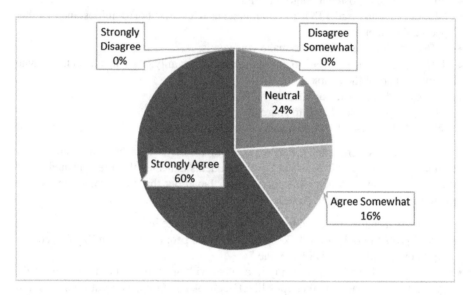

Fig. 4. I understand the concept of *Kawaii* culture better now than I did at the start of the course.

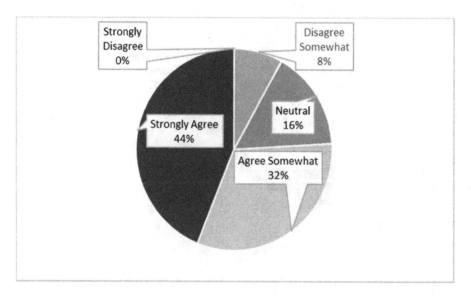

Fig. 5. Using LINE contributed to my understanding of *Kawaii* culture.

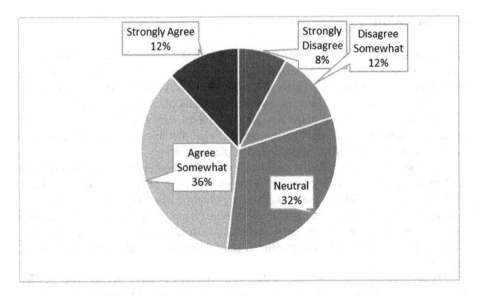

Fig. 6. I was more likely to notice examples of *Kawaii* culture in Japan because we had experienced *Kawaii* culture using LINE before departing for Japan.

Another set of Likert scale questions asked students to evaluate LINE with respect to both user-experience and usability. These questions, along with summaries of the associated answers, follow below. Respondents who "agreed somewhat" and those who "strongly agreed" are aggregated as "agreed" in this summary.

- 100% agreed that LINE was useful for receiving update messages sent by the instructors to the whole class.
- 99% agreed that LINE was useful for exchanging messages with small groups.
- 96% agreed that LINE was useful for exchanging messages with other individuals.
- 92% felt more connected to the group because we used LINE.
- 92% agreed that LINE stickers are cute.
- 92% agreed that they enjoyed seeing their classmates' stickers during the course.
- 92% agreed that they were glad we used LINE instead of a social media tool such as Facebook that is more common in the United States.
- 90% agreed that they felt more comfortable exploring Japan because they could use LINE to contact instructors or classmates if needed.
- 88% agreed that they enjoyed using LINE stickers to express their feelings about experiences they had during this course.
- 88% agreed that LINE notes posted by the instructors were useful.
- 75% agreed that the LINE notes posted by students about the places we would visit were useful.

4   Discussion

As seen in the previous section, we found that LINE was a useful tool in several different ways. First, LINE was helpful in facilitating communication between the students, faculty and Japanese hosts who were involved in our course. Additionally, using LINE helped students learn about Japanese culture, especially the *Kawaii* design principle.

Instead of simply reading about *Kawaii*, the students were able to experience *Kawaii* culture first-hand using LINE. The students reported that this experience helped them understand the Japanese *Kawaii* design principle more deeply.

The students reported that they enjoyed expressing their emotions and mood using stickers that carried their messages in the condensed form of cuteness. We found that students were more likely to use stickers during the time when we were in Japan. Additionally, the students indicated that they were more observant of different forms of cuteness in Japan as a result of regularly interacting with LINE's *Kawaii* design. In other words, LINE itself served as instructional scaffolding to learn about the aesthetic of cuteness.

The authors also observed that enabling the students to use LINE as soon as they joined the group helped create a sense of belonging and a group learning environment. LINE provided users with the virtual space to share their messages embedded in visuals that soften negative emotions and magnifies positive emotions.

Students were better able to help each other with problems because of our use of LINE. Often a student would post a question to our LINE group and another student would answer the question before either of the instructors had a chance to answer. It was rewarding to see the group helping each other out, although this approach was also potentially problematic as described below.

There were a couple of minor downsides of using LINE as a communication tool. As in using any social media platform, students may use it to rely on others with regard to getting information about details and logistics. This can lead the students to become less responsible, because they are aware that they can get help from others if it is needed. In other words, because the social media tool can become their information source, students may be less diligent about keeping track of important logistical issues. Additionally, some of our students did not know how to turn data roaming on and were not able to use their phones immediately upon arrival in Japan and others did not know how to monitor their data usage to ensure they stayed under the limits imposed by their international phone plans.

Overall, incorporating LINE had multiple benefits, making group communication easier, helping create a sense of belonging, and serving as instructional scaffolding to learn about usability, user-experience and cross-cultural design principles. In addition, because LINE is popular with Japanese people, our students were better able to communicate with their homestay families and others who we met in Japan. In several cases, students have continued to use LINE to stay in touch with people they met in Japan.

Acknowledgements. The initial offering of the course described in this paper was supported by a grant from the Japan Foundation.

References

1. Aoki, S.: Kyarakutā Powa: Yurukyara Kara Kokka Burandingu Made. (Character Power: From Yurukyara to National Branding). NHK Shuppan, Tokyo (2014)
2. Berque, D., Chiba, H.: Exposing American undergraduates to *Monozukuri* and other key principles in Japanese culture, design, technology and robotics. In: Stephanidis, C. (ed.) HCI 2016. CCIS, vol. 617, pp. 3–8. Springer, Cham (2016). doi:10.1007/978-3-319-40548-3_1
3. Bloomberg. www.bloomberg.com/graphics/2016-line-ipo/. Accessed 4 Nov 2016
4. LINE. https://line.me/en-US/. Accessed 4 Nov 2016
5. Yomota, I.: Kawaii Ron (The Theory of *Kawaii*). Chikuma Shobō, Tokyo (2006)

Research on Car Gesture Interaction Design Based on the Line Design

Jing Chunhui[⊠] and Jing Zhang

Sichuan University, Chengdu, China
unknownboy@163.com

Abstract. There are a series of problems in the interaction design of car gestures, such as the weak consistency of interior interaction and external modeling, and the less contact between gesture design and cultural perceptual factors. In order to solve the above problems, from the perspective of feature line design, user experience experiment is used to extract the long path and short path features of car gesture interaction. According to these characteristics, combining with the knowledge of car modeling feature lines and the rules of line design in Chinese calligraphy, a HUD map display gesture application is designed for the target car based on the service design rule. The preliminary evaluation results show that the design method can improve the user's interest and pleasure, and is helpful to the integrity and consistency of car design.

Keywords: Line · Experience design · Car styling · Car gesture interaction · Service design

1 Introduction

Gesture belong to the natural way of human interaction like language and has been an important part of human-computer interaction [1]. For more than a decade,, researchers have been advocating a new interface that will allow drivers to operate smoothly while driving without increasing cognitive load [2]. According to the study of Wahl, in the environmental interaction era which we'll face right away, the traditional ways of interaction rely on the display and keyboard to communicate with the user may will be eliminated, we need a Interactive mode which will be able to link the technology and the users without the third party [3]. As a natural way of interaction, gestures can greatly reduce the cost of cognitive and visual communication, which have great potential for development.

Driving modern cars is a complex task. Drivers must constantly observe traffic and instrumentation while dealing with various random distracted driving tasks, such as telephone rings or conversation with passengers, etc. [2]. However, the number of in-car devices has reached the limits of the driver can bear, especially a large number of traditional input devices such as knobs, buttons and handles [4]. Therefore, safety and cognitive load reduction are the primary concerns for all car interaction designs. Compared with the traditional visual interaction, gesture interaction can keep the driver's visual attention on the driving task [5]. At the same time, Geiger et al. found that

© Springer International Publishing AG 2017
P.-L.P. Rau (Ed.): CCD 2017, LNCS 10281, pp. 624–633, 2017.
DOI: 10.1007/978-3-319-57931-3_50

gesture interaction can effectively reduce the driver's distraction [6]. As a result, a number of studies have attempted to bring gestures into car design [7, 8].

However, there are still some problems in the design of interactive gesture. For example, the vast majority of car interior interaction design and external styling design are basically independent of each other, which has resulted in the design of car interior design and external design split. On the other hand, the current interactive design research is relatively concentrated in the parametric test [9], but pay little attention to cultural and natural factors. Therefore, in order to solve the above problems, this paper intends to study the car gesture interaction design by drawing on the knowledge of car styling and culture rules.

2 Lines and Car Gestures

In the early period of car styling design, it is often used to construct the car styling with the line sketch, and the car styling feature line is also considered as an important representation of car styling [10]. Zhao has characterized the car styling line summarized as 20 [11], and used it to guide the car shape design. In order to keep interior styling and car exterior styling coordinated, designers often look for the modeling feature from the external modeling characteristic line and apply it to the configuration of various parts of the interior (Fig. 1). Therefore, the lines can be used to characterize the knowledge of car modeling.

Fig. 1. Car exterior and interior styling lines

For the "Whole-hand gestures" [12], people usually perceive gesture behavior by capturing the movement of the hand, i.e., by observing the "fingertip curve" [13]. This finger movement forms a dynamic line on a time dimension. At the same time, lines are also an important way to construct various cultural products in the world [14], especially in China, which emphasizes image culture. Therefore, taking the line as the design ontology, it is possible to make the car gesture design conform to the cultural aesthetic characteristics and to benefit the whole design of the car by drawing the rules of the car modeling and cultural field.

3   Gesture Feature Experiments

The purpose of the service design is to make the properties of the design product converted from the "Useful" and "Available" and other basic needs to the "Satisfaction" and "Easy to use", and other high-level needs. In order to provide satisfactory services, in the service design the designer needs to focus on the user experience inspection and understanding. The commonly used hand movements in the car reflect the behavior patterns and cognitive habits of users in driving situations. Take these hand movements as the gesture design reference object, you can design interactive products which are more suitable for user habits. In order to obtain the types and characteristics of hand behavior in the car, the feature experiment was carried out.

3.1   The Experimental Process

20 users (9 females) were selected in the experiment. The flow of the experiment is as follows: 1. First of all, through the questionnaire to obtain the user's basic information and driving tasks make the hand position changes (relative to the normal driving hand position). 2. Based on the driving tasks obtained through the questionnaire, a number of major test scenarios were designed to allow the user to complete the relevant driving behavior in the test scenario. The researchers used the observation and video recording methods to capture their behavior. 3. Got typical hand behavior characteristics through the behavior classification statistics.

In the experiment, 3 common driving tasks were identified by questionnaire: over-taking; answering telephone calls; adjusting (audio or air conditioning, etc.). Then, according to the experimental design of Pellegrino [15], we selected a straight road section in Sichuan University. The experiment scene of overtaking was simulated by the auxiliary car of the experimental staff, and simulated the experimental scenarios of answering phone calls and adjusting. After that, we found that users have two typical characteristics of hand movements through observation and video analysis. The first feature occurs in the hand movement of a long path, such as when the driver shifts, the right hand leaves the steering wheel to the vicinity of the gear lever, and then back to the steering wheel; When the driver adjusts the volume knob, the right hand will also reach the center position, then back to the steering wheel; In answering the phone, the driver also takes the phone from the central position of handrail to the head position and so on. The common feature of these behaviors is that the trajectory of the hand is long; the driver will not have long-term eye-tracking (without looking at the movement of the hand, or looking at it and immediately returning to watching the road); In the experiment, the users adopt random, comfortable and inaccurate hand movement; Eventually, the hands return to the steering wheel position (which is determined by the primacy of the driving task); All users use the right hand to perform tasks. The second feature occurs in the hand movement of a short path. For example, the driver's right hand leave the steering wheel to press the horn; Hand movement in the shift; And, after answering the phone many users will not directly put the phone back in situ, but holding the phone from the ear shift to the steering wheel position to pause (then the right hand will contact the steering wheel for a short driving time), and then return the phone to the center armrest and so on. The common features of these hand movements are short trajectories; And the iterative repetitive movement often occurs. For example, the driver often presses the horn of the car more than once; After the phone, some users will once again lift the phone back to the ear to listen to confirm and then put it back; As well as the fine-tuning of reciprocating motion and so on.

3.2 Experimental Results

It can be found that the basic gesture behavior can be divided into two categories through the experiment: Long path gestures and short path gestures.

3.2.1 Long Path Gesture Design Features

The main design features of long path gestures are: As the driver in the driving process will not give a lot of visual attention to hand behavior, the hand can not be too close to the center console and other entities, so the designer should give the gesture to a large redundant space to avoid interference. At the same time, in order to facilitate the capture of sensors, Akyol et al. have found that car hand movements need to be limited to higher than gearshift [7]. Thus, in very limited space, long-path gestures that are highly variable are unlikely to occur; Secondly, because of the long path gestures with casual, comfortable features, therefore, the gesture design needs to meet the ergonomic requirements of the human body. In McNeill's study, the comfort of a series of gestures has been summarized, Such as "when the elbow flexion more than 90° the muscles will be uncomfortable; try to avoid the wrist and arm rotation" and so on [16], these can be used as the reference of long path gesture design. In addition, the hand will eventually return to the steering wheel, so the end of the path should be located in the vicinity of the right side of the steering wheel, which means that the end of the gesture design should also be located near the right side of the steering wheel, so the gesture designer only needs to consider the starting position.

3.2.2 Short Path Gesture Design Features

The main features of short path gestures are as follows: Short path gestures often occur in iterative and repeated paths. Through the user interviews we know that the main reason for this phenomenon is due to the ower cost of conduct of short hand gesture. And many users doubt the accuracy of the sensor, so the users always do a few more repeated action to confirm. At the same time, there are users that only do short-path gesture for one time feel "too little work," so subconsciously repeated several times. In short, both for the user's psychological needs or task requirements, iterative short-path gesture design needs to be taken seriously.

4 Implementation

Most of the time the service is invisible, but the user will feel the full range of services from multiple sensory channels. and the invisible service can also be displayed based on the subconscious experience design of the line. The main purpose of the design practice part is to design a gesture product for a target model (see Fig. 2). Based on the Loehmann study, the content of car gestures can not be too much [17]. At the same time, because the most important purpose of car interaction is to drive safely, our design goal is to design a car-assisted driving products with no more than 5 kinds of gestures. Based on this goal, the following sections detail how to design long path and short path gestures.

Fig. 2. Target model

4.1 Long Path Gesture Experience Design

Usually, straight line trajectories with long distances and gesture behavior with sharp kink traces will result in discomfort, so gesture lines are usually designed with smooth over-curves. Curves tend to give people the feeling of soft and elastic, but car styling often pursue the image of muscle, strength and speed, which requires a more gentle curve adjusted to a tension curve. This requires a curve with a sense of tension. Tension is a psychological effect, which is a important way to create strength of the car modeling line. Arnheim argues that the purpose of tension is to make "the static object has a dynamic posture" [18]. Bangor created the flame surfacing for BMW because Aristotle said that "the shape of the flame is the most active of all shapes, because the shape of the flame is most conducive to produce a sense of movement."

Arnheim describes the way in which tension is constructed as "a temporary equilibrium or dynamic equilibrium with a thrust, thrust, and pull against each other" [18]. In the car styling line, designers tend to use the appropriate tilt and bending deformation to create imbalances, so as to provide tension to lines. Similar to car styling features, dynamic gesture path lines also require tension. However, it should be noted that the inclination and deformation are the consequence of the interaction between the applied force and the resistance force. Appropriate deformation and tilt like a bow, can be used to accumulate strength, But the excessive deformation means that the resistance is too weak, which is detrimental to the tension; On the contrary, not enough deformation means that the force is not strong enough.

In order to design a gesture that matches the car body shape image, it is necessary to study the characteristics of car body modeling. Therefore, according to the characteristic line theory, the researchers extracted the main feature lines of the target model from the front and side view angles, and analyzed and integrated the local variation of the lines. As shown in Fig. 3, to make gestures more natural, the gesture trajectory must be smooth and excessive without straight-line angle, so the straight line angle added

Bezier curve. Therefore, the straight-line corners are changed to over-curves based on the Bezier curve. The results show that the lines can be divided into three categories (Fig. 4): Class A is asymmetric large-curvature lines; Class B is symmetrical large-curvature lines; and Category C is acute-angle small-curvature lines. In order to further obtain the optimal degree of deformation of each type of line, we set 5 deformation degree of different curves in each type of deformation curve (Fig. 4). The Likert scale questionnaires were designed from three aspects: the degree of visual tension, the degree of matching with exterior shapes, and the esthetic level of strength and speed. On the Internet, 50 users (24 women) were scored, and the highest score was obtained: A3. A3 curve is a kind of Class A curve, and the deformation degree is in power savings and restraint. It is also fit with the body waist line. Therefore, A3 curve is taken as the basic path form of the long path gesture.

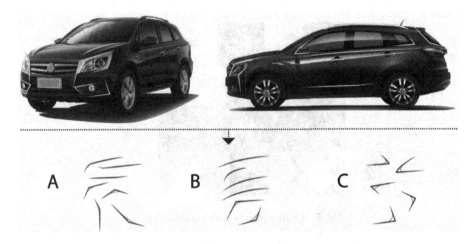

Fig. 3. Target car modeling line feature extraction

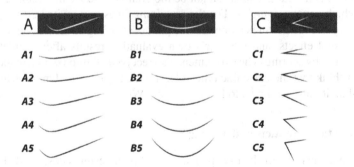

Fig. 4. Three types of basic lines

4.2   Short Path Gesture Experience Design

Similar to the gesture, a traditional culture - Chinese calligraphy is also used lines to build aesthetic [14]. It depicts emotions and images through the lines with the movement of the nib that is squeezed with ink. It uses lines to build beauty in many ways. Because short-path gestures often use repeated lines to enhance its sense of presence, in order to find out the factors that help to construct the short path gestures, the researchers analyzed more than 20 famous works of calligraphy, It is found that there are a lot of works in the use of repeated ways to enhance the performance of local lines of the phenomenon like short path gestures. In Liang's study, this phenomenon is called a mass effect [19]. Based on this, the researchers drawn and summarized the repeated features of the lines in the calligraphy works, and obtained a series of local characteristics of the calligraphy lines (Fig. 5).

Fig. 5. Characteristics of calligraphy lines

Next, the researchers also need to carry out these lines for further screening and improvement. As the car gestures can not be too complex, so we first remove some of the lines which are too complex. For the remaining lines, we invited 20 users in the laboratory to simulate gestures along the line path. According to the smoothness of the operation, visual effects, and the user's own evaluation results after simulation, the optimal line is B by scoring. The experiment also received additional information: most of the users think that the basic line type at least need to be iterated more than 2 times (Fig. 4, B-line iterative 3 times) to form a gesture. While the upper limit is 5 times.

4.3   Car Gesture Products and Testing

Based on the acquisition of the long path and short path gestures described above, the designers devised a car gesture product. The main purpose of this product is to be able to use gestures to interactively switch the map on the HUD and the central control screen display, and can manually adjust the display brightness. Service design not only needs to consider user needs, but also take into account the needs of the designer. Through the face-to-face communication with the typical designers and users, to record the key processes in the service. At the same time, detail is the key to the service design, so the first need is to sort out the touching points. The contact points between the user and the product were used as the touching points. In order to reduce the driver's operating frequency and reduce cognitive load in the driving situation, the number of touching points were reduced as far as possible without affecting the user's operation. Finally, through a series of comparisons and design iterations. The number of the touching points were reduced to 3. Based on the contact, the designer has designed the product tasks. And because the Sequencing of the tasks is very important in the service design, the designer also considered the order of the three functions. The final three tasks are: open; stow; adjust the brightness. Since the function of opening and stowing is the opposite, in order to reduce the cost of learning and cognition, the gestures of stowing and opening are also designed as opposite lines, so that users can learn one kind of gesture and then deduce the other. In addition, since the right hand needs to return to the steering wheel position after completing the gesture, the end point of the gesture points to the right side of the steering wheel. The starting point is located in the original picture of the transferred image in the position of the central control display screen, gesture trajectory design using long path gestures (Fig. 6). Conversely, the hand gesture is reversed when the opposite "stow" task is performed (Fig. 6).

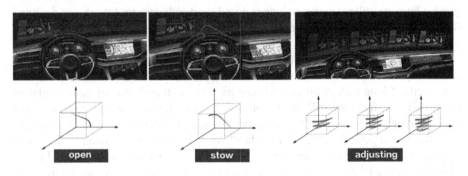

Fig. 6. Gesture design

Similarly, using the resulting short path gesture, the adjusted luminance gesture is designed as shown in Fig. 6. And because the required degree of brightness is different, brightness adjustment function includes three modes: bright, normal and dark, It is switched by the number of basic iterations. With reference to previous studies, the minimum number of iterations is twice, at most 4 times.

Subsequently, the researchers conducted user research. As the prototype has not yet been produced, it is impossible to perform accurate quantitative testing. But we let users to simulate the operating experience in the car. That means, after the action is performed, the feedback is given on the screen of the car, which is controlled by the experimenter. The main purpose is to obtain the user's response and information which can optimize the product. First, let the user in accordance with the gestures we designed to simulate the operation, and then let the user in accordance with their own ideas to design their own gestures, the final interview, eventually interviewed them. Through the experiment we found that the gesture interactive products can significantly stimulate the user's interest and concern, and they can learn in a short period of time, most of the tasks have been completed. Users believe that gesture design and car styling and cultural factors are more fit, and get a great sense of satisfaction and pleasure. However, there are also problems such as a deviation in the position of the user's operation when performing the brightness adjustment gesture. Someone like to operate in the vicinity of the right side of the steering wheel, and someone like to operate in the center console position. These require further user research; There are some users have doubts of the implementation ability of non-contact gesture interaction, so some users keep giving visual attention in the operation. Although most users feel the gesture track is very beautiful, but if you do not tell this is related to calligraphy and car styling, most users can not find on their own. These need further consideration of the follow-up design.

5   Conclusion and Future Works

As Donald Norman said, "Good behavior comes from careful design." In this study, we propose the design of car gesture interaction based on line experience design. In order to make the car interaction design consistent with the external design, as well as to meet the user's cultural and cognitive habits, the modeling principles of car styling lines and calligraphic lines are utilized to design long path and short path gestures for car, and designed the interactive product based on experience design and service design, which provides a possibility for the design of hand gesture and the design of car interactive products.

Through the current design and testing, the research has found some factors that should be paid attention to. Such as iterative design features of short path gestures; spatial constraints of long path gestures; and final hand position problems of gestures and so on. In addition, there are still some problems, such as the continuing interest of users mentioned by Coskun et al. [20]. After 2 months, when the freshness subsided, can users still stick to the gesture interaction product? As well as the above mentioned, how to conduct a unified gesture design for users with different behavior habits? And how to make the user feel the content and image of the gesture is more intuitive and interesting? At the same time, the current research is mainly qualitative exploratory research, and further work is needed to enhance the credibility and availability of the study. These subsequent quantitative tests will have to wait until the prototype is finished. Will there be new discoveries with the participation of quantitative data? And whether the current findings will be amended? All of these need to be further studied.

Acknowledgments. This work was supported by Young Teachers Fund of Sichuan University Grant Number 2082604194264; and the Open Research Subject of Research Center of Industrial Design GY-16YB-11.

References

1. McNeill, D.: Hand and Mind: What Gestures Reveal About Thought. University of Chicago Press, Chicago (1995)
2. Riener, A.: Gestural interaction in vehicular applications. Computer **45**(4), 42–47 (2012)

3. Wahl, H., Groh, R.: User interface and interaction design in future auto-mobility. In: Marcus, A. (ed.) DUXU 2016. LNCS, vol. 9746, pp. 161–171. Springer, Cham (2016). doi: 10.1007/978-3-319-40409-7_17

4. Ecker, R., Broy, V., Butz, A., et al.: pieTouch: a direct touch gesture interface for interacting with in-vehicle information systems. In: Conference on Human-Computer Interaction with Mobile Devices and Services, Mobile HCI 2009, Bonn, Germany, 1–10 September 2009 (2009)

5. Alpern, M., Minardo, K.: Developing a car gesture interface for use as a secondary task. In: Extended Abstracts of the 2003 Conference on Human Factors in Computing Systems, CHI 2003, Ft. Lauderdale, Florida, USA, 5–10 April 2003 (2003)

6. Geiger, M., Zobl, M., Bengler, K., et al.: Intermodal differences in distraction effects while controlling automotive user interfaces. In: Conference on, pp. 5–10 (2001)

7. Akyol, S., Canzler, U., Bengler, K., et al.: Gesture control for use in automobiles. In: IAPR Conference on Machine Vision Applications, DBLP, pp. 349–352 (2000)

8. Zobl, M., Geiger, M., Schuller, B., et al.: A real-time system for hand gesture controlled operation of in-car devices. In: Proceedings of the International Conference on Multimedia and Expo, ICME 2003, vol. 3, pp. 541–544 (2003)

9. Newell, A., Card, S.K.: The prospects for psychological science in human-computer interaction. Hum.–Comput. Interact. 1(3), 209–242 (1985)

10. Jing, C., Zhao, J.: Research on vehicle shape optimization design based on evolutionary thinking. China Mech. Eng. 25, 1517–1523 (2014)

11. Zhao, D., Zhao, J.: Automobile styling and feature line. Packag. Eng. 28, 115–117 (2007)

12. Riener, A., Rossbory, M., Ferscha, A.: Natural DVI based on intuitive hand gestures. In: Workshop User Experience in Cars, INTERACT, p. 5 (2011)

13. Kandinsky, W., Rebay, H.: Point and Line to Plane. Dover Publications, Mineola (1947)

14. Zong, B.: Aesthetic Walking. Shanghai People's Publishing House, Shanghai (2000)

15. Pellegrino, O.: An analysis of the effect of roadway design on driver's workload. Baltic J. Road Bridge Eng. 4(2), 45–53 (2009)

16. Silpasuwanchai, C., Ren, X.: Designing concurrent full-body gestures for intense gameplay. Int. J. Hum.-Comput. Stud. 80, 1–13 (2015)

17. Loehmann, S., Knobel, M., Lamara, M., Butz, A.: Culturally independent gestures for in-car interactions. In: Kotzé, P., Marsden, G., Lindgaard, G., Wesson, J., Winckler, M. (eds.) INTERACT 2013. LNCS, vol. 8119, pp. 538–545. Springer, Heidelberg (2013). doi: 10.1007/978-3-642-40477-1_34

18. Arnheim, R.: Art and visual perception: a psychology of the creative eye. Am. J. Psychol. 68(2), 330 (1955)

19. Peixian, L.: Analysis of dots, lines, and the "faxiang". Orient. Art 4, 98–105 (2012)

20. Coskun, A., Zimmerman, J., Erbug, C.: Promoting sustainability through behavior change: a review. Des. Stud. 41, 183–204 (2015)

The Role of Trust with Car-Sharing Services in the Sharing Economy in China: From the Consumers' Perspective

Shang Gao[1(✉)], Jia Jing[2], and Hong Guo[3]

[1] School of Business, Örebro University, Örebro, Sweden
shang.gao@oru.se
[2] School of Business Administration,
Zhongnan University of Economics and Law, Wuhan, China
joel10207@163.com
[3] School of Business Administration, Anhui University, Hefei, China
homekuo@gmail.com

Abstract. The development and advancement of ICT enable people to share excess capacity (e.g., car, apartment). In this paper, we focus on Didi Chuxing, which is one of the most prominent examples of car-sharing services in the sharing economy in China. This study aims to investigate the role of trust with car-sharing services in sharing economy from the consumers' perspective. Based on the literature review, a research model with eight research hypotheses is proposed. The research model is empirically tested with Didi Chuxing by using survey data collected from a sample of 309 subjects. Six research hypotheses are significant supported, while two research hypotheses are rejected in this study. The results indicate that the most important determinant for the consumers' trust in the car-sharing service platform is platform reputation. In addition, increased degree of the consumers' familiarity with the car-sharing service platform has a positive impact the consumers' trust in the car-sharing service platform. However, the perceived car-sharing service platform reputation has a positive impact on the consumers' trust in drivers on the platform.

Keywords: Trust · Familiarity · Car-sharing service · Reputation · Didi chuxing

1 Introduction

Along with the development of ICT, the sharing economy marketplace is growing rapidly, particularly in the travel industry [4]. The sharing economy refers to the phenomenon of turning unused or under-used assets owned by individuals into productive resources [35]. The sharing economy generates value by matching unused and underused assets with consumers willing to pay for the services those assets could provide. And online peer-to-peer platforms (e.g., Airbnb, Uber [14], Didi Chuxing) plays a more and more important role in the sharing economy and is expected to further impact consumer behavior in the travel industry in the future [30]. Online services offered in these platforms enable people to share cars, accommodation, bicycles, and other items with others who are willing to pay to use them.

© Springer International Publishing AG 2017
P.-L.P. Rau (Ed.): CCD 2017, LNCS 10281, pp. 634–646, 2017.
DOI: 10.1007/978-3-319-57931-3_51

Sharing economy start-ups of the travel industry gain market share by setting themselves apart from their competitors by supporting property owners to establish a C2C relationship and easily share excess capacity in an often unregulated environment [4]. Consumers found out that services (e.g., car-sharing) provided by these platforms in the sharing economy are often more convenient and less expensive [16]. While economic benefits and convenience are likely to be the important factors for the adoption of car-sharing services, there are also other potential factors (e.g., Trust) might influence users' intention to use the services. Previous research (e.g., [17, 18]) indicated the importance and relevance of trust in the sharing economy. For instance, Botsman regarded trust as the sharing economy's currency in TED talks in 2012. Trust is very important to build relationships and facilitate interactions among product owners, platform, and consumers in this sharing process. Consumers may perceive some potential risks when they are using online sharing economy services. These perceptions generated due to many reasons, such as uncertainty about platform reputations and sharing services providers. However, to our knowledge, there has not been much research on the role of trust with car-sharing services in the sharing economy in developing countries (e.g., China).

In this research, we focus on Didi Chuxing, which is one of the most prominent online peer-to-peer platforms in the sharing economy in China. The objective of this research is to better understand the role of trust on the online sharing economy platforms in China. In an attempt to gain new insights into the role of trust in the sharing economy, we propose a theoretical research model that augments and integrates the theory of trust with a consideration of reputation and familiarity based on previous research. And the research model is empirically evaluated using survey data collected from a sample of 309 subjects in China.

The remainder of this paper is organized as follows: the literature review is provided in Sect. 2. The research model and hypotheses are presented in Sect. 3. The empirical study with Didi Chuxing is described in Sect. 4. This is followed by a discussion of the findings and limitations of this study in Sect. 5. Section 6 concludes this research and suggests directions for future research.

2 Literature Review

2.1 The Sharing Economy

The sharing economy has emerged as alternative suppliers of goods and services traditionally provided by long-established industries [37]. The sharing economy can be defined as a socio-economic ecosystem that commonly uses information technologies to connect different stakeholders-individuals, companies, governments, and others, in order to make value by sharing their excess capacities for products and services [16]. Moreover, Botsman and Rogers [7] indicated that sharing the economy underlies the business model in the operation of collaborative consumption, where people offer and share underutilized resources in creative, new ways. The emerging "sharing economy" is particularly interesting in the context of big cities that struggle with population growth and increasing density [9]. There are some other names implies the similar concept as the sharing economy, such as "collaborative consumption" [5], "commercial sharing systems" [23] and "access-based consumption" [4].

The sharing economy market allows people to easily share their excess capacity with the rest of the world. The advanced ICT makes the matching of supply and demand less expensive and more convenient. For example, intelligent terminals, GPS, maps and satellite positioning can help us look for available vehicles nearby. Electronic payment systems on online peer-to-peer platforms provide a convenient way of billings and making payments.

2.2   Trust and Reputation

Building consumer trust is a strategic imperative for online vendors because trust strongly influences consumer intentions to interact with unfamiliar vendor online [26]. The lack of consumer trust has been a barrier for the wide diffusion of mobile services [11–13] and e-commerce [19]. Since car-sharing services can be seen as one kind of mobile services, it is believed that the lack of trust applies to consumers for car-sharing services in the sharing economy. Consequently, many consumers may hesitate to engage in using car-sharing services. Consumers are frequently interacting with the following two actors in car-sharing services in the sharing economy: online peer-to-peer platforms and drivers. Therefore, it is critical to build consumer trust to facilitate interactions among actors (e.g., drivers, platforms, riders) involved in car-sharing services in the sharing economy. Trust can help consumers overcome perceived risk and uncertainty, and then affect their behavior intentions on using some online services [29].

Reputation and trust are deeply intertwined in e-commerce. However, they are two different concepts. In [33], the authors defined trust as a psychological state comprising the intention to accept vulnerability based upon positive expectations of the intentions or behavior of another. Reputation is a public opinion that represents a collective evaluation of a group regarding the characteristic of an entity or a person [36]. In previous research (e.g., [8, 27]), reputation has been identified as one of important factors influencing consumers' initial trust with online transaction behavior.

Since car-sharing services platform are responsible for recruiting competent drivers to provide riding services to consumer, we believe that the consumer's trust on both drivers and the platform is likely to be influenced by the platform reputation.

2.3   Familiarity and Disposition to Trust

Trust is significantly affected by both familiarity and peoples' disposition to trust in e-commerce [15]. Familiarity deals with an understanding of the current actions of other people or of objects, while trust deals with beliefs about the future actions of other people [25]. Familiarity can build trust by continuous ongoing interactions between two parties [15]. The familiarity with the concept of car-sharing services is of help to build a good trust relationship between consumers and the car-sharing service platform. Familiarity can be served as an antecedent of trust. Disposition to trust is a general inclination to display faith inhumanity and to adopt a trusting stance toward others [27]. The former inclination deals with the belief that people in general are trustworthy; the latter deals with the belief that better results will be obtained by giving people credit and trusting them, regardless of whether this trust is justified [27]. This factor is closely associated with personal educational background, personal characteristic, and personal experience [21]. According to previous research, disposition to trust can be seen as a complementary precondition of trust [15].

3 Research Model and Research Hypotheses

The research model and research hypotheses are presented in this Section.

3.1 Research Model

Drawing upon the literature presented in Sect. 2, we proposed a theoretical research model that augments and integrates the theory of trust with a consideration of reputation and familiarity. Figure 1 presents the research model and associated eight research hypotheses. The eight research hypotheses are illustrated in the next sub-section.

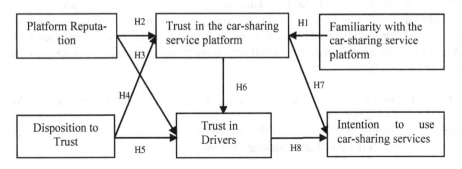

Fig. 1. Research model

3.2 Research Hypotheses

As indicated in Sect. 2.3, familiarity is an antecedent of trust. Increased degree of familiarity with a car-sharing service platform can be seen as a way to alleviate, uncertainty and complexity of the platform [15, 21]. As a result, this may accumulate consumers' trust in the car-sharing service platform. Previous research also found that increased degree of familiarity with Airbnb.com would increase the accommodation providers' trust in Airbnb.com [28]. Thus, we propose the following hypothesis:

H1:   Increased degree of the consumers' familiarity with the car-sharing service platform has a positive impact the consumers' trust in the car-sharing service platform.

Reputation is an important attribute of a company, which is a key factor that affects consumers' trust. A good reputation is a symbol of the company's ability, honesty and goodwill, which is particularly important for increasing initial trust, because in the initial stage of trust, consumers often have no direct interaction experience [27]. In e-commerce, previous research found that perceived reputation has a significant impact on the trust of online companies and their products [22, 24]. To make a trusting decision in using car-sharing service in the sharing economy, we believe that reputation of both the service platform and drivers on the platform is very important. If the car-sharing service platform is well-reputed, peoples' trust in both the service platform and drivers is likely to be enhanced. Therefore, we propose the following two hypotheses.

H2:   The perceived car-sharing service platform reputation has a positive impact on the consumers' trust in car-sharing service platform.
H3:   The perceived car-sharing service platform reputation has a positive impact on the consumers' trust in drivers on the platform.

The disposition to trust is a trend that a person can believe in the goodness of other individuals based on a lifelong socialization [15]. Previous studies indicated that peoples' disposition to trust have a direct impact on the formation of e-commerce trust [21, 31]. In this study, we believe that disposition to trust is closely associated with trust in both the service platform and drivers on the platform. Thus, we put forward the following assumptions:

H4:   The stronger the consumers' disposition to trust is, the more they will trust inthe car-sharing service platform.
H5:   The stronger the consumers' disposition to trust is, the more they will trust in drivers on the car-sharing service platform.

Car-sharing service platform has some mechanisms to restrict and block the drivers who are not serving consumers in a professional manner. For instance, the platform asks consumers to rate and review drivers' services. We assume that the perceived trustworthiness of listed drivers on the car-sharing service platform is reliant on the perceived trustworthiness of the car-sharing service platform. Previous research also indicated that increased degree of trust in Airbnb.com would increase the accommodation providers' trust in potential renters [28]. Thus, the following hypothesis is proposed:

H6:   Increased degree of the consumers' trust in thecar-sharing service platformhas a positive impact on the consumers' trust in drivers.

Previous studies found that the higher the consumers' trust in online retailer websites is, the stronger they would have intention to purchase goods on the websites [15, 20]. In this study, we think such relationships could also apply to car-sharing services in the sharing economy. Trust has been recognized as a crucial enabling factor in relations in an online environment where there is uncertainty, risk, and fear of opportunism [15]. The consumers' trust in the car-sharing service platform and drivers on the platform can reduce their uncertainty in the online environment and make them feel comfortable interacting with the platform and drivers on the platform. As a result, they are more likely to have the intention to use car-sharing services. These arguments lead to the following hypotheses:

H7:   Increased degree of trust in the car-sharing service platforms will increase the consumers' intentions to use car-sharing services.

H8:   Increased degree of trust in drivers on the car-sharing service platforms will increase the consumers' intentions to use car-sharing services.

4   An Empirical Study with Didi Chuxing

To understand the role of trust with car-sharing services in the sharing economy, the proposed research model were empirically tested with Didi Chuxing in China.

4.1   Car-Sharing Service: Didi Chuxing

Didi Chuxing is a typical peer-to-peer marketplace in the sharing economy. Didi Chuxing, founded in 2012 in China, is the world's largest car-sharing company. Didi Chuxing incorporated Uber's China unit in Aug 2016. Didi Chuxing is able to provide real-time, and location based car-sharing service. Consumers can use Didi Chuxing app on their smart devices to submit a trip request which is then routed to drivers on Didi Chuxing platform who use their own cars. The Didi Chuxing app on the smart devices allows consumers to indicate when and where they need a pickup, and drivers on the other side of the platform respond to the request. Consumers need to store payment information on Didi Chuxing app. Neither the rider nor the driver deals with payments. Didi Chuxing takes a percentage of the fare, and the rest goes to the driver.

4.2   Instrument Development

The validated instrument measures from previous research were used as the foundation to create the instrument for this study. All the items were adopted from prior studies [1, 10, 15, 20–22, 26, 34]. In order to ensure that the instrument better fit this empirical study, some minor words changes were made to ensure easy interpretation and comprehension of the questions. A questionnaire was developed first in English and then translated into Chinese. Back-translation was conducted by bilingual third parties to improve the translation accuracy. To further ensure that instrument were clearly articulated, we conducted a pilot test of the survey instrument with 25 consumers of DiDi ChuXing in Spring 2016. According to their feedback, the questionnaire was modified and the ambiguity of the problem was further refined.

As a result, 20 measurement items[1] were included in the questionnaires. In addition, a seven-point Likert scale, with 1 being the negative end of the scale (strongly disagree) and 7 being the positive end of the scale (strongly agree), was used to examine participants' responses to all items in the survey.

4.3   Samples

The data for this study was collected through paper-based questionnaires from 23rd Oct 2016 to 31th Dec 2016 in the biggest city in the central China. People were asked to participate in the survey voluntarily. Firstly, we explained who we were, and the purpose of the survey. The participants were also informed that the results would be reported only in aggregate and their anonymity would be assured. 350 completed questionnaires were collected, among which 309 of them were valid answers (i.e., valid respondent rate 88.3%). For instance, the persons who had never used Didi Chuxing were regarded as invalided answers. Among the participants, 129 of the respondents were male, and 180 were female. The majority of those participants between 18 to 30 years old (96.8%).

4.4   Measurement Model: Reliability and Validity

The quality of the measurement model is determined by (1) Content validity, (2) Construct reliability and (3) Discriminant validity [2]. To ensure the content validity of our constructs, a pretest with 3 Chinese researchers in E-business was carried out. And we found that the questionnaire was well understood by all the researchers.

To further test the reliability and validity of each construct in the research model, the Internal Consistency of Reliability (ICR) of each construct was tested with Cronbach's Alpha coefficient. As a result, the Cronbach's Alpha values range from 0.829 to 0.907. A score of 0.7 is marked as an acceptable reliability coefficient for Cronbach's Alpha [32]. All the constructs in the research model were above 0.70. Consequently, the scales were deemed acceptable to continue.

Convergent validity was assessed through composite reliability (CR) and the average variance extracted (AVE). Bagozzi and Yi [3] proposed the following three measurement criteria: factor loadings for all items should exceed 0.5, the CR should exceed 0.7, and the AVE of each construct should exceed 0.5. As shown in Table 1, all constructs were in acceptable ranges.

The measurements of discriminant validity were presented in Table 2. According to the results, the variances extracted by the constructs were more than the squared correlations among variables. The fact revealed that constructs were empirically

---

[1] The measurement items are available at this link: https://tinyurl.com/h9g6qlo.

Table 1. Factor loadings, composite reliability, and AVE for each construct

Construct	Item	Factor loading	CR	AVE	Cronbach's alpha
Familiarity	Fam1	0.747	0.881	0.714	0.890
	Fam2	0.911			
	Fam3	0.868			
Disposition to trust	Dis1	0.787	0.855	0.664	0.829
	Dis2	0.900			
	Dis3	0.750			
Platform reputation	Rep1	0.768	0.882	0.653	0.870
	Rep2	0.825			
	Rep3	0.789			
	Rep4	0.846			
Trust in DiDi	Tr_Di1	0.865	0.909	0.770	0.907
	Tr_Di2	0.887			
	Tr_Di3	0.880			
Trust in driver	Tr_dr1	0.813	0.896	0.682	0.849
	Tr_dr2	0.833			
	Tr_dr3	0.809			
	Tr_dr4	0.848			
Intention to use	Int1	0.806	0.865	0.682	0.857
	Int2	0.858			
	Int3	0.812			

Table 2. Discriminant validity

Variables	Familiarity	Disposition	Reputation	TrustDiDi	Trust in driver	Intention to use
Familiarity	**0.714**					
Disposition	0.471	**0.664**				
Reputation	0.461	0.570	**0.653**			
Trust DiDi	0.104	0.019	0.797	**0.770**		
TrustDriver	0.038	0.339	0.418	0.365	**0.682**	
Intention	0.067	0.115	0.556	0.649	0.303	**0.682**

Note: Diagonals represent the average variance extracted, while the other matrix entries represent the squared correlations.

distinct. As good results for convergent validity and discriminant validity were achieved, the test result of the measurement model was good.

Furthermore, AMOS 21.0 was used to investigate the fitness of the data to the model. As recommended by [6], CFI was one of the primary fit-statistics for the purposes of this study. A CFI above 0.90 is indicative of a well-fitting model. According to the results, CFI is 0.959 in this study. This means that the resulting measurement model has good model-to-data fit.

4.5   Structural Model and Hypotheses Testing

The structural model was tested using AMOS 21.0. Figure 2 presents the structural measurement model. Table 3 presents the path coefficients, which are standardized regression coefficients. Six (H1, H2, H5, H6, H7, H8) of the eight research hypotheses were significantly supported. Amos 21.0 is used to test the structural model in this study.

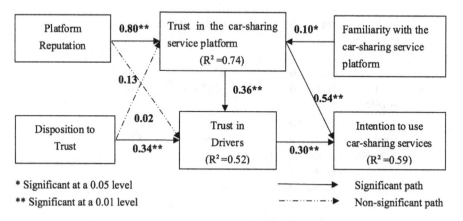

* Significant at a 0.05 level
** Significant at a 0.01 level

Fig. 2. Structural measurement model

Table 3. Test of hypotheses based on path coefficient for both the age groups

Hypotheses	Path coefficient	Hypothesis result
H1	0.10*	Supported
H2	0.80**	Supported
H3	0.13	Rejected
H4	0.02	Rejected
H5	0.34**	Supported
H6	0.36**	Supported
H7	0.54**	Supported
H8	0.30**	Supported

*$p < 0.05$; **$p < 0.01$

The R^2 (R square) in Fig. 2 denotes to coefficient of determination. It provides a measure of how well future outcomes are likely to be predicted by the model, the amount of variability of a given construct. In our analysis, the R^2 coefficient of determination is a statistical measure of how well the regression coefficients approximate the real data point. According to the results, the amount of variance in the consumers' intention to use car-sharing services explained by the model was 0.59.

5 Discussion

The contribution of this study is twofold. Firstly, we proposed a research model to study the role of trust in the sharing economy platforms based on previous research. This contributes to the literature in the sharing economy. Secondly, the results of the empirical study with Didi Chuxing in China provided some practical implications for actors involved in the car-sharing services in the sharing economy.

The results indicated that the most important determinant for the consumers' trust in the car-sharing service platforms was platform reputation. This implied that the consumers paid more and more attention to the reputation of the car-sharing service platform before formulating trust in the platform. Moreover, the results demonstrated that increased degree of the consumers' familiarity with the car-sharing service platform would have a positive impact the consumers' trust in the car-sharing service platform. This is in line with the findings with the apartment sharing service (Airbnb) in the sharing economy from [28]. Furthermore, both the consumers' trust in the car-sharing service platform and drivers on the platform had a positive impact on their intention to use car-sharing services.

However, according to the results, the perceived car-sharing service platform reputation did not have a positive impact on the consumers' trust in drivers on the platform. Riders and drivers are two important actors in car-sharing service marketplace. Information asymmetries may arise between riders and drivers since they often knew little about each other before. A good car-sharing platform reputation does not necessarily build the consumers' trust on the drivers on the platform. A possible explanation might be that the sharing economy markets is loosely regulated. It might be difficult to build trust between riders and drivers since they information asymmetries regarding each other's behavior in the process of car-sharing services.

Another interesting finding was that the stronger the consumers' disposition to trust did not lead to their trust in the car-sharing service platform. A possible reason was that disposition to trust was a kind of trust preference, which reflected a psychological tendency whether a person is willing to trust another person. Drivers are real individuals, while Didi Chuxing app is a virtual online platform. Some consumers might be more likely to trust real individuals who they can have face-to-face communications in the physical world.

This study also provided some practical implications. The car-sharing service platform providers need to further build platform reputation. Moreover, they can provide good tutorials to help consumers use their platform more effectively. To attain a good car-sharing service market, it is very important for the platform to work a good mechanism to build trust relationships between drivers and riders. Riders do expect that car-sharing service marketplace can be better regulated by relevant governmental agencies.

However, we were also aware of some limitations of this study. Firstly, we only tested the research model and research hypotheses with samples from one of the big cities in China. This sample might not be fully representative of the entire population in China. Secondly, all the data were collected using self-reported scales in the research. This may lead to some caution because common method variance may account for some of the results. Thirdly, we only examined the research model with one of car-sharing service platforms in China. Therefore, the generalizability of the results remains to be determined. Last but not least, the subjects in this study were young people in China.

6 Conclusion and Future Research

We have examined the role of trust in car-sharing services in the sharing economy from the perspective of consumers in this study. Based on literature review, a research model with eight research hypotheses was proposed in the study. And the research model was empirically tested with Didi Chuxing in China. According to the results, six of the eight research hypotheses were significantly supported. The results indicated that the most important determinant for the consumers' trust in the car-sharing service platform was platform reputation. In addition, increased degree of the consumers' familiarity with the car-sharing service platform would have a positive impact the consumers' trust in the car-sharing service platform. However, the perceived car-sharing service platform reputation did not have a positive impact on the consumers' trust in drivers on the platform.

Continuing with this stream of research, we plan to examine the applicability of the research model with other services in the sharing economy. Future research is also needed to empirically verify the research model with samples from other countries in the world. Furthermore, some mediating factors (e.g., age, gender) may provide fresh insights and offer new directions for future research.

References

1. Andersson, M., Hjalmarsson, A., Avital, M.: Peer-to-peer service sharing platforms: driving share and share alike on a mass-scale. In: International Conference of Information Systems 2013, Milan, Italy (2013)
2. Bagozzi, R.P.: The role of measurement in theory construction and hypothesis testing: toward a holistic model. In: Ferrell, O.C., Brown, S.W., Lamb, C.W. (eds.) Conceptual and Theoretical Developments in Marketing, pp. 15–32 (1979)
3. Bagozzi, R.P., Yi, Y.: Specification, evaluation, and interpretation of structural equation models. J. Acad. Mark. Sci. 40(1), 8–34 (2012)
4. Bardhi, F., Eckhardt, G.M.: Access-based consumption: the case of car sharing. J. Consum. Res. 39(4), 881–898 (2012)
5. Belk, R.: You are what you can access: sharing and collaborative consumption online. J. Bus. Res. 67(8), 1595–1600 (2014)
6. Bentler, P.M.: On the fit of models to covariances and methodology to the Bulletin. Psychol. Bull. 112(3), 400 (1992)
7. Botsman, R., Rogers, R.: What's Mine is Yours: The Rise of Collaborative Consumption. Collins, London (2010)
8. Chen, Y.-H., Barnes, S.: Initial trust and online buyer behaviour. Ind. Manag. Data Syst. 107(1), 21–36 (2007)

9. Cohen, B., Kietzmann, J.: Ride on! Mobility business models for the sharing economy. Organ. Environ. **27**(3), 279–296 (2014)
10. Davis, F.D.: Perceived usefulness, perceived ease of use and user acceptance of information technology. MIS Q. **13**(3), 319–340 (1989)
11. Gao, S.: High Level Modeling and Evaluation of Multi-Channel Services. Norwegian University of Science and Technology (2011)
12. Gao, S., Krogstie, J., Siau, K.: Adoption of mobile information services: an empirical study. Mob. Inf. Syst. **10**(2), 147–171 (2014)
13. Gao, S., Yang, Y.: The role of trust towards the adoption of mobile services in China: an empirical study. In: Li, H., Mäntymäki, M., Zhang, X. (eds.) I3E 2014. IAICT, vol. 445, pp. 46–57. Springer, Heidelberg (2014). doi:10.1007/978-3-662-45526-5_5
14. Gao, S., Zhang, X.: Understanding business models in the sharing economy in China: a case study. In: Dwivedi, Y.K., et al. (eds.) I3E 2016. LNCS, vol. 9844, pp. 661–672. Springer, Cham (2016). doi:10.1007/978-3-319-45234-0_59
15. Gefen, D.: E-commerce: the role of familiarity and trust. Omega **28**(6), 725–737 (2000)
16. Hamari, J., Sjöklint, M., Ukkonen, A.: The sharing economy: why people participate in collaborative consumption. J. Assoc. Inf. Sci. Technol. **67**(9), 2047–2059 (2015)
17. Hawlitschek, F., Teubner, T., Adam, M.T.P., et al.: Trust in the sharing economy: an experimental framework. In: The 2016 International Conference on Information Systems (ICIS 2016) (2016)
18. Hawlitschek, F., Teubner, T., Gimpel, H.: Understanding the sharing economy–drivers and impediments for participation in peer-to-peer rental. In: 2016 49th Hawaii International Conference on System Sciences (HICSS), pp. 4782–4791. IEEE (2016)
19. Hoffman, D.L., Novak, T.P., Peralta, M.: Building consumer trust online. Commun. ACM **42**(4), 80–85 (1999)
20. Jarvenpaa, S.L., Tractinsky, N., Vitale, M.: Consumer trust in an internet store. Inf. Technol. Manag. **1**(1–2), 45–71 (2000)
21. Kim, D.J., Ferrin, D.L., Rao, H.R.: A trust-based consumer decision-making model in electronic commerce: the role of trust, perceived risk, and their antecedents. Decis. Support Syst. **44**(2), 544–564 (2008)
22. Koufaris, M., Hampton-Sosa, W.: The development of initial trust in an online company by new customers. Inf. Manag. **41**(3), 377–397 (2004)
23. Lamberton, C.P., Rose, R.L.: When is ours better than mine? A framework for understanding and altering participation in commercial sharing systems. J. Mark. **76**(4), 109–125 (2012)
24. Lu, Y., Zhou, T.: A research of consumers' initial trust in online stores in China. J. Res. Pract. Inf. Technol. **39**(3), 167–180 (2007)
25. Luhmann, N.: Trust and Power. John Willey & Sons (1979)
26. McKnight, D.H., Choudhury, V., Kacmar, C.: The impact of initial consumer trust on intentions to transact with a web site: a trust building model. J. Strateg. Inf. Syst. **11**(3–4), 297–323 (2002)
27. McKnight, D.H., Cummings, L.L., Chervany, N.L.: Initial trust formation in new organizational relationships. Acad. Manag. Rev. **23**(3), 473–490 (1998)
28. Mittendorf, C.: What trust means in the sharing economy: a provider perspective on Airbnb.com. In: The 22nd Americas Conference on Information Systems (2016)
29. Njite, D., Parsa, H.: Structural equation modeling of factors that influence consumer internet purchase intentions of services. J. Serv. Res. **5**(1), 43 (2005)
30. Pizam, A.: Peer-to-peer travel: blessing or blight? Int. J. Hosp. Manag. **38**, 118–119 (2014)
31. Ridings, C.M., Gefen, D., Arinze, B.: Some antecedents and effects of trust in virtual communities. J. Strateg. Inf. Syst. **11**, 271–295 (2002)

32. Robinson, J.P., Shaver, P.R., Wrightsman, L.S.: Criteria for Scale Selections and Evaluation. Academic Press, San Diego (1991)
33. Rousseau, D., Sitkin, S., Burt, R., et al.: Not so different after all: a cross-descipline view of trust. Acad. Manag. Rev. **23**(3), 393–404 (1998)
34. Tussyadiah, Iis P.: An exploratory study on drivers and deterrents of collaborative consumption in travel. In: Tussyadiah, I., Inversini, A. (eds.) Information and Communication Technologies in Tourism 2015, pp. 817–830. Springer, Cham (2015). doi:10.1007/978-3-319-14343-9_59
35. Wallsten, S.: The competitive effects of the sharing economy: how is Uber changing taxis? Technology Policy Institute (2015)
36. Wang, Y., Vassileva, J.: A review on trust and reputation for web service selection. In: 27th International Conference on Distributed Computing Systems Workshops, ICDCSW 2007, p. 25. IEEE (2007)
37. Zervas, G., Proserpio, D., Byers, J.: The rise of the sharing economy: estimating the impact of Airbnb on the hotel industry. Boston University School of Management Research Paper (2013-16) (2015)

A Critique on Participatory Design
in Developmental Context: A Case Study

Ulemba Hirom[1(✉)], Shyama V.S.[1], Pankaj Doke[1], Sylvan Lobo[1],
Sujit Devkar[1], and Nikita Pandey[2]

[1] Tata Consultancy Services Limited, Mumbai, India
{ulemba.h,shyamav.s,pankaj.doke,
sylvan.lobo,sujit.devkar}@tcs.com
[2] Tata Institute of Social Sciences, Mumbai, India
nikita.pandey2015@tiss.edu

Abstract. The dimensions of understanding and involving users and their context while constructing a system have become important. Participatory Design has shown promising success in recent times. The concept of Participatory Design originates from developed countries [11, 13, 16, 17]. Its nature and methods are more oriented toward the Western setting where there is more privilege in terms of economy, education, and technology and a different socio-economic context. However, in the Developmental context, these presumptions may operate differently. In this paper, we critique the operationalization of Participatory Design in a healthcare case study in a developmental context. The study was conducted in urban-poor areas in a metropolitan city in India with 5 users individually, by a Designer and Public Health policy student. All users were recruited on the basis of their education (not more than 8th standard) and the age of their child (below 18 months). This paper reports findings on various factors such as social-cultural barriers, family power hierarchy, language barriers, power distance issues which affect and limit an attempt to facilitate Participatory Design in a developmental context.

Keywords: Participatory design · ICTD · Participant observation · Healthcare · Service design

1 Introduction

In recent years, the need for involving users and their perspectives in developing a system [17] has gained a much larger audience. With this increasing focus on human-centric approaches, the scope of Participatory Design has engulfed a wider spectrum of design and developmental processes [14]. Participatory Design (PD), in its nature, practices and principles, is still confined towards the Western context [11, 17] where it has been used successfully for decades [13]. Until now the arguments about PD have been more within the context of developed countries where the application was mainly to meet the business end [14]. Although attempts have been extended toward including PD in a developmental context [11], limited research has been recorded about its successes or failure in such a setting [13].

© Springer International Publishing AG 2017
P.-L.P. Rau (Ed.): CCD 2017, LNCS 10281, pp. 647–658, 2017.
DOI: 10.1007/978-3-319-57931-3_52

We have attempted PD in a developmental context with less-literate female users living in lower economic conditions, for designing a vaccination service. We studied how PD works through passive participant observations while the PD sessions were taking place. From our observations and comparison with literature, we would like to critique and comment on which aspects of PD seem to work and which do not in a developmental context. We initially highlight key studies in PD for a developmental context where we highlight the known challenges faced, followed by explaining the setting and method of our study, and proceed with highlighting and discussing the key findings of our study.

2   Literature Survey

2.1   Participatory Design in Developmental Context

Originating in Scandinavian academic and trade unions, PD has been popularly discussed and adopted since the 1990's and 2000's. It has been viewed both as a methodology, where methods need to be strongly defined, and as an orientation or design approach, where methods are loosely defined. In either way, the idea is to democratize and involve the workers/users into the design or research process, to cooperatively arrive at designs and artefacts that are grounded in their own context. PD allows to bridge users' tacit knowledge and researchers analytical knowledge. It provides a democratic environment empowering users, while designers play a facilitating role. The PD is hence beneficial although it has limitations such as being too grounded with users perspectives possibly prevents radical change; lacking rigour in the methods in practice and a tendency to focus on artefacts rather than overall workflows. Some of the key challenges of PD are to elicit users' tacit knowledge effectively and ensuring effective participation and representation of the users [16].

Much of the exploration of methods have been in the Western context [2, 6]. However, PD in developmental context has been recently attracting a lot of interest from Researchers, Practitioners and Design community [11, 19]. With its methods based on the human-centered approaches, the process of PD has extended towards including the lower economic sections of people in designing systems for them [8, 11, 13, 15]. In the Western context, PD has mainly evolved from practices in organizations [14] for developing innovative products and services internally or between organizations, business partners and people associated with the product or services such as customers and consumers.

Most views about PD come from "Design Thinking" which is popular among the Business and Design community [14]. Consequently, the methods are more oriented toward the corporate culture of telling, making and enacting, using tools and techniques like maps, models, diaries, used of cards, etc. [14]. In the past few years, researchers have increasingly emphasized on including PD in multidisciplinary and multicultural dimensions, the claim being that it should not be limited to corporate organizational context alone. Thus attempts have been made to extend PD in various scenarios whether in developmental or cross-cultural contexts. Some of the factors that affect PD in a developmental context are, power distance, cultural and language barriers, incompatible values of PD techniques, uncertain methods and techniques, organizational culture differences between users and designers, low literacy levels, and high costs due to dispersed geographical locations [11]. These factors have been categorized into: human; social, cultural and religious; financial and timeframe [14]. Shorter sessions with flexible scheduling were found essential for recruitment taking into account the users social obligations and work commitments [14]. In conventional methods of PD the stakeholders, users and designers interact with each other and design together. However [14] suggests an alternative where the Designer interacts with stake holders and users separately to ensure better participation from both sides and to solve problems of interaction.

For a developmental context, the discourse is more on the culture bias and how social-cultural factors and their understanding leads to adaption of PD and its uses [11, 13, 15, 17]. Kensing and Blomberg [9] mentioned three major issues which exist in PD (1) politic of design, (2) the nature of participants and (3) the methods, tools and techniques in implementing PD. In developing countries such issues come from various factors such as cultural background, socio economic and political situation [13]. Moreover, there are other various unique issues which arise within a developmental context such as the roles of power distance, communication barriers, incompatibility of methods and tools and the role of culture on which participants' behavior depends [11]. The interpretation process of a group of people requires cultural context as it is grounded in their experiences, knowledge, interest, social values and emotions [18].

From a Western perspective the assumption of democratized workspace, high literacy, good infrastructure, and better technology could be questioned while conducting PD in a developing country context [13]. The assumptions need to be studied further in the actual context within a developing country.

Spinuzzi [16] also describes criteria for evaluation PD, namely: "Quality of life for workers", "Collaborative development", and "Iterative process", where users and researcher are involved and collaboratively develop solutions with common aims and a shared sense of ownership and agreement, leading to a democratic development of the users.

Increasingly participatory design is also moving towards designing for services [1, 3, 5, 7], which is away from the earlier tool perspectives [16] or creation of tangible products. This also has its own set of challenges and approached. For instance [3] have explored participatory design for healthcare services, through experience based design, where users' experiences are captured through storytelling, one on one interview, video diaries and audio recordings. Researchers later create emotion maps and plat customer journey maps, and participants help to improve. A common challenge is the need for a lingua-franca for all stakeholders to communicate effectively. Researchers have explored the use of Patterns, Pattern languages and pattern cards for participatory design [10].

3   Method

3.1   Objective

The objective of the study was to examine the phenomenon of participatory design (PD) in a developmental context. We wished to study the limitations and challenges of

PD in the context of users from a lower socio-economic background, with lesser-literacy, in re-designing a vaccination service. We observed how established methods and adaptions performed in the field and we report our experiences accordingly.

3.2   Participants and Setting

For the participatory design sessions, we selected 5 female users from urban-poor areas within a metropolitan city in India. The participatory design sessions were conducted by a Designer and a Public Health Policy student who was also a qualified Dentist, with one user at a time. Three users were from Chembur, a suburban area, and two users were from Govandi, a slum area in Mumbai. The users were selected through a door-to-door recruitment strategy followed by convenience sampling on the basis of their education background and age of their youngest child. We recruited users who were migrants to the city, less-literate (i.e. education qualification below 8th standard), and had a child within the past 18 months. We arrived at the criteria of 18 months as vaccination is done frequently with this period.

The location and timing for the session were decided according to user convenience, in their own house. Most of the house where the PD sessions took place, had only a single room where they performed their daily activities. Each house had a family of 5 to 6 members (including in-laws). All the five families had migrated from various places in India such as Karnataka, Tamil Nadu, and Uttar Pradesh and have been living in Mumbai for around more than 30 years. The common language chosen for communication was Hindi, as all participants spoke different languages natively.

3.3   Participatory Design Session

The Designer and Public Health Policy Student conducted the PD sessions with the 5 users, over a time span of two weeks. A silent observer was also present during the sessions, who only observed and did not participated. Each user was visited once before the session to schedule the session at a convenient location. The sessions included the Designer, Public Health Policy student, the less-literate female user and occasionally family members (children, mother-in-law) who were not main participants but influenced the discussions. The sessions lasted for a minimum of 30 min to a maximum of 90 min and were mostly performed in the afternoon (post lunch) as per users' preferences. The designer, public health policy student and observer were dressed down to suit the surrounding. Due to lack of space in the houses/living areas, most of the activities were carried out on the bed or in the small open spaces outside of the house.

In the beginning of the session the Designer and the Public Health Policy student started with very basic demographic questions. Then the session progressed to open ended questions asking user to describe how they prepared their favourite food. This would help the user articulate processes that were familiar to them before starting with breaking down the vaccination process. Then the session moved towards various tasks like creative exercises and puzzles to help the user warm up towards creative thinking. The session gradually moved towards photo elicitation and storytelling about vaccination process. This was followed by stakeholder mapping and empathy mapping. The session ended with a role-play where the user enacted the service provider and described what the ideal interaction would be with this healthcare service. Users also gave inputs on how they would design aspects of the service. During the process, the Designer and the Public Health Policy student used different materials which were familiar to the users such as pen, paper, colour sketch pens, matchsticks, pictures of smileys, etc. Small goodies like color sketch pens were gifted to the kids as a token of appreciation to the users.

3.4   Fly-on-the-Wall and Non-participant Observation [4, 12]

The passive observer noted down the PD sessions using Fly-on-the-wall technique. The observer maintained a distance without disturbing or suggesting any ideas and silently captured observations, actions and feelings in the form of written notes, sketches and doodles.

When the session was going on, the observer tried to maintain at least a meter distance away from participants. Most of the time the observer was sitting next to the door of the room. The observer also tried not to catch users' attention through any of his actions.

Though field notes were the primary data collection tool, audio recorder and camera (videos and images) were also used to capture the dynamics of interactions, body language and gestures especially in-between the activities. The field notes broadly covered what was happening in the session, who were involved, and observer's thoughts and ideas. The criteria for observations and notes were based on:

- *Physical surrounding.* The observer noted the physical nature of the surrounding where the users resided. The houses in Govandi were very close to the metropolitan city's open air dumping ground. The houses in Chembur were close to a research institute.
- *Room description.* At the beginning, the observer made notes describing the physical nature of the rooms such as number of rooms, estimated size and objects present inside it. The observer also noted any available visual cues which reflected users' economic status, religion and belief system and aspiration through by simply looking at the type of appliances user s' have, the kind picture on the wall, the accessories which the users used.
- *Physical appearance of the participants.* The observation was extended for all the participants to understand their aspirations, goals and intentions. This includes observing different skills, their speech and vocabulary, dresses and jewelry, hand and eye gestures.
- *Break points (other people intervention during the session).* Each break point was also noted down, such as outsiders interrupting in the session, conditions where the session had to pause, the involvement of other audience, etc.
- *Designer and the Public Health Policy student.* The effectiveness of the activities attempted by the designer and student were also noted while the session was progressing. At the same time, the impact of prior skills and languages with the designer and Public Health Policy student, were addressed using their activities and body language.

3.5   Post-session Interview and Analysis

The observer also held a short interview the designer and healthcare student, to summarize the whole process after the PD session and their overall experiences. The raw data was then analyzed using inductive content analysis and reported in the form of themes and models.

4   Findings and Discussion

4.1   Cultural Factors Influencing in Participatory Design

We noticed certain cultural factors that affected the PD process, as described below.

Family Hierarchy. There seemed to be a strong power hierarchy system in the families, and this influenced the sessions, where the user refrained from expressing herself freely. All our users were housewives and had moved to their husband's residence post marriage, where they typically lived with their in-laws. During the PD session, the presence of her in-laws or husband often resulted in her not voicing her opinions freely. The sessions were formal and rigid if the mother-in-law or husband were present. We observed that users tended to participate more confidently in the absence of family members, other than children. Often the mother-in-law got involved in the session, which led the users to agree to her opinions rather than state their own. In one case, when asked to user who the most important person in the entire vaccination process was, the mother-in-law instead replied *"Ma (mother) ka responsibility hai"*. The user simply agreed to her statement. The presence of the sister-in-law also seemed to prevent a user from fully expressing herself freely, despite the sister-in-law too having a baby and familiar with vaccination. They tended to compare each other's experiences and validate each other's stories. This however prevented the user from expressing her own story or opinions. Users were reluctant to disagree with their family members. Figure 1 shows how mother-in-law and sister-in-law also engaged in the PD session.

Fig. 1. The image shows mother-in-law, in right corner, involved in PD

Scheduling. Timing also played an important cultural role in conducting the participatory sessions. Choosing a time that was convenient to the user was important, so that the user could participate in the PD session openly. Most of the users invited us post-lunch around time window of 14:00 to 15:00, as they could finish their household work by then. Also particularly at this timing there would be lesser family members as the husbands would be out for work. Thus, usually it remained as a free time for them and there would be less interruption from outside. One of the users described the session as "time-pass for her, as she did not have any work at that time". She treated the session as a fun activity. Another user also brought to our notice that they sometimes missed vaccination as it was during the lunch time, and they had to prepare lunch for their husband before they left for work.

Gender Issues. There seem to be an outlook of discomfort with women interacting with an (unknown) opposite gender during the sessions. In one of the sessions, the mother-in-law showed and often interrupted the session if the observer sat next to the user (which was due to the limitation of space during the session). The mother-in-law also seemed suspicious and uncomfortable with the (male) observer taking down notes.

4.2 Communication Barriers

Language for PD. As the participants were migrants, i.e. the users as well as the designer and student, they chose Hindi as a commonly known language to communicate during the sessions. They lacked native proficiency in the language. They both faced some difficulties in communicating and expressing ideas. For example due to a lack of common terminology, both the designer and student could not easily explain certain technical term such as process, involvement, registration etc. to the user. On the other hand, the designer and student could not understand the local terms which the user used during the PD session. This communication barriers sometime led to not understanding each other with unclear information communicated among the participants and thus hampering the whole process of PD. Hence it would be ideal to have mediators with proficiency with the users' or local language, who can also communicate technical ideas from the designers and other stakeholders. Alternatively, designers should strive towards engaging with users using mechanisms that act as *lingua-franca*.

4.3 Pen and Paper Relating to Literacy

Users were reluctant to use pen and paper. One of the exercises that the designer and student requested the users to do involved drawing an object out of a circle on a sheet of paper. This was planned as a warm-up exercise, however, the users usually got nervous and hesitated to draw, and repeated that they are not educated. After insisting for a while, some of the users attempted and drew very tiny drawings (Fig. 2). Sometimes they enquired whether whatever they have drawn are correct or not. One of the user asked if we were taking their exams.

Fig. 2. The baby interrupting the session

The users seemed to associate pen and paper with higher literacy of a person, and might have brought forward fear and embarrassment regarding their literacy status. Instead of drawing or using pen and paper, they were more comfortable with verbal conversations. Artefacts that suggest the need for higher literacy should be avoided in a PD session. Alternate more accessible/amenable forms should be explored.

> Field note – *The moment the designer showed the pen and paper, the user said she couldn't do it and kept saying she hardly know how to draw.*

> Field note – *User said she doesn't know how to draw the cup in which she prefers to make tea but pinpoint toward the cup from the kitchen (for one of the PD exercises)*

> Field note – *After much probing by the designer and student, the user started drawing roti, milk packet and match box but often asking the designer and student whether it was ok or not.*

4.4 Cognitive Ability on Articulation and Abstraction

Awareness of Vaccination Process. We observed that the users from the Govandi (slum area) had very little knowledge about the vaccination process as compared to the Chembur, possibly due to less exposure to hospital and healthcare facilities at Govandi (we found that users seems to not always have childbirth at the hospitals, for instance). They also often interchangeably used the term Polio injection and Calcium injection with the vaccination process. Due to which the process of the PD was usually limited to only their woes and not about them designing the process.

Abstraction of Vaccination Process. We found that users were facing difficulties in understanding the vaccination as a 'process'. They were unable to easily express what they would prefer the process should have been, which hampered their attempt to redesign the service. They were unable to easily express who were involved in the process as stakeholders. They kept saying that they would do whatever the hospital people told them to, and found it difficult to understand they could come up with (hypothetical) alternatives.

With some triggers (e.g. role playing as doctors or the health workers, or providing an analogy of explaining the cooking process and then explaining the vaccination process similarly) from the designer and the student, some of the users were able to express some ideas that would alleviate the issues they faced: e.g. vaccination at their home so that they could massage and comfort the baby to prevent them crying; or about the importance of mother-child card as they usually forgot to take it to the healthcare center.

We found that users tend to accept the Vaccination service top-down as is, and it was something they had to mandatorily follow without questions. It seemed unfamiliar to them to think about redesigning the service, they felt they did not have the authority to do so.

4.5   Gender Role in PD

Gender seems to play an important role in doing the PD especially in a context of less-literate and culturally rooted context. Since all the participants were female and there were no male involved in any of the session (other than the observer), the users seemed more active during the session and more free and open in the discussion. However in the few interactions with the male observer, users and their family seemed to express discomfort. This suggests that there could be more difficulties if male participants were included in PD sessions (as designers or other stakeholders).

4.6   External Factors

There were a variety of external factors that affected the PD sessions. Since the PD sessions were held in users' houses, there were lot of external breakdowns. For example, the baby was not getting much attention during the session, so it would often play or tear up the artefacts (Fig. 2). Many times the participants could not resume the sessions till the baby was pacified. Neighbors or other people appearing during the sessions caused distraction to the participants. The observer and users taking notes also to some extent made the users slightly conscious and might have affected the sessions. Current affairs, such as demonetization and cash crunch at the period when we conducted the study, also caused certain amount of stress with the users, which again affected their participation.

4.7   Discussion

The above case study provided glimpse of pros and cons of participatory design in a developing country.

Participation. We felt that some basic preparation is required for participants before conducting the Participatory design. To some extent both the parties need to adjust to be in a common group. From designer and healthcare student they had to dress up to fit in with the users, whereas some preparation had to be provided to the user before introducing abstract concepts like vaccination. The limitations of the participant's ability and skill also needs to be considered along with their context.

Participatory Session. Although past literature mentioned power distance within the participants as a major observation in developmental context, we did not face such an issue in our study. This could be due to the small group size of participant (3 members) and also the location and timing as in our cases it was more driven by the user preferences, and that the group mainly consisted of female participants driving the discussion. Another points to be noted is having a participatory session with only one user at a time, with lesser stakeholders. This kind of a session created sufficient opportunity for each individual user to their feelings and opinions, as all the participants were in the same or near to same context. Though the dynamicity of the session being conducted in the local environment is something appreciable, it has its own breakdowns and challenges such the external factors mentioned earlier, the limitations and dilemmas out of cultural incompetency, and communication barriers.

Tool and Techniques for the PD. Although some of the tools and techniques were created from Western setting, they can be still be applied toward the developmental context if it can be translate to their local context such as Storytelling and Photo elicitation. But at the same time there are few existing tools which were hard to implement due to its limitation in the given context such as user journey maps. As in [3], such abstract steps would be suitable to be conducted separately by other stakeholders after sessions like storytelling, and then in another iteration improved by feedback from the users.

5   Conclusions and Future Work

In this study, we have attempted to outline the operational challenges and limitations in adopting participatory design in a developmental context. We have broadly discussed our finding in three parts (1) Participants (2) the Participatory session and the Tools and Technique used in it. At the same time we have to recognize the other factors which are needed to critically analyze for conducting participatory design for developing countries. The work also needs to address the role of the gender of the participants in participatory design session in the culturally rooted context. For example, whether to conduct the participatory design with same genders or opposite genders or a mix of both genders. The scope could be extended to comparison of doing participatory design with one user or multiple users. The external factors which hamper the session need to be addressed more elaborately. Designing for the end user would depend on many aspects: user experience, need, requirements, usability etc. and all other aspects of value creation. As a direct consumer of the products and services, users are grounded to their context and are well aware of requirements. Considering the users for design process would be an essential in near future. In order to elicit the user experience, emotions and value, participatory design would play an important role.

Acknowledgments. We would like to express our gratitude toward all the users and facilitators for their willingness and support in this project. This project is sponsored by TCS Innovation Labs Mumbai.

References

1. Blomkvist, J., Holmlid, S., Sandberg, F., Westerlund, B.: Workshop: exploring participatory prototyping of services. In: Proceedings of the 12th Participatory Design Conference: Exploratory Papers, Workshop Descriptions, Industry Cases, vol. 2, pp. 151–152. ACM (2012)
2. Bødker, S.: Creating conditions for participation: conflicts and resources in systems design. DAIMI Rep. Ser. **13**, 215–236 (1994)
3. Bowen, S., Dearden, A., Wright, P., Wolstenholme, D., Cobb, M.: Participatory healthcare service design and innovation. In: Proceedings of the 11th Biennial Participatory Design Conferenc, pp 155–158. ACM (2010)
4. Cooper, J., Lewis, R., Urquhart, C.: Using participant or non-participant observation to explain information behaviour. Inf. Res. **9**(4), 9–14 (2004)
5. Gangadharan, G.R., Jain, A.N., Rajshree, N., Hartman, A., Agrahari, A.: Participatory service design for emerging markets. In: Proceedings of 2011 IEEE International Conference on Service Operations, Logistics, and Informatics, pp 68–73 (2011)
6. Halskov, K., Hansen, N.B.: The diversity of participatory design research practice at PDC 2002–2012. Int. J. Hum.-Comput. Stud. **74**, 81–92 (2015). doi:10.1016/j.ijhcs.2014.09.003
7. Holmlid, S.: Participative; co-operative; emancipatory: from participatory design to service design. In: Conference Proceedings ServDes 2009; DeThinking Service; ReThinking Design, Oslo, Norway, 24–26 November 2009, no. 059, pp. 105–118. Linköping University Electronic Press (2012)
8. Katjivirue, M.: Participatory design in Namibia. In: Proceedings of the 13th Participatory Design Conference: Short Papers, Industry Cases, Workshop Descriptions, Doctoral Consortium Papers, and Keynote Abstracts, vol. 2, pp 127–128. ACM, New York (2014)
9. Kensing, F., Blomberg, J.: Participatory design: issues and concerns. Comput. Support. Coop. Work **7**, 167–185 (1998). doi:10.1023/A:1008689307411
10. Khambete, P., Athavankar, U., Doke, P., Shinde, R., Roy, D., Devkar, S., Kimbahune, S., Chaudhary, S.: A case study in participatory service design for rural healthcare system in india using a pattern language. In: Chakrabarti, A. (ed.) ICoRD'15 – Research into Design Across Boundaries Volume 1. SIST, vol. 34, pp. 3–13. Springer, New Delhi (2015). doi:10. 1007/978-81-322-2232-3_1
11. Oyugi, C., Nocera, J.A., Dunckley, L., Dray, S.: The challenges for participatory design in the developing world. In: Proceedings of the Tenth Anniversary Conference on Participatory Design 2008, pp. 295–296. Indiana University, Indianapolis (2008)
12. Parke, J., Griffiths, M.: Participant and non-participant observation in gambling environments. Enquire **1**, 1–14 (2008)
13. Puri, S.K., Byrne, E., Nhampossa, J.L., Quraishi, Z.B.: Contextuality of participation in IS design: a developing country perspective. In: Proceedings of the Eighth Conference on Participatory Design: Artful Integration: Interweaving Media, Materials and Practices, vol. 1, pp 42–52. ACM, New York, (2004)
14. Sanders, E.: Perspectives on participation in design. In: Wer Gestaltet die Gestaltung? Praxis, Theorie und Geschichte des Partizipatorischen Designs, vol. 1 (2014)

15. Hussain, S., Sanders, E.B.-N., Steinert, M.: Participatory design with marginalized people in developing countries: challenges and opportunities experienced in a field study in Cambodia. Int. J. Des. **6**(2), 91–109 (2012)
16. Spinuzzi, C.: The methodology of participatory design. Tech. Commun. **52**, 163–174 (2005)
17. Winschiers, H.: The challenges of participatory design in a intercultural context: designing for usability in Namibia. In: PDC, pp. 73–76 (2006)
18. Yasuoka, M., Sakurai, R.: Out of Scandinavia to Asia: adaptability of participatory design in culturally distant society. In: Proceedings of the 12th Participatory Design Conference: Exploratory Papers, Workshop Descriptions, Industry Cases, vol. 2, pp 21–24. ACM, New York, (2012)
19. Participatory Design with Marginalized People in Developing Countries: Challenges and Opportunities Experienced in a Field Study in Cambodia. Int. J. Des. http://www.ijdesign. org/ojs/index.php/IJDesign/article/view/1054/455. Accessed 1 Dec 2016

Understanding Users' Acceptance of Money Gifting in a Social Game

Hanjing Huang and Pei-Luen Patrick Rau[✉]

Department of Industrial Engineering, Tsinghua University, Beijing, China
huanghj15@mails.tsinghua.edu.cn, rpl@tsinghua.edu.cn

Abstract. The explosive growth of social media has created new opportunities for social games and social payments. This study investigates users' acceptance of the money gifting social game. The experiment was conducted on WeChat lucky money, a social game bringing the tradition of giving cash-filled lucky money into digital. WeChat lucky money becomes an immediate hit and boosts the usage of WeChat payment in China. Eight North Americans and eight Koreans were recruited to experience the WeChat lucky money. The results showed that international users enjoyed giving and receiving lucky money on WeChat. Most users preferred to play the WeChat lucky money with their close families and friends. Compared with North Americans, Koreans cared more about the extending meaning of the lucky money. Koreans also felt more social pressure when receiving a large amount of money from others.

Keywords: Social games · Money gifting · Cross-culture

1 Introduction

Social media have begun creating an ecosystem for businesses and entertainment. For example, Facebook plans to transform Messenger into a platform where users can communicate with business and buy things [1]. Indeed, the cashless economy is already popular in China. Released in 2011, WeChat is a mobile instant messaging application developed by Tencent. It has added various functions such as online-to-offline services, advertising, e-commerce, social games, and finance. In 2016, there exist over 800 million monthly active users in WeChat [2]. About a third of WeChat users apply WeChat payments to make regular online purchases [3].

WeChat also brings the tradition of giving cash-filled lucky money into digital. Giving lucky money is a Chinese tradition for certain festive occasions. People send lucky money to families and friends on festivals or some other special events such as weddings. WeChat lucky money is designed as an in-app function. People can send lucky money to an individual or a group through WeChat lucky money. On 2016 Spring Festival Eve, more than 400 million users sent 8 billion packets of digital lucky money to their families and friends [4]. WeChat lucky money also turns out to be a useful marketing tool for Internet services such as taxi and food delivery apps. These apps use lucky money as coupons to attract customers.

© Springer International Publishing AG 2017
P.-L.P. Rau (Ed.): CCD 2017, LNCS 10281, pp. 659–668, 2017.
DOI: 10.1007/978-3-319-57931-3_53

Meanwhile, WeChat sees a shift in the demographics of the user base and sets its sights on globalization. A quarter of WeChat users are already non-Chinese [5]. On 2016 Spring Festival, WeChat brought the Chinese custom of lucky money to New York pedestrians [6]. This event thrilled passers-by and educated people from all over the world about this joyful custom and festive atmosphere. Other social media also try to involve in the online gift services. However, Facebook shut down the gift services, which allowed users to send digital cards to their friends [7]. Facebook still explores new ways to help businesses drive sales on Facebook. It is critical to explore how international users use social media in China.

This study used WeChat lucky money as an example of social gifting in social media. The behavior of giving money is rare in other social media. Some researchers has already used Wechat lucky money platform to investigate users' gifting behaviors [8]. The current study offers new insights to the globalization of social media. Social media help users adapt to new environment through communication. Previous research reveals that interpersonal communication is essential to the outcome of the adjustment process [9]. When people start new life in a new culture, they will receive challenges from language barriers, relational issues, loneliness and racial discrimination [10, 11]. Prior research also demonstrates the great potential of social media to help international students adapt to a new culture. For example, exchanging and viewing messages in online newsgroups and on bulletin boards helped Chinese immigrants adapt to the new life in the United States [12]. The frequency of using Facebook was also found to positively predict Chinese students' bridging social capital [13].

Do international users accept the lucky money in social media? Does international users' cultural background influence their acceptance of the lucky money in social media? This study aims at answering these questions and offering suggestions for the design of global social media and social games.

2   Literature Review

2.1   Culture and Social Media Usage

Individual motivations are culture bound. Previous research highlighted the effect of culture on everything from attitudes to motivations to needs and how to fulfil needs, as well as people's behavior on social media [14]. Correa et al. defined the social media as "a mechanism for the audience to connect, communicate, and interact with each other and their mutual friends through instant messaging or social networking sites." [15]. Previous study work has supported the view that online cultures mirror the offline cultures of which they are a product [16, 17].

Recent research has indicated the effect of culture on user behavior on social media. Qiu et al. [18] took China and the United States as examples of the East–West distinction. They compared Renren and Facebook and found that Renren culture was perceived as more collectivistic than Facebook culture. For example, Renren users were found more benevolent in in-group sharing. Facebook users were found more self-talk and self-interested.

Previous studies also explored the effect of culture on the motivations and usage of social media games. Culture directly affects players' expected outcome from playing social games and indirectly affects players' usage pattern [19]. Collectivism-oriented players play social media games to seek social outcomes. They aim at maintaining or improving a relationship. They are more likely to engage in reciprocal gifting behavior. Individualism-oriented players play games to seek personal status through competition. They prefer the behavior of advancement.

2.2 Culture and Gift Giving Behavior

The motivations and patterns of gift giving also vary from culture to culture [20]. North Americans typically have independent self-construal, focusing on the attractiveness of the gift rather than the extending meaning of the gift [21–23]. Their gift giving is often motivated by the desire to make the recipient happy. North Americans also have more flexibility in the gift budget. In contrast, Koreans typically view themselves through the relation to others. Their gift giving is often motivated by the desire to enhance the reputation. Koreans are more careful in the selection of gift budget. They are more sensitive to the obligation to reciprocate. They have strong motivations to keep conformity with others. When Koreans receive a gift without being able to reciprocate, they will feel indebted [23]. Koreans fell more social pressure to reciprocate. Thus, Koreans are less inclined to accept a gift than North Americans [24, 25].

3   Methodology

The purpose of this study is to investigate international users' experience and acceptance when they receive digital lucky money from Chinese friends. To achieve this purpose, we took North Americans and Koreans to compare cultural differences. Questionnaires and interviews were used to investigate international users' experience of WeChat lucky money.

3.1 Participants

Eight North American and eight Korean college students were recruited. They had stayed in China for less than 1 year. Eight Korean participants aged from 20 to 29 years old ($M = 23.75$, $SD = 3.01$) and eight North American participants aged from 22 to 26 years old ($M = 24.38$, $SD = 1.77$) participated in the experiment. There was no significant difference in the ages between two samples ($p > .1$). Each sample was gender balanced. All participants were WeChat users. They were get used to applying WeChat to contact with their Chinese friends. But none of them had tried WeChat lucky money before the experiment. Participants spent an average of 98.13 min per day on WeChat ($SD = 86.27$) and had an average of 106.75 friends on WeChat ($SD = 95.94$). Participants mainly used WeChat to communicate with others or express their feelings in China. The results from the t-tests showed that North American participants and Korean participants did not have significant difference in the adaption and satisfaction of the life in China (all p-values $>.50$).

3.2 Procedures

Before the experiment, participants were provided written informed consent and asked to fill in questionnaires on demographic information, usage of WeChat, adaption and satisfaction of the life in China. In the beginning of the experiment, experimenters used slides to introduce cultural traits of lucky money and usage of WeChat lucky money.

The experiment was taken on the platform of WeChat lucky money. There are two different types of WeChat lucky money: (1) an individual transfer of money, and (2) a competitive game among multiple users, where the goal is to win an allotment of lucky money. For example, when people decide to give away 100 yuan to 10 people, WeChat will automatically divide the 100 yuan into 10 sets randomly.

In the experiment, participants experienced both types of WeChat lucky money. One was from an individual. In this scenario, participants received the lucky money with a fixed amount from their Chinese language partner. The Chinese language partner sent lucky money to participants to celebrate the coming New Year. The other one was from a WeChat group, a group doing a class project together. The scenario was that students in the group were giving and receiving lucky money to celebrate "We got an A in the final presentation" and the coming New Year. The sequence of the scenarios was randomized. Figure 1 showed an example of participants' receiving a random amount of money from the group.

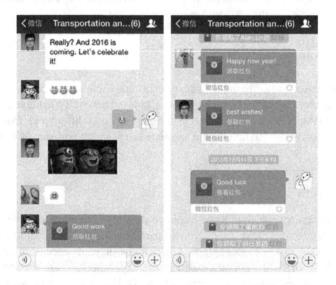

Fig. 1. Example of WeChat lucky money interface from a group

When participants received lucky money from an individual or a group, they were asked to fill in the questionnaire about their experience. The measurement items were adapted from previous Internet uses and gratifications research [26, 27]. The questionnaire included four dimensions: entertainment, information seeking, social support and acceptance (see Table 1). The agreement to each statement was measured by a seven-point Likert scale ranging from 1-completely disagree to 7-completely agree.

Table 1. Questionnaire of user experience of receiving group lucky money

Category	Statement
Entertainment	• The lucky money in the group one keeps me entertained • I have fun receiving the lucky money from the group • I think the function that I can receive lucky money from the group is interesting
Information seeking	• The group lucky money helps me learn more information about Chinese culture
Social support	• I feel more connected with Chinese • I feel receiving the emotional support when I receive the group lucky money • I feel respected by Chinese
Acceptance	• I can accept the group lucky money function • I would send lucky money to a group • I would tell my friends the group lucky money function on WeChat

A semi-structured interview was followed. They needed to talk with the experimenter about their experience. The questions of interview (see Table 2) were generated under three categories: feelings, money issues and usage.

Table 2. Questions of interview

Category	Question
Feelings	• What's your feeling when you receive the lucky money?
Money issues	• Do you care about the amount of money that you receive? • Will the amount of money affect your feelings?
Usage	• Would you like to send this type of lucky money? • When will you send this type of lucky money? • Who will you send lucky money to? • How much will you send?

4 Results

Using the questionnaire and semi-structured interview, we explored international users' experience of WeChat lucky money. The findings were organized in the following sections:

4.1 Questionnaire

The results of participants' experience on the lucky money from questionnaires were shown in Fig. 2. On average, participants gave an average score between 3 to 4 on the seven-point Likert scale. The results suggested that participants had neutral to positive attitudes toward WeChat lucky money. The results from the paired t-tests showed that there did not exist significant differences between user experience of group lucky money and that of individual lucky money in the dimension of entertainment, information seeking and acceptance (all p-values >.40). But participants felt significantly more social support from receiving individual lucky money (t = −3.162, p = .006). Korean participants and North American participants did not have significant differences in these four dimensions (all p-values >.50).

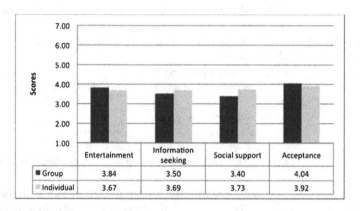

Fig. 2. Participants' Experience of WeChat lucky money

4.2   Interview

Feelings. *How do North Americans and Koreans feel when they receive lucky money from a group or an individual?*

For the group lucky money, most Korean participants (6 out of 8) considered it as a way to share happiness and celebrate some achievements. For example, "I am happy. I can share with my friend" (K4), "I think, it is like one sharing emotional things" (K3). Most North American participants (7 out of 8) thought that the group lucky money was funny, like a game. For example, "It's good, it's a funny tool" (A6), "Rich, very rich. I think that maybe I can buy food. Money can be used now" (A7), "I think it is kind of funny, interesting" (A2), "It is like a game. Try to see who can get the higher" (A3). One Korean participant and one North American participant pointed out that their feelings about the group lucky money still depended on the closeness between themselves and the senders, "I would be more comfortable getting it from my close friends" (A4). And one Korean participant thought that it was a convenient way to give others money, "It is convenient. Because giving friends or families money is a little bit rare. But using this program, it's more convenient to give other guys money" (K6).

For the individual lucky money, most Korean participants (7 out of 8) felt happy and friendly. For example, "It is pretty good" (K6), "I feel like Chinese are very friendly, and they want to contact with other people. To me, I feel so friendly with her" (K5), "I am thankful to him" (K3), "I think it's better than real money, it's more convenient" (K8). The other one Korean participant felt strange, "Really strange, because friends rarely give others money, I need to send them back" (K1). Half of the North American participants (4 out of 8) felt excited and considered it as a gift. For example, "I think it is really a nice gift" (A2), "A little surprised" (A4). The other North American participants felt uncomfortable and focused on the people who gave them, the time and the aim of the lucky money, for example, "I feel so uncomfortable, because it is too much, usually friends don't give money to each other" (A5).

In all, most participants thought that the group one was like a game, and the individual one had more extending meanings in it. Participants were more likely to accept group lucky money. Some participants focused on the closeness between themselves and the senders, the sending time and the aim of sending lucky money.

Money-Issues. *How does the amount of money that participants receive affect their feelings?*

For the group lucky money, half of Korean participants (4 out of 8) thought that the behavior that people gave them lucky money was more important. Most of North American (6 out of 8) thought that group lucky money was like a lottery.

For the individual lucky money, half of Korean participants (4 out of 8) thought that the behavior was more important. Three Korean participants (3 out of 8) claimed that they would feel pressure if they received too much money. Five North American participants (5 out of 8) claimed that they did not care about the amount of money. Two North American participants believed that the more, the better. One North American participant claimed that it depended on the sender and the occasion.

From the above, people's attitudes toward the money were different in group one and individual one. Participants were more focused on the amount of money in individual lucky money. Korean participants claimed that too much money from individual would generate pressure on them.

Usage. *When will participants send the lucky money? How much will they send?*

Most participants reported that they would send the group lucky money for fun and used the individual lucky money to express their own feelings, such as expressing thanks to someone. Most participants would only give a small amount of money in a group. For example, "I am a student, so I am poor, so I would send, maybe, I don't know, but 40 yuan for 60 people" (A8), "Probably, usually, I don't give my friends money, I will give them up to 10 yuan for fun, but not more than that" (A7), "Probably not much money, maybe 20 yuan" (A6). For the individual one, participants would be more careful about the amount of money. The closeness would affect their selection of the budget. For example, "For my best friends, I would give them 100 RMB, for others, maybe 40 to 50 RMB" (K5), "In Korean, coffee or ticket, it depends on who she is, roughly from 50 to 300 RMB, 50 RMB for unfamiliar friends, 300 RMB for my families or very close friends" (K8).

5 Discussion

Overall, participants had neutral to positive attitudes toward WeChat lucky money. The group lucky money with a random amount of money was perceived as a game.

The individual lucky money with a fixed amount of money was considered as a way to express one's feelings to others. Participants felt significantly more social support from the individual lucky money. Participants were more likely to enjoy the process of giving and receiving the group lucky money. The randomness and entertainment of the group lucky money increase users' acceptance of money gifting social games. Before the experiment, none of the participants had ever tried the function of lucky money on WeChat. But after the introduction of the experimenter, they expressed great interest in this function. In the design of global social media, clear guides should be provided for international users. WeChat lucky money also helped participants know more about Chinese culture. Participants also felt social support from Chinese through receiving WeChat lucky money. Thus, social media can help users adapt to new culture. Participants also considered the payment on WeChat as a convenient tool for person-to-person trade and e-commerce. Social media can add the efficient payment function to create larger ecosystem.

This study found small cultural differences on the acceptance and usage of money-gifting social games. Korean participants cared more about the extending meanings of the lucky money and felt more pressure when they received too much money from others. This result is consistent with prior studies that showed a small effect of culture on user behaviors in social media games [19]. Influenced by the interdependent self-construal, Koreans are more likely to feel more pressure about giving gifts even in online social games. Koreans will feel uncomfortable when they receive a large amount of money from others. Although the effect is small, designers should consider carefully about the cultural difference because of the large population of potential users. Some North American and Korean participants focused on the closeness with the senders. They preferred to send more money to the families or friends who have close ties with them. Compared with other online games, social media games are unique in its relationship to users' off-line interaction. This study can help designers understand users' motivations and usage pattern.

This study was limited in several aspects. First, the sample size was small. The sample was also skewed toward specific ages (20–30 s) and restricted to college students. Although it is sufficient to gain some insights on cultural differences for an exploratory study, the conclusions cannot be properly applied to general populations. Second, this study used WeChat lucky money as an example. More researches should be done to investigate the effect of culture on different types of social games.

6   Conclusion

This study found that most international participants felt happy and accepted the function lucky money on WeChat. The group lucky money with a random amount of money was like a game. The individual lucky money with a fixed amount of money was considered as a way to express one's feelings to others. But none of the participants had tried the lucky money function before the experiment. In the design of global social media, a clearer introduction of function should be offered to international users.

Moreover, designers should consider more about cultural differences when social media explores opportunities to expand overseas. Compared with North Americans, Koreans were more likely to feel more pressure about receiving gifts even in online social games. The culture difference would affect users' experience of global social media.

References

1. Chowdhry, A.: Facebook messenger rolls out payment service across the U.S. http://www.forbes.com/sites/amitchowdhry/2015/06/30/facebook-messenger-rolls-out-payment-service-across-the-u-s/-56f0a7052e84
2. Statista. Number of active WeChat messenger accounts 2010–2016. https://www.statista.com/statistics/255778/number-of-active-wechat-messenger-accounts/
3. Jaivin, L.: WeChat: a new Chinese empire? http://www.sbs.com.au/news/feature/wechat-new-chinese-empire
4. Wang, H.H.: It's time for Facebook to copy WeChat. http://www.forbes.com/sites/helenwang/2016/08/11/its-time-for-facebook-to-copy-wechat/?yptr=yahoo-79dcefba27a4
5. China Channel. More WeChat lucky money data for Chinese new year 2016. http://chinachannel.co/wechat-lucky-money-data-for-chinese-new-year-2016/
6. Tencent. WeChat hands out lucky money on New York's times square billboards during Chinese new year. http://www.prnewswire.com/news-releases/wechat-hands-out-lucky-money-on-new-yorks-times-square-billboards-during-chinese-new-year-300215938.html
7. Constine, J.: Facebook is shutting down gifts to focus on its buy button and commerce platform. https://techcrunch.com/2014/07/29/an-obituary-for-facebook-gifts/
8. Chen, N., Rau, P.L.P.: Reciprocal norms moderate the influence of guanxi on feelings and behavior of closeness. Soc. Behav. Personal.: Int. J. 44(7), 1099–1114 (2016)
9. Gudykunst, W.B.: Theorizing About Intercultural Communication. SAGE, Thousand Oaks (2005)
10. Al-Sharideh, K.A., Goe, W.R.: Ethnic communities within the university: an examination of factors influencing the personal adjustment of international students. Res. High. Educ. 39(6), 699–725 (1998)
11. Ying, Y.W., Liese, L.H.: Emotional well-being of Taiwan students in the US: an examination of pre-to post-arrival differential. Int. J. Intercult. Relat. 15(3), 345–366 (1991)
12. Ye, J.: Acculturative stress and use of the Internet among East Asian international students in the United States. CyberPsychol. Behav. 8(2), 154–161 (2005)
13. Chen, L., Yang, X.: Nature and effectiveness of online social support for intercultural adaptation of mainland Chinese international students. Int. J. Commun. 9, 21 (2015)
14. Gudykunst, W.B.: Bridging Differences: Effective Intergroup Communication. SAGE, Thousand Oaks (2004)
15. Correa, T., Hinsley, A.W., De Zuniga, H.G.: Who interacts on the Web? The intersection of users' personality and social media use. Comput. Hum. Behav. 26(2), 247–253 (2010)
16. Marcus, A., Krishnamurthi, N.: Cross-cultural analysis of social network services in Japan, Korea, and the USA. In: Aykin, N. (ed.) IDGD 2009. LNCS, vol. 5623, pp. 59–68. Springer, Heidelberg (2009). doi:10.1007/978-3-642-02767-3_7
17. Morling, B., Lamoreaux, M.: Measuring culture outside the head: a meta-analysis of individualism–collectivism in cultural products. Personal. Soc. Psychol. Rev. (2008)
18. Qiu, L., Lin, H., Leung, A.K., Tov, W.: Putting their best foot forward: emotional disclosure on Facebook. Cyberpsychol. Behav. Soc. Netw. 15(10), 569–572 (2012)

19. Lee, Y.H., Wohn, D.Y.: Are there cultural differences in how we play? Examining cultural effects on playing social network games. Comput. Hum. Behav. **28**(4), 1307–1314 (2012)
20. Park, S.Y.: A comparison of Korean and American gift-giving behaviors. Psychol. Mark. (1998)
21. Hoppe, M.H.: Introduction: Geert Hofstede's culture's consequences: international differences in work-related values. Acad. Manag. Exec. **18**(1), 73–74 (2004)
22. Singelis, T.M.: The measurement of independent and interdependent self-construals. Pers. Soc. Psychol. Bull. **20**(5), 580–591 (1994)
23. Shen, H., Wan, F., Wyer Jr., R.S.: Cross-cultural differences in the refusal to accept a small gift: the differential influence of reciprocity norms on Asians and North Americans. J. Pers. Soc. Psychol. **100**(2), 271 (2011)
24. Miller, J.G., Bersoff, D.M.: Cultural influences on the moral status of reciprocity and the discounting of endogenous motivation. Pers. Soc. Psychol. Bull. **20**(5), 592–602 (1994)
25. Miller, J.G., Bersoff, D.M.: The role of liking in perceptions of the moral responsibility to help: a cultural perspective. J. Exp. Soc. Psychol. **34**(5), 443–469 (1998)
26. Ko, H., Cho, C.H., Roberts, M.S.: Internet uses and gratifications: a structural equation model of interactive advertising. J. Advert. **34**(2), 57–70 (2005)
27. Rayburn, J.D., Palmgreen, P.: Merging uses and gratifications and expectancy-value theory. Commun. Res. **11**(4), 537–562 (1984)

The Role of Socially Assistive Robots in Elderly Wellbeing: A Systematic Review

Reza Kachouie[1(✉)], Sima Sedighadeli[1], and Amin B. Abkenar[2]

[1] Monash Business School, Monash University, Melbourne, Australia
{reza.kachouie,sima.sedighadeli}@monash.edu
[2] La Trobe University, Melbourne, Australia
a.abkenar@latrobe.edu.au

Abstract. The population of the world is aging and one of the main concerns of the aged care industry is to provide appropriate care for elderly people as their health and independent functioning declines. This paper reports a systematic review of the roll of Socially Assistive Robots (SAR) in elderly wellbeing, based on Cochrane principles. Relevant publications from diverse databases, including healthcare, engineering, and robotics were sourced and screened. Ninety-five studies in forty-two study groups have been synthesized. The reported outcomes have been categorized based on five PERMA constructs (Positive emotion, Engagement, Relationships, Meaning, and Achievement) in addition to a sixth category (other effects). The findings indicate that SAR has the potential to enhance elderly wellbeing and decrease the workload of caregivers. Based on concerns that emerged during the quality appraisal process, several significant recommendations are made to improve future research and its applicability. Furthermore, acknowledging individuals' needs, expectations, and preferences alongside multi-modal interaction and data collection translates into improvement of personalization of care. The development of new approaches such as web-based interfaces and cloud computing are highly recommended as the means of overcoming the constraints of the limited computing and storage capabilities of SAR. Moreover, human-like engagement characteristics of socially assistive robots should be seamlessly integrated with other assistive technologies such as tele-health, e-health, and smart homes.

Keywords: Socially assistive robots · Elderly wellbeing · Assistive technologies · Aged care · Systematic review

1 Introduction

A decline in birth rates and extended longevity have resulted in an increase in the elderly population worldwide. Consequently, the ratio of the number of people aged between 15 and 64 to one elderly person (aged 65 years or above) dropped dramatically from 12 to 9 between 1950 and 2000 and is forecasted to decrease to 4 in 2050 [1]. One of the main concerns of the aged care industry is the provision of appropriate care for the elderly as their ability to function independently declines.

© Springer International Publishing AG 2017
P.-L.P. Rau (Ed.): CCD 2017, LNCS 10281, pp. 669–682, 2017.
DOI: 10.1007/978-3-319-57931-3_54

Researchers are working on the development of different technologies such as biomedical devices, nano-medicine, tele-health, smart homes, and robots to support the process of care giving and keeping the elderly at home longer. However, research in the interdisciplinary area of Socially Assistive Robots (SAR) is increasingly interested in overcoming the missing human element and the issue of human-robot engagement.

Systematic reviews of past studies help us to better understand what is already known [2] and unites current research and existing knowledge in the literature [3–5]. This research aims to synthesize existing knowledge in the field of SAR and its effects on elderly wellbeing. In line with existing literature [e.g., 89], this systematic review mostly follows the principles explained in the Cochrane Handbook for Systematic Reviews of Interventions [6], and integrates evidence from qualitative and quantitative studies. Critical appraisal frameworks for the analysis and interpretation of evidence from qualitative and quantitative research have been adopted [i.e. 7, 8]. We have not excluded any of the studies that did not meet a minimum quality threshold, since the exclusion of such studies would lead to the loss of valuable information.

This systematic review summarizes the reported effects of socially assistive robots on elderly wellbeing, and reveals the potential opportunities and drawbacks of the design of field trials in this domain. It attempts to address the following question: "What does existing research tell us about socially assistive robots?" In total, 1231 potentially relevant publications were found and screened, which resulted in 95 publications meeting the inclusion criteria. In synthesizing these studies, we had the opportunity to consider similarities, differences, and limitations. The review also sheds light on how SAR has the potential to improve the wellbeing of elderly people, and reveals the areas that have been neglected. All in all, this systematic review intends to offer a better foundation for the design of future research.

The applications of SAR need to be reviewed for the purpose of future development in the field, and several researchers have begun to do so. In a very valuable review which was carried out in September 2009, Bemelmans et al. [9] outlined the effectiveness of SAR and its effects on the elderly and observed that, while there are reported positive effects, the scientific value of the evidence is inadequate. This review was carried out in 2009 and includes 41 publications, reporting on 17 studies, and involving four robot systems and one undefined robot. Another valuable review was conducted by Broekens et al. [10] who summarized the effects of assistive social robots on the health and psychological wellbeing of elderly people. This review was undertaken in 2007 and includes 43 studies and the application of eight different robots in elderly care. A more recent review has addressed the role of social commitment robots in the care of elderly people with dementia [11]. This review was conducted in 2012 and includes a total of 21 studies. Several other recently-published reviews can be found in the literature [e.g. 12–14] although these are neither systematic nor focused on socially assistive robots.

One major contribution of this research is that it is holistic and includes almost all the studies reported in previous reviews. Because it is a comprehensive review, it may prove to be a valuable reference for future researchers. Some of the previous reviews focused only on specific databases or did not cover all the related research areas (e.g. healthcare, engineering, and robotics). Moreover, they rarely cite studies from 2009 onwards; however, according to our finding if we select the latest publication as the representative of each group, the number of studies has doubled since 2009. Apart from the increase in the number of related studies, several recent studies have conducted field trials with significantly larger samples [e.g. 15 which had 80 participants]. Moreover, some recent studies carried out trials in other geographical regions such as Khosla et al. [16] in Australia, and Jayawardena et al. [17] in New Zealand. Furthermore, some robots such as Brian, Ifbot, and Matilda have been used in elderly care since 2009. Additionally, the number of home trials has increased dramatically in recent years and the results have been more conclusive since human-robot interaction has taken place without the presence and intervention of researchers.

Another contribution of this review is that, by comparing previous reviews, it links the findings to wellbeing theory and PERMA, which enables future studies be designed with a stronger focus on wellbeing. The existing reviews have drawn general conclusions regarding the positive effects on the elderly or reported positive effects of SAR in terms of (socio) psychological and physiological parameters. However, this review explicitly mentions the reported effects of SAR and summarizes the effects according to PERMA.

2 Background

Researchers broadly categorize assistive robots for the elderly into two major groups, rehabilitation and assistive social robots [10]. Rehabilitation robots are intended for physical assistive purposes and are typically not communicative; these types of robots include artificial limbs and exoskeletons [18], robotic walker [19, 20], and smart wheelchairs [21]. There are two sub-categories of assistive social robots: service robots for supporting basic tasks of independent living, and companion robots for enhancing the health and psychological wellbeing of the elderly. In another study, healthcare robots are classified into health and safety monitoring, physical assistant, and companion robots [22].

Researchers in the field of SAR are trying to assist elderly people to experience objectively healthy living standards and to feel subjectively satisfied. It could be presumed that the eventual goal of SAR is to enhance the wellbeing and quality of life of elderly. Many researchers agree that wellbeing is a multifaceted concept [e.g. 23–26] and a large range of wellbeing definitions exist [27], although there is disagreement about which components to take into account [28]. Thus, there is a need for methods to collect and merge subjective and objective information. According to a group of researchers, wellbeing is "the dynamic process that gives people a sense of how their lives are going through the interaction between their circumstances, activities, and psychological resources" [24].

Diener and Seligman [29] state, "Current measurement of well-being is haphazard, with different studies assessing different concepts in different ways" (p. 2). In some studies [e.g. 30–32] the effects of robots were classified according to three inter-related groups: psychological, physiological, and social effects. Also, in another study, Khosla et al. [33] chose five constructs including positive engagement, acceptability through reciprocity, personalization of care, encouragement for healthy living, and usefulness through mental activity engagement, to determine the impacts of robots on elderly wellbeing. A new approach to wellbeing suggests that there are five constructs of which one or more should be nurtured in order for people to experience wellbeing [34]. These constructs are recognized by the acronym PERMA (Positive emotion, Engagement, Relationships, Meaning, and Accomplishment).

Forgeard et al. [35] state "these five elements are the best approximation of what humans pursue for their own sake[1], which is why they have a place in wellbeing theory". In a highly cited article, Forgeard et al. [35] summarized various domains of wellbeing measures and highlighted wellbeing theory defined by PERMA. Moreover, PERMA has been validated in various settings and contexts such as universities [36], adventure tourism [37], and institutional leadership and culture change [38].

3   Review Design

In this systematic review, the authors followed the principles in the Cochrane Handbook for Systematic Reviews of Interventions [6]. Elderly care and human-computer inter-action are multifaceted and convoluted, so most prior studies in these fields adopted a mixed-methods approach. Hence, the authors incorporated evidence from qualitative, quantitative, and mixed-methods studies.

A list of potentially related studies was compiled in January 2013, based on a search of various databases, and was updated in December 2013. In the first phase, related conference proceedings and journal articles were systematically searched in a broad range of databases including ACM digital library, IEEE digital library (Xplore), ProQuest, SCIRUS, JSTOR, the Cochrane library, the MEDLINE and PubMed, BioMed, and CINAHL. Moreover, a free search was carried out in Google Scholar and La Trobe university library. Only English publications were included, without any limi-tation regarding date of publication.

The search term included the subject ("robot*", "assis* device*", "assis* technolo*", "self-help device", "AIBO", "Care-o-bot", "CERO", "Feelix", "Hug", "iCat", "Ifbot", "Matilda", "Meka", "NAO", "NeCoRo", "PaPeRo", "Paro", "Pearl", "Robocare", "PR2", and "Sparky") in any conjunction with the context ("aged", "elder*", "senior*", "old person*", "old people", and "dementia") and their associated Medical Subject Headings (MeSH) terms, their database-specific thesaurus equivalent and subheadings. The asterisk (*) character was used to replace any other possible character(s) in the search term; as a result, "elder*" stands for the terms "elder", "elders", "elderly" and "elderliness". Usually, existing reviews assist to detect potentially related references [39]; hence, references to existing reviews were scanned and related studies were added to the list.

Edwards et al. [40] state that during the review process, the possibility of excluding relevant studies will be minimized by engaging at least two reviewers. Two authors independently scored each study on a three-point scale (zero = not relevant, one = relevant, two = very relevant) based on the relevance of the title to the subject of socially assistive robots in elderly care. After adding the scores from two reviewers, publications

---

[1] Emphasis was in original text.

that scored zero were excluded. Decisions were made regarding the eligibility of publications with a score of one. Subsequently, abstracts of the remaining publications were extracted and then subjected to the same screening process. After this stage, full texts of the remaining publications were obtained and independently assessed by two reviewers. When there were discrepancies between the reviewers' opinions, these were addressed in face-to-face discussions.

The frameworks developed by Thomas et al. [8] and Spencer et al. [7] were used to appraise the quality of quantitative and qualitative studies respectively. Authors did not exclude any studies because of poor methodological quality.

4   Search Results

After discarding identical publications, a total of 1231 potentially relevant publications were found. In total, two hundred and ninety-six and then 127 publications remained after screenings based on title and abstract respectively. Inter-related agreement between two reviewers were calculated using Cohen's kappa coefficient [41] and resulted in 0.67 and 0.81 which shows good and very good agreement strength between two raters [42]. After a comprehensive review, 94 publications remained which met the inclusion criteria.

The inclusion criteria were: the publications had to be in English, the participants had to be elderly, and the study reported a field trial or human-robot interaction. Technical descriptions of robot characteristics were excluded. None of the publications was excluded based on the location of the interaction; therefore, the interaction could occur in places such as the participant's home, a nursing home, medical center, or retirement village. No robot was excluded based on low level of autonomy or intelligence.

After data extraction, publications were clustered into study groups because many of the screened publications are just republished versions of previous research with some changes. These changes included publishing only some parts of the study, merging and mixing new and old data, or just changing the title. If any study was published more than once with some changes, a study cluster synthesis and a report was conducted based on the one which is most complete or of the longest duration. For example, if two studies are similar, but one included more tests and measures and/or the study lasted longer, we based the report on this study.

5   Quality Appraisal

During the quality appraisal process, several issues emerged, which threaten the generalization of outcomes. One major limitation is the inadequacy of the research methodology. Most of the studies used uncontrolled trials, and there was infrequent use of control groups. Moreover, most of the studies were not long enough to eliminate the novelty effect (e.g. interest or stress in facing new technology) and Hawthorne effect (e.g. in case of supervised interactions), thereby compromising external validity [e.g. 43, 44]. Other limitations include small sample sizes, cultural bias (most of the studies have been carried out in Japan), and gender imbalance.

Research in the field of socially assistive robots is in the early stages and therefore has limitations. Several recommendations have been made to overcome these limitations and improve future research applicability. Innovative research strategies are required in order to address the shortcomings. The quality of observational studies would be improved with the application of methodological approaches such as Randomized Controlled Trial (RCT) to reduce allocation bias [45], triangulation-use of multiple data sources- for rigorous qualitative research [46], and Propensity Score Matching (PSM) to correct for sample selection bias [47]. To improve the quality of studies, trials should be long enough to eliminate the novelty effect, and the sample size should be adequate enough so that the findings can answer the research questions effectively.

Several of the studies overcame some of these limitations. For example, Banks et al. [48] used a control group; Wada et al. [49] implemented very good measures; Wada, Shibata [50] applied a more solid research methodology; Libin, Cohen-Mansfield [51] applied a good methodology and their findings are, arguably, very reasonable. Moreover, Khosla et al. [52] linked each robot service to one aspect of the emotional wellbeing of elderly people.

6   Findings

Although virtually all of the included studies report the positive effects of SAR on the wellbeing of elderly people, there are few studies which tested and reported the effects of SAR on nursing staff, although there is evidence of positive effects such as a decrease in nursing staff's mental poverty [53] and stress [54]. In order to acquire comprehensive and more organized information about the reported effects, we based our discussion on PERMA constructs and tried to link the reported effects with one of the PERMA constructs. However, these constructs are highly interrelated and mapping the effects mentioned in some of the studies to these constructs is difficult. In addition, there is no explicit construct for mapping the physical and physiological wellbeing of elderly people. Keeping these perspectives in view, the following section reviews the reported effects. Some of the reported effects were too general or could be linked with more than one construct, so we created a new category for them - 'Other effects'.

6.1   Positive Emotion

To experience wellbeing, individuals need positive emotion in life such as peace, satisfaction, hope, and love. Positive emotions influence how individuals perceive their overall happiness. In most of the included studies, it is reported that SAR has the potential to produce positive emotions in the elderly (e.g. [51, 54–60]). Some studies pointed out that the feelings and moods of the elderly improved [54, 55, 59, 61, 62], while others stated that SAR increased the sense of security and joy in life of elderly people [62, 63]. Furthermore, it has been observed that elderly people became calmer [64], revealed richer expressions [65], increased laughter [54, 65], and their stress level decreased [55–57] during trials. Moreover, several other studies confirmed that the trials improved the emotional state of elderly people [59, 66].

6.2 Engagement

Engagement is a self-reported psychological state of individuals who are immersed in and are concentrating on an activity [35]. When an individual has clear objectives, is interested in the ongoing activity and receives feedback, s/he is experiencing a high level of engagement [35].

It is reported that elderly people who participated in trials had an evocative experience and could externalize their internal emotions more easily [64]. Some research shows that the daily activities of elderly people increased [67, 68] and they performed movements actively, especially in outdoor activities [69]. In some studies, researchers used a robot to motivate physical exercise and to encourage the elderly to engage in activities [70].

6.3 Relationships

'Relationship' refers to the condition of connection among individuals who are related to, or deal with, each other. Individuals who establish a positive relationship can relate to others and perceive other people in their lives who care about them. It was found that by taking part in field trials and using SAR, elderly people increased their social interactions and activities, networks, and ties [68, 71, 72]. Moreover, it decreased the loneliness experienced by the participants [48, 67]. Researchers have found that using SAR facilitates the establishment of a friendly relationship and encourages communication among elderly people [64, 65, 69]. Moreover, in some cases, participants developed a friendship with the robot [73].

6.4 Meaning

Meaning can be defined in several ways from "the ontological significance of life from the point of view of the experiencing individual" [74] to "feeling of belonging and serving something larger than the self" [34]. Researchers mentioned that robots decreased depression in the elderly who participated in trials [54]. According to Hamada et al. [75], when elderly people engage with SAR, their perception of the external world is more positive.

6.5 Accomplishment

'Accomplishment' means the highest degree of success, attainment, or mastery in a specific area [76]. At an individual level, accomplishment means achieving a desired status and progression toward goals [77]. Accomplishment is strongly related to competence. During a field trial, by winning in one-on-one or group games supervised by the robot, the elderly experienced a sense of achievement [16, 33]. Achieving, achieving perceived autonomy [78] and improvement in response time [79, 80] can be considered as two accomplishments resulting from SAR.

6.6 Other Effects

In this review, the 'other effects' group was added as a category for those outcomes that were too general or could be associated with more than one construct. Some studies reported that the wellbeing of the elderly increased after engaging with robots (e.g. [33, 81]). One study found that using a robot led to improvement in the personalization of care [16, 33]. Moreover, some researchers reported that engaging with robots reduced physically disruptive behavior and overall agitation in elderly people [51, 82]. Several studies (e.g. [61, 83]) reported the positive psychological effects of SAR on the elderly. Tapus [79, 80] refers to improvement in SMMSE (Standardized Mini–Mental State Examination) score, and in another research, Tanaka et al. [84] discuss possible improvement of cognitive function of the elderly by engaging with SAR. However, some studies revealed that SAR could have some negative effects on the elderly; for instance, it could increase the level of anxiety due to fear of breaking or doing something wrong with the robot [85] as well as negligible improvement in users' health [86].

7 Conclusion

Finding and addressing the impacts of SAR on the wellbeing and quality of life of the elderly is important for a variety of stakeholders, from the elderly themselves to health sector policymakers, and from elderly family members to nursing home managers and nurses. Policy makers and practitioners can use this work for health economics evaluation, long-term impact on health care costs and quality of life of the elderly. In total, ninety-five studies in forty-two study groups have been examined and synthesized in this systematic review. Our review revealed that a variety of robots have been developed with different designs, attributes, and applications; however, there is not a single ideal design of SAR.

The results of this systematic review indicate that SAR potentially can enhance the wellbeing of the elderly and decrease the workload of nurses. Because wellbeing is multifaceted, and in order to acquire more organized knowledge, we categorized the reported outcomes according to PERMA (Positive emotion, Engagement, Relationships, Meaning, Accomplishment) [34]. In addition, we included a sixth category for more general or physiological effects. This review revealed that SAR could improve all six sub-categories of elderly wellbeing, especially their positive emotions and relationships. The different aspects of wellbeing are strongly interrelated, and an improvement in wellbeing overall does not necessarily occur as a result of improvement in one aspect only; hence there is a need for a balanced improvement. Therefore, robots which are capable of improving all or most aspects of elderly wellbeing are potentially more beneficial and effective compared to ones with fewer applications; hence, future studies should consider wellbeing from different perspectives. This review also revealed that most of the studies that were examined have focused on the first three aspects of PERMA (positive emotions, engagement, and relationship) and the other two aspects (meaning and accomplishment) have been under-studied. There is still a need for further studies regarding the potential application of SAR.

Furthermore, if consideration is given to individuals' needs, expectations, and preferences, this may lead to improved personalization of care. For example, Wu et al. [87] found that older people and young adults perceived robot expressions differently. They argue that robots should be designed to match the target population. In addition, concentration on person-centered care, multi-modal interaction and data collection translate into a better SAR design. In line with Mayer and Panek [88], we also propose that human-like engagement characteristics of socially assistive robots could be exploited by integrating them seamlessly with other assistive technologies such as tele-health, e-health, and smart homes. Moreover, the development of new approaches such as web-based interfaces and cloud computing is highly recommended in order to overcome the impact of the limited computing and storage capabilities of SAR.

References

1. United Nations Report: world population ageing, 1950–2050. In: United Nations. Department of Economic and Social Affairs. Population division (2002)
2. Levy, Y., Ellis, T.J.: A systems approach to conduct an effective literature review in support of information systems research. Inf. Sci.: Int. J. Emerg. Transdiscipline **9**, 181–212 (2006)
3. Marshall, C., Rossman, G.B.: Designing Qualitative Research, 4th edn. Sage Publications Inc., California (2006)
4. Cooper, H.M.: The Integrative Research Review: A Systematic Approach. Sage Publications Inc., Beverly Hills (1984)
5. Creswell, J.W.: Research Design: Qualitative, Quantitative, and Mixed Methods Approaches, 3rd edn. SAGE Publications Inc., Thousand Oaks (2009)
6. Higgins, J.P.T., Green, S.: Cochrane handbook for systematic reviews of interventions, Version 5.1.0 (2011). The Cochrane Collaboration www.cochrane-handbook.org. Accessed Mar 2011
7. Spencer, L., Ritchie, J., Lewis, J., Dillon, L.: Quality in Qualitative Evaluation: A Framework for Assessing Research Evidence. National Center for Social Research. Government Chief Social Researcher's Office, London (2003)
8. Thomas, H., Ciliska, D., Dobbins, M., Micucci, S.: Quality assessment tool for quantitative studies. In: Effective Public Health Practice Project. McMaster University, Toronto (2003)
9. Bemelmans, R., Gelderblom, G.J., Jonker, P., de Witte, L.: Socially assistive robots in elderly care: a systematic review into effects and effectiveness. J. Am. Med. Direct. Assoc. **13**(2), 114–120.e111 (2012). doi:10.1016/j.jamda.2010.10.002
10. Broekens, J., Heerink, M., Rosendal, H.: Assistive social robots in elderly care: a review. Gerontechnology **8**(2), 94–103 (2009). doi:10.4017/gt.2009.08.02.002.00
11. Mordoch, E., Osterreicher, A., Guse, L., Roger, K., Thompson, G.: Use of social commitment robots in the care of elderly people with dementia: a literature review. Maturitas **74**(1), 14–20 (2013). doi:10.1016/j.maturitas.2012.10.015
12. Nejat, G., Sun, Y., Nies, M.: Assistive robots in health care settings. Home Health Care Manage. Pract. **21**(3), 177 (2009)
13. Shibata, T., Wada, K.: Robot therapy: a new approach for mental healthcare of the elderly – a mini-review. Gerontology **57**(4), 378–386 (2011)
14. Shibata, T.: Therapeutic seal robot as biofeedback medical device: qualitative and quantitative evaluations of robot therapy in dementia care. Proc. IEEE **100**(8), 2527–2538 (2012). doi: 10.1109/jproc.2012.2200559

15. Wada, K., Takasawa, Y., Shibata, T.: Robot therapy at facilities for the elderly in Kanagawa prefecture - a report on the experimental result of the first week. In: RO-MAN, IEEE 2013, pp. 757–761. IEEE (2013)

16. Khosla, R., Chu, M.T., Kachouie, R., Yamada, K., Yoshihiro, F., Yamaguchi, T.: Interactive multimodal social robot for improving quality of care of elderly in Australian nursing homes. In: Proceedings of the 20th ACM International Conference on Multimedia, Nara, Japan 2012, pp. 1173–1176. ACM, 2396411 (2012)

17. Jayawardena, C., Kuo, I., Datta, C., Stafford, R.Q., Broadbent, E., MacDonald, B.A.: Design, implementation and field tests of a socially assistive robot for the elderly: HealthBot version 2. In: 4th IEEE RAS & EMBS International Conference on Biomedical Robotics and Biomechatronics (BioRob), 24–27 June 2012, pp. 1837–1842 (2012)

18. Kazerooni, H.: Exoskeletons for human power augmentation. In: IEEE/RSJ International Conference on Intelligent Robots and Systems, (IROS 2005), 2–6 August 2005, pp. 3459–3464 (2005)

19. Glover, J., Holstius, D., Manojlovich, M., Montgomery, K., Powers, A., Wu, J., Kiesler, S., Matthews, J., Thrun, S.: A robotically-augmented walker for older adults. Technical Report, Carnegie Mellon University, School of Computer Science (2003)

20. Morris, A., Donamukkala, R., Kapuria, A., Steinfeld, A., Matthews, J.T., Dunbar-Jacob, J., Thrun, S.: A robotic walker that provides guidance. In: IEEE International Conference on Robotics and Automation, Proceedings. ICRA 2003, 14–19 September 2003, pp. 25–30 (2003)

21. Gomi, T., Griffith, A.: Developing intelligent wheelchairs for the handicapped. In: Mittal, V.O., Yanco, H.A., Aronis, J., Simpson, R. (eds.) Assistive Technology and Artificial Intelligence. LNCS, vol. 1458, pp. 150–178. Springer, Heidelberg (1998). doi:10.1007/BFb0055977

22. Broadbent, E., Stafford, R., MacDonald, B.: Acceptance of healthcare robots for the older population: review and future directions. Int. J. Soc. Robot. 1(4), 319–330 (2009). doi:10.1007/s12369-009-0030-6

23. Diener, E.: Subjective well-being. In: Diener, E. (ed.) The Science of Well-Being. Social Indicators Research Series, pp. 11–58. Springer, Netherlands (2009)

24. Michaelson, J., Abdallah, S., Steuer, N., Thompson, S., Marks, N., Aked, J., Cordon, C., Potts, R.: National Accounts of Well-being Bringing Real Wealth Onto the Balance Sheet. NEF (The New Economics Foundation), London (2009)

25. Pollard, E.L., Lee, P.D.: Child well-being: a systematic review of the literature. Soc. Indic. Res. 61(1), 59–78 (2003). doi:10.1023/a:1021284215801

26. Stiglitz, J.E., Sen, A., Fitoussi, J.P.: Report by the Commission on the Measurement of Economic Performance and Social Progress. Commission on the Measurement of Economic Performance and Social Progress, Paris (2009)

27. Gasper, D.: Understanding the diversity of conceptions of well-being and quality of life. J. Socio-Econ. 39(3), 351–360 (2010)

28. Diener, E., Scollon, C., Lucas, R.E.: The evolving concept of subjective well-being: the multifaceted nature of happiness. Adv. Cell Aging Gerontol. 15, 187–219 (2003)

29. Diener, E., Seligman, M.E.P.: Beyond money: toward an economy of well-being. Psychol. Sci. Public Interest 5(1), 1–31 (2004). doi:10.1111/j.0963-7214.2004.00501001.x

30. Wada, K., Shibata, T.: Living with seal robots; its sociopsychological and physiological influences on the elderly at a care house. IEEE Trans. Robot. 23(5), 972–980 (2007). doi:10.1109/tro.2007.906261

31. Wada, K., Shibata, T., Saito, T., Tanie, K.: Relationship between familiarity with mental commit robot and psychological effects to elderly people by robot assisted activity. In: IEEE International Symposium on Computational Intelligence in Robotics and Automation, 16–20 July 2003, pp. 113–118 (2003)

32. Wada, K., Shibata, T.: Robot therapy in a care house - results of case studies. In: The 15th IEEE International Symposium on Robot and Human Interactive Communication, ROMAN, 6–8 September 2006, pp. 581–586 (2006)

33. Khosla, R., Chu, M.T., Kachouie, R., Yamada, K., Yamaguchi, T.: Embodying care in Matilda – an affective communication robot for the elderly in Australia. In: ACM SIGHIT International Health Informatics Symposium (IHI 2012), Florida, USA, 28–30 January 2012 (2012)

34. Seligman, M.: Flourish: A Visionary New Understanding of Happiness and Well-being. Free Press, Nariman Point (2011)

35. Forgeard, M.J.C., Jayawickreme, E., Kern, M.L., Seligman, M.E.P.: Doing the right thing: measuring well-being for public policy. Int. J. Wellbeing 1(1), 79–106 (2011)

36. Oades, L.G., Robinson, P., Green, S., Spence, G.B.: Towards a positive university. J. Positive Psychol. 6(6), 432–439 (2011)

37. Dominey-Howes, D., DeLacy, T.: A study of well-being of adventure tourists. In: Taylor, S., Varley, P., Johnson, P. (eds.) Adventure Tourism: Meanings, Experience and Learning. Routledge (2013)

38. Slavin, S.J., Schindler, D., Chibnall, J.T., Fendell, G., Shoss, M.: PERMA: a model for institutional leadership and culture change. Acad. Med. 87(11), 1481 (2012)

39. Littell, J.H., Corcoran, J., Pillai, V.K.: Systematic Reviews and Meta-Analysis. Oxford University Press, Oxford (2008)

40. Edwards, P., Clarke, M., DiGuiseppi, C., Pratap, S., Roberts, I., Wentz, R.: Identification of randomized controlled trials in systematic reviews: accuracy and reliability of screening records. Stat. Med. 21(11), 1635–1640 (2002). doi:10.1002/sim.1190

41. Cohen, J.: Weighted kappa: nominal scale agreement provision for scaled disagreement or partial credit. Psychol. Bull. 70(4), 213 (1968)

42. Altman, D.G.: Practical Statistics for Medical Research. Chapman and Hall, London (1991)

43. Bracht, G.H., Glass, G.V.: The external validity of experiments. Am. Educ. Res. J. 5(4), 437–474 (1968)

44. Bernstein, I.N., Bohrnstedt, G.W., Borgatta, E.F.: External validity and evaluation research. Sociol. Methods Res. 4(1), 101–128 (1975). doi:10.1177/004912417500400106

45. Jadad, A.R.: Randomised Controlled Trials: A User's Guide. BMJ Books, London (1998)

46. Cohen, D.J., Crabtree, B.F.: Evaluative criteria for qualitative research in health care: controversies and recommendations. Ann. Fam. Med. 6(4), 331–339 (2008). doi:10.1370/afm.818

47. Dehejia, R.H., Wahba, S.: Propensity score-matching methods for nonexperimental causal studies. Rev. Econ. Stat. 84(1), 151–161 (2002). doi:10.1162/003465302317331982

48. Banks, M.R., Willoughby, L.M., Banks, W.A.: Animal-assisted therapy and loneliness in nursing homes: use of robotic versus living dogs. J. Am. Med. Dir. Assoc. 9(3), 173–177 (2008). doi:10.1016/j.jamda.2007.11.007

49. Wada, K., Shibata, T., Musha, T., Kimura, S.: Effects of robot therapy for demented patients evaluated by EEG. In: International Conference on Intelligent Robots and Systems, IROS, 2–6 August 2005, pp. 1552–1557 (2005)

50. Wada, K., Shibata, T.: Living with seal robots—its sociopsychological and physiological influences on the elderly at a care house. Robot. IEEE Trans. 23(5), 972–980 (2007)

51. Libin, A., Cohen-Mansfield, J.: Therapeutic robocat for nursing home residents with dementia: preliminary inquiry. Am. J. Alzheimer's Dis. Dement. 19(2), 111–116 (2004)

52. Khosla, R., Chu, M.T., Nguyen, K.: Enhancing emotional well being of elderly using assistive social robots in Australia. In: International Conference on 2013 Biometrics and Kansei Engineering (ICBAKE), pp. 41–46. IEEE (2013)
53. Saito, T., Shibata, T., Wada, K., Tanie, K.: Examination of change of stress reaction by urinary tests of elderly before and after introduction of mental commit robot to an elderly institution. In: 7 International Symposium on Artificial Life and Robotics, pp. 316–319 (2002)
54. Shibata, T., Wada, K., Saito, T., Tanie, K.: Psychological and Social Effects to Elderly People by Robot-Assisted Activity. John Benjamins Publishing Company, Amsterdam (2008)
55. Saito, T., Shibata, T., Wada, K., Tanie, K.: Relationship between interaction with the mental commit robot and change of stress reaction of the elderly. In: IEEE International Symposium on Computational Intelligence in Robotics and Automation, 16–20 July 2003, pp. 119–124 (2003)
56. Giusti, L., Marti, P.: Interpretative dynamics in human robot interaction. In: The 15th IEEE International Symposium on Robot and Human Interactive Communication, ROMAN 2006, Hatfield, UK, 6–8 September 2006, pp. 111–116 (2006)
57. Marti, P., Bacigalupo, M., Giusti, L., Mennecozzi, C., Shibata, T.: Socially assistive robotics in the treatment of behavioural and psychological symptoms of dementia. In: The First IEEE/RAS-EMBS International Conference on Biomedical Robotics and Biomechatronics, BioRob, 20–22 February 2006, pp. 483–488 (2006)
58. Suga, K., Sato, M., Yonezawa, H., Naga, S., Shimizu, J.: Effects of robot-assisted activity on senior citizens-Indicators of HVA, MHPG, and CS concentrations in saliva. J. Anal. Bio-Sci. 26(5), 435–440 (2003)
59. Sakairi, K.: Research of robot-assisted activity for the elderly with senile dementia in a group home. In: SICE Annual Conference, 4–6 August 2004, pp. 2092–2094 (2004)
60. Heerink, M., Krose, B., Evers, V., Wielinga, B.: Influence of social presence on acceptance of an assistive social robot and screen agent by elderly users. Adv. Robot. 23(14), 1909–1923 (2009)
61. Saito, T., Shibata, T., Wada, K., Tanie, K.: Change of stress reaction by introduction of mental commit robot to a health services facility for the aged. In: Joint 1st International Conference on Soft Computing and Intelligent Systems and 3rd International Symposium on Advanced Intelligent Systems (2002)
62. Sabelli, A.M., Kanda, T., Hagita, N.: A conversational robot in an elderly care center: an ethnographic study. In: The 6th International Conference on Human-Robot Interaction, New York, NY, USA 2011, pp. 37–44. ACM (2011)
63. Yamamoto, H., Miyazaki, H., Tsuzuki, T., Kojima, Y.: Entertainment and amusement robot technologies. A spoken dialogue robot, named wonder, to aid senior citizens who living alone with communication. J. Robot. Mechatron. 14(1), 54–59 (2002)
64. Nakashima, T., Fukutome, G., Ishii, N.: Healing effects of pet robots at an elderly-care facility. In: 9th International Conference on Computer and Information Science (ICIS), IEEE/ACIS 18–20 August 2010, pp. 407–412 (2010)
65. Hamada, T., Okubo, H., Shimada, Y., Watanabe, Y., Onari, H., Kagawa, Y., Hashimoto, T., Akazawa, T.: Effective method of robot therapy in a nursing home-study on intervention of therapy. In: International Joint Conference SICE-ICASE, 18–21 October 2006, pp. 3391–3394 (2006)
66. Shibata, T., Wada, K., Ikeda, Y., Sabanovic, S.: Cross-cultural studies on subjective evaluation of a seal robot. Adv. Robot. 23(4), 443–458 (2009)
67. Kanamori, M., Suzuki, M., Oshiro, H., Tanaka, M., Inoguchi, T., Takasugi, H., Saito, Y., Yokoyama, T.: Pilot study on improvement of quality of life among elderly using a pet-type robot. In: IEEE International Symposium on Computational Intelligence in Robotics and Automation, 16–20 July 2003, pp. 107–112 (2003)

68. Tamura, T., Yonemitsu, S., Itoh, A., Oikawa, D., Kawakami, A., Higashi, Y., Fujimooto, T., Nakajima, K.: Is an entertainment robot useful in the care of elderly people with severe dementia? J. Gerontol. A Biol. Sci. Med. Sci. **59**(1), M83–M85 (2004)

69. Sasama, R., Yamaguchi, T., Yamada, K.: An experiment for motivating elderly people with robot guided interaction. In: Stephanidis, C. (ed.) UAHCI 2011. LNCS, vol. 6766, pp. 214–223. Springer, Heidelberg (2011). doi:10.1007/978-3-642-21663-3_23

70. Fasola, J., Mataric, M.: Robot exercise instructor: a socially assistive robot system to monitor and encourage physical exercise for the elderly. In: 2010 Citeseer (2010)

71. Kawaguchi, Y., Shibata, T., Wada, K.: The effects of robot therapy in the elderly facilities. Alzheimer's Dement. **6**(4 Suppl.), S133 (2010). doi:10.1016/j.jalz.2010.05.416

72. Kidd, C.D., Taggart, W., Turkle, S.: A sociable robot to encourage social interaction among the elderly. In: IEEE International Conference on Robotics and Automation, ICRA 15–19 May 2006, pp. 3972–3976

73. Heerink, M., Krose, B., Evers, V., Wielinga, B.: The influence of social presence on enjoyment and intention to use of a robot and screen agent by elderly users. In: The 17th IEEE International Symposium on Robot and Human Interactive Communication, RO-MAN, 1–3 August 2008, pp. 695–700 (2008)

74. Crumbaugh, J.C., Maholick, L.T.: An experimental study in existentialism: the psychometric approach to Frankl's concept of noogenic neurosis. J. Clin. Psychol. **20**(2), 200–207 (1964)

75. Hamada, T., Hashimoto, T., Akazawa, T., Matsumoto, Y., Kagawa, Y.: Trial of robot therapy in elderly people using a pet-type robot. In: Joint 2nd International Conference on Soft Computing and Intelligent Systems and 5th International Symposium on Advanced Intelligent Systems (SCIS&ISIS) (2004)

76. Ericsson, K.A.: Attaining excellence through deliberate practice: insights from the study of expert performance. In: Desforges, C., Fox, R. (eds.) Teaching and Learning: The Essential Readings. Blackwell Publishers Ltd, Oxford. doi:10.1002/9780470690048.ch1

77. Heckhausen, J., Wrosch, C., Schulz, R.: A motivational theory of life-span development. Psychol. Rev. **117**(1), 32 (2010)

78. Mival, O., Cringean, S., Benyon, D.: Personification technologies: developing artificial companions for older people. Paper Presented at the Human Factors in Computing Systems, CHI2004, Vienna, 24–29 April

79. Tapus, A.: Improving the quality of life of people with dementia through the use of socially assistive robots. In: Advanced Technologies for Enhanced Quality of Life. AT-EQUAL 2009, 22–26 July 2009, pp. 81–86 (2009)

80. Tapus, A.: The role of the physical embodiment of a music therapist robot for individuals with cognitive impairments: longitudinal study. In: Virtual Rehabilitation International Conference, Haifa, Israel, 29 June–2 July 2009

81. Hutson, S., Lim, S.L., Bentley, P.J., Bianchi-Berthouze, N., Bowling, A.: Investigating the suitability of social robots for the wellbeing of the elderly. In: D'Mello, S., Graesser, A., Schuller, B., Martin, J.-C. (eds.) ACII 2011. LNCS, vol. 6974, pp. 578–587. Springer, Heidelberg (2011). doi:10.1007/978-3-642-24600-5_61

82. Libin, A., Cohen-Mansfield, J.: Robotic cat NeCoRo as a therapeutic tool for persons with dementia: a pilot study. In: 8th International Conference on Virtual Systems and Multimedia 2002, pp. 916–919 (2002)

83. Saito, T., Shibata, T., Wada, K., Tanie, K.: Change of stress reaction of the elderly by interaction with robot seal in health services facility for the aged. In: Joint 2nd International Conference on Soft Computing and Intelligent Systems and 5th International Symposium on Advanced Intelligent Systems (SCIS&ISIS) (2004)

84. Tanaka, M., Ishii, A., Yamano, E., Ogikubo, H., Okazaki, M., Kamimura, K., Konishi, Y., Emoto, S., Watanabe, Y.: Effect of a human-type communication robot on cognitive function in elderly women living alone. Med. Sci. Monit. **18**(9), CR550–CR557 (2012)
85. Heerink, M., Krose, B., Evers, V., Wielinga, B.: The influence of a robot's social abilities on acceptance by elderly users. In: The 15th IEEE International Symposium on Robot and Human Interactive Communication, ROMAN, 6–8 September 2006, pp. 521–526 (2006)
86. Klamer, T., Ben Allouch, S.: Acceptance and use of a social robot by elderly users in a domestic environment. In: Pervasive Computing Technologies for Healthcare (PervasiveHealth), 2010 4th International Conference on-NO PERMISSIONS, 22–25 March 2010, pp. 1–8 (2010)
87. Wu, Y.-H., Wrobel, J., Cristancho-Lacroix, V., Kamali, L., Chetouani, M., Duhaut, D., Le Pévédic, B., Jost, C., Dupourque, V., Ghrissi, M.: Designing an assistive robot for older adults: the ROBADOM project. IRBM (2013)
88. Mayer, P., Panek, P.: A social assistive robot in an intelligent environment. Biomed. Tech. **58**, 1 (2013)
89. Kachouie, R., Sedighadeli, S., Khosla, R., Chu, M.-T.: Socially assistive robots in elderly care: a mixed-method systematic literature review. Int. J. Hum.-Comput. Interat. **30**(5), 369–393 (2014)

A New Method for OTAs to Analyze and Predict Users' Online Behavior Patterns and Preferences

Rui Kang and Pei-Luen Patrick Rau[✉]

Department of Industrial Engineering, Tsinghua University, Beijing 100084, China
rpl@mail.tsinghua.edu.cn

Abstract. OTAs use traditional statistics models to analyze huge number of data that is generated by the users, and then make predictions on their behavior patterns and preferences. In online tourism industry, statistics models were deeply studied and widely used by many big business companies. However, the author proposed a new model that is able to "freely" analyze and predict users' online behavior patterns. It constructed a framework that is able to build and modify behavior models for different users in varied environments. Every single action conducted by the customer initiates an update of the existing model, which generates changes of parameters in quantity and/or quality. These changes get fed back to the environment where the customer faces, and cause changes of environment parameters in quantity and/or quality. The changes of the environment parameters stimulate another update cycle of the behavior model. In addition, the results of this study, which were based on the real data, demonstrated how users' booking behavior affects the OTA's products recommendations.

Keywords: OBPM model · Online Travel Agency (OTA) · Online behavior pattern · Affordance · Perception · Decision making

1 Introduction

In the global online tourism market, Online Travel Agency (OTA) companies usually provide recommendations on hotels and other tourism products to online customers based on their previous purchase history. In other words, OTAs use traditional statistics models to analyze huge number of data that is generated by the users, and then make predictions on their behavior patterns and preferences. As one of the two branches of statistics, Descriptive Statistics quantitatively describes the main features of collections of information [1]. Inferential Statistics, as the other branch, draws conclusions from data that are subject to random variation [2]. Statistics modeling methodology helped the entire online tourism industry to effectively analyze and predict the customers, and provide recommendations to them. Statistics modeling methodology was commonly recognized as one of the most successful application in this field. Yet, with the development of e-commerce and online tourism industry, it is founded that online customers' preferences are becoming difficult to be predicted comparing to the past. Meanwhile, the author found three bottlenecks that statistics models fail to solve. First of all, if online users generate data that does not at all reveal their own information for reasons, such as

© Springer International Publishing AG 2017
P.-L.P. Rau (Ed.): CCD 2017, LNCS 10281, pp. 683–692, 2017.
DOI: 10.1007/978-3-319-57931-3_55

privacy concerns, the predictions coming out off from statistics models are inevitably wrong and sometimes misleading. Second of all, it is difficult, and in some cases impossible, to find a sample cluster that is large enough to do sampling for statistics models. For example, it is very easy to find angel investors in capital market in the US because there are lots of qualified angel funds and investors, however, because of the financial development stage, there are very limited number of investors that make angel level investment in China. It is hard to find a pool of samples that is large enough to build statistics models. Third of all, statistics model presents overall characters that are common to the majority of the samplings, yet hotel booking behaviors and preferences are always caused by individual characters that are usually impossible to be revealed by statistics models. This is especially true for OTA platforms that are selling products and services to middle and high class level customers. Due to the definition of probability, statistics models inevitably cause these problems but fail to solve them.

2 Literature Review

In academia globally, there is whole bunch of paper studying OTA industry, spreading over lots of areas. For example, Lee et al. [3], studied how online user's decision making pattern may vary according to the user's personal innovativeness level. Wen [4] examined the factors affecting online travel customers' purchasing decision by exploring the literature on the theoretical foundation of factors influencing the travel's online purchasing intentions in general and in tourism industry specifically. Christou and Kassianidis [5] revealed the relationship between consumers' perception of OTAs' characteristics and their intentions to adopt online travel shopping. Austin et al. [6] studied the consumer trust against the transactions on OTA's site, with a view to improving overall understanding of the key influences of an OTA firm's online performance. Mayr and Zins [7] did research in broadening the scope of revealing factors influencing either the benefits and service quality of traditional travel agencies or those of online travel agencies by taking into account various distribution channel options. However, there are very limited amount of research located in how OTAs react to online users' actions. Loh et al.'s work is one of the very few research papers. Loh et al. [8] presented a recommendation system that is aiming to help travel agencies, be them traditional agencies or electronic facilities, to discover what products to recommend to their customers, by seriously utilizing text mining technology. Yet, the author found this recommendation system laboring and time consuming. The system that Loh et al. presented acts as a system that supports the decision making but not directly providing solutions to customers who are not professional and are awaiting for expertise answers.

In this paper, the author proposes a new modeling method to analyze and predict the customers' online behavior patterns and preferences and hence provide them with direct solutions. OTA platforms that embed this model do not necessarily need the customers to have booked hotels or flights or other tourism products in the past. Running this model does not necessarily need large number of statistically similar customers. This is to say, the model proposed in this paper avoids the three bottlenecks that bother the statistics models.

3   Proposal of Model

The author's model is able to "freely" analyze and predict users' online behavior patterns. Hence the author names his model Online Behavior Prediction Modeling (OBPM) model. OBPM model was given birth by human behavior modeling. It constructed a framework that is able to build and modify behavior models for different users in varied environments. Every single action conducted by the customer initiates an update of the existing model, which generates changes of parameters in quantity and/ or quality. These changes get fed back to the environment where the customer faces, and cause changes of environment parameters in quantity and/or quality. The changes of the environment parameters stimulate another update cycle of the behavior model as illustrated in Fig. 1.

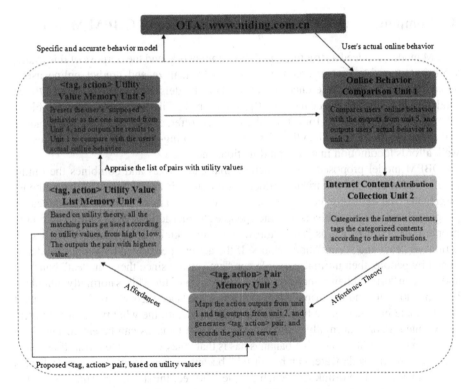

Fig. 1. Updating circle of users' behavior modeling

When the customer finishes his/her online behavior, OBPM model terminates the update circle accordingly. This process explains why the same user was given to different hotel recommendations when they had differed needs or preferences in their mind. To speak in more general way, different mind set generates different needs, which accordingly leads to different actions and performances; different actions cause different types and/or amount of changes of the OTA's platform contents, which would be perceived by the customer, who then performs different actions to satisfy his/her needs, initiating another update circle.

As shown in Fig. 1, all the data needed in this model, comes from the online actions directly and indirectly performed by the user. This, indeed, guarantees the real-time modeling update. This methodology adopted Observe, Orient, Decide, and Act Loop concept (OODA Loop) [9]. The actions executed by the user initiates a new round of OODA loop, i.e. a circling of <tag, action> matching pair update. With each cycle, the user's model in the back end "gets to know" more accurately about what can be done on the hotels on OTAs' website. This is to say, the new model uses the <tag, action> pair to categorize the hotels as well as actions that can be done onto these hotels. Each action stimulates an update circle of the model in the back end. This emboldens that the prediction accuracy grows with the number of customer's actions.

4   Components and the Running Mechanism of OBPM Model

OBPM model is indeed a structural modeling framework, and the purpose of this framework is to provide best-of-breed models, and to analyze and predict online users' behavior patterns and preferences by using these models. The base theory of OBPM model is Gibson's affordance theory [10]. According to Gibson, people perceive objects in terms of the possibilities for actions these objects offer, or afford, people. The contour and shape of a coffee mug handle affords people grasping–lifting–drinking, and a sidewalk affords locomotion in a general direction, and so on.

OBPM model proposed a new method that categorizes and combines the online hotels, flights and other tourism products based on their attributes. Affordance theory asserts that the actions executed on objects by people are in fact not determined by people-selves but by the objects on which people conduct actions. For example, normally people take actions such as "sit", "throw out", and "kick" upon chairs, but not such actions as "eat" and "drink" upon chairs. If the actions performed by people are determined by people, then normally people can "eat" chairs since they can "eat" bananas, and they can "drink" chairs since they can "drink" soda water. This is normally ridiculous if people do "eat" and/or "drink" chair actions. Affordance theory explains to us why it is not people but the objects that have the rights to determine what types of actions to be executed. People normally "eat" bananas because bananas can be eaten. This is to say that one of the attributes that bananas has is that "they can be eaten to stuff people". And likewise, the soda water can be "drunk" because it has the attribute that indicates the soda water can be drunk to quench people who feel thirsty. In the author's model, when people observe contents on OTAs' website they actually perceive the attributes of these contents. As long as they perceive the objects' attributes, they see the <tag, action> matching pairs and realize what set of actions they can execute on the objects. The adoption of Affordance Theory forms the solid ground for the author's creative new model.

Based on Gibson's Affordance theory [10], the author established the perception module, the first kernel module, inside the model. The perception module permits online users to monitor the tourism products to find out what actions they can do to or with those tourism products. The perception is based on "affordiances" which is a form of distributing perception tags so that they can be easily categorized and combined. These tags hold ways that customers see the tourism products, actions that can be conducted onto the products under a given perception tag, and what these actions afford the users in terms of filling their needs. The online users only need to be aware of their needs. When they scan the OTA's websites they pick the tag with the action that best satisfies their need structure (highest utility action choice).

The affordance approach was taken to satisfy engineering constraints rather than theoretical concerns, but there is no shortage of theoretical justification for making such a move. In his landmark literature, The Perception of the Visual World [11], Gibson argued that people perceive the objects in their environment in terms of their affordances, or the opportunities for action that they provide. In this model, the <tag, action> pair memory categorizes the the internet contents based on perceptions they afford people, and use different tags to differentiate various categorizations. At the same time, the whole set of tags can be recombined freely in real time, and recorded on the server. In other words, the <tag, action> pair memory (Unit 3 in Author's model) first determines the mapping between the online tourism products and actions that can be performed onto them, which provides solutions to following questions: (1) how these tourism products are perceived, (2) what set of actions can be executed onto the objects, and (3) what and how much the action executors can obtain if they perform the actions on these tourism products. Figure 2 illustrates the mechanism of semantic markups of perceptions that online tourism products afford people.

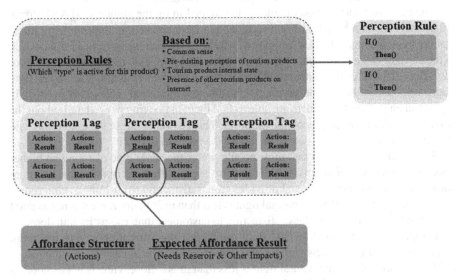

Fig. 2. Semantic markup of online tourism products

Another innovation worth mentioning in this model is that it borrows the idea of utility theory. The author does not inherit deep from utility theory because in the current version model he uses dualistic structure to indicate the model's prediction on the user's preferences. The author uses the following formula

$$I = \begin{cases} 1, \text{ if the activation of the action gives positive utility} \\ 0, \text{ others} \\ -1, \text{ if the activation of the action gives negative utility} \end{cases}$$

where the value of the utility V_Utility = I, to process the data that OTA's platform presets and updates.

5   Real Data Example

The author collected the real data from Niding (www.niding.com.cn), an Online Travel Agency (OTA) website that is mainly serving Chinese travelers. Niding has been running in the industry for more than six years and is up to now the largest pre-pay platform of four- and five-star hotels in China. The website has more than 10000 four and five star hotels in China, which cover 100% first and second tier Chinese cities and 95% of third tier (and lower tiers) cities. This platform also provides flight booking services for airlines from any city in the world to any city in the world. The author embedded his model in the back end of the platform, so that online users' preferences and behavior pattern can be better analyzed and managed.

One customer wanted hotel booking and logged in on the author's OTA platform. After categorization based on his criteria the platform showed up the following information about the hotels to the customer: (1) the hotel has 6 elevators and 41 floors, each of the elevators takes customers right up to the top floor, (2) club rooms starts from floor 21 to floor 30, and (3) the restaurant for club room customers is in floors 25 and 26 (two floors are connected by inside stairs). All the above information is clearly showed up in more than one place. Customers are able to find them in booking page, details about the hotel, as well as other places on the platform. This customer chose the club room, and specifically marked that he wanted to choose the room in floor 21.

Statistical data indicates that most people prefer the same type of rooms in higher floors. Particularly, club rooms in 30th floor are tagged with the attribution that has more natural lights and better view, and provides more satisfaction to customers; club rooms in 21st floor are tagged that the natural light is less than in 30th floor, view is not as good as in 30th floor, and provide less satisfaction to customers than rooms in 30th does.

Particularly, club rooms in 30th floor are tagged the attribution saying has more natural lights and better view, and provides more satisfaction to customers; club rooms in 21st floor are tagged that natural light is less than in 30th floor, view is not as good as in 30th floor, and provide less satisfaction to customers than rooms in 30th does. When the customers see multiple choices of the club rooms in the sense of in multiple floors, internet content attribution collector 2 and <tag, actions> pair memory 3 automatically combine and organize the content tags in the following structure, and pass the <tag, actions> pair into <tag, actions> utility value list memory 4 (Table 1).

Table 1. Structure of perception tags on Club rooms of the hotel

30th floor, more natural light, better view, more satisfaction to customers	21st floor, less natural light, no better view, less satisfaction to customers
Club rooms	

Usually people prefer rooms with more natural light and better window view, thus <tag, actions> utility value list that memory 4 presets, and activates the content tags in the following way (Table 2).

Table 2. Pre-set activation of perception tags on Club rooms of the hotel

30th floor, more natural light, better view, more satisfaction to customers	21st floor, less natural light, no better view, Less satisfaction to customers
Club rooms	

We presumably believe that taking the action "choose on the hotel that is tagged 30th floor, more natural light, better view, more satisfaction to customers" provides the online user with higher utility score than "choosing the room in 21st floor"; taking the action "choose on the hotel that is tagged 21st floor, less natural light, no better view, Less satisfaction to customers" provides the online user with lower utility score. This is to say, <tag, actions> utility value list memory 4 output the following three pieces of information to highest <tag, actions> utility value memory 5, and meanwhile feedback the above activation status into <tag, action> pair memory 3.

- <30th floor, more natural light, better view, more satisfaction to customers, choose, $U = A$>
- <21st floor, less natural light, no better view, Less satisfaction to customers, choose, $U = B$>
- $(A > B)$

Highest <tag, actions> utility value memory 5 receives the order from <tag, actions> utility value list memory 4 and set <30th floor, more natural light, better view, more satisfaction to customers, choose> as the standard <tag, actions> pair for online users booking club rooms and passes the results into the online behavior comparison unit 1, so that the results from Highest <tag, actions> utility value memory 5 would be compared with the user's actual online behavior.

Yet, the information that online behavior comparison unit 1 actually receives from the platform is that the user chooses the club room that is on 21st floor, which has less natural light and less quality of window view, and thus outputs <21st floor, less natural light, no better view, Less satisfaction to customers, choose> pair into internet content attribution collector 2. Internet content attribution collector 2 receives the order from online behavior comparison unit 1, and finds that although club rooms on 30th floor with more natural light and better window view are statistically preferable to most customers, the less height of floor in which the club rooms are located is what this particular customer does need. With this piece of information noted, Internet content attribution collector 2 transmits the following data into <tag, actions> pair memory 3 (Table 3).

Table 3. Updated activation of perception tags on Club rooms of the hotel

30th floor, more natural light, better view, more satisfaction to customers	21st floor, less natural light, no better view, Less satisfaction to customers
Club rooms	

<tag, actions> pair memory 3 updates the analysis and predictions about this customer, and outputs this piece of information to the OTA platform via <tag, actions> utility value list memory 4 and highest <tag, actions> utility value memory 5. Thus the entire system of the author's model gets updated.

Next, we see how this mechanism works when more than one seats in business class flight are available (note that both the size and space of the seats in business class are large enough so that the possibility of seats being tight is ruled out). Internet content attribution collector 2 and <tag, actions> pair memory 3 automatically combine and organize the content tags in the following structure (Table 4).

Table 4. Structure of perception tags on seats on international flight seats

Window seat, good window view, not suitable for passengers suffering from acrophobia	Aisle seat, no window view, suitable for passengers suffering from acrophobia
International flight, first and business class seats	

and pass the following tag combination into <tag, actions> utility value list memory 4 according to the set of tags that are already attributed to the customer (Table 5).

Table 5. Updated activation of perception tags on international flight seats

Window seat, good window view, not suitable for passengers suffering from acrophobia	Aisle seat, no window view, suitable for passengers suffering from acrophobia
International flight, first and business class seats	

Hence the author's platform would be able to provide this seat recommendation to this customer and choose services that is more suitable to this customer, i.e. the aisle seat with no window view, which might be preferable to most other customers though. In this way, the model "knows" the customer's preference and hence becomes able to analyze and predict this customer's other behaviors and preferences.

6 Conclusion and Future Work

- OBPM model constructed a framework that is able to build and modify behavior models for different users with different behaviors in different environments. Every sub-model and module deserves research work on it. None of the Emotion Module, and Decision Making Module would be able to sustain without solid academic adoption on theories and systematic reasoning. Future work would include the specific research on each of the sub-models and their base theories.

- The calculation of the utility value in this proposed algorithm is rough and simplified. The author processes the utility values as binary structured digit. How to use values from 0 to 1 to replace the binary values to make the algorithm and model more precise is one of the areas that future work locates.

- Two real data example is presented in this paper, yet whether this model and base algorithm can be utilized in more instants and even the whole internet in China deserves more future research work. And if the answer is yes, what modifications should be made accordingly also deserve deep research work.

Acknowledgments. We wish to thank Niding (www.niding.com.cn) for providing the real data, and the relevant employees for openly discussing their opinions.

References

1. Mann, P.: Introductory Statistics, 2nd edn. Wiley, Hoboken (1995). ISBN 0-471-31009-3
2. Upton, G., Cook, I.: Oxford Dictionary of Statistics. Oxford University Press, Oxford (2008). ISBN 978-0-19-954145-4
3. Lee, H.Y., Qu, H.L., Kim, Y.S.: A study of the impact of personal innovativeness on online travel shopping behavior—a case study of Korean travelers. Tour. Manag. **28**, 886–897 (2007)
4. Wen, I.: Factors affecting the online travel buying decision: a review. Int. J. Contemp. Hosp. Manag. **21**(6), 752–765 (2009)
5. Christou, E., Kassianidis, P.: Consumer's perceptions and adoption of online buying for travel products. J. Travel Tour. Mark, **12**(4), 93–107
6. Austin., N., Ibeh., K.I.N., Yee., J.C.C.: Consumer trust in the online travel marketplace. J. Internet Commer. **5**(2), 21–39
7. Mayr, T., Zins, A.: Acceptance of online vs. traditional travel agencies. Anatolia: Int. J. Tour. Hosp. Res. **20**(1), 164–177
8. Loh, S., Lornzi, F., Saldana, R., Licthnow, D.: A tourism recommender system based on collaboration and text analysis. Inf. Technol. Tour. **6**
9. Boyd, J., Richard, J.: Destruction and creation. US Army Command and General Staff College (1976)
10. Gibson, J.: The Ecological Approach to Visual Perception. Houghton-Mifflin, Boston (1970)
11. Gibson, J.: The Perception of the Visual World. Houghton-Mifflin, Boston (1950)
12. Silverman, B., Bharathy, G., Johns, M., Nye, B., Eidelson, R., Smith, T.: Sociocultural games for training and analysis. IEEE/SMC Trans., 1113–1130 (2007). IEEE Press, New York
13. Cornwell, J., O' Brien, K., Silverman, B., Toth, J.: Affordance theory for improving the rapid generation, composability, and reusability of synthetic agents and objects. In: 12th Conference on Behavior Representation in Modeling and Simulation (BRIMS, formerly CGF), pp. 12–15. SISO (2003)
14. John, B.: Reducing the variability between novice modelers: results of a tool for human performance modeling produced through human-centered design, behavior representation in modeling and simulation. In: 19th Conference on Behavior Representation in Modeling and Simulation (BRIMS) (2010)
15. Saaty, T.: Decision making with the analytic hierarchy process. Int. J. Serv. Sci. **1**(1) (2008)

16. Silverman, B., Johns, M., Cornwell, J., O' Brien, K.: Human behavior models for agents in simulators and games: part I–enabling science with PMFserv. Presence **15**(2), 139–162 (2006)
17. McCarthy, C., Mejia, L., Liu, H.: Cognitive appraisal theory: a psychoeducational approach for understanding connections between cognition and emotion in group work. J. Spec. Group Work **25**(1), 104–121 (2000)
18. Richards, C.: Certain to Win: The Strategy of John Boyd, Applied to Business. Xlibris Corporation, Bloomington (2004). ISBN 1-4134-5377-5
19. Norman, D.: The Design of Everyday Things: Revised and Expanded Edition, p. 11. Basic Books, New York City (2013). ISBN 978-0465050659
20. Neisser, U.: Introduction: the ecological and intellectual bases of categorization. In: Neisser, U. (ed.) Concepts and Conceptual Development: Ecological and Intellectual Factors in Categorization, chap. 1, p. 12. Cambridge University Press (1989). ISBN 9780521378758
21. Gibson, J.: The theory of affordances. In: Shaw, R., Bransford, J. (eds.) Perceiving, Acting, and Knowing (1977). ISBN 0-470-99014-7 (1977)

A Pilot Study of Mining the Differences in Patterns of Customer Review Text Between US and China AppStore

Lisha Li[(⊠)], Liang Ma, Pei-Luen Patrick Rau, and Qin Gao

Department of Industrial Engineering, Tsinghua University,
Beijing, People's Republic of China
li-ls15@mails.tsinghua.edu.cn

Abstract. With the fast growing of AppStore market and the developing of techniques in opinion mining, this study was aimed to investigate the sentiment and opinions of customer reviews in both China AppStore and US AppStore, and identify the difference of key term and patterns of apps reviews among different genres and between China AppStore and US AppStore. Results showed that there were small differences in using adjective words used or expressing key opinions. The result of this study could help publisher to extract useful customer feedback from customers reviews when publishing apps in foreign countries.

Keywords: Cross-cultural product and service design · Cultural differences · Review mining

1 Introduction

In recent years, mobile services and platforms have achieved critical mass in the information and communications technology industry. The key to their success has been mobile app services, including naive softwares and platforms that offer internet-based services with good user experiences [9]. With iOS being one of the major mobile phone operation systems, its app service platform, Apple's App Store (henceforth, AppStore) also prosper in app service market with a growing number of publishers and users. Since AppStore launched with only 500 apps and a dozen developers in July 2008, the market increased to over 2,281,240 apps and 529,078 active app publishers in April 2016 [11]. By April 2016, there were 155 AppStore territories that are available for apps to be sold in the corresponding countries or regions [1]. And up to September 2016, a total of 140 billion of apps were downloaded by users from all over the world [13]. In this rapidly growing market, for publishers that have their apps published in multiple AppStore territories, it is very important to adapt to the local market, and adjust contents of apps accordingly.

AppStore provide a rich source of information about apps, including one app's price, description, technical information, and customer ratings and reviews, which could provide both qualitative and quantitative data about the customer

© Springer International Publishing AG 2017
P.-L.P. Rau (Ed.): CCD 2017, LNCS 10281, pp. 693–702, 2017.
DOI: 10.1007/978-3-319-57931-3_56

perception of the apps, and is very important for both customers and apps publishers. On the one hand, customers' ratings and reviews of apps would affect other customers' purchase decisions, this effect is equivalent to the persuasive effect studied in the advertising literature [6]. Meanwhile, online customer review system is one of the most powerful channels to generate online word-of-mouth [5], and earlier studies have found that word-of-mouth may affect others' decisions in different social contexts [10]. According to previous studies, online reviews have significant impact on sales [4,6]. On the other hand, for publishers, customer review is a major source for the feedback. Other feedback source for apps including e-mail feedback and blogs. Feedback could reveal bugs or features of the current version that need to be fixed or improved.

Customer review in AppStore is spontaneous customer feedback, which has rich sources of information. However, these sources are much less structured than traditional surveys for customer satisfaction studies. The information is contained in free-style text, not in a set of answers elicited for a specific set of questions. With the advent of automatic techniques for text mining such as clustering and key term extraction, free-form customer opinions can be processed efficiently and distilled down to essential topics and recurring patterns of content. Researchers have begun to focus on the analysis of opinion typically using supervised machine learning techniques [8]. For example, by analyzing online reviews of computer game, the characteristics of computer games and user experience in game play could be identified [14]. By using linguistic techniques, researchers have extracted and analyzed the most important factor a moviegoer considers when rating a movie online, and found that reviewers mainly discuss their personal evaluation rather than discouraging or encouraging readers to see the movie [12]. By clustering rare textual opinions based on point-wise mutual information and using externally imposed review semantics on a data set from Amazon containing sales data and consumer review data for digital cameras and camcorders over a 15-month period, researchers have analyzed the consumers' relative preferences for different product features and use the textual data to predict future changes in sales [2].

With the fast growing of AppStore market and the developing of techniques in opinion mining, this study was aimed to investigate the sentiment and opinions of customer reviews in both China AppStore and US AppStore, and identify the difference of key term and patterns of content in apps reviews among different genres and between China AppStore and US AppStore. The result of this study could help publisher to extract useful customer feedback from customers reviews when publishing apps in foreign countries, and provide a insight of cultural differences in writing apps reviews between Chinese and American. To be specified, the research questions of this study were:

RQ1. Between America AppStore and China AppStore, and among different genres, is there any difference of patterns in customer review for top-selling apps?

RQ2. What is the portion of app-review relevant words in the review text for top selling apps, is there any difference among different genres, and between China AppStore and America AppStore?

2   Method

Data Collection

Review text and relative data were collected from the following four genres in both US AppStore and China AppStore: Social Networking, Photo & Video, Games, and Entertainment. The reason of choosing these four genres was that in the top chart for each genre there were enough common apps in both US AppStore and China AppStore, and there were enough reviews for apps in the top chart. For each genre, apps in the top 200 free apps chart and top 200 paid apps chart were collected, therefore the total number of apps that were included in this study were 3200. A web crawler was developed to collect the app information, review text, and other relative data. For each app, the collected app information including region (US or China), app name, genre, release date, overall average rating, overall number of ratings, and app price for paid apps. Fifty most recent reviews were collected for each app, or all of the reviews if total number of reviews was less than 50. Review title was collected together with review text for each review. Apart from the most recent reviews, all reviews of some selected apps were collected as well.

Natural Language Processing

For reviews wrote in English, processing raw review text including the following steps: removing irregular characters, converting to lower case, word tokenization and part-of-speech tagging, stemming and lemmatizing, and removing stop words, calculating word frequencies, and generating term frequency-inverse document frequency (TF-IDF) matrix. For reviews in Chinese Store, steps of processing raw text were similar to processing English text, with the lack of converting to lower case, and stemming and lemmatizing. We used Natural Language Toolkit (NLTK) [3] for English word tokenization and part-of-speech tagging, and Jieba [7] for Chinese word tokenization and part-of-speech tagging. When generating TF-IDF matrix, each review was treated as a document.

Reviews Clustering

We selected k-means clustering algorithm to cluster the reviews. This algorithm is widely used in document clustering and text-mining for it's simplicity. Considering the fact that online reviews have a wide variance in lengths, we chose cosine distance for k-means algorithm so that the cluster results would be independent to the lengths of reviews. The cosine distance were calculated from TF-IDF matrix, which were calculated during the natural language process

Noise Point Detection

The density-based spatial clustering of applications with noise (DBSCAN) algorithm views clusters as areas of high density separated by areas of low density. Clusters found by DBSCAN can be any shape, as opposed to k-means which assumes that clusters are convex shaped. This algorithm can be used to detect noise point, but the result is heavily related to the input parameters. In this study, we used DBSCAN to find noise reviews which were less relevant other reviews.

3   Results

The number of apps and reviews collected were showed in Table 1. The rest of this section showed the results of frequent terms analysis, clustering analysis, and noise review detection. All Chinese have been translated into English for understanding and comparison.

Table 1. Number of reviews collected

Genre	Number of reviews collected	
	US	CN
Social networking	13,533	11,865
Photo & video	16,024	14,096
Games	16,771	16,871
Entertainment	14,952	12,651

3.1   Frequencies of Adjectives

Figures 1 and 2 showed the top 20 frequent adjective words of US reviews and Chinese·reviews in the whole review collection. Words like "good", "great", "fun", and "easy" were most frequent in both US and Chinese reviews. For US reviews there was no adjectives with negative sentiment in the top frequent adjective words. Similarly, for Chinese reviews, only one adjective with negative sentiment, which was "boring", occurred in the 20 most frequent adjective words. For Chinese reviews, the term of "not bad" was the most frequent adjective words and had much higher frequency than the rest of adjectives. In US reviews, "great" and "good" were top two frequent words, and compared with Chinese reviews, the gap between the frequence of the most frequent adjective and the frequencies of the rest of the adjectives was smaller. The results suggested that customers in both AppStores were more likely to express positive sentiments. And the high frequent of the term "not bad" in China AppSore may caused by the habit of using "not bad" as a common pet phrase among Chinese people.

For both US reviews and Chinese reviews, top 20 frequent adjective words of the reviews of four genres were similar to that of the whole review collection, Tables 2 and 3 showed the top frequent adjective words of four genres of US reviews, the words that were not common among the four genres were presented in boldface type. For US reviews, the number of common adjective words among four genres was 16, and the number of that for Chinese reviews was 10, which suggested that customers in China AppStore wrote their reviews more specific according to the genre of the app.

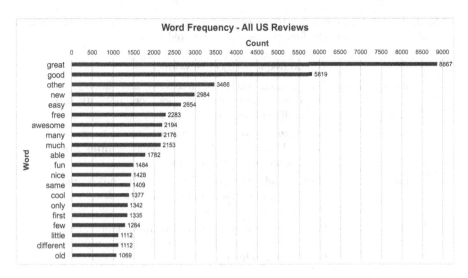

Fig. 1. Adjestive frequency, all US reviews

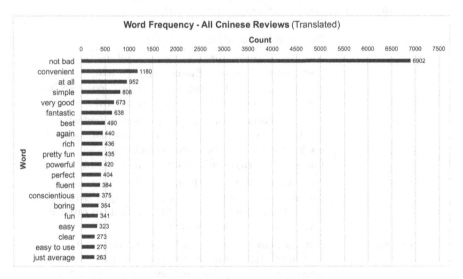

Fig. 2. Adjestive frequency, all Chinese reviews

3.2   Cluster Results

K-means clustering algorithm was performed on both US reviews collection and Chinese reviews collection. We ran multiple k-means with k various from 2 to 16 for both US reviews collection and Chinese reviews collection, and extracted top 50 terms in each cluster for each ran. Then we inspected the results for each ran manually to see if the reviews were clustered by topics or features. The final k

Table 2. Top 20 frequent adjective words of four genres of US reviews, words that were not common among the four genres were presented in bold

Genre	Top 20 frequent adjective words
Social networking	Great, good, other, new, free, easy, able, many, much, **nice**, same, awesome, few, cool, only, **update**, **bad**, different, **old**, first
Photo	Great, good, easy, other, awesome, free, new, many, much, able, **nice**, cool, only, different, **simple**, first, same, **amazing**, few, **perfect**
Games	Great, good, other, new, **fun**, awesome, much, many, free, first, same, **hard**, **little**, only, able, few, different, easy, cool, **bad**
Entertainment	Great, good, other, new, free, many, awesome, much, easy, able, cool, **old**, few, same, only, first, **nice**, **bad**, **little**, different

Table 3. Top 20 frequent adjective words of four genres of Chinese reviews, words that were not common among the four genres were presented in bold

Genre	Top 20 frequent adjective words
Social networking	Not bad, **convenient**, very good, at all, fantastic, best, simple, fun, rich, **fluent**, **easy to use**, **powerful**, **clear**, **boring**, again, perfect, **concise in visual**, **pretty fun**, **beautiful**, **successful**
Photo	Not bad, **convenient**, simple, **powerful**, fantastic, at all, best, very good, perfect, **easy to use**, again, **easy**, **special effects**, **clear**, **concise in visual**, fun, **just average**, rich, **blurred**, **important**
Games	Not bad, at all, **pretty fun**, **conscientious**, simple, **boring**, again, fantastic, very good, simple, rich, **perfect**, fun, **just average**, **fluent**, best, **exquisite**, **important**, **delicate**, **severe**
Entertainment	Not bad, **convenient**, at all, **fluent**, very good, rich, best, fantastic, simple, **clear**, again, perfect, **powerful**, **boring**, fun, **just average**, **pretty fun**, **conscientious**, **easy to use**, **concise in visual**

values were both 12 for US reviews collection and Chinese reviews collection. The extracted top terms and clustered reviews focus were showed in Tables 4 and 5.

Both US reviews and Chinese reviews contained clusters of reviews for complains about compatible and crushes or bugs. Top terms of US reviews contained large amount of "great", "like/love", and "fun", and top terms of Chinese reviews had more specific adjectives or descriptions. Customers in US AppStore complained about the advertisements in apps, while similar complain was not found

Table 4. *K*-means result for US reviews collection

Cluster	Number of reviews	Top 10 terms	Key feature
1	188	Upgrade loved app, app recently compatible, app past really, upgraded app recently, unusable, loved app past, upgraded app, made much, spoiled, app past	Compatible
2	839	Way many ad, every, ad pop, play, fun, ad every, good, time, get, great	**Advertisements in app**
3	855	Game, try, app crash, crashing, work, even, play, keep, time try, crash every	Crash
4	563	Pretty, cool game, app cool, really, game, game cool, seems cool, pretty cool app, cool good, really cool app	Cool game
5	1067	App love, much, fun, use, awesome, really, love love, like, like app, app much	love this app
6	668	Fun play, much, game fun, great fun, really fun, play, super fun, fun fun, nice game, fun use	Fun game
7	917	Great app use, great app work, app use, app work great, great great, work great, app work, great app easy, use, app easy	Great app
8	542	Awesome game, ever played, game much, played, game addicting, game best, addicting, love game addicting, much	Addicting game
9	57	Really, good, like, great original, new feature way, adding new feature, feature way playing, way playing, feature way, playing make	Feature
10	54058	Time, amazing, really, easy, one, would, make, best, please, play	Need fix or update
11	252	Actually work, love work, work perfectly, perfectly, love work great, actually, really, get work, work like, even work	App works good
12	1274	Time, work, refund, buy, work waste, get, even, get money, app waste, want refund	Waste of money, **want refund**

in Chinese reviews. Customers in US AppStore directly complained about "waste of money" and "want refunding", while customers in Chinese AppStore expressed dislike for charging for membership. This results suggested that customers in US AppStore were more used to ask customer services for refunds than customers in China AppStore.

Noise Review Detection

We were also interested in finding "noise" reviews in the review collection. If we consider most reviews were about the apps, then we could use DBSCAN to detect "noise" reviews that had little relevance to the reviewed app. We ran multiple times with different combinations of minimum number of points and distance, and recorded the estimated number of clusters and noise points, and extracted the review text of noise points. The final settings of the two input parameters were that *minimum number of points* = 5, and *distance* = 0.8 for both US reviews collection and Chinese reviews collection. Results showed that in genres of Social Networking and Photo, proportion of irrelevant reviews in US Store would be larger than that in Chinese Store (4.91% and 3.23% for US, 2.82 %

Table 5. K-means result for Chinese reviews collection (translated)

Cluster	Number of reviews	Top 10 terms (translated)	Key feature
1	36648	Live video, software, like, phone, good, fun, photo, game, effect, easy	Display, UI
2	1670	Version, endless, update, case, phone, photo, bug, album, reason, log in	Compatible
3	1237	First time, download, great, display, functions, good, recommend, find, really, work	Good use experience
4	1293	Update, good, can't open, things, display, uninstall, write reviews, delete, like	Can't use
5	836	Uninstall, free, video player, disgusting, really, annoying, app, wish, right away, bad	**Membership, charging**
6	692	First try, work good, friends, fun, trustworthy, app, really, display, like, simple	Easy use, interesting
7	1138	Feel, support, indeed, game, childhood, can't stop playing, recommend, originality, real, cute	Playability
8	984	Fun, filter, friends, app, wish, stickers, display, work great, support, recommend	Usability of photo editing
9	3323	Wish, support, friends, great, functions, utility, powerful, really, phone, reviews	Utility
10	789	Trash, effect, supper, friend, fun, support, useful, app, download, live video	Try this app out
11	2370	Wait for, fix it, support, every time, bug, can't log in, trash, system, can't open, video	Crash, bugs
12	4503	Crash, really, good, classic, interesting, time-killer, can't use, player, support, great	Time-killing game

and 2.65% for China), while in genres of Games and Entertainment, proportion of irrelevant reviews in US Store would be larger than that in Chinese Store (2.43% and 2.74% for US, 3.23 % and 3.42% for China), as showed in Table 6. However this difference in number of noise reviews was not that great, as we set same input parameters for both US reviews collection and Chinese reviews collection.

Table 6. Number of noise review detected

Genre	Number of noise reviews		Percentage of noise reviews (%)	
	US	CN	US	CN
Social networking	664	334	4.91	2.82
Photo & video	518	374	3.23	2.65
Games	408	545	2.43	3.23
Entertainment	410	433	2.74	3.42

Discussion

This study investigated the difference of key term and patterns of content in apps review text among different genres and between China AppStore and US AppStore. We presented a preliminary method for mining customer opinions from free-style review text. This review text mining technique could be used in customer opinion mining and customer satisfaction survey for mobile app publishers and other interested producers with further modification and improvement. The results showed that in general the key term used and opinion expressed in reviews of China AppStore and US AppStore were similar, only minor difference was found. One of the differences was that the reviews wrote by customers in China AppStore were more specifically related to the genres of the reviewed apps. The other differences was that customers in US AppStore were more used to ask customer services for refunds. This differences may caused by the fact that the internet-based services were relatively new to Chinese customers than US customers, and the return policy was more mature in US. As Chinese customers were less used to ask or complain to customer services, they may complain more in the reviews, hence the result of their reviews were more specifically related to the genres. This study was a pilot study, there is still more to explore with review text in this manner, and the comparison between two review collections needed to be more quantified, and works related to culture differences were still needed to investigate further.

Acknowledgement. This research was supported by the National Natural Science Foundation of China (NSFC, Grant Number 71471095). This study was also supported by Tsinghua University Initiative Scientific Research Program under Grant Number: 20131089234.

References

1. Apple: Apple - choose your country or region. https://www.apple.com/choose-your-country
2. Archak, N., Ghose, A., Ipeirotis, P.G.: Deriving the pricing power of product features by mining consumer reviews. Manage. Sci. **57**(8), 1485–1509 (2011)
3. Bird, S., Klein, E., Loper, E.: Natural language processing with Python: analyzing text with the natural language toolkit. O'Reilly Media Inc., Sebastopol (2009)
4. Chen, Y., Fay, S., Wang, Q.: Marketing implications of online consumer product reviews. Bus. Week **7150**, 1–36 (2003)
5. Dellarocas, C.: The digitization of word of mouth: promise and challenges of online feedback mechanisms. Manage. Sci. **49**(10), 1407–1424 (2003)
6. Duan, W., Gu, B., Whinston, A.B.: Do online reviews matter?-An empirical investigation of panel data. Decis. Support Syst. **45**(4), 1007–1016 (2008)
7. fxsjy: Jie ba - Chinese text segmentation. https://github.com/fxsjy/jieba
8. Gamon, M., Aue, A., Corston-Oliver, S., Ringger, E.: Pulse: mining customer opinions from free text. In: Famili, A.F., Kok, J.N., Peña, J.M., Siebes, A., Feelders, A. (eds.) IDA 2005. LNCS, vol. 3646, pp. 121–132. Springer, Heidelberg (2005). doi:10.1007/11552253_12
9. Kim, J., Park, Y., Kim, C., Lee, H.: Mobile application service networks: Apple's app store. Serv. Bus. **8**(1), 1–27 (2014)
10. McFadden, D.L., Train, K.E.: Consumers' evaluation of new products: learning from self and others. J. Polit. Econ. **104**, 683–703 (1996)
11. PGbiz: app store metrics. http://www.pocketgamer.biz/metrics/app-store/

12. Simmons, L.L., Mukhopadhyay, S., Conlon, S., Yang, J.: A computer aided content analysis of online reviews. J. Comput. Inf. Syst. **52**(1), 43–55 (2011)
13. Statista: cumulative number of apps downloaded from the apple app store from July 2008 to September 2016 (in billions). http://www.statista.com/statistics/263794/number-of-downloads-from-the-apple-app-store
14. Zhu, M., Fang, X.: A lexical approach to study computer games and game play experience via online reviews. Int. J. Hum.-Comput. Interact. **31**(6), 413–426 (2015)

The User's Performance Study for Different Layouts of Car's Dashboards

Linghua Ran[⊠], Xin Zhang, Huimin Hu, Chaoyi Zhao,
and Taijie Liu

Ergonomics Laboratory, China National Institute of Standardization,
Beijing 100191, China
ranlh@cnis.gov.cn

Abstract. The automobile driving interface pictures are designed and simulated, including 4 kinds of different layout designs and 3 kinds of different color designs, which are served as the simulation system interface to implement the prototype evaluation. Tobii X2-30 screen-type eye tracker and Ergolab man-machine circular simultaneous platform system are adopted in the experiment to gather and record the users' eye movement data. There are totally 30 participants in 20–45 years old who participated in the experiment. In the formal experiment process, the participators are required to read out the data shown on the picture. The task accomplishment time and recognition accuracy by the participators are selected to be served as the evaluation indexes. After completing the experiment, the mean searching time, mean recognition and reading time and total time are calculated. The difference on recognition and reading efficiency among single picture, pictures with different layout schemes and pictures with different colors are compared, and the influence on identification performance by coding of dashboards and colors are analyzed.

Keywords: User's performance · Layouts · Colors · Coding

1 Introduction

The meters on the car's dashboard are important display components for automobile's normal operation and fault alarm. As one of most important man-machine interfaces in the automobile, the reasonable design of dashboard directly influences driver's recognizing and reading efficiency and also indirectly influences the performance of whole automobile and market competitiveness [1]. In order to ensure that the driver can rapidly and accurately acquire the required information and improve driver's recognizing and reading efficiency, how to properly deal with the man-machine work efficiency problem in this system becomes the emphasis in the meters design.

In complicated and variable driving environment, the cognitive resources with maximal consumption by the driver are visual recognition. Meter's structure and their scribed line as well as size dimension and color of figure and symbol greatly influence

© Springer International Publishing AG 2017
P.-L.P. Rau (Ed.): CCD 2017, LNCS 10281, pp. 703–712, 2017.
DOI: 10.1007/978-3-319-57931-3_57

driver's visibility [2]. The coding of information is the main factor influencing the communication efficiency. Current study on information coding is mainly focused on visual coding, including the character coding, color coding, shape coding and location coding, etc., therein, more common study refers to the study on character coding and color coding. Foreign ergonomics researchers tend to study the influence on decision-making performance by single information coding mode [3–8]. The study mostly focuses on flight and aerospace fields [9, 10], and the study on automobile's dashboard tends to shape coding and character coding [11] and there are seldom studies on color coding and location coding.

Currently, the domestic scholars have implemented some study on information coding, mainly pertaining to optimization on information display mode under certain specified conditions [13, 14]. The study direction refers to the optimization study on piloting operation interface normally [15–17], or tends to the influence on identification performance by single information coding [18–22]. Relevant definitions have been defined in series of national standards and ISO standards for different coding elements and coding principles. The domestic scholars have implemented relevant summarization and elaboration. Bai Rui summarize the design principles and requirements for visual signal's layout, color and mark [23]; Xiuli et al. narrate the design stipulations for color coding and alarm characters [24]; Chunping and Tao narrate the setting requirements and basic design principles for automobile meters based on man-machine engineering [25, 26].

The layout and color coding for main elements on the automobile driving interface are studied and analyzed in this paper based on eye tracking technology, and the subjective feeling on use interface by users is discussed in combination with user's subjective evaluation.

2 Method

2.1 Experimental Instrument

Tobii X2-30 screen-type eye tracker and Ergolab man-machine circular simultaneous platform system are adopted to gather and record participator' s eye tracking data. The problem on layout and design for automobile's dashboard interaction interface is explored.

2.2 Experimental Materials

In the current design of automobile's dashboards, there are four kinds of meters frequently used by drivers, the speedometer, engine tachometer, fuel meter and water thermometer. There are four kinds of layout mode for common meter: left and right symmetrical structure on the left and right; the speedometer and tachometer are larger and locating on both left and right side; the fuel meter and water thermometer are smaller and are placed adjacent to speedometer and tachometer; the speedometer

Table 1. Pictures used for experiment

Lay-out Type	Layout Description	Description on Colors	Picture
Type A	Left and right structure	The ground color of Type A dash-board is black, the dashboard verge, scale and icon are white; Partial scales for Type E are marked with red; the background color of dashboard for Type F is black and apricot, the dashboard verge is grey, the scale is blue and partial scales are marked with red.	
Type B	The tachom-eter and speedometer and distribute on both left and right sides of dashboard	The ground color of Type B dash-board is the same to Type A ; Partial scales for Type E are marked with red; the ground color of dashboard for Type F is black and apricot, the dashboard verge, scale and icon are white, the pointer is blue and par-tial scales are marked with red.	
Type C	The speed-ometer lo-cates at the central loca-tion of dash-board	The ground color of Type C dash-board is the same to Type A; Partial scales for Type E are marked with red; the ground color of dashboard for Type F is black, the dashboard verge, scale and icon are orange.	
Type D	The tachom-eter and speedometer and distribute on both left and right sides of dashboard	The ground color of Type D dash-board is black, the dashboard verge, scale and icon are white; Partial scales for Type E are marked with red.	

locates in the center of dashboard, the speedometer, fuel meter and water thermometer distribute on both sides of speedometer. Based on different meter locations, four categories and 14 kinds of layout schemes are summarized totally. All layout modes are adopted with black-background and white-word character. In addition, one piece is taken from four categories of layouts respectively to make its scale red and three kinds of more special colors was designed. Table 1 show the pictures used in this experiment.

2.3   Experiment Design

The automobile dashboard models adopted in the experiment process are displayed on the computer display in random sequence. The participators are required to recognize and read the readings on the dashboard. The screen brightness and indoor illumination are stable, and the distance between participators and screen is 0.55–0.65 m.

2.4   Experiment Procedure

The participators are required to sufficiently understand the experiment procedures and requirements before the experiment. Each participator is required to recognize and read dashboard models four times. After completing one recognition and reading, the participator should take a rest for half minute to eliminate the error caused by fatigue effect. In the process of experiment, the eye tracker remains the real-time recording. After completing the experiment, the participator is required to complete an available test record sheet.

2.5   Selection for Participators

The experiment participators include 30 teachers and students at school, with 1:1 for male and female proportion, and the age group is 20–45 years old. All participators are right handedness, normal eyesight or corrected eyesight and without severe astigmatism.

3   Results and Discussion

3.1   Searching and Recognition Time for Different Meter Interfaces

The statistics of mean searching time and mean recognition time for each type of meter are as shown in Table 1.

3.2   Recognition and Reading Accuracy for Different Meter Interfaces

The recognition and reading accuracy is as shown in Table 2.

For speedometer, the picture with lowest recognition and reading accuracy is No. 21 with the accuracy of 86.7%. For tachometer, the picture with lowest recognition and reading accuracy is No. 9 p with the accuracy of 83.3%. For fuel meter, the picture with lowest recognition and reading accuracy is No. 11 with the accuracy of 70.0%. For water thermometer, the picture with lowest recognition and reading accuracy is No. 6 with the accuracy of 70.0%.

Table 2. Searching time and recognition time for each type of meter

	Classification	Type A	Type B	Type C	Type D	Type E	Type F
Speedometer	Mean searching time (s)	0.659	0.653	0.368	0.648	0.705	0.683
	Mean recognition and reading time (s)	1.143	1.257	1.215	1.047	1.162	1.408
	Total time consumption (s)	1.802	1.910	1.582	1.695	1.867	2.091
Tachometer	Mean searching time (s)	0.846	0.859	1.117	1.020	0.998	1.132
	Mean recognition and reading time (s)	1.005	1.043	1.133	0.995	1.193	0.974
	Total time consumption (s)	1.851	1.902	2.250	2.015	2.191	2.106
Fuel meter	Mean searching time (s)	0.935	0.925	1.053	1.168	0.927	1.057
	Mean recognition and reading time (s)	0.881	0.983	1.180	0.971	0.969	1.160
	Total time consumption (s)	1.816	1.908	2.233	2.139	1.896	2.217
Water thermometer	Mean searching time (s)	0.860	0.873	2.624	1.062	0.829	3.482
	Mean recognition and reading time (s)	0.816	0.943	0.938	0.801	1.448	0.981
	Total time consumption (s)	1.676	1.816	3.561	1.863	2.277	4.463

3.3 Questionnaire on User's Subjective Preference

The participators should implement the sequencing for the four kinds of meters according to observation frequency during actual driving. The sequencing for four kinds of meters are counted as 4 points, 3 points, 2 points and 1 point. Final total points for four kinds of meters are as shown in Table 3. The observation frequency during

Table 3. Statistics on recognition and reading accuracy for each meter (%)

Meter type	1	2	3	4	5	6	7	8	9	10	11
Speedometer	100	100	100	96.7	100	100	100	90	93.3	100	93.3
Tachometer	93.3	100	96.7	96.7	100	100	100	100	83.3	96.7	96.7
Fuel meter	96.7	90	90	93.3	100	96.7	86.7	96.7	96.7	86.7	66.7
Water thermometer	90	96.7	93.3	76.7	96.7	70	90	93.3	90	96.7	80
Meter type	12	13	14	15	16	17	18	19	20	21	
Speedometer	100	90	100	93.3	100	96.7	100	100	100	86.7	
Tachometer	96.7	96.7	96.7	96.7	100	96.7	96.7	100	96.7	100	
Fuel meter	100	90	96.7	93.3	96.7	100	96.7	90	90	70	
Water thermometer	93.3	90	83.3	93.3	90	93.3	93.3	80	96.7	100	

driving is speedometer, the tachometer, fuel meter and water thermometer rank the second respectively.

In the subjective interviews, the participators are invited to implement the marking on satisfaction for layouts of the several meters, and 5-point system is adopted to calculate the data. Results are as shown in Table 4. The picture with highest point is Nos. 5–6 pictures, the next ones are No. 1–4 pictures and No. 13–14 pictures. The point for left and right layout design is generally higher than the one of symmetrical layout design (No. 8–12 pictures), and the design in No. 7 picture that the tachometer is placed underneath is unpopular.

Table 4. Statistics on observation frequency point for four kinds of meter

	Speedometer	Tachometer	Fuel meter	Water thermometer
Observation frequency	66	47	35	19

4 Analysis

4.1 Meters Layout

The significant difference analysis on total time is implemented for the different layout designs. On 0.05 confidence level, the significant inspection results are as shown in Table 5. It may be observed that the layout design of Type A meter and Type C meter have significant difference on recognition for speedometer and water thermometer. The layout design of Type B meter and Type C meter have significant difference on recognition for speedometer, tachometer and water thermometer and the layout design of Type C meter and Type D meter have significant difference on recognition for tachometer and water thermometer.

Table 5. Statistics on satification point for each meter design

	No. 1–4	No. 5–6	No. 7	No. 8	No. 9	No. 10 and 12	No. 11	No. 13–14
Satisfaction point	3.77	4.30	2.73	2.83	2.73	2.97	2.74	3.63

For speedometer, the picture with shortest total time is Type C, which is 1.582 s. The picture with longest total time is Type F, which is 2.091 s. For tachometer, the picture with shortest total time is Type A, which is 1.851 s. For fuel meter, the picture with shortest total time is Type A, which is 1.816 s. For water thermometer, the picture with shortest total time consumption is Type A, which is 1.676 s. For the speedometer, the design that the speedometer locates in the middle location on Type C picture may shorten the mean searching time. During recognition of tachometer, mean searching time designed for Type A is the shortest. The design for Type F may cause the disturbance for searching and it has a longer searching time. Type C picture's design enables that the tachometer locates on one side of speedometer, the scale presents the longitudinal setting to be unfavorable for recognition so as to cause that the mean searching time for examinee is longer. The fuel meter and water thermometer on Type B picture locate in the upward center the location, the eye movement path is shorter and the searching time may be reduced. The time on recognition and reading designed to be located inside speedometer and tachometer of Type A picture is shorter. The design for Type F may also enable recognition time more longer which reduced examinee's recognition and reading efficiency.

In conclusion, when the speedometer is served as main recognition object, the layout design adopted for Type C is optimal, but it is unfavorable for the other three kinds of meter's recognition and reading. If the consideration is implemented by synthesizing other three kinds of meters, the layout design for Type A and Type B may also be selected.

4.2   Color Matching for Meters

Meter pictures with scale marked with red and special color matching are compared with their original pictures. On 0.05 confidence level, the significant difference analysis on total time is implemented. The significant inspection results are as shown in Table 6. It may be observed that, in the picture with red marking scale, the recognition on speedometer for No. 15 and No. 2 as well as No. 18 picture and No. 14 picture have significant difference. The picture with special colors has significant difference on recognition time with the color of black background and white characters. There is significant difference on water thermometer between on No. 19 picture and No. 4 picture.

Table 6. Significant inspection results to reaction time with different layout

Meter type	Speedometer	Tachometer	Fuel meter	Water thermometer
Type A–Type B	0.296	0.972	0.117	0.279
Type A–Type C	0.135	0.008*	0.311	0.000*
Type A–Type D	0.911	0.972	0.632	0.176
Type B–Type C	0.012*	0.009*	0.575	0.010*
Type B–Type D	0.351	0.944	0.273	0.784
Type C–Type D	0.109	0.007*	0.592	0.020*

Note: "*" indicates P < 0.05, the difference is notable on 0.05 grade.

5   Design Suggestions

The analysis and suggestions for Type A–Type F meters are as shown in Tables 7 and 8.

Table 7. Statistical results to different color interfaces

Factors	Picture No.	Speedometer	Tachometer	Fuel meter	Water thermometer
Mark with red	No. 15- No. 2	0.353	0.006*	0.133	0.608
	No. 16- No. 6	0.648	0.121	0.638	0.538
	No. 17- No. 8	0.696	0.086	0.265	0.155
	No. 18- No. 14	0.177	0.011*	0.686	0.950
Special color matching	No. 19- No. 4	0.004*	0.565	0.126	0.022*
	No. 20- No. 7	0.004*	0.202	0.209	
	No. 21- No. 10	0.000*	0.112	0.159	

Note: "*" indicates $P < 0.05$.

Table 8. Analysis and Suggestions for Type A–Type F

Design type	Analysis and suggestions
Type A	It is suggested that the use for No. 2 picture layout is optimal, the tachometer and fuel meter are located on the left side, and the speedometer and water thermometer are located on the right side
Type B	It is suggested that the use for No. 6 picture layout is optimal, the speedometer and water thermometer are located on the left side, and the speedometer and fuel meter are located on the right side; the layout for No. 7 picture is suggested to be unavailable
Type C	It is suggested that the use for No. 10 picture and No. 12 picture layout is optimal, the speedometer is located in the middle, the tachometer is located on the left side, the fuel meter is located on the right side; it is suggested that the layout for No. 11 picture isn't used; the water thermometer may be located inside identical dashboard together with fuel meter in the mode of easy distinguishing, or the water temperature is displayed on the display screen
Type D	It is suggested that the use for No. 13 picture layout is optimal, the tachometer and water thermometer are located on the left side, and the speedometer and fuel meter is located on the right side
Type E	During recognition for speedometer and tachometer, this color have no obvious effect to improve the recognition speed and accuracy
	During recognition for fuel meter and water thermometer, this color reduces driver's recognition and reading speed, however, the accuracy rate may be improved effectively
Type F	The color of No. 19 and No. 21 picture may reduce the identification efficiency; it is suggested not to use two kinds of color matching
	The color of No. 20 picture may shorten the recognition and reading time, the similar color may be considered to be employed to improve driver's recognition and reading speed

6   Conclusions

- Based on the meter's use frequency, the speedometer should be placed in the most obvious location where the recognition and reading are easy. The speedometer may be placed in the middle location of dashboard (namely, Type C layout design), if other three kinds of meters are required to be synthesized for consideration, the layout design for Type A picture and Type B picture may also be available.
- With the scale for fuel meter and water thermometer with red marking, the accuracy for driver's recognition and reading may be improved effectively. The scale for speedometer and tachometer may be marked with red.
- In the process of meter recognition, the special design for colors easily influences driver's recognition and reading speed and the recognition and reading is prolonged. During design, the use of special colors should be avoided.
- In the experiment, partial examinees regarded the fuel meter as water thermometer. In order to avoid that this kind of mistakes, the fuel meter and water thermometer may be placed separately, and the obvious identification mark should be marked on the dashboard.

Acknowledgment. This work is supported by the National Key Technology R&D Program project number: 2014BAK01B01.

References

1. Chunping, Y., Qi, Y.: Automobile meter design and ergonomics evaluation based on human factor. J. China Safety Sci. **17**(10), 62–66 (2007)
2. Tullis, T.S.: An evaluation of alphanumeric, graphic, and color information displays. Hum. Factors **23**(5), 541–550 (1981)
3. Van Orden, K.F., Divita, J., Shim, M.J.: Redundant use of luminance and flashing with shape and color as highlighting codes in symbolic displays. Hum. Factors **35**, 195–204 (1993)
4. Yeh, M., Wickens, C.D.: Display signaling in augmented reality: effects of cue reliability and image realism on attention allocation and trust calibration. Hum. Factors J. Hum. Factors Ergon. Soc. **43**(3), 355–365 (2001)
5. Yeh, M., Wickens, C.D.: Attentional filtering in the design of electronic map displays: a comparison of color coding, intensity coding, and decluttering techniques. Hum. Factors **43**(4), 543–562 (2001)
6. Destefano, D., Lefevre, J.A.: Cognitive load in hypertext reading: a review. Comput. Hum. Behav. **23**(3), 1616–1641 (2007)
7. Roodenrys, K., Agostinho, S., Roodenrys, S., et al.: Managing one's own cognitive load when evidence of split attention is present. Appl. Cogn. Psychol. **26**(6), 878–886 (2012)
8. Luke, T., Brook-Carter, N., Parkes, A.M., Grimes, E., Mills, A.: An investigation of train driver visual strategies. Cogn. Technol. Work **8**, 15–29 (2006)
9. mance in flight decks equipped with synthetic vision information system displays. Int. J. Aviation Psychol. **14**(1), 79–102 (2004)

10. Wickens, C.D.: Display Formatting and Situation Awareness Model (DFSAM): An Approach to Aviation Display Design. Lähde2 (2003)
11. Iqbal, B.M., Suzianti, A., Nurtjahyo, B.: Military vehicle dashboard design using semantics method in cognitive ergonomics framework. In: Harris, D. (ed.) EPCE 2015. LNCS (LNAI), vol. 9174, pp. 152–163. Springer, Cham (2015). doi:10.1007/978-3-319-20373-7_15
12. Zulizwan S.: Design of Ergonomics Car Instrument Panel and Dashboard (2011)
13. Wei, L., Yuchun, T.: Visual performance on colorful encoding displayed by character. J. Beijing Inst. Technol. 20(4), 485–488 (2000)
14. Damin, Z., Rui, W.: Study on target identification based on cognition characteristic. J. Beijing Univ. Aeronaut. Astronaut. 29(11), 1051–1054 (2003)
15. Qingxin, Z., Damin, Z.: Target identification for different tasks of weighting under multi-interface and multi-task. J. Beijing Univ. Aeronaut. Astronaut. 32(5), 499–502 (2006)
16. Deqian, Z., Zhijun, Z., Hezhi, Y.: VDT visual ergonomics for interface: influence on visual performance by tone factor. Psychol. Sci. 31(2), 328–331 (2008)
17. Zhuang Damin, Z., Xiaoru, W.: Information color encoding based on different mental workload and task type. J. China Ordnance 30(11), 1522–1526 (2009)
18. Jie, Z.: Study on Cognitive Ergonomics for Colorful Character Encoding. Fourth Military Medical University (2012)
19. Yingwei, Z., Zhuang Damin, W., et al.: Design and analysis on character encoding ergonomics for display interface. J. Beijing Univ. Aeronaut. Astronaut. 39(6), 761–765 (2013)
20. Lei, Z., Damin, Z.: Word and location encoding on man-machine display interface. J. Beijing Univ. Aeronaut. Astronaut. 37(2), 185–188 (2011)
21. Jing, L.: Information Encoding Method for Man-Machine Interface with Equilibrium Cognition Loading. Southeast University (2015)
22. Qun, W., Fang, X., Zhongliang, W., Liang, L., Sijuan, Z., Xue, S.: Experimental study for word encoding ergonomics on cockpit display interface. Veh. Power Technol. 1, 27–30 (2015)
23. Rui, B., Tao, Y., Yanyan, Z.: Designed visual encoding on operator interface. Modern Decoration Theory 05, 83–84 (2015)
24. Xiuli, S., Dayong, D., Wenjun, D.: Analysis on basic requirements for visual warning signal in aircraft cockpit. Progress Aeronaut. Eng. 6(4), 512–518 (2015)
25. Chunping, Y., Qi, Y.: Automobile meter design and ergonomics evaluation based on human factor. China Saf. Sci. J. 17(10), 62–66 (2007)
26. Tao, Z., Liming, C.: Design and manufacturing on automobile dashboard. Coach Technol. Study. 32(6), 34–36 (2010)

Do Consumption Values and Environmental Awareness Impact on Green Consumption in China?

Lebohang Sekhokoane, Nan Qie$^{(\boxtimes)}$, and Pei-Luen Patrick Rau

Department of Industrial Engineering, Tsinghua University, Beijing, China
malatsa@gmail.com,
qienan14@mails.tsinghua.edu.cn, rpl@tsinghua.edu.cn

Abstract. This research explores the relationships between the following aspects: (1) Green product purchase intention and green consumption behaviours; (2) Consumption values and green product purchase intention; (3) Environmental awareness and green product purchase intention. The research made use of questionnaires that were physically administered around university campus. There were two groups of respondents in this study: electric motorcycle users and mobile phone users. The following findings were obtained from the study; (1). Behavioural intention are significantly correlated with green consumption behaviours. (2). Consumption values effect on behavioural intention. (3). Environmental awareness significantly impacts on behavioural intention. The findings can guide green product design and production towards a more effective direction.

Keywords: Green consumption · Consumption values · Environmental awareness

1 Introduction

In recent decades, environmental issues have received substantial global attention, so countries and organizations are striving towards promotion of environmentally friendly practices. Due to various development drivers and mainly industrial manufacturing, environmental degradation has been reported to be on the increase. In particular, China has realized the magnitude of environmental degradation relatively later compared to western countries [1]. As a consequence, the country has been experiencing declines in many critical resources in addition to deteriorating air pollution situation. Although environmental laws have been put in place to address environmental issues, the issue that remains under scrutiny is whether their implementation is effective or not.

Despite all the laws and efforts countries make, success can rarely be achieved if individual citizens do not also participate. Individual citizens are the consumers who buy, use and recycle/dispose products of all types. The products can be loosely classified into environmentally friendly products and environmentally unfriendly products, dependent on their manufacturing, usage and disposal features. Adoption of sustainable consumption habits and practices is regarded as the main remedial action. Consumers

© Springer International Publishing AG 2017
P.-L.P. Rau (Ed.): CCD 2017, LNCS 10281, pp. 713–723, 2017.
DOI: 10.1007/978-3-319-57931-3_58

are said to practice environmentally friendly lifestyles if they could buy green products and engage in recycling practices. Green consumers are believed to possess an understanding that the security of the world is under threat from the prevailing situation of deteriorating environmental conditions. As a result, they are willing to pay more for environmentally friendly products.

As a result, the idea of green consumption has emerged as a key element in both academic and policy debates. In order to understand the consumers' desires to engage in green consumption behaviour and intention, numerous studies have been conducted to establish the influencing factors thereof [2–5]. China's role in environmental protection is being keenly watched by the whole world, as a result of prevalent air pollution levels in large cities such as Beijing. The objective of this study is to establish a model for understanding green purchase in China. The knowledge that is going to be obtained from this study would mainly be valuable in manufacturing, policy-making and marketing.

2 Understanding Green Consumer Behaviors

The interest of this research lies with an answer to the question, "What are the motivating factors for consumers to engage in green consumption behavior?" There are two theories that are commonly used in understanding green consumption behavior, including the Theory of Planned Behavior (TPB) and the Theory of Consumption Value.

The TPB is based on a foundation that the consumers' intention lead to their respective behavioral actions [6]. A lot of studies [7, 8] show that the use of the TPB has been a major contributor in the research trying to understand what influences green consumption behaviors. However, there is also some understanding that consumers' attitudes do not always translate into engagement in actual green consumption behaviours. Homer and Kahle [9] proposed inclusion of values in attitude-behaviour models. They found that values are more related to attitudes than they are to behaviours.

If, as suggested above, values are to be incorporated into the research of consumption behavior, the Theory of Consumption Values seems the most appropriate to use. Sheth et al. [10] propose that this theory should be able to explain why consumers choose to buy or not to buy any particular product. Five different consumption values form the basis of this theory. Functional value concerns how a customer views and expects a product to function. Social value conceptually addresses how purchasing or using a product will affect the way the consumer perceives to be acknowledged in a social context. Emotional value is derived from the inner-self of a customer, which is based on personal feelings associated with buying or using a product. Epistemic value is driven by a desire from a customer to learn or experience new things from a product. Conditional value is associated with how the product can meet the consumer's expected level of possibilities given alternating circumstances.

Besides consumption values, environmental awareness is another factor that can influence green purchase intention. Environmental awareness is a construct that has been found to directly influence pro-environmental behavioural intention, which in turn influences actual pro-environmental behaviours. Kollmuss and Agyeman [13] define environmental awareness as "knowing of the impact of human behaviour on the environment". They go further to posit that it has two distinct components based on knowledge (cognitive) and perception (affective). Among environmental awareness factors, most commonly referred to are environmental concern (EC) and perceived consumer effectiveness (PCE). Environmental concern is one of the significant role-players in pro-environment purchase decisions [14]. As for PCE, Antil [17] defines it as the consumer's assessment of how effective his/her abilities could be in facilitating change to environmental problems. PCE has been tested and found to be a significant predictor of environmentally friendly behaviors in various studies [2, 11, 12]. Previous study showed that if consumers' environmental knowledge (EK) could be increased, their credibility towards being environmentally friendly could be established [15]. Value orientation (VO) can also influence green purchase attitude. Collectivism and individualism are the two commonly used constructs to assess consumers' VO. Individualism is said to be exhibited by those consumers who value personal gratification. On the other hand, collectivist consumers are said to ignore personal gratification by showing cooperation and willingness to work towards societal goals [16].

With an emphasis on both environmental awareness (perceived consumer effectiveness, environmental concern, and clothing environmental attitude) and product consumption value, Yoo et al. [11] applied the Theory of Consumption Values to identify the factors that influence bamboo textile purchase intention. The variables used in this study emanate from both the Theory of Consumption Values (emotional, social, epistemic, price, and functional) and constructs from green consumption literature (perceived consumer effectiveness and environmental concern). In the study, they found three consumption values (price, epistemic and emotional) to be significantly correlated to bamboo product purchase intention. All of the ecological consumer awareness variables (perceived consumer effectiveness, environmental concern and clothing environmental attitude) were found to positively influence bamboo product purchase intention. To a large extent, this study also confirms the applicability of the Theory of Consumption Values in establishing an understanding of how green consumption behaviours are influenced by consumption values.

By incorporating the consumption values and the environmental awareness variables in this manner, their study has provided the motivation and inspiration to the current study. In the current study, both the consumption values and the environmental awareness will be assessed against green purchase intention as well as green consumption behaviours. Green consumption behaviours can be roughly understood to include activities such as buying environmentally friendly products, practising energy-efficient ways of doing things, re-using some products instead of disposing of, practising recycling, and many others.

3   Research Questions and Hypotheses

Drawing from the preceding discussion on commonly used research frameworks on green consumption behavior research, the current study's research questions are

- Does consumer environmental awareness have an impact on green purchase intention and green consumption behaviour in China?

- Do consumption values have an impact on green purchase intention and green consumption behaviour in China?

In the context of this study, green consumption behaviours will be used to mean consumers' behavioural activities that involve the consumption of products to avoid causing harm to the environment. Although many conceptual frameworks exist that aim to explain the value-attitude-behaviour relationship in green behaviour studies, a general consensus is that such behaviours are influenced by related behavioural intention. Taking this assumption into consideration, the following hypothesis was made.

H1: *Green product purchase intention will have a positive impact on green consumption behaviour.*

For the purposes of this study, a selection of environmental awareness measures was designated as follow: environmental concern (EC), environmental knowledge (EK), value orientation (VO) and perceived consumer effectiveness (PCE). EC and PCE have been mentioned in Yoo et al.'s study [11]. EK concerns the credibility and VO influences the attitude of the consumer towards green purchase. On the basis of environmental awareness being widely accepted as an effective predictor of pro-environmental behaviours, the following hypothesis is formulated:

H2: *Environmental Awareness (defined in terms of EC (H2a), EK (H2b), VO (H2c) and PCE (H2d)), will positively influence green product purchase intention.*

When making green purchase decisions, choices have to be made by consumers regarding which products to buy and which brands to choose. Sheth *et al.* [10] propose the Theory of Consumption Values to explain how these choices are influenced by behavioural indicators. The theory consists of five distinct value constructs, namely functional value, social value, emotional value, epistemic value and conditional value. In that respect, hypotheses based on consumption values were formulated as follows:

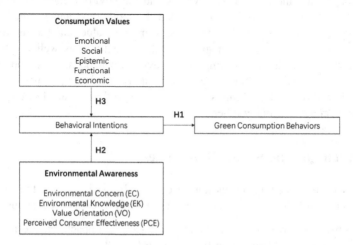

Fig. 1. Research framework

H3: *Consumption values (H3a functional, H3b social, H3c emotional, H3d epistemic, H3e economic) will directly affect green product purchase intention.*

The overall research framework is illustrated in Fig. 1. The three hypotheses will be tested one by one, and altogether provide a basic understanding of green consumer behaviours.

4 Methodology

In this study, data was collected from two population samples: electric motorcycle consumers and mobile phone consumers. There might exist differences in environmentally-driven behavioral as well as consumption patterns between the two groups. To carry out the exercise, a pair of questionnaires were formulated and distributed accordingly. There were specific questions focusing on different behavioral items for each group. Additionally, both questionnaires also had similar questions addressing general environmental issues.

The sample for the electric motorcycle users comprised 133 students of ages ranging from 17 to 35 years (M = 22, SD = 2). Males accounted for 42 per cent. One hundred and thirty students, of age range from 17 to 30 years (M = 20, SD = 2), participated in the mobile phones users' survey. Seventy-six percent of them were males.

The questionnaire sets began with a brief introduction and a declaration that the information gathered through the questionnaires would only be used for the purposes of this study. The questions in the questionnaires were grouped into three parts. The first part sought personal information. The second part sought personal feelings towards owning an environmentally-friendly product as well as views on environmentally-related issues. Information pertaining to participants' behavioral intention, along with actual behaviors were also in part two. Environmental knowledge was tested at the last part of the questionnaires.

The questionnaires were designed in such a manner that the variables discussed in the hypotheses formulation section could be obtained. Each variable would be made up of an aggregation of at least two items. Except for the personal and environmental knowledge information, the scales of measurements were 7-point Likert type ranging from 1 (strongly disagree) to 7 (strongly agree). Both sets of questionnaires were originally drafted in English and were later translated into Chinese (See Appendix, questionnaire design for electrical motorcycle group).

A primary analysis was conducted on each factor. Epistemic and functional factors were combined into one factor due to low Cronbach alpha. Economic and EK were eliminated from further analysis due to Cronbach alpha less than 0.50.

5 Results

By analyzing the questionnaire data, the three hypotheses were tested. Correlation and regression were conducted. T-tests were used to compare between the two groups. The two samples will be referred to as group one for electric motorcycle consumers and group two for mobile phones consumers.

5.1   Testing Hypothesis One

It was hypothesized that green purchase intention would lead to behaviors. Correlation analysis between intention and behaviors was conducted. Although no cause and effect relationship can be confirmed through simply correlation analysis, it can still indicate relationship between the two variables. The results were shown in Tables 1 and 2. Intention and behaviors were highly correlated for both groups with $p < .01$.

Table 1. Pearson's r correlations between variables (electric motorcycles group)

Variable	E	S	EF	PCE	EC	VO	I	B
Emotional	1	.632**	.440**	.259**	.154	.164	.643**	.284**
Social		1	.545**	.317**	.107	.034	.424**	.206*
Epistemic-functional			1	.297**	.236**	.177*	.354**	.174
PCE				1	.491**	.432**	.270**	.363**
EC					1	.518**	.325**	.383**
VO						1	.296**	.368**
Intention							1	.457**
Behaviors								1

**. $p < 0.01$, *. $p < 0.05$

Table 2. Pearson's r correlations between variables (mobile phones group)

Variable	E	S	EF	PCE	EC	VO	I	B
Emotional	1	.602**	.449**	.418**	.282**	.347**	.433**	.320**
Social		1	.359**	.274**	.225*	.260**	.413**	.296**
Epistemic-functional			1	.519**	.419**	.545**	.471**	.510**
PCE				1	.536**	.690**	.613**	.605**
EC					1	.447**	.418**	.441**
VO						1	.598**	.595**
Intention							1	.769**
Behaviors								1

**. $p < 0.01$, *. $p < 0.05$

5.2   Testing Hypothesis Two

It was hypothesized that environmental awareness in terms of environmental concern (EC), value orientation (VO) and perceived consumer effectiveness (PCE), will positively influence green product purchase intention. As an overview step prior to regression analysis, reference will be made to correlation results shown in Tables 1 and 2. Incidentally, analyses are performed on both sets of population samples.

Correlation. For group one, a small correlation coefficient was obtained between PCE and intention $[r = .270, N = 124, p < .01]$ while medium correlation coefficients were obtained for the remaining two pairs, between VO and intention $[r = .296, N = 127,$

p < .01] and between EC and intention [r = .325, N = 124, p < .01]. Interestingly, EC and VO yielded a large correlation coefficient [r = .518, N = 124, p < .01] (See Table 1). Group two variables showed substantially higher correlations between the variables and intention. There were strong correlations between VO and intention [r = .598, N = 117, p < .01], and also between PCE and intention [r = .613, N = 117, p < .01]. A medium correlation was observed between EC and intention [r = .418, N = 117, p < .01] (See Table 2).

Regression. In order to assess the ability of environmental awareness measures (PCE, VO, EC) to predict levels of intention, a standard multiple regression analysis was performed with intention as a dependent variable while PCE, VO, and EC were independent variables in the model. For group one, the total variability explained by the model was 11.2% [$F(3, 123) = 6.32, p < .01$]. Of the total contribution to the variance in the model by the three measures, EC appeared to have contributed the most judging from its beta value (beta = .186, $p = .08$). For group two, the above procedure produced a regression model which 41.3%, [$F(3, 121) = 30.1, p < .01$] of the intention can be predicted by the environmental awareness variables. VO (beta = .349, $p < .01$) appeared to contribute the most, followed by PCE (beta = .303, $p < .01$). The least contribution came from EC (beta = .094, $p = .254$) which is not a significant contribution.

5.3 Testing Hypothesis Three

It was hypothesized that consumption values in terms of functional, social, emotional, epistemic, economic, will positively influence green product purchase intention. Still correlation and regression were conducted to test the hypothesis.

Correlation. The results for group one indicates that emotional had a strongest correlation with intention [r = .643, N = 124, p < .01] followed by social [r = .424, N = 124, p < .01]. Epistemic-functional also had a significant correlation with intention [r = .354, N = 124, p < .01]. Amongst the independent variables, emotional and social had a high correlation with the Pearson's correlation coefficient value of .632 [N = 124, p < .01] (See Table 1). Correlations between independent variables and the dependent variable were loosely similar for group two with the highest observed between epistemic-functional and intention [r = .471, N = 117, p < .01]. Emotional and intention yielded the second-largest correlation [r = .433, N = 117, p < .01] while social and intention produced the lowest of the three correlations [r = .413, N = 117, p < .01]. Amongst the independent variables, social and emotions were the most correlated [r = .602, N = 117, p < .01] (See Table 2).

Regression. Having observed the correlations that exist between the independent variables and the dependent variable, multiple regression analysis was used to assess how much of the variability in the dependent variable can be predicted by the independent variables. For group one, the regression model suggests that 43.2% of the variability in Intention can be predicted by the consumption values measures [$F(3, 127) = 34, p < .01$]. Observing the beta values resulting from the model, emotional appears to have the largest significant contribution in the prediction (beta = .60, $p < .01$) while social contributes the least (beta = −.012, p = .894), which is not a significant contribution. The regression model for group two suggests that 27.2% of the variability in intention can be significantly predicted by the independent variables combined together [F(3, 119) = 16.2, p < .01]. The beta values from the model suggest that epistemic-functional has the most significant contribution of the three independent variables (beta = .304, p < .01).

5.4 Comparison Between Two Groups

As discussed previously, the contents in the two questionnaire sets used in this study were neither entirely the same nor entirely different. To compare between the two groups, only variables that contain the same items can enter the model, including value orientation (VO), environmental concern (EC), and behaviors.

In order to explore the differences in means of the variables for the two sample groups, an independent-sample t-test was performed using the three variables (VO, EC, and Behaviors). The results showed that there was no significant difference in EC means for the two sample groups. Comparing VO scores in group one (M = 22.58, SD = 2.76) and group two (M = 21.40, SD = 2.51) resulted in a significant difference t(253) = 3.56, p < .001. There was also significant differences in the scores of behaviors in group one (M = 20.67, SD = 3.67) and group two (M = 18.81, SD = 3.04) under conditions (t(248) = 4.39, p < .001). This means that the mean scores for both VO and behaviors were significantly higher for group one sample than for group two sample.

6 Discussion and Conclusion

The results of analysis confirmed all the hypotheses. For both groups, green purchase intention can be significantly predicted by environmental awareness variables (PCE, VO and EC) and consumption values. Since green purchase intention is highly correlated with green purchase behaviour (Hypothesis 1), it follows that increasing consumers' environmental awareness (Hypothesis 2) and consumption values (Hypothesis 3) will ultimately result in an increase in green consumption behaviour. Environmental awareness can be increased through marketing, in which case it might deem essential to highlight the environmental friendliness of products. With use of appropriate legislation, governments can enforce and regulate marketing of green products thereof. Another way of influencing green product purchase intention is through enhancement of consumption values. Knowledge of consumers' perceived values can assist in the design and production of environmentally friendly products as a way to ensure that they appeal to customers' expectations. Again, legislation can play a major role in controlling how products are manufactured, and also how they are marketed. The idea would be to highlight the values that are deemed appealing to consumers. If done properly, the ultimate result would be an increase in green consumption behaviours.

In addition, it has to be mentioned that in increasing consumers' environmental awareness, efforts have to be made to understand consumers' value orientations (collectivistic or individualistic). An ideal scenario would be that consumers are more collectivistic. Perceived consumer effectiveness also needs to be duly considered, as consumers with high PCE tend to engage in green consumption activities more. Enhancing consumption values associated with green products on the other hand must be approached mostly from the emotional view of the consumers. It has to be established which emotions consumers attach to green products. Addressing such emotional attributes associated with green products can then lead to an increased interests towards green products.

Based on similar questions from the questionnaire sets, three variables (VO, EC, and behaviors) were subsequently used to test the differences across the two sample groups. Electric motorcycle users showed a significantly higher level of collectivism than their mobile phones counterparts. This then implies that electric motorcycle users are likely to engage more in environmentally friendly activities as a result of their collective orientation. Also, the behaviors mean for the electric motorcycle group was found to be significantly larger than for the mobile phones group.

Appendix: Survey Questionnaire

Emotional
Purchasing an electric motorcycle will make me feel I am doing something good for the environment
Purchasing an electric motorcycle will make me feel I am a good person
Purchasing an electric motorcycle will make me feel I am making a wise choice
Purchasing an electric motorcycle will make me feel I have seen a great deal of life
Purchasing an electric motorcycle will make me feel I have a unique personality
Social
It can reflect my level of knowledge and consciousness
It can reflect my care and sympathy
It can reflect my social status
It can reflect my income level
It can reflect my achievements
Epistemic
It can arouse my curiosity of new things
It can provide me with a new experience
Functional
It can provide me with the functions that a I need in a motorcycle
It can make my transportation convenient
Economic
It is worth purchasing an electric motorcycle
Electric motorcycles should be more expensive than other motorcycles powered by oil
I'd still like to buy an electric motorcycle even it costs more
Perceived Consumer Effectiveness (PCE)
Customers can have a positive influence on the environment and society through purchasing green products

When purchasing products, I will try to consider what it will bring to the environment and other people using these products

Because individuals cannot have any influence on the whole environment, pollution and natural resources, my behaviour won't make anything change

Every consumer should make efforts to protect and improve the environment

If other people are careless about the environment, a single person's efforts can have make no difference

I think I have the ability to help solve environmental problems

Every consumer can have a positive influence on society by purchasing products from a responsible company

Ecological Concern (EC)

I am very concerned about the world environment

Humans are abusing and destroying the environment badly

I don't think recycling is important

Humans intervening in the environment usually produces fatal consequences

To keep economic development benign, we need to develop stable economics that can control increases in industry

Earth is like a spaceship with limited room and resources

Development has limitations in terms of range. Going beyond this range will make our industrial society lose the ability to develop

Value Orientation (VO)

In life I pursue self-dignity

In life I like to help people

In life I pursue independence

In life I will work hard for the goal of a group or organization

In life I am willing to cooperate with others in the group

In life I pursue authority

In life I can sacrifice my own benefits for those of the group

In life I pursue social power

Behavioural Intention

I am sure I will consider purchasing an electric motorcycle

Because of the environmental function, I will buy an electric motorcycle

When purchasing a motorcycle, among all the choices meeting my needs, I am more willing to buy an environmental friendly one

I think I will buy another electric motorcycle in the future

When purchasing a motorcycle, I will consider purchasing an electrical one as my first priority

Consumption Behaviours

I do my best to buy and use products made of recyclable material

Between two products, I will choose the one which does less harm to the environment and other people

For environmental or ecological reasons, I have changed my previous products

Compared to a shower, I prefer a bath

I never mind recycling paper bags or plastic bags

I have avoided purchasing products that will be of potential harm to the environment

References

1. Chan, R.Y.: Determinants of Chinese consumers' green purchase behavior. Psychol. Mark. **18**, 389–413 (2001)
2. Zhao, H., Gao, Q., Wu, Y., Wang, Y., Zhu, X.: What affects green consumer behavior in China? A case study from Qingdao. J. Clean. Prod. **63**, 143–151 (2014)
3. Akehurst, G., Afonso, C., Martins Gonçalves, H.: Re-examining green purchase behaviour and the green consumer profile: new evidences. Manag. Decis. **50**, 972–988 (2012)
4. Chan, R.Y.: Consumer responses to environmental advertising in China. Mark. Intell. Plan. **22**, 427–437 (2004)
5. Awad, T.A.: Environmental segmentation alternatives: buyers' profiles and implications. J. Islam. Mark. **2**, 55–73 (2011)
6. Ajzen, I.: The theory of planned behavior. Organ. Behav. Hum. Decis. Process. **50**, 179–211 (1991)
7. Runyan, R.C., Foster, I.M., Park, J., Ha, S.: Understanding pro-environmental behavior: a comparison of sustainable consumers and apathetic consumers. Int. J. Retail Distrib. Manag. **40**, 388–403 (2012)
8. Chung, J.-E., Stoel, L., Xu, Y., Ren, J.: Predicting Chinese consumers' purchase intention for imported soy-based dietary supplements. Br. Food J. **114**, 143–161 (2012)
9. Homer, P.M., Kahle, L.R.: A structural equation test of the value-attitude-behavior hierarchy. J. Pers. Soc. Psychol. **54**, 638 (1988)
10. Sheth, J.N., Newman, B.I., Gross, B.L.: Why we buy what we buy: a theory of consumption values. J. Bus. Res. **22**, 159–170 (1991)
11. Yoo, J.-J., Divita, L., Kim, H.-Y.: Environmental awareness on bamboo product purchase intention: do consumption values impact green consumption? Int. J. Fash. Des. Technol. Educ. **6**, 27–34 (2013)
12. Kim, Y., Choi, S.M.: Antecedents of green purchase behavior: an examination of collectivism, environmental concern, and PCE. In: NA-Advances in Consumer Research, vol. 32 (2005)
13. Kollmuss, A., Agyeman, J.: Mind the gap: why do people act environmentally and what are the barriers to pro-environmental behavior? Environ. Educ. Res. **8**, 239–260 (2002)
14. Hartmann, P., Apaolaza-Ibáñez, V.: Consumer attitude and purchase intention toward green energy brands: the roles of psychological benefits and environmental concern. J. Bus. Res. **65**, 1254–1263 (2012)
15. Laroche, M., Bergeron, J., Barbaro-Forleo, G.: Targeting consumers who are willing to pay more for environmentally friendly products. J. Consum. Mark. **18**, 503–520 (2001)
16. Cheah, I., Phau, I.: Attitudes towards environmentally friendly products: the influence of ecoliteracy, interpersonal influence and value orientation. Mark. Intell. Plan. **29**, 452–472 (2011)
17. Antil, J.H.: Socially responsible consumers: profile and implications for public policy. J. Macromarketing **4**, 18–39 (1984)

A User Experience Study for Watching Delay Interrupted Video in the Context of Mobile Network

Hao Tan[1], Jiahao Sun[2(✉)], Bin Wang[3], Qiyong Zhao[3], Wei Li[2], and Zhengyu Tan[2]

[1] State Key Laboratory of Advanced Design and Manufacturing for Vehicle Body,
Hunan University, Changsha, China
htan@hnu.edu.cn
[2] School of Design, Hunan University, Changsha, China
{sunjiahao2015,liwei2014}@hnu.edu.cn
[3] MBB Lab, Huawei Technologies Co. Ltd., Shanghai, China
{i.wangbin,zhaoqiyong}@huawei.com

Abstract. The development of mobile application in our daily lives has changed our way of receive various of information, the way people use mobile devices to receive information has become whenever and wherever based on the mobile network technique. End user experience in the context of Internet services is also depend on the waiting time in the beginning of service and the intervals during the service caused by the system delays. We use several factors buffer, stalling time) to investigate the relationship between the video QoE and delay. We used the results of these analyses to inform the construction of the user's satisfaction influenced by time delay. Given by the experiment results, we have conclusion some factors-based contexts which could influence the user's satisfaction and some changeable QoE-related trends based on those three factors.

Keywords: User experience · Delay · Video quality assessment · Mobile network service

1 Introduction

Nowadays, VoIP is very common in IP networks, and the important trend of video traffic has increased rapidly, meanwhile, the wide use of mobile devices with video display support and the application of wireless networks (WLANS and 3G/4G) have contributed to this scenario. In a few years, the contents related to videos transmitted through the network will be 90% (Begen et al. 2011; Cisco Systems Inc. 2013). To provide a satisfactory video service to users in real time is a certain challenge to the internet and multimedia providers.

The video streaming service is a typical internet service in which the video contents need to be encoded and stored in multimedia database, then transmitted to the customers through the core network, finally displayed on user's devices like a smartphone or a tablet PC. Based on this model of video streaming service, there are many factors such as bandwidth, delay, jitter, packet loss and so on will influence the quality of video contents which could not afford each customer. Moreover, when the customer uses

© Springer International Publishing AG 2017
P.-L.P. Rau (Ed.): CCD 2017, LNCS 10281, pp. 724–735, 2017.
DOI: 10.1007/978-3-319-57931-3_59

mobile devices, the scenario here becomes more complicated and produces more difficulties, such as wireless signal coverage and wireless channel instability. such situation is one kind of system delays which makes users spend time on waiting for the system's response.

Also, in research field, such delays are commonly defined as system delays (Selvidge et al. 2002; Szameitat et al. 2009) or system response times (Dabrowski and Munson 2011; Schleifer and Amick 1989). System delays are caused by two parts, one is about the system itself, such as processing speed, network bandwidth or the computation on the complexity requests. Another one is about the transient factors, such as network congestion, background processes and so on (Seow 2008). From the research on Human Computer Interaction (HCI) in the past decades, system delays can evidently influence the users' experience (Ceaparu et al. 2004; Nah 2004; Thum et al. 1995).

2 Proposed Technique

2.1 QoE

The study on the quality of experience (QoE) has played an important role in the increasing popularity of various video services (Cisco Documentation 2014). Quality of Experience (QoE) is a concept commonly used to describe user's whole satisfaction reflecting the degree of delight or annoyance of a user with a (multimedia) system, service or application (Le Callet et al. 2012). In concise explanation, QoE is an assessment of the user satisfaction with the contents shown on different kinds of devices (Zepernick et al. 2011; Raake et al. 2014). Thus the network infrastructure used for the video streaming requires an evolution method to assess the video QoE. The ITU-T made a definition of QoE as an assessing system to evaluate the service quality based on users in 2007. There are many factors affect this quality measure system, including different kinds of technical and non-technical (Brooks and Hestnes 2010). These factors are related to service preparation, delivery and presentation, which makes challenge to maintaining QoE at an acceptable level. Many solutions have been introduced to tackle the challenge of video traffic quality. However, the realistic situations are required to meet the satisfaction of users and preserve the interest of service providers.

Given by the investigations above, delays lead user to wait for the system response, the waiting time here plays an important roll in user experience, although there have been many studies on how user react to delays before (Larson 1987; Clemmer and Schneider 1989; Dube et al. 1989, 1991; Hui and Tse 1996).

2.2 Delay

Given by system delays are caused by system itself and transient factors (Selvidge et al. 2002; Szameitat et al. 2009), users are influenced by these delays then lead to have bad experience or low performance (Ceaparu et al. 2004; Nah 2004; Thum et al. 1995).

Recently, many studies focus on the whether the negative effects of delays can be managed or avoided by interface design (Branaghan and Sanchez 2009; Galletta et al. 2006; Krejcar 2009). There are two elements that can effects user experience and performance during delays, the one is delays' lengths, the other one is delays' variability (Kuhmann 1989; Kuhmann et al. 1987; Schaefer 1990). It is an almost universal view that long waiting times are harmful to users' performance and experience which will have bad influence on users' overall satisfaction (Martin and Corl 1986; Schaefer 1990; Seow 2008; Simoens et al. 2011).

However, it should be noticed that only the impact of a single delay or short delay on the user have been considered in the former articles instead of multiple delay. In our study, we want to evaluate the users' experience of different kinds of delays occurred in video streaming. The main goal of this paper is to evaluate the quality of user experience in different delay context of mobile network. Therefore, delay factors are divided into initial buffer (video initial buffer time) and stalling time (video playing time of the stall) to allow users to evaluate. The experiment applies methods related to QoE in the assessment of uer satisfaction which influenced by delay factors. A typical process of video service quality evaluation is detailed and the assessment methods are divided into subjective and compared in the context of mobile network.

The study is devoted to concluded the standard of QoE which can help internet and multimedia providers plan and construct the internet, which core is video QoE, from the perspective of human factors and provide the best experience under wireless internet environment.

As the user experience is the primary productive forces, video QoE plays a very important role in improving the video service. With the trend of decreasing the traffic rate, the consumption of video traffic has become the key measure to enhance the revenue of the global internet and multimedia providers and the user experience of the video service has become the key to measure the quality of the internet and multimedia providers' network. Thus, the video QoE in our study can help them keep abreast of the user experience and adjust the network to improve quality of service. Moreover, with the consumer's subjective scores in emotional scales, a correlation model between different inquiring feedback delaying and the different emotional experience levels in online e-commerce platform was designed, which produced a trial guide of feedback delaying service design in online e-commerce platform and help to promote the online e-commerce service experience.

3   Implementation

There were lots of factors may impact to the video QoE. Baraković et al. were divided many factors into five factor categories: technological performance, usability, subjective evaluation, expectations, and context. Xue et al. reported the influence factors of the user perception also included screen size, viewing distance, lighting, and user movement when viewing videos on mobile devices. Thus, the laboratory equipment for an iPhone 6 Plus mobile phone (5.5 in., 1920 * 1080p), used to play the experimental video clips; A camera to record the process; The video subjective scoring table for experimental material used to the user to score for each experimental video clips; A video editing software to mimic the video buffer and stalling in the mobile network, allowing users to feel the real network delay. In order to test the time delay, we asked participants to perform the paradigm under one situation. We investigated the time delay during the video with the user experience. Further, we divided the time delay into the buffering time and stalling time and analyzed how these two factors influenced the video QoE.

4   Experiments

4.1   Participants

In this study, there were 38 participants (21 male/17 female) took part in. The age ranged between 18 and 55 (M = 21, SD = 10) years. They were experienced mobile device users and all had use network for 6 years on average. Prior to the study, all participants were required to accept the visual fatigue testing and fill in the individual basic information table. Finally, 30 participants (15 male/15 female) were qualified to join in this study. And 80% of the participants often use mobile device to watch the video.

4.2   Method

Thus, to assess for the experience quality of video we used a subjective modified approach. The method we use and the criterion the users relay on as a practical way to objectively measure the quality of video is MOS that is one of the subjective quality evaluate methods (ITU-T P.910 1999; ITU-R BT.500-10 2000; Jones and Atkinson 1998; Caramma et al. 1999; Watson and Sasse 1998) which is the most commonly method to assess the video quality.

We use the quality scale which included "bad", "poor", "fair", "good", and "excellent", and they are translated to the values 1, 2, 3, 4 and 5 (Fig. 1) when calculating the mean opinion score (ITU-T recommendation P-910). According the ITU-T recommendation BT 500-13, it reported that the MOS is a prevalent used metric. The observer selected a score from 1 to 5 in the quality scale to evaluate every video.

Quality scale.

5	Excellent
4	Good
3	Fair
2	Poor
1	Bad

Fig. 1. Quality scale

In this experiment, we had two tasks to research the video QoE and the time delay. In the first task, we investigated the time delay. Moreover, we compared the influence of the initial buffer time and the stalling time on the video QoE to users. In the task two, we researched that when the user watched 6 min video, other conditions in the same situation, whether playing long time shorter or increasing the stalling time have impact to the user QoE to watch video.

4.3 Tasks

Task 1

In this task, we experimented on an iphone6 plus. Please users to sit in the most comfortable position, holding the phone and adjust it to the most comfortable distance. Next, the participant was informed the experiment testing process and the purpose of the experiment.

In this experiment, we took several measures eliminate the user negative sentiment from the video clips content. Firstly, the participant selected one video that he or she was most interested in. Next, the participant selected one type of video about 20 s in length and clicked the play button. Next, there was a buffer of T seconds in every video. The participant then need to assess a MOS score from 5 to 1 in this experience. When the MOS score reached 1 score, all trials were finished by default (Fig. 2). The buffer time T included: 0.1 s, 0.5 s, 1 s, 2 s, 1 s, 3 s, 4 s, 5 s, 6 s, 7 s, 8 s, 9 s, 10 s (Table 1).

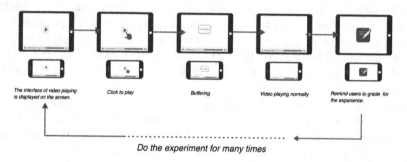

Fig. 2. The experimental process of buffer

Table 1. The video clip material about buffer.

	T1	T2	T3	T4	T5	T6	T7	T8	T9	T10	T11	T12
Buffer (s)	0.1 s	0.5 s	1 s	2 s	3 s	4 s	5 s	6 s	7 s	8 s	9 s	10 s

This step also selected one type video about 20 s in length primarily, then, the participant clicked the play button. The video clip started playing 5 s fluently, after the staling appearing T seconds. After stalling, the video clip playing continued. According this situation, the participant gave a MOS score to assess it (Fig. 3). The stalling time included (Table 2): 0.1 s, 0.5 s, 1 s, 2 s, 1 s, 3 s, 4 s, 5 s, 6 s, 7 s, 8 s, 9 s, 10 s.

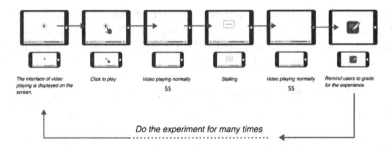

Fig. 3. The experimental process of stalling time

Table 2. The video clip material about stalling.

	T1	T2	T3	T4	T5	T6	T7	T8	T9	T10	T11	T12
Stalling (s)	0.1 s	0.5 s	1 s	2 s	3 s	4 s	5 s	6 s	7 s	8 s	9 s	10 s

Task 2

In this task, we experimented on an iphone6 plus. Ask users in the most comfortable sitting position holding the phone and adjust to the most comfortable distance. Then, the participant was informed the experiment testing process and the purpose of the experiment.

The participant selected one type video about 6 min in length, and clicked the play button to watching the video clips. In this task, we aimed to research the influence of multiple buffering and stalling during in the video viewing influence to the user QoE. After the video buffering T seconds, the video continued to play X seconds. Then, stalling was appeared during T seconds. The video continued playing X seconds until the next stalling happened. Moreover, the delay times *(T + X) was a stalling segment (e.g. the video clip had one time delay, 1 * (T + X) = 1 stalling segment) (Fig. 4). The participant finished watching the video clips, rated the MOS, besides, they started to test

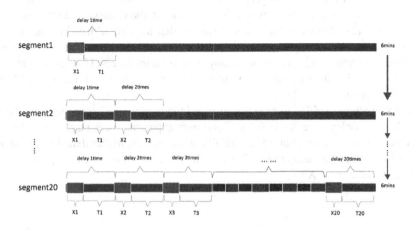

Fig. 4. The experiment material processing

the next stalling segments. We would examine each of these segments in turn. There were 20 stalling segments according to the stalling time. When the participant rated 1 score, this test was finished. The T included 0.1 s, 0.5 s, 1 s and 3 s. The X index was 2 s, 4 s, 8 s, 16 s, 32 s, 64 s and 128 s (Table 3).

Table 3. The ratio of video clip material about stalling segment

Delay time (T)	X1	X2	X3
MOS	5	4	3
Interval playing	2 s, 4 s, 8 s, 16 s, 32 s, 64 s, 128 s		
Stalling times	1, 2, 3, 4, 5, 6, 7, 8, 9, 10, 11, 12, 13, 14, 15, 16, 17, 18, 19, 20		

When the interval playing time get 32 s, 64 s and 128 s,
If the stalling times was more than 11, 6, 3 times, the next segment don not need test, respectively

Debriefing of participants revealed that the video they chose had a proper content and experimental materials were close to the actual situation. Most participants were patient enough to finish all the tasks. This fits with the fact that all participants won money in excess of the guaranteed bonus of 200RMB.

5   Results

5.1   Task 1

In task one, participants were asked to watch videos with different delay on a smart phone which is in the mobile network, and then assess the user experience using the MOS scale.

We investigated whether initial buffer time and stalling time have difference effect on user experience in the context of mobile network. For this, we average the scores of initial delays and stalling time on the phone. Results showed in Fig. 5 revealed that under the same length of waiting time, the scores of initial time were generally higher than those of stalling time, which indicated that user has a higher tolerance of initial delay than stalling time when they were watching a video in the context of mobile network. However, results showed in Fig. 5 also revealed that the overall trend of initial delay and stalling time are nearly the same. We then conducted a repeated measure one-way ANOVA including all 12 lengths of waiting time as factor levels. This analysis showed a significant main effect of these two factors on user experience ($F_{(2, 30)}$ ¼ 11.105; $p = 0.001$; partial Z2 ¼ .425).

The users have positive user experience and the participants' score reached the top at 5 when the delay time X1 = 0.1 s. Good user experience was suggested when the initial delay was no more than 0.5 s, with all the scores were higher than 4.5. The scores dropped to 4 when the delay time X2 = 1 s. Then, the scores dropped to approximately 3 when the delay time X3 = 3 s.

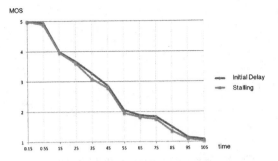

Fig. 5. The MOS's scores of initial delay and stalling time

5.2   Task 2

To test whether lengths of play duration and times of intervals exert an effect on watching experience in the context of mobile network, we conducted a repeated measures 2-way analysis of variance (ANOVA) including 7 different lengths of play duration (2 s, 4 s, 8 s, 16 s, 32 s, 64 s and 128 s) and times of intervals ranged from 1 to 15 as factor levels on three length of stalling time ($X1 = 0.1$ s, $X2 = 1$ s and $X3 = 3$ s) respectively. Figures 6, 7 and 8 respectively show the mean MOS scores on these three buffer levels.

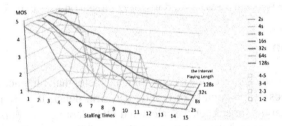

Fig. 6. Mean MOS scores with 0.1 s initial delay

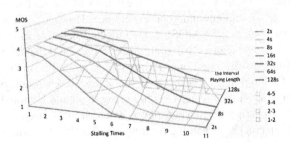

Fig. 7. Mean MOS scores with 1 s initial delay

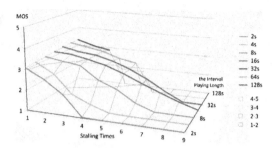

Fig. 8. Mean MOS scores with 3 s initial delay

For watching experience reflected by MOS scores of users in the context of mobile network, when the single stalling time is 0.5 s, analysis showed a significant main effect of play duration and times of intervals, as well as interaction between play duration and times of intervals with [$F(1,29) = 8.114$, $p < 0.001$, $R2 = 0.727$]. When the initial delay is 1 s, there was also a significant main effect of play duration ($p < 0.001$), times of intervals ($p < 0.001$) and interaction between play duration and times of intervals with [$F(1, 29) = 7.145$, $p = 0.000$, $R2 = 0.684$]. Same conclusion can be obtained from the analysis of 3 s-stalling-time with [$F(1, 29) = 8.024$, $p = 0.000$, $R2 = 0.519$]. Thus, the results revealed that both the decrease of single play duration time and increase of times of intervals while watching a video had negative effects on user experience.

6   Conclusion

In this paper, we firstly analyzed the most significant factor that influences the experience of watching videos in the context of mobile network: delay. It is divided into initial buffer time and stalling time. Then we calculated MOS score giving consideration of all these factors and compared the results depending on different conditions. Given by the experiment we performed, it can be figured out clearly that the MOS score is very similar in initial buffer time and stalling time. When the delay was shorter than 0.5 s, the users' MOS scores indicated excellent and good experience. However, when the delay was longer than 4 s on average, the MOS scores reflected negative emotions. All users showed a zero tolerance and an awful experience to the video if the delay was over 10 s in length. According to the emotional rating scores, after the participants finished experiment, all of them pointed out that they feel annoyed when delays occurred and they disliked delays when they were watching video. It should be noted that the effect of dislike the delays was significant when they were watching a video on a mobile device, although the participants prefer waiting for longer buffer time to endure single stalling time in the processing of video playing.

But it is worth noting that in the video playing duration ranged from 2 s to 16 s, the shorter the length of playing time, the lower the users tolerance to the times of single stalling. For example, when the video playing time is 2 s, the length of single stalling is 500 ms, the times of single stalling which the participants could tolerated is 7. However, when the video playing time was extended to 15 s, the times of single stalling which the participants could tolerated increased to 15. Meanwhile, when the video playing time was extended to 32 s, the video MOS scores of participants will not decline with the increase of the times of single stalling rapidly. For example, when the video playing time is 2 s, the times of single stalling increased from 1 to 3, the MOS score fell 0.64 points, while in 128 s' video playing duration, the score only fell 0.1 points. Moreover, at the condition of fixed playing time, the longer the single stalling time is taken, the less user want to continue watching the video. Take the 32 s playing time as an instance, when a single stalling takes only 0.1 s, user can tolerate 10 times single stalling and the MOS score is 10 points, however, when a single stalling takes 3 s, user's tolerance of stalling decrease to 8 times meanwhile MOS score decrease to 1 points. So in certain case of watching short video of 6 min or less and a fixed delay totals, we can draw two conclusions from the experiment, (1) the more delay time gathers in the initialization of the video instead of playing the better, (2) higher frequency and less single stalling time introduces worse experience than more single stalling time and lower frequency.

7 Future Work

For the future study, we want to add more factors in our investigation and compare with different video contents, and compare the QoE under different watching environments, like when the users are not single, or the video streaming service platform have some social functions in real time.

Acknowledgments. We would like to express our gratitude to Xiao Tan and Hui Yang who helped us during the experiment with his professional skill. The research was supported by Huawei Wireless Supported Projects.

References

Begen, A.C., Akgul, T., Baugher, M.: Watching video over the web: part 1: streaming protocols. Internet Comput. IEEE **15**(2), 54–63 (2011)

Cisco Systems Inc.: Cisco Visual Networking Index: Forecast and Methodology, 2012–2017, White Paper, May 2013

Selvidge, P.R., Chaparro, B.S., Bender, G.T.: The world wide wait: effects of delays on user performance. Int. J. Ind. Ergon. **29**, 15–20 (2002)

Szameitat, A.J., Rummel, J., Szameitat, D.P., Sterr, A.: Behavioral and emotional consequences of brief delays in human–computer interaction. Int. J. Hum Comput Stud. **67**, 561–570 (2009)

Dabrowski, J., Munson, E.V.: 40 years of searching for the best computer system response time. Interact. Comput. **23**, 555–564 (2011)

Schleifer, L.M., Amick III, B.C.: System response time and method of pay: stress effects in computer-based tasks. Int. J. Hum. Comput. Interact. **1**, 23–39 (1989)

Seow, S.C.: Designing and Engineering Time: The Psychology of Time Perception in Software. Addison Wesley, Upper Saddle River (2008)

Ceaparu, I., Lazar, J., Bessiere, K., Robinson, J., Shneiderman, B.: Determining causes and everity of end-user frustration. Int. J. Hum. Comput. Interact. **17**, 333–356 (2004)

Nah, F.F.-H.: A study on tolerable waiting time: how long are Web users willing to wait? Behav. Inf. Technol. **23**, 153–163 (2004). http://dx.doi.org/10.1080/01449290410001669914

Thum, M., Boucsein, W., Kuhmann, W., Ray, W.J.: Standardized task strain and system response times in human–computer interaction. Ergonomics **38**, 1342–1351 (1995)

Le Callet, P., Möller, S., Perkis, A.: Qualinet white paper on definitions of quality of experience. In: European Network on Quality of Experience in Multimedia Systems and Services (COST Action IC 1003) (2012)

Zepernick, H., Engelke, U.: Quality of experience of multimedia services: past, present, and future. In: Adjunct Proceedings of the 9th European Interactive TV Conference (EuroITV 2011), pp. 115–119 (2011)

Raake, A., Egger, S.: Quality and quality of experience. In: Möller, S., Raake, A. (eds.) Quality of Experience: Advanced Concepts, Applications and Methods, pp. 11–34. Springer, New York (2014)

Brooks, P., Hestnes, B.: User measures of quality of experience: why being objective and quantitative is important. IEEE Netw. **24**(2), 8–13 (2010)

Larson, R.C.: Perspectives on queues: social justice and the psychology of queuing. Oper. Res. **35**, 895–905 (1987)

Clemmer, E.C., Schneider, B.: Toward understanding and controlling customer dissatisfaction with waiting. Report no. 89-115. The Marketing Science Institute, Cambridge, MA (1989)

Dube, L., Schmitt, B.H., Leclerc, F.: Consumers' reactions to waiting: when delays affect the perception of service quality. In: Srull, T.S. (ed.) Advances in Consumer Research, vol. 16, pp. 59–63. Association Consumer Research, Provo (1989)

Dube, L., Schmitt, B.H., Leclerc, F.: Consumers' affective response to delays at different phases of a service delivery. J. Appl. Psychol. **21**, 810–820 (1991)

Hui, M.K., Tse, D.K.: What to tell consumers in waits of different lengths: an integrative model of service evaluation. J. Mark. **60**, 81–90 (1996)

Branaghan, R.J., Sanchez, C.A.: Feedback preferences and impressions of waiting. Hum. Factors **51**, 528–538 (2009). http://dx.doi.org/10.1177/0018720809345684

Galletta, D.E., Henry, R.M., McCoy, S., Polak, P.: When the wait isn't so bad: the interacting effects of website delay, familiarity, and breadth. Inf. Syst. Res. **17**(1), 20–37 (2006). http://dx.doi.org/10.1287/isre.1050.0073

Krejcar, O.: Problem solving of low data throughput on mobile devices by artefacts prebuffering. EURASIP J. Wirel. Commun. Netw. **2009**, 802523 (2009). http://dx.doi.org/10.1155/2009/802523

Kuhmann, W.: Experimental investigation of stress-inducing properties of system response times. Ergonomics **32**, 271–280 (1989)

Kuhmann, W., Boucsein, W., Schaefer, F., Alexander, J.: Experimental investigation of psychophysiological stress-reactions induced by different system response times in human–computer interaction. Ergonomics **30**, 933–943 (1987)

Schaefer, F.: The effect of system response times on temporal predictability of work flow in human–computer interaction. Hum. Perform. **3**, 173–186 (1990)

Martin, G.L., Corl, K.G.: System response time effects on user productivity. Behav. Inf. Technol. **5**, 3–13 (1986)

Simoens, P., Vankeirsbilck, B., Deboosere, L., Ali, F.A., De Turck, F., Dhoedt, B., Demeester, P.: Upstream bandwidth optimization of thin client protocols through latency-aware adaptive user event buffering. Int. J. Commun. Syst. **24**, 666–690 (2011). http://dx.doi.org/10.1002/dac.1188

ITU-T P.910: Subjective video quality assessment methods for multimedia applications. International Telecommunication Union, September 1999

ITU-R BT.500-10: Methodology for the subjective assessment of the quality of television pictures. In: International Telecommunication Union, March 2000

Jones, C., Atkinson, D.J.: Development of opinion-based audiovisual quality models for desktop video-teleconferencing. In: International Workshop on Quality of Service (1998)

Caramma, M., Lancini, R., Marconi, M.: Subjective quality evaluation of video sequences by using motion information. In: Proceedings of International Conference on Image Processing, ICIP 1999, October 1999

Watson, A., Sasse, M.A.: Measuring perceived quality of speech and video in multimedia conferencing applications. In: Proceedings of ACM Multimedia 1998, September 1998, pp. 55–60 (1998)

Cisco Documentation: Cisco visual networking index: forecast and methodology 2013–2018, Cisco White Paper, June 2014

Driver's Information Needs in Automated Driving

Huining Xing[1], Hua Qin[1(✉)], and Jianwei Niu[2]

[1] School of Mechanical-Electronic and Automobile Engineering,
Beijing University of Civil Engineering and Architecture,
Beijing 100044, People's Republic of China
qinhua@bucea.edu.cn
[2] School of Mechanical Engineering, University of Science and Technology
Beijing, Beijing 100083, People's Republic of China

Abstract. The purpose of this paper is to study the drivers' information needs in automated driving. Virtual reality and simulation techniques were used to simulate the automated driving in different scenarios, and drivers need to fill in the information needs assessment questionnaires after completing the task. In automated driving, the eye tracker recorded the fixation behavior. The experimental results showed that, regardless of whether drivers focused on automated driving system or not, it is necessary for the system to feedback some general information to the driver, such as vehicle-related information (such as the current speed, blind spots), road-related information (such as the surrounding traffic, condition around, etc.), the auxiliary system state (on or off) and the ability of the auxiliary system to process the current scene etc..

Keywords: Drivers' information needs · Automated driving · Urban roads · Decision information

1 Introduction

At present, unmanned machinery has become a hot spot not only in the field of vehicle driving [1], but also in the military field, manned spaceflight, agricultural production and other fields [2]. For example, the UAV can perform many tasks that people couldn't complete, and then to reduce casualties, enhance the combat capability [3]; at the same time, automated driving system could make the vehicle driving at desired speed stably, it could also realize the functions, navigation etc. [4, 5]. However, there were still many problems in the process of switch from automatic control of machinery to manual control [6]. Therefore, the switch between automated driving and manual driving involved many aspects of the problems which included drivers' reaction time, vehicle performance, human-computer interaction and so on [7, 8].

In some cases of automated driving, when the automated driving system couldn't make the right decision on the current situation, the driver needed to take over the vehicle in time and make decisions. The driver played the role of the supervisor in automated driving [9], however, due to excessive trust to the automated driving system [10], the driver's vigilance and behavioral adaptation decreased, which caused the

© Springer International Publishing AG 2017
P.-L.P. Rau (Ed.): CCD 2017, LNCS 10281, pp. 736–744, 2017.
DOI: 10.1007/978-3-319-57931-3_60

e.g. slower reaction times or misinterpretation etc., that means that the driver are not good at supervising [11, 12]. The driver will do some other things that nothing to do with driving, such as listening to music, calling and so on, under these circumstances, the driver cannot fully understand the vehicle condition and the surrounding environment, compared to manual driving in which the driver was absorbed in driving. Therefore, when drivers need to take over the vehicle, the driver will need some information about the parameters of the car, the environment and so on, in order to successfully take over the vehicle to ensure the safety of the vehicle.

Currently, the urban traffic in China mainly has the following features [13]:

(1) With the acceleration of China's urbanization, urban population increased, the number of vehicles rose sharply, which caused traffic congestion, the reducing of the traffic capacity of the road.
(2) The traffic flow is mixed and disordered, there are various types of traffic participants in the road.
(3) The driver's behavioral intentions are difficult to predict, and the phenomenon that the vehicle is not according to the traffic rules exists.

Therefore, based on the characteristics of urban roads in China, this paper studied the information needs of drivers under different level of intention in automated driving.

2 Experimental Design

In order to study the driver's information needs in automated driving, and evaluate the level of drivers' information needs in automated driving, virtual reality and simulation technology was used to test participants. According to the characteristics of urban roads in China, 6 kinds of common scenes in city were selected and designed, participants simulated automated driving in each scenario, and filled in information needs assessment questionnaires at the end of the experiment.

2.1 Automatic Driving Simulation Platform and Experimental Scenario

The experiment was completed in the virtual reality and simulation laboratory of China National Institute of standardization. The experimental scenario is shown in Fig. 1. Participants in the vehicle simulated automated driving through the scene on the screen.

Fig. 1. Driving simulator

The participants' eye fixations can be used as behavioral instruction to drivers' information needs in automated driving, subjects' fixation behavior was tracked by ahead-mounted eye tracker, and it was recorded into video through the iView X software, then participants' fixation time were obtained through video analysis by the BeGaze3.3 analysis software.

The design of the scenes was in conformity with the traffic condition of urban road in real world. In this experiment, the following were six typical scenes, (1) traffic jam in which the drivers need to repeatedly start and brake; (2) crossroads that vehicles mixed; (3) a scene that the forward vehicle changes lanes frequently; (4) the bus forcibly occupied the driveway; (5) traffic accident appeared in front of the car; (6) a scenario that the forward vehicle makes an emergency braking.

2.2 Experimental Tasks and Processes

In this study, 12 participants participate in the experiment, included 10 males and 2 females, aged between 22 and 47 years of age. The participants' driving experience between 1 years and 16 years, they do not have any automated driving experience before. The 12 were randomly divided into 2 groups, 6 subjects in each group. The first group of participants did not have secondary tasks and was required to supervise the automated driving system absorbedly, named as supervision group. The second group of participants had secondary tasks, named as secondary-task group.

This experiment is carried out by automated driving simulation platform. Before the experiment, firstly, the researchers introduced the experimental content and the experimental task to the participants, so that the participants could understand the purpose of the experiment. Secondly, the participants signed a written informed consent and fill in the personal information questionnaire. Prior to conducting a formal experiment, each participant had ten minutes to familiarize themselves with the experimental environment and the automated driving simulator. Participants wore eye tracker equipment before the start of the experiment.

In the formal experiment, the participants' fixation behavior was tracked by the head-mounted eye tracker in real time, and was recorded by iView X software. The participants were required to complete a questionnaire survey after completing an automated driving simulation scene, and evaluate the importance of the required information of the automated driving based on the current scene. After completing the questionnaire of the current scene, we start the experiment of the next scene, until all the experiments were completed, the end.

3   The Results and Analysis of the Experiment

3.1   Questionnaire Analysis and Discussion

The scores of each parameter evaluated by the participants in each scene were collected, and then the collected data were processed by Pareto chart and Pareto principle. The following will be analyzed from three aspects of vehicle-related information, environment-related information and system-related information. The results are shown in Table 1, 2 and 3.

Table 1. Vehicle-related information

Supervision group			Secondary-task group		
Information parameter	Scores	Cumulative percentage	Information parameter	Scores	Cumulative percentage
The reflector	143	20.66%	The current speed	168	23.17%
The current speed	137	40.46%	The reflector	150	43.86%
The rearview mirror	136	60.12%	The blind spot of the vehicle	136	62.62%
The blind spot of the vehicle	122	77.75%	The rearview mirror	100	76.41%
Instrument board	71	88.01%	Instrument board	62	84.97%
Speed of revolution	47	94.80%	Speed of revolution	58	92.97%
The fuel	36	100.00%	The fuel	51	100.00%

Vehicle-Related Information. For the supervision group, Table 1 showed that when the subject is in the state of supervision, it is considered that the situation of the reflector, the current speed of the vehicle, the rearview mirror and the blind spot of the vehicle are very important decision-making information. They need to watch the ongoing scene all the time when they were supervising, so that it can make the appropriate decisions quickly and timely. Drivers could make corresponding decision based on observing the surrounding conditions of road and vehicle conditions through the reflector and the rearview mirror, and clearly knowing their own vehicle blind spot situation. In fact, we pay little attention to the instrument board, speed of revolution and the fuel of the vehicle in our daily life, only when the vehicle is started, we will pay attention to that information. In addition, if the car is in long distance running, the amount of oil will become particularly important, but because all the scenes are based on the city road, so the information about the staff became not so important for the subjects.

For the secondary-task group, Table 1 shows that the driver believes that the current speed of the vehicle, the reflector, the blind spot of the vehicle and the rearview mirror is very important. It can be found that, the important information that the driver thought is the same as it in supervision group, although the driver's attention is dispersed. It also shows that the information needed to be provided as general information to the driver in automated driving so that the driver can make the right decision in time.

Environment-Related Information. For the supervision group, Table 2 showed that the participants thought information as those were very important, which were the risk level of the current scene, distance between the vehicle to two lanes, vehicle headway, changing lane and personnel, vehicles speed on both sides, traffic signals on the current road and the number of lanes. They need to pay attention to these aspects of real-time information. These scenes are based on the city road, and the speed of the vehicles is very slow, so it rarely needed driver overtaking, so the information of overtaking lane

Table 2. Environment-related information

Supervision group			Secondary-task group		
Information parameter	Scores	Cumulative percentage	Information parameter	Scores	Cumulative percentage
Risky level of the scene	128	7.69%	Traffic signs on the current road	152	7.15%
Distance between the vehicle to two lanes	124	15.14%	Risky level of the scene	145	13.98%
Vehicle headway	120	22.36%	The front obstacle	142	20.66%
Changing lanes and personnel	111	29.03%	Changing lanes and personnel	140	33.88%
Vehicles speed on both sides	110	35.64%	Change lanes on both sides	138	40.38%
Traffic signs on the current road	108	48.68%	Vehicle and personnel status of current lane	136	46.78%
Change lanes on both sides	104	54.93%	Vehicle headway	133	53.04%
Vehicle and personnel status of current lane	100	60.94%	Vehicles speed on both sides	131	59.20%
The number of lanes	93	66.53%	Distance between the vehicle to two lanes	128	65.22%
Current vehicle speed	90	71.94%	Current vehicle speed	124	71.06%
Current speed limit	89	77.28%	Current speed limit	111	76.28%
Overtaking lane distance	81	82.15%	The number of lanes	110	81.46%
Driving conditions of the road ahead	80	86.96%	Driving conditions of the road ahead	109	86.59%
Distance to the obstacle	77	91.59%	Distance to the obstacle	108	91.67%
The front obstacle	73	95.97%	Overtaking lane distance	106	96.66%
Weather condition	67	100.00%	Weather condition	71	100.00%

distance is not so important. In addition, the questionnaires showed that only a small number of participants will take into account the weather conditions when they made decisions. Because the driver was able to observe the road condition in time, it is not so important to make a decision on the distance to the problem section and the distance to the front obstacle.

For the secondary-task group, we can see from Table 2 that when the driver's attention is dispersed, that some environmental information is very helpful for driving decision: (1) traffic signs on the current road; (2) the risky level of the current scene; (3) the front obstacle; (4) changing lanes and personnel; (5) change lanes on both sides; (6) vehicle and personnel status of current lane; (7) vehicle headway; (8) vehicles speed on both sides; (9) distance between the vehicle to two lanes; (10) current vehicle speed; (11) the current speed limit.

Table 3. System-related information

Supervision group			Secondary-task group		
Information parameter	Scores	Cumulative percentage	Information parameter	Scores	Cumulative percentage
Vehicles speed around	127	8.21%	The current speed and braking distance	160	7.92%
The current speed and braking distance	124	16.22%	The state of the assistant system (on or off)	159	15.79%
Vehicles and personnel on both sides	121	24.05%	The ability of auxiliary system to deal with the current situation	150	23.22%
Driving scheme for the current status provided by auxiliary system	119	31.74%	Driving scheme for the current status provided by auxiliary system	147	30.50%
The ability of auxiliary system to deal with the current situation	113	39.04%	Vehicles speed around	141	37.48%
The display of the vehicle speed	108	46.02%	Vehicles and personnel on both sides	138	44.31%
The current road traffic marking (solid line, dotted line)	102	52.62%	Lane-changing on both sides	129	50.69%
Lane-changing on both sides	97	58.89%	Tips of the level of problem occurred on the front road	127	56.98%
The state of the assistant system (on or off)	88	64.58%	Speed of the front obstacles	126	63.22%
Speed of the front obstacles	82	69.88%	The display of the vehicle speed	120	69.16%
Tips of distance to destination	81	75.11%	Display of distance to accident section	115	74.85%
Tips of the level of problem occurred on the front road	81	80.35%	Driving scheme of the vehicle	113	80.45%
Driving scheme of the vehicle	80	85.52%	The reason of driving scheme provided by auxiliary system	110	85.89%
The reason of driving scheme provided by auxiliary system	79	90.63%	The current road traffic marking (solid line, dotted line)	106	91.14%
Display of distance to accident section	74	95.41%	Tips of distance to destination	96	95.89%
Details of the travel plan provided by the auxiliary system	71	100.00%	Details of the travel plan provided by the auxiliary system	83	100.00%

Although the subjects performed secondary tasks when they were driving in the experiment, the demand to environmental information was still high when the subjects were asked to make decisions in different urban road scenarios. For this automated driving vehicle, the driver cannot always supervise the automated driving system, driver will generally do something that nothing to do with driving, so the automated driving system should provide the surrounding traffic and vehicle condition information in real time as much as possible, because of the secondary task, the driver cannot detect the front obstacle, the current road traffic sign and speed limit timely. Therefore, the automated driving system should also be timely feedback to the driver about these kinds of information, to assist the driver to make appropriate decisions quickly and correctly.

System-Related Information. For the supervision group, Table 3 showed that the participants would pay little attention to system-related information, but pay more attention to the surrounding traffic information, pedestrians around the vehicle itself, braking distance and so on when they were supervising. Although participants can observe traffic condition and pedestrian and vehicle condition, they still hope that the automated driving system provided some information such as the current speed, current situation of lane line, the surrounding condition of vehicle and some other observable information to help them make decisions quickly. At the same time the information provided by the system could release drivers' workload, so that the driving process becomes relatively comfortable.

For the secondary-task group, Table 3 showed that the cumulative percentage accounted for 80% of the decision information, the information is the highest score of the participants, which is the most important, as follows: (1) the current speed and braking distance; (2) the state of the assistant system (on or off); (3)the ability of auxiliary system to deal with the current situation; (4) driving scheme for the current status provided by auxiliary system; (5) vehicles speed around; (6) vehicles and personnel on both sides; (7) lane-changing on both sides; (8) tips of the level of problem occurred on the front road; (9) speed of the front obstacles; (10) the display of the vehicle speed; (11) distance to accident section.

The subjects in the experiment has been the implementation of the second tasks, so the system parameters of the decision information, auxiliary system state, the ability of auxiliary system to process the current situation accounted for the main position in the drivers' mind, this is because that most of the drivers' attention will focus on the secondary task when the driver is in the implementation of the second tasks. Therefore, when the vehicle meets the corresponding conditions on the road, the drivers generally only need to be aware of whether the automated driving system can solve the current situation or not, so that they could make corresponding decision.

The statistical results showed that if a person the more trust on the automated driving system, less information he will need, he only thought that information related to the auxiliary system is the most important, for them, they believed that the automated driving system can replace them to supervise the road condition. Therefore, it is enough for them to get the feedback from automated driving system. But if a person does not trust on the automated driving system, then he will consider more traffic condition and vehicle condition.

3.2   Analysis and Discussion of Eye Movement Results

For supervision group, Table 4 showed that participants need to dothe tedious task of supervision, so that 99.85% of the fixation time was on the driving task, but some subjects occasionally see the hands of the questionnaire and the other has nothing to do with the driving task when they were under the supervision, so for the second tasks at the time accounted for 0.15% of total time.

Table 4. Fixation time

Types of tasks	Supervision group		Secondary-task group	
	Fixation time	Percentage	Fixation time	Percentage
Driving task	2725.6	99.85%	78.1	8.62%
Secondary task	4.1	0.15%	827.5	91.38%

In the secondary-task group, participants performed secondary tasks, however, participants' distribution of attention will be also affected by the level of trust on the automated driving system. Participants would occasionally look down at the current scene and observe the road condition while they were doing the secondary task, Table 4 showed that about 91.38% fixation time of participants was focused on secondary tasks, and 8.62% fixation time was on driving task.

4   Conclusion

The purpose of this project is to study the decision-making process of the driver in automated driving vehicle in the urban road scene, as well as the tendency of decision-making and the information content of drivers when they were taking over from the automated driving system. The decision information required by different participants in different scenarios is different. If a person has a high level of trust on the automated driving system and is fully involved in the experimental simulation scenario, he would need only a small amount of decision information in automated driving. The following information should be provided to the driver whether the driver is supervising the automated driving system or not:

1 vehicle-related information (such as current speed, blind spots, etc.)
2 road-related information (such as the surrounding traffic condition, vehicle condition around, etc.)
3 status of auxiliary system (on or off)
4 the ability of the auxiliary system to deal with the current scene.

Acknowledgement. The research project presented in this paper is a part of the Project "Research on the Technology and Standard of Ergonomics Design for Information Display Interface", which was supported by the China National Institute of Standardization. The authors would like to acknowledge the support of the China National Institute of Standardization for this project (2014BAK01B01).

References

1. Wang, C.: Parameter identification and application of automatic train control model. Beijing Jiaotong University (2015)
2. Austin, R.: Unmanned Aircraft Systems: UAVs Design, Development and Deployment. Wiley, Hoboken (2011)
3. Franklin M.: Unmanned combat air vehicles: opportunities for the guided weapons industry? Royal United Services Institute for Defense and Security Studies (2008)
4. Yi, J., Li, Y., Zheng, L., et al.: Integrated control of longitudinal and lateral motion of vehicle automated driving system. China J. Highw. Transp. 23(5), 119–126 (2010)
5. Guo, J.: Design and implementation of GPS autonomous navigation system for unmanned aerial vehicle. Chang'an University. (2014)
6. Zeeb, K., Buchner, A., Schrauf, M.: Is take-over time all that matters? The impact of visual-cognitive load on driver take-over quality after conditionally automated driving. Accid. Anal. Prev. 92, 230–239 (2016)
7. Körber, M., Gold, C., Lechner, D., Bengler, K.: The influence of age on the take-over of vehicle control in highly automated driving. Transp. Res. Part F: Traffic Psychol. Behav. 39, 19–32 (2016)
8. Banks, V.A., Stanton, N.A.: Keep the driver in control: automating automobiles of the future. Appl. Ergon. 53, 389–395 (2015)
9. Merat, N., Lee, J.D.: Preface to the special section on human factors and automation in vehicles designing highly automated vehicles with the driver in mind. Hum. Factors: J. Hum. Factors Ergon. Soc. 54(5), 681–686 (2012)
10. Kazi, T.A., et al.: Designer driving: drivers' conceptual models and level of trust in adaptive cruise control. Int. J. Veh. Des. 45, 339–360 (2007)
11. Martens, M.H., et al.: Human factors' aspects in automated and semiautomatic transport systems: state of the art. Eur. Comm., CityMobil Deliv. D3.2.1. (2008)
12. Jamson, A.H., et al.: Behavioural changes in drivers experiencing highly-automated vehicle control in varying traffic conditions. Transp. Res. Part C: Emerg. Technol. 30, 116–125 (2013)
13. Zhang, S., Che, L., Huang, J.: Understanding of traffic congestion in big cities in China. Sci. Technol. (25) (2016)

Retraction Note to: Design for Meaningful Materials Experience: A Case Study About Designing Materials with Rice and Sea-Salt

Liang Yin[1,2(✉)], Ziyu Zhou[1], and Hang Cheng[2]

[1] Politecnico di Milano, Via Durando 38a, Milan, Italy
liang.yin@polimi.it, ziyu.zhou@mail.polimi.it
[2] Jiangnan University, No. 1800, Lihu Road, Binhu District,
Wuxi, Jiangsu Province, China
chenghangchloe@gmail.com

Retraction Note to:
Chapter "Design for Meaningful Materials Experience: A Case Study About Designing Materials with Rice and Sea-Salt" in: P.-L.P. Rau (Ed.): Cross-Cultural Design, LNCS 10281, https://doi.org/10.1007/978-3-319-57931-3_21

"The authors have retracted this article [1] because the work of other researchers was included without their permission. Work was mainly reused from two articles by E. Karana et al., 2015 [2–3]. All authors agree to this retraction.

1. Yin, L., Zhou, Z., Cheng, H.: Design for Meaningful Materials Experience: A Case Study About Designing Materials with Rice and Sea-Salt. In: Rau, P.-L. P. (ed.) CCD 2017. LNCS, vol. 10281, pp. 258–268. Springer International Publishing (2017). doi:10.1007/978-3-319-57931-3_21

2. Karana, E., Barati, B., Rognoli, V., Zeeuw van der Laan, A. Material driven design (MDD): A method to design for material experiences. International Journal of Design, 9(2), pp.35–54.(2015). http://www.ijdesign.org/ojs/index.php/IJDesign/article/view/1965/687

3. Karana, E., Pedgley, O., Rognoli, V. On Materials Experience. Design Issues, Summer (31:3), pp.16–27. DOI:10.1162/DESI_a_00335 (2015)"

The retracted online version of this chapter can be found at
https://doi.org/10.1007/978-3-319-57931-3_21

Author Index

Abkenar, Amin B. 669
Ahmed, Pervaiz K. 582
An, Dadi 301

Beringer, Robert 605
Berque, Dave 614
Bryan-Kinns, Nick 241

Cao, Xiaoqin 133
Chan, Alan H.S. 582
Chan, Edwin H.W. 301
Chang, Jiaxin 521
Chang, Tzu Chiang 3
Chen, Hsiao-Hua 469
Chen, Li-Yu 37, 232, 312
Chen, Xue 49
Chen, Yue 509, 592
Chen, Zhe 521, 554
Cheng, Hang 258
Cheong, Soon-Nyean 582
Chhor, Jimmy 531
Chiaia, Bernardino 15
Chiba, Hiroko 614
Chu, Junjie 216
Chuang, Miao-Hsien 324
Chunhui, Jing 624

Deng, Shunong 521
Devkar, Sujit 647
Doke, Pankaj 647
Dong, Lili 546

Fang, Shijing 192
Fang, Wen-Ting 25, 356
Fang, Xing 133
Fantilli, Alessandro 15
Fu, Zhiyong 385, 495

Gao, Jing 565
Gao, Qin 509, 592, 693
Gao, Shang 634
Gao, Ya-Juan 37, 181, 312
Germak, Claudio 565
Gong, Miaosen 171

Gong, Yun 531
Guo, Hong 634

He, Canqun 146
He, Shushu 334
He, Xue 385
Hirom, Ulemba 647
Hu, Huimin 703
Huang, Ching-Hui 312
Huang, Hanjing 659
Huang, Shu Hui 3
Hwang, Shyh-Huei 204

Ji, Zhangyu 146
Jiang, Chenhan 345
Jin, Yige 37, 356
Jin, Ziliang 49
Jing, Jia 634

Kachouie, Reza 669
Kang, Rui 683
Kao, Yi-Fang 121
Kilina, Elena 76

Lai, Ka-Hin 546
Lan, Taihua 181
Lee, Sandy 37
Lei, Tian 49
Li, Jing 554
Li, Lisha 693
Li, Wei 192, 724
Li, Ya-jun 269
Li, Zhengsheng 146
Liang, Qiao 171
Lien, Chun-Ming 121
Lin, Po-Hsien 25, 181
Lin, Rungtai 25, 37, 356
Linder, Chelsea 369
Liu, Feng 521
Liu, Heng 133
Liu, Long 399
Liu, Taijie 703
Liu, Xu 49
Lobo, Sylvan 647

Long, Ren   49
Lou, Yongqi   345
Lupetti, Maria Luce   565

Ma, Jin   59
Ma, Jui-Ping   324
Ma, Liang   693
Ma, Lin   521, 554
Ma, Qi   582
Mahmood, Farez   441
Mamtimin, Adila   521
Mi, Haipeng   565
Ming, Chew Kien   161
Mohd Saman, Fauzi   441

Ni, Minqing   412
Ni, Shuya   146
Ni, Tong-Fang   324
Niu, Jianwei   736
Noor, Nor Laila Md   441

Pandey, Nikita   647
Peruccio, Pier Paolo   15
Phang, Chee Wei   582
Putrevu, Jagannadha Sri Harsha   369

Qian, Fengde   356
Qie, Nan   713
Qin, Anran   171
Qin, Hua   736

Ran, Linghua   703
Rau, Pei-Luen Patrick   531, 546, 659, 683,
        693, 713
Ren, Lei   232

Sedighadeli, Sima   669
Sekhokoane, Lebohang   713
Sheridan, Jennifer G.   241
Shi, Jintian   432
Sun, Jiahao   724
Sun, Xiaohua   288, 432

Tan, Hao   192, 724
Tan, Zhengyu   192, 724
Tang, Da-Lun   94
Tassi, Roberta   76
Teh, Pei-Lee   582
Thiry, Jeffery Yeow Teh   161

V.S., Shyama   647
Valsecchi, Francesca   76

Wakkary, Ron   451
Wan Adnan, Wan Adilah   441
Wang, Bin   724
Wang, Chu   399
Wang, Jiaojiao   146
Wang, Man-Ying   94
Wang, Ming-Shean   204
Wang, Shu-Huei   204
Wang, Wei   241
Wang, Xiaoge   181
Wang, Xiaolan   451
Wang, Yanyun   216
Wong, Ju-Joan   469
Wu, Cecile Ching-yi   482
Wu, Jun   356
Wu, Xin   554
Wu, Yan   232
Wu, Yongmeng   241

Xie, Chunhui   369
Xing, Huining   736
Xu, Shihui   192
Xu, Xiang   241

Yang, Ning-Hsien (aka Vincent)   104
Yang, Xu   146
Yao, Yuan   565
Yao, Ziying   399
Yap, Wen-Jiun   582
Yeh, Mo-Li   121
Yen, Wun-Cong   312
Yin, Liang   258
Yuan, Quan   509, 592

Zhang, Binhui   288
Zhang, Jing   624
Zhang, Linghao   171
Zhang, Xin   703
Zhao, Chaoyi   703
Zhao, Qiyong   724
Zhao, Yi-qian   269
Zheng, Yangshuo   133
Zhou, Bo   288
Zhou, Ping   495
Zhou, Qian   399
Zhou, Ziyu   258
Zou, Yongzhen   133

Printed in the United States
By Bookmasters